Rock-cut Temples of South India

Architectural Dimensions

Rock-cut Temples of South India

Architectural Dimensions

Preeti Sharma
Professor & Head, Department of History & Indian Culture
Banasthali Vidyapith, Rajasthan

Aryan Books International
New Delhi

ROCK-CUT TEMPLES OF SOUTH INDIA
Architectural Dimensions

ISBN: 978-81-7305-510-2

Published in **2015** by

Aryan Books International

Pooja Apartments, 4B, Ansari Road, New Delhi-110 002 (India)
Tel.: 23287589, 23255799; Fax: 91-11-23270385
E-mail: aryanbooks@gmail.com
www.aryanbooks.co.in

Designed and Printed in India by
ABI Prints & Publishing Co., New Delhi

Dedicated to the Revered 'Master'
Shri Parthasarathi Rajagopalachariji

Preface

Temple making is generally a movement of the creator's idea from within to the exteriors through the medium of stones. He projects the mass frontally, elevated vertically in three-dimensional forms and creates a structural edifice. In contrast, the rock-cut temples present the spectrum of life moving from outside to inside to create a world of their own. Rock-cut shrines are nothing but fountains of creativity where ideas of art evolved as sapling and were later nurtured into trees.

My visits to South India as a student of Art History initiated me to the enigmatic world of cave temples, a fascinating amalgamation of human ingenuity and divine mythology. These visits proved a budding ground for a number of questions in my mind to be contemplated upon in the course of future study. For instance, historically speaking, the practice of cave excavations was popular among the non-theistic religious sects like Buddhism and Jainism, which required a secluded place to meditate upon and seek the self, or even before that, as safe retreats for the wandering monks, *bhikshus*, during rainy season. But the ritual-oriented Brāhmanical sects did not necessitate such exclusion. Then, what led the Śaivite and Vaiṣṇavite followers to chisel cave temples in the rocks, both hard and soft, involving a rigorous process and tremendous technical expertise? Was it sectarian rivalry? Or, an urge to proclaim supremacy over seemingly indefatigable mountains? Were the creators motivated by some nobler inner instincts? Or, were they moved by their own aesthetic sensibilities? Did they intend to herald some novelty in the prevailing cultural set up? Or, was it an endeavour to seek divine grace for some material incentives? Was the activity linked to political aggrandizements by the reigning dynasties? Or else, does the actual rationale lie beyond all such assumptions and comprehensions?

The symbolism latent in the excavated shrines as well as the chiseled forms are equally baffling. Besides, to what an extent the caves replicated their structural prototypes, as they betray minutest details of wooden architectural components? How was the technique of excavating, carving and sculpting, both in softer and hard stones, devised? Above all, what actually prompted their royal patrons who, despite incessant military campaigns, actively patronized them? Was the activity a manifestation of or legitimization of political authority disguised under religious affiliations? What propelled the equally enthusiast artists who measured steps with their mentors in undertaking such vulnerable, enormously challenging, time-consuming and patience-testing enterprises. The manner of their creation, the magnitude of scale on which executed, lavish sculptural embellishments brimming with conventionalized iconographic representation, bespeaks upon the artistic expertise as well as the desire of the creators to endow their creations with immortal fame and enduring life span. These were some of the queries and observations enticing me to work on the rock-cut architecture of South Indian cave temples.

To me the rock-cut temples revealed themselves as hidden treasures of art inside the mountain. They are the creations of space through architectural projection of divine drama through sculptures. They rather signify a unique world or cosmos of Gods where they play, dance, marry, eliminate the evil, i.e. indulge in interplay of creation and annihilation within the cave premises, and manifest themselves in hierarchies and a variety of manifestations. Herein the soft, elegant, rhythmic forms of deities, emerging from the heart of the hard granite or soft trap stone, are a spectator's delight. The spontaneity and dynamism underlying these figures render them lifelike. The reflection of images, particularly in bright and fading sunlight, is indeed a matter of supreme vision or divine revelation. For me, the experience of moving within the inscrutable environs from one cave to another was analogous to Alice moving in the wonderland.

Although a number of European and Indian archaeologists and art historians have studied these monuments through the years, their attempts remained primarily descriptive and survey-oriented accounts. The few detailed studies undertaken were region specific or dynasty centric. Such being the state of affairs, a systematic study of Indian cave temple architecture as a whole remains a *desideratum*.

The present work is a humble effort to map out the sequence of and highlight the architectural components of the rock excavations in South India beginning from the Cālukyan caves through Pallava *rathas* and *maṇḍapams* up to the climax of such ventures in the form of Rāṣṭrakūṭa Kailāśanātha temple at Ellorā. I have also attempted to discuss the current status of Indian heritage sites, exposed to multiplicities of vulnerabilities, both natural as well as human, and recommended certain measures that might help in mitigating the threat looming large over these treasures of our adorable past.

In planning the study, emphasis has been given on two significant aspects of cave excavations: (i) Temple architecture constitute first part of the excavation wherein the deity resides. Without the presence of religious sculptures, the abode of God and the art of rock-cut temples would be incomplete. Thus, sculptural art and iconography are not separate but comprise the second and indispensable part of the compact rock-cut architectural whole; (ii) The monolithic temples chiseled and separated from the hill have to be treated as the culmination of the art of cave excavations.

The methodology adopted for the study involved both consulting extant material for reference as well as undertaking extensive field visits to the Brāhmanical excavation sites in Karnataka, Tamil Nadu and Maharashtra to get a first-hand information about the excavations. Consultations with subject experts for technical know-how, and locals for place-related myths and legends were also resorted to.

In the writing of this work, some oft occurring references have been given in abbreviated forms. In describing Pallava shrines' technical terminology, K.R. Srinivasan's convention has been adopted, while for those in Cālukyan and Rāṣṭrakūṭa territories, K.V. Soundara Rajan's usage has been followed. The inscriptions have been quoted *in situ* or as given in the *Epigraphia Indica, Indian Antiquary, Corpus Inscriptionum Indicarum* and *South Indian Inscriptions.*

Dating of the rulers or temples has not been delved upon much, as in the absence of reliable epigraphic evidences it can never be conclusively ascertained. For a similar reason, the controversy regarding authorship of Pallava Mahābalipuram monuments has been deliberately avoided. On stylistic grounds, Elephanta caves are being assigned Rāṣṭrakūṭa origin. Regarding art styles and iconographic specifications, only relevant and select portions have been cited from the *śilpaśāstras.* Of the plethora of forms and manifestations classically assigned to Hindu divinities, only those frequently or sparsely portrayed in the rock-cut shrines have been chosen for analysis.

A uniform scheme of italicized words has been used for the words from languages other than English, i.e. Sanskrit, Hindi, Tamil, etc., as well as for book titles and references. The use of diacritical marks in modern place-names is being refrained from, but these have been used for ancient place names, dynastic nomenclatures and technical terminology of Hindi, Sanskrit or Tamil languages.

Despite my best efforts, there will certainly be several errors in the text, for which I accept all responsibility.

P.S.

Contents

Preface *vii*
Acknowledgements *xiii*
Abbreviations *xvii*
List of Illustrations *xix*

1. A Survey of Rock-cut Architecture in India 1
2. Political History of South India (From Fourth to Ninth Centuries AD) 31
3. Cālukya, Pallava and Raṣṭrakūṭa Art Activities 69
4. Evolution of Rock-cut Cave Architecture: The Cālukyan Phase 111
5. Origin of Monolithic Architecture during the Pallavas 155
6. Development of Monolithic Architecture: Contribution of the Rāṣṭrakūṭas 199
7. South Indian Rock-cut Temples: Sculptures and Their Iconography 247
8. The Epistemology of Conservation: Mapping Challenges of Preserving Rock-cut Heritage Monuments in South India 305
9. Conclusion 329

Appendices 343
Glossary 359
Bibliography 367
Index 387

Acknowledgements

I am indebted to many individuals and institutions for completing this book. First of all, I express deep gratitude and reverence towards my esteemed guru and eminent art historian, Dr. S.K. Gupta, former Head, Department of History and Indian Culture, University of Rajasthan, Jaipur. It was a privilege to be trained under his enlightened guidance. It was indeed because of his illuminating insight that I could see through the basics, as also the technicalities of the topic. But for his encouragement and sustenance to my enthusiasm, peeping into these wonder creations of South Indian cave temples while sitting in Rajasthan could be never initiated nor culminated. Moreover, his earnest efforts to make the text 'picture perfect' evoke all my respect for him. Discussions with Shri M.A. Dhaky, distinguished Indian art expert, proved quite fruitful and informative in clarifying technical details. Shri R.C. Agrawala, former Director, Department of Museums and Archaeology, Government of Rajasthan, Jaipur, very affectionately provided valuable tips and related articles that came to his notice. I owe heartfelt thanks to both the scholars. Mr. Shilakanth Pattar's learned insights about the technicalities of Bādāmī caves were really very useful in grasping the minutiae of the excavated sites as also their existing status.

I also wish to thank the Librarians of: Central Library, Banasthali University; Central Library, University of Rajasthan, Jaipur; Library, University Maharani's College, Jaipur; Central Library, Jawaharlal Nehru University, New Delhi; M.S. University, Baroda (Gujarat); Central Library, Aligarh Muslim University, Aligarh (U.P.); Department of Museums and Archaeology Library, Albert Hall, Jaipur; Library, Information Centre, Govt. of Rajasthan, Jaipur; Radha Krishnan Library, Jaipur; Government Maharaja's Public Library, Jaipur; Indian Council of Historical Research Library, New Delhi; and Library, National Museum, New Delhi; for extending their kind co-operation. My thanks are also due to the Archaeological Survey of India staff at Delhi, Ellorā, Aurangābād and Chennai for facilitating my site visits and useful information. The library staff at the Indian Institute of Advanced Study (IIAS), Shimla deserves appreciation for all the assistance provided in procuring relevant data.

I am indebted to the general administrative and library staff at the American Institute of Indian Studies (AIIS), Gurgaon for not only providing all facilities possible during my visits to the Institute, but also for making my stay quite comfortable. My heartfelt thanks are due to Sh. J.S. Yadav, former Director, Centre for Art & Archaeology, AIIS, for his constant help and personal assistance throughout the process of data collection there. Dr. Bilimale's kind gesture for arranging my daily commutation from home to the Institute also evokes admiration; so does Dr. Vandana Sinha's (Director – Academic) promptness in providing me the required photographs.

Photographs of the monuments; ground plans of Cālukyan caves at Aihoḷe; Ellorā, and Bādāmī, Pallava *ratha* and *maṇḍapam* plans, Rāṣṭrakūṭa cave plans; and line figures reproduced in the text are courtesy the American Institute of Indian Studies (AIIS) Photo Archives, Archaeological Survey of India (ASI) website, K.R. Srinivasan (1993), K.V. Soundara Rajan (1981), and Susan Huntington (1985). The author duly acknowledges all sources at the place of citation. My technical assistant at Banasthali, Surgyan Gurjar, extended valuable assistance in finalizing the photographs.

I owe gratefulness to my parents, Sh. R.S. Sharma and Smt. Vimla Sharma, for blessing me with this life. Satish 'Bhai Saab', who initiated my academic life as a fatherly figure, cannot be thanked in words. My siblings, Bhawana Didi, Manohar, Akash, Manju and Ravi, have been enormously supportive. I am grateful for Deepak and Sunil jijaji's inspiration too. My *bhabhis*—Kamana, Manju, Sunita and Meena—always catering to my miscellaneous requirements and creating congenial surroundings at home, have contributed towards this work, in their own manner. Divyam deserves special thanks for his immense, ungrudging contribution in the formative and technical stages of the writing. Dear Tanushree, Atul, Aditi, Ruchita, Kunal, Anirudh and dearest Aryaman, Apoorv and Anany, always acted as stress relievers. Appaji and dear Pammi were a great company during field visits. Shobha Bhabhi and Naveen Bhaiya deserve special mention for their generosity in taking care of all the travel and stay arrangements for facilitating my trip to Bādāmī and Ellorā sites.

Kumkum aunty's relishing pleasantries, redeeming me of all the strains of journeys from Banasthali to Jaipur, would always be cherished. Amongst friends, Prof. Vinay Sharma's constant motivation was always stimulating for academic advancement. Ishwar Singh Brar, quite generously, 'bore the burden' of my reading stuff from Delhi. Sivadasan too responded quite munificently to my request for photographs. Fond gratitude is due to my dear husband Sanjeev, not only for his constructive criticism, valuable suggestions for scholastic perfection, great inputs for theoretical constructions and reinvigoration of my energy from time to time, but also for the patience and perseverance with which he faced my work pressures, unruly demands and quelled my fears to meet self professed deadlines for winding up the work.

I also thank my institution, Banasthali Vidyapith, for providing research oriented atmosphere in the campus, thereby facilitating stimulus to such works.

I extend special thanks to Mr. Vikas Arya of Aryan Books International for his meticulous way of organizing this publication and for his insightful suggestion to add a relevant chapter on heritage conservation.

Above all, my heartiest thanks reach out to the 'MASTER' for being with me, always!

Abbreviations

AA	:	*Artibus Asiae*
ABORI	:	*Annals of the Bhandarkar Oriental Research Institute*, Poona
ARASI (also ASIR)	:	*Annual Report of Archaeological Survey of India*
ASI	:	Archaeological Survey of India
ASSI	:	Archaeological Society of South India
ASWI	:	Archaeological Survey of Western India
BMC	:	*Bulletin of Museums and Archaeology in U.P.*
BORI	:	Bhandarkar Oriental Research Institute
BS	:	*Bṛhat-Saṁhitā*
CTD	:	*Cave Temples of the Deccan* by K.V. Soundara Rajan
CTI	:	*Cave Temples of India* by James Fergusson and James Burgess
CTP	:	*Cave Temples of the Pallavas* by K.R. Srinivasan
DOS	:	*Discourses on Śiva* edited by Michael W. Meister
ECSA	:	*Ellorā Caves: Sculpture and Architecture* edited by Ratan Parimoo *et al.*
EI	:	*Epigraphia Indica*
EHI	:	*Elements of Hindu Iconography* by Gopinatha Rao
GOS	:	*Gaekwad's Oriental Series, Baroda*
HCIP	:	*The History and Culture of the Indian People*
IA	:	*Indian Antiquary*
ISGDP	:	*Iśāna Śiva Guru Dev Paddati*

JBBRAS	:	*Journal of the Bombay Branch of the Royal Asiatic Society*
JRAS	:	*Journal of the Royal Asiatic Society of Great Britain and Ireland,* London
LK	:	*Lalit Kala*
MASI	:	*Memoirs of Archaeological Survey of India*
OA	:	*Oriental Art*
SII	:	*South Indian Inscriptions*
TASSI	:	*Transactions of the Archaeological Society of South India*
TOI	:	*Times of India*
VA	:	*Vaikhānasa Āgam*

List of Illustrations

MAPS

1. Cālukya and Rāṣṭrakūṭa cave temple sites (after Soundara Rajan 1981). 8
2. Pallava cave temple and monoliths sites (after Srinivasan 1993). 9
3. The Cālukyan territories (after mapsofindia.com). 33
4. The Pallava Empire Expansion (after mapsofindia.com). 37
5. The Rāṣṭrakūṭa regions (after mapsofindia.com). 42
6. Aihoḷe: Site plan (after AIIS). 72
7. Bādāmī: Site plan (after AIIS). 78
8. Elephanta Island (after AIIS). 227
9. Mahābalipuram: City map (after mapsofindia.com). 319

MONOCHROME PLATES (FIGURES)

1. Bādāmī: Cave I, chisel marks on the exterior wall. 10
2. Mahābalipuram: Rock cutting remains near *rathas*. 10
3. Mahābalipuram: Rock chiselling marks, pilaster and sculptural carving details in Dharmarāja *ratha*. 11
4. Ellorā: Cave XVI (Kailāśa), excavated monument replica in courtyard. 11
5. Bādāmī: Cave III, pillar top rafting intersections. 12
6. Mahābalipuram: Chiselled *ratha* pillar capitals . 12
7. Ellorā: Cave XVI (Kailāśa), timber roofing reproduction in rock, (with painting marks), details. 13
8. Mahābalipuram: Bhīma *ratha*, east façade, second storey, wooden architecture technique, details (after AIIS). 13
9. Mahābalipuram: Bhīma *ratha*, *candraśālā*, north façade, *mādala* details (after AIIS). 9

10. Mahābalipuram: Dharmarāja *ratha*, view across the façade. 15
11. Elephanta: Cave 4, façade, pillar attached to the parent rock (after AIIS). 16
12. Ellorā: Cave XVI, southern side cloister niche, protrusion grooves. 17
13. Aihoḷe: Durgā temple, ground plan (after AIIS). 73
14. Aihoḷe: Megutī temple, ground plan (after AIIS). 74
15. Aihoḷe: Megutī temple (after AIIS). 74
16. Aihoḷe: Durgā temple (after AIIS). 75
17. Aihoḷe: Lāḍ Khān temple (after AIIS). 76
17 (i). Aihoḷe: Lāḍ Khān temple, roofing details (after AIIS). 76
18. Bādāmī: Loval Śivālaya temple (after AIIS). 77
19. Mahābalipuram: Shore temple, ground plan (after AIIS). 89
20. Mahābalipuram: Shore temple with *prākāra* (after AIIS). 90
21. Kāñcīpuram: Kailāśanātha temple (after AIIS). 91
22. Aihoḷe: Rāvaṇa Phaḍi, side-shrine (after AIIS). 113
23. Aihoḷe: Rāvaṇa Phaḍi, shrine pillars (after AIIS). 114
24. Aihoḷe: Rāvaṇa Phaḍi cave, ground plan. 115
25. Aihoḷe: Rāvaṇa Phaḍi, pillar (after AIIS). 116
26. Aihoḷe: Rāvaṇa Phaḍi pillars, details (after AIIS). 117
27. Aihoḷe: Rāvaṇa Phaḍi pillar, shaft details (after AIIS). 117
28. Aihoḷe: Rāvaṇa Phaḍi cave, doorframe fragment (after AIIS). 117
29. Aihoḷe: Rāvaṇa Phaḍi, Varāha, *antarāla*, north wall (after AIIS). 119
30. Aihoḷe: Rāvaṇa Phaḍi cave, *Mahiṣāsurmardinī*, *antarāla*, south wall (after AIIS). 120
31. Bādāmī: Rock-cut cave nos. I, II, III, plan (after Huntington 1985). 124
32. Bādāmī: Rock-cut cave no. II, plan (after Soundara Rajan 1981). 124
33. Bādāmī: Cave IV, *mukhamaṇḍapa* interior, (pillars with standing *jina*), from east (after AIIS). 125
34. Bādāmī: Cave IV, *mukhamaṇḍapa* interior, pillar details (after AIIS). 126
35. Bādāmī: Cave I, *mukhamaṇḍapa*, frontal pillar *potikā* details (after AIIS). 126
36. Bādāmī: Cave I, *maṇḍapa*, interior pillar details (after AIIS). 126
37. Bādāmī: Cave I, *maṇḍapa*, interior view (after AIIS). 127
38. Bādāmī: Cave I, *maṇḍapa*, pillar details (after AIIS). 128
39. Bādāmī: Cave II, pillar detail (after AIIS). 128
40. Bādāmī: Cave I, *mukhamaṇḍapa* pillar, pecking geese and swag, details (after AIIS). 128
41. Bādāmī: Cave I, *maṇḍapa*, interior view (after AIIS). 129
42. Bādāmī: Cave I, *maṇḍapa* pillar, cushion capital, detail (after AIIS). 129
43. Bādāmī: Cave II, *prastara* and pillar capital, detail (after AIIS). 129
44. Bādāmī: Cave III, *mukhamaṇḍapa* pillar, type 1. 130
45. Bādāmī: Cave III, *mukhamaṇḍapa* pillar, type 2. 130
46. Bādāmī: Cave III, pillar cushion, detail (after AIIS). 130
47. Bādāmī: Cave III, façade, bracketed pillars. 131
48. Bādāmī: Cave I, pillar, details (after AIIS). 132

49. Bādāmī: Cave II, *kīrtimukha* and swag motif, *mukhamaṇḍapa* (after AIIS). 132
50. Bādāmī: Cave III, fore-pillar capital and bracket (after AIIS). 133
51. Bādāmī: Cave I, *maṇḍapa* pillars (after AIIS). 134
52. Bādāmī: Cave I, *mukhamaṇḍapa,* interior view (after AIIS). 134
53. Bādāmī: Cave III, *maṇḍapa,* fore-pillar base (after AIIS). 135
54. Bādāmī: Cave I, pilaster, base, east end (after AIIS). 136
55. Bādāmī: Cave III, *adhiṣṭhāna, gaṇā* frieze, left of steps (after AIIS). 136
56. Bādāmī: Cave I, entablature of entrance to *maṇḍapa* (after AIIS). 137
57. Bādāmī: Cave I, *prastara,* detail (after AIIS). 137
58. Bādāmī: Cave I, entrance to *maṇḍapa,* details (after AIIS). 138
59. Bādāmī: Cave II, pilaster and doorframe, left (after AIIS). 138
60. Bādāmī: Cave III, *garbhagṛha* (after AIIS). 139
61. Bādāmī: Cave II, *mukhamaṇḍapa,* west wall, *Trivikrama* (after AIIS). 140
62. Bādāmī: Cave III, west wall, *Trivikrama* (after AIIS). 140
63. Bādāmī: Cave I, ceiling, coiled *nāga* (after AIIS). 141
64. Bādāmī: Cave II, series of ceilings (after AIIS). 142
65. Bādāmī: Cave II, ceiling with *matsya-cakra* (after AIIS). 143
66. Ellorā: Cave XVII, rear aisle sculptured pillars (after AIIS). 144
67. Ellorā: Cave XVII, first pillar to left of shrine, details (after AIIS). 145
68. Ellorā: Cave XXI, pillar and *adhiṣṭhāna,* details. 146
69. Mahābalipuram: Varāha *maṇḍapam,* ground plan (after Srinivasan 1993). 161
70. Mahābalipuram: Mahiṣamardinī *maṇḍapam,* ground plan (after Srinivasan 1993). 161
71. Mahābalipuram: Trimūrti *maṇḍapam,* ground plan (after Srinivasan 1993). 162
72. Mahābalipuram: Kōṇēri *maṇḍapam,* ground plan (after Srinivasan 1993). 162
73. Mahābalipuram: Varāha *maṇḍapam, garbhagṛha* entrance (after AIIS). 163
74. Mahābalipuram: Ramanuja *maṇḍapam, alpavimāna* view (after AIIS). 164
75. Mahābalipuram: Unfinished Pañcapāṇḍava *maṇḍapam,* ground plan (after Srinivasan 1993). 165
76. Mahābalipuram: *Adhiṣṭhāna* types in Pallava cave temples (after Srinivasan 1993). 165
77. Mahābalipuram: Pillar types in Pallava cave temples (after Srinivasan 1993). 166
78. Mahābalipuram: Ramanuja *maṇḍapam,* façade pillar, details (after AIIS). 167
79. Mahābalipuram: Pañcapāṇḍava *maṇḍapam,* view (after AIIS). 167
80. Mahābalipuram: Pañcapāṇḍava *maṇḍapam,* pillar (after AIIS). 168
81. Mahābalipuram: Varāha *maṇḍapam,* façade, through central pillars (after AIIS). 169
82. Mahābalipuram: Mahiṣamardinī *maṇḍapam,* inner façade, pillar capital details (after AIIS). 170
83. Mahābalipuram: Koneri *maṇḍapa*, inner pillars, southern end (after AIIS). 171

84. Mahābalipuram: Mahiṣamardinī *maṇḍapam*, façade on east, *somakānta stambha* (after AIIS). 171
85. Mahābalipuram: Mahiṣamardinī *maṇḍapam*, *maṇḍapa*, inner façade, *siṁhapāda staṁbha* (after AIIS). 172
86. Mahābalipuram: Varāha *maṇḍapam*, façade, *vyāḷapāda* pillar, details (after AIIS). 172
87. Mahābalipuram: Varāha *maṇḍapam*, façade, *vyāḷapāda* pillar capital, details (after AIIS). 173
88. Mahābalipuram: Varāha *maṇḍapam*, pillar capital, section details (after AIIS). 173
89. Mahābalipuram: Adi Varāha (Paramesvara) cave, façade pilaster, rear view (after AIIS). 174
90. Mahābalipuram: Koneri *maṇḍapa*, *haṁsamālā* above *garbhagṛha* doorway (after AIIS). 174
91. Mahābalipuram: Trimurti *maṇḍapam*, elevation details (after AIIS). 175
92. Mahābalipuram: unfinished Pidari *ratha* (after AIIS). 178
93. Mahābalipuram: Pañcapāṇḍava *rathas*, site location. 179
94. Mahābalipuram: Pañcapāṇḍava *rathas*, plan (after Huntington 1985). 179
95. Mahābalipuram: Draupadī *ratha*, ground plan (after AIIS). 180
96. Mahābalipuram: Arjuna *ratha*, ground plan (after AIIS). 180
97. Mahābalipuram: Dharmarāja *ratha*, west elevation. 181
98. Mahābalipuram: Dharmarāja *ratha*, *adhiṣṭhāna* details. 183
98 (i). Mahābalipuram: *Pādabandha adhiṣṭhāna.* 184
98 (ii). Mahābalipuram: Arjuna and Draupadī *rathas*, *pādabandha adhiṣṭhāna.* 184
99. Mahābalipuram: Dharmarāja *ratha*, *gaṇāvarī* beneath the *kapota* (after AIIS). 185
100. Mahābalipuram: Dharmarāja *ratha*, *haṁsamālā* beneath the *kapota* (after AIIS). 185
101. Mahābalipuram: Dharmarāja *ratha*, prostrate monkey chutes, east side (after AIIS). 186
102. Mahābalipuram: Draupadī *ratha*—detail of *toraṇa* and *bhūtamālā* (after AIIS). 186
103. Mahābalipuram: Dharmarāja *ratha*, *karṇakūṭa* (after AIIS). 187
104. Mahābalipuram: Valaiyankuṭṭai *ratha*, *śikhara* details (after AIIS). 188
105. Mahābalipuram: Valaiyankuṭṭai *ratha* (after AIIS). 188
106. Mahābalipuram: Bhīma *ratha*, second storey, north façade, gable roof (after AIIS). 189
107. Mahābalipuram: Bhīma *ratha*, second storey, north façade, sala miniature (after AIIS). 190
108. Ellorā: Gaṇeśa Leṇa, Cave No.1, ground plan (after Soundara Rajan 1981). 200
109. Ellorā: Gaṇeśa Leṇa, Cave Nos. 2, 3, 4, 5, ground plan (after Soundara Rajan 1981). 200

110. Ellorā: Gaṇeśa Leṇa, Cave No. 6, ground plan (after Soundara Rajan 1981). 201
111. Ellorā: Gaṇeśa Leṇa, Cave Nos. 8, 9, 10, 11, ground plan (after Soundara Rajan 1981). 201
112. Ellorā: Gaṇeśa Leṇa, Cave No. 12, ground plan (after Soundara Rajan 1981). 202
113. Ellorā: Gaṇeśa Leṇa, Cave Nos. 13, 14, 15, 16, ground plan (after Soundara Rajan 1981). 202
114. Gaṇeśa Leṇa, Cave No. 17, ground plan (after Soundara Rajan 1981). 203
115. Ellorā: Gaṇeśa Leṇa, Cave No. 18, ground plan (after Soundara Rajan 1981). 203
116. Ellorā: Gaṇeśa Leṇa, Cave No. 19, ground plan (after Soundara Rajan 1981). 204
117. Ellorā: Cave XVI (Kailāśa), Lankeśvara cave, ground plan (after Soundara Rajan 1981). 204
118. Ellorā: Cave XV (*Daśāvatāra*), ground plan (after Soundara Rajan 1981). 204
119. Ellorā: Cave XVI (Kailāśa), Lankeśvara section, interior row of pillars, square *Brahmakānt*, octagonal *Indrakānt* (after AIIS). 205
120. Ellorā: Cave XV (*Daśāvatāra*), lintel detail, east wall, doorway (after AIIS). 211
121. Ellorā: Cave XVI (Kailāśa), elephant caryatids. 214
122. Ellorā: Cave XVI, Lankeśvara section, pillar details. 215
123. Ellorā: Cave XVI, Lankeśvara, pillar capital details. 216
124. Ellorā: Cave XVI (Kailāśa), *śikhara vimāna* as visible from exteriors. 217
125. Ellorā: Cave XVI (Kailāśa), projecting *gopuram kakshāsana.* 219
126. Ellorā: Cave XVI (Kailāśa), *Nandimaṇḍapa.* 220
127. Ellorā: Cave XVI (Kailāśa), Jaṭāyu's attack on Rāvaṇa, southern façade (after ASI). 223
128. Ellorā: Cave XVI (Kailāśa), Kārtikeya and *Dikpālas*, outer screen wall (after ASI). 225
129. Elephanta: Main cave (Cave 1), ground plan. 228
130. Elephanta: Main cave (Cave 1), *liṅga* shrine (after ASI). 228
131. Elephanta: Main cave, *liṅga* shrine and *dvārapāla* (after AIIS). 229
132. Elephanta: Main cave, façade (after AIIS). 230
133. Elephanta: Main cave, façade pillar (after AIIS). 230
134. Elephanta: Main cave, main hall, pillar shaft details (after AIIS). 231
135. Elephanta: Main cave, main hall, pillar capital details (after AIIS). 232
136. Elephanta: Main cave, main hall, pillar capital details (after AIIS). 233
137. Elephanta: Cave 2, façade, unfinished pillars (after AIIS). 234
138. Elephanta: Cave 3, doorway (after AIIS). 235
139. Elephanta: Cave 4, façade (after AIIS). 236
140. Elephanta: Main cave, *Maheśamūrti* (after ASI). 238
141. Elephanta: Main cave, entrance *dvārapāla*, pillars in hall (after AIIS). 240
142. Ellorā: Cave XXIX (Sitā ki Nahani/Dhumar *Leṇa*), *Kalyāṇasundara* panel (after AIIS). 253

143. Ellorā: Cave XXIX (Sitā ki Nahani/Dhumar *Leṇa*), west wall, Śiva Pārvatī panel (after AIIS). 254
144. Ellorā: Cave XIV (*Rāvaṇa kā Khāi*), Śiva Pārvatī *akshakrīḍā* panel (after AIIS). 256
145. Bādāmī: Cave I, standing *Ardhanārīśvara* (after AIIS). 258
146. Aihoḷe: Rāvaṇa Phaḍi cave, rightside wall, Harihara and *Dvārapāla* (after AIIS). 260
147. Ellorā: Cave XXVII (Milkmaid's cave), Brahma, Viṣṇu and Śiva in niches (after AIIS). 261
148. Ellorā: Cave XVI, (Kailāśa), east court, east corridor gallery, *Liṅgodbhavamurti* (after AIIS). 262
149. Ellorā: Cave XVI (Kailāśa), east court, south corridor gallery, Rāvaṇa offering his nine heads to Śiva (after AIIS). 263
150. Bādāmī: Cave I, façade, right wall, *Naṭarāja* (after AIIS). 265
151. Mahābalipuram: Varāha *maṇḍapam, Naravarāha.* 270
152. Mahābalipuram: Varāha *maṇḍapam, Trivkrama.* 272
153. Bādāmī: Cave III, *Mukhamaṇḍapa*, east wall, *śeṣāsana* Viṣṇu. 274
154. Mahābalipuram: Mahiṣamardinī *maṇḍapam, maṇḍapa*, south wall, *śeṣaśayī* panel (after AIIS). 275
155. Ellorā: Cave XXI (Rameśvara), *Mahiṣamardinī* (after ASI). 278
156. Adi Varāha *maṇḍapam: Antarāla*, backwall, south extreme, *Mahiṣamardinī* (after AIIS). 279
157. Mahābalipuram: Draupadī *ratha, garbhagṛha*, Durgā panel (after AIIS). 280
158. Mahābalipuram: Draupadī *ratha* (after AIIS). 281
159. Ellorā: Cave XVI (Kailāśa), Lankeśvara section, *Mahiṣamardinī* panel (after AIIS). 281
160. Aihoḷe: Rāvaṇa Phaḍi cave, Śiva-Naṭarāja panel, Mātṛkā and Gaṇeśa (after AIIS). 283
161. Aihoḷe: Rāvaṇa Phaḍi cave, *mātṛkā* group (after AIIS). 283
162. Mahābalipuram: Adi Varāha (Paramesvara) cave, Gajalakshmī, north extreme (after AIIS). 284
163. Ellorā: Lankeśvara, entrance, Gajalakshmī panel (after AIIS). 285
164. Bādāmī: Cave II, *samudramanthana* motif above *prastara* (after AIIS). 286
165. Bādāmī: Cave II, *matsya-cakra* in ceiling, details (after AIIS). 287
166. Bādāmī: Cave I, *bhūmakara* bracket (after AIIS). 287
167. Ellorā: Cave XVII, first pillar to right of shrine, details (after AIIS). 288
168. Ellorā: Cave XVII, first pillar to right, capital detail (after AIIS). 288
169. Ellorā: Cave XXIX (Sita Ki Nahani/Dhumar *Leṇa*), pillar-capital, *Kumara* (after AIIS). 289
170. Ellorā: Cave XXI, bracket sculpture (after AIIS). 290
171. Bādāmī: Cave III, *mukhamaṇḍapa*, entrance pillar bracket, Śiva Pārvatī (after AIIS). 291
172. Bādāmī: Cave III, *mukhamaṇḍapa*, entrance pillar, *mithuna* on bracket. 292

173. Mahābalipuram: Adi Varāha (Parameśvara) *maṇḍapam*, portraits of Mahendravarman II and Queens (after AIIS). 293
174. Bādāmī: Cave II, *mukhamaṇḍapa* pillar, amorous couple (after AIIS). 294
175. Ellorā: Cave XIV (Rāvaṇa kā Khāi), *maṇḍapa*, pillar details, *mithuna* (after AIIS). 294
176. Bādāmī: Cave III, pillar shaft, *mithuna*. 295
177. Bādāmī: Cave III, pillar shaft, *mithuna*. 296
178. Ellorā: Cave XVI (Kailāśa), Kāma and Rati (after ASI). 297

COLOUR PLATES

1. Bādāmī: Cave I, chisel marks on the exterior wall.
2. Mahābalipuram: Rock cutting remains near the *rathas*.
3. Mahābalipuram: Rock chiselling marks, pilaster and sculptural carving details in Dharmarāja *ratha*.
4. Ellorā: Cave XVI (Kailāśa), courtyard, incising and carving of left wards façade.
5. Ellorā: Cave XVI (Kailāśa), left façade, pillar carving, rudimentary stage.
6. Ellorā: Cave XVI (Kailāśa), courtyard, semi-finished pillars.
7. Ellorā: Cave XVI (Kailāśa), Lankeśvara section, excavated stairs leading to first floor.
8. Mahābalipuram: Dharmarāja *ratha*, cutting of pillars from the rock, ceiling details.
9. Ellorā: Cave XVI (Kailāśa), ceiling painting, group of elephants (after ASI).
10. Aihoḷe: Rāvaṇa Phaḍi cave, exterior view.
11. Aihoḷe: Rāvaṇa Phaḍi cave, *garbhagṛha*.
12. Aihoḷe: Rāvaṇa Phaḍi cave, *garbhagṛha*, *praṇāla* outlet.
13. Bādāmī: Exterior view outside Cave I.
14. Bādāmī: Cave I, view from site entrance.
15. Bādāmī: Cave II, façade, details.
16. Bādāmī: Cave III, *mukhamaṇḍapa*, octagonal, square and fluted pillar types.
17. Bādāmī: Cave III, façade view.
18. Bādāmī: Cave III, façade, bracketed pillars.
19. Bādāmī: Cave III, *mahāmaṇḍapa*, view from the *garbhagṛha*.
20. Bādāmī: Cave III, façade, *mukhamaṇḍapa*, *mahāmaṇḍapa*, *garbhagṛha* view.
21. Bādāmī: Cave III, façade *prastara*, brackets, and the *kapota*, details.
22. Bādāmī: Cave III, *trivikrama* panel, details.
23. Ellorā: Cave XVII A, exteriors.
24. Ellorā: Cave XVII B, façade view.
25. Ellorā: Cave XVIII, entrance.
26. Ellorā: Cave XXI, façade.
27. Mahābalipuram: Cut out niche.
28. Mahābalipuram: Unfinished rock carving.
29. Mahābalipuram: Pañcapāṇḍava *rathas*.

30. Mahābalipuram: Bhīma *ratha*, façade and elevation details.
31. Mahābalipuram: Bhīma *ratha*, octagonal *vyāḷapāda* pillars in façade.
32. Mahābalipuram: *Siṁhapāda* pillar.
33. Mahābalipuram: Dharmarāja *ratha*, *vyāḷapāda* pilaster.
34. Mahābalipuram: Dharmarāja *ratha*, *kapotabandha adhiṣṭhāna*, details.
35. Mahābalipuram: Arjuna and Draupadī *rathas*, *adhiṣṭhāna*, projecting *mahāpaṭṭī* with animal busts.
36. Mahābalipuram: Dharmarāja *ratha*, *kapota* details, *haṁsāvarī* over *valabhī* moulding.
37. Mahābalipuram: Dharmarāja *ratha*, elevation details, *āditala hāra pañjara*.
38. Mahābalipuram: Bhīma *ratha*, gable roof.
39. Ellorā: Cave XVI (Kailāśa), Lankeśvara cave, *garbhagṛha*.
40. Ellorā: Cave XVI (Kailāśa), Lankeśvara cave, *maṇḍapa* pillar *pīṭha* base with mouldings.
41. Ellorā: Cave XVI (Kailāśa), exterior view.
42. Ellorā: Cave XVI (Kailāśa), view from Lankeśvara, with bright painting remnants.
43. Ellorā: Cave XVI (Kailāśa), a complex of different edifices, view from *yajñaśālā*.
44. Ellorā: Cave XVI (Kailāśa), the *vimāna* emerging alongside the hill's slope.
45. Ellorā: Cave XVI (Kailāśa), *nandīmaṇḍapa*.
46. Ellorā: Cave XVI (Kailāśa), courtyard view.
47. Ellorā: Cave XVI (Kailāśa), surrounding cloisters' inside view.
48. Ellorā: Cave XVI (Kailāśa), surrounding cloisters, external view.
49. Ellorā: Cave XVI, Lankeśvara, pillar details.
50. Ellorā: Cave XVI, Lankeśvara, pillar shaft details.
51. Ellorā: Cave XVI, Lankeśvara, pillar shaft ornamentation.
52. Ellorā: Cave XVI, Lankeśvara, pillar.
53. Ellorā: Cave XVI (Kailāśa), ground storey pillar detail.
54. Ellorā: Cave XVI (Kailāśa), ground storey, pilaster detail.
55. Ellorā: Cave XVI (Kailāśa), pilaster capital details.
56. Ellorā: Cave XVI (Kailāśa), *dhvajastaṁbha*.
57. Ellorā: Cave XVI (Kailāśa), courtyard pillar shaft, sculptured panel.
58. Ellorā: Cave XVI (Kailāśa), animal caryatids, *adhiṣṭhāna*.
59. Ellorā: Cave XVI (Kailāśa), *adhiṣṭhāna* caryatids, motif details.
60. Elephanta: Main cave, *liṅga* shrine (after ASI).
61. Ellorā: Cave XVI, Lankeśvara, amorous couples on adhiṣṭhāna.
62. Bādāmī: Cave III, erosion of ceiling paintings.
63. Bādāmī: Cave III, water seepage effects over pillar base.
64. Bādāmī: Monkey scaring visitors outside the caves.
65. Ellorā: Cave XVI, Lankeśvara, first floor left corridor, scratch marks.
66. Ellorā: Cave XVI, Lankeśvara, scratch marks.
67. Ellorā: Cave XXXIV, preservation initiatives, renovation drive.

1

A Survey of Rock-cut Architecture in India

'Rock-cut architecture' conveys the twin terms—'rock-cut' and 'architecture'. The former is related to the cutting of rock either in excavating or sculpting modes and the latter symbolizes the creation of form in space. Together, they signify the making of space inside the rock in the form of a cave.

Caves are primarily of two types: (i) natural shelters used by the primitive man for habitation, (ii) man-made caves excavated in the likelihood of natural caverns. India has had an antiquity of caves. Here the caves not only served as physical shelters but as symbols for the psychic also. They were treated as sacred for contemplation, exploring the self and realization of the Absolute in their secluded, dark environs. Caves within the mountains represented the most apt metaphor to demonstrate the fundamental relationship of the Absolute with the self. Perhaps this very fact urged the followers of various sects towards natural as well as excavated caves. Though the exact motive behind excavating rocks to create caves is still an enigma, religious considerations must have been a potent cause.

NOMENCLATURE FOR CAVE EXCAVATIONS

The Sanskrit term for cave, *guhā*[1] was derived from the root *guh*, i.e. 'to conceal, keep secret'. Therefore, *guhā* conveyed the 'concealed, secret and mysterious'.[2] The *guhā* was a place wherein the knower, knowledge and knowable were hidden, or the soul secreted in it.[3] *Jñānaguhā* was a name of *Prakṛti* in the *Bhāgavata Purāṇa*.[4] Cave was also designated as *layaṇa* or *leṇa*. In the *Upaniṣads*, the cave, identified with the heart, was the resting place of the *ātman*.[5]

The process of rock-excavation or making a cave inside the rock has been termed *kṛti*, derived from the Sanskrit root *kṛī*, meaning to cut or chisel out.[6] The Buddhists called the excavation work *selakamma* while their master stonemason was *selavaddhakī*.[7]

Initially, the excavations were likened to caves as they resembled natural caves.[8] The designation, though, was not unanimously accepted. Rather, the making of a cave was often put under the category of either architecture or sculpture. As most of them were spacious, well-planned shrines, skillfully wrought and chiseled out of the solid cliff, their adequate designation, therefore, was 'rock-architecture'.[9] Benjamin Rowland[10] also upheld the term 'cave' to be rather misleading as it implied a natural grotto serving as home to wild beasts or savages whereas these man-made mountainous recesses were actually among the most refined examples of Indian religious art history. He called these rock-hewn imitations of free-standing architectural types as 'rock-cut sanctuaries'. They were also typed as 'construction by excavation'.[11]

Another viewpoint placed the rock structures in a class of sculptures. Percy Brown[12] held that they involved no constructional principles or functional properties. Therefore, rock architecture, to all intents and purposes, was sculpture on a grand and magnificent scale. From excavating interior caves to carving out entire temple complex, as at Ellorā, the activity rather assumed form of architectural sculpture. However, G.C. Pande[13] highlighted that the Ellorā shrine, despite excavated from the mountain, remained attached to it, and thus became a cave and temple in one. Therefore, use of the nomenclature 'cave' for the rock-cut creations does not appear altogether inappropriate.

CAVES AS IMAGES AND SYMBOLS

Various images associated with the cave also conveyed its symbolism. Firstly, the image of the 'mountain' as a temple was mentioned in ancient Indian texts.[14] Merū, Mandara and Kailāśa[15] were amongst the twenty types of temples mentioned in the *Bṛhat Saṁhitā* whereas the *Matsya Purāṇa* described them as types of the mountain, the axis of the world. Several inscriptions also extolled eloquently the temple as the mountain. For instance, the Mandasor Sūrya temple inscription (437-38 AD) described the shrine with its broad and lofty spires as resembling a mountain.[16] The Gaṅgādhar stone inscription of Vishvavarman in Jhālāwār referred to a Viṣṇu temple bearing affinity to the lofty peak of Kailāśa.[17] Vijayasena's Deopārā inscription compared the Pradyumneśvara shrine to the (central) mountain on which the sun rests at midday, the only mountain worth mention amongst all.[18]

The temple as mountain also found an echo in the art. The Pārvatī temple, Nacnā Kuṭharā,[19] had the outer face of its walls covered with carved rock shapes. Architecturally, the *śikhara* cluster symbolized the final shape of all the 'mountain peaks'. This aspect of the temple preserved the memory of a cult, the cult of caverns, and corresponded to the immediate realization of the cavity of the heart.[20] Thus, the mountain temple image linked the temple abode of gods to another abode of cave within the mountain.

Secondly, the *guhā* denoted an inner or enclosed space. In the Vedic traditions, the image of *guhā* in the cosmogonic myth of Indra and Vṛtra[21] rendered an ambiguous implication where the cave either concealed the light as the 'cows'[22] or revealed the inner light.[23] The closed cave was associated with oppression and darkness where the hidden demon was slain by Indra.[24] The open cave variously became the 'seat of *Ṛta*', the 'rock of heaven' (*divo adrim*), the womb of the mountain (*parvatasya garbha*), or the stone house (*harmya*). In the *Atharva Veda*, *guhā* assumed the mystical meaning of a 'secret, mysterious or concealed place'.[25] In the hidden recesses of the external and interior cave, the seer had the vision of the unity of all things.

Thirdly, *guhā* was likened to the *garbha* or womb. The *bīja*, i.e. god, as a seed developing inside the womb, was in the *garbhagṛha* that was to be excavated. The cave temples and also the structural shrines comprised of *garbhagṛha*, the symbolic inner 'cave' of the temple 'mountain'. Entering into it was like entering into the darkness to find the light. Thus, the cave became a place of spiritual rebirth.[26] 'Return to the mother's womb' was often indicated by narrow entrance to the sacred caves. By entering the cave, the external cave became a sacrament of his own interior cave for the devotee. Hence, *guhā* as *garbha* must have assumed great symbolism.

Fourthly, cave was also conceptualized as a treasure chest, *nidhi* or *koṣa*. *Divasprstādguhā nidhi nihitau Brāhmaṇasya* connoted that the treasures of sacred lore of a Brāhmaṇa are hidden in a cave.[27] Another related notion was that the most precious mystery must be protected like a treasure.[28]

The *Śatapatha Brāhmaṇa* equated the *guhā* with the heart.[29] The 'cavity of the living being', its heart, was the place where the self or the God was believed to be present. This space, therefore, had to be left empty for its real occupant, the *Ātman* or *Puruṣa*.[30] Terms such as *guhācara* and *guhām praviśya* suggested that the presence of the *Ātman* in the *guhā* was not merely static but also dynamic. The individual soul and the supreme *Ātman* were said to have entered the 'secret cave of the heart and the highest upper sphere'. The *Śvetāśvatara Upaniṣad* described the macrocosmic and microcosmic soul as residing in the *guhā* or the depth of beings.[31] This image gave rise to *guhā* as a symbol of withdrawal, or the innermost secret recess where sense impressions were excluded and the innermost Being was revealed[32] to the ascetics meditating therein.

Above all, the *guhā* served as the abode of gods. The *Vāyu Purāṇa* mentioned various kinds of residences on different mountains.[33] Śiva was called *guhāśaya* in the *Śvetāśvatara Upaniṣad*. In the *Śatarūdrīya*, he was praised as the 'one who has entered the cavity or the depth'[34] and also as the *hṛdaya*. He was called *guheśvara*,[35] i.e. the lord of the external and interior caves. The famous Kandariyā Mahādeva temple at Khajuraho exemplifies this aspect of Śiva. Furthering the symbolism, *Bhāgvata Purāṇa* suggested that the divine Being, the lord of all beings, dwells in the *guhā*.[36] Brahmā was conceived as residing in the *guhā*.[37] Guhārāja was held to be the best temple form by Varāhamihira.[38] The imagery, however, was not confined to Vedic thought. The name Guhāgupta for a Bodhisattva in the *Mahāvyutpatti* and the *Ṣaḍdharmapuṇḍarīkasūtra* signified *guhā* as the angelic guardian of a person. Divinities within a *stūpa* were located in a cave. For example, in the *Sādhanamālā*, Goddess Uṣṇīśa-vijayā sat inside a cavern in the *caitya*.[39]

Indian thought and symbols explicitly proved that cave was the archetypal symbol of the meditator's heart where he withdrew to seek inner light. The essential process was one of recovering a form or idea *avyakta* or latent in material in conscience. The *gahā*, i.e. home, symbolized the psychic matrix of bondage in early Buddhist parlance. Therein the monk left his home behind and retreated within, from *gahā* to *guhā*.[40]

Thus, it is apparent that the cave was the solitary vision beyond reflections. The intimacy of concentration within led to the light on the far horizon that could be realized as nothing but: *O Licht in Schlafenden Haus*—O Light in sleeping house.[41]

EXCAVATION ACTIVITIES OUTSIDE INDIA

Cave excavations were not restricted to India alone. The early Brāhmī inscriptions of Srī Lankā have mostly been recovered in caves. A total of 1,234 inscriptions have been inscribed in caves, mostly natural rock-shelters.[42] These included the inscriptions of Uttiya, younger brother of Devānāmpiya Tissā, under whom Buddhism was introduced into Srī Lankā.[43]Ashoka's son Mahendra, on his arrival in Ceylon, erected a *vihāra* on Mihintala mountain, where sixty-eight cells, still existing at Ambustella dagoba, were cut out of rock.[44]

In China, the Ming-oi caves at Kizil commenced in second century AD. Bāmiyān (Afghanistan) was honey-combed with scores of rock-cut caves, *vihāras* and shrines, while interior galleries provided access to the sculpted head of the colossal Buddha. In Tibet too, caves near *vihāras* served as meditation retreats. Rock-cut monuments also existed in ancient Egypt and Greece. This wide global presence has made the origin of Indian rock excavations a contentious issue.

ORIGIN OF INDIAN CAVE ARCHITECTURE

It is a debatable issue with contrary claims of foreign and indigenous origin being advocated. The exponents of foreign origin held that rock-cut monuments were the most ambitious examples of the development of monumental stone carving following Alexander's invasion and the establishment of relations with Western Asia.[45] Though no direct resemblance to sculptural architecture in Egypt, Asia Minor or Iran could be detected yet the *caityas* were treated as reproduction of actual Achaemenid buildings as the Naqsh-i-Rustam tombs. Percy Brown,[46] on the basis of the affinity between façade of the tomb of Darius at Persepolis and the Lomaś Ṛṣi cave, opined that the fully mature nature of Indian stone architecture was a derivation from the art repertory of a more advanced people. Fergusson expounded a similar idea that nothing properly called architecture was to be found in India until after Alexander's invasion.[47]

The indigenous origin of rock excavations has also been suggested. Burgess explained the phenomena on the basis of geological factor, i.e. availability of rocks suitable for the purpose.[48] Certain rock-cut tombs at Mennapuram, near Tellicerry in Kerala were believed by Dubreuil to be the remains of a Vedic fire-altar in a cave form.[49] Refuting the popular notion of antiquity of Mauryan caves at Barābar and Nāgārjunī as most primitive specimens of rock-cut architecture, S.P. Gupta[50] held that they marked the culmination and not the beginning of Indian cave architecture. Another view[51] highlighted the coincidence in the rise of Sātavāhana kingdom and consequent expansion of overseas trade with the first cutting of rock monasteries in Western India. The mobility of the artist and his subsequent exposure to new ideas within the country must have helped in shaping of the art.[52] Therefore, the indigenous origin of Indian rock art holds substantial credence.

LOCATION

As the ancient cave sites were mostly located on major trade routes, their mutual relation attracts obvious attention.[53] Their location[54] perhaps depended on a combination of factors. Seeking donations from merchants and traders for the rock-cut complexes might have been the primary motive. Besides, if they were conveniently located, the architects and sculptors could be easily cajoled to work on the caves. The monks could easily resume their wanderings from such locations once rains were over. Soon, however, these temporary settlements acquired permanent character, especially, after being endowed with fields, villages and their perpetual gifts.[55]

EARLIEST CAVES

Originally associated with Buddhism, the phase of rock architecture in India extended approximately over a period of thousand years. The caves in Barābar and Nāgārjunī hills, near Patna, excavated during Ashoka and Dasharatha for Ājīvikā monks as *varṣā niṣidiya* dwellings, are generally believed to be the earliest known examples of Indian rock-cut art.[56] However, S.P. Gupta has held that the high quality of polish, multi-chambered plan and the variety in conception goes against this theory.[57]A clear-cut hiatus between the natural cave dwellings of pre-historic times and the Mauryan man-made caves has been detected, tracing their roots to the natural caves of Rāmgarh, Budhāni, Son Bhaṇdār, etc.[58]

The Buddhist excavations categorized into early (*Hīnayāna*) and later (*Mahāyāna*) phases represented the *vihāra*[59] and *caitya*[60] types. However, the antiquity of the latter, prior to Buddhism, is well established.[61] The development of Buddhism from the isolated practice of asceticism to a monastic organization must have necessitated enlargement of the single rock-cut cell[62] to monumental rock-cut assembly halls as found in Western India.[63] This may have led to the replacement of the single cell rock-cut model for the forest ascetic by *bhikshu-gṛhas* or clusters of cells for wandering monks.[64] Hence, the gradual evolution of monastic cells into monastery courts and finally into monastic shrines. The *vihāra* of Pāli canon might have been the structural prototype of rock-cut *vihāras*.[65] The *vihāra* was a main hall supported on pillars while the typical *caitya* consisted of a round apse containing the solid stone *stūpa*[66] with an aisle or *pradakshiṇāpatha* on its two sides. In the early *vihāras*, the architectural plans were simple. But from about second century AD, they became quite complex. In the accounts of Hieun Tsang and Fahien elaborate *sanghārams* were mentioned, sometimes having five storeys, each diminishing by hundred cells and the lowermost storey comprising five hundred cells.[67]At Kanherī, an elaborate system of inter-connected canals and aqueducts, *panādī*, is suggestive of water arrangements in such structures.[68]

The *caitya* probably arose out of ritualistic needs of Buddhism, for with the emergence of the *stūpa* as a cult object, a building for its display and accommodation of the congregation was required.[69] Hitherto religious rites were conducted in the open and no tradition for a temple was in vogue.[70] Still further, the ambitious plan of producing an exclusive rock-cut temple may have led to the excavation of the *caitya-vihāra* consisting of a shrine with attached cells. The long process of evolution of *Hīnayāna caitya* form may be traced from third century BC Barābar excavations. Passing through Bhājā, Koṇḍane, Pitalkhorā and Ajantā, the activity continued at Bedsā, Nāsik to its culmination at Kārle. The progress, though slow yet steady, may be recognized in its gradual emancipation from wooden conventions.[71] The early phase of rock excavations ceased virtually in second century AD. From fifth century AD, stimulated by the cultural conditions and congenial atmosphere created during the Gupta age, the Buddhists revived their rock-cut architectural activity. The new, *Mahāyāna* rock excavations emerged at specific localities, such as Ellorā, Aurangābād and Ajantā in Western India.[72]

Changes in the nature of Buddhism also led to alteration in the stylistic treatment of excavated halls. The form of *vihāra* though retained, its inner cells were converted into shrines for the installation of Buddha images. In *caityas* too, Buddha images were introduced on the façades and interior walls. The apsidal *caitya* form disappeared with removal of the *stūpa* as the primary object of reverence. After seventh century AD, as far as the Buddhists were concerned, rock-cut form of expression ceased. The induction of *Vajrayāna*, elements of tantricism, magic, sexual mysticism, etc. heralded a transformation. By the end of eighth century AD, Buddhism itself was declining while a reformed and revived Hinduism began excavation of a series of pillared halls in identical style, though adapted to its own ritualistic creeds.

Thus, rock excavations in India developed as visual architectural forms. Beginning as simple excavations, the activity under the Buddhists and Jainas reached culmination in form of multi-storey projected like buildings inside the caves. The Vaiṣṇava and Śaiva sects carried the process further. However, they did not fully copy the *caitya* or *vihāra* models, but excavated their own types of cave temples.

Cave temple signified a different meaning in the new ideology. The Hindus identified the cave as a *guhā* with *garbhagṛha*. Thus, it pronounced a living place for the god, i.e. new form for a temple.

TEMPLE

Known variously as *devālaya*, *devāyatana*, *devakula*, *devagṛha*, etc., temple implied a residence of the god. It was also looked upon as an image of god and, therefore, worshipped by *pradakshiṇā*, circumambulation.[73] In all likeness to the *Puruṣa*, the temple had its various components[74] named as *janghā*, *mastaka*, *kaṇṭha*, *grīvā*, *nāsikā*, etc., after human body parts. Making of temples, both structural and excavated, has been a long tradition under various Indian regional dynasties including the Guptas, Cālukyas, Pallavas, and Rāṣṭrakūṭas. Subsequently, several *śilpaśāstras* and *vāstuvidyā* texts were compiled as canons of temple architecture providing a theoretical insight into their foundation principles.

Pl. 1. Bādāmī: Cave I, chisel marks on the exterior wall.

Pl. 2. Mahābalipuram: Rock cutting remains near the *rathas*.

Pl. 3. Mahābalipuram: Rock chiselling marks, pilaster and sculptural carving details in Dharmarāja *Ratha.*

Pl. 4. Ellorā: Cave XVI (Kailāśa), courtyard, incising and carving of left wards façade.

Pl. 5. Ellorā: Cave XVI (Kailāśa), left façade, pillar carving, rudimentary stage.

Pl. 6. Ellorā: Cave XVI (Kailāśa), courtyard, semi-finished pillars.

Pl. 7. Ellorā: Cave XVI (Kailāśa), Lankeśvara section, excavated stairs leading to first floor.

Pl. 8. Mahābalipuram: Dharmarāja *Ratha*, cutting of pillars from the rock, ceiling details.

Pl. 9. Ellorā: Cave XVI (Kailāśa), ceiling painting, group of elephants (after ASI).

Pl. 10. Aihoḷe: Rāvaṇa Phaḍi cave, exterior view.

Pl. 11. Aihoḷe: Rāvaṇa Phaḍi cave, *garbhagṛha*.

Pl. 12. Aihoḷe: Rāvaṇa Phaḍi cave, *garbhagṛha*, *praṇāla* outlet.

Pl. 13. Bādāmī: Exterior view outside Cave I.

Pl. 14. Bādāmī: Cave I, view from site entrance.

Pl. 15. Bādāmī: Cave II, façade, details.

Pl. 16. Bādāmī: Cave III, *mukhamaṇḍapa*, octagonal, square and fluted pillar types.

Pl. 17. Bādāmī: Cave III, façade view.

Pl. 18. Bādāmī: Cave III, façade, bracketed pillars.

Pl. 19. Bādāmī: Cave III, *mahāmaṇḍapa*, view from the *garbhagṛha*.

Pl. 20. Bādāmī: Cave III, façade, *mukhamaṇḍapa*, *mahāmaṇḍapa*, *garbhagṛha* view.

Pl. 21. Bādāmī: Cave III, façade *prastara*, brackets, and the *kapota*, details.

Pl. 22. Bādāmī: Cave III, *trivikrama* panel, details.

Pl. 23. Ellorā: Cave XVII A, exteriors.

Pl. 24. Ellorā: Cave XVII B, façade view.

Pl. 25. Ellorā: Cave XVIII, entrance.

Pl. 26. Ellorā: Cave XXI, façade.

Pl. 27. Mahābalipuram: Cut out niche.

Pl. 28. Mahābalipuram: Unfinished rock carving.

Pl. 29. Mahābalipuram: Pañcapāṇḍava *Rathas.*

Pl. 30. Mahābalipuram: Bhīma *Ratha*, façade and elevation details.

Pl. 31. Mahābalipuram: Bhīma *Ratha*, octagonal *vyāḷapāda* pillars in façade.

Pl. 32. Mahābalipuram: *Siṁhapāda* pillar.

Pl. 33. Mahābalipuram: Dharmarāja *Ratha*, *vyāḷapāda* pilaster.

Pl. 34. Mahābalipuram: Dharmarāja *Ratha*, *kapotabandha adhiṣṭhāna*, details.

Pl. 35. Mahābalipuram: Arjuna and Draupadī *Rathas*, *adhiṣṭhāna*, projecting *mahāpaṭṭī* with animal busts.

Pl. 37. Mahābalipuram: Dharmarāja *Ratha*, elevation details*, āditala hāra pañjara*.

Pl. 36. Mahābalipuram: Dharmarāja *Ratha*, *kapota* details, *haṁsāvarī* over *valabhī* moulding.

Pl. 38. Mahābalipuram: Bhīma *ratha*, gable roof.

Pl. 39. Ellorā: Cave XVI (Kailāśa), Lankeśvara cave, *garbhagṛha.*

Pl. 40. Ellorā: Cave XVI (Kailāśa), Lankeśvara cave, *maṇḍapa* pillar *pīṭha* base with mouldings.

Pl. 41. Ellorā: Cave XVI (Kailāśa), exterior view.

Pl. 42. Ellorā: Cave XVI (Kailāśa), view from Lankeśvara, with bright painting remnants.

Pl. 43. Ellorā: Cave XVI (Kailāśa), a complex of different edifices, view from *yajñaśālā.*

Pl. 44. Ellorā: Cave XVI (Kailāśa), the *vimāna* emerging alongside the hill's slope.

Pl. 46. Ellorā: Cave XVI (Kailāśa), courtyard view.

Pl. 45. Ellorā: Cave XVI (Kailāśa), *nandīmaṇḍapa*.

Pl. 47. Ellorā: Cave XVI (Kailāśa), surrounding cloisters' inside view.

Pl. 48. Ellorā: Cave XVI (Kailāśa), surrounding cloisters, external view.

Pl. 49. Ellorā: Cave XVI, Lankeśvara, pillar details.

Pl. 50. Ellorā: Cave XVI, Lankeśvara, pillar shaft details.

Pl. 51. Ellorā: Cave XVI, Lankeśvara, pillar shaft ornamentation.

Pl. 52. Ellorā: Cave XVI, Lankeśvara, pillar.

Pl. 53. Ellorā: Cave XVI (Kailāśa), ground storey pillar detail.

Pl. 54. Ellorā: Cave XVI (Kailāśa), ground storey, pilaster detail.

Pl. 55. Ellorā: Cave XVI (Kailāśa), pilaster capital details.

Pl. 56. Ellorā: Cave XVI (Kailāśa), *dhvajastaṁbha.*

Pl. 57. Ellorā: Cave XVI (Kailāśa), courtyard pillar shaft, sculptured panel.

Pl. 58. Ellorā: Cave XVI (Kailāśa), animal caryatids, *adhiṣṭhāna*.

Pl. 59. Ellorā: Cave XVI (Kailāśa), *adhiṣṭhāna* caryatids, motif details.

Pl. 60. Elephanta: Main cave, *liṅga* shrine (after ASI).

Pl. 61. Ellorā: Cave XVI, Lankeśvara, amorous couples on adhiṣṭhāna.

Pl. 62. Bādāmī: Cave III, erosion of ceiling paintings.

Pl. 63. Bādāmī: Cave III, water seepage effects over pillar base.

Pl. 64. Bādāmī: Monkey scaring visitors outside the caves.

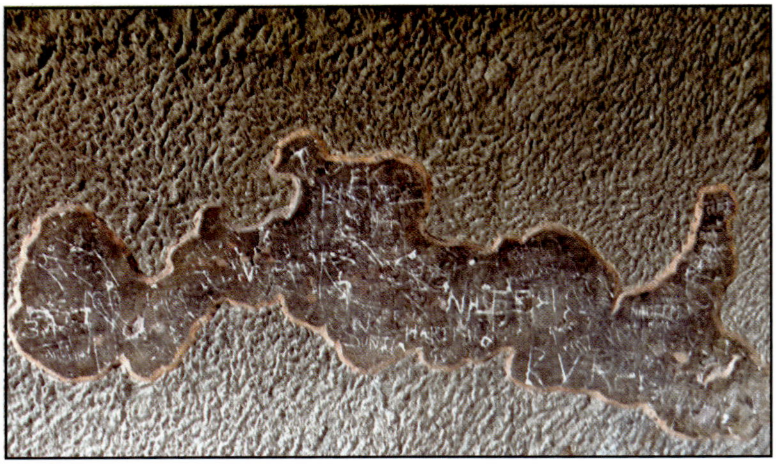

Pl. 65. Ellorā: Cave XVI, Lankeśvara, first floor left corridor, scratch marks.

Pl. 66. Ellorā: Cave XVI, Lankeśvara, scratch marks.

Pl. 67. Ellorā: Cave XXXIV, preservation initiatives, renovation drive.

Amongst prominent South Indian *vāstu* texts, the *Aṁśumadbhedāgama, Kāmikāgama, Kāraṇāgama, Vaikhānasāgama, Suprabhedāgama, Mayamatam, Viśvakarmaśilpa, Viśvakarmaprakāśa, Śilpasaṁgṛha, Bṛhat Saṁhitā, Pāñcarātra*[75] *Āgamas, Mānasāra, Samarāngaṇa Sūtradhāra, Īśānaśivagurudevapaddhati, Śilparatnam*, etc., primarily elaborated upon structural temple architecture.

The earliest classification of structural styles given in the *vāstuśāstras*[76] comprised of the schools of Viśvakarmā and Maya. Later temples were variously grouped as geographical divisions, after a tribe or a dynasty. Geographically, Nāgara, Draviḍa and Vesara conveyed threefold classification.[77] Nāgara denoted the region between the Himālayas and Vindhyas, while Draviḍa signified the territory between river Kṛṣṇā and Kanyākumārī.[78] The region Vesara was not clearly defined, though sometimes suggested between the Vindhyas and the Kṛṣṇā. Thus, geographically Nāgara in North India and Draviḍa in Deccan and South India constituted the earliest temple orders. However, the large sub-varieties[79] given in the *vāstuśāstras* could not be applied to the existing temples; as such it did not prove to be a scientific classification.

Fergusson classified Indian temples as Indo Āryan, Draviḍian and Cālukyan types on ethnic grounds.[80] A somewhat more rational distinction was recommended on the technical basis of temple ground plan and elevation. Plan wise, the North Indian *prāsāda* temples were almost always *caturārṣa*. The South Indian temples had a *caturārṣa garbhagṛha* within a bigger square *pradakshiṇā* enclosure.

Elevationally in North India, the *śikhara* was gradually inclined inwards in a convex curve. The projections in the plan were also carried upwards to the top emphasizing verticality. The *āmalaka, āmalasāra* or *āmlaṣmhī* under the *kalaśa* was also characteristic of Nāgara temples. The South Indian *vimāna* had a pyramidal elevation consisting of multi-storeyed *talas*, each a replica of the *garbhagṛha*, ending in *stūpikā* with *kalaśa*. The *kapota* with *caitya kūḍūs* and miniature *śālās* around the upper *talas* remained other features of the style. Thus, the classification of structural temples, either on type of ground plan or elevation *śikhara*, seems to be the most appropriate one as it conveyed their stylistic distinctness accurately.

However, classification of the excavated cave temples was a more difficult task. They did not consist of the *śikhara* or other architectural elements as seen in a structural edifice. Rather, in the early forms, they were merely interiors, with a façade. It was only in a few later instances, as at Mahābalipuram or Ellorā, that partial or full replicas of structural shrines were attempted in rock. So they could only be classified on the basis of their plan and religious/sectarian affiliations, as Buddhist or Brāhmanical.

CHRONOLOGY AND EXTENT

While the Buddhist *Hīnayāna* and *Mahāyāna* excavations were created from third century BC to seventh century AD, the Brāhmanical cave temples in Deccan commenced between fifth-sixth centuries AD.[81] Down south, the earliest suggested date for an excavated shrine is seventh century, given in Maṇḍagappaṭṭū

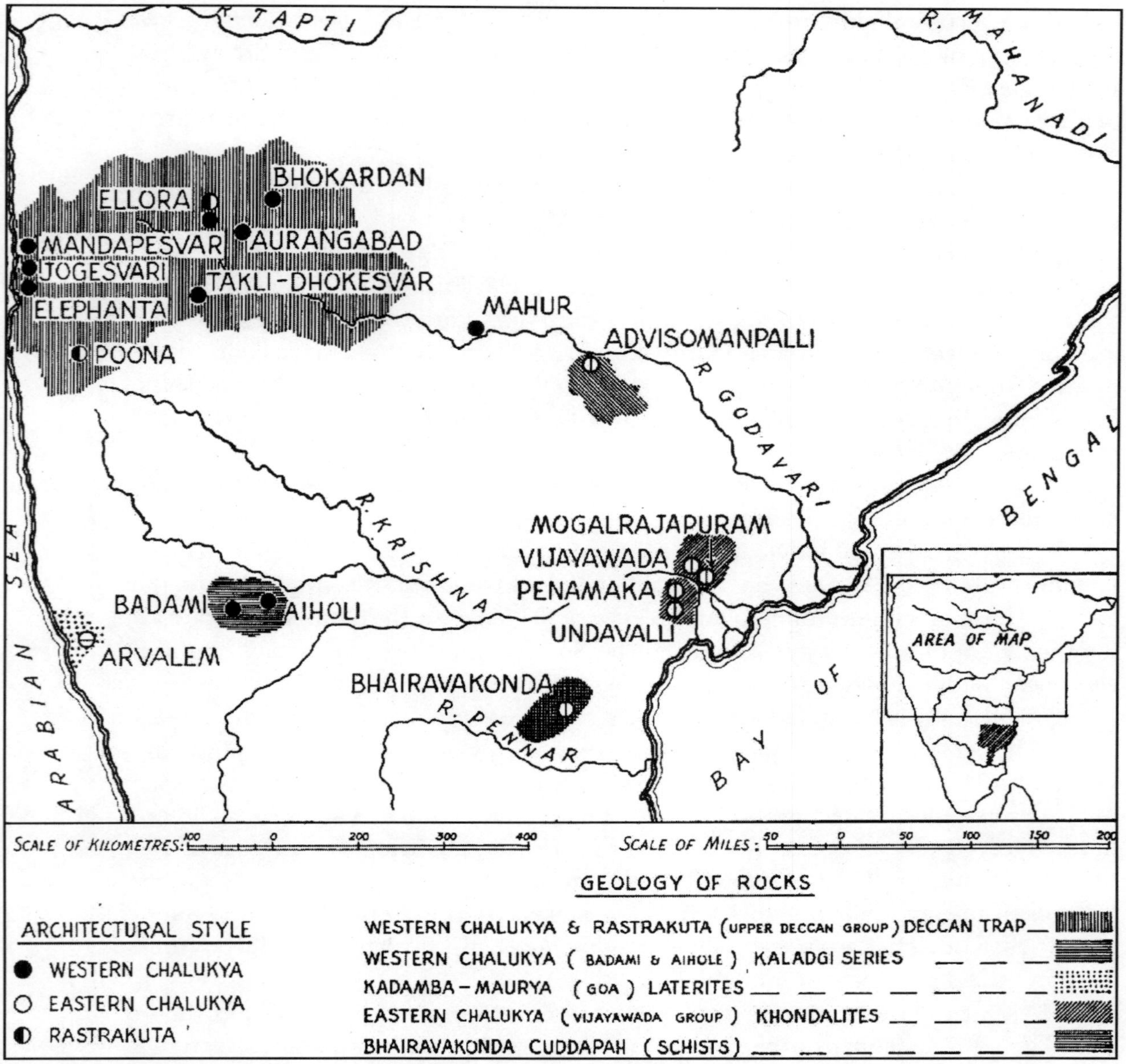

Map 1. Cālukya and Rāṣṭrakūṭa cave temple sites (after Soundara Rajan 1981).

inscription.[82] The Jainas also began excavations around the same time. The extent of rock excavations may be seen in Western, Eastern and Southern India. Of a total of around 1,200 excavations, the Buddhists claimed nearly 75%, Brāhmanical caves constituted 18%, while Jainas had 4% to their share.[83] The prominent Buddhist sites included Kārle, Koṇḍane, Bhājā, Ajantā, Bāgh, Ellorā, Aurangābād, Kanherī, Udaigiri, etc.

The Brāhmanical shrines were excavated in Deccan by Cālukyas and Rāṣṭrakūṭas at Aihoḷe, Bādāmī, Elephanta, and Ellorā (Map 1); and down South, in and around Mahābalipuram, Uṇḍāvallī, etc., by the Pallavas and Paṇḍyas (Map 2).

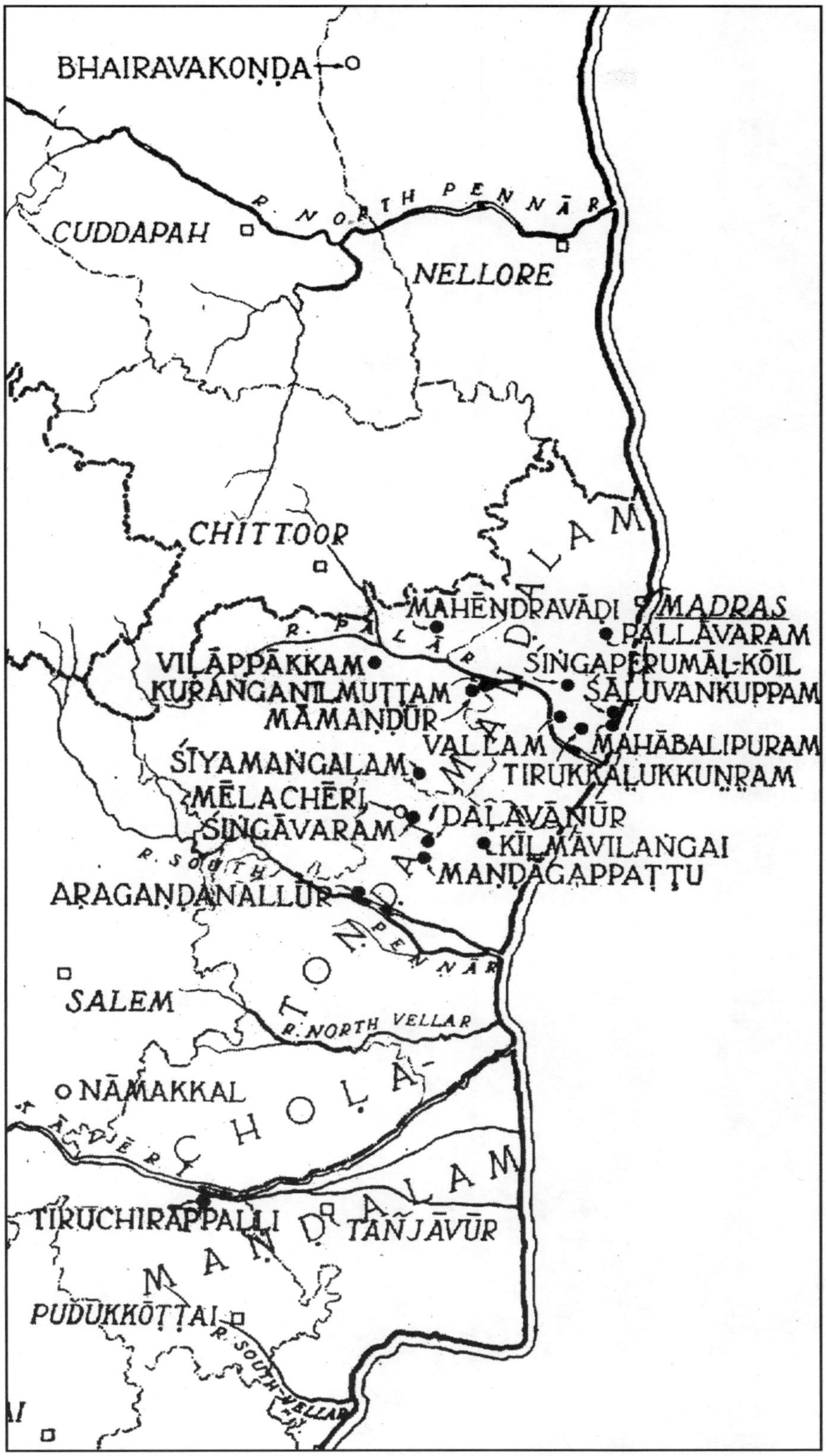

Map 2. Pallava cave temple and monolith sites (after Srinivasan 1993).

Fig. 1. Bādāmī: Cave I, chisel marks on the exterior wall.

ROCK TYPES

The earliest caves in Barābar and Nāgārjunī hills were quarried out of hard quartzite gneiss forming this range. Those in Eastern and Western regions were constituted from softer trap formations as Deccan basalt, Goṇḍwānā sandstone, Cretaceous sandstone and Vindhyan sandstone.[84] Burgess explained that trap rocks lying horizontally in Western India were singularly uniform in their conformation with alternating strata of harder and softer rocks[85] facilitating excavation of caves. Elephanta and Ellorā caves were carved from Deccan basalt.[86] Towards south, the Cālukyan caves were cut into finely grained, horizontally stratified soft sandstone, while down south the Pallavas utilized the very hard, close grained granite rock for their excavations.

TOOLS

No written information survives about the nature of tools or the process of rock-excavations. Accordingly, we have to rely exclusively on observations made in the unfinished caves. The traces therein help inference that the main tools used were pointed chisel (Pls. 1-3) and iron mallet.[87] Flat chisels of varying width were employed to polish the rock face. A pick-axe was resorted only if the rock was very soft.[88] Thus, for the purpose of excavations, especially in soft rocks, simple tools like pick-axe, chisel and hammer were used (Figs. 1-3). An idea of the tools and excavation process can be had from the copingstone relief from Bharhūt.[89]

Fig. 2. Mahābalipuram: Rock cutting remains near *rathas.*

TECHNIQUES OF CAVE EXCAVATIONS

The technique of excavation was quite significant in the development of cave temple architecture. The Buddhist caves were replicas of wooden models. Similarly, the Brāhmanical cave temples were monument-oriented temples (Fig. 4). They were unable to initially adapt their forms and technique to the rock medium and built the interior parts in wood. The main medium known till then was wood, while *tṛṣṭā* was one of the foremost artists. Therefore, the arch, railings, ribs to strengthen curved wooden roof, pillars to support roof, *kīrtimukha* to provide light inside the cave, designs and techniques indispensable to the woodworker were all exactly reproduced in stone (Figs. 5-6). Even the smallest details of structural forms were recreated in rock, correctly aligned, mathematically straight and superbly finished (Figs. 7-9). The relief of Indra's Paradise at Bharhūt accurately reproduced a wooden *caitya* hall.[90] However, in the cave temples architecture was not as important as sculptural/decorative components. The techniques and tools were mostly the ones used by the Buddhists for early excavations.

The technique of rock excavation primarily involved two methods: (i) *Stepped Method*: The method of enlarging an initial working platform. Under this, first the rock face was polished and the façade sketched in and incised (Pls. 4-6). If a high chamber was to be hewn out, the workmen commenced by digging a tunnel into the rock beneath the stipulated ceiling (Figs. 10-11). This was first widened and then deepened by cutting steps (Pl. 7). On each level an artisan followed the stonemason, to polish the walls. The rough work with the pickaxe and pointed chisel was, perhaps, carried out by the same artisan. While he worked

Fig. 3. Mahābalipuram: Rock chiselling marks, pilaster and sculptural carving details in Dharmarāja *ratha.*

Fig. 4. Ellorā: Cave XVI (Kailāśa), excavated monument replica in courtyard.

Fig. 5. Bādāmī: Cave III, pillar top rafting intersections.

his way deeper into the mountain, plasterers and painters followed along behind to work in the front part of the chamber.

(ii) *Method of Digging Shafts*: Under this, the stone masons dug trenches into the ground on the levels where they were working, leaving ribs of rock standing between the trenches, which were roughly the same width. Breaking through these ribs from both sides simultaneously, using several chisels as wedges was relatively an easy matter.

The advantage of stepped method over digging one was that wedges could be driven in vertically, so that the rock broken away fell down on to the step immediately below and could then easily be carried over the lower steps to the exit. The *caitya* halls were apparently always hewn out in this way.

The excavation work always proceeded in stages. Firstly, the stonemasons penetrated from a tunnel downwards to the top of the proposed colonnade. The rubble was removed through the *caitya* window. With the barrel roof having obtained its final appearance, work would begin on hewing out the lower zone, in the second stage. The last stage was the working of the pillars, which were initially in a rough state.

Fig. 6. Mahābalipuram: Chiselled *ratha* pillar capitals.

Some early Pallava caves at Mahābalipuram provide first-hand information about the technique used to hollow out low chambers.[91] The artisans incised the colonnade on the polished rock of the façade and divided the remaining areas that had to be worked into square panels (Pl. 8). Deep grooves were then cut along the incised lines with a pointed chisel so that regular bosses were left. These protrusions could then easily be hewn off by striking them from the side (Fig. 12). When the first layer had been removed, squaring lines were drawn and another layer of hard granite chiseled away. The process was repeated in the interior of the cave until the chamber reached its desired size. In this case, unlike the Buddhist caves, the rough work was done separately from the sculpturing of the detail. Only after the entire rock-cut temple had been given a roughly hewn surface, did the artisans begin to cut away the final layer of the protrusions, to polish the walls and finish the pillars. The remarkable manipulative skill displayed in fashioning these architectural forms implies that the workmen employed were by no means mere beginners.

Fig. 7. Ellorā: Cave XVI (Kailāśa), timber roofing reproduction in rock (with painting marks), details.

DIFFERENCES IN SOFT AND HARD ROCK EXCAVATIONS

The techniques of excavations (both cut-in caves and carve-out monoliths) in hard granite rock had naturally to be different from that employed in softer rocks as sandstone, trap, limestone, etc. No traces of methods of early excavations in the hard gneiss rock caves of Barābar group exist presently. Towards south the Pallava and Pāṇḍya specimens of a later period, left off at different stages from commencement to completion, throw light upon the hard rock excavation technique. That the whole must have been a laborious hammer and chisel work is apparent from a study of such unfinished instances by Srinivasan.[92]

Initially, the chosen face of the hard rock was cut into, to an appropriate depth till a vertical scarp of the desired height could be obtained. In these rocks with a straight cleavage, this process, called *aravaḍiṭṭal* in Tamil, was perhaps done by marking a line of wedge-shaped holes about 1″ square and as much deep at short intervals, with hammer and chisel. A number of flat-edged iron wedges (*āppu*) of the same thickness were inserted into these holes and driven in with a heavy hammer. The pressure and the concussion of the enclosed air split the rock to a considerable extent downwards, which could thus be removed in sizable pieces.

Fig. 8. Mahābalipuram: Bhīma *ratha*, east façade, second storey, wooden architecture technique, details (after AIIS).

Having obtained the desired surface of suitable dimensions, the actual quarrying was made by blocking out the face of the prepared scarp into large squares of about 2′ and cutting grooves all round the squares to a depth of about 2-3″ so that the squares themselves projected out as relief. The projecting material of these squares was, subsequently, chiseled off by lateral and centripetal strokes. The

Fig. 9. Mahābalipuram: Bhīma *ratha*, *candraśālā*, north façade, *mādala* details (after AIIS).

process was repeated. The progress of the quarrying was kept uniform over the entire region, thus maintaining an even depth of excavation at every stage. While doing so, the positions of the façade pillars, etc., which were to be left intact, were roughly marked and the excavation in the above manner continued into the intervening spaces. The general architectural components as pillars, beams, cornices were finished finally by a more careful chiseling in which work the 'feathering' strokes predominated so that smooth, even surfaces were obtained according to the granulation and texture of the rock. It also appears that while the rough quarrymen went excavating inside, a second set followed finishing the details from outside inwards and from above downwards.[93]

The hardness of material also entailed greater time to work on it. Therefore, these excavations could only be of lesser depth, height and width in comparison to the softer specimens. Besides, the hard stone carving and sculptural embellishments had to be limited in quantity and executed in semi-relief and large size in contrast to the numerous, smaller intricate carvings and relief of softer medium where the worker, rooted in traditions of wooden-carving, exhibited the same tendency for embellishment even at the cost of architectural effect. Against this, the South Indian cave temples and monoliths present greater architectural effect, less ornamented pillars, more plain faces, etc.

TIME TAKEN

As to the amount of time taken by the craftsmen to accomplish work on a cave, scholars express divergent opinions. For early Buddhist caves as at Kārle, the stipulation ranges from sixty years[94] to 'just a few years'.[95] Kosambi opined, 'The formidable undertaking, chipped by patient hand labor out of the most refractory of stone must have taken several generations.'[96] However, while sixty years' time seems excessive, a few years appear inadequate.[97] The symmetrical plan reveals influence of a single master craftsman and to extend work to generations, beyond his own life span, is again inappropriate. A period of ten to fifteen years seems to be more acceptable.[98]

Fig. 10. Mahābalipuram: Dharmarāja *ratha*, view across the façade.

Fig. 11. Elephanta: Cave 4, façade, pillar attached to the parent rock (after AIIS).

Though there is a complete lack of evidence regarding the amount of time and number of workers involved in excavations at any early cave site in India, the early Chinese caves furnish interesting information. The inscribed throne of the gigantic Buddha in the Feng Hsien Su excavation at Lungmen mentions that the cave work began on 1st April 672 and was completed on 30th December 675 covering a period of 3 years and 9 months.[99] This evidence indicates that it was physically possible for colossal caves to be excavated in a surprisingly short period of time. Therefore, it cautions us against exaggerated time recommendations for Indian excavations.

Among the later excavations, for Ellorā shrine complex it is surmised that thousands of expert masons had worked upon it for a period of about hundred years.[100]

ECONOMICS OF CAVE TEMPLE EXCAVATIONS

Although the later cave temples in Deccan and South India were mainly royal enterprises, the early caves are mainly assignable to generosity by the traders and laity. We get inscriptional evidences[101] revealing the tendency of benefactions, among cross-sections of society.

Donations did play an important role in bearing the architectural expenses and craftsmen's wages. With commencement of the monument work, devotees must have come forth with their contributions. Another surmise is that after the cave excavation plan was finalized, donations were invited. In this context, social changes such as emergence of a wealthy trader class, a general increase of wealth and the rise of great families may explain proliferation of this artistic patronage. Such factors described as 'useful satellites of architectural history'[102] might have contributed towards this development along with ancillary factors.

Payment was considered especially important for ecclesiastical work, for a patron could acquire merit if only he bore its cost. This spirit was exhibited when the Ruvaṇveli *stūpa* in Ceylon was built by Duttha Gamini (161-137 BC).[103] Donations to a religious establishment were usually referred to as *deya-dhamma,* i.e. meritorious gift. Such gifts were given by cross-sections of the society. For instance, fairly substantial donations towards the excavation of Western caves came from a class of people from whom such gifts were not usual. A *lohavāṇiya* from Karādh donated a cave at Kudā, while another was given by *mālākāra*; at Nāsik, a cave was donated by a fisherman, *dāsakas,*

Fig. 12. Ellorā: Cave XVI, southern side cloister niche, protrusion grooves.

while at Kanherī by a blacksmith, *kamāra*. Joint donations were not unknown. A Kārle pillar was given by the traders' association, *vāṇiya gāma*, from Dhenukākaṭa[104] and a Junnār cave by a guild of corn-dealers. In the Western Indian caves, apart from such donations, large perpetual endowments by the rulers and the donations of *mahārathīs* and *mahābhojas* were also made.[105] However, the majority of endowments came from the merchant class[106] while the monks and nuns themselves formed the next largest group, excluding royalty and higher officials.[107]

SOCIOLOGY OF THE EXCAVATIONS

Excavations into a mountainside could have been no easy task. In the absence of any related evidence, it is difficult to surmise whether the artisan-craftsmen of these excavations belonged to any specific castes and possessed any special expertise. However, the technique and process taken up suggest that they were not novices.[108] Initially, they did adopt wooden forms and incorporated details inappropriate for rock-cut structures. Later, it seems that having perceived their incongruity, they evolved a style of their own, remedying their defects. The choice of appropriate sites manifests efforts of extensive search and substantial climbing, considerations of the rock properties and geological availability before final selection.[109] The successive excavation stages also entailed a lot of pre-planning. The initial conception of any cave could, probably, be the work of a single master craftsman executed with the help of his team. Those who did the preliminary stone cutting knew the exact number of large blocks to be left standing for later conversion into pillars. They also calculated the number of blocks to be left on an apsidal plan and the exact height and width of the roof. An accurate system of measurement, therefore, must have been employed.

The exact location probably depended on choice of a suitable mass of rock with no visible or probable faults. The *navakārmika*,[110] i.e. the monk in charge of new works, himself could not have been an expert in such technical matters. Several classes of stone-workers have been suggested epigraphically. For instance, an inscription from Sāñcī[111] refers to the *āvesanin*, probably the master craftsman; a Kanherī inscription describes *selavadhakins* (stone masons) and *mithikās* (polishers) among other unidentified craftsmen.[112] The sculptures and painting were, perhaps in different hands; the *rūpakāra* of Bharhūt[113] and the *lūpadakhe* of Ramgarh[114] being sculptors. Carpenters (*vardhakis*) were employed to help, no doubt, with the various wooden additions to the early *caityas*. All these evidences suggest the predominance of technical expertise.

As revealed by certain Cālukyan and Pallava inscriptions, it is quite likely that the craftsmen moved from place to place for new assignments. For instance, short label inscriptions at Bādāmī, record some 200 names mostly in Telugu and Kannada characters of sixth century AD.[115] Their purpose was evidently to record names or epithets of individuals. Numerous inscribed vertical strokes accompanying names probably suggest the number of days worked by respective craftsman.[116] They represent heterogeneous grouping comprising artisans from Andhra and Northern regions though locals were not excluded.

It is also likely that the architect sculptors of early Buddhist caves were not necessarily connected with Buddhism and worked readily for both Buddhist and non-Buddhist patrons.[117]

DEVELOPMENT OF THE BRĀHMANICAL ROCK-CUT CAVES

The resurgence of Brāhmanism began with the Guptas in the north and Cālukyas and Pallavas in the south.[118] The Guptas were, perhaps, the first to patronize Brāhmanical cave excavations at Udaigiri[119] near Vidiśā. The Vākāṭakas and Kalacuris emulated them. It is quite significant that unlike Buddhism, in Brāhmanism neither monasticism nor rituals were indispensable. Therefore, from ritualistic or utilitarian viewpoint caves were not required therein. Still large-scale excavation projects were undertaken. Beginning from Bādāmī and Aihoḷe in early sixth century AD, they soon boldly entered into the erstwhile Buddhist strongholds like Ellorā and Aurangābād. Eighth century Kailāśa temple at Ellorā proclaimed their triumph. By ninth century the feat was almost final as Buddhist rock activities virtually ended by this time. Therefore, the Brāhmanical excavations may be seen as a bid or challenge[120] to garner popular support by imitating the Buddhist tactics.

Besides theistic, the development was geographical too, advancing from North to South India. Religious creeds and cults from the north had infiltrated into South India as early as fourth century BC.[121] The *Nayanmār* and *Ālvār* saints proved instrumental for the creation of large number of temples. Seventh century onwards, architectural history of South India entered a new phase. Probably the rise of *Bhakti* against the heterodox Buddhism led to both structural and rock excavated temples. Though they imitated the Buddhist models the *caitya* form was not deemed suitable for either Śaivism or Vaiṣṇavism. They rather preferred the *Mahāyāna vihāra* form.

In south, rock-cut temples ranged from shallow pillared *maṇḍapams* of one or more cells cut in interior walls to the shaping of monolithic *rathas* and finally, an entirely rock-cut structural replica temple, a shrine in living rock with all accessories. Hence, the development proceeded from cut-in to cut-out specimens. This also entails an evolutionary process underlying the Brāhmanical cave temples. They signified more ambitious, large dimensional endeavours, potent with greater symbolism than their Buddhist counterparts. Their magnitude leaves no doubt regarding popularity of the medium.

Rock architecture might have appealed to the Indians for its stability[122] and adaptability to Indian conditions. The desire for permanence[123] as well as climatic utility may have also induced a shift from wooden to stone medium. The *guhā* with its *svayaṁbhū* nature easily struck chord of Indian spirituality.[124] The notion of an unchangeable and immutable godhead and his abode was perhaps better expressed in rock-hewn than masonry creations.[125] Hence, the quasi-eternity of the medium offered advantages in such climate over any ephemeral structure, with its general adoption almost setting a trend.

HISTORIOGRAPHY

For centuries the rock monuments thus created remained enigmatic. A lot has been written about them since sixteenth century up to the current times. The historiography of cave temples may be classified in three groups. In the beginning, the European travellers, fascinated by the magnificent art of South Indian caves, but ignorant about the myth, culture and spirit of Indian art, which was responsible for their creation, wrote about them. They saw these monuments from a European viewpoint and failed to analyze them as the product of Indian art genius. For instance, sixteenth-century accounts of Elephanta by Portuguese Garcia Da Orta (1534),[126] the first European to record his visit; Castro (1538),[127] first to measure an Indian monument; or Van Linschoten (1585),[128] who described Elephanta images as monstrous. Seventeenth-century accounts of the site by Coutto (1616)[129] or Ovington (1689)[130] proved inadequate as they had no knowledge of Hindu iconography. Capt. Pyke's (1712) article in the *Archaeologia*[131] probably carried the first ground plan of the site. He attributed its sculptural panels to Chinese, Egyptian, or Alexandrian origin. Gough (1785) was the first to compile foreign accounts of Elephanta.[132] Erskine's (1813) monograph[133] comprised the panels' iconographic study, while Stevenson (1852) cited *paurāṇic* references.[134]

Interest was also exhibited in Ellorā from an early period. Malet (1794) wrote an essay, illustrated with well-made drawings, on Ellorā.[135] Wilford presented fancied interpretations of the site.[136] Similar interest was displayed by early European travellers like Balbi, Manucci, Hamilton, Chambers, Goldingham, etc.[137] in the Mahābalipuram rock monuments. However, the travellers' accounts remained mostly sketches and anecdotes.

Historiography of rock monuments received a boost by the efforts of James Fergusson. His very first publication was the illustrated *Rock-cut Temples of India* (1845). Rock architecture was also covered partly in the *History of Indian and Eastern Architecture* (1876). But his most comprehensive account proved to be the *Cave Temples of India*, co-authored with Burgess (1880). It was a general, descriptive monumental history of cave architecture in Western, Eastern and South India, highlighting Buddhist, Jaina and Brāhmanical affiliations. Though Fergusson succeeded in elaborating upon the architectural principles, yet he failed to grasp the symbolism of the excavated forms. The *śilpaśāstrīya* knowledge could not be utilized by him, depriving his works of the inner spirit latent in Indian art creations.

Significant contributions followed the interest shown by the second group of archaeologist historian officials as Burgess, Alexander Rea, Longhurst and Cousens. Burgess' *The Rock Temples of Elephanta or Gharāpuri* (1871) remains the best guidebook yet written. It has architectural and iconographic details with Sanskrit terms and Hindu concepts but lacks analytical content. Burgess, who discovered the inscribed Cālukyan cave III at Bādāmī (1876), wrote its detailed illustrated account.[138] *Rock Cut Temples of Elurā* (1877), *Cave Temples of India*, (1880) and *Report on Elurā Cave Temples and the Brāhmanical and Jaina Caves in Western India*[139] (1883) were his other publications on cave architecture, besides his detailed volumes on temple architecture. Meticulous architectural and epigraphic analysis was remarkable in his writings. Still, he could not imbibe the conceptual symbolism of the monuments or their sculptures.

Archaeological historiography tradition under Rea produced two works, viz. *Cālukyan Architecture of the Bellari District* (1896) and *Pallava Architecture* (1909). Longhurst delved upon Pallava architecture in his ASI Memoirs,[140] while Cousens wrote about Cālukyan caves in *Cālukyan Architecture of the Kanarese Districts* (1926). All these works remained descriptive. Besides, they were not exclusively concerned with cave architecture. Cousens was initially inclined towards Indian *śilpa* texts but he failed to capitalize their details into his works.

Meanwhile, the general European cave temple historiography progressed further after Fergusson. Carr (1869)[141] compiled an account of earlier writings on Mahābalipuram. Havell (1913)[142] highlighted the 'Indian-ness' of architecture and its symbolism. Still cave architecture was not his forte. Vogel,[143] Dubreuil,[144] Brown,[145] Kramrisch,[146] Zimmer,[147] etc., contributed occasionally towards cave art writings. However, theirs were quite generalized works devoid of specific cave art analysis.

In due course, some American scholars were also drawn by Indian cave art leading to both European and American publications. In 1962, Boner in *Principles of Composition in Hindu Sculpture-Cave Temple Period* produced a scientific, geometric analysis of selected sculptures in Bādāmī, Mahābalipuram and Ellorā caves. She tried to interpret the principle of composition underlying the relief from the live rocks on the walls of these cave temples of Western and Southern India. But she could not highlight the inner meaning or else the symbolism of the forms. Willetts (1966) compiled an exhaustive bibliography on Mahābalipuram monuments. Benjamin Rowland included rock architecture as a chapter, devoid of any insight into its philosophical aspects, in his *The Art and Architecture of India* (1970). Lockwood (1974) published a collection of studies on Mahābalipuram[148] and related themes in the history and art of the Pallavas, based on his field studies. Kail,[149] Markel,[150] Chatham,[151] Tarr,[152] amongst others, furthered the process of discussing Indian cave art. Harle included description of rock art in the *Art and Architecture of the Indian Subcontinent* (1986). Another American after Boner and Chatham, Rabe dealt with the chronology of the Mahābalipuram *Rathas*[153] classifying them into archaic, severe, classical and embellished categories. Iconographic analysis of Mahābalipuram rock sculptures was attempted by Marilyn Hirsch,[154] who tried to fill in the gaps noticeable in Pallava art at Mahābalipuram between fourth to seventh centuries AD by an analysis of the major and minor stylistic developments seen in the figural and sculptural art of Andhra Pradesh, which she held as the source of Pallava art.

Berkson in *Ellorā: Concept and Style* (1992) discussed a relationship between the environment and the temples. She also examined the architectural and compositional features unifying the caves. It was mainly a sculptor's assessment account totally different from Boner's approach. But the symbolism of form still remained unattended to.

Thus, we comprehend that the European, American scholars and the archaeologists were instrumental in bringing the Indian monuments to light, but they could not grasp the real significance or purport of these edifices. This was due to their failure in exploring Indian *śilpas* or studying them just as ornamental motifs without imbibing their inner form or religious, cultural background.

The third group of historians consisted of Indian scholars who were well acquainted with Indian mythology and who wrote from an Indian viewpoint. But their writings, too, were mostly descriptive sans symbolic details and analytical approach.

Ram Raz's *Essay on the Architecture of the Hindus* (1834) was the first systematic Indian work on architecture. He, however, did not cover cave architecture. Bhandarkar,[155] Aiyanger,[156] and Krishna Sastri[157] provided pace to Indian art historiography. R.D. Banerji was the first to highlight the bas-reliefs of Bādāmī in his work.[158] Ramanayya[159] discussed rock architecture in the context of South Indian shrines. A fresh approach towards the aesthetics of Elephanta and its nearby caves, including literary references and photographs, was adopted by Kanaiyalal Vakil[160] and later by Hirananda Sastri,[161] who also provided panel descriptions and cave measurements. Another authentic account came forth from Yazdani (1937).[162] Goswami made some references to rock-cut architecture in the *Art of the Pallavas* (1957) and *The Art of the Rāṣṭrakūṭas* (1958). Deshpande[163] did pioneering works in the field of rock art analysis. Pramod Chandra[164] and C. Sivaramamurti[165] also worked on some aspects of the art. In 1962, Nagaswamy initiated a new theory[166] by assigning authorship of all the rock-cut monuments at Mahābalipuram to Rajasimha. The idea was carried further in his later writings.[167] He, however, did not bother to discuss their art or symbolism much. Gupte[168] also contributed towards descriptive study and some analysis of erotic figures seen in Ajantā, Ellorā and Aurangābād cave art. Buddhist caves, in particular, were studied by Sukumar Sen and Vidya Dehejia.[169] Srinivasan also did commendable work in the architectural analysis of Pallava rock-cut edifices.[170] Similarly, K.V. Soundara Rajan in several pioneering works[171] compiled a comprehensive, *śilpaśāstrīya* account of the Deccan caves.

Ramaswami[172] did an appreciable job of collecting all possible aspects related to the Mahābalipuram rock-cut temples. However, his work was somewhat general and descriptive lacking any originality of thought or analytical content. Partha Mitter[173] countered the European misconceptions about Elephanta shrines in 1977. The origin of Indian rock-cut art was revised by S.P. Gupta (1980).[174] Fascinations with Ellorā continued further. Besides, T.V. Pathy[175] and M.K. Dhavalikar,[176] contemporary scholars like Ratan Parimoo,[177] Deepak Kannal,[178] and several art oriented scholars[179] are currently working on Indian rock-cut architecture and its related aspects.

Besides individual scholarly efforts, there have been publications of special issues of art journals such as *Mārg*[180] devoted to rock architecture. These were brought out, respectively, under Muriel Neff, Walter Spink, T.N. Ramachandran and S. Settar, all renowned art scholars' guidance. The occasional publication of research articles by both foreign and Indian scholars in reputed journals and magazines[181] has also brought to light newer aspects of rock-cut art.

Despite such a long list and numerous contributions, it is discernible that even the Indian writings on rock-cut art, mostly descriptive and generalized in contents, are devoid of insights and analytical viewpoint. The symbolism or comparative analysis has seldom been attempted therein. Therefore, the Cālukyan, Pallava and Rāṣṭrakūṭa rock-cut creations need to be assimilated at one place to overview the development of art and architecture in them.

NOTES AND REFERENCES

1. *Cf.* V.S. Agrawala, 1965, *Indian Art*, Varanasi, p. 186.
2. As defined by Lokesh Chandra, 1988, 'Ellorā as Śūnyata and Rūpam', in Ratan Parimoo *et al.* (eds.), *Ellorā Caves: Sculptures and Architecture (ECSA)*, New Delhi, p. 131; *also see* Baumer, 1988, 'From Guhā to Akāsa: The Mystical Cave in the Vedic and Saiva Traditions', *Ibid.*, p. 78.
3. *gūdhājñātr-jñāna- jñeya-padārthāh asyām*
   gūhate 'syām ātmā iti vā. Cf.Vācaspatya Lexicon.
4. *Bhāgavata Purāṇa*, 3. 26. 5.
5. 'Rest' in the spiritual sense connoted retreat from the world. *Cf. Bṛhadāraṇayaka Upaniṣad.* IV, 1, 7.
6. *Vide* V.S. Agrawala, *op. cit.*, p. 206.
7. Pradip S. Meshram, 1991, *Early Caves of Maharashtra: A Cultural Study*, Delhi, p. 1.
8. *See* Owen C. Kail, 1975, *Buddhist Cave Temples of India*, Bombay.
9. Opined by Percy Brown, 1965, *Indian Architecture: Buddhist and Hindu*, Bombay, p. 19.
10. In 1970, *The Pelican History of Art: The Art and Architecture of India-Buddhist-Hindu-Jain*, p. 113.
11. *See* Louis Frederic, 1959, *Indian Temples and Sculpture*, London, p. 143.
12. *Cf.* Percy Brown, *op. cit.*, p. 19.

13. G.C. Pande, 1984, *Foundations of Indian Culture: Spiritual Vision and Symbolic Forms in Ancient India*, New Delhi, p. 312.
14. *Cf.* Stella Kramrisch, 2002, *The Hindu Temple*, Vol. I. Delhi (rpt.), p. 161.
15. *Meru*, the pole of earth; *Mandara*, the churning rod planted on *Kūrma* Viṣṇu; and *Kailāśa*, the Himālayan abode of Śiva.
16. Mandasor Stone Inscription of Bandhuvarman, in 1963, *Corpus Inscriptionum Indicarum*, III, p. 83.
17. *Ibid.*, p. 76.
18. *Epigraphia Indica*, I, pp. 310-14.
19. *Archaeological Survey of India*, Vol. XXI, p. 95.
20. Stella Kramrisch, *op. cit.*, p. 167.
21. It shows a stage where the living space containing life, water, and light had to be conquered and freed from the oppressing enclosure, *vṛtra* or *vala*. Indra pierces the 'primordial hill' and creates an opening to release the light called the 'Sun in the rock'- *Svar yad aśman*. *Vide* F.B.J. Kuiper, 1983, *Ancient Indian Cosmogony*, New Delhi, pp. 70 f., 84.
22. *Guhā*, *Ṛg Veda*, I: 6, 5.
23. 'I found the shining (face of the Gods) at the seat of Order (*Rtasya pade*) in secret (*guhā*)...' *Cf. Ṛg Veda*.
24. *Ṛg Veda*, II: 11, 5.
25. *Paramam Dhāma hymn*, *Atharva Veda*, II: 1, 1-2.
26. The description about inner sanctum in early religious structures of Tamil Nadu—*karuvodu peyariya Kanbu in nāl il*—taking its name after the womb, corresponds to the Sanskrit *garbhagṛha*, which literally means the abode of creation. *Cf. Nedunalvādai*, p. 144.
27. *Atharva Veda*, XI: 5, 10.
28. *See Chandogya Upaniṣad*, III: 15, 1.
29. *Tasmād idam guheva hṛdayam*, XI: 2, 6, 5.
30. *Cf. Katha Upaniṣad*, IV: 6-7, 12.
31. *Anor anīyān mahato mahīyān ātmā guhāyām*. 3.20.
32. *Katha Upaniṣad*, II: 12.
33. 'On the Viśākhā mountain there is a great dwelling belonging to Guha, the secret one (Karttikeya), the God who is very fond of living in caves' – *Guha*; *Vāyu Purāṇa*, XXXIX, 55.
34. *Gahvaresthāya Namah*, 44, *Cf. Yajur Veda*, XVI.
35. *Cf.* A.K. Ramanujam, 1979, *Speaking of Śiva*, New York, pp. 47, 149-51, and 153-61.
36. *Bhagavān-Sarva-bhūtānām adhyaksho vasthito guhām*. II: 9, 24.
37. *Brahmā-yo veda nihitam guhāyām parame vyoman*; *Indische Studien*, 2. 217.
38. *Cf. BS*, 56.18.25; According to Utpala, it is shaped as a *guhā*. *Cf.* Commentary on *Bṛhat Saṁhitā*, LV.25.
39. *Caitya-guhā-garbha-sthitām*.*Cf. Sādhanā* 191, in *Sādhanā Mālā*, 2. 394.
40. *Cf.* G.C. Pande, *op. cit.*, p. 372.
41. Richard von Schaukal quoted by Lokesh Chandra in 'Ellorā as Śūnyatā and Rūpam', *op. cit.*, p. 132.
42. They are edited in the first volume of S. Parnavitana, 1970, *Inscriptions of Ceylon*, Colombo.
43. Lokesh Chandra, *op. cit.*, p. 132.
44. *Cf.* Turnour's *Mahāvano*, pp. 103, 123; Emerson Tennent's *Ceylon*, Vol. II, p. 607; *Cf.* James Fergusson and James Burgess, 1969 (repr.), *The Cave Temples of India*, pp. 19-20, footnote no. 1.

45. Benjamin Rowland, *op. cit.*, p. 113.
46. *Cf.* Percy Brown, *op. cit.*, p. 8.
47. *Vide* James Fergusson and James Burgess, *op. cit.*, p. 31.
48. *Ibid.*, p. 166. He traced the Western Indian Buddhist caves to wooden origin without detecting any foreign influence. See also, p. 398.
49. *Cf.* O.C. Gangoly, 1954, *Indian Architecture*, Bombay, p. 70.
50. In 1980, *The Roots of Indian Art*, Delhi, p. 194.
51. Vidya Dehejia, 1972, *Early Buddhist Rock Temples*, London, pp. 17-18.
52. For instance, the innovation at Bedsā in the form of tall, slender columns with elaborate 'bell' capitals with a stepped abacus supporting animal and rider crowning figures might have been inspired by the artist's visit to the Ashokan pillar at Sāñcī.
53. *Cf.* K.de.B. Codrington, 1930, 'Ancient Sites near Ellorā, Deccan', *IA*, LIX, pp. 10-13; *Also* Reverend J.E. Abbott, 1891. 'Recently Discovered Buddhist Caves at Nadsur and Nenavli in the Bhor State' in *IA*, XX, p. 121; D.D. Kosambi, 1955, 'Dhenukākaṭa', *Journal of the Asiatic Society of Bombay*, 30, pp. 51-52.
54. Sukumar Sen discussing the rise of the western caves thus suggested the process: A monk's primary mission being the spread of the Buddha's word, long journeys must have been undertaken along the established trade routes with merchants and traders. During these long, slow journeys, their mutual acquaintance and possible conversion of some could also be likely. On reaching the western coastal area, the monks, tired of wandering, must have wanted a place to settle down for the three months of rainy season. Their merchant trader friends would have been willing to contribute towards the building of monasteries to gain spiritual merit on them and their families and 'divine' favour on their business enterprises—As described in 1962, *Buddhist Monks and Monasteries of India*, London, p. 138 f.
55. Vidya Dehejia, *op. cit.*, p. 146.
56. Percy Brown, *op. cit.*, p. 19; *Cf.* Benjamin Rowland, *op. cit.*, p. 113; K.R. Srinivasan, *op. cit.*, p. 23; M.W. Meister, 1981, 'Sub-urban Planning and Rock-cut Architecture in India', in M.S. Nagaraja Rao (ed.), *Madhu (M.N. Deshpande FestSchrift)*, Delhi, p. 157.
57. *Vide* 1980, *The Roots of Indian Art*, pp. 194-95.
58. Rāmgarh-hills of Lakhanpur in Sirguja State on Calcutta Nagpur line; Budhānī-45 Rock Shelters in Distt. Sehore, M.P. (discovered in 1975 by K.D. Bannerji and Bhopardikar); Son Bhanḍār-near Rājgir, (discovered in 1812 by Buchanan).
59. Originally a cell or dwelling of a monk, the word later denoted a full monastic establishment (*Sanghārama* of *Bhikkhu Saṁghā*). *Cf.* V.S. Agrawala, *op. cit.*, p. 189. It was one of the five kinds of buildings, viz. *Addhayoga*, *Vihāra*, *Prāsāda*, *Harmya*, and *Guhā*, allowed by the Buddha to be used by his disciples. *Vide Cullavagga*.
60. Pali *cetiya* translated as a 'sepulchral monument'; A derivation of *citi*, the Vedic fire-altar, grammatically it is not possible to connect it with *citā* though both share the common root *ci*- *Cf.* Giuseppe Tucci, 1988, *Stūpa: Art, Architecture and Symbolism*. New Delhi, p. XIV; Used as an object of veneration, *Mahācaitya* was one of the four sites related to Buddha's birth, enlightenment, first sermon and *parinirvāṇa*. *Cf. Mūlasarvāstivada-Vinaya, Gilgit Mss*, 2. 113. 9f.
61. As dedicated to *yakshas* and *devas*, *Vide Atharvaveda*, X, 8.15; Sacred Buddhist halls. *Cf. Dīghanikāya Aṭṭhakathā*, 2.596, *Anguttara Nikāya*, 5.6; Also meant sacred trees, *caitya tarū*, *caitya dru*, *caitya ḍruma*, *caitya vrksha-Cf. Var. Br.*, 5; Referred to in epics also—*caitya prāsāda*. *Cf. Rāmāyaṇa*, 5.15; *caitya-yūpa- śatānkitāh* in *Mahābhārata*, 1.109.13.
62. Cave cells for monks were known from Ashokan times. The Lomas *Ṛṣi* and Sudāmā caves replicated in their interiors both the hut and the clearing of a forest ascetic's retreat- *Cf.* J.C. Huntington, 1974-75, 'The Lomas Ṛṣi: Another Look', *Archives of Asian Art*, XXVIII,

pp. 34-56; At Udaigiri in Orissa, the Jaina caves of Kharvela's period are scattered around a low scarp. *See* Debala Mitra, 1975, *Udaigiri and Khaṇḍagirī*, New Delhi. In simpler ones like the Tiger cave, a boulder has been turned into gaping jaws enclosing the ascetic's cell. *Cf.* M.W. Meister, 'Sub-urban Planning and Rock-cut Architecture in India', *op. cit.*, p. 157.

63. Benjamin Rowland, *op. cit.*, p. 113.
64. Vidya Dehejia, *op. cit.*, pp. 92-113.
65. Suggested by Tarapada Bhattacharyya, 1963, *The Canons of Indian Art*, Calcutta, p. 65.
66. A memorial enshrining a relic (*dhātu*) symbolising the Buddha, erected at *Cātummahāpathe* *Cf. Dīgha Nikāya*, XVI, 5, 11. Three primary meanings associated with *Stūpa* are: (i) 'Topknot, crest, tuft or lock of hair' for supremacy. In *Taittirīya Saṁhitā*, 3.3.6, 5; *See also Pañcaviṁśa Brāhmaṇa*, 13.4.4; *Vājasaneyī Saṁhitā*, 2.2., 25.2; *Śatapatha Brāhmaṇa*, 3.5.3.4; *Atharvaveda*, 7.74.2. (ii) 'Stem, tree, pillar, post' for stability. *Cf. Ṛgveda*, 1.24.7. (iii) 'Heaped, piled up' as a form of monument, *Vide Dhātupatha*, 26.127, 32.133; *Vācasptya Lexicon*, 3.5.19; *Srīdhānyakamaka*, literally meaning 'heap of grain', was a famous *caitya* in South India. *Cf. Mañjusrī–Mūlakalpa* 88.10-*dakshiṇāpatha samjñake Srī-dhānyakamake caitye jina dhātudhare bhuvi.*
67. *Cf.* 'Dakshiṇa and the Pigeon Monastery', Nilakanta Sastri (ed.), 1939, *Foreign Notices of South India*, Madras, p. 66f; *See also* James Legge, [1886] 1965, *A Record of Buddhistic Kingdoms*, New York, pp. 96-98.
68. V.S. Agrawala, *op. cit.*, p. 187.
69. *See* Owen C. Kail, *op. cit.*
70. Also suggested by the bas-reliefs of Bharhūt and Sāñcī of second to first centuries BC. *Cf.* Percy Brown, *op. cit.*, p. 47.
71. *Vide* S.K. Saraswati in R.C. Majumdar (ed.), *The History and Culture of the Indian People*, Vol. II, pp. 495-99.
72. At Ajantā, a beginning had already been made, while at Ellorā an entirely new undertaking was initiated by the Buddhists, later developed by the Jainas and Brāhmaṇas into the most comprehensive range of rock monuments in India.
73. A temple is also visited for *darśana*, one of the six traditional methods of cognizing truth, viz. *Nyāya, Vaiśeṣika, Sāṁkhya, Yoga, Mimānsa* and *Vedānta*. *Darśana* presupposes *yoga*. *See* Stella Kramrisch, 2002, *The Hindu Temple*, Delhi, p. 8.
74. *Vide Agni Purāṇa*, Chap. 61, verses 19-27. *See also* Manmohan Ganguli, *Orissa and Her Remains*, and Ram Raz, 1834, *Essay on the Architecture of the Hindus* for technical terms revealing analogy of temple parts with the human body; *Agni Purāṇa* also identified its parts with attributes of Śiva such as *pīmha* or pedestal, i.e. *brahmāṇḍa; janghā*, i.e. *pañcabhūtas; kaṇṭha*, i.e. *māyā* with Rūdra; *amalasāra*, i.e. *vidyā; śūla*, i.e. *ardha candra* and three *śaktis*. *Vide* Chapter 102, 17 ff.
75. In chapter 7, footnote no. 10.
76. The school of Maya is referred to in the *BS*, Chap. 56, verse 29; its Chap. 58, verse 4 refers to *Drāvida* School; to these were later added *Lāṭa, Virāṭa* and *Bhūmija* types.
77. *Vide Mayamata*, Chaps. XIX and XXI. *See also Iśānaśivagurudevapaddati, Paṭala* XXX; *Tantra Samuccaya, Paṭala* II; *Suprabhedāgama*, Chap. XXX; *Kāmikāgama Paṭala* XLIX; *Kasyapa āilpa*, Chap. XXV, etc.
78. *Kṛshṇādi-Kanyanta*, in *Kāmikāgama*.
79. Described as 45, 64,100 and 96 in different texts. *Cf. Appendix* (I) a, b, c.
80. *See History of Indian and Eastern Architecture*, Vol. II, p. 21.
81. Dated inscription of AD 578 in Bādāmī cave III. For related details, *see* Chapter 2; *Cf. EI*, XXVII, p. 8.
82. *Vide EI*, XVII, p. 17.

83. As suggested by Burgess in the *Cave Temples of India*, pp. 169-70.
84. *Cf. Appendix* II.
85. *Cf.* James Burgess, *CTI*, p. 167.
86. Thick pile of *lāvā* (basalt) flow originated from volcanic activity in the geological past after consolidation gave rise to this trap rock. It is mostly amygdaloidal in nature, containing vesicles filled with chalcedony and zeolite, and traversed by veins of quartz in many places. The joints—wide spaced and not open in nature—helped excavation of many large chambers even without support.
87. Andreas Volwahsen, 1969, *Living Architecture: Indian*, Calcutta, p. 178.
88. *See* Percy Brown, *op. cit.*, p. 21.
89. Carved on one side only. Central right portion of the slab depicts two male figures carrying dagger-like sharp instruments in their hands. They may represent forest dwellers evident from their garments (*parṇavastra*); on their backs they are carrying baskets of implements and weapons to chisel the rocks; they have actually cut off the rock and even prepared steps. A very interesting example as it represents the process of carving rocks with sharp instruments for the building of rock-cut structures, domestic or religious. *Cf. Coping stone, No 68.163. Mason's at Work, Bharhūt Lintel, 2nd-1st century* BC. R.C. Agrawala, 1961, 'Unpublished Bharhut Reliefs in the National Museum, New Delhi', *Lalit Kalā*, No. 14, Bombay, Plate XX, Fig. 11, p. 51.
90. *See* Benjamin Rowland, *op. cit.*, p. 113.
91. *Cf.* K.R. Srinivasan, 1993, *Cave Temples of the Pallavas*, Delhi, plate I (a, b).
92. *Cf. Ibid.*
93. Indicated by finished façades in some cave shrines with still incomplete interiors and comparatively more finished tops and less finished bases.
94. *Vide* Karl Khandalavala and Moti Chandra (eds.), 1956 (April) - 1957 (March), Editorial article, 'Date of the Kārle *Caitya*'. *LK* ¾, p. 23.
95. *Cf.* Walter Spink, 'On the Development of Early Buddhist Art in India', *Art Bulletin*, XL, p. 99.
96. *See Introduction to the Study of Indian History*, 1956, Bombay, p. 251.
97. Vidya Dehejia, *op. cit.*, p. 137.
98. D. Barrett. 1959 (Oct.), 'Correspondence', *LK*. 6, p. 77, suggesting a period of 10 years.
99. *Cf.* Seiichi Mizuno and Tosio Nagahiro, 1941, *A Study of the Buddhist Cave Temples at Lung-Men*, Tokyo.
100. *Vide* Subinoy Gangopadhyay, *op. cit.*, p. 25; for details see Chap. 6.
101. *Cf. Appendix* III.
102. Geoffrey Scott in 1961, *The Architecture of Humanism*, London, p. 25f.
103. 'The king took extraordinary precautions to prevent any voluntary work being done lest any of the merit should be lost to himself...' *Cf.* A.K. Coomaraswamy, 1956, *Medieval Sinhalese Art*, New York, p. 57.
104. The town Dhenukākaṭa has not been identified though Kosambi relates it to Devgadh on the opposite curve of hills from Kārle; *see* D.D. Kosambi, 1955, 'Dhenukākaṭa', *Journal of the Asiatic Society of Bombay*, 30, pp. 59-60.
105. Vidya Dehejia, *op. cit.*, p. 142.
106. Owen C. Kail has suggested that the portrayal of amorous couples and adoption of female forms for sculptural ornamentation outside caves at Bhājā, Koṇḍane, Ajantā, Pitalkhorā, etc. depicted not merely decorative character, but represented the world 'outside the temple, of the merchants, traders travelling along ancient trade routes and supporting their creations'. *See Buddhist Cave Temples of India*, p. 26.

107. Though Buddha forbade monetary accumulations for them, various gifts of fields and permanent endowments made this possible. Eg., Nahapana inscription mentioned the village of Karajika given to ascetics in Kārle caves; Kosambi, *op. cit.*, p. 52 ff. Also hinted- 'Monks deviated from the spirit of the law without deviating from the letter of the law: forbidden to touch money, they used a piece of cloth as insulation'. Some rich men on joining the *saṁgha* are said to have donated large sums. *See* Vidya Dehejia, *op. cit.*, p. 145.
108. Requirement of special experience exhibited from failed attempts at Mahābalipuram due to ignorance of the nature of granite and inexperience of forms necessary to meet out difficulties consequent on the nature of the mass, while long experience in sandstone and basalt at Ellorā yielded more success as seen in the form of the Kailāśa.
109. It is a matter of wonder that even in that distant past, experimental digging (test-pit) was done on the face of the hill slope for finding the quality of the rock as suggested by a test pit found nearly 15 m below the present level of Ajantā caves. The rocks in the pit appear to be affected by exfoliation, bedding joints, innumerable quartz vein intrusion and presence of zeolite, chlorophaeite, thus the alignment for construction was, perhaps, shifted to the present level where the basaltic rock is of better quality evident from physical and microscopic test - *Vide* Subinoy Gangopadhyay, *op. cit.*, p. 20.
110. *See Lüders' List* no. 773 (Bharhūt); no. 154 (Sonārī Stūpa I); no. 1250 (Amarāvatī).
111. On the inner face of top architrave of southern gateway, *see also Lüders' List* no. 346.
112. Inscription no. 4, on the right gatepost of the *Caitya*, *ASWI*, Vol. V.
113. *Cf.* B.M. Barua and K.G. Sinha, 1929, *Bharhūt Inscriptions*, Calcutta, No. 92.
114. *See* Bloch, 'Caves and Inscriptions in Ramgarh Hills', *ARASI*, 1903/04, pp. 123-31.
115. *Vide South Indian Inscriptions*, XV, Nos. 277-400; XX, Nos. 258-273; XV, Nos. 415-477.
116. *Cf.* Srinivas V. Padigar, 'Craftsmen's Inscriptions from Bādāmī: Their Significance', in Ratan Parimoo (ed.), *ECSA*, pp. 398-99.
117. Percy Brown, n.d., *Indian Painting*, Çalcutta, p. 9. Kramrisch has also thrown light upon the Indian craftsmen in, 1983, 'Traditions of the Indian Craftsman', in Miller (ed.), *Exploring India's Sacred Art*, Philadelphia, pp. 59-68.
118. *Refer to* Chapter 2 for details.
119. *Cf.* S.K. Saraswati, 1957, *HCIP*, Vol. V, Bombay, p. 488. A Śaiva inscription recorded the excavation of the cave as a temple of Śiva Śambhū by Vīrasena Śāba. *See* J.F. Fleet, 'Udaigiri Cave Inscription of Chandragupta II, No. 2', *Corpus Inscriptionum Indicarum*, Vol. III; *cf.* A. Cunningham, *Archaeological Survey of India*, Vol. X, p. 57 ff.
120. The cave art of the Brāhmanical faith was a self-imposed essaying in stonecutter's art with the chief purpose of providing a counter blast to the Buddhist creations of the past. *Cf.* K.V. Soundara Rajan, 1981, *CTD*, New Delhi, p. 2.
121. *See* K.A. Nilakanta Sastri, 1963, *Development of Religion in South India*, p. 28.
122. Percy Brown has suggested that it was as immovable as the mountain of which it formed a part, 1965, *op. cit.*, p. 19; *also* Naudou, *Indian Temples and Sculpture*, p. 54 for a similar opinion.
123. A Kanherī inscription certainly expressed this spirit when the donor claimed the erection of a *caitya* that would endure until the end of the *kalpa*: *cf.* James Burgess, 1970, *ASWI*, Vol. V, New Delhi, p. 75; *cf. also* Benjamin Rowland. 'In the Indian examples there was probably already the idea of preserving the Buddha's law through the bad times at the end of the *kalpa*', *op. cit.*, p. 113.
124. *Cf.* J.C. Harle, 1986, *The Art and Architecture of the Indian Sub-Continent*, London, p. 45.
125. *Cf.* S.K. Saraswati, 1968, *HCIP*, Vol. II, Bombay, p. 494.
126. *Cf.* 1563, *Coloquious dos simples e drogas... da India*, Goa.

127. *Vide* 1843, *Primeiro Roteiro da Costa da India desde Goa ate Dio.*
128. *Cf. Itinerario*, 1596, Amsterdam.
129. *See* 1841 (July) – 1844 (July), *Of the Very Remarkable and Stupendous Pagoda of Elephanta*, Decade VII, Book III, Chapter XI in *JBBRAS*, Vol. I.
130. *See* 1696, *A Voyage to Suratt in the Year 1689*, London.
131. 1785, 'Account of a Curious Pagoda Near Bombay', in *Archaeologia*, Vol. VII, London.
132. *See* 1785, *A Comparative View of the Ancient Monuments of India*, London.
133. *See* his 1819, 'Account of the Cave Temple of Elephanta...' in *Transactions of the Literary Society of Bombay*, Vol. I, London.
134. *See* 1850-52, 'The Theory of the Great Elephanta Cave', *JBBRAS*, Vol. IV, No. XVI, pp. 261-75.
135. *Cf.* 1799, *Asiatic Researches*, Vol. VI, p. 389.
136. *Cf. Asiatic Researches*, 1798, Vol. V, p. 136.
137. For their details, *see* W. Willetts, 1966, *An Illustrated Annotated Annual Bibliography of Mahābalipuram* (1582-1962), Kualalumpur, pp. 9-12.
138. *Cf.* 1877, 'Rock Cut Temples at Bādāmī in Dekhan', *IA*, VI.
139. *Vide* 1883, *ASWI*, (1877-1880), Vol. V, London. This was preceded by *Report on the Buddhist Cave Temples and Their Inscriptions, ASWI* (1876-79), Vol. IV.
140. 1924-30, *MASI*, Nos. 17, 33 and 40, Calcutta.
141. *Cf.* 1869 (ed.), *The Seven Pagodas on the Coromandel Coast*, Madras. It was a compilation of early accounts, mainly descriptive in character.
142. 1913, *Indian Architecture*, London.
143. 1914, 'The Seven Pagodas', *ASIAR*, 1910-11, Calcutta.
144. *Vide* 1914, *Archaeologie du Sud de L' Inde*, Paris; 1917, *Draviḍian Architecture*, Madras; 1937, *Iconography of South India*, Paris.
145. *Cf.* 1942, *Indian Architecture, Buddhist and Hindu*, Bombay.
146. Her writings, 1946, *Hindu Temple*, Calcutta and *Indian Sculpture* consisted of several references to cave art.
147. 1955, *The Art of Indian Asia*, 2 vols., had occasional mention of cave monuments.
148. M. Lockwood, Gift Siromoney *et al.*, 1974, *Mahābalipuram Studies*, Madras.
149. *See* 1975, *Buddhist Cave Temples of India*, Bombay and 1984, *Elephanta—The Island of Mystery*, Bombay.
150. 1980, '*An Iconological Assessment of the Great Relief at Māmallapuram*', Master's Essay, Michigan University.
151. 1981, *Stylistic Sources and Relationships of the Kailāśa Temple at Ellorā* (Ph.D. thesis, Univ. of California, Berkeley), U.M.I., Michigan.
152. *Cf.* 1969, *Architecture of the Early Western Chalukyas*, U.C.L.A.
153. *See* 1988, *The Monolithic Temples of the Pallava Dynasty: A Chronology* (Vols. I-III) (Ph.D. Thesis, Univ. of Minnesota, U.S.A.), U.M.I. Michigan. He has also published 2001, *Great Penance at Māmallapuram*, Chennai.
154. *Cf.* 1988, *Sources for the Figural Sculptures of Māmallapuram* (Ph.D. thesis, New York Univ. 1986), U.M.I. Michigan.
155. *See* 1911, *The Guide to Elephanta Island*, Bombay.
156. *Cf.* 1917, 'The Antiquities of Mahābalipuram', *IA*, XLVI, Bombay.
157. *See* 1926, 'Two Statues of Pallava Kings and Five Pallava Inscriptions in a Rock Temple at Mahābalipuram', *MASI*, No. 26, Calcutta.
158. *Cf.* 1928, *Bas Reliefs of Bādāmī, MASI*, No. 25, Calcutta.
159. *Cf.* 1992, *An Essay on the Origin of the South Indian Temple*, New Delhi.

160. *Cf.* 1932, *Rock-cut Temples around Bombay at Elephanta and Jogeshwari, Mandapeshwar and Kanheri.*
161. *See* his 1934, A *Guide to Elephanta*, Delhi for details.
162. *Cf.* 1937, *The Rock Hewn Temples of Aurangābād*, (repr. from) *Indian Art and Letters*, Vol. XI, No. 1, London.
163. Some of his works included 1954, 'Places of Buddhist Pilgrimage: Rock-cut Sanctuaries around Bombay', *Indo Asian Culture*, Vol. III, No. 1; 1955, 'Rock-cut Caves in Western India', *Buddhist Remains in India*; 1959, 'The 'Rock-cut Caves of Pitalkhara', *Ancient India*, No. 15.
164. *Cf.* 1957, *A Guide to Elephanta Caves*, Bombay.
165. *See* 1961, *Kalugumalai and Early Pandyan Rock-cut Shrines*, Bombay.
166. *Cf.* 1962, 'New Light on Mamallapuram', Reprint from the Silver Jubilee Vol. of the *ASII*, for an insight into the theory.
167. *See* 1968, *Mamallai* (Tamil), Madras; and 1985, 'The Author of Māmallapuram Monuments: A Fresh Look', in Asher M. Frederick & G.S. Gai (eds.), *Epigraphy: Its Bearing on the History of Art*, Delhi.
168. *Cf.* 1962, *Ajantā, Ellorā and Aurangābād Caves*, Bombay.
169. *Cf.* S. Sen, 1962, *Buddhist Monks and Monasteries of India*, London; V. Dehejia, 1972, *Early Buddhist Rock Temples: A Chronological Study*, London.
170. *Cf.* 1964, *Cave Temples of the Pallavas*, Delhi; 1972, *Temples of South India*, Delhi; 1975, *The Dharmarāja Ratha and Its Sculptures: Mahābalipuram*, New Delhi. He has also contributed in Meister and Dhaky, 1983 (eds.), *The Encyclopaedia of Indian Temple Architecture, South India*, Vol. 1, pts. 1, 2, 3, Delhi.
171. Touched upon the subject in 1965, 'The Matrix of South Indian Architecture', (repr.) from *Journal of Indian History*, Vol. XLIII, Pt. III, No. 129; 1969, *Early Temple Architecture in Karnataka and its Ramifications*, Dharwar. Besides 1978, *Art of South India: Tamil Nadu and Kerala*, Delhi; 1980, *Art of South India: Deccan*, Delhi; 1981, *Cave Temples of the Deccan*, Delhi; and portions contributed to Meister and Dhaky, 1983 (eds.), *The Encyclopaedia* of Indian *Temple Architecture, South India*, Vol. 1, pts. 1, 2, 3, Delhi testifies to his range of contribution in the study of rock architecture.
172. *See* his 1970, *Seven Pagodas: The Art and History of Mahābalipuram*, Madras.
173. *Cf.* 1977, *Much Maligned Monsters: A History of European Reactions to Indian Art.*
174. *See* 1980, *The Roots of Indian Art.*
175. *Cf.* 1980, *Elurā—Art and Culture*, New Delhi.
176. His monograph 1983, *Masterpieces of Rāshtrakūta Art—The Kailas*, Bombay; 2003, *Monumental Legacy—Ellora*, Delhi.
177. He has created numerous writings under the influence of the Vienna school. Prominent ones are - 1988 (ed.), *Ellorā Caves: Sculpture and Architecture*, Delhi; 1991, (ed.), *The Art of Ajantā: New Perspectives*, 2 vols., Delhi; *A New Light on the Sculptures of Ellorā*; 2000, *Studies in Indian Sculpture: Regional Genres and Interpretations, Essays on New Art History*, 2 vols., Delhi.
178. He has co-edited the *ECSA* and *The Art of Ajantā: New Perspectives*. His 1996, *Ellorā—An Enigma in Sculptural Styles*, Delhi, traces evolutionary pattern and historical continuity in art creations at the site. He also wrote under the influence of Vienna school of thought, especially Riegl, Wofflin and Stella Kramrisch.
179. Such as, Pradip S. Meshram, 1991, *Early Caves of Maharashtra: A Cultural Study*, Delhi; Leila Ghosh and Dalia Roy, 1986, *Ajantā and Ellorā*; Shivaji Panikkar, Kirit Mankodi, S.K. Maity and S.K. Saraswati have discussed aspects of their sculptures in their writings.

180. For instance, *Mārg* issues on: 1960 (Sept.), 'Elephanta', Vol. XIII, No. 4, 1967 (March); 'Ajanta to Ellorā', Vol. XX, No. 2, Bombay; 1970 (June-Sept), 'Hymn to Mahābalipuram', Vol. XXIII, Nos. 3-4, Bombay; 1979, 'In Praise of Aihoḷe, Bādāmī, Mahākūṭa and Paṭṭaḍakal'.

181. To mention a few, *cf.* Gary Tarr, 1970, 'Chronology and Development of the Chalukya Cave Temples', *Ars Orientalis,* Vol. 8, Michigan; Aschwin Lippe, 'Early Chalukya Icons', *Artibus Asiae,* Vol. XXXIV; *cf.* his 1967, 'Some Sculptural Motifs on Early Chalukya Temples', *AA.* Vol. XXIX, No. 1; Doris C. Chatham, 1981, 'Pratihāras from Paṭṭaḍakal to Ellorā', in Anand Krishna (ed.), *Chhavi-2;* Susan Huntington, 1981, 'Iconographic Reflections on the Arjuna Ratha', in Joanna Williams (ed.), *Kalādarshana;* M. Meister, 1981, 'Sub-urban Planning and Rock-cut Architecture in India', in Nagaraja Rao (ed.), *Madhu;* Carmel Berkson, 1982, 'An Approach towards Examining Style in the Cave Temples', in Bettina Baumer (ed.), *Rupa-Pratirupa;* Gift Siromoney *et al.,* 1983, 'Iconometric Analysis of the Sculptures of the Dharmarāja Ratha', in K.V. Ramesh (ed.), *Srinidhih;* Odile Divkaran, 1970, 'Le Temple de Jambuliṅga a Bādāmī', *Arts Asiatiques,* 20; 1987, 'Some Characteristics of the Early Brāhmanical Caves in the Pāṇḍyan Country', in M.S. Nagaraja Rao (ed.), *Kusumānjali,* etc.

2

Political History of South India
(From Fourth to Ninth Centuries AD)

EARLY BACKGROUND

From the earliest times, the political history of South India was shaped up by some small kingdoms. In the very beginning, the three *vendārs*, i.e. crowned kings of the Cēra, Cola and Pāṇḍya dynasties, constituted the chief political powers. The Cēra or Kerala Empire with capital Vañgī comprised the west coast up to Konkaṇ in the north. The Cola kingdom, with its capital Uraiyūr, embraced the Kāverī delta and adjoining regions. Territory to the south of the Cola kingdom up to Kanyākumārī, cited in Kautilya's *Arthaśāstra*, Megasthenes's *Indicā*, and other Greek writings, was the Pāṇḍya country with its capital at Madurai̅. They were all mentioned in the Ashokan inscriptions[1] as his independent neighbours. However, the historical chronology of these three kingdoms remained quite uncertain. Their first tangible account is found in the early Tamil *Saṅgam* literature generally dated from first century to third century AD.[2]

Politically, the Cola ascendancy began from about first century BC till the rise of the Pāṇḍya and Cēra dynasties in the first century AD. Nonetheless, military skirmishes to establish their hegemony became order of the day among the upcoming powers. Still benevolent, hereditary monarchy; highly developed arts; affluent economy; and brisk trade emerged as the general features of the times. The great port-cities of Puhār (Cola), Śāliyūr (Pāṇḍya) and Bandar (Cēra) were the emporia of foreign trade. The author of the *Periplus* (AD 75) described the lucrative trade between India and the Roman Empire. The discovery of a Roman 'factory' where textiles were processed for export; several Roman amphorae vessels; and large quantities of gold and silver

Roman coins from Arikāmeḍu, near Pondicherry, has provided material confirmation of the literary evidences.

This bliss did not continue for long and was eclipsed by the Kālabhras, a warlike race encroaching from the northern borders. Any definite information about the Kālabhras is lacking though some later sources have several references to them. Around third century AD, the power of the kings mentioned in the *Saṅgam* literature was perhaps dying out as suggested by *Śirupānārruppadai*. This decline is attributed to the Kālabhras. The Velvikuḍī grant[3] of Pāṇḍya Nedunjadaiyan denounced them as *kali-araśar* or evil kings, the terrible conquerors of the Pāṇḍya country, whose invincible arms uprooted many *adhirājas* and upset the social order by confiscating all charitable *devadānas* and *brahmadeyas*. The *devadānas* and *brahmadeyas* were revenue free gifts or land-grants made to the temples and Brāhmaṇas, respectively.

The Kālabhras probably occupied the areas along the northern border of the Tamil land. It is quite likely that events as the southward advance of the Āndhras and the invasion of *Dakshiṇāpatha* by Samudragupta might have brought about a change in their location. Possibly dislodged from their position they, in turn, subverted the dynasties ruling around Kāñcī. Further south they established themselves in the Cola and Pāṇḍya kingdoms and thus brought about a complete change in the ancient political conditions of South India at the commencement of the fourth century AD. It has also been surmised that the political revolution attributed to the Kālabhras was perhaps due to religious antagonisms leading to the dominance of the heretical orthodoxy. The revocation of benefactions to Brāhmaṇas, patronage to Buddhist monks and scholars, and the ascendancy of the heretical sects during the period under consideration in South India exemplify the Kālabhras' anti-Brāhmanical stance.[4]

Whatever be the real causes behind their rapacious raids, the Kālabhras nearly eliminated the Cola power, which could later revive in ninth century only. The southern territories of the Pallavas and Pāṇḍyas were also similarly overrun.

There is almost a total lack of information regarding life pattern in the Tamil areas during the next two centuries. But the Deccan proper, i.e. region to the north of the Kṛṣṇā, witnessed emergence of the Vākāṭaka, Ikshavāku, Sālankāyana and Viṣṇukuṇḍin dynasties that divided the erstwhile Sātavāhana Empire amongst them and also perpetuated its artistic and cultural traditions. Religiously, this period marked the ascendancy of Buddhism and Jainism. Buddhism exerted an artistic influence and inspired the art of Ajantā and Andhra regions,[5] suggested by the caves excavated at Ajantā and the images and *stūpas* at Amarāvatī, Bhaṭṭiprolu, Nāgārjunākoṇḍā, etc. Jainism received popular acceptance among the kings of Western Deccan and the Tamil lands.[6]

Finally, the political order was restored in the latter half of the sixth century by the almost simultaneous emergence of the mighty Pallavas[7] of the Simhavishnu line, the Pāṇḍyas in the Tamil land and of the Cālukyas of Bādāmī across the Tungabhadrā in Western Deccan (Map 3). The overthrow of the Kālabhras heralded the first step towards this revival. Both Simhavishnu Pallava and Kadungon Pāṇḍya claimed to have uprooted the Kālabhras.[8] For the succeeding two-and-a-half centuries, these two dynasties divided the entire Tamil country between them. Ruling from their respective capitals, Kāñcīpuram and Madurai, they engaged in constant warfare among themselves. Besides the Pāṇḍyas, the Pallavas had to contest the Cālukyas of Bādāmī and later their successors, the Rāṣṭrakūṭas of Mānyakheṭa. The division of the Southern Peninsula into the plateau kingdoms on the west and the coastal kingdoms on the east perhaps enhanced the desire of each power to control the entire waterway,[9] particularly the Godāvarī and Kṛṣṇā rivers. Vengī, lying between the Godāvarī and Kṛṣṇā deltas and identified with modern Pedda Vegi, the capital of the Sālankāyanas and other Eastern Deccan dynasties, was frequently the bone of contention. In these conflicts the enemies of the Pallavas served as the natural allies of the Pāṇḍyas, their southern adversaries while the rulers of Ceylon being the neighbours of the Pāṇḍyas got more inclined towards their foes, i.e. the Pallavas.

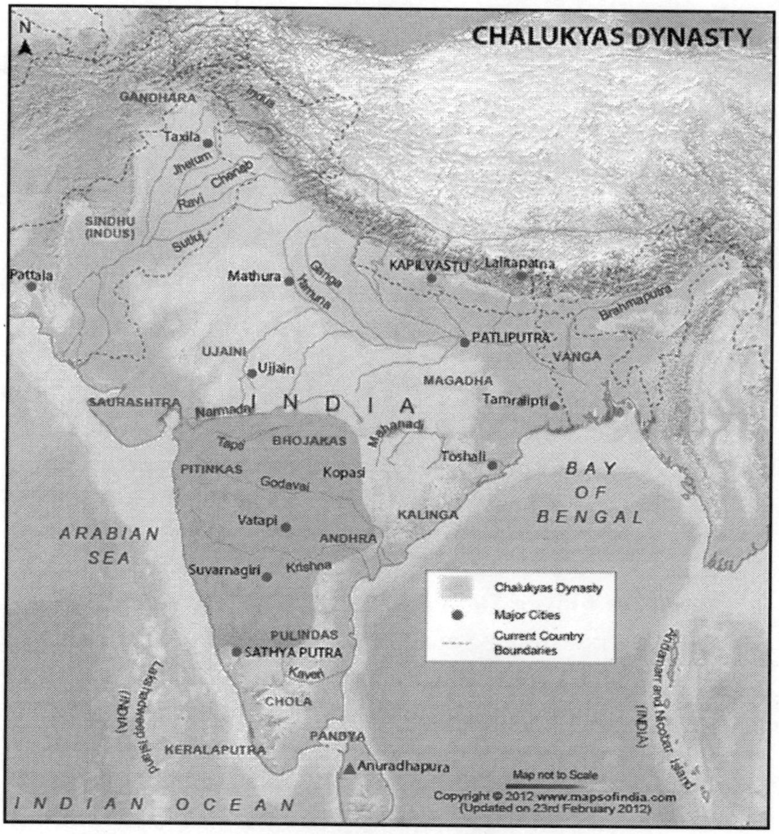

Map 3. The Cālukyan territories (after mapsofindia.com).

With this early background, the political history of each of the three dynasties, viz. the Cālukya, Pallava and Rāṣṭrakūṭa, may be discussed independently to comprehend the background for development of art and architecture under them.

1. THE CĀLUKYAS OF BĀDĀMĪ[10]

There were two branches of the Cālukyas: Western and Eastern. The history of the Cālukyas of Bādāmī, also known as the Early Western Cālukyas, is mainly known through inscriptional sources. Their early inscriptions addressed them as Calkya, Calikya, Culukya or Cālukya: (i)...*Chalikyo Vallabhēśvaraḥ*... (Bādāmī Vallabheśvara Inscription) and (ii) *Chi (Cha) lukyānām- an (V) avāye*... (Ciplun Plates of Pulakeshin II).[11] The name was possibly derived from an ancestor Calka, Calika, or Caluka.

Cālukyas, who claimed the status of *kshatriyas*, were probably an indigenous Kanarese family, their mother tongue being Kannada and majority of inscriptions issued in Kanarese. Their origin has been a matter of much speculation. Their own inscriptions assign them legendary origin. They called themselves *Hāritiputras* of the *Mānavyagotra* in their epigraphs: *padaṁ Vishṇōḥ Mānavyasagōtrāṇ (ā) m Hāriti-putrāṇā (ḥ)*... (Ciplun

Plates). The Handarike inscription and *Vikramānkadevacarita* stated that the Cālukyas were born in the *culka* of sage Hāriti Pañcaśikha. The records of later Cālukyas of Kalyāṇī link their origin to Brahmā and his descendants, assigning a mythological elaboration to their *Hāritiputra* and *Mānavasyagotra* epithets.

However, these versions of the origin and rise of the early Cālukyas appear to be *paurāṇic* legends and myths to exalt their authority and obviously carry no historical value. Their earliest authentic kings were Jayasimha and Ranaraga, as given in later genealogical records,[12] who probably held a subservient position. The first independent ruler of the dynasty was Ranaraga's son Pulakeshin I (AD 535-566), the first *Mahārāja* in the family and perhaps its real founder also. His Bādāmī inscription informs that he laid foundations of the Vātāpī fort and entered it like a bridegroom:

Śaka-varṣēśhu caṭuṣ-śatēshu pañca-ṣaṣṭi-yutēshu
... Calikyo vallabhēśvaraḥ
Dharādharēndra-Vātāpim = ajēyam= bhūtayē bhuvaḥ
adhastād = uparishṭāch = ca durggam = ētad = acīkarat. (Vallabheśvara Inscription)

This infers that he probably ruled the region roughly comprising modern Bijapur with its capital at Bādāmī. The site with strategic importance may have been chosen as a possible base against their rival neighbouring Kadamba and Kalacuri dynasties. The Mahākūṭa pillar inscription[13] of Mangalesha project Pulakeshin as performing several sacrifices including *hiraṇyagarbha* and *aśvamedha.* These may have been in commemoration of his military successes.

Pulakeshin's son Kirtivarman I (AD 566-597) expanded the empire. The Mahākūṭa inscription assigns him victory over Vaṅga, Aṅga, Kaliṅga, Magadha, Mādraka, Kerala, Gaṅga, Pāṇḍya, Coliya, Dramila, Āluka and Vaijayantī. The list appears exaggerated. A more reliable account by Kirtivarman's son Pulakeshin II described him as the *kālarātri* to the Nalas, Mauryas and Kadambas. The subjugation of the Kadamba capital Vanavāsī (Vaijayantī) in North Kanara district (in modern Bombay) was specifically recorded in Cālukyan *dānapatras.* Due to his military feats, the political influence of the Cālukyas must have extended over vast regions in Deccan. He bore the title of *prathama vidhātur* of Vātāpī in the Ciplun Plates.

After Kirtivarman, Pulakeshin II being a minor, his uncle Mangalesha (AD 597-610) acted as regent. He sustained the policy of empire expansion and gained victories against the Kalacuris and Revatīdvīpa. It seems that Mangalesha wanted to secure the throne for his own son. Therefore, towards the end of his reign he faced a civil war with his nephew Pulakeshin, who must have put forth his claim as the rightful heir. Mangalesha was killed and the throne of Bādāmī passed on to Pulakeshin 'Satyāśraya' (AD 610-642). He found the empire engulfed in confusion and anarchy, and successfully combated the dual challenge of external aggressions, and subjugation of the alienated subordinates. He subdued the Kadambas of Vanavāsī, the Gaṅgas, the Ālupas of South Kanara and the Mauryas of Konkaṇ. The Haidarabad Grant of Pulakeshin (dated AD 612) suggest that he acquired the imperial title of *Parameśvara* by defeating hostile kings, saving his homeland from enemies, and restoring Cālukyan sovereignty in the territory of the disaffected neighbours.[14]

Further north he vanquished the Lāṭas, Mālavas and the Gurjaras and extended the northern frontier of his empire at one bound up to Māhī. His greatest triumph was over Harsha *sakalauttarādhipati* (sometime between AD 630-34), the Maukharī ruler of Kanauj as described in the Aihoḷe *praśasti* and verified by Hiuen Tsang in *Si Yu Ki* or *Buddhist Records of the Western World*. These conquests established the sovereignty of Pulakeshin over the three *Mahārāṣṭrakas* or great kingdoms, i.e. Maharashtra, Konkaṇ and Karnāṭa. By a campaign directed towards Eastern Deccan, he humbled Kosala and Kaliṅga. Moving along the coastal route towards south, he next took over Piṣṭāpuram (in Godāvarī district). His brother *yuvarāja* Kubja Vishnuvardhana was put in charge of the newly acquired territory thus founding the Eastern Cālukyan branch, which lasted till AD 1070 when Kulottunga merged it into the Cola family.

By his southward advancement, Pulakeshin henceforth initiated a struggle that was to bring him to utter ruin. Down south he came into conflict with Pallava Mahendravarman I, whom he forced to seek shelter behind the ramparts of Kāñcīpuram as per Aihoḷe *praśasti*. This heralded a struggle that turned into a family feud carried on with full vigour by both the sides. The prolonged series of Cālukya-Pallava wars was apparently precipitated by Pulakeshin overthrowing the Kandara and the Viṣṇukuṇḍin powers located on borders of the Pallava Empire. This might have whetted the empire expansion appetite of both Pallava and Cālukya dynasties. The struggle became so usual that the Pallavas were addressed as their *prakṛtyamitra*[15] in the Cālukyan epigraphs.

Pulakeshin next befriended the Colas, Keralas and the Pāṇḍyas in a possible encirclement move against the Pallavas. Having thus acquired vast regions between the Bay of Bengal and the Arabian Sea, he returned to Bādāmī as 'Lord of the Eastern and Western Waters' (Lohaner Plates). In his Pallava expedition against Narasimhavarman *Māmalla* pitched battles were fought at Sūramāra (Anantapur district), Pariyāl (Kurnool district), and Maṇimaṅgala (Cingleput district), as mentioned in the Kūram plates of Parameshvaravarman.[16] Initially, Pulakeshin seems to have the upper hand as indicated by Aihoḷe *praśasti*. Later Narasimha occupied Bādāmī (Vātāpī), as suggested by his title *Vātāpīkoṇḍā*.[17] Pulakeshin possibly fell fighting. He was undoubtedly the greatest Cālukyan monarch of Bādāmī whose influence spread even beyond India. The Muslim historian Tabari mentioned sending of an embassy by *Prmesha*, a possible derivation of Parameshvara, another name of Pulakeshin to Khusru II, king of Persia. Nilakanta Sastri, giving AD 625-26 as the date of this event, held that this courtesy was possibly reciprocated.[18]

After Pulakeshin the Cālukya power remained in abeyance for about an interregnum of thirteen years (AD 642-655) with a possible Pallava hold of Bādāmī and its surrounding areas. Finally, Vikramaditya I (AD 655-681) restored the Cālukyan fortunes. His Gaḍval plates mention him successively fighting against Pallava rulers Narasimhavarman I, Mahendravarman II and Parameshvaravarman I.[19] Sathianathaier has related Vikramaditya's title *Rājamalla* to his victory over Pallava *Māmalla*, i.e. Narasimhavarman I.

Vikramaditya also attacked and killed Mahendravarman II in alliance with the Western Gaṅga ruler Durvinita. As hinted earlier, the contending powers in these struggles followed the policy of befriending the enemy's enemy. Therefore, the Cālukyas could garner the support of the Gaṅgas and Pāṇḍyas against the Pallavas. The defeat of Parameshvara and the capture of Kāñcī, though short-lived, were Vikramaditya's greatest victory. In the meantime, the advancement of the Cālukyan forces was checked at Peruvalanallur by Parameshvaravarman I's general Siruttondar.

Vikramaditya's death in AD 681 was followed by a lull in the Cālukya-Pallava conflicts. His successor Vinayaditya (AD 681-696) claimed the subjugation of *trairājya Pallavapati* or *trairājyakāñcīpati*, the adversary being Narasimhavarman II. Vinayaditya, with son Vijayaditya, also earned victory over the lord of entire *uttarāpatha* and seizure of the 'Gaṅgā and Yamunā *pālidhvaja*'.

Vijayaditya's reign (AD 696-733) was the longest among the Cālukyas of Bādāmī. The first Kāñcī expedition of Vikramaditya II as *yuvarāja*, resulting in the defeat of Pallava Parameshvaravarman II, was undertaken during his 35th regnal year (AD 730-31).

Vikramaditya II's (AD 733-744) reign was marked by two significant events: (i) Arab raids on the northwestern parts of Cālukyan Empire and, (ii) renewed struggle with the Pallavas. After successful Arab repulsion, Vikramaditya began wars with the Pallavas. His queen Lokamahadevi's inscription[20] refers to his triple victory over Kāñcī. The Vakkalerī plates also mention the Cālukyan conquest of *Tuṇḍakarāṣṭra*. Vikramaditya bestowed the war booty on the Kāñcī Kailāśanātha temple[21] and thus wiped the disgrace that had befallen the Cālukyas by Narasimha I's Bādāmī occupation. Vikramaditya is also credited with victories over the Pāṇḍyas, Colas, Keralas and Kālabhras and erection of a *jayastaṁbha* on the southern ocean to mark his achievements.

Kirtivarman II (AD 745-757) was the last ruler of the Western Cālukyas. His power was steadily undermined by Rāṣṭrakūṭa Dantidurga (AD 742). Having occupied Ellorā and gradually strengthened his position in the Deccan, Dantidurga went down south to Kāñcī and after some struggle entered into a matrimonial alliance with Nandivarman by marrying his daughter Reva to Nandi.[22] Having deprived Kirtivarman of his outlying provinces and consolidating his own position, Dantidurga finally struck the Cālukyas sometime in AD 752-53 and proclaimed his sovereign power in Deccan. In this manner the great dynasty of the Cālukyas of Bādāmī, which once held sway from the Tāptī to the Godāvarī-Kṛṣṇā regions, disappeared from the pages of history.

2. THE PALLAVAS OF KĀÑCĪPURAM

The second powerful dynasty of the times was that of the Pallavas, who had built a fairly extensive empire to the south of the Kṛṣṇā and Tungabhadrā rivers with Kāñcīpuram as their capital (Map 4). The origin of the Pallavas has been quite enigmatic. The term 'Pallava' itself connotes a totemistic origin. Tradition in *Śilappadikāram* and *Maṇimēkalai* described Cola Killi Valavan as having a liaison with the Nāga princess of Maṇipallavam (Jaffna peninsula). Their son Toṇḍaimān Ilandiraiyan was made king of Toṇḍaimaṇḍalam (2nd century AD). One view held that *Toṇḍai* was the name of a creeper and 'Pallava' in Sanskrit meant a sprout, hence the connection between the Pallavas and the rulers of Toṇḍaimaṇḍalam. Another legend suggested the founder of the line, the son of *Mahābhārata's* hero Arjuna and a *apsarā*, was cradled at his birth in a litter of sprouts.[23]

Pallavas are also held as Sanskrit variant of Pahlava (Parthian) who settled in the Indus region and Western India alongside the Śakas. They supposedly occupied Toṇḍaimaṇḍalam in the wake of Sātavāhana downfall. The theory of Parthian origin is also substantiated by elephant scalp shaped crowns (similar to those of Demetrius) in the Vaikuṇṭha-perumāl temple sculptures.[24] They are also assumed to be immigrants from non-Tamil lands whose kingdom was not within limits known to Tamil traditions. Their earliest inscriptions were in Prākṛt while later ones in Sanskrit, unlike those of the Tamil rulers of *Saṅgam* age who patronized Tamil literature. Besides, they assumed titles like *Dharmamahārāja* and *Aśvamedhayajin*. Hence, it can be surmised that they were from a different region. However, their origin as an indigenous people of south has also been put forth.[25]

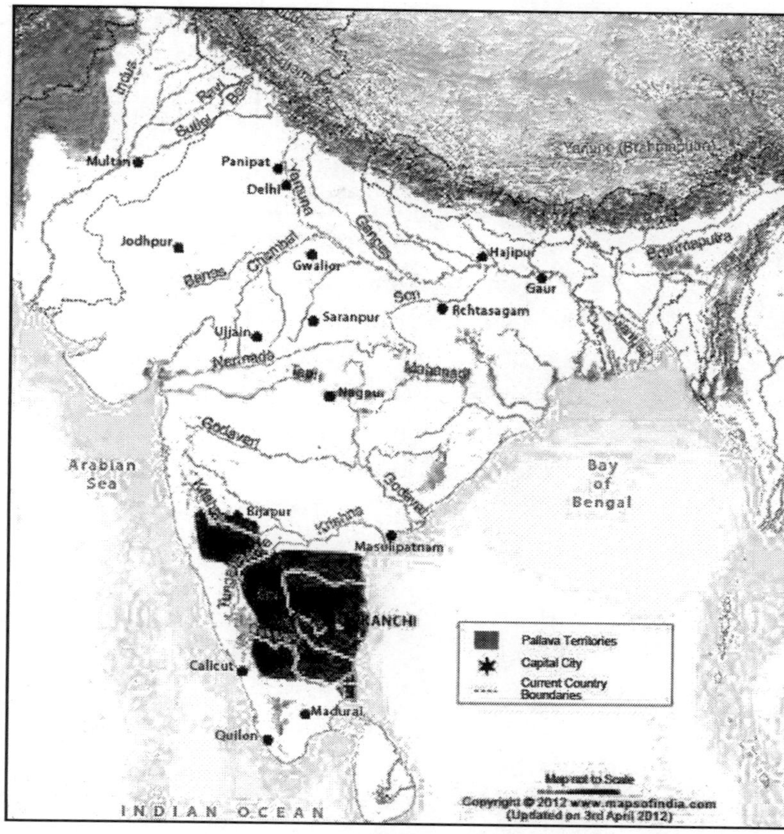

Map 4. The Pallava Empire Expansion (after mapsofindia.com).

A majority of the scholars support the southern origin of the Pallava dynasty. This is quite likely that as natives of Toṇḍaimaṇḍalam, the Pallavas ruled Kāñcī as a local dynasty under Toṇḍaiman Ilandiraiyan during *Saṅgam* age. The possible Sātavāhana acquisition of Toṇḍaimaṇḍalam in about second century AD might have reduced the Pallavas to be their feudatories. Exact information is lacking; still it may be conjectured that after the Sātavāhana collapse, the Toṇḍaiman chieftain reasserted independence as *Toṇḍaiyar* (a Tamil rendering of Pallavas). The Mayiḍavolu grant of *yuvarāja* Shivaskandavarman and Hīrahaḍagalli grant of his 8th regnal year, and an inscription of Simhavarman recovered from Guntur district, all prove their expansion from Kāñcī to Kṛṣṇā (all issued during AD 250-350). This view of Sātavāhana affinity probably also explains the earliest Pallava epigraphs being in Prākṛt and Sanskrit, or the non-Tamil character of their earlier administrative system. Still, in the absence of any reliable historical evidence, the exact chain of events or the relation between the early Toṇḍaiyar kings and the later Pallavas remains uncertain. Nothing is known about Ilandiraiyan's predecessors or successors.

The earliest known Pallava king, probably also the greatest of the early Pallavas, was Shivaskandavarman (beginning of fourth century AD). Vishnugopa of Kāñcī[26] was one of the twelve kings of *Dakshiṇāpatha* defeated by Samudragupta. This Gupta invasion perhaps resulted in Vishnugopa losing his western territories to the Kadambas and the Gaṅgas.[27] Several Sanskrit copper-plates provide the names and mutual relations of more than sixteen rulers who ruled over the diminished kingdom, the last being Simhavarman I (AD 436). Thus, continuity in the Pallava lineage till fifth century AD may be ensured. However, after Simhavarman I there is again a lack of information up to the reign of Simhavarman II. This political oblivion may also be due to the Kālabhra incursions.

Simhavishnu (AD 555-590), son of Simhavarman II, revived the Pallava power in the latter half of the sixth century AD. A copper-plate grant dated in the sixth regnal year of the latter described the achievements of the former as *yuvarāja* omitting any historical details about Simhavarman, the reigning king. This indicates that Simhavishnu was the virtual founder of the restored Pallava power. The Kāśākuddi plates[28] acknowledge his victories over Kālabhra, Mālava, Cola, Pāṇḍya and Siṁhala (Ceylon). Thus, it is likely that Simhavishnu, as eulogized by his son Mahendravarman I in the *Mattavilāsa-prahasana*, ushered in the age of Pallava greatness as the rulers of Tamilakām, i.e. the land of the Tamils or land with Tamil as the current language of the classes as well as the masses. Its geographical limits were Venkaṭam (Tirupati hills) in the north, Kumārī (a river now lost in the Indian Ocean) in the south, and the sea on the east and the west.[29]

Mahendravarman I (AD 590-630) had a fairly long reign. The most significant political event of his period was the resumption of the Pallava-Cālukya struggle. As narrated earlier, Mahendravarman had a vast empire, bordered by the Kandaras and Viṣṇukuṇḍins. In his southward advancement, after vanquishing these border kingdoms, it was but natural for Pulakeshin to come into conflict with the Pallava monarch. He acquired the northernmost portions of the Pallava Empire in the Pullalūr encounter. Still, Pallava hold towards the southern part up to Kāverī was intact even late in Mahendra's reign.[30] He thus appears to have laid the foundations of the Pallava imperialism and also safeguarded his empire against any further Cālukya encroachment.

Mahendravarman's achievements were versatile. Being bestowed with an artistic temperament he, as *vicitracitta*, initiated rock architecture in South India, besides engraving of stone inscriptions. *Mattavilāsa-prahasana*, the drama on Buddhist *bhikshus*, exemplified his prolific writing skills. He, thus, represented a truly myriad personality.

Narasimhavarman I (AD 630-668) was the most remarkable sovereign of his dynasty with multi-faceted achievements. His military feats, including four victories against the traditional Cālukyan foes, were amplified in his epithet *Māmalla*. The Kūram plates[31] of Parameshvaravarman inform about Narasimha's memorable victory over Pulakeshin II in the battles of Pariyala, Maṇimaṅgala and Suramāra. According to Mallikārjuna temple inscription,[32] his general Siruttonda invaded Bādāmī in about AD 642. Narasimha assumed the title *Vātāpīkoṇḍā* in commemoration of this victory, which led to the death of Pulakeshin and occupied the southern parts of Cālukyan Empire, including the capital Bādāmī. For the next thirteen years, while the Cālukya kingdom was sunk in abeyance, Narasimha established his supremacy among the southern Colas, Cēras, Kālabhras and the Pāṇḍyas, although no details of these wars are available.

He also sent two naval expeditions to Ceylon to restore Manavarma, a deposed Ceylonese prince who fought with him against Pulakeshin. The second larger and successful expedition was dispatched from Mahābalipuram port and has been compared in the copper grants with Srī Rāma's *Lankāvijaya*.[33] His political and military entanglements notwithstanding, Narasimha made great contributions to South Indian rock-architecture and sculpture through monolithic *rathas* and excavated *maṇḍapams*. Thus, the Pallava Empire undoubtedly reached its zenith under him.

Both Mahendravarman II (AD 668-72) and his successor Parameshvaravarman I (AD 672-700) retained the strained relations with the Cālukyas. Parameshvara fought with Vikramaditya I and allies Pāṇḍya Arikesari Parankusa and Gaṅga Bhuvikrama. As already mentioned the Gaḍval plates reveal that Vikramaditya conquered Kāñcī, destroyed *Māmalla*'s family and camped near Uragapura (or Uraiyūr) on the Kāverī on 25th April AD 674. But this success was short-lived. Though he had reached as far as Lalgudi near Peruvalanallūr, Vikramaditya could neither demolish Pallava might nor eliminate *Māmalla*. As described epigraphically,[34] Parameshvara defeated Vallabha Vikramaditya's army in the battle of Peruvalanallūr and made him flee. Another military combat of his times was the Pallava-Gaṅga feud indicated by the battle of Vilandai. The battle went against Parameshvara, who lost the Pallava jewel *ugrodaya* to the Gaṅga adversary. The jewel was taken back later by Nandivarman II in the third battle of Vilandai. In spite of his constant warfare, Parameshvara took active interest in art activities and patronized several *rathas* and *maṇḍapams*.

Narasimhavarman II Rajasimha's reign (AD 700-728) was marked by peace and prosperity. Being comparatively free from dynastic wars, he scored notable artistic progress. Credited with the beginnings of structural temples, he also carried further the tradition of excavated *maṇḍapams*. He is believed to have patronized poets Daṇḍī and Bhāsa and sent embassies to China[35] while his queen Rangapataka was a Cambodian princess. Thus, it is apparent that Rajasimha's reign must have been quite eventful. His son Mahendravarman III, who constructed a shrine in the Kailāśanātha temple at Kāñcī[36] and perhaps ruled jointly as a *yuvarāja* (AD 720-25), probably did not survive his father. It was possibly he who was represented as a wounded person brought from the battlefield to the presence of Rajasimha and his queen in relief panel XVIII of the Vaikuṇṭha-perumāl temple[37] at Kāñcīpuram.

Parameshvaravarman II (AD 728-731) ruled for about three years. In AD 731 Cālukya *yuvarāja* Vikramaditya II invaded Kāñcī in alliance with the Gaṅga prince Ereyappa and levied tribute. The invasion caused great confusion and anarchy in the Pallava state. The Gaṅga king Sripurusha claimed to have won the Pallava *chatra* and assumed the title *Permānaḍī* after killing *Kāḍuveṭṭi*, i.e. the king of Kāñcī when the latter waged a war of retaliation, at Vilandai.

Parameshvaravarman's death must have led to chaos in the Pallava dominions with no immediate successor. The Vaikuṇṭha-perumāl temple sculptures narrate the selection of Nandivarman II Pallavamalla (AD 732-796), son of Hiranyavarman of a collateral branch, by the *ghaṭikā*, sort of a corporate body constituted by prominent ministers, courtiers, Brāhmaṇas and traders. His accession to the throne was obviously not a peaceful one. Besides, during his long reign of about 65 years, Nandivarman faced several challenges, the most crucial being of the Pāṇḍya and Cālukya powers. His general Udayachandra aided him in the encounters. Sometime around AD 741-742 Cālukya Vikramaditya II invaded Kāñcī.[38] Nandivarman was defeated and fled from Kāñcī. The victor, however, spared the city from ravages. Nandivarman recovered Kāñcī soon, though how, it is uncertain to say.

He maintained amicable relations with Rāṣṭrakūṭa Dantidurga, who had occupied Kāñcī and consolidated his position in the Deccan following Vikramaditya's death in AD 744. Sometime back, Nandivarman had subordinated the Gaṅgas, who assisted the Pallava against the Rāṣṭrakūṭa. Some territory was taken and handed over to Jayanandivarman, the Bāṇa[39] feudatory of Nandivarman. Meanwhile, renewing the Pallava-Pāṇḍya skirmishes, Varagunamaharaja I defeated the Pallava forces at Pennāgadam (AD 767). Nandivarman tried hard in vain to restrain the Pāṇḍya imperialism. His long reign was not devoid of art creations. He built the Vaikuṇṭha-perūmāl and Mukuteśvara temples. The former edifice artistically depicted Pallava history in narrative sculptures while the latter temple was originally named *Dharma-mahādēvī-gṛham*, probably after his queen Dharma-mahādēvī.

Dantivarman (AD 796-846) was also unable to resist the Pāṇḍya aggressions under Varaguna and Srimara Srivallabha. From his 21st to the 49th regnal years, lack of inscriptions indicates a temporary eclipse of power. This is confirmed by a recently discovered Pāṇḍyan copper-plate *dānapatra* stating that Toṇḍaimaṇḍalam had passed on to the Telugu Cola ruler Srikantha[40] of the Poṭṭappi family. Three inscriptions discovered from Vaikuṇṭha-perumāl temple (Kāñcīpuram), Taṇḍalam and Sumangalī village (both in North Arcot) respectively, assignable more or less to ninth century AD, suggest that when Dantivarman lost control over Toṇḍaimaṇḍalam temporarily, some Pallava scions carved out independent, short-lived principalities of their own, and were finally overcome by Nandivarman III.

How Dantivarman reoccupied Toṇḍaimaṇḍalam is not specifically known. He also had to face the hostility of Rāṣṭrakūṭa Govinda III. The latter probably occupied Kāñcī (AD 802) after defeating the former and retired to his camp at Rāmeśvara-*tīrtha*, on the bank of Tungabhadra in about 804-05.[41] His territories probably extended till the Cola-maṇḍalam as suggested by the excavation of a cave temple at Malayadippaṭṭi by his Muttaraiyan chieftain Kuvavan Sattan.

Nandivarman III (AD 846-859) had matrimonial relations with the Rāṣṭrakūṭas and perhaps, Colas.[42] He organized a strong confederacy of the Gaṅgas, Tamil Colas and Rāṣṭrakūṭas. While the Gaṅgas were Pallava feudatories, the Cola and Rāṣṭrakūṭa alliance must have been facilitated by marital ties. Together they fought the battle of Tellarū against Pāṇḍyan Srimara. A victorious Nandivarman assumed the title

Tellarerinda and later reached as far as the Vaigai River, in the heart of the Pāṇḍya Empire. This way, he restored the Pallava power to its former glory.

Nripatunga (AD 859-99) secured a decisive victory against Srimara in the battle of Arisil[43] near Kumbakoṇam (AD 860-61). He also supported a successful expedition, sent by the Ceylonese king Sena II, to help Srimara's son Varagunavarman II ascend the throne (AD 862). The prince sought aid of Sena II of Ceylon when his stepbrother Viranarayana was made the *yuvarāja* (AD 860) overlooking his rightful claim. A grateful Varaguna acknowledged Nripatunga's overlordship, putting an end to the prolonged series of Pallava-Pāṇḍya feuds. However, at this juncture all was not well within the Pallava Empire itself.

Differences arose between Nripatunga and his brother Aparajitavarman whereby the Pāṇḍyas assisted Nripatunga while the Colas besides Gaṅgas supported Aparajita, born of a Cola princess. Their armies met at Srīpurambiyam near Kumbakoṇam (about AD 885) in a decisive battle. Aparajita won, though his Gaṅga ally lost his life. This was perhaps the end of Nripatunga's and the beginning of Aparajita's reign. Inscriptions subsequent to Nripatunga's 26th and prior to 41st year, i.e. AD 899 at Madavalam in northern Toṇḍaimaṇḍalam, have not been found anywhere. This gap suggests the reign of Aparajita, whose inscriptions from 3rd to 18th years issued almost annually are available. After AD 899, Nripatunga was totally unheard of. He could have been the Pallava king slain by Aditya Cola according to the Kanyākumārī inscription.[44] Aditya's role in Srīpurambiyam battle has not been clearly stated though he may have aided Aparajita (AD 885-903) in restoring order in the Pallava country as suggested by his title *Toṇḍai-nāḍu-pāviya.*[45]

In return for his services, an indebted Aparajita granted Aditya some territory in Toṇḍaimaṇḍalam suggested by his continuous stay there. Till AD 885 Aditya was not known epigraphically in his home country; rather, the inscriptions of overlord Nripatunga and his ally Varaguna were found there. Meanwhile, his regular inscriptions from places as Tirumālpuram, Takkolam, Ukkal, Uttiramerūr, Tirukkaḷukkuṇṛam, etc., in Toṇḍaimaṇḍalam ranged from AD 890-91 to 897, i.e. 21st to 27th year. This is a clear evidence of his sojourn in the Pallava territory. Maybe his subordinate position prompted Aditya to plan the overthrow of his suzerain. The Kanyākumārī inscription of Virarajendra Cola mentions the killing of a Pallava king by his ancestor Aditya, while the Tiruvālangādu plates[46] of Rajendra Cola describe how Aditya fought against Aparajita and took possession of his territories.

This makes it apparent that Aditya Cola ultimately defeated Aparajita to terminate the Pallava power and expanded Cola influence further north in Toṇḍaimaṇḍalam sometime around AD 903. In spite of this incursion, the Pallava power reasserted itself for some more time under Nandivarman IV and Kampavarman, as suggested by their numerous inscriptions. Nandivarman is also referred to in an extant Tamil work *Nandikkalambakam*, written in praise of *Tellarrū Nandi*. Kampavarman began his rule of 32 years in AD 948, according to his Uttiramerūr record[47] until the empire was finally taken over by Cola Parantaka.

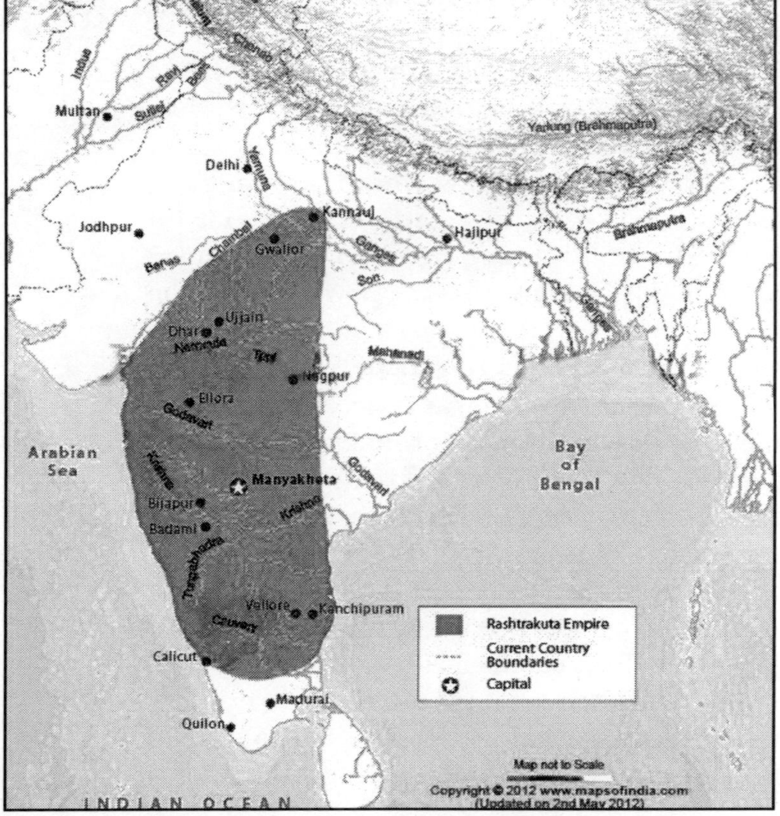

Map. 5. The Rāṣṭrakūṭa regions (after mapsofindia.com).

3. THE RĀṢṬRAKŪṬAS OF MĀNYAKHEṬA

The Rāṣṭrakūṭas of Mānyakheṭa or Mālkheḍ had founded their empire on the ruins of the Western Cālukyan Empire of Bādāmī. They were probably an indigenous people of the Deccan. Several Rāṣṭrakūṭa families were known to be ruling in different parts of the Deccan since fifth century AD: two in Satara, and one with capital at Ellicpur (Berar) as a Cālukya feudatory in the first half of seventh century. This family ultimately established a powerful empire (Map 5).[48] The Rāṣṭrakūṭas' origin is also contentious.

They themselves claimed descent from Yadu while scholars held variant views linking them respectively, to a Tuṅga family, Rājpūtānā-Kanauj regions, Telugu lineage, and Maraṭhi family. Altekar traced their antiquity in the term *Rathikā* (i.e. westerners) found in Ashokan inscriptions.[49] He also highlighted their occupation of Maharashtra, Berar and parts of Karnataka besides close ties with Kanarese families. The earliest known Rāṣṭrakūṭa was Dantivarman (AD 650-70). Little is known historically about his successors Indra, Govinda I and Karka I. Karka's eldest son Indra I was probably a feudatory of Cālukya king in his campaign against the king of Valabhī (AD 725). His marriage with the Cālukya princess Bhavanaga resulted in Dantidurga's birth. Danti also began his career as a Cālukya feudatory and probably assisted Vikramaditya II against the Pallavas and the Arab invaders. Gradually, his ambition seems to have grown and after Vikramaditya II's death, he launched upon a career of conquest on his own.

Dantidurga occupied Ellorā (AD 742) when Cālukya Kirtivarman II was reigning. The former strengthened his position by depriving the latter of his outlying provinces. He subdued the Gurjaras of Malwā, the rulers of Kosala, Kaliṅga and Telugu Colas of the Srīśailam country. After invading Kāñcī, he formed an alliance with Nandivarman. Thus, consolidating his prestige and power, he sounded the death knell of the Cālukyan Empire and proclaimed himself the sovereign power in the Deccan. The Samangad plates (AD 754) record his acquisition of Khāndesh, Nāsik, Poonā, Satārā and Kolhāpur.

As Dantidurga died issueless, his uncle Krishna ascended the throne (AD 756) and foiled an attempt by Kirtivarman II to reassert his supremacy (AD 757).[50] He also dispatched an expedition under *yuvarāja* Govinda against Vishnuvardhana IV of Vengī, who was defeated[51] and parts of his empire annexed to the Rāṣṭrakūṭa dominions. Krishna also defeated the Gaṅgas of Mysore. While the Rāṣṭrakūṭa power was being militarily consolidated, Krishna undertook the excavation of the monolithic Kailāśanātha temple at Ellorā.[52]

Govinda II (AD 772-75) was addicted to sensual pleasures, hence his ambitious brother Dhruva planned to seize the throne. He first subdued Govinda (AD 780) and then proceeded against his allies. He incarcerated Gaṅga Sivamara[53] and annexed the whole of Gaṅgavādi. Similarly, Pallavamalla had to pay a tribute of elephants.[54] Eastern Cālukya Vishnuvardhana IV had to part with some territories, besides marrying off his daughter Silamahadevi to Dhruva. Thus settling affairs in the south, Dhruva began the tripartite struggle for empire between the Pālas, Gurjara Pratihāras and Rāṣṭrakūṭas by undertaking an elaborate campaign towards North India. The struggle, beginning sometime after AD 785-86, continued for about a century and its keynote seems to have been the possession of the imperial city of Kanauj for which each of these dynasties tried and succeeded in turn.

Dhruva defeated both Dharmapala of Gauda and Vatsaraja (of Rājputānā and Central India) and carried his victorious army to the Gaṅgā Yamunā doab. The symbols of these two rivers were incorporated in the Rāṣṭrakūṭa banner as a mark of his victory. The northern campaign was perhaps a mere plundering raid, as no effort was made to consolidate his conquests. Still, it enhanced the power and prestige of the Rāṣṭrakūṭa Empire and there was probably no challenge to his authority from the Himālayas to Kanyākumārī.

Govinda III had to face the hostility of his disinherited brothers, particularly Kambha, the eldest, in alliance with Nandivarman Pallavamalla and Gaṅga Sivamara. Govinda defeated the confederacy of twelve rulers. He adopted a conciliatory policy towards his brothers while their allies were subdued. Using his victory with moderation, Govinda reinstated Kambha as viceroy of Gaṅgavādi and gained his lifelong loyalty. Govinda's second brother Indra, who stood by him, was rewarded with the viceroyalty of Lāṭa.

Next he led a military expedition towards North India. His success was as illustrious as that of his father. However, events in the south enforced his return (AD 800) in about two years' time. Taking advantage of his absence, Vijayaditya II of Vengī had raised arms. Govinda put his younger brother Bhima on the throne (AD 802) after defeating Vijayaditya. He is credited victory over the hostile confederacy of the Gaṅga, Pallava, Pāṇḍya and Kerala rulers.[55] He even occupied Kāñcī for some time after defeating Dantivarman (AD 802). Once again all the major powers between Himālayas to Kanyākumārī were vanquished and practically the whole of India acknowledged Rāṣṭrakūṭa suzerainty. Govinda's achievements aptly justify the claims of his court-poets that after his birth the Rāṣṭrakūṭas became as unassailable as the Yādavas had become after Srī Kṛṣṇa Murārī's birth.[56]

After Govinda III's death (AD 814), decline set in this high watermark of power and glory. His successor Amoghavarsha was a minor; therefore, Govinda's nephew Karka, the viceroy of Lāṭa and Malwā, was appointed his regent. Rebellions broke out on all sides assuming such serious proportions that Amoghavarsha had to flee (AD 818). But Karka gradually restored order and helped Amoghavarsha in recovering his throne within three years. Vengī was reoccupied from Vijayaditya II in AD 830. In about 850 AD war resumed with the Eastern Cālukyas. Amoghavarsha emerged a decisive victor in the battle of Viṅgāvalli (district Kurnool). But Gaṅgavādi was lost. After almost continuous war of twenty years, the Rāṣṭrakūṭa forces had to evacuate Gaṅgavādi and an alliance was fostered by the marriage of Amoghavarsha's daughter Chandrobelabba with the Gaṅga crown prince Butuga.

Thus, Amoghavarsha's reign of about sixty-six years saw virtually no peace. Although he maintained peace and order in his empire, the Rāṣṭrakūṭa power did suffer a visible decline. Despite regular military entanglements, he indulged in peaceful pursuits too. Himself an author, he composed the *Kavirājamārga*, a work on poetics. He is also applauded as the maker of Mānyakheṭa city.[57] The reign of Krishna II (AD 880-914) proved to be a disastrous one. Besides others, he received a crushing defeat at Vallāla while espousing the cause of his Cola grandson Kannaradeva.

Indra III succeeded Krishna. Taking advantage of succession disputes in Vēngī, he brought bulk of it under Rāṣṭrakūṭa occupation. His campaign towards North India was very successful. Indra was succeeded by Amoghavarsha II (AD 927), who became a victim to the foul play of his ambitious younger brother Govinda IV. But Govinda's tyranny, inefficiency and oppressive rule alienated the people and his officials alike, who bestowed the kingdom on Baddega Amoghavarsha III, a half-brother of Indra III. Amoghavarsha had a short reign of three years during, which the administration was, in fact, carried on by his son *yuvarāja* Krishna III.

Krishna finally ascended the throne in AD 939. Soon he set to punish the Cola king for sheltering Govinda IV. His Bāṇa and Vaidumba feudatories assisted him, as also Butuga II, the ruler of Gaṅgavādi. They captured Kāñcī and Tanjore (AD 943). Having invaded the Cola kingdom they won a decisive victory (AD 949) in the battle of Takkolam[58] wherein Butuga killed the Cola *yuvarāja* Rajaditya. The Cola resistance notwithstanding, Krishna occupied a large part of Toṇḍaimaṇḍalam, i.e. the northern half of their empire[59] thus dealting a rude shock towards the end of Parantaka's reign.

Krishna was also successful in Vengī where he set up his brother Danarnava and two princes, Badapa and Taila II, against King Amma II, fomenting trouble there. He also advanced towards Northern India (AD 963) in keeping with the practice of his predecessors, assisted by Gaṅga Marasimha II. They compelled Paramāra Harsh Siyaka of Malwā to acknowledge Rāṣṭrakūṭa suzerainty. In retaliation, Harsh sacked Mānyakheṭa (AD 972-73) during his successor Khottiga's reign. Although Mānyakheṭa was reoccupied, Khottiga did not live long. His death (AD 973) saw his nephew Karka II enthroned. Situation worsened by his inefficiency. Taking advantage of the chaos and confusion, Cālukya Taila II, a feudatory chief of Tardavādi rebelled against the king and defeated him. Karka fled and continued to rule a small principality in Mysore till AD 991 while Taila seized the Rāṣṭrakūṭa kingdom. Gaṅga Marasimha made an unsuccessful attempt to regain it for Indra IV. Marasimha and Indra IV both committed *sallekhana*[60] in AD 975 and 982, respectively. Thus, the mighty Rāṣṭrakūṭa dynasty that once held sway over almost the whole of India was finally overthrown.

Taila's success was the beginning of the later Cālukyas of Kalyāṇī. He ruled Mānyakheṭa for nearly twenty-four years and was followed by Satyasraya and Somesvara I. Vikramaditya VI was the most illustrious king of this branch. In about AD 1162, their commander-in-chief, Bijjala, revolted usurping a greater portion of the empire. The Yādavas of Devagiri and the Hoysalas of Dvārasamudra who absorbed considerable part of the Cālukyan kingdom continued the process of usurpation. After AD 1190, the *rājās* of the line were reduced to petty chiefs marking a final end to their sovereignty.

Thus, the period from the later half of the sixth to the first half of the tenth century AD witnessed the rise to power and the decline of the Cālukyas of Bādāmī, the Pallavas of Kāñcīpuram and the Rāṣṭrakūṭas of Mānyakheṭa.The Pāṇḍyas, Gaṅgas, Bāṇas, Colas and other smaller powers sided with any of these three dynasties. Politically, it remained an era of conflicts for an extension of their influence and territories. Such conflicts, however, did not deter the growth of art, religion and culture in these regions. Rather, the contending political parties appear to have vied with one another in producing artistic creations, as indicated by the large number of edifices erected under them. Before discussing their contribution towards art, it is desirable to have an idea of the prevailing cultural conditions as cultural milieu is the prime force permeating all walks of life.

CULTURAL MILIEU

Like its political history, the earliest cultural history of South India may also be gleaned from the *Saṅgam* literature. Historically, these poems and texts written in praise of their kings, though not exactly accurate, provide vital insights into social life. The South Indian culture was an assimilated form of the indigenous traditions and the Āryan influence making inroads gradually across the Vindhyas.[61] For a long time the Vindhya range denoted roughly the southern limit of the extent of Āryan settlements. A *Ṛgvedic* hymn[62] referred to *Dakshiṇāpāda* as the 'region where the exiled Āryan betook himself'. According to some scholarly opinions,[63] it simply meant the 'South' beyond the limits of the recognized Āryan world. Pāṇinī[64] and Baudhāyana,[65] respectively, mentioned *Dakshiṇātya* and *Dakshiṇāpatha*. The *Aitreya Brāhmaṇa*[66] stated that Viśvāmitra condemned his fifty sons, who were jealous of Śunahṣepa, to live on the borders of *Āryāvarta*. Their descendants were to be *dasyus* like the Āndhras, Puṇḍras and Pulindas. Though the Āryans' gradual progress into South India is not clearly traceable, the process of 'Āryanization' of the south can be surmised through literature and legends.

Legends related to Agastya[67] preserve the memory of the percolation of Āryan culture into South India. The legend of his encounters with Ilvala[68] and Vātāpī[69] marks the beginning of Agastya's connection with the south. The *Mahābhārata* records his southward journey on some unspecified business[70] when he asked the Vindhyas to stop getting higher till he returns and, never returned. An allied tale is of Agastya drinking up the waters of the ocean to expose the demons hidden underneath.[71] The deal with the Vindhyas and the drinking of the ocean waters were probably allegorical representations of the expansion of the Aryan culture towards the south, and later across the seas.[72] The way he fought against the *asuras*, Agastya symbolized the early Āryan fighters in South India who must have met resistance at the hands of the early non-Āryan inhabitants there.[73] The Āryan expansion involved not only subduing resistance but also clearing of the forests as suggested by the legend of Videgha Māthava in the *Śatapatha Brāhmaṇa*.[74] This idea is also suggested in the *Mahābhārata*.[75] Agastya has also been hailed as the initiator of agriculture,[76] and the originator of Tamil language and grammar in South.[77] Tradition has that he served as the Pāṇḍyas' *purohita*.[78] Thus, Agastya appears as an active agent in the north-south cultural contact.

Āryans' southward expansion is also indicated by the Parśurāma legends; be it creation of the Kerala country after his twenty-one expeditions against the *kshatriyas*,[79] or the exchange of his mother's head with a *pariyā*, i.e. tribal woman. This aspect of the legend was probably a befitting instance of the cultural synthesis between the Āryan and non-Āryan races. Similarly, Kauṇḍiṇya *ṛṣi* supposedly had intimate relations with the south. Several South Indian inscriptions and copper-plates record land-grants to *Brāhmaṇas* of Kauṇḍiṇya *gotra*. A song of Āvūr Mūlam Kilār portrays the life of a Kauṇḍiṇya *Brāhmaṇa* family of Pūnjārrūr village in Tanjore, in second and third centuries AD.

Whatever be the pace of the cultural synthesis, the later Brāhmanical texts, such as the *Aitreya Brāhmaṇa*, *Vāyu Purāṇa*, *Matsya Purāṇa*, *Epics*, etc.,[80] suggest that by the time of their composition, having crossed the Vindhyas, the Āryans had founded several states from Narmadā or Revā to Godāvarī. Vidarbha[81] was one such state. The adoption of Āryan traditions is also hinted by the mention of *cērapādāh* in *Aitreya Brāhmaṇa* as one of three peoples to transgress certain ancient injunctions.[82] That the people of the extreme south were known to Baudhāyana[83] or Ashoka[84] suggest their increased proximity with the northerners.

Probably some teachers also expedited the process of establishing Āryan influence. The description of *āsramas* in the *Daṇḍakāraṇya* in the *Rāmāyaṇa*[85] conveys this notion. The *Sutta Nipāta* also records southern movement of teachers. For instance, Bavari, a teacher, left Kośala and settled at Aśmaka. However, his pupils going north to Magadha to meet Buddha, through Paiṭhan, Mahiṣamatī and Ujjain rather suggest reversal of the usual Āryan southbound destination. Tamil literature, as the earliest evidence from the south, suggests that the new influences were heartily welcomed and the changes effected in a peaceful manner. However, *Rāmāyaṇa* stories regarding hostility of the *rākshasas* towards Āryan *yajñas* and *ṛṣis*; the dire need for Rāma to curb their excesses, etc., when historically proven, may provide some evidence of initial opposition to the incoming culture.[86] Till then it is inferred that with their tribal moorings continuing, the locals needed a formalized religious system and social norms in the process of evolution.

Several Vedic concepts, as *ṛṇatraya*, respect to *Brāhmaṇas*, performance of *yajñas*, chastity of Arundhati, etc.; as well as *epic* stories were incorporated into the *Saṅgam* texts. The early Cēra, Cola and Pāṇḍya kings claimed to have fed the opponent forces of the *Mahābhārata* war. Furthermore, the destruction of *tripura* by Śiva; story of King Śibi; the struggle between Kṛṣṇa and the *asuras*, etc., were well known to them. Marriage, as a sacrament attended by ritual, was introduced in the Tamil country by the Āryans.[87]

The northern influence was perhaps most marked in the field of religion and ethics. *Saṅgam* texts mentioned Karikala escorting a departing guest by walking seven steps with him, as a probable observance of the practice of *saptapadī*. Regarding killing of a cow, Brahmaṇ, or a foetus as heinous crime was likely Āryan impact. During the *Saṅgam* times, popularity of various features of Vedic religion such as the veneration of Vedic deities; worship of Viṣṇu with *tulsī* and bell as mentioned in *Padirruppaṭṭū*; custom of fasting in temples; temple of Saraswati mentioned in *Maṇimēkalai*; belief in the concept of *avatāra*; the effect of *karma* in next births, etc., were indicative of northern infiltration. This impact was, however, not overwhelming and may be regarded as reciprocal as suggested by Upinder Singh. In a way it was not imposition of Sanskritic influences upon a passive south or a simple story of 'Aryanization' of South India. Therefore, while worship of their primitive deities sustained, various Āryan deities were adopted with local adaptation. For instance, Kārtikeya as Murugan or Subramaṇya, Viṣṇu as Māyōn, Indra and Durgā as Vēndan and Kotravai, respectively, were identified with their southern godheads as mentioned in *Saṅgam* and post-*Saṅgam* texts. Such status prevailed till the *Saṅgam* age.

Towards the end of the third century AD, the political rise of the Kālabhras and overthrow of the established social order by them brought in important repercussions. This period also witnessed the ascendancy of heretical sects leading to an upheaval, particularly in the Tamil regions. Fearing largescale conversions to Jainism and Buddhism,[88] Śaivite and Vaiṣṇavite followers began to counter the rising tide of heresy with a twofold strategy: (i) the growth of an intense *Bhakti* towards Śiva and Viṣṇu and, (ii) posing challenges for public debates, testing doctrines through ordeals, etc.[89] The *Nayanmār*[90] and the *Ālvār*[91] saints (7th-9th centuries AD) roused the people in the Tamil land with their soul-stirring compositions, and proved instrumental in popularising Śaivism and Vaiṣṇavism. Such religious intensity filled the artists too, with a deep spiritual bonding. The upcoming Brāhmanical religions necessitated the erection of religious edifices as abodes for the deities and *mūrtis* represented in *avatāras* and *līlās*. Apart from royalty, the feudal chiefs and nobles vied with each other in sponsoring temples and endowing them for various services. In fact, the rise of the temple to a pivotal place in the religious and social life was perhaps the direct outcome of this revivalist movement.

DYNASTIC RELIGIOUS AFFILIATIONS

A brief insight into the religious condition under the Cālukyas, Pallavas and the Rāṣṭrakūṭas may explain how the revival of Hinduism was a contributory factor in the emergence of new art forms in South India between seventh to ninth centuries AD.

Cālukyan

The rise of the Cālukyas was associated with *paurāṇic* resurrection. They revitalized sacrificial rituals proved by the performance of *srauta yajñas* as *vājapeya, agniṣṭoma, agnicayana, pauṇḍrika, aśvamedha, hiraṇyagarbha, bahusuvarṇa*, etc. by the Cālukyan kings, as recorded in their epigraphs. Śaiva *Āgamas* and *Purāṇas* were assigned prominence. From the beginning, the Cālukya kings worshipped both Vaiṣṇava and Śaiva deities. The varāha-*lañchana* indicated their Vaiṣṇavite affiliation while Śaivite leanings were apparent from the worship of Kārtikeya and *Saptamātṛkās*. They claimed protection by the former and nourishment by the latter.[92] Pulakeshin I, who bore the titles of *Srī-pṛthvī-vallabha, Srī-vallabha* or *vallabha* and *hiraṇyagarbha-prasūta*, performed the *aśvamedha*:

> *Aśvamēdh-ādi yajñānāṁ yajvā śrauta-vidhānataḥ*
> *Hiraṇyagarbhasambhūtaś=CalikyoVallabhēśvaraḥ* (Vallabheśvara Inscription).

Mangalesha got excavated the Vaiṣṇavite cave III at Bādāmī and gifted the village Lāñjigēśvara for Viṣṇu worship.[93] He was a *mahābhāgavata*. Thus, the Bhāgavata religion received great impetus under the early rulers.

The later rulers perhaps embraced Śaivism. Vikramaditya I, the restorer of the Cālukyan Empire, called himself *param-maheśvara*.[94] Vijayaditya patronized the Saṅgameśvara temple at Paṭṭaḍakal. A large number of temples, structural and rock-cut, were dedicated to Śiva, at Aihoḷe, Bādāmī, Paṭṭaḍakal and Mahākūṭa. The Lokeśvara[95] and Trailokeśvara[96] temples enshrined the Śiva *liṅga*. The Lakulīśa or Pāśupata sect seems to be quite popular. The Lakulīśa sculptures in the Virupāksha and Mallikārjuna temples at Paṭṭaḍakal, a seated Lakulīśa image of the Bhūtanātha group at Bādāmī, and another sculpture in the Makuṭeśvara at Mahākūṭeśvara, are all evidences of the prevalence of the Lakulīśa cult. The existence of Kāpālikas has also been suggested on the basis of two goblin sculptures carved at Makuṭeśvara temple compound.[97]

The cult of Śakti-worship also flourished. Mahiṣamardinī sculptures in the Cālukyan shrines at Rāvaṇa Phaḍi and Durgāda-guḍī (Aihoḷe), Bādāmī cave I, and Tārābasappā temples attest this fact. The Gaudarguḍī (Aihoḷe) dedicated to Bhagvatī or Lakshmī further indicated the popularity of Śakti worship. The worship of Gaṇapati was also popular. Gaṇeśa images found in Bādāmī cave I, in the Tārābasappā and Hucchimallī temples, Aihoḷe conveys this notion. The Bādāmī Gaṇeśa with Durgā and Kārtikeya has been suggested by Aschwin de Lippe to be the first appearance of the deity in South India.[98] Architectural evidences, such as the Aihoḷe Badigerguḍī and Sūryanārāyaṇa Saūra temples signifies the worship of Śūrya. Veneration towards the trinity of Brahmā, Viṣṇu and Maheśa was also known. The usual practice was to have them carved in the *maṇḍapa* ceiling with the main deity shown in the middle. Thus, the five main Brāhmanical cults, viz. Śaiva, Vaiṣṇava, Śākta, Saura and Gaṇapātya co-existed amicably in the Cālukyan period. Composite images of *Harihara* in Rāvaṇa Phaḍi and Durgāda-guḍī (Aihoḷe) and Bādāmī cave III; *Ardhanārīśvara* in Rāvaṇa Phaḍi and Bādāmī cave I; installation of Brahmā, Viṣṇu, Maheśvara images in the

Jambūkeśvara temple, Bādāmī are testimonials to the prevailing spirit of co-existence. The *pañcāyatana* worship advocated by Shankaracarya was, perhaps, also a move to foster unity amongst these sects.

The Cālukya rulers usually observed religious toleration. For instance, Mangalesha, a *bhāgavata*, donated ten villages[99] to the Makuṭeśvara Śaiva temple, already enjoying rich endowments by Pulakeshin I and Kiritivarman. Popularity of Buddhism[100] in the Cālukyan territory is also apparent.[101] That Jainism had taken deep roots is indicated by the erection of Megutī Jinālaya, attributed to the famous Jaina scholar and composer of Aihoḷe *praśasti*, Ravikirti; and the excavated Jaina cave at Aihoḷe. The Jainas also received gifts for the worship of their deities, although none of the Cālukya rulers had formally adopted Jainism. For instance, Vinayaditya made a gift to a Jaina monk belonging to *Mūlasaṁgha* and *Devagaṇa*; Vijayaditya gifted the village Sembalūru to Jayadeva Pandita for worship at the *Śankhajinālaya*; Vikramaditya II also gave away a land-grant for the worship of a *Jina* while camping at Raktapura, i.e. Paṭṭaḍakal. This reflects upon the spirit of toleration as well as the popularity of Jainism in the Cālukyan regions.

The royal consorts did not lag behind their husbands in pursuing their religious inclinations. As already mentioned, Vikramaditya II's wives Lokamahadevi and Trailokya Mahadevi erected temples to commemorate his achievements. Vijayaditya's mother Vinayavati and sister Kumkum Mahadevi, respectively, built the trinity temple at Bādāmī[102] and the *Anesejje basadī* at Puligere.[103]

Thus, on the whole, religious life under the Cālukya kings was marked by the revival of Hinduism, the erection of and endowments to numerous edifices, and peaceful co-existence of different Brāhmanical and non- Brāhmanical sects.

Pallavas

Under the Pallavas, both Vaiṣṇavism and Śaivism gained popularity. Names as Shiva Skandavarman, Skandavarman, Parameshvara, Nandivarman, etc. suggest that some of the rulers were Śaivite. The *vṛṣabha lāñchana* and *khaṭvāṅga* banner further corroborate this. The use of *vṛṣabha lāñchana* throughout Pallava rule signified Śaivism as the state religion irrespective of the personal faith of individual king. Their inscriptions[104] in Atiraṇacanda and Dharmarāja *maṇḍapams* or Gaṇeśa and Dharmarāja *rathas*, giving different names of Śiva as Īśvara, Rūdra, Śaṁbhū, Bhava, Dhurjaṭi, Śaṁkara, Paśupati, Hara, etc., also reveal their Śaiva leanings. Mahendravarman I *Guṇabhāra* was converted from Jainism to Śaivism[105] by saint Appar or Tirunavukkaraiyar. Rajasimha was spoken of as *Srī-vṛṣabha-darpaḥ*. He used to wear the figure of Śiva or his *liṅga* symbol on his head.[106] This indicates the provenance of the Liṅgāyat sect.[107] Narsimhavarman I, Parameshvara I, etc. were other prominent followers of Śaivism. Parameshvara has been described as *khaṭvāṅgaketuḥ*. The Brāhmanical reformation brought about by the *Nayanmār* and *Ālvār* saints also led to the popularity of Śaivite sects as the Kālāmukhas,[108] Pāśupatas,[109] Mahēśvaras, Śāktas and Kāpālikas.[110]

Charters[111] issued by Simhavishnu, Vishnugopa, etc. project them as adherents of the Vaiṣṇava faith. Vaiṣṇavism was, perhaps, deeply rooted in the Tamil land from the earliest times as suggested by *Saṅgam* and post-*Saṅgam* texts like *Paripādal*, *Śilappadikāram*, etc. The earliest epigraphic enumeration of the ten *avatāras* could be seen in the Pallava Mahābalipuram Ādivarāha cave temple: *Matsyaḥ Kūrmō Varāhaś-ca Nārasiṁhaś-ca Vāmana (ḥ) Rāmo Rāmaś-ca Rāmaś-ca Buddha (ḥ) Kalkī-ca tē daśa.*[112] Among the later rulers, Nandivarman Pallavamalla was a Vaiṣṇavite who worshipped Viṣṇu at Kāñcī, Srīraṅgam, Nandipuram and Tiruvallikkeni.

The prevalence of Durgā worship is suggested by the shrines and sculptures found throughout the Pallava Empire. The instances of *nava kaṇḍam*, i.e. head offering to Durgā, have also been cited.[113] A panel inscription[114] of the 20th year of Kampavarman records the act of head offering to Durgā by a warrior and a subsequent land-endowment to his relative and an inscribed *nāḍukal* (stone monument) in his memory.[115] Besides, human sacrifice offering to Durgā was also rife. Exhibited at the Mahābalipuram Varāha *maṇḍapam*, it was clearly an act different from self-immolation. It had a man in the act of offering another man's head to the deity.[116] In addition, the cult of *mātṛgaṇas* or *saptamātṛkās* also flourished in the later Pallava period. Though their representations are lacking in the monolithic cave temples around Toṇḍaimaṇḍalam, they do appear in the Kailāśanātha temple, Kāñcī. A temple dedication to *Saptamātṛkās* was made during Dantivarman's reign at Ālaṁbākkam, known as Dantivarma-caturvēdi-maṅgalam.[117] The Virattaneśvara temple at Tiruttani built under Aparajita also enshrined the *Saptamātṛkā* group.

The cult of *Jyēṣṭhā* had a parallel recognition. *Nanndikkalambagam* (9th century) described her as the elder sister of Lakshmī and a cause of evil, poverty and unhappiness. She was probably propitiated by her devotees for warding off evil. The Kailāśanātha temple, Kāñcī showed *Jyēṣṭhā* representation for the first time. She was quite popular in Pāṇḍya and Muttaraiyār regions in eighth ninth centuries AD. Pāṇḍya Sadaiyan Maran got a cave temple excavated for *Jyēṣṭhā* at Tirūpparankunram.[118] Toṇḍaradippoḍi mentioned her in derision in *Tirumalai*:

> *Garuḍavāhana numniṛka-Cēṭṭai tan maḍi,*
> *Yahattucbchelvam-pārttu-irukkinrire.* (*Tirumālai*. v.10)

(The saint ridiculed the worship of *Jyēṣṭhā* by devotees in the vain hope of fulfilling their desires forgetting Viṣṇu who could confer all boons.)

Besides the Brāhmanical cults, evidences[119] of Buddhists and Jainas living under the Pallavas also abounded. Early *Saṅgam* anthologies indicated that Buddhism and Jainism were among the religious faiths prevailing at Puhār, Vañcī and Madurai. In the post-*Saṅgam* period, they gained strongholds among merchant communities and craftsmen.

The Pallava rulers are often charged with religious persecution. Mahendravarman I is said to have persecuted *Nayanmār* Appar[120] when he was a Jaina. After his conversion to Śaivism, he was charged with[121] persecution of the Jainas, Vaiṣṇavas and the Buddhists. Open and strong condemnation of Jainism and Buddhism by Vaiṣṇava saints during Nandivarman Pallavamalla and supposed royal patronage to Vaiṣṇavism by him also convey this impression. Toṇḍaradippoḍi held:

Veṛuppoḍu Śamaṇarmuṇḍar
Vidiyil Śākkiyargal, ninpāl
Poruppariyanagal pēśil pōvadēnōyadāgi... (*Tirumālai*, 8)

Tirumangai condemned the sacred books of the Pāśupatas, Jainas and the Buddhists as false: *Velliyār-piṇḍiyār bōdhiyār-enṛu-ivar-ōdum kallanūl*.[122] Another instance cited to indicate the religious intolerance of Pallavamalla is the impalement panel, found in the lower row of sculptures on the western wall and to the right of the entrance to the *maṇḍapa* in Vaikuṇṭha-perumāl temple. The sculpture is described as a representation of two men being impaled.[123] The Udayendiram grant[124] is interpreted as the expulsion of owners of certain lands and their transfer to Brāhmaṇas.

However, these charges lack historical content. Mahendravarman not only patronized several Vaiṣṇavite cave temples including the monolithic Viṣṇu temple at Mahēndravāḍī,[125] but was perhaps also responsible for the making of the first[126] stone temple in South India dedicated to the trinity. The Udayendiram grant records of property seizure, may be instances of their owners' undesirable activities inimical to the state.[127] Likewise, the impalement panel does not prove that the penalised belonged to the heretical sects. Thus, religious persecution by the Pallava rulers seems to be unfounded. Rather, the Pallava rulers, from the outset, were generous towards different faiths. Along with *devadāna* and *brahmadeya* grants, the *palliccandam* endowments,[128] and land-grants to Jaina sects were also made. Royal patronage was an important component of the religious life of the times. The Pallava kings were instrumental in the erection of numerous religious edifices, both rock-cut and structural, despite their constant military struggles.

Mahendravarman I claimed initiation of rock-cut architecture by excavating *maṇḍapams* in several parts of his empire. Narasimha *Māmalla* got excavated the *maṇḍapams* and *rathas* at Mahābalipuram. Parameshvaravarman I being regularly engrossed in wars, his reign was marked by a paucity of any major monuments. Still the excavation of Rāmānuja and Dharmarāja *maṇḍapams* exhibit his interest in building art. He is assigned creation of the Ganeśa *ratha*, besides completion of the Draupadī *ratha* and Ādi-varāha *maṇḍapam* at Mahābalipuram. He was, perhaps, also responsible for the *Vidyāvinita Pallava Paramēśvaragṛham* at Kūram representing an early attempt at structural temples.[129]

Rajasimha is credited with some of the most outstanding structural monuments, such as the Kailāśanātha and Airāvateśvara (Kāñcī),[130] Shore (Mahābalipuram) and the Talagiriśvara temples (Panamalāi).[131] He also carried further the tradition of excavated cave-temples by the two caves at Śāḷuvankuppam. His queen Rangapataka is credited with a shrine in the Kailāśanātha.[132] Nandivarman Pallavamalla patronized the Vaikuṇṭha-perumāl[133] (*Paramēśvara-Viṇṇagaram*) and Mukteśvara temples, at Kāñcī.[134] Dantivarman built the Kailāśanātha temple at Ālaṁbākkam.[135] The Viṣṇu temple at Kiliyanūr is perhaps the only monument known from Nandivarman III's times. Under Aparajitavarman, the Vīrattāneśvara temple was constructed at Tiruttani by Nambi Appi,[136] while the reign of the last Pallava ruler Kampavarman witnessed erection of shrines at Śolāpuram,[137] Tiruvarriyūr,[138] and Kavantaṅdalam.[139] Thus, the

Pallava monarchs indulged in extensive architectural patronage, especially temple-erections. They were also largely responsible for extension of temple activities by making endowments and benefactions for its maintenance. These occasionally included whole village or large units of arable lands granted for different services of the temple. The services could be related to *Nandāvilakkuppuram* (lighting perpetual lamps), expenses for *Tiruvilāpuram* (festivals), *Nandavanāppuram* (flower gardens), *Pudukkuppuram* (annual repairs), etc.

Among royal ladies, besides Rangapataka, Reva erected the *Dharmamahadeviśvaragṛham* at Mukteśvara. Nripatunga's wife Prithvimanikkam is credited with the construction of Bhuvanamaṇikka *Viṣṇugṛham*, while his second wife Viramahadeviyar performed *tulābhāra* and *hiraṇyagarbha* ceremonies at Tirukkodikkaval and also gifted fifty *kaḷañjus* of gold to the local temple. Thus, the religious affiliations of the Pallavas contributed towards the enrichment of their aesthetic as well as spiritual life.

Rāṣṭrakūṭas

The Hindu religious renaissance, expressed architecturally under the Cālukyas and followed by the Pallavas, seemingly reached its final phase of most fertile development under the Rāṣṭrakūṭas. Their plates contained homage to both Śiva and Viṣṇu, and the royal seal was either eagle or *yogeśvara* Śiva. However, the inscriptions extolled an inclination towards Śaivism. They boasted replacement of Vaiṣṇavism by Śaivism as the transformation of the great boar (emblem of Viṣṇu) into a deer (insignia of Śiva): *Mahā-varāhaṁhāriṇīchakāra*.[140] Dantivarman recorded his devotion to Śiva through *hiraṇyagarbha mahādāna*[141] to Mahākāleśvara Śiva at Ujjain. Krishnaraja I got excavated the Ellorā Kailāśanātha temple. He is also credited with erection of a *devakula*-Kanneśvara where *śaivācāryas* and scholars could reside, propagate and popularize their faith. The custom of founding a Śaiva temple in memory of an ancestor and of naming the deity after the dead has also been hinted at.[142] The Dakshiṇā Śiva temple with a Pāśupata custodian Jaṭabhara, Maheśamūrti at Elephanta and Ellorā, manifestations of Śiva from different Rāṣṭrakūṭa regions, give evidence to the wider prevalence of Śaivism.

In the later times, Viṭhobā or Viṣṇu of Paṇḍhārapura became the most dominant deity in the Rāṣṭrakūṭa territories. Among other sects, Sun and Navagraha worship was popular.[143] Worship of Śakti, Durgā, Mātṛkās, and divine consorts as Saraswatī, Lakshmī, Pārvatī was also prevalent. Amoghvarsha I, himself a Jaina, cut off one of his fingers as offering to Mahālakshmī to ward off an epidemic[144] inflicting his kingdom.

Besides *paurāṇic* sects, Jainism and Buddhism also flourished.[145] Dantivarman of Gujarat branch, a Hindu by faith, donated a village to a Buddhist *vihāra* or *Ārya saṁgha*, at Kāmpilya.[146] Buddhist establishments flourished under the Rāṣṭrakūṭas at Kanherī and Dambal. The records of the Raṭṭas of Saundatti describe *Mahāsāmanta* Prithvirama as having erected a Jaina temple in AD 875. These instances suggest the prevalence of Buddhism and Jainism in the Rāṣṭrakūṭa territories and also attest to the spirit of religious toleration prevailing therein.[147] The masses followed *smārta* section of

Brāhmanical faith. Prayers, performance of *sandhyā, prāyascitta*, pilgrimages, etc. were attached due importance. Village deities as Mahāśobā, Ellamā, *Vīrāgal* or deified stones, *yakshas, kinnaras*, inscribed talismans, etc. were also popular.

Gradually, the cult of public temples was gaining ground. Somadeva, a Jaina writer from Karnataka, declared that the endowments to feeding and drinking houses, and for the erection of temples and rest-houses was the most important duty of the *vaiśya* or moneyed class.[148] They might have been substitutes for the *srauta* sacrifices, or a possible influence of the Buddhist *vihāras* and *caityas* as congregation centres.

These religious inclinations of the Cālukya, Pallava and Rāṣṭrakūṭa monarchs stimulated the process of temple erection. While the lead was taken up by the royalty, the laity also did not lag behind in making benefactions for construction, renovation or maintenance of the temples.[149] The temple did not remain a mere place of worship but in due course emerged as a centre of great wealth.[150] Evidences suggesting hoarded wealth in temples of Deccan proper are not forthcoming although in north, the wealthy temples yielded the highest plunder to Mahmud Ghaznavi. In the Tamil regions too, large endowments were bestowed upon the temples by the ruling dynasties. This makes imperative a brief perusal of the economic condition of the period, as money serves as the strength behind all architectural activities right from construction to the maintenance and conducting of daily routine in the edifices.

ECONOMIC STATUS

South Indian Economy

Sound economy is the primary requirement for extending patronage to art and related activities. South India being a land of rivers—Godāvarī, Kṛṣṇa and Kāverī were the three main rivers; Mahānadī, Pennār, Palār, Vaigai and Tāmraparṇī constituted minor rivers; while Tungabhadrā, Narmadā and Tāptī were other important rivers—agriculture was a major occupation of its inhabitants from early times. The earliest *vendārs* emerged in the fertile agricultural tract, *marutam tiṇai*, of the major river valleys. The early *tiṇais* were dominated by the Cēras (Periyār valley), Colas (Kāverī valley) and the Pāṇḍyas (Vaigai and Tāmraparṇī valleys) as described in the early *Saṅgam* literature.[151] *Marutam* was an inland town while a coastal town of commercial importance, for instance, Uraiyūr of the Colas, Madurai of the Pāṇḍyas and Vañci of the Cēras, was known as *neiṭal*.[152] These three powers struggled to gain control over the resources of the others.[153] The *Saṅgam* texts describe the transformation of these powers from tribal groups into farming societies.[154]

The bulk of the land was owned by *vēḷāḷar*, the agriculturists. The richer among them also held official administrative positions and enjoyed titles as *vēl* and *araśu* in Cola and *kāvidi* in the Pāṇḍya Empire. They hired labour to plough their lands while the poorer *vēḷāḷar* worked themselves on their farms. The agricultural operations were mostly carried on by women of the lowest class *kaḍaiśiyar*.[155] Trade was glorified as one of the two 'esteemed pursuits', the other being agriculture in *Saṅgam* texts.[156] Evidences, such as the *Saṅgam* literature, classical writers and archaeological findings, describing brisk trade, both inland and foreign, are abundant. Caravans of merchants carrying their merchandise from place to place conducted internal trade. Foreign maritime trade was even more lucrative. Traders from various countries, as far as Rome, Srī Lankā, China, etc. reached Tamil ports, while the seafaring instincts of the Tamils themselves are also referred to in literature.[157]

South India had trade links with Srī Lankā,[158] Rome,[159] and countries of Southeast Asia.[160] The foreign trade apparently stressed the export and import of luxury items as gold, gems, horses, etc. meant mainly for elite consumption.[161] The major articles of export included silk,[162] cotton fabric,[163] pearls,[164] ivory, spices,[165] pepper,[166] and fragrant woods.[167] The imports primarily consisted of coins, mainly Roman coins received in large quantities in exchange for *kari*, i.e. pepper, beryl and cotton textiles. Gold and silver coins, struck by all Roman emperors from Augustus to Nero, have been found in the Tamil areas. Topaz, coral, wine,[168] lamps,[169] horses,[170] etc. remained other items of trade.

Such expanding commerce during the early Christian centuries was carried on by different types of traders, such as *umaṇār* (salt merchant), *paratavār* (fishermen turned traders), *māṇikkuyinār* (gem or jewel makers), *kañca-kārār* (bronze sellers), etc. It must have led to affluence and prosperity in the south. But around third century AD, the political breakdown created by the Kālabhras led to the decline of the Cēra, Cola and Pāṇḍya *vēndārs*, followed by a subsequent clash of interests among new aspirants to social and political authority. The *Kural* extols the importance of agriculture and refers to the breakdown of political ethics causing strain on the cultivators due to forcible demands.[171] This crisis must have affected the volume of trade[172] as well. Due to the lack of any contemporary records, nothing certain can be stated about this phase. Authentic records pointing towards the genesis of a new socio-economic formation under the Pallava and Pāṇḍyas are available only from the seventh century AD.[173]

Agriculture

Agriculture still remained the main occupation of bulk of the village people. Rather, this period marked the tendency to extend agricultural activities. Apart from the *marutam* regions, attempt to introduce large-scale agriculture in non-*marutam* or drier areas is also hinted upon.[174] This task was made possible by the *brahmadeya* and the *devadāna* grants under the aegis of the Pallava-Pāṇḍya dynasties. The *brahmadeya* grants and the temple evolved as institutional forces in the new framework of Brāhmaṇa-Kshatriya alliance wherein the ruling families claiming Kshatriya status and divine descent sponsored the brahmanical ideology and allocated land-grants to the Brāhmaṇas and temples. In the *brahmadeya* land, production was taken care of by the Brāhmaṇas while in *devadāna* land, the *vēḷāḷars* or land owning peasants managed the cultivation. Both the settlements were, perhaps, marked by advanced farming methods as the seasonal regulation of cultivation and irrigation technology.[175] Cultivable lands in the region depended mostly on seasonal rains. Therefore, the provision of a network of irrigation canals, tanks, lakes, and large wells had to be undertaken partly by the state and partly by private initiative to keep famine at a bay. Thus, better and effective management made considerable difference in the farming societies of the period under consideration in comparison with the earlier ones.[176]

Another feature of agricultural expansion was the emergence of agricultural regions or units like the *kōṭṭam, nāḍu* and *kūrram*. Although they predated the Pallava Pāṇḍya period, they emerged as viable units of socio-economic and political importance during seventh to ninth centuries AD only. The *kōṭṭam* was probably a pastoral-cum-agricultural region while the other two were mainly agricultural regions. Twenty-four *kōṭṭams* were traditionally assigned to the Pallava region; about 50 *nāḍu* and *kūrram* localities were listed in the Pāṇḍya country.[177] In a way, it seems that agrarian development during this period was not an isolated process but an outcome of an integrated framework of land relationships. Relations developed around the Brāhmaṇa, *vēḷāḷar* and the temple. The integrated approach was perhaps also exhibited by the numerous *brahmadeyas* and *devadānas* of seventh-ninth centuries AD, emerging in the form of religious architecture like rock-cut caves, monoliths and structural edifices in the Pallava-Pāṇḍya regions.[178]

Trade

Trade constituted an important aspect of economic life. The markets or commercial centres, *nagarams*, usually situated at the confluence of rivers or in delta areas, enjoyed a pivotal position in the trade-network. It was, in fact, an era of organized commerce with merchants forming powerful guilds and corporations, transcending political divisions and probably also unaffected by the ongoing wars or struggles around them. They were of varied types, viz. *svadeśabehārulu* (merchants of the home country), *paradeśabehārulu* (of another country), and *nānādeśī* (of different countries). The most renowned guild was the *Aiññūrruvar* or Five Hundred *Svamis* of Ayyāvoḷe (Aihoḷe). It was also called *Ayyāvoḷe, Nānādeśī,* and *Valañjīyar*. Founded in Aihoḷe in about eighth century AD, by 500 *mahājanas* of Aihoḷe *mahāgrahāra*, it was probably a heterogeneous group of merchants from different countries associated together for a common purpose, i.e. trade.[179] Its members, famed for their daring spirit, are said to have visited the Cēra, Cola, Pāṇḍya, Magadha, Kośala, Saurashtra, Kurumba, Kamboja, Lāṭa, Pārasa (Persia), Nepāl, and many more regions, conducting both inland and foreign trade.

Maritime trade flourished considerably as countries of South Asia developed an extensive maritime commerce by ninth century AD. India probably had trade contacts with China, Jāvā and Malāyā, besides Srī Lankā. The main trade items included sapphires, moonstones, pearls, rubies, diamonds, lapis-lazuli, onyx, and other precious articles; spices as cloves, cardamoms, pepper; sandal, camphor, musk, saffron and other perfumes; various industrial products and elephants. Amongst the industries, spinning and weaving were in a flourishing state. Carpet making, metal works, jewellery industry, salt manufacturing, pearl fishing, etc. were a few prominent industries. It seems that all the crafts, arts and industries were organized in castes and guilds[180] leading to an integrated commercial network.

In brief, the general economic condition in the Pallava realm; their constant warfare with Cālukya and other contemporary powers; the artistic inclinations of monarchs;

and numerous religious endowments suggest their treasuries must have been substantial and well maintained to bear all these expenses. This rather confirms the saying in *Mahābhārata* that 'treasury is the support of kings'.[181] Thus, South Indian economy was in a thriving condition from the very early times except an interlude of about three centuries marking the end of the *Saṅgam* age.

Deccan Economy

Towards the Deccan, the hub of Cālukyan and Rāṣṭrakūṭa empires, certain distinct factors could be traced. The Deccan plateau was conducive for only relatively smaller areas of agriculture, due to its river system, and more suitable for the growth of transport networks and communications. The passes in the Western Ghats linked the coast to the interior and relatively drier zones, thereby helping uninterrupted travel and movement.[182] Another peculiarity was a symbiotic relationship between the political factions, the commercial groups and Buddhism[183] from the Sātavāhana period onwards. The parallel sponsoring of Buddhist institutions by kings and merchants[184] and the rise of mercantile establishments served as 'symbolic integrative media for a dominant politico mercantile elite'.[185] Overseas trade was also in a flourishing state in the Deccan region conducted through the ports of Bharoch, Kalliāna (Kalyāṇa), Naosārī, Sibor (Sopārā), Thānā, Dābhol, etc. The chief means of livelihood were agriculture and trade. The crops cultivated included cotton (Gujarat and Berar), barley and jowar (Maharashtra and Karnataka), rice, coconut and betelnuts (Konkaṇ).

Trade

Trade, both inland and foreign, was quite brisk. The principal items of export were cotton yarn and cloth, rough and fine muslins, mats, hides, indigo, incense, perfumes, betelnuts, coconut, sandalwood, teakwood, sesame oil and ivory, thus consisting of both natural resources and industrial products. Bronze, sesame and varieties of cotton were exported from Kalyāṇa. Gujarat, Berar and Telengana were renowned for cotton textiles. The forests of Mysore and Western Ghats yielded rich quantities of sandalwood, teak and ebony wood and their timber was exported from Western Indian ports since early historic times. Deccan was also rich in minerals. Evidences of copper extracted from the mines at Bellary, Cudappah, Bijapur, Dharwar, Canda, etc. are also available.[186] Diamond mines yielding rich harvests in diamonds till a later period were located at places as Golcunda, Bellary, Anantpur and Cudappah. Mālkheḍ in close proximity to these sites could have led to a lucrative jewellery market while diamonds were possibly also available for export.

The articles of import were probably silk from China; aloes and sandalwood from Malay archipelago; ivory and emeralds from Africa; inferior pearls from the Persian Gulf; dates, gold, slaves, Italian wine, copper, tin, lead, topaz, flint glass, antimony, coins, etc. The various crafts and industries of the times were organized in guilds or corporations, though their detailed functions or constitution are yet to be compiled. Besides, the productive economic activities, the regular military campaigns must have also added to their wealth.[187] Lakshmī, the goddess of prosperity, was a significant motif on the Rāṣṭrakūṭa seals.

On the whole, economic life in the Deccan also appears to be as sound and flourishing as down south during the period under consideration.

Thus, it is apparent that despite constant political strife, the prevailing religious-cultural environment coupled with economic affluence provided an impetus to great activity and vigour in the field of art and architecture, especially erection of religious edifices. The temple was no longer a mere place of worship. Besides itself participating in economic activities as pointed out earlier, its construction and maintenance offered employment to numerous artisans, craftsmen, etc., engaged in bold planning and skilful execution of their projects. In a way, it seems that the political, military campaigns set the pace for cultural exchanges across widely separated areas. The movements of the armies, setting of communication networks, merchants or commoners and, above all, the *Bhakti* saints propagating their message across the land must have facilitated the emergence of a common heritage in the form of art.

The tendency of artists migrating and getting employment in different kingdoms or regions has already been hinted in chapter one. In some exceptional cases, the victor king hired the artists of the vanquished country for the creation of magnificent edifices. For instance, Cālukya Vikramaditya II hired services of artisans from Kāñcī. Moreover, the matrimonial alliances between various ruling families may have also been instrumental in the flow of cultural and artistic traditions from one region to another. Thus, motivated by the prevailing conditions, each of the dynasties included in this study fervently indulged in architectural activities; although it sometimes raises a doubt too that how could they spare time for peaceful pursuits like arts while engaged in political maneuvering or regular warfare. It almost is proven that peaceful atmosphere and freedom from warfare enabled the kings to indulge more in other pursuits, for instance, the magnitude of buildings raised under Pallava Rajasimha's tranquil reign while paucity of edifices during war-stricken Parameshvara I is quite contrasting.

A deep yearning for recording their faith and to immortalize their devotion towards the deity might have been responsible for the patronage. Whatever their real sentiments, motives and the factors underlying the creation of religious structures in such large numbers, it is certain that the individual contribution of kings and royal patronage was quite crucial in the rise of independent art styles of the period. It is also revealed by art styles named after individual kings, for instance Mahendra style, *Māmalla* style, Rajasimha style, etc. To accord the various art monuments a place in time or to reconstruct the chronological sequence of the art of the period concerned, perusal of political history proves quite handy.

NOTES AND REFERENCES

1. Rock Edict II, *vide* Alexander Cunningham, 1961, *Corpus Inscriptionum Indicarum*, Vol. I, Varanasi, p. 66.
2. The union or academy of scholars and poets at the Pāṇḍya court was famed as *Saṅgam*. The eight *Eṭṭuttogai* (anthologies) and *Paṭṭuppāṭṭu* (ten idylls) survive the vast literature created by them. Pliny the elder; the anonymous author of the *Periplus of the Erythrean Sea* (both of late first century AD) and Ptolemy, the second century geographer from Alexandria

wrote about them. For further details *cf.* V. Kanakasabhai Pillai, 1966, *The Tamils 1800 years Ago,* Tirunelveli; *also* P.T. Srinivasa Iyengar, 1929, *History of the Tamils*, Madras; K.A. Nilakanta Sastri, 1964, *The Culture and History of Tamils*, Calcutta; N. Subrahmanian, 1966, *Saṅgam Polity*, New York; K.A. Nilakanta Sastri, 1999, *A History of South India*, Delhi, pp. 104-31.

3. *Aḷav-ariya ādhirājarai agala nīkki agal- iḍattai=*
kkaḷabhraṇ= eṇṇuṅ= kali-araiśaṇ Kaikkoṇḍ = adaṇai iṛakkiyapiṇ (*Velvikuḍī Grant*).
4. *See* K.A. Nilakanta Sastri, 1964, *The Culture and History of the Tamils*, p. 19.
5. *Cf. also* Ludwig Bachhofer, 1973, *Early Indian Sculpture*, Vol. 1 (Indian Ed.), Delhi.
6. The Gaṅgas of Mysore were associated with Jainism. *Cf.* Saletore, *Medieval Jainism*, p. 7. Amongst the Gaṅgas of Talwad Rachamalla made endowments to Jaina establishments in Coorg, *vide IA*, VI, p. 103. He also erected a Jaina shrine upon Valhmalai hill. *See EI,* IV, p. 140; The Kadambas of Banavāsī though performed *aśvamedha yajña* showed unusual favour towards Jainism. *Cf.* Sharma, *Jainism and Karnataka Culture*, p. 9; Ravikirti of Aihoḷe inscription constructed the *Jinendra* Megutī temple at Aihoḷe. Besides, the Bādāmī Jaina caves were indicative of Jaina inclinations of Cālukyas. For further details, *see* Nahar and Ghosh, 1917, *Epitome of Jainism,* Calcutta; M.S. Ramaswami Ayyangar and B.S. Rao, 1922, *Studies in South Indian Jainism,* Madras; P.B. Desai, 1957, *Jainism in South India and Some Jaina Epigraphs,* Sholapur.
7. For their political history, *refer to* Jouveau-G. Dubreuil, 1917, *The Pallavas,* Pondicherry; R. Gopalan, 1928, *History of the Pallavas of Kāñcī*, Madras; P.T. Srinivasa Iyengar, 1929, *History of the Tamils*, Madras; H. Heras, 1933, *Studies in Pallava History*, Madras; K.A. Nilakanta Sastri, 1948, *The Tamil Kingdoms of South India*, Bombay; R. Sathianathaier, 1956, *Studies in the Ancient History of Toṇḍaimaṇḍalam*, Madras; T.V. Mahalingam, 1969, *Kāñcīpuram in Early South Indian History*, Bombay; K.K. Pillay, 1969, *A Social History of the Tamils*, Madras.
8. Kadungon recovered territories from Kālabhras, *EI*, XVII, p. 306.
9. *See* Romila Thapar, 1992, *A History of India*, Vol. I, New Delhi (repr.), p. 168; *See also* A.L. Basham, 1990, 'Geographical Factors in South Indian History', in H.M. Nayak and B.R. Gopal (eds.), *South Indian Studies*, Mysore, pp. 17-22.
10. For their detailed political account *see*, K.A. Nilakanta Sastri, 1960, 'The Cālukyas of Bādāmī', in G. Yazdani (ed.), *The Early History of the Deccan*, Parts I-VI, pp. 201-32; *Cf.* D.C. Sircar, 1962, 'The Chālukyas of Bādāmī' in R.C. Majumdar (ed.), *The Classical Age*, Bombay, pp. 227-49; N.L.N. Rao, 1967, 'The Chālukyas of Bādāmī', *Maharashtra State Gazetteer*, History, Pt. I, Bombay, pp. 201-31; H.V.S. Murthy and R. Ramakrishnan, 1977, *A History of Karnataka*, New Delhi; B.A. Saletore, 1936, *Ancient Karnataka*, Vol. I, Poona.
11. (i) *EI*, XVII, p. 8; and (ii) *EI*, III, p. 5.
12. 'Aihoḷe Inscription of Pulakeshin II' in R.B. Pande, 1962, *Historical and Literary Inscriptions*, Varanasi, p. 241.
13. 1890, *IA*, XIX, p. 17.
14. *Vide* 1877, *IA*, VI, p. 78.
15. For instance, the Vakkaleri Plates of Kirtivarman II:
prakṛty-amitrasya Pallavasya samūl-ōnmūla-
nāya kṛta-matir = atitvarayā Tu (ṁ) ḍaka-viṣayaṁ ...
16. *SII*, I, No. 151.
17. *See* Mallikārjuna Temple Inscription, *IA*, IX, p. 199; The Kāśākuddi Plates suggested that he imitated *kumbhodbhava* Agastya by his conquest of Vātāpī. *Cf. SII*, II.

18. *Cf.* 1999, *A History of South India*, 4th ed., Delhi, p. 136; A painting in Ajantā cave I depicting welcome of Persian envoys by a king probably represented this event. *See* R.S. Gupte and B.D. Mahajan, 1962, *Ajantā, Ellorā, and Aurangābād Caves*, p. 62; Madanjeet Singh, 1965, *The Cave Paintings of Ajantā*, London, pp. 173-74.
19. As described by T.K. Seshadri, 1978, 'The Chālukya-Pallava Conflict', in M.S. Nagarajarao (ed.), *The Chālukyas of Bādāmī* (Seminar Papers), Bangalore, p. 209; this fact gets epigraphic corroboration by the Gaḍval Plates, *EI*, X, p. 103.
20. 1881, *IA*, X, p. 164.
21. *Vide* Vikramaditya's Kāñcī Inscription, *EI*, III, p. 360.
22. *Cf. SII*, II, No. 98, v.16.
23. (i) *Cf.* R.C. Majumdar and A.S. Altekar, 1946, *New History of the Indian People*, Vol. VI, Lahore, p. 222; (ii) *Vide* K.A. Nilakanta Sastri, *The Culture and History of the Tamils*, p. 18.
24. *Vide* B.L. Rice, 1909, *Mysore and Coorg from Inscriptions*, London, p. 53; *Cf. also* Jouveau G-Dubreuil, *Ancient History of the Deccan*, p. 47; V. Venkayya, 'The Pallavas', *ARASI for 1906-07*.
25. *Cf.* Iravatham Mahadevan, 1971, 'Pallavas and the "Jar" Legends', in Saw Ganesan (ed.), *Prof. K.A. Nilakanta Sastri Felicitation Volume*, Madras, pp. 84-88. *See also*, Saw Ganesan, 'Fresh light on Pallava History', *Ibid.*, pp. 474-78.
26. *Prayāg Praśasti. Cf.* Fleet, *Corpus Inscriptionum Indicarum*, III, I, p. 6 ff.
27. Held sway over a greater part of Karnataka and territory of the Kāverī basin known as Gaṅgavādi, from about second century AD till eleventh century AD. They served as feudatories of the Cālukyas as their hereditary servants, *IA*, VII, p. 303. They were perhaps also subservient to the Pallavas, who claimed to enthrone the Gaṅga kings, *SII*, XIV, pp. 332-33; probably accepted Rāṣṭrakūṭa suzerainty after the fall of Cālukyas, *Epigraphia Carnatica*, IX, No. 60. For further details, *refer* P.B. Desai, 1970, *History of Karnataka*, Dharwar; *Cf. also*, H.M. Nagaraju, *Gaṅga Prabhu Durvinita* (in Kannada); M.V. Krishna Rao, 1936, *The Gaṅgas of Talakad*, Madras.
28. *SII*, II, No. 73, v. 20.
29. *Cf.* K.R. Srinivasa Iyengar, in R.C. Majumdar, 1968, (ed.), *HCIP*, Vol. II, p. 290.
30. Suggested by his Tirucirāpallī Cave Inscription, *cf. SII*, I, Nos. 33-34.
31. *Cf. SII*, I, No. 151.
32. Refer *IA*, IX, p. 199.
33. *Vide* Kāśākkudi Plates, *SII*, II, No. 73.
34. *Cf.* Kūram Plates in *SII*, I, No. 151; also Udayendiram Plates, *SII*, II, No. 74.
35. He sent an embassy to China in AD 720 (*Ts'o-fou-yuan-kouei*, dated 1013). *Vide* K.A. Nilakanta Sastri in 1939, *Foreign Notices of South India*, Madras, pp. 116-17; *Cf. also*, his *A History of South India*, p. 139.
36. Kailāśanatha Inscription in *SII*, I, No. 27.
37. As described by C. Minakshi, 1941, *The Historical Sculptures of the Vaikuṇṭhaperumāl Temple*, *MASI*, No. 63, Delhi, p. 62 and plate, XII, 6.
38. Vikramaditya conquered Kāñcī thrice as revealed by Paṭṭaḍakal Inscription in *IA*, X, p. 164. His first invasion in AD 730 as *yuvarāja* led to exacting of tribute from Parameshvara II. *Cf.* Ulchhala Inscription, *Ancient India*, No. 5, p. 54. The Nārwan plates dated Śaka 664 (i.e. AD 741-742) inform about his second invasion, *vide EI*, XXVII, pp. 126ff. The third expedition led by *yuvarāja* Kirtivaman II took place towards the end of his reign (AD 744-45).
39. A Bāṇa chief ruling over Gaṅgavādi 6000 with Pallava support, *cf. Epigraphia Carnatica*, X, p. iv; and a chief Mahāvali Vānarāya, subordinate to Nandivarman in his 62nd regnal

year, mentioned in *SII*, III, p. 91, lend credence to this event; Bāṇas feudatories of the Pallavas influenced South Indian politics from fourth to sixteenth centuries AD. They first figured in the Tālagunta inscription (AD 600) of Kadamba Kākustavarman. Their influence area Perumbānappādi stretched from Kolar in the north down to North Arcot in the south. For details, *see* M.S. Govinda Swamy, 1965, *The Role of Feudatories in Pallava History*, Annamalai; V. Balambal, 1978, *Feudatories of South India* (800–1070 AD), Allahabad, pp. 33-65; T.V. Mahalingam, *The Banas in South Indian History*.

40. *Cf.* R. Anandasivan and K.K. Ramamurthy, 1984, 'Three Inscriptions of the Pallava Period: A Study', in K.V. Ramesh (ed.), *Svāsti-Srī*, Delhi, pp. 145-49.
41. For the inscription *see* British Museum Plates of Govinda III in *IA*, XI, p. 126.
42. Marambavai, figuring as a donor in a couple of Cola Aditya I's inscriptions, was probably his elder sister and a queen of Nandivarman III who bore his son Aparajitavarman. *Cf.* K.R. Srinivasan, *CTP*, pp. 12 and 17.
43. Bāhūr Plates, *EI*, XVIII, p. 10; *also* in *SII*, II, pp. 513-17, v. 16-17.
44. *Cf. EI*, XVIII, p. 42, v. 55; *see also*, *Travancore Archaeological Series*, III, pp. 142 ff.
45. Tillaisthānam Inscription, *SII*, III, No. 89.
46. *See SII*, III, No. 205, v. 49.
47. *Vide SII*, VI, No. 371.
48. For Rāṣṭrakūṭa political history, *cf.* A.S. Altekar, 1967, *Rastrakutas and Their Times*, Poona; V.V. Mirashi also discussed their history. *See* 'Rashtrakutas of Mānapura' in *ABORI*, XXV, pp. 36-50; Rudra Kavi, 1917, 'Rāshtraudha-vamsa', *GOS*, Baroda; J.F. Fleet, 1899, 'The Dynasties of the Kanarese Districts of the Bombay Presidency', *Bombay Gazetteer*, I, Pt. 2, Bombay.
49. A.S. Altekar, 1967, *Rastrakutas and Their Times*, p. 19.
50. Yewoor Inscription, *IA*, VIII, p. 11 ff.
51. Alas Plates of Yuvarāja Govinda II (AD 769), *EI*, VI, p. 208 ff.
52. Karhad Plates of Krishna III in *EI*, IV, p. 282.
53. *See* Wāni Dindori Plates, *IA*, XI, p. 157.
54. *Cf.* Rādhanpur Plates, *EI*, VI, pp. 242 ff.
55. As held by R.C. Majumdar in *Ancient India*, p. 366.
56. *Vide*, Wāni Dindori Plates, *op. cit.*; *Cf.* R.C. Majumdar (ed.), *HCIP*, Vol. III, p. 198.
57. K.A. Nilakanta Sastri, A *History of South India*, p. 146.
58. *Cf.* Altekar, 1967, *op. cit.*, p. 117.
59. Various epigraphs as: Solapuram Inscription, *EI*, VII, p. 195; Ukkala Viṣṇu Temple Inscription, *EI*. IV, p. 82; Karhad Plates, *EI*, IV, p. 278; Siddhaliṅgamādam Inscription in *Madras Epigraphical Collection for 1909*, No. 375—all hailing from territory usually governed by Colas and Pallavas and dated in Krishna's reign suggest his direct rule over Toṇḍaimaṇḍalam.
60. *IA*, XXIII, p. 124. In Jaina tradition, it meant death by starvation or fasting. The royal instances of *sallekhana* are indicative of Jaina influence in the region.
61. The earliest Āryan settlements were on the river banks in Punjab. During the later Vedic period extending till about sixth century BC, they expanded gradually towards the east and the south. It seems that by fourth century BC, their spread over the whole of India was complete. The new eastern kingdoms were Kurus, Pāñcālas, Videhas, etc. For more details, *see* R.P. Chanda, *Indo Aryan Races*; N.K. Dutt, *Aryanization of India*; F.E. Pargiter, *Ancient Indian Historical Tradition*.
62. *Ṛgveda*, X. 61. 8; *see also Vedic Index*, I. 337.

63. Suggested by H.C. Raychaudhuri, 2002, *Political History of Ancient India*, Delhi (repr.), p. 76.
64. *See* Pāṇinī's *Aṣṭādhyāyī*, IV. 2. 98.
65. *Baudhāyana Sūtra*, I. 1. 29.
66. *See Aitreya Brāhmaṇa*, II. 3. 33.6.
67. Known variously as Maitravaruṇī, Mānya, Kuṁbhasambhava, Ghaṭoṭdhava, or Vātāpīdvita, he was a Vedic *mantradṛṣṭā ṛṣi*. *Cf*. *Ṛgveda*, I. 23. 165 - I. 24. 191. Credited with the Aryanization of South India, his supposed headquarter was the Podiyil hill in Western Ghats. Several *Agastyāsramas* and *tīrthas* found in south lend historicity to his movement towards and settlement in that part of the country.
68. The legendary *daitya* king of Maṇimatī approached by Agastya seeking wealth to fulfill his wife's wishes. *Mahābhārata*, III. 94. 4. He used to kill the Brāhmaṇas treacherously with his brother Vātāpī. *Ibid*., III. 94.10.
69. Brother of Ilvala killed by Agastya. The region Vātāpī (Bādāmī), the assumed abode of the *daitya* duo, might have derived its name after him, marking Agastya's first connection with the south. A later epigraph from Nandivarman Pallavamalla's reign compared Narasimhavarman's conquest of Vātāpī (Bādāmī) with Agastya's feat: *Agastya iva vimathita Vātāpiḥ Pariya (Bhū) Maṇimaṅgalasūramāraprabhṛitiṣhu jetā bahuśo Vallabharājasya Narasimhavarmmā*. *Vide* Nandivarman Pallavamalla's Grant in 1879, *IA*, VIII.
70. A legend referred to by Nilakanta Sastri has it that on the occasion of Śiva's marriage with Pārvatī, Agastya had to be sent to the south to redress the balance of the earth, disturbed by the assemblage of all the gods and sages in the north. *See* 1999, *A History of South India*, p. 64.
71. *Mahābhārata*, III. 103. 2-3.
72. It spread to the Southeast Asian countries like Malāyā, Campā, Annām, Jāvā, Borneo, Sumātrā forming 'Greater India' as also Srī Lankā. For the process of expansion, refer to B. Ch. Chhabra, 1965, *Expansion of Indo-Aryan Culture during Pallava Rule (As Evidenced by Inscriptions)*, Delhi; K.K. Pillay, 1976, *South India and Sri Lanka*, (rev. ed.); and T.N. Subramanian, 1967, *The Pallavas of Kāñcī in South East Asia*.
73. *Rāmāyaṇa*, *Araṇya Kāṇḍa*, 11: 71-72; On their way to Agastya's *āsram*, Rāma narrated to Lakshmaṇa how the sage rendered the earth habitable by overpowering the demons. Deriving inspiration from Agastya's success against the *asuras* it seems that Daṇḍakāraṇya was made fit for human, i.e. Āryan habitation by both the brothers. The writers of *Purnānūru* and *Tolkappiyam* related Agastya as a northern *ṛṣi* to Dwārikā. He is said to have led eighteen kings, eighteen *kulas* of *vēlir* and *aruvālar* southwards from Dwārikā. *Vide* D.N. Jha and K.M. Srimali, 2000, *Prachīn Bhārata Kā Itihāsa*, Delhi, pp. 270-71.
74. The legend symbolically suggested the eastern advancement of the Āryans only in areas that had been cleared, i.e. purified by fire. *Śatapatha Brāhmaṇa*, I.4.1.10-18.
75. For instance, the burning of Khāṇḍava forest by Arjuna and Kṛṣṇa to eliminate its miscreant inhabitants. *Vide Mahābhārata*, I. 216.32.
76. Several anecdotes of destroying southern forests and cultivating lands, in the *Mahābhārata* and *Purāṇas*, are associated with Agastya. *Cf*. G.P. Upadhayaya, 1976, 'Origins and Functions of *Tīrthas*—Some Epic *Paurāṇic* Testimonies', *Proceedings, Indian History Congress*, Calicut, p. 128.
77. K.A. Nilakanta Sastri, 1963, *Development of Religion in South India*, p. 15. He is credited with composition of a Tamil work on grammar *Agastiyam* in the first Saṅgam.

78. Mentioned in later epigraphs as the Velvikuḍī grant, *EI*, XVII, p. 300. Agastya as the family priest of the Pāṇḍyas was also mentioned in Kālidāsa's *Raghuvaṁśa*, VI. 61.
79. *Mahābhārata*, III. 117.9; III. 117.14.
80. *Aitreya Brāhmaṇa*, VIII. 14 alluded to princes of south who were called *Bhojas*.
81. Extended from modern Berar and Wardha to Payoṣiṇī, a tributary of Tāptī in the north, *vide. Mahābhārata*, III. 61. 22-23; its kings claimed Yadu lineage, *Matsya Purāṇa*, 44. 36, *also Vāyu Purāṇa*, 95. 35-36; It was famous for tiger killing dog Mācalās - *Cf. Journal of the American Oriental Society*, 19, p. 100. *Bṛhadāraṇayaka Upaniṣad* (*Vedic Index*, II. 297) mentioned sage Vidarbhi Kauṇḍiṇya, probably derived from Kuṇḍina, capital of Vidarbha (as given in *Mahābhārata*, III. 73. 1-2), i.e. modern Kauṇḍiṇyapura in Amarāvatī. The association of Vidarbha with Kuṇḍina suggests that Vidarbha of the Vedic texts lay in the Deccan only. Kālidāsa in *Raghuvaṁśa* (v. 39-40) called the king of Vaidarbha *Bhoja*, i.e. a southern prince; Agastya's wife Lopāmudrā was a princess of Vidarbha, *Mahābhārata*, III. 95. 7.
82. Nilakanta Sastri held that the statement could mean the customs and habits of Cēra or Malabar region diverged from the rest of the south from very early times. *Cf. A History of South India*, p. 62.
83. Baudhāyana mentioned customs peculiar to the southerners like: dining with women, dining with one who is not initiated—*anupeta*, eating food kept overnight, marry one's maternal or paternal cousin, etc. *Baudhāyana Dharmasūtra*, I. 2. 2-3.
84. Refer to *footnote no. 1*. The edicts in Brāhmī script and Prākṛt idiom in places as far as Mysore and Kurnool could not have been illegible to their natives.
85. *Rāmāyaṇa, Araṇya Kāṇḍa*, 1.1.
86. *See Rāmāyaṇa, Ayodhyā Kāṇḍa*, 116.14, 15 and 17.
87. *Cf. Tolkappiyam* as referred to by Nilakanta Sastri, *A History of South India*, p. 117.
88. During this so-called period of dominance of heterodoxy, Jainism in particular received great patronage under Kālabhras, the new political sovereigns. *Cf.* K.V. Raman. *Pāṇḍiyar Varalāru* (Tamil), pp. 263-64. The great upsurge in popularity of Jainism and Buddhism obviously worried the followers of the Brāhmanical sects.
89. The *Periyapurāṇam* (v. 1410-11) refers to plenty of disputes and debates between the *Nayanmārs* and the Jainas and the suppression or conversion of the latter to Hinduism. *Cf.* D. Dayalan, 1992, *Early Temples of Tamil Nadu*, p. 16; *cf.* A.K. Nambi, 1977, *Glimpses of Tamil Culture Based on the Periya Purāṇam*, Madurai; R. Champakalakshmi, 1996, 'From Devotion and Dissent to Dominance: The *Bhakti* of the Tamil *Alvar* and *Nayanar*', in R. Champakalakshmi and S. Gopal (eds.), *Tradition, Dissent and Ideology*, Delhi, have also discussed the trend.
90. *Nayanmārs*, i.e. leaders, sixty-three in all, were canonical Śaivite saints. Appar, Sambandar, Mānikkavācakar and Sundarar were most renowned ones. From 6th-7th centuries AD, they propagated Śaivism through devotional songs. For more details, *see* C.V. Narayana Ayyar, *The Origin and Early History of Śaivism in South India; also* Kingsbury and Philips, *Hymns of the Tamil Śaivite Saints*; M. Rajamanickam, 1972, *The Development of Śaivism in South India (AD 300-1300)*. Dharmapuram; I.C. Tyagi, 1982, *Shaivism in Ancient India*, Meerut.
91. Vaiṣṇava saints were twelve in number. *Ālvār* meant 'one diving in deep wisdom'. They, together with the *Nayanmārs*, restrained Jaina influence and provided a secure footing to the twin edifices of Vaiṣṇavism and Śaivism in the south. *Cf.* J.S.M. Hooper, *Hymns of the Ālvārs. See also*, M. Srinivasa Iyengar, *Tamil Studies*; Susmita Pande, 1982, 'Contribution of the *Ālvārs* and *Nayanmārs*', *Birth of Bhakti in Indian Religions and Art*, New Delhi, pp. 112-40; Suvira Jaiswal, 1967, *The Origin and Development of Vaiṣṇavism (from 200 BC to 500 AD)*. Delhi.

92. Bādāmī Cave III Inscription, 1877, *IA*, VI, p. 363.
93. *Ibid.*; *cf.* A.M. Annigeri, 'Religion under the Chālukyas of Bādāmī', *The Chālukyas of Bādāmī* (Seminar Papers), p. 234.
94. *Cf. JBBRAS*, XVI, p. 1.
95. Built by Lokamahadevi, Vikramaditya II's chief queen: *Haihaya vaṁśa-sambhūta priya mahādevī Umā bhagavat=īva lōkamātāyā sthāpito mahā śaila prāsāda-srī Lokeśvara... srī Lokamahadevyayāḥ*. *Vide* Kirtivarman II's Paṭṭadakal Inscription in *EI*, III.
96. *Sri Trailōkymahādēvyāyāh sthāpito mahā-śaila prāsāda-Srī Trailokyeśvara (Ibid.)*; Trailokyamahadevi was Vikramaditya II's second queen.
97. *Cf.* A.M. Annigeri, *op. cit.*, p. 236.
98. 1978, *Indian Mediaeval Sculpture*, p. 138.
99. Villages as Kisuvolal, i.e. Paṭṭadakal, Āryapura or Aihoḷe, Kendurumāṇya, were granted to the temple with the consent of his stepmother Durlabhadevi. *Cf.* Mahākūṭa pillar inscription, 1890, *IA*, XIX, pp. 16-20.
100. It had entered the regions probably during the Ashokan times as inferred from his rock-edicts found at Māskī, Koppal, Brahmagirī, Jatingarāmeśwar, etc. *Cf.* E. Hultzsch (ed.), *Corpus Inscriptionum Indicarum*, Vol. 1, *Inscriptions of Ashoka*, ASI, Delhi. *Mahāvaṁśa* and *Dīpavaṁśa* describe Moggaliputta Tissa, who had converted Ashoka to Buddhism, deputing Mahadeva to Mahiṣamaṇḍala (modern Mysore) and Rakhkhita to Varanasi for the propagation of Buddhism.
101. A sculpture of *Bodhisattva* Padmapāṇi was carved in a natural cavern between Bādāmī caves II and III. Besides, Aihoḷe cave IV, partly structural and partly rock-cut, has been assigned to the Buddhist faith. *Cf.* S. Settar. 'A Buddhist *Vihāra* at Aihoḷe', *East and West*, Vol. 19. Hiuen Tsang (AD 641) described more than 100 Buddhist *vihāras* and more than 5,000 monks of both *Hīnayāna* and *Mahāyāna* sects in the Cālukyan territory. *Cf.* T. Watters, *On Yuan Chuang's Travels in India*, Vol. II, 1905, p. 239. However, Buddhism does not seem to have a stronghold in the Deccan region at any given point of time.
102. *Refer* to R.S. Panchamukhi, *Karnatak Inscriptions*, Vol. 1, No. 2, p. 3.
103. Gudigere Inscription in *SII*, XX, No. 46; *also IA*, XVIII, pp. 37-39.
104. *Cf.* N.S. Ramaswami, 1970, *Seven Pagodas*, Madras, pp. 86-88.
105. *SII*, Vol. 1, No. 33, v.2.
106. Adjunct '*Maheśvara Śikhāmaṇidīptimauli*' in Vayalur Pillar Inscription in *EI*, XVIII, p. 150.
107. *Cf.* B.G.L. Swamy, 1978 (Jan-June), 'The Religion of the Pallavas of Kanchi', *Quarterly Journal of the Mythic Society*, Vol. LXIX, Nos. 1-2, pp. 73-78.
108. Called so as they adorned their faces with the caste mark of black streak. *Cf.* Gopinatha Rao. *Elements of Hindu Iconography*, Vol. II, Pt. 1, p. 25; became influential mainly in the 8th-9th centuries and imbibed several features of the *Āgamas*. *Vide* R.N. Nandi, *Religious Institutions and Cults in the Deccan*, p. 84. For more about the Kālāmukhas, *see* David N. Lorenzen, 1972, *The Kāpālikas and Kālāmukhas – Two Lost Śaivite Sects*, New Delhi.
109. Earliest references to Pāśupata sect in Tamil Nadu are found in the *Mattavilāsa Prahasana* of Mahendravarman I though *liṅga* findings from Gudimallam (Amarāvatī) indicate its entry in the region around second century BC. *Cf.* D. Dayalan, 1992, *Early Temples of Tamil Nadu*, p. 14.
110. Also found mention in *Mattavilāsa Prahasana* as living at Ekambam. Post-*Saṅgam* texts like *Maṇimēkalai*, too, contained reference to them as living in the Kāverīpumpaṭṭinam cemetery, and as being worshippers of *Bhairava* and Kotravai. *Cf.* 6: 86-91; for further readings *refer* David N. Lorenzen, *op. cit.*

111. For instance, the Taṇḍantoṭṭam *Dānapatras* indicative of the Vaiṣṇava affiliation of Pallava kings. *Cf. SII*, II, Pt. V, p. 530, v. 12.
112. *Vide* H. Krishna Sastri, *Two Statues of Pallava Kings and Five Pallava Inscriptions in a Rock Temple at Mahābalipuram, MASI*, No. 26, p. 5.
113. A sculpture on the back wall of the Draupadī *Ratha* has *padmāsana* Durgā with a devotee kneeling at her feet, in the act of cutting his head; another panel in the Varāha *maṇḍapam* with similar figures; yet another in Tirucirāppaḷḷī cave shows the devotee putting his sword to his neck. The Śiva temple at Pullamangai has a sculpture of the goddess standing on the head of a buffalo. Vogel was the first scholar to notice the significance of head offering in these sculptures. *Cf. Bulletin of the School of Oriental Studies*, Vol. VI, London, pp. 539-43.
114. Discovered in Mallam (Nellore distt.), *cf. SII*, XII, No. 106 with illustration. It depicts the first stage of *navakaṇḍam* as cutting left wrist and final act of *tavam* or decapitation.
115. According to K.R. Srinivasan, the vow of *navakaṇḍam* was taken by the warriors who desired victory for their kings in battles and even for cattle raids and hunts. It was a prizable act. *Vide* 1960, *Religion as Revealed in Early Monuments and Literature of the South*, Madras, pp. 29-30. Such head offerings are described in *Kaliṅgaṭṭu Paraṇi* and *Daśakumāracarita* while the rituals connected with such self-immolations are described in the *Kalikā Purāṇa*, chapter 70.
116. *See* Gopinatha Rao's *EHI*, Vol. 1, Pt. 2, p. 342 for an illustration.
117. *Cf.* C. Minakshi, 1977, *Administration and Social Life under the Pallavas*, Madras, p. 221.
118. *Cf. IA*, XXII, p. 67; *SII*, XIV, No. 3.
119. *Cf.* D. Dayalan, *op. cit.*, p. 16. For more about Buddhism and its centres in the region, *see* P.R. Srinivasan and Ayyappan, *Story of Buddhism; also* T.N. Vasudevarao, 1979, *Buddhism in the Tamil country*; C. Minakshi, 'Buddhism in South India', *South Indian Studies II*, pp. 83-131. Quite strangely, Buddha was held to be an incarnation of Viṣṇu in a Mahābalipuram inscription; *see footnote no. 112*. Likewise, Jainism existed rather in a more forceful manner. It attracted even royals like Mahendravarman I. The hold of Buddhism and Jainism over the masses is suggested by the contemptuous references of *Nayanmārs* and *Ālvārs* who finally restricted their popularity. Even Hiuen Tsang regretted his creed Buddhism yielding ground to Digambara Jainism. *See* K.A. Nilakanta Sastri, *Culture and History of the Tamils*, p. 114.
120. Although the real name of Appar's persecutor is not given but his title *Guṇadhara* bears affinity with *Guṇabhara*, another name of Mahendravarman I. The *Periya Purāṇam*, a Tamil text narrating the life of 63 *Nayanmārs*, mentions Guṇadhara who first persecuted and later patronized Appar. *Cf.* V. Venkayya, *EI*, III, p. 278. *Also* A.H. Longhurst, 1998, *Pallava Architecture, MASI*, No. 17, Delhi (repr.), p. 4.
121. Indicated also by the location of his later rock-cut Śaiva temples. For instance, at Tirucirāppaḷḷī, it was a famous Jaina resort below a noted Jaina cavern, while those at Daḷavāṇūr and Śīyamaṅgaḷam located near Jaina centres suggest their conversion into Hindu shrines. *Vide* K.R. Srinivasan, 1998, *CTP*, New Delhi, p. 31.
122. *Cf. Periyatirumoli*, IX, 7-9. He is said to have stolen a Buddha image of solid gold from the Nāgapaṭṭinam *vihāra* for the renovation of the Srīraṅgam temple. *See* Sastri in *The Culture and History of the Tamils*,p. 112.
123. *Vide* C. Minakshi, *The Historical Sculptures of the Vaikuṇṭha-perumāl Temple.*
124. *Cf. IA*, VIII, p. 281.
125. *Refer* to *EI*, IV, pp. 152-53 for epigraphic evidence of the making of this MahendraViṣṇugṛha by *Guṇabhara*, i.e. Mahendravarman.

126. *See* Maṇḍagappaṭṭū Inscription, *EI*, XVII, p. 17; *see also SII*, XII, Nos. 8 and 13.
127. C. Minakshi, 1977, *Administration and Social Life under the Pallavas*, Madras, p. 207.
128. *Vide* T.N. Subramaniam (ed.), 1967, Pallankōvil Copper Plates Grant, *Thirty Pallava Copper Plates*, Madras, p. 1 ff.
129. *Cf.* K.R. Srinivasan, *CTP*, p. 7.
130. *SII*, I, p. 14; XII, p. iii.
131. *Ibid.*, XII, No. 29.
132. N.S. Ramaswami, *op. cit.*, p. 25 suggesting so on the basis of an inscription in the Kailāśanātha temple.
133. Longhurst assigned its building to Parameshvaravarman II. *Cf.* 1998, *Pallava Architecture, MASI*, Pt. III, Delhi, p. 16. Dantivarman's epigraph, however, assigns it to Nandivarman Pallavamalla's reign. *See SII*, XII, No. 43.
134. *Cf. SII*, IV, No. 827.
135. K.R. Srinivasan, *CTP*, p. 11.
136. *Vide SII*, XII, Nos. 94-95.
137. In *EI*, VII, p. 193.
138. *See SII*, XII, No. 105.
139. *Cf. Ibid.*, VII, Nos. 420-21.
140. *Cf.* Fleet, 1883, 'Sanskrit and Old Canarese Inscriptions', *IA*, XII, p. 159.
141. *See* Ellorā Daśāvatāra Cave Inscription, *ARASWI*, V.
142. The Hebbal Inscription (AD 975) refers to a Bhujjabbeśvara temple built to commemorate Bhubbarasi, the grandmother of Gaṅga ruler Marasimha II.
143. The Kāvi Plates describe the restoration of the Jayaditya temple, situated in Kotipura by Govindaraja Prabhutavarsha. *Cf.* 1876, *IA*, V, p. 147. The Ragholi Plates of Jayavardhana also testify to prevalence of solar cult. *Cf. EI*, IX, p. 42. The Pathari Pillar Inscription mentions temple of Saurī. *Cf. EI*, IV, p. 250.
144. Sanjan Copper Plates, *EI*, XVIII, p. 248, v. 47.
145. In his *Pārśvābhyudaya*, Jinasena calls himself the *paramaguru* of Amoghavarsha. *Cf. IA*, XII, pp. 216-18. Similarly, the Jain mathematical work *Sārasaṁgṛha* also mentioned Amoghavarsha as a follower of *syādvāda*. *See* Winternitz, 1920, *Geschichte der Indischen Litteratur*, Leipzig, III, p. 575. Karka's Sūrat Plates record grants by Amoghavarsha to Jaina establishments. *Cf. EI*, XXI. These references highlight royal patronage to Jainism.
146. Plates of Dantivarman of Gujarat. *EI*, VI, p. 292, v. 53-67.
147. A solitary instance of sectarian narrowness can also be seen in the Sūrat Plates (AD 821) of Karka stating that Indra, the donor's father, did not bow his head before any deity, except Śaṁkara, *vide EI*, XXI, p. 143. Barring this, on the whole, the Rāṣṭrakūṭas were rather tolerant. Despite chiefly being Śaivites, they made grants to Brāhmaṇas for all purposes as described in the Cambay Plates of Govinda IV, *EI*, VII, pp. 40-41.
148. *Cf. Nītivākyāmṛta*, VII, 83; Shikarpur Inscription no. 284, contemporary to Krishna II, recorded the construction of a temple and a tank by a private individual who also granted a piece of land for their maintenance. *Cf. Epigraphia Carnatica*, VII.
149. *Refer* to *Appendix* IV.
150. An instance of Krishna I gifting gold and jewels to the Śiva image in Ellorā shrine:
māṇikya- kāñcana- purassara- sarvvabhūtyā
tatra sthitaḥ punar= ābhūshyata yēna Śambhūḥ. *Vide IA*, XII, p. 159. The Cambay Plates of Govinda, IV (AD 930) informs that he donated 400 villages and 32 lakhs of *drammas* for different temples in his dominions. *See EI*, VII, p. 26.

151. *Refer* to R. Champakalakshmi, 1999, *Trade, Ideology and Urbanization—South India 300* BC *to* AD *1300*, Delhi, p. 26.
152. *Cf.* R. Champakalakshmi, 1991, 'Urban Processes in Early Medieval Tamil Nadu', Indu Banga (ed.), *The City in Indian History: Urban Demography History and Politics*, (UHAI) Manohar, New Delhi, p. 48.
153. *Cf. Purananūru*, 7-9, 23, 25, 31-32; *cf.* K.A. Nilakanta Sastri, 1975, *The Colas*, Madras, p. 30. The pearl rich Pāṇḍya coastal region and the pepper rich hilly tracts of the Cēras might have been a constant source of conflict among the three *vendārs*.
154. *Cf. Purananūru*, 29, 123, 125; *cf.* Rajan Gurukkal, 1981, 'Early Iron Age Economy', *Proceedings, Indian History Congress*, 42nd session, p. 75.
155. K.A. Nilakanta Sastri, *A History of South India*, p. 128.
156. *See Maduraikkāñci*, 1.122.
157. Instances as a Pāṇḍya prince who was drowned in the sea. *Vide Purananūru*, 182; It also cites legend of a Cola king plying a fleet across the seas and controlling the high winds. *Cf. Ibid.*, 66; *Maṇimēkalai* suggested that the Tamils were familiar with the experience of being trapped in a mid-ocean storm. *Cf.* IV, 29-34.
158. The megalithic cultural remains of Srī Lankā and South India depict common symbols suggesting early contacts. *Cf.* Champakalakshmi, *Trade, Ideology and Urbanization*, p. 114. The Northern Srī Lankan Brāhmī inscriptions (3rd-4th centuries BC) mention names of Tamil *velirs* (land-owners) and presence of Tamil merchants in Srī Lankā. Recorded by Parnavitana, 1970, *Inscriptions of Ceylon*, Vol. 1. Early Brāhmī Inscriptions, Colombo. Likewise Srī Lankan merchants were also known in early Tamilakām. *Vide* Tirupparankunram Brāhmī Inscription. *See* Mahadevan, 1968, 'Corpus of Tamil Brāhmī Inscriptions', in Nagaswamy (ed.), *Seminar on Inscriptions*, Madras. The use of Ceylonese forms of Brāhmī in potsherds at Arikāmeḍu also indicate their mutual relations, which might have included trade. *Cf.* Mahadevan's, 1981, 'An Old Sinhalese Inscription from Arikamedu', *Seminar on Epigraphy, Kuppuswami Sastri Birth Centenary*, Madras.
159. Suggested by archaeological findings and literary references as R.E.M. Wheeler, A. Ghosh and Krishna Deva, 1946 (July), 'Arikamedu: An Indo-Roman Trading Station on the East Coast of India', *Ancient India*, No. 2; E.H. Warmington, 1974, *The Commerce between the Roman Empire and India*, Delhi; K.S. Ramachandran, 1980, *Archaeology of South India*, Delhi. The distribution pattern of Roman coins highlight the shift from western coasts of early centuries before Christ to the Tamil and Andhra coasts from first-second centuries AD. *Cf.* S. Suresh, 1993, 'A Study of the Roman Coins and Other Antiquities in India with Special Reference to South India', Ph.D. Thesis (unpublished), JNU, Delhi.
160. Suggested literally. *Maṇimēkalai* described several parts of the story beyond the seas in South and South-East Asian regions like Sāvakam and Maṇipallavam, i.e. Java and Jaffna. *Cf.* Chaps. XIV, XV, XXI, XXV. For an early Sanskrit inscription from Laos mentioning a Pāṇḍya and a copper coin with tiger emblem, see I. Mahadevan, 1994, 'Ancient Tamil Contacts Abroad: Recent Epigraphic Evidence', *Journal of the Institute of Asian Studies*, Vol. XII, No. 1, Colombo, pp. 136-55. References of Chinese visiting the Buddhist sites in Andhra regions are also available. *Cf.* Amita Ray, 1983, *Life and Art of Early Andhradesa*, Delhi. The influence of Amarāvatī's Buddhist art upon the early sculptural art of Campā has also been pointed out by R. Champakalakshmi to highlight the relations of the two regions. *Cf. Trade, Ideology and Urbanization*, p. 116.
161. Used perhaps for enhancing their social status, such precious things were also offered as gifts. For instance, by a Pāṇḍya king recorded in *Maduraikkāñci*, 766; or bestowed upon the visitors by the Cēra king in *Purananūru*, 343: 8; sometimes gifted away to the bards and

kinsmen who, gratefully, would sustain the position of their patron. *Cf.* R. Champakalakshmi, *ibid.*, p. 190.

162. Probably a transit good from China en route to Rome. *Cf.* McCrindle, 1973, *The Commerce and Navigation of the Erythraean Sea and Ancient India as Described by Ktesias, the Knidian*, Amsterdam, Calcutta (repr.). Referred to as *paṭṭū* in Tamil texts. *Cf. Akanānūru*, 236: 11, *Paṭṭinappālai*, 1.107.
163. The only manufactured, exportable item. Produced in Cola region, argaritic muslins of Uraiyūr were mentioned in *Periplus*, 59; *Arthaśāstra*, II. 11: 115 referred to its production in the Pāṇḍya land; *Śilappadikāram*, VI. 88 described 32 varieties of cotton fabrics.
164. South Indian pearls, *muṭṭū*, were counted among the most highly valued ones in ancient times. *Cf.* Clarence Maloney, 1968, 'The Effect of Early Coastal Sea Traffic on the Development of Civilization in South India', Ph.D. Thesis (unpublished), Pennsylvania. The Pāṇḍyan coast was particularly rich in pearls and gems—*maṇi*.
165. Mainly procured from the Cēra country, from 1st-2nd centuries AD. Under the impetus of lucrative spice trade and increased demand, Tamil merchants sought new areas like the spice rich South-East Asian islands to meet the requirement, *cf. Śilappadikāram*, XIV. 104-12.
166. Known also as *Kari*, it made up almost 3/4th of the average total of Rome bound cargo. *See* E.H. Warmington, *op. cit.*, p. 181. Sacks of black pepper reached Kāverīppumpaṭṭinam from the west coast, i.e. Cēra region.
167. All types of woods, ornamental or aromatic, were included for trade purposes. Most prevalent were sandalwood, teak, ebony, etc., growing around Coimbatore, Malabar regions. *Cf.* G. Watt, 1966, *The Commercial Products of India*, New Delhi. Fragrant woods also constituted a part of the transit trade as besides the hilly regions of South India, they also came from South-East Asian lands. *Vide* Maloney, *op. cit.*, pp. 162-63. *See also*, *Śilappadikāram*, XIV. 104-12.
168. Roman wine *tēral* was very popular in South India as suggested by V. Kanakasabhai Pillai in 1966. *The Tamils Eighteen Hundred Years Ago*, Tirunelveli, p. 87. Amphorae sherds have been found from Arikāmeḍu, Kāraikkāḍu, etc., some of which reveal traces of incrustation caused by wine resin on the inside. *Cf.* R.E.M. Wheeler, 1955, *Rome beyond the Imperial Frontiers*, London, p. 177.
169. The *yavana* lamp with wick giving out a steady flame was much in demand. *Cf.* R. Champakalakshmi, *Trade, Ideology and Urbanization*, p. 188. Some lamps were like statues bearing the *takalī* or lamp container in their folded palms; see *Neṭunalvāṭai*, 101-03.
170. The southern climate not being favourable for breeding, horses were imported into South India mainly from the Arab countries. *Cf.* R. Champakalakshmi, *Trade, Ideology and Urbanization*, p. 189. Milk white steeds imported into Puhār are referred in *Paṭṭinappālai* while *Maduraikkāñcī* describe their import at the Pāṇḍyan ports. *Cf. Paṭṭinappālai*, 1.185; *Maduraikkāñcī*, 1. 323.
171. *Cf.* R. Champakalakshmi, *Trade, Ideology and Urbanization*, p. 81; footnote no. 76.
172. *Cf.* B.N.S. Yadava, 1978 (July) – 1979 (Jan), 'The Accounts of the Kali Age and the Social Transition from Antiquity to the Middle Ages', *Indian Historical Review*, Vol. V, Nos. 1-2, p. 61. R.S. Sharma has suggested the decay of towns following the decline of trade in third century AD. Refer to 1972, *Proceedings, Indian History Congress*, 33rd Session, pp. 92-104.
173. *Cf.* R. Champakalakshmi, *Trade, Ideology and Urbanization*, p. 37.
174. Pūlānkuriccī record of *brahmadeya* granted in the semi-arid Ramanathapuram district (5th century AD). *Cf.* R. Nagaswamy, 1981, 'An Outstanding Epigraphical Discovery in Tamil Nadu'. *Fifth International Conference Seminar on Tamil Studies*, Madurai.

175. With each of the *brahmadeya* or *devadāna* settlements, an irrigation system in form of tanks, canals and wells was usually appended. *See* T.M. Srinivasan, 1970, 'A Brief Account of the Ancient Irrigation Engineering Systems Prevalent in South India', *The Indian Journal of History of Science*, Vol. 5, No. 2. An inscription from Bādāmī records the guild of 'Five Hundred' setting apart the proceeds of an impost that belonged to them for the purpose of maintaining a tank at Kattageri. *Cf.* 1877, *IA*, VI, p. 138. It is also believed that the Brāhmaṇas with their specialized astronomical knowledge might have facilitated predictability of yields based on seasonal sowing and cropping patterns.
176. For details *see* D. Ludden, 1985, *Peasant History in South India*, Princeton; *see also* Rajan Gurukkal, 1986 (July-Dec), 'Aspects of the Reservoir System of Irrigation in the Early Pandya State', *Studies in History*, N.S., Vol. II, No. 2.
177. *Cf.* R. Champakalakshmi, *Trade, Ideology and Urbanization*, p. 85; footnote no. 94.
178. *See* K.R. Srinivasan, 'Pallava Architecture', in *Ancient India*, No. 14, 1958.
179. For details *refer to* K.R. Venkatarama Ayyar, 1947, 'Medieval Trade, Craft and Merchant Guilds in South India', *Journal of Indian History*, pp. 268-80. *See* also Abraham, 1988, *Two Medieval Merchant Guilds of South India*, New Delhi; for trade under Cālukyas, *see* Kamat, 1978, 'Social Life and Economic Conditions under the Chalukyas of Bādāmī', in M.S. Nagaraja Rao (ed.), *The Chalukyas of Bādāmī* (Seminar Papers), pp. 181-85.
180. As suggested by K.A. Nilakanta Sastri in *A History of South India*, p. 299.
181. *Śāntiparva*, XII, 130: 35.
182. As H.P. Ray suggested in 1986, *Monastery and Guild: Commerce under the Sātavāhanas*, Delhi, chapter 1.
183. The Sātavāhanas probably realized the advantage of acknowledging the dominance of Buddhist ideology over merchants and classes involved in commerce and production activities. *Cf.* Romila Thapar, 1982, *A History of India*, Vol. 1, pp. 111-12; *see also* Vidya Dehejia, 1972, *Early Buddhist Rock Temples*.
184. The spread of Buddhism and Jainism coincided with a rise in trade and commercial activity. This introduced an element of heterogeneity in the urban centres. *Vide* R. Champakalakshmi, *Trade, Ideology and Urbanization*, p. 101. The Tamil Brāhmī inscriptions also support the Buddhist and Jaina bias of the merchants seen as making gifts to the two sects. *Cf.* I. Mahadevan, 1968, 'Corpus of Tamil Brāhmī Inscriptions', *Seminar on Inscriptions*.
185. *See* J. Heitzman, 1989 (March), 'Early Buddhism, Trade and Empire', *Journal of Southeast Asian Studies*, Vol. XX, No. 1, pp. 121-37.
186. *Cf.* Touche, 1917, *A Bibliography of Indian Geology and Physical Geography*, Calcutta, pp. 113-37. Copper was also mentioned as an article of export from Bharoch in the *Periplus*. *See* Schoff, p. 36.
187. Suggested by Rāṣṭrakūṭa epigraphs: *lakshmtr=atmakalamkam=ahita-malam nindyaih kubhup asrayaih*, (i.e.) Lakshmī abiding in the waters of his sword. *Vide* 1883, *IA*, XII, p. 265. *Aṛinrpati-makuṭa-ghaṭṭita-caraṇas* (i.e. whose feet were rubbed by diadems and crowns of lofty people). *IA*, *ibid.*, pp. 218-19; for trade details *also see* Dikshit, 1994, 'Trade under the Rashtrakutas', in B.R. Gopal (ed.), *The Rāshtrakūṭas of Malkhed: Studies in their History and Culture*, Mysore.

3

Cālukya, Pallava and Raṣṭrakūṭa Art Activities

From the fifth to ninth centuries AD, a spurt could be noticed in South Indian stone temple erection activity. The inauguration of the process of temple construction commenced with the consolidation of the powers of the Cālukyas of Bādāmī and the Rāṣṭrakūṭas of Mānyakheṭa in the Deccan and the Pallavas in Kāñcī. The best and maximum output in this field came during AD 550-850. It was the time when these three kingdoms were keen political rivals as well as close competitors in the patronage of art, architecture and literature.

The use of stone for building sacred edifices was rather a novel phenomenon. Especially in South India, it has been suggested that there was a taboo on the use of stone for sacred and secular structures because of its long local association with funerary erections.[1] This may have deterred stone as a building material in temples till the close of the sixth century and in carving images of deities till the first half of the seventh century.[2] The *Āgamas* and *Śilpaśāstras* preferred and recommended wood, then mortar, and lastly, stone for making images.[3] Stone shrines had no place even in Vedic rites wherein the altars were mainly brick-piles. The *svaya matṛṇṇa* or the naturally perforated 'bricks' placed in the centre of *yajña* or Agni[4] were most probably a special kind of stone.[5] However, evidences disprove this supposed taboo on the use of stone in the Vedic era itself. The *Śatapatha Brāhmaṇa* mentions stone castles and ramparts, *aśmapura*,[6] and houses with safest roofs.[7] But generally in those times the architecture, whether secular or religious, was primarily wooden. The large scale use of wood may be assigned to the availability of timber in abundance.[8] Houses of big dimensions were constructed of timber.[9] Even the dwellings of divine beings were believed to have been made up of wood. For instance, the house of Parameśṭhī Prajāpati, whose model was adopted by human beings.[10] Later, however, stone as an art medium seems to have gained ascendancy. *Śilpaśāstras* as *Rūpa-maṇḍana*[11] and *Viṣṇudharmottara Purāṇa*[12] consists of details for the carving of stone icons.

In, south, the imperishable stone medium was firstly adopted by Cālukya Mangalesha and his contemporary Pallava monarch Mahendravarman I almost simultaneously. Mangalesha excavated the Vaiṣṇavite cave III at Bādāmī, in association with the *srāddha* of Kirtivarman in AD 578.[13] Mahendravarman excavated the first Pallava cave-temple at Maṇḍagappaṭṭū, held to be the first cave-temple in the Tamil country associated with Brāhmanical religion.[14] His Maṇḍagappaṭṭū inscription[15] holds great significance in this regard. Herein he, as *vicitracitta*, claimed to have created a brickless, timberless, metalless and mortarless temple—*lakshitāyatana*—dedicated to Brahmā, Īśvara and Viṣṇu.

While the Cālukyan shrines were cut in soft sandstone, the Pallava monuments were created out of hard granite. Thus, the Cālukyas and the Pallavas, in their respective regions, inaugurated two parallel traditions of stone architecture. These political powers generously patronized structural shrines, sculptures, art of painting, etc.

1. THE CĀLUKYAN ART ACTIVITIES

The Early Western Cālukya temples concentrated at Aihoḷe, Bādāmī, Mahākūṭa and Paṭṭaḍakal are amongst India's most fascinating sacred monuments. They constitute the largest group of stone buildings belonging to sixth, seventh and eighth centuries AD. Besides, they are the earliest extant shrines, grouped together by their patronage, period and style. An artistic analysis reveals bewildering variety of their forms. The royal patronage was perhaps directly responsible for this intense building activity,[16] promoting the transition from the rock-cut medium to structural stone techniques and thereby forming one of the most creative phases in the history of Indian architecture and sculpture.

Origin of Early Cālukyan Temples

The Cālukyan enthusiasm for constructed, freestanding buildings has not been correctly interpreted so far. Therefore, the origin of their early temples is unsettled. Henry Cousens[17] traced their origin to the Pallava Draviḍian temples. However, Longhurst[18] held that no Pallava monument has been found prior to seventh century AD. The earliest Pallava monuments were all rock-cut and the construction of structural temples began only in the Rajasimha period (AD 674-800). Stella Kramrisch has also pointed out that not only in the Draviḍa country itself in seventh century AD, but also in the Kanarese part of the Deccan, where Aihoḷe, Mahākūṭeśvara, Bādāmī and Paṭṭaḍakal are located, such temples were built at an earlier date.[19] Although various temples had been mentioned in several copper-plate inscriptions,[20] recording gifts made by the early Pallava kings to temples, the temples themselves are not extant. Therefore, any idea of their form becomes the subject of mere imagination. Thus, any theory seeking to trace the origins of the Cālukya temples of sixth century AD to the Pallavas is untenable.[21]

Therefore, Cousens' theory of Pallava origin of Cālukyan temple architecture evokes no serious thought. On the contrary, Gupte[22] has suggested that it was the art of Aihoḷe and Bādāmī that had influenced the art forms in the Tamil lands.

The Gupta origin of Cālukyan architecture has also been similarly rejected.[23] It is quite likely that the Cālukyan art was indigenous and independent in origin. However, this is equally correct that in the process of its evolution, Cālukyan art did imbibe several features,[24] both architectural and sculptural from the Vākāṭaka, Kalacuri, Gupta and the Pallava styles.

TEMPLE SITES

From second half of sixth century with the cave-shrines at Aihoḷe and Bādāmī[25] to the beginning of the seventh century, the Cālukyan architecture was on its way to transition from the rock-cut to structural techniques. The Gaudarguḍī at Aihoḷe and the Kumāra Brahmā at Ālampur were amongst the earliest Cālukya shrines.[26]

Their extant monuments are mainly at two centres: (i) clusters of shrines or isolated temples mostly in the valley of the Mālaprabhā, particularly between Bādāmī and Aihoḷe, at the sites of Bādāmī, Nagral, Cikka Mahākūṭa, Mahākūṭa, Paṭṭaḍakal, Siddhankolla, Aihoḷe, etc.; (ii) between the banks of the Tungabhadrā and the Nallamalai, at the sites of Ālampur, Pañcaliṅgala, Kudaveli, Mahānandī, Turimella, etc.[27] At these centres, Aihoḷe, Bādāmī and Paṭṭaḍakal are the main sites that flourished with a series of fabulous monuments.

AIHOḶE

Of these sites, Aihoḷe (Map 6)[28] consisted of shrines numbering nearly a hundred,[29] most of them clustered in large or small groups. It has not been possible so far to explain the construction of so many temples at this particular secluded place.[30] Five rock-cut caves are also seen in the vicinity of the structural temples.

The entire temple building activity at Aihoḷe synonymous with a movement, considering the number and variety of forms erected, is assignable to four Cālukyan monarchs, viz. Pulakeshin I, Kirtivarman, Mangalesha and Pulakeshin II.[31] The process initiated with the Konṭi-guḍī group[32] in early sixth century and culminated with the Megutī temple in seventh century. In accordance with the observations of Gupte,[33] it may be held that the Cālukyan shrines evolved gradually through the following stages:

1. The appearance of a veranda-shaped temple with a transverse plan and the *garbhagṛha* built in the back wall, firstly seen in the Konṭi-guḍī group. A wall did not as yet enclose it.
2. The temple plan with a pillared *mukhamaṇḍapa*, *sabhāmaṇḍapa* and *garbhagṛha* in the back wall. This pattern found in the Lāḍ Khān temple marked an advance over the Konṭi-guḍī group. One of its façade pillars depicted the varāha *lāñchana*.[34]
3. Pattern of the temple with a *mukhamaṇḍapa* and a *sabhāmaṇḍapa* datable to mid-sixth century as seen in the temples of Tārabasappā, the main temple of the Galaganātha group, the Nārāyaṇ temple and the temple adjoining Hucchimallī guḍī.

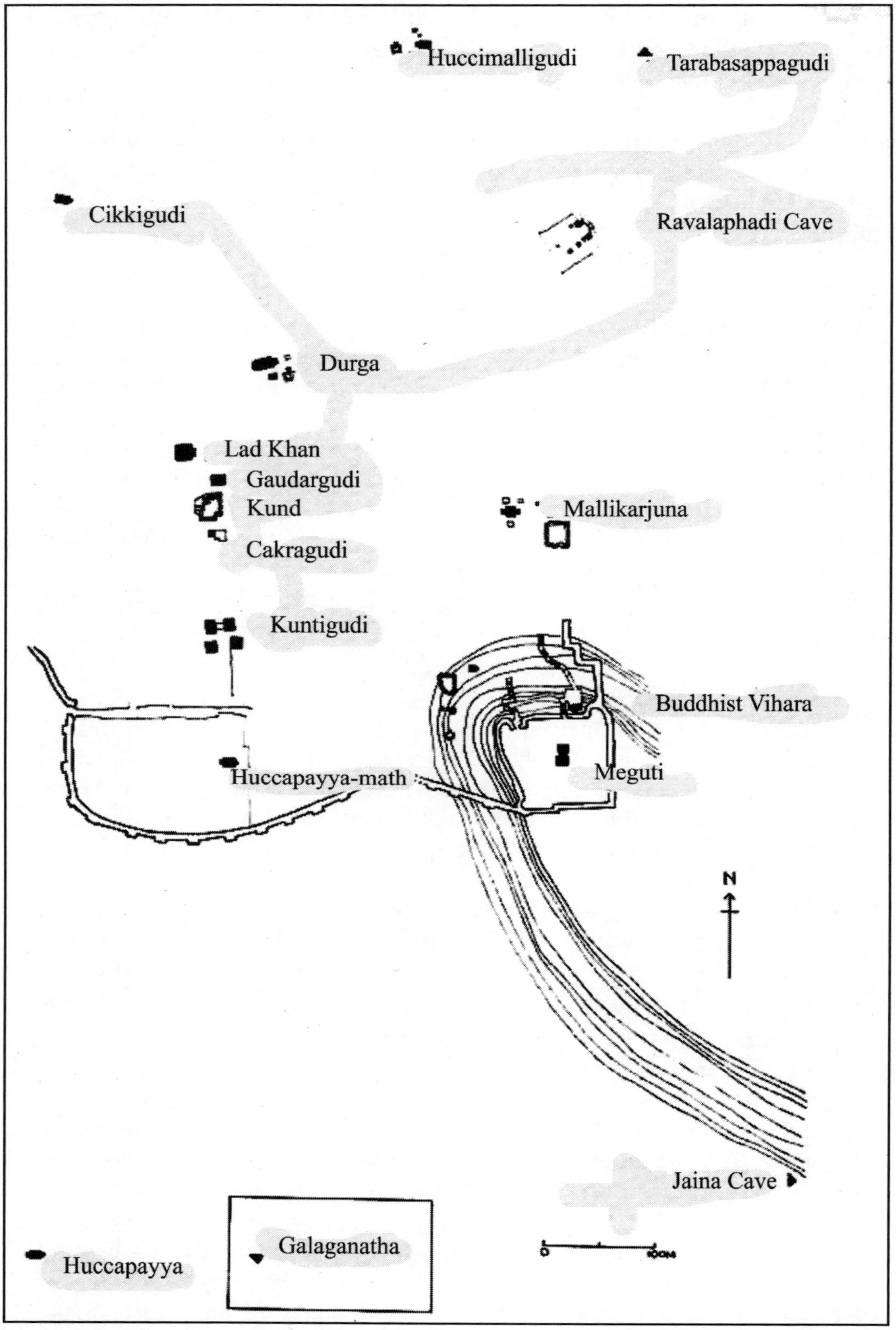

Map. 6. Aihoḷe: Site plan (after AIIS).

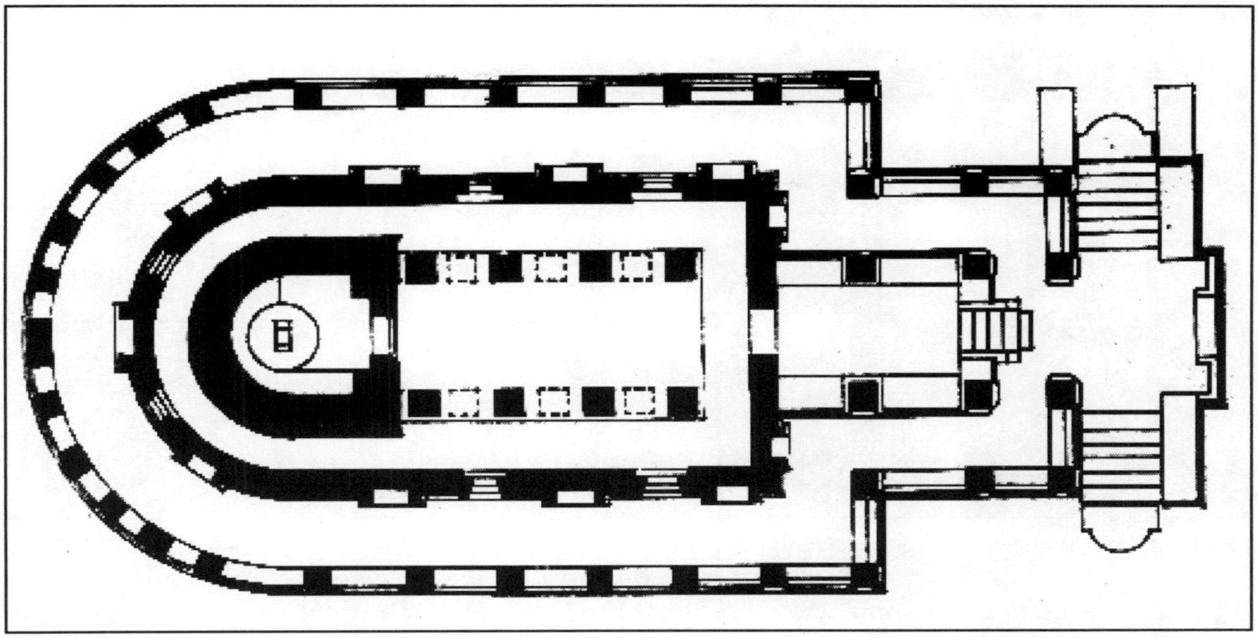

Fig. 13. Aihoḷe: Durgā temple, ground plan (after AIIS).

4. The appearance of *pradakshiṇāpatha* in temples as Gaudar-guḍī, Durgā temple (Fig. 13), Aṁbiger guḍī, Cakra guḍī, etc. These shrines are usually placed after AD 560.
5. The final evolution of the Cālukyan temple was form with a *mukhamaṇḍapa, sabhāmaṇḍapa, antarāla* and *garbhagṛha,* with or without *pradakshiṇāpatha.* The *antarāla*[35] was present in most of the rock-cut architecture of the fifth century AD. At Aihoḷe, besides the Rāvaṇa Phaḍi cave, in the structural temples, *antarāla* was firstly provided for in the Hucchimallī guḍī. Its early stage was signified by its place in the *sabhāmaṇḍapa* itself. The temple in Galaganātha group having the *antarāla* separated from the *sabhāmaṇḍapa* marked an advance over Hucchimallī guḍī. The Jaina Megutī[36] temple built during Pulakeshin II presented an evolved form of Cālukyan temple. It had a *mukhamaṇḍapa* in front of an *antarāla* and a *garbhagṛha* surrounded by a *sandhāra pradakshiṇāpatha* (Fig. 14).

Thus, in the course of over two centuries, the temple construction progression at Aihoḷe produced forms that became elemental to Hindu temple architecture. From the rock-cut architectural activity that preceded it, a significant transition was made with stone medium.[37] In the early Cālukyan temples, blocks of stone were used for building. For instance, the Megutī temple was constructed by stone blocks assembled without use of mortar. This stimulated a new technique of placing the blocks as desired in the plan and executed by the stone carvers accordingly. They were not simple rectangular or cubical stone blocks but mostly had some projections on one side so that when placed in a row, the desired form could be projected. This rendered the process of placing slabs as equivalent to sculptures, each slab having its own identity in the

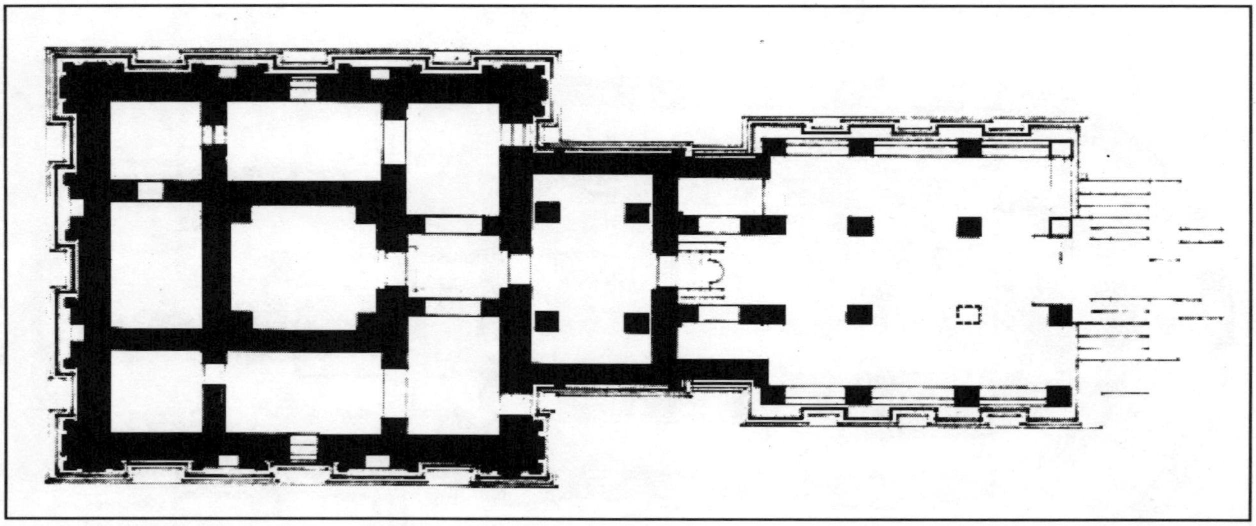

Fig. 14. Aihoḷe: Megutī temple, ground plan (after AIIS).

projection of temple walls, sculptures and verandah. Thus, the early Cālukya temple architecture was not plain construction. As it was a new kind of architecture, the form of the Hindu structural temple could emerge only gradually (Fig. 15).

Experimental Ventures

The seeming confusion due to inexperience in the stone medium was reflected in individual buildings with their different parts often executed in contrasting styles. Stylistic evolution, therefore, could not follow a straight linear path. It obviously posed problems to the architects who tried to solve them in their own manner. This led to the rise of several artistic innovations. For instance, the heavy outline of the Lāḍ Khān temple emphasized its experimental nature.[38] Unusual in both plan and form, the simple layout, flat roof, walls with disproportionate strength, imitation of wooden forms, etc. suggested that the architects of Hindu dressed stone buildings were still finding their way.

Fig. 15. Aihoḷe: Megutī temple (after AIIS).

Fig. 16. Aihoḷe: Durgā temple (after AIIS).

The Durgā temple with its apsidal *garbhagṛha* resembling a Buddhist *caitya*, external *mukhamaṇḍapa*, an open-sided *pradakshiṇāpatha* and an embryonic *śikhara* also signified the emerging form of early Cālukyan temple. Its overall appearance seemed somewhat unusual. The form related it to Buddhist shrines while its high base and open bays conferred an airy quality on it. Moreover, the partly ruined small *śikhara* was quite unassertive. These features placed the Durgā temple in a class of its own. It was actually an architectural experiment with few parallels (Fig. 16).

The main temple in the Hucchappayya Maṭha group with its almost entirely blank walls and elaborately sculptured corner pilasters and *dvāraśākhās* was also notable for want of a definite plan.

Development of Aihoḷe Temple Architecture

Among its early temples, the Lāḍ Khān[39] comprised several remarkable features. It marked the first appearance of a 'cushion' capital on its slightly tapering plain square pillars with *potikās*. This capital, with an expanded floral *phalaka* supporting the bracket, later on became familiar in the South Indian architecture. The introduction of the *kakshāsana*[40] was also noticed herein. The masonry blocks, placed one upon the other sans any binding component, reveal the primitive character of the temple. The walls displaying disproportionate strength signified inexperienced workmanship. The inside pillars exhibited exultant strength with their ponderous *potikās*, low *kapota*, etc. The exterior carving portrayed an unrefined beauty.

With the erection of more shrines, however, the architects made relative progress, symbolized by the Megutī temple. Besides well-defined architectural features, it marked an improvement in the quality of the masonry. Smaller blocks of stone were used

Fig. 17. Aihoḷe: Lāḍ Khān temple (after AIIS).

while ornamentation was treated with more delicacy, as suggested by the design of the *potikā* capitals on the exterior pilasters. Still, on the whole, the temple did not show any marked advance in planning or general arrangements. Hence, from the simple structure consisting of a crudely made *garbhagṛha* in a veranda like structure, to the mature form with a *mukhamaṇḍapa*, an enclosed *sabhāmaṇḍapa*, *antarāla* and *pradakshiṇāpatha*, the Cālukya temple at Aihoḷe finally acquired an evolved plan.

Śikhara

The Aihoḷe *śikhara* form also evolved in a gradual manner. Like the Gupta temples,[41] those at Aihoḷe had flat or slightly sloping roofs and in some instances, were surmounted by a small upper shrine or *śikhara*, possibly a subsequent addition. Almost three temples at Aihoḷe originally had no *śikhara* or had it as a later addition.[42] The Lāḍ Khān temple had a very low roof with huge slabs laid almost flat (Figs. 17-17(i)). Stone battens between the roofing stones rendered the surface of the roof watertight. This roofing

Fig. 17 (i). Aihoḷe: Lāḍ Khān temple, roofing details (after AIIS).

technique seemed to be a primitive effort to replace the conventional thatched roof on a wooden frame with a stone roof. It consisted of large flat slabs near whose joints grooves were chiselled with a corresponding ridge at the edges. Long, narrow stones were fitted into the grooves, covering the entire length of the joints. The shape of the stone ribs suggests timber origin while the overhanging cornices were probably derived from thatch.

Roofing stones were common in Aihoḷe but were subsequently replaced by successive layers of horizontal corbelling. The pillars bearing weight of the roof by an arrangement of capitals with four *potikās* in an intersecting cross shape also represented wooden art influence. Over the roof, a small square shrine symbolized *śikhara*, more developed in later shrines. The Hucchappayyā main temple was also flat-roofed with large slabs. Some other smaller, flat roofed temples had simple Nāgara *śikhara* over their *garbhagṛha*. Of them, some were initially Vaiṣṇava shrines, later converted into Śaivite ones and their *śikhara* also being subsequent additions.[43]

Fig. 18. Bādāmī: Loval Śivālaya temple (after AIIS).

Thus, from the simple beginnings in the Konṭi guḍī group and the Lāḍ Khān to the more evolved forms in the Durgā, Hucchimallī guḍī, or the Galaganātha temples, the early Cālukyan temples throw ample light on the evolution of Nāgara Hindu temple *śikhara*. One of the earliest attempts at the *śikhara* form was over the Durgā[44] temple. After completion, instead of being curved in outline, it appeared almost straight sided, like an elongated pyramid, inclined inward at the apex to support the *āmalaka*. This placement of a distinct *śikhara* on an apsidal structure derived from a *caitya* appears as an interesting instance. The *śikhara* in the Hucchimallī guḍī temple was raised over a square end. On its front or eastern face, a portion was projected and shaped like a *caitya* arch with a central panel. This panel contained a carved figure of Śiva dancing the *tāṇḍava*. Later, the projected part gradually extended into a kind of gable and became the roof of the *antarāla*.[45]

It may be seen that most of the *śikharas* at Aihoḷe were in Nāgara style though marked with primitive simplicity of design.[46] The Tārābasappā and Hucchimallī guḍī offered good examples of the evolution of the Nāgara *śikhara* type at Aihoḷe as Mallikārjuna and Virūpāksha at Paṭṭaḍakal, of the southern *vimāna* type. A distinct local type, known as Kadamba Nāgara, with receding and multi-tiered roof was exemplified in the Mallikārjuna temple at Aihoḷe.[47]

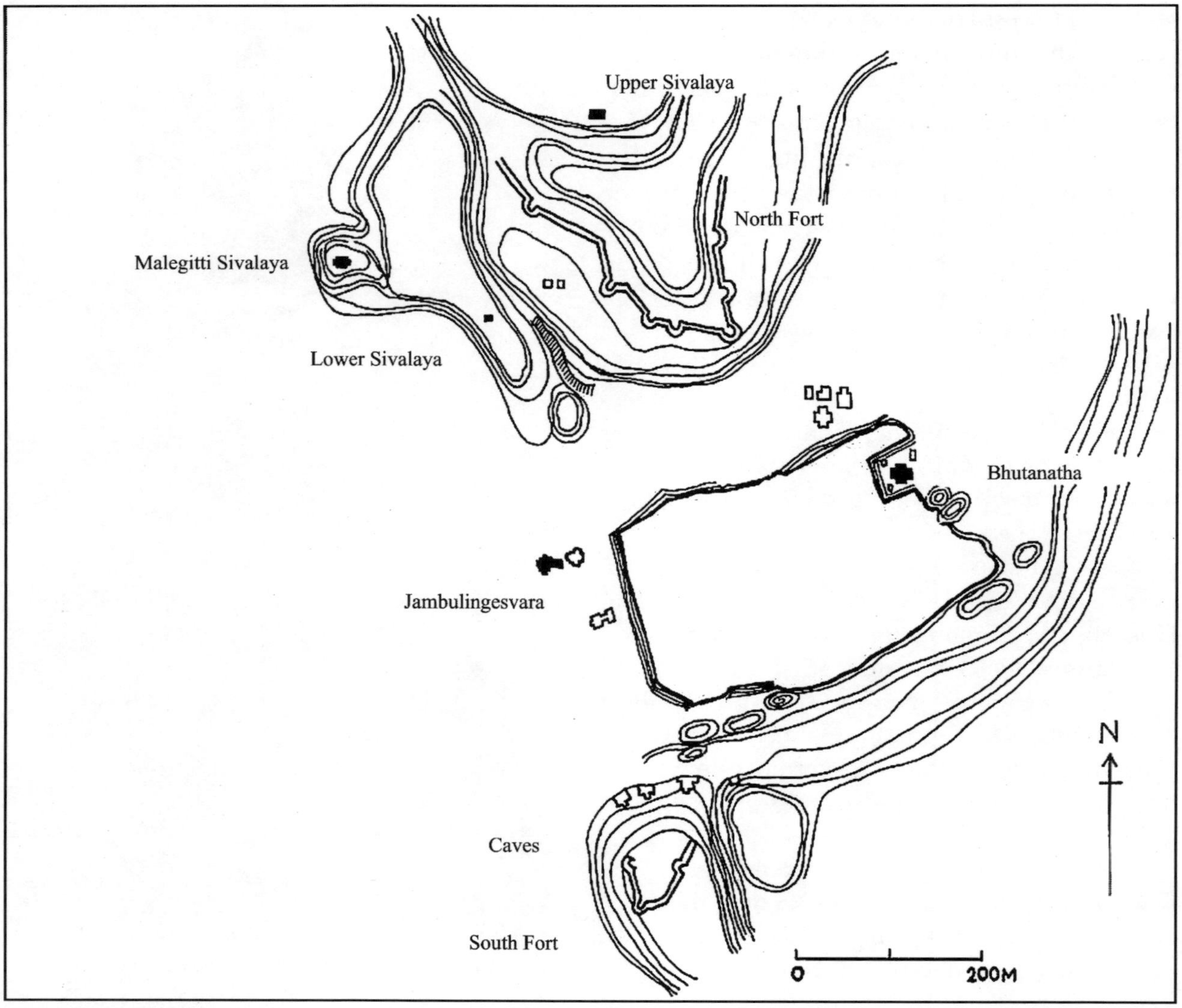

Map 7. Bādāmī: Site plan (after AIIS).

BĀDĀMĪ

The Dravidian style was far more noticeable at Bādāmī,[48] a site signifying further evolution of Cālukyan temple architecture (Map 7). Located in the southeast Bijapur, it was an early capital of the Cālukyas. It comprised some of the most interesting early Cālukyan architectural remains including a series of cave temples, both Hindu and Jaina, some old structural temples and fortifications.

Out of the three-Śaiva temples at Bādāmī:

(i) upper or the Azar Śivālaya (possibly seventh century) was remarkable for its imposing *śikhara*, now partly ruined. It originally had a *caturārṣa garbhagṛha*, *pradakshiṇāpatha* and *sabhāmaṇḍapa*. Its vigorous *śikhara* marked a stylistic transition between the Malegittī and the Loval Śivālayas. The reliefs carved on plinth, wall panels illustrating Kṛṣṇā scenes, and the *gaṇa* friezes on the temple *adhiṣṭhāna* depicted influence of the nearby cave temples.

(ii) The Mālegittī Śivālaya, located on a gigantic sandstone boulder, presented a more compact and harmoniously proportioned elevation. It was clearly divided into the *garbhagṛha, sabhāmaṇḍapa* and *mukhamaṇḍapa*. The first two being square in plan, its heavy monolithic pillars, *potikā* capitals, overhanging *kapota*, all suggestive of possible influence of rock-cut tradition. Its octagon to dome form *śikhara*, supported by a series of smaller *śālās* or shrines, was illustrative of an early phase in the evolution of the Draviḍian *śikhara*. The Mālegittī's compact structure was clearly Draviḍian in style as suggested by the sturdy pillars in *mukhamaṇḍapa*, the massive capitals with crossed *potikās* and the recurrence of the *kūḍū* motif. Its weighty roof structure reproduced in stone the features of a timber frame roof, a probable Pallava influence.[49]

(iii) Loval Śivālaya temple, of a similar date, has only the *garbhagṛha* and its roof left intact. It is held that its *maṇḍapa* was carried away in a land slide.[50] The *śikhara* dominated by an octagonal *stūpī* and miniature *śālās* rose from a rocky outcrop high above Bādāmī (Fig. 18).

In addition to the early shrines, Bādāmī also consisted of the Dattātreya, Bhūtanātha[51] and Jambūliṅga temples ranging from ninth to thirteenth centuries.

PAṬṬAḌAKAL

The third Cālukyan site of Paṭṭaḍakal signified a shift in the field of temple erections. The Cālukyan art activities are likely to have suffered setbacks in the wake of the civil war between Mangalesha and Pulakeshin II (AD 609-10)[52] and later the occupation of Bādāmī (AD 642) by Pallava Narasimhavarman I.[53] Cālukyan hegemony was re-established after a hiatus of thirteen years. Vikramaditya I revived Śaiva[54] temple building process at Paṭṭaḍakal, their new power centre.

Paṭṭaḍakal or ancient Paṭṭaḍa Kisuvolal near Bādāmī, on the banks of the Mālaprabhā, had Cālukyan shrines of both Draviḍian and Nāgara styles [55] erected side by side. Of the ten temples of consequence, four, i.e. the Pāpanātha, Jambūliṅga, Karsiddheśvara and Kāśīnātha represented Nāgara style, whereas the Saṅgameśvara, Virūpāksha, Mallikārjuna, Galagnātha, etc. were based on the Draviḍian style.

The Pāpanātha seems to be a dedication to Viṣṇu, later converted into a Śaivite shrine. There has been much speculation over its date suggested to be AD 650,[56] AD 680,[57] and AD 735,[58] etc. Located to the south of the Virūpāksha, it had a very ornate structure and Nāgara *śikhara*. Both in plan and elevation, the temple indicated the uncertainity still prevailing as to the appropriate demarcation of its main components and their relation to each other. It appeared as a long, low composition with a flat roof and rather small and stunted *śikhara*. Frequent repetitions of the same sculptural motifs suggested a dearth of ideas as also ignorance of accurate allotment of space. The *antarāla* was made so large that it became almost a supplementary *maṇḍapa*. The massive and solid interiors conveyed a possible rock-cut influence.[59] It also appears to have undergone major architectural alterations at least twice.[60]

The Śaivite Saṅgameśvara temple bore striking resemblance to the Arjuna *ratha* at Mahābalipuram. The only difference being that Saṅgameśvara was of dressed stones rather than rock-cut. It marked several significant modifications, as the absence of a *śukanāsā* on the *antarāla*, the first appearance of the *pañjara* in the *hāra*, lack of *karṇakūṭas* in the *hāra* of the top *tala*, etc. This absence was perhaps the first step[61] towards the elimination of the *hāra* itself and its replacement by the *vāhanas* and *lāñchanas* of the shrine deity at the corners.[62] It also introduced two side shrines in the *ardhamaṇḍapa* walls dedicated to Durgā and Gaṇeśa. It was an indication of the Vaiṣṇavite Cālukyas' emerging Śaivite leanings.

In about AD 745 the Virūpāksha and Mallikārjuna temples were built by Lokamahadevi[63] and Trailokyamahadevi,[64] queens of Vikramaditya II, commemorating his victory over the Pallavas.[65] Both edifices were in Draviḍian style. The Virūpāksha or Lokeśvara temple was very symmetrical in plan. It symbolized a correction of the inconsistencies apparent in Pāpanātha's plan and also marked advancement upon the Saṅgameśvara.[66] It consisted of a frontal detached *nandimaṇḍapa*. Its various parts appeared as a coherent group. The architectural details of the pillars, pilasters, *kapota*, brackets or floral scrollwork on window *jālīs*, the bold animal supports, the intricate bas-reliefs or the lifesize sculptures in the panels and niches, all testified to expertise applied in their creation. The introduction of *gopuram* as an entrance was also seen herein. The temple *śikhara* with a *stūpī* reflected Draviḍian character.

The nearby Mallikārjuna or Trailokyeśvara temple with several unfinished parts[67] was similar in general plan and design to the Virūpāksha, suggesting both to be the work of one architect. It had a circular *grīvā* and *śikhara* on top of the square *talas*. The topmost *tala* had no *hāra* at all, marking the total elimination of this component and heralding the advent of the *vāhanas* instead.[68] On clearing the *adhiṣṭhāna* and *nandimaṇḍapa*, S.R. Rao has dated the Mallikārjuna prior to the Saṅgameśvara and Virūpāksha temples in about seventh century.[69]

At Mahākūṭeśvara, Nāgara and Draviḍa styled major and minor shrines were noticeable. Of them, the Makuṭeśvaranātha[70] was probably the first in a sequence of temples having a Draviḍian *śikhara*. The *dvāraśākhā* decoration depicted Gupta influence.[71] Therefore, the temple bore both Draviḍian and Nāgara features.

A group of nine temples called Nava Brahmā, within an enclosure at Ālampur (Andhra Pradesh), revealed affinity with the Paṭṭaḍakal shrines, suggesting their Cālukyan origin. The Ālampur shrines became remarkable for marking a shift of emphasis from interior decoration, especially of the ceilings, as at Bādāmī and Paṭṭaḍakal, to that of the exterior walls.

Thus, it is apparent that at these sites, the Cālukyan patronage led to the creation of numerous edifices offering great variety of forms ranging from simple *maṇḍapa* types to typical *vimāna* and *prāsāda* instances,[72] paving way for the organized Hindu temple form.

Development of Cālukyan Temple Components

Orientation

Besides their individual characteristics, the Cālukyan temples also exhibited certain common components revealing evolution of their forms. Orientationwise most of them faced east or west though some were north facing too. For instance, at Aihoḷe two temples in Konṭi guḍī group faced east, one faced west while the Megutī faced north.

Lalāṭabiṁba

The *garbhagṛha dvāra lalāṭabiṁba* usually carried some cognizance of the shrine deity as a mark of identification. For instance, Vaiṣṇava temples had Lakshmī, Viṣṇu or Garuḍa and Śaiva shrines showed anthropomorphic form of Śiva. At Aihoḷe, the Vaiṣṇava Galaganātha shrine *lalāṭabiṁba* depicted Garuḍa holding snakeheads in his hands.

Dvāraśākhās

They were carved profusely. Vertical bands of frieze work were delicately chiselled while pilasters with decorative motifs and mouldings could be seen on either side. *Caitya kūḍū* was a popular motif on cross beams, architraves and *prastara*. Above the lintels, tiny *śikharas* of the Nāgara and Draviḍian types with *kūḍū* were carved. The Gaṅgā and Yamunā, often accompanied by attendants, were a regular *dvāra* motif. The Durgā temple provided one of the most impressive *dvāraśākhā* versions while less sophisticated composition was seen in the Konṭi guḍī and the Galaganātha temples. The Gauda temple at Aihoḷe preserves one of the most elaborate and beautifully carved *dvāraśākhās* in the northern style. Herein, pilasters supporting three miniature niches created by *kūḍūs* frame the opening. Garuḍa, holding serpents appear ready to fly out of the *lalāṭabiṁba*. The southern style pattern replaced the niches with foliated *makara* motif. In between their open jaws they held a jewelled garland, that in the Virūpāksha and Pāpanātha temples at Paṭṭaḍakal was furnished with a central medallion. The Virūpāksha *dvāraśākhā* with *toraṇa, devakoṣṭhas*, multiple accessory figures and southern style *dvārapālas* indicated the increasing complexity and elaboration of architectural forms. Similarly, Svarga Brahmā shrine *dvāraśākhā* also appeared quite elaborative in form with manifold divisions in both jambs and lintel.

Windows

Perforated stone windows or *jālīs* in early Western Cālukyan shrines provided examples of super carving. In several shrines, the windows demonstrated their timber origin with criss-cross bars. In the Lāḍ Khān temple, such bars were decorated with full lotus flowers, whereas in the Durgā temple the windows were framed by pilasters surmounted by mouldings including *makaras*. The Nagral Nāganātha temple had superbly carved windows with ornamental framing on its exterior walls. Prominent window motifs included the *svāstika* in Durgā and Kadaśiddeśvara temples, foliation in Virūpāksha and Mallikārjuna temples, geometrical and fish patterns in Lāḍ Khān temple windows, etc.

Adhiṣṭhāna

The early Cālukyan *adhiṣṭhānas* were deeply moulded and sculpturally carved. Several temples at Bādāmī, Aihoḷe and Paṭṭaḍakal had *vyāḷa* and *makara* figures positioned at top of the *adhiṣṭhāna*. At Paṭṭaḍakal, beneath the porches and *nandīmaṇḍapa adhiṣṭhāna*, lions and elephants appeared, often engaged in violent struggle. Narrative friezes depicting courtly scenes or Kṛṣṇā episodes were carved in Durgā temple and on some slabs from Bādāmī and Mahākūṭa temple *adhiṣṭhāna*.

Gateways

Sometimes ornamental gateways were erected as entrance to a group of temples as seen at Galaganātha and Veṇīyāvar groups. These early temple-complexes with multiple shrines enclosed within walls and entered by imposing gateways became the forerunners of later great walled temples with towered *gopurams* in South India.

Pillars

They were mostly square in section and sometimes profusely carved. In shape and variety, they resembled those in the rock-cut temples.[73]

Thus, it seems that the Cālukya architects quickly seized upon the possibilities offered by the structural techniques and evolved a number of temple types at various sites.

Sculptures

Sculptural ornamentation was an integral component in the growth of temple architecture. The temples at Aihoḷe, Paṭṭaḍakal, Bādāmī and Mahākūṭa consisted of rich and diversified sculptures. The Cālukyan art spirit was outward and worldly unlike the inward, contemplative spirit of Gupta art. Their artistic development is assignable to two phases: (i) extending from about fifth to mid-seventh centuries AD, and (ii) from mid-seventh to mid-eighth centuries AD.

The first phase began at Aihoḷe and continued at Mahākūṭa. The reliefs in Lāḍ Khān, Durgā, Hucchappayya Maṭha, Konṭi group temples, representing sculptures of Gajalakshmī, Brahmā, Umā-Maheśvara, Nārāyaṇa, Viṣṇu, etc. were notable for their poise and balance. The emphasis was mainly on the gesture and delicacy of form rather than details of the appearance. The Mālegittī sculptures, though delicately carved, lacked the elongation and compactness of Paṭṭaḍakal sculptures. The form was not yet idealised and retained its human, earthly quality. At Mahākūṭa, the Aihoḷe style continued, though with a marked trend towards refinement, grace and elegance. The compactness of form and elongation of limbs began to emerge as seen in the *Ardhnarīśvara* figure on northern wall of Mahākūṭeśvara temple. The gigantic figures of Bhairava and Bhairavī echoed the naturalness of form that began at Aihoḷe. The *Mahiṣamardinī* in Durgā temple *pradakshiṇāpatha devakoṣṭha* was particularly noteworthy for the naturalness depicted in the *aṣṭabhujī* deity.

Although the slow infiltration of Pallava style began after AD 643, i.e. after the Pallava occupation of the empire, the Cālukya artists strove to transform it with their indigenous genius.[74] The influence became more evident when the local tendency of balance and simplicity was combined with the Pallava elongation of forms during the second phase.

The second phase, which also began at Aihoḷe in Rāvaṇa Phaḍi cave and reached its culmination at Paṭṭaḍakal, was marked by Pallava influence.[75] The elongation of form and the attenuation of limbs were integrated so gradually that by the time it reached Paṭṭaḍakal, the local style was developed into a compactness of elegance and charm, making the figures quite enchanting. Linearism became prominent while roundness gradually moved out. The *tribhaṅga Mahiṣamardinī* in Virūpāksha temple *antarāla* expressed realism and dynamism. Mahiṣa's facial expressions, when her sword pierced his body, were aptly conveyed.

Overall, the Cālukyan sculptural art appeared as a beautiful blending of the earthly and the spiritual as it represented both religious and secular traditions. The female form fascinated the artist the most. It has been rightly suggested that the purpose of art was not to convey divinity but to render the female form in all its inherent charms.[76]

Sculptural Placements

The varied sculptural representations of gods and goddesses, celestial couples, friezes, mythical animals, *mithunas*, etc. adorned various parts of the temple.

Maṇḍapa Sculptures

The early Western Cālukyan temple *maṇḍapas* had balcony *kakshāsana* backs' carved with auspicious *padma ghaṭas*. *Maṇḍapa* sculptures in Lāḍ Khān and Hucchappayya Maṭha temples at Aihoḷe depicted *mithunas* embracing beneath trees. In the Durgā and Konṭi group temples, *mithunas* were carved in graceful swaying postures. Horse-headed or partly animal-bodied women, sometimes in violent embraces with male consorts, were also sculpted. The *mithunas* carved on *maṇḍapa* pillars of the Virūpāksha and Pāpanātha temple were almost three-dimensional. Women accompanied by small children were depicted on the *nandīmaṇḍapa* in Virūpāksha temple. *Dvārapālas* with *gadās* as seen in Durgā and Hucchppayya temples constituted yet another category of forms sculpted.

Pillars, Potikās and Uttira Sculptures

The pillar shafts in the *maṇḍapas* and *sabhāmaṇḍapas* of the early Cālukyan temples depicted lavish intricate relief decoration. Framed in projecting bands, medallions and circles, they consisted of narrative reliefs, mythological scenes and ornamental motifs. The Lāḍ Khān *maṇḍapa* pillars consisted of large variety of motifs, whereas the Durgā temple comprised *gaṇa* friezes and *mithunas*. Pillars of the Cikkī temple, Aihoḷe, were delicately carved with rearing animals while the Virūpāksha and Mallikārjuna temples' pillars portrayed narrative reliefs, birds and animals embellished with foliation, and jewelled garlands, etc.

The *potikās*, supporting the *uttira* above the pillars in several temples, were fashioned into rearing mythical animals. Sometimes they served as leafy shelters for *mithunas* beneath. At Pāpanātha and in some Aihoḷe shrines, *potikās* were transformed into mythical beasts emerging out of *makara mukhas*.

The *uttira*, supporting roof slabs, was also decorated in many temples with lotus creepers and flower motifs. In the Hucchappayya temple, a *gaṇāvarī* frieze was carved on the *uttira*.

Ceiling Panels

They were carved with great skills. The Konṭi-guḍī and Hucchappayya Maṭha temples had divinities like Brahmā, Viṣṇu, and Maheśa carved on their *sabhā maṇḍapa* ceilings. Śiva-Pārvatī with nandī were carved at the Mallikārjuna, Nagral Nāganātha and Bādāmī Jambūliṅga temples in a series of compositionally and stylistically identical ceilings. Varied forms of Viṣṇu like on Garuḍa in a small medallion at Aihoḷe; surrounded by *aṣṭadikpālas* in Bādāmī Cave III; seated in an octagonal frame in Bādāmī Jambūliṅga; and his various *avatāras* on the ceiling panels in the Cikkī temple at Aihoḷe were also sculpted. Kārtikeya in Hucchimallī, Aihoḷe and Sūrya riding his chariot in Virūpāksha temples appeared quite impressive.

Sculptures, not cultistic and generally decorative in character, were also found on the ceiling panels. Flying couples were an extremely popular ceiling motif. The most renowned examples are of the Durgā temple portraying billowing garments suggestive of rapid flight of the figures through space. *Svāstika* and *matsyacakra* were other common motifs seen in Bādāmī cave II and Jambūliṅga. A coiled serpent with a human torso at its centre was one of the most striking of all ceiling motifs.[77]

Wall Panels

The Cālukyan temple exteriors were generally profusely sculpted though the plainness of Megutī walls offered a contrast. The Svarga Brahmā at Ālampur reflected great articulation on its walls in form of *devakoṣṭhas* and latticed windows flanked by figural sculptures. The pilastered wall projections depicted mythological representations of Śiva and Viṣṇu. Śiva was represented in iconic, aniconic and dancing forms. The dynamic dance icon was often put in the *kūḍūs* placed against the front of the *śikharas* of the Paṭṭaḍakal temples. Lakulīśa image in Mālegittī Śivālaya, standing Śiva figures at Saṅgameśvara and Jambūliṅga, Śiva Pārvatī with nandī and *ardhanārīśvara* images, were also carved. The relaxed posture and gentle feminine quality of Saṅgameśvara temple *ardhanarīśvara* figure was very prominent. The depiction of these figures in transparent garments seems to glorify the body. *Liṅgodbhava* Śiva figure in a magnificient composition on the east wall of the Paṭṭaḍakal Virūpāksha temple was quite remarkable.[78]

Viṣṇu was portrayed mostly in his *avatāra* forms in the wall panels. The Varāha was carved in Bādāmī caves II and III and in Rāvaṇa Phaḍi, Aihoḷe, and Kālakāleśvara at Mahākūṭa, etc., almost always in an identical posture. The *Trivikram* in Bādāmī cave III modelled almost three-dimensionally was superior to its rather flat version in the Virūpāksha. The Mālegittī north wall panel consist of a standing Viṣṇu flanked by two *āyudhapuruṣas*, in a rare occurrence of the concept.[79] The parallel relief on the south wall was of standing Śiva dressed in a revealing loincloth and an ornate jewelled head dress.[80] In stylistic details, the reliefs have been related to the Gupta sculptures of Malwā, Central and North India.[81]

Mahiṣāsurmardinī, as an icononographic form, was indeed a significant figure in Cālukyan sculptural art. It was in the structural panels of the Aihoḷe Durgā and Paṭṭaḍakal Virūpāksha temples that the force of killing the demon was fully expressed.

The Aṁbikā of the Megutī temple was exceptional for its composition and refined carving. The importance accorded to *Saptamātṛkās* is proved by huge sculptures at Aihoḷe. The Mālegittī Śivālaya panel showed a double *makara toraṇa* sheltering two mothers nursing their babies while the *makaras* carried *nidhi* or *gaṇas*. Below was a frieze of *yāḷis* and elephants, betraying influence of wooden architecture.[82]

The Cālukyan period was, in a way, characterized by iconographic transition similar to architectural and stylistic changes. This could be seen in the development of the concept of *dikpālas*. Evolution of iconographic formulae is illustrated by the position of *aṣṭadikpālas* that kept alternating till their definite positions were fixed. Similarly, the *anugraha* and *dakshiṇa* aspects of Śiva form had not been crystallized while Cālukyas were the first to carve the image of *sthāṇu* Nṛsiṁha as tearing open Hiraṇyakaśipu's abdomen. The concept of *āliṅganāmūrti* of Śiva emerged at Aihoḷe while the *Somaskandamūrti* was firstly carved in the Kāśīviśveśvara temple. Śaivite mythology was further enriched with the creation of forms as *Kālārimūrti* at Paṭṭaḍakal. Carving of *tāṇḍava* Śiva in the *śukanāsā kūḍūs* continued at Tāraka Brahmā and Bāla Brahmā temples (Alampur).

Although Cālukyan art was basically religious in nature, it also had a secular aspect. The numerous *mithunas* in various erotic postures were a popular motif.[83] However, they were not always depicted as loving couples. A couple carved in Durgā temple had a *yakshī* holding a kneeling man by his hair, ready to kill him. *Maithuna* motif was firstly carved in Paṭṭaḍakal. The orgiastic scenes in Mahākūṭa and Aihoḷe[84] probably appeared during 7th century AD. The so-called shameless goddess or *Lajjā gaurī*[85] in *uttānapāda* pose frequently found at Bādāmī, Mahākūṭa and Ālampur, perhaps symbolized fertility rites. Thus, it was a period of transition from early to medieval times in the depiction of the erotic motif. The *gaṇas* in varying dance pose, expression and hair styles seen in the caves and Mālegittī Śivālaya at Bādāmī illustrated the comical aspect of Cālukyan art.

Influence of Other Art Styles

Although the Cālukyan art was mainly a local growth, it apparently borrowed several elements of the Northern and Southern Indian art traditions. At Aihoḷe and Bādāmī, the cave temples signified continuation of the heritage of the Vākāṭakas, Kalacuris, etc., who patronized the rock-cut shrines at Ajantā, Ellorā and Elephanta, pervading with Gupta and post-Gupta influences. This fact necessitates an analysis of the northern influence on Cālukyan art.

Northern/Gupta Influence

The Cālukyas played the same role in reviving Hinduism and rejuvenating art in their territories as the Guptas did prior to them. Therefore, the Cālukyan art offers affinity to the Gupta specimens. In their art compositions, the over crowding of figures was avoided as in Gupta art. Like the Gupta artists, the Cālukyan artists also displayed an imaginative mind in the selection of religious themes.[86] They were probably inspired by the dramatic romantic portrayals by classical poets as Kālidāsa is inferred by the mention of Kālidāsa's name in Ravikīrti's *praśasti*.[87]

The Gupta influence was markedly noticeable in the first phase of Cālukyan art. Elaboration of Gupta motifs was frequent. For instance, the concept and form of Sūrya holding two lotuses prevalent in Gupta times was elaborated by depicting Uṣā and Pratyuṣa as shooting arrows in Hucchimallī guḍī temple and as being drawn by seven horses in the Virūpāksha shrine. In a way, Cālukyas even outclassed the Guptas in revealing the spirit of their sculptures. For example, the Gupta *ardhanārīśvara* form was lacking in spirit but the Cālukyan artists brought out both the feminine and masculine aspects pretty well. The sublimation of mildly erotic couples also occurred in the Cālukyan period. Although the Gupta-Vākāṭaka artists at Ajantā were primarily responsible for the depiction of *mithunas*, their depiction in the *kāmaśāstrīya* poses may be attributed to the Cālukyas.

Thus, a considerable influence of Gupta classicism was apparent in the subtlety of expressions and postures, and the refinement of Cālukya sculptures. Architecturally speaking, the structural temples with the Nāgara *śikhara, pūrṇa kalaśa, nāsikā,* perforated windows in *pradakshiṇāpatha* as seen in Gupta shrines at Nacnā kuṭharā and Cārcomā, besides various sculptural details, signified a strong northern influence. The earliest urge towards the use of Nāgara style may be found in the Bhadravaliṅga temple, Mahākūṭa.

Southern Influence

In the Cālukyan shrines, the *śikhara* crowned by *caṭuṣkoṇīya* or *aṣṭakoṇīya stūpī kūṭa-śālā pañjara*; a detached *nandīmaṇḍapa,* imposing gateways; a group of related *parivārālayas* within an enclosure; *kūḍū* and sculptural motifs reflected southern art influence. It has also been held that the Cālukyas probably hailed from a part of Karnataka, now in Andhra Pradesh, in the vicinity of Ālampur and Srīśailam.[88] Therefore, their familiarity with the earlier traditions of Amarāvatī, Nāgārjunākoṇḍā consisting of storeyed *śikharas*, *śālās* and *kūṭas*, apsidal shrines, pillared halls, *gaṇas, nidhis, aṣṭabhujī Viṣṇu*, etc. was but obvious. The *Lajjādevī* popular at Mahākūṭa, Nāganātha Siddhankolla, Ālampur, Pañcaliṅgala, etc. was probably a Sātavāhana type derivation.[89] Thus, the convergence of influences in the form of Cālukyan art signified the architectural variety of its monuments.

Cālukya Paintings

The art of painting under the Cālukyas is suggested by the paintings in Bādāmī Cave III. Discovered by Stella Kramrisch[90] on the front *maṇḍapa* ceiling, these painting fragments may be placed amongst the earliest Brāhmanical specimens. The cave inscription described its dedication to Viṣṇu by Mangalesha[91] and applauded its wonderful workmanship, ceiling and sides, all extremely beautiful to behold: *Paramabhāgavatolayana mahāviṣṇugṛham atid vaimānushyakam atyadbhutakarmaviracitam bhūmibhāgopabhāgopariparyantā tiśayadarśanīyatamam kṛtvā*.[92]

The fragments included a scene of Indra in his palace Vaijayanta watching dance performance by two artists. The next panel projected a royal person in the *mahārājalīlā* pose. Surrounded by several crowned princes sitting around,[93] he had his queen on the left attended by *prasādhikās*. The figures are identifiable as Kirtivarman with his queen comparable to Indra in his glory. The prevalent belief was that a departed king goes to heaven to be in the company of Indra himself. Accordingly, Kirtivarman shown as sharing the glory of Indra in his Sudharma Devasabhā: *avanimavanatārir yaśchakārātmasamsthām pitari surasakhitvam prāptavatyātmaśaktyā.*[94] Perhaps this representation of Kirtivarman side by side with Indra and placed near the Varāha sculpture[95] inspired the Varāha sculpture at Mahābalipuram. There the royal portraits of Simhavishnu and Mahendravarman with their queens were carved close to the Varāha panel.[96]

The painted fragments of two flying *vidyādhara mithunas* were also noticeable in the cave. One panel had them in *kaṇṭhāśleṣa* pose, i.e. hands around each other's necks. The second showed the *vidyādhara* playing the *vīṇā* while his consort sat nearby. Hence, the extant painted remains at Bādāmī are a clear evidence of the prevalence of this fine art during the Early Cālukya rulers, especially under Mangalesha.

2. THE PALLAVA ART ACTIVITIES

The Pallava artistic productions, commencing with the rock-cut architecture under Mahendravarman (AD 610-640), provided the foundations of the Draviḍian style. While with the Cālukyas the construction of stone temples had started almost simultaneously with their cut-in cave temples, in the Pallava kingdom of Kāñcī, the structural phase perhaps started later to their cut out monoliths, from the times of Rajasimha (AD 700-728).[97] The art of structural building accorded greater freedom to the architect and was easier too.

Their temples being largely granitic and plain, it is likely that during the intense political competition with Cālukyas, the Pallava rulers may have also realised the advantages of softer rocks to create more aesthetic temples.[98] The difficulties faced such as requirement of greater labour, new tools and skills involved in the quarrying and sizing of the very hard granite, gneiss and charnockite rocks, might have also inspired Rajasimha to experiment with different kinds of stones from the rocks of Toṇḍaimaṇḍalam. Above all, rock architecture had implied the creation of monuments only in places with abundant rocks or hills. Rock-cut temples could not be created everywhere, for instance, in Kāñcī. But its abundance of sandstone facilitated the use of softer medium for all building as well as sculptural activity.[99]

Selection of Stone

The structural phase began with a series of experiments with different kinds of hard and softer stones. The blackish hard leptimite (Shore temple), the hard reddish gneiss (Mukundnāyanār temple), the softer greyish white granite (Olakkanneśvara temple), and hard pinkish gneiss (Talagiriśvara at Panamalāi) were types of harder rocks in temples raised during this period. However, the construction in such hard stones being difficult and time consuming, Rajasimha ultimately resorted to the softstone medium. The shift was to softer brown local sandstone, quite coarse and of an inferior quality. The fragility of the new stone was perhaps well realised by the *sthāpatis*. Therefore, granitic flat slabs were introduced at the *upāna* or *pāda* level, and *pratī* and *paṭṭikās* above the *jagati* to check the corrosiveness of sandstone from ground salts. The Kailāśanātha temple in Kāñcī,[100] built of locally quarried sandstone and supported by granite slabs at the *adhiṣṭhāna* mouldings for strength and standing, represented such type of a shrine.

The selection of stone though largely depended on its nearby availability,[101] was not always determined by that. Later, Pallava monarchs succeeding Rajasimha reverted to harder granites at Kāñcī itself.[102]

Origin of the Pallava temple

Dubreuil[103] has suggested the Pallava temple origin from the primitive hut. In fact, Pallava stone specimens made into beams and planks looked like wooden ones. Thus, the Draviḍian art inspired by them was, undoubtedly, of an indigenous origin.

TEMPLE SITES

Mahābalipuram

The earliest Pallava monuments were those at Mahābalipuram.[104] Situated about 59 km south of Chennai, it was an important sea-port in ancient India. *The Periplus of the Erythraen Sea* and Ptolemy's account described it as Malange.[105] Renowned for its rock-cut monuments, the place has always been shrouded in mystery. A belief prevalent is that there is a city or temples offshore, under the sea which, being covered with copper tops, were particularly visible at sunrise, their shining surface reflecting sunrays.[106] This is further corroborated by the enigmatic term 'seven pagodas', an old name for the site. The Shore temple is believed to be one of the seven shrines, the remaining six still being under the sea. Conscious efforts in the past, for instance by Mackenzie and Ellis (1830) through careful soundings taken offshore to discover these submerged buildings, proved a failure. However, the Tsunami devastation in December 2004 unveiled a line of rocks with man-made features about 500 metres from the Shore temple. Another structure, perhaps a temple, located about 100 metres northeast besides several relics depicting lion and elephant carvings, has also been recovered lending credence to the legend of the 'seven pagodas', besides boosting up the excavation and exploration mission of the ASI ongoing since 2001. The archaeologists claim to have found a round *gopuram*-shaped top, rocky walls, a temple close to the shore and a slab believed to be the pedestal for installing the deity. A square structure resembling a *garbhagṛha* and covered with marine growth and its centre buried under silt has also been found. All these revelations, in a way, authenticate the theory of 'submerged city and temples'.[107]

Mahābalipuram site has about fourteen rock-cut caves, nine monolithic shrines, three structural stone temples and four relief-sculptured rock-panels, all Pallava creations.[108]

Kāñcīpuram

Kāñcīpuram or Kāñcī,[109] the Pallava capital, 72 km from Chennai, was known from a very early date for the number and beauty of its temples.[110] According to an estimation,

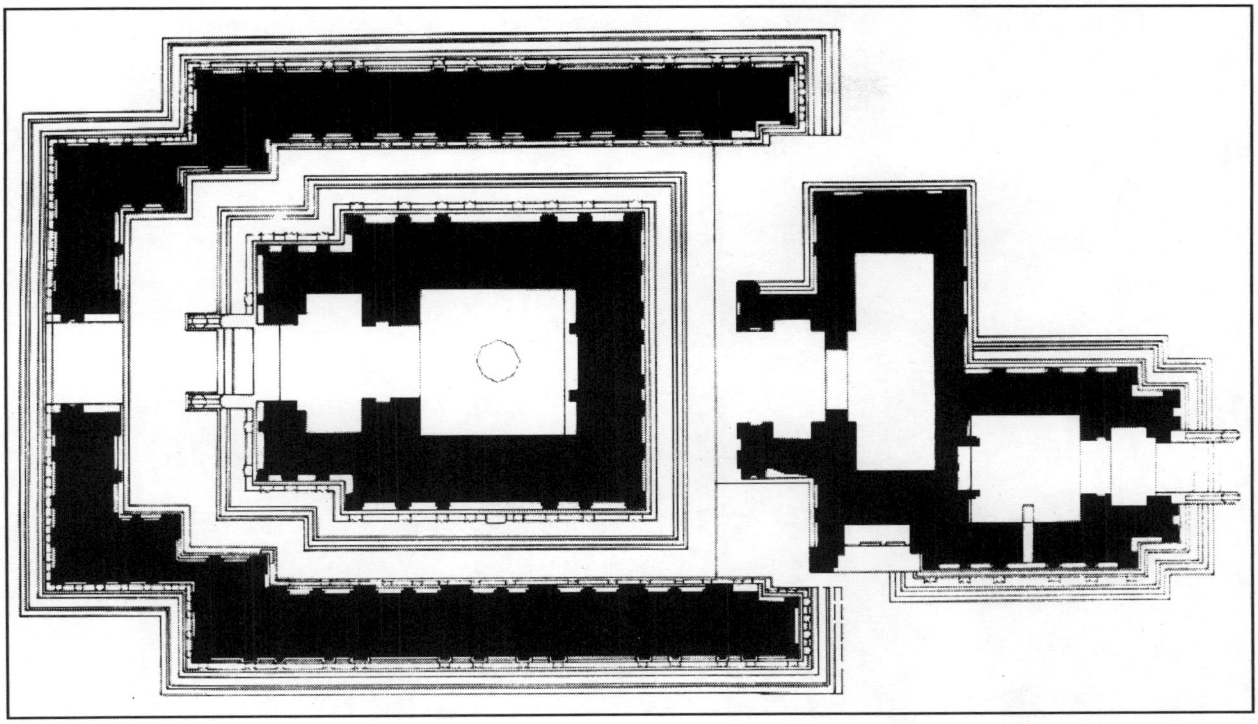

Fig. 19. Mahābalipuram: Shore temple, ground plan (after AIIS).

as many as 170 temples,[111] both big and small, existed within Kāñcīpuram, which was 8 km long and 3 km broad. Hiuen Tsang (AD 639) mentioned 80 *deva* temples[112] while local legends assigned 108 sanctums to Śiva and 18 to Viṣṇu,[113] mostly known from the seventh century AD.

The various Pallava temples erected at these twin sites set the pace for the growth of Draviḍian architecture.

GROWTH OF TEMPLE ARCHITECTURE

The first Pallava building of dressed stone was the Mahābalipuram Shore temple, named so as it stood on the extreme shore of the ancient port. Though the earliest Pallava masonry production, it did betray some experience in the art of building construction. For over a thousand years, despite the ceaseless activity of the sea or the menace of the drifting sands, its twin towers stood erect and the shrines have remained intact.

The plan of the Shore temple (Fig. 19) was not usual. The underlying idea, perhaps, was that the *garbhagṛha* should face east, overlooking the sea so as to be illuminated by the first rays of the rising sun and be visible to the mariners as a lighthouse by the night.[114] The shrine's location on the shore left no space for a frontal *maṇḍapa* or *gopuram*, which was finally placed at the rear. The central *vimāna* Kshatriyasiṁheśvara was, therefore, surrounded by a massive *prākāra* with an opening from the west. Two additional *vimānas*, i.e. the Rājasiṁheśvara and the Narapati Siṁha Pallava Viṣṇugṛha, were attached rather unsymmetrically to its western end. These two supplementary

Fig. 20. Mahābalipuram: Shore temple with *prākāra* (after AIIS).

shrines converted the Shore temple into a double-towered, unconventional monument, the whole complex enclosed by a common rectangular *prākāra* (Fig. 20).

The *catuṣtala* Kshatriyasiṁheśvara was of a *samacaturārṣa* plan up to the *grīvā* that, with the *śikhara* and basalt *stūpī* above, was *aṣṭakoṇīya*. The *hāra* of *kūṭa* and *śālās* were confined to the second and third *talas* and the top of the *ardhamaṇḍapa* in front of the *āditala*, which carried figures of squatting lions at the four corners. The top *tala* had four squatting *gaṇas*[115] blowing conches, symbolizing a Śaiva temple. The *prākāra*, closely set, was of a lower height than the *āditala* and carried *karṇakūṭas* at the corners and *śālās* over the lengths of the sides. The central *śālā* over the seaward entrance on the eastern length of the *prākāra* was made larger than the rest to simulate a *dvāraśālā* or lesser *gopuram* scheme.[116] Its proportionately tall storeys and the elimination of the *hāra* elements over the lowest and topmost *talas* lend a distinct grace to this edifice, while the close set *prākāra* of a lesser height surrounding the *āditala*, with *hāra* elements over

Fig. 21. Kāñcīpuram: Kailāśanātha temple (after AIIS).

its coping, simulated the appearance of a *pañcatala*. Besides the usual rearing lion based pilasters, the walls and *prākāra* pilasters had *gaja, vṛṣa, nāga* and *gaṇa* at their bases.

The *tritala samacaturārṣa* smaller Rājasiṁheśvara *vimāna* with *aṣṭakoṇīya grīvā, śikhara* and *stūpī* on top had the *āditala* devoid of the *hāra* elements on top. It, like the top *tala*, had four seated conch-blowing *gaṇas* placed at the corners. The *hāra* elements were placed over the second *tala* on all four sides and also over the *ardhamaṇḍapa* in front of the *āditala*. The *talas* were proportionately tall and the *stūpī* over *grīvā* and *śikhara* was made of polished black basalt. The wall pilasters had characteristic rearing lion bases. It showed a rock-cut *adhiṣṭhāna* towards the *Viṣṇugṛha* rear wall.

The Shore temple, for its square lower storey and the pyramidal *śikhara* in diminishing *talas*, has been likened to the Dharmarāja *ratha*.[117] The design of its *śikhara* and appearance of the rearing lion pilaster constituted important original components in structural art. Besides, it seems that portions of the ground plan of the outer *prākāra* consisted of a system of shallow cisterns, which were filled occasionally so as to make it a type of water temple. Thus, the architectural proportions and the natural setting on the sea made the Shore temple one of the finest monuments in India.

The Olakkanneśvara temple, Mahābalipuram, now devoid of its original *śikhara talas*, retains only the outer shell of its *āditala* and *ardhamaṇḍapa*. The Talagiriśvara temple at Panamalāi, square in base and *talas* had smaller oblong shrines with cells attached to the middle of its south, west and northern sides over corresponding offset extensions of the *adhiṣṭhāna*, in its east-facing *āditala*. In its elevation, the *vimāna* was *catuṣtala* and the *śālā* superstructures of the *dvitala ayatārṣa* side shrines merged into the *hāra* of *karṇakūṭa* and were *aṣṭakoṇīya*. The *āditala* and attached shrines' wall-corners were cantoned by bold rearing *vyāla* pilasters. The top *tala* carried *gaṇa* forms at the corners. Otherwise the temple walls lacked sculptures probably due to the hard reddish granite.

The Mukundanayanār temple was a plain edifice with a *dvitala vimāna, caturārṣa* in plan and an *aṣṭakoṇīya grīvā śikhara* constituting its Draviḍa form.

The Kāñcīpuram Kailāśanātha temple (Fig. 21) was a possible joint venture of Rajasimha and Mahendravarman III.[118] The east-facing main *vimāna* Rājasiṁheśvara was *catuṣtala, samacaturārṣa* up to the *grīvā*, which like the *śikhara* above, was *aṣṭakoṇīya*. In elevation, the *śikhara talas* were built over a bridge of slabs spanning the tops of the two walls of the *āditala* in *kadalikā karaṇa* mode. The double walling and the additional buttressing by smaller *vimānas* on the sides and corners were evidently measures to support the *vimāna śikhara*, the largest one of the period and at the same time to provide a pleasing base, height, ratio and a balanced proportion to the edifice.

Apart from its main structure, the temple had certain distinct arrangements, possibly later additions, in relation to the entrance. The eastern opening of the surrounding *prākāra* was occupied by a *āyatārṣa dvitala śālā* type *vimāna*, Mahendravarmeśvara, which looked like a *gopuram* when viewed from afar. Both its *talas* were devoid of the *hāra*. It contained the usual fluted *liṅga* and *somaskanda* panels in its *garbhagṛha*. Thus, although a place of worship, with its accompaniments it appeared to be a *gopuram*. The open area in its front had eight *dvitala, samacaturārṣa,* and Draviḍa *śikhara vimānas* with *somaskanda* carved inside. One of these was contributed by Rangapataka,[119] wife of Rajasimha. Thus, inference that the Kailāśanātha was built in several stages.

That the masons were realizing the adequacy of building materials was implicit from the fact that in the Kailāśanātha, while the foundations of the temple were granitic, its upper portions were of sandstone. This might have been done to ensure a hard and firm foundation to carry its weight and a better plastic substance for the sculptures.

The Vaiṣṇavite Vaikuṇṭha-perumāl temple in Kāñcīpuram, built by Nandivarman Pallavamalla, was another Pallava masterpiece of the larger variety. Facing west, it was built of sandstone with an admixture of granite in its *adhiṣṭhāna*'s *upāna* and *paṭṭikā* mouldings. It was a *sandhāra, samacaturārṣa, catuṣtala vimāna* with all the *talas*, except the topmost, containing the superposed *garbhagṛha*, enshrining the *sthānaka, āsana* and *śayana* forms of Viṣṇu. The triple *talas* were created by an arrangement of three concentric walls forming three concentric squares, one inside the other with *sandhāra pradakshiṇāpatha* in between. The temple was also remarkable for a series of panelled sculptures narrating the Pallava history from their legendary ancestors' up to Nandīvarman Pallavamalla, its patron.[120]

Several other temples built in Kāñcīpuram, despite smaller proportions, became remarkable for their architecture and iconography. These included Mukteśvara, Mātaṅgeśvara, Airāvateśvara, Valiśvara, Irāvataneśvara, Pirāvataneśvara, etc. They were built mainly of sandstone with granite slabs forming the *adhiṣṭhāna upāna* and *paṭṭikā* and also the *upapīṭha*, wherever added, to raise the height of the edifice. Nearly all of them present composite varieties of the *caturārṣa vimāna* with varying *talas*, the upper *talas* being non-functional and provided with the *hāra* over the *prastara* of the *tala* below, and with different plans in the *grīvā śikhara*. The Irāvataneśvara and Tripurāntakeśvara were *dvitala, samacaturārṣa*, including the *grīvā* and *śikhara* and hence, were Nāgara. The Mātangeśvara and Mukteśvara were *tritala*, with square *talas*, but circular *grīvā* and *śikhara*. The Pirāvataneśvara and Valiśvara were *dvitala* and *tritala* respectively, with *caturārṣa talas* and *aṣṭakoṇīya grīvā* and *śikhara* making them Draviḍian in form. The Kailāśanātha at Tiruppaṭṭur was a larger *vimāna* in sandstone akin to the Kāñcīpuram Kailāśanātha though displaying a provincial variety of the Pallava *vimāna*.[121]

In the later part of the eighth century, granite blocks, cut, moulded, carved and sculptured, were extensively used in temples. For instance, in the smaller temples or the granite *adhiṣṭhāna* of large brick temples of Vaikuṇṭha-perumāl and Sundarāvarada-perumāl at Uttiramerur and Chingleput during Dantivarman's reign. In the former, the *devakoṣṭhas* were to enshrine stucco figures while in the latter slab reliefs were to be placed. The *tritala* brick shrine of Sundarāvarada-perumāl over the stone *adhiṣṭhāna* was unique in having all the three *talas* functional with the *śālās* dedicated to Viṣṇu's *sthānaka, āsana* and *śayana* forms, while the abutting smaller shrines on the three sides (south, west and north) of its lower two *talas* contained six other principal forms of Viṣṇu as Satya, Acyuta, Anirudha, Naranārāyaṇa, Nṛsiṁha and Varṣa, thus incorporating the *navamūrtis* or nine forms in accordance with the *Vaikhānāsāgama*.

The Virāttaneśvara temple at Tiruttani (Cingleput), built of hard black stone in the ninth century during Aparajitavarman, was *ektala vimāna*, square in *adhiṣṭhāna* and *āditala* that carried an apsidal *grīvā śikhara*. It exemplified the definite polarisation of Gaṇeśa and Durgā respectively, in the southern and northern outer wall *devakoṣṭhas* of the *ardhamaṇḍapa*, and Dakshiṇāmūrtī, Viṣṇu and Brahmā respectively, in the south, west, and north outer wall *devakoṣṭhas* of the *āditala* wall. The introduction of a projected *praṇāla* outlet from the northern side of the *garbhagṛha* floor to carry away the *abhiṣeka* water was another notable feature in this temple.[122]

This group of later temples marked not only the end of the artistic productions but also indicated a decline in the might of the Pallava dynasty.

Development of Pallava Structural Temples

An account of the Pallava structural shrines makes it explicit that theirs was a phase of elaborately planned and meticulously built edifices. Their ground plan and elevation schemes marked several advancements upon preceding rock-cut monuments.[123] The larger temples were particularly noteworthy for the *devakoṣṭhas* around the main *vimāna*. In plan, the earlier smaller *mukhamaṇḍapa* became a proper *ardhamaṇḍapa*, the archaic *padmabandha adhiṣṭhāna* type made its first appearance in the Shore temple,[124] while the hitherto plain *adhiṣṭhāna* components such as the *jagati, padma* or *tripaṭṭakumuda* were embellished. *Gajamuṇḍas* appeared at the corners in the *kaṇṭhavājana* portion of *adhiṣṭhāna* for the first time as in the Kāñcīpuram Kailāśanātha and Panamalāi Talagirīśvara temple.[125] The wall pilasters in the *vimānapāda,* particularly the corner ones, had *vyāḷapāda.* An instance of *nāgapāda* occurred at Shore temple. The wall decoration showed panels or niches containing *alaṁkāradevatās* with several subservient figures.

In elevation, the *āditala hāra* consisted of *ṣaḍvargakūṭas* and *śālās* such as at Kailāśanātha and Validvara temples, Kāñcī. The *śālās* were now a little longer than the previous ones and the gap between two *śālās* in *hāra* series also lessened in this period.

The *hāra* for an *anarpita vimāna āditala* was completely given up. It was also given up in the uppermost *tala* and instead, *gaṇa* or *vṛṣa* figures were placed at the corners. *Grīvādevatās* appeared for the first time at the cardinal points, particularly in the larger temples. The *grīvā* for an *aṣṭakoṇīya śikhara* was sometimes prismatic as in the Shore temple, Mahābalipuram and the minor shrines in the Kailāśanātha, Kāñcī. In such cases, the *grīvādevatās* were omitted. The *aṣṭakoṇīya śikhara* type as that of Arjuna *ratha* continued with minor modifications as seen at the minor shrines of the Kailāśanātha or the Airāvateśvara and Pirāvataneśvara temples, Kāñcī. The *śikharas* of Shore temple, Mahābalipuram and the Kailāśanātha and Valiśvara temples at Kāñcī had a distinctly different form, being a little indrawn in contour. The *stūpīs* were now elongated rather than globular.

Thus, from the somewhat compressed forms of the monolithic *rathas* to the loosely assembled elements of the Shore temple to the refined Kailāśanātha temple, we come across efforts by the Pallava artisans to present the *śikhara* in a coherent architectural form, well proportioned, substantial, at the same time rhythmic in its mass and elegant in its outlines. They acquired perfect maturity finally in the Vaikuṇṭha-perumāl temple. Besides architectural, the numerous structural edifices manifested the flowering genius of the Pallava artists in the realm of sculptural art also.

Pallava Sculptures

Built of dressed stone often without any form of mortar, the temples and their surroundings were bedecked with sculptures and reliefs representing mythical scenes and at times, also the struggles of the Pallava dynasty. For instance, the walls of the Vaikuṇṭha-perumāl temple *pradakshiṇāpatha* were comprised of relief panels illustrating the Pallava and Cālukya battles.[126]

Pallava sculptural specimens have been recovered from various sites. Out of these, Mahābalipuram and Kāñcīpuram were certainly the most important centres where images of various deities and saints affiliated with Śaivism, Vaiṣṇavism and Śāktism as well as royal portraits were carved out in the seventh and eighth centuries AD.

In the seventh century, sculptural representations undertaken at Mahābalipuram consisted of *ardhanarīśvara*, Gaṇeśa, Gajalakshmī, Mahiṣamardinī and the varāha, *trivikram, śeṣaśāyin, govardhandhārī* forms of Viṣṇu. The early eighth century shrines are a veritable treasure-house of Śaivite iconographic forms. The Śaivite sculptures of Shore temple have mostly been eroded by the moist and saline winds from the sea, but the Kāñcīpuram Kailāśanātha temple with its sculptural creations appear as the richest of all the Pallava shrines in terms of figural decoration. Herein, a wide variety of sculptures depicting Śiva as *Naṭeśa, Tripurāntaka, Gajāsurasaṁhāra, Andhakāri, Jalandhara, Kankāla, Brahmāśīrṣacedaka, Yogeśa, Kālārī, Bhairava*, in *ūrdhvatāṇḍava, saṁhāratāṇḍava* (all *ugra* forms) and *Kalyāṇasundara, Gaurī-Śankara, Umāsahita, Bhikshāṭana, Dakshiṇamūrti, Liṅgodbhava, Gaṅgādhara, Rāvaṇānugraha, Arjunānugraha, Caṇḍeśānugraha, Brahmānugraha, Indrānugraha, Kāmānugraha, Viṇādhara, Somaskanda*, etc. (all *saumya, anugraha* forms) were created. The *Somaskanda* relief was usually placed on the rear wall of the *vimāna garbhagṛha*. Besides, Durgā, Gaṇeśa, various forms of Viṣṇu as

Nṛsiṁha, *Trivikrama*, Varāha, *garuḍārūḍha* Viṣṇu, Viṣṇu with Srīdevī and Bhūdevī, as Mohinī, *gaṇas*, and *samudramanthana*, were depicted.

The Vaikuṇṭha-perumāl temple consisted of the *sthānaka*, *āsana* and *śayana* forms of Viṣṇu. A number of subservient figures occurred along with the main *alaṁkāradevatās*. *Gaṇas*, *kinnaras* and *cāmaradhārīs* may be seen in large numbers. Animal forms also occupied a place in the Pallava sculptures. Figures as *nandī*, *gaja*, *siṁha* and *vṛṣa* were carved on the Shore and Kailāśanātha temples' *prākāra* coping. The Kailāśanātha *prākāra* section had Pārvatī in the Himalayan environs and the thirty-two *pādadevatās* including eight *dikpālas*.[127] Thus, the Pallava sculptures abounded in religious themes.

Technique

The sculptures were created both in relief and round. They were carved out of the living rock as well as sculpted from dressed stones, both hard granites as well as softer sandstone. When sculpted in hard granite, the relief sculptures on the walls and *devakoṣṭhas* were given stucco modelling for the finer elements like coiffure, ornaments, facial details, etc., to achieve better decorative effects. From eighth century onwards, carved granitic slabs were assembled[128] as seen at Irāvattaneśvara and Kailāśanātha shrines. Under Dantivarman, the standard technique used in Olakkaneśvara, Jalanātheśvara temples, etc., was to have relief panels of sculptured granite slabs inserted in the masonry construction.[129] Thus, the sculptured panels were generally in relief, whereas sculptures were sunken reliefs carved after re-erection. The scooped out method in contrast to the bold relief of Pallava carving recalled the cave temple technique.[130]

The sculptures were usually placed on the walls around the *garbhagṛha*, *maṇḍapas*, *bhadradevakoṣṭhas*, *prākāra devakulikās* and coping; *adhiṣṭhāna* mouldings; as *grīvādevatās*; on the *śikharas*; as pillar and pilaster bases, in friezes, etc.

Religious Sculptures

The diversity of divine forms in Pallava sculptures is suggested by varied representations of Śiva and Viṣṇu. Deities were shown with multiple hands[131] and *āyudhas* and overall indicated a lack of spontaneity and naturalness at Kāñcīpuram as compared to the earlier artistic creations at Mahābalipuram.[132] Amongst the new representations, Śiva's *nṛtyamūrtis* and incidents depicting *harakṛīdā* were graphically portrayed. Verticality was created in the images with tall crowns, elongated limbs and long faces, etc., emphasized perhaps more in frontal view.[133] In the *Rāvaṇānugraha* image, Rāvaṇa, depicted bigger than Śiva, indicated a sense of perspective on part of the sculptor. The *Gajāsurasaṁhāra* Śiva was carved dancing with *gajacarm* in his two hands symbolizing his triumph. The *gaṇas* in Kailāśanātha temple in multitudes portrayed diverse forms rarely found elsewhere, except in the early caves at Bādāmī. In the same shrine, *Naṭeśa* Śiva represented the Pallava[134] specific *lalāṭatilaka* pose while Pārvatī's pose expressed shyness and awe. On the outer walls and the *prākāra*, all covered with stuccoed and painted sculptures, the *Saptamātṛkās*, Gaṇeśa, Caṇḍeśa and the *dikpālas* made their first appearance in the Pallava art.[135]

A *caturbhujī* Viṣṇu image from Perangur, holding *śaṁkha* and *cakra* in the upper two hands, lower right hand in *abhaymudrā* and left in *kaṭihasta* is held[136] to be the largest known Viṣṇu image of the Pallava period.

The Tiruvural Mahādeva or Jalanātheśvara temple (Takkolam) marked rather a deviation from the standard practice. Representing perhaps a local tradition,[137] it had no *garbhagṛha* image, rather a small *somaskanda* relief placed in the *lalāṭabiṁba*. Similarly, the Virattaneśvara temple, Tiruttani, also dateable to Aparajitavarman, instead of any *Somaskanda* relief behind the *liṅga*, had *Umāsahita* relief in the *kūḍū* over its *vṛttāyat śikhara*.

Secular Sculptures

Pallava artists also carried out secular sculptures in large numbers. A dancer in specific classical pose was portrayed in the Bāhūr temple. The Vaikuṇṭha-perumāl consisted of panels of group dance. Rajasimha himself was depicted as watching dance performances. The same temple had war scenes with elephant riders and other figures engaged in various fight poses. These relief figures were quite dynamic reflecting free flow of lines. Later, *caturbhujī dvārapāla* images were also carved. Animal figures were represented in a lively manner. A monkey family in the Bāhūr temple appears to be an extension of the same in Mahābalipuram relief panel. Besides, the *vyāḷapāda* bases for Pallava pillars and pilasters appeared very graceful. Sometimes the couchant lion had a forepaw raised, while at times its front legs were placed on the ground. *Gaja*, *nāga* and *vṛṣa* bases were also carved. *Gajamuṇḍas* were generally put in the *adhiṣṭhāna* mouldings though animal sculptures were also carved on the *prākāra* coping and *śikhara*. The Pallava sculptural art probably lost its vitality during Aparajitavaraman only to be revived later under the Colas in a new form.

Pallava Bronzes

This period also witnessed creation of some of the greatest bronze masterpieces especially under Rajasimha and Aparajita. The bronze traditions that took shape under the Sātavāhanas and Ikshvākus in the Kṛṣṇā valley evolved further down south under the Pallavas marking the earliest phase of art in Tamil regions.

The usual characteristics of these images comprised of the *yajñopavīta* over the right arm, a heavy undergarment worn in the *hastisauṇḍika* style, the absence of *srīvatsa* and presence of Lakshmī figure symbolic of the early type of the *srīvatsa* symbol, etc. The Viṣṇu and Śiva images generally were made in *sthānaka* mode. In anatomical details, the images were usually marked by stability rather than dynamism. Characterized by these and several other features, the finest miniature and medium-sized Pallava bronzes included the *Viśāpaharaṇa*,[138] *Tripurāntaka*,[139] *Naṭeśa*,[140] *Somaskanda*,[141] *Vṛṣabhāntika* Śiva-Pārvati, *Naṭarāja*, Viṣṇu and Durgā images—all counted amongst the greatest productions of the times.

The Pallava bronze art, in its turn, seems to have influenced the prevailing and even later art traditions of the Colas,[142] Cēras,[143] and the Pāṇḍyas[144] also. Its intermingling with the Cālukyan tradition has also been suggested.[145] Thus, it is quite apparent that the ancient[146] art of casting metal images assumed considerable importance under the Pallava dynasty.

Art of Pallava Painting

The rare surviving fragments in the monuments of Rajasimha furnish splendid examples of the flourishing art of Pallava painting. Traces of line and colour in cave temples as at Māmaṇḍur hinted towards the art of painting. The structural temples at Panamalāi and Kāñcīpuram also consisted of painting remains. A painting from Panamalāi depicted Pārvatī watching the dance of Śiva. Her pose of standing gracefully with one leg bent has been likened to the *lalāṭatilaka* pose of dancing Śiva portrayed in a relief at the Kailāśanātha shrine.[147] The charming remains of a princely figure and a *somaskanda* in the Kailāśanātha, discovered by Jouveau Dubreuil, further illustrated the Pallava painter's art. Daubs of paint and traces of line have been discerned in several cells in the *pradakshiṇāpatha*, some bearing similarity with those in the Bādāmī caves.[148] The *somaskanda* theme was a great favourite in the Pallava art and its only painted representation survived in cell no. 41. It was a lovely theme of fond parents and a frolicsome child, of ideal mates and the object of their love: *Tathānganāmmoriva bhāvabandhanam babhūva yat prema parasparārṣayam vibhaktamapyekasutenatat tayoh paraparasyopari paryacīyata.*[149] Thus, it is evident that the Pallava period bloomed with multifaceted art forms and activities.

3. RĀṢṬRAKŪṬA ART ACTIVITIES

Although the political history of the Rāṣṭrakūṭas has been clearly delineated up to a large extent, very little is known about the artistic developments that took place under them. The extant monuments testify that both excavated and structural edifices were created under them. Still, for a long time only the rock-cut art of Ellorā and Elephanta remained synonymous with Rāṣṭrakūṭa art and no sincere efforts were put in to trace their structural monuments in the Deccan and South India. This persisted despite the discovery of many Rāṣṭrakūṭa structural temples belonging to their period of occupation of the Cālukyan Deccan regions in Karnātaka and Andhra as well as the Tamil Cola regions down south. In the Deccan, the Rāṣṭrakūṭa phase witnessed a steady increase in the building of temples and *basadīs*. References to temples became increasingly greater in number from mid-ninth century suggesting an outburst in building activity.

TEMPLE SITES

Deccan (Karnāṭa/Andhra Regions)

The Rāṣṭrakūṭa temples and their remains have been found in Deccan at various sites. These include shrines at Aihoḷe, Paṭṭaḍakal, Mahākūṭa, Hallur, Bachanagudda, Gudur, Yankacī, etc. (Bijapur Distt.); Gadag, Ron, Konnur, Rājur, Naregal, Kukkanur, Mevundī, Asundī, Lakshmesvar, Adaraguncī, etc. (Dharwar Distt.); Huli, Sogala, Savaditti, etc. (Belgaum Distt.); Kudaṭini, Hampī, Kolgal, etc. (Bellary Distt.); Jatinga Rāmeśvara, Adnur, Cikka Madhure, etc. (Citradurg Distt.); Bhavanāsī Saṅgam, Ālampur, Pāpanāsī, etc. Aihoḷe and Sirivala sites each yielded over more than twenty temples of the period.

Southern Regions

Kāverīpakkam, Peraṅgiyur, Bāhūr, etc. have yielded evidences of shrines belonging to the period of occupation.

Medium

The architects initially built shrines of red sandstone but later used granite. Temples at Aihoḷe, Paṭṭaḍakal, Mahākūṭa, Gudur and Hampī were erected in red sandstone while those at Gulbarga, Bellary and the neighbouring regions were mostly granitic. Towards the closing years of their rule, temples in schist were also built. Schist, being softer and finely grained than sandstone or granite, offered the artists more opportunities.[151]

DEVELOPMENT OF RĀṢṬRAKŪṬA TEMPLE STYLE

(A) Karnāṭa Region

Plan

Temples of different dimensions and varied plans were erected. In plan, nearly all the temples, except the Jaina *basadīs* at Paṭṭaḍakal and Hallur, were of *nirandhāra* types. Basically, the Rāṣṭrakūṭa temple consisted of the *garbhagṛha*, *ardhamaṇḍapa* and *navaraṅga* or *sabhāmaṇḍapa*. A variant of this plan found in the Mārkaṇḍeśvara temple, Sirivala had a nandi shrine also. The Kāśīviśveśvara temple (Paṭṭaḍakal), though depicted Cālukyan influence, yet explicitly symbolized a style of its own. It consisted of the *prāsāda*, *gūdamaṇḍapa*, *mukhacatuṣkī* and *nandīmaṇḍapa*.[152] Its *pañcabhūma śikhara*, with its height, shape and intricate *jāla*, presented an advanced form. The Parameśvara temple at Konnur, like the Brahmeśvara temple at Savadi, exhibited a stellate plan. Its *adhiṣṭhāna* as well as *garbhagṛha* walls presented about thirteen angles. In two Rāṣṭrakūṭa temples at Aihoḷe, the Cālukyan *maṇḍapa* type plan was adopted.

The Rāṣṭrakūṭa architects, probably in a bid to maintain their distinct identity, deviated from the Cālukya idiom but did not completely dissociate themselves from the established trends. They did introduce new ideals, motifs, new set of plans, innovative wall patterns, and pillar types. The preceding Cālukyan norms were modified to suit their aesthetic sense and purpose. Though *ekakūṭas* constituted the bulk of the temples, *dvikūṭas* and *trikūṭas* were also created.[153] The Nārāyaṇa temple, Savadi and Jodukalaśa temple, at Sudi, both *dvikūṭa* type, had two *garbhagṛhas* each while the Kundargi group at Aihoḷe, being of *trikūṭa* type, had three *garbhagṛhas*. The *Traipuruṣa* concept probably resulted in the consecration of the *trimūrtis*, either in separate or in the same cell. The Navaliṅga temples (Kukkanur) led to the grouping of nine temples. Thus, the Karnāṭa temples under the Rāṣṭrakūṭa monarchs attained a diversity of plans and rapid progress in execution of their details.

Adhiṣṭhāna

Use of the *upāna, jagati* and *tripaṭṭa kumuda* mouldings of the Cālukyan *adhiṣṭhāna* was continued while the deep *galā* was given up. Dentil heads became a regular feature in the *upāna* towards the later phase. The Jaḍarguḍī *adhiṣṭhāna* at Aihoḷe projected a complete Cālukyan influence in the form of the *upāna, jagati*, plain but deep *galā*, and a *kūḍū kapota*. The Sirivala temples depicted two types of *adhiṣṭhāna*: (i) very simple and (ii) more ornate, especially over *tripaṭṭa kumuda*. The *adhiṣṭhāna* was generally not too high though the *trikūṭa* Kundargī group (Aihoḷe), built on a high plinth probably to elevate the low height temples, offered a deviant.

Walls

They were usually simple in decoration with recesses and projections mainly in the *garbhagṛha* wall. The plainness of the wall was occasionally broken with narrow, tetragonal pilasters. The Rāmaliṅgeśvara shrine at Kudaṭinī and the Viśveśvara at Hallur represented such type of wall decoration. At times, *pañjar* topped by *śikharas* were also added in the pattern as seen in the Jaina *basadī* at Paṭṭaḍakal and Kalleśvara at Kukkanur. The walls of temples near Galaganātha group (Aihoḷe), at Rājur, Savadi and Hallur also consisted of small reliefs. A more ornate type of wall decoration in the form of pilasters, *pañjaras* with *śikhara*, sculptural reliefs and *makara toraṇas* was created in the Navaliṅga group, Kukkanur and Candraśekhara temple, Paṭṭaḍakal. The wall of Baleśvara temple, Lakshmeśvara was divided vertically into a number of sections by tetragonal pilasters and niches crowned by chiselled *caityas* and *makara toraṇas*.

The temples at Sirivala, Hallur, Huli, Ron, Kudaṭinī, etc. comprised of *haṁsamālā* motif above the wall and below the *kapota* as a regular feature.

Pillars

Rāṣṭrakūṭa temples consisted of a variety of pillars, some plain and others embellished. The earliest type in the Konṭi guḍī temple, Aihoḷe, was square at bottom with a designed *tripaṭṭa* at the top. Above it, the indented square section was decorated with a carved *caitya*. Its upper square section designed with *puṣpāvallī* was topped by a triangle-shaped *caitya* while the lower part showed figure sculptures and *muktāvallī*. The shaft was topped by a massive *āmalaka* while brackets represented *taraṅga* type.

The Allibasappā, Jadaraguḍī, and Konṭi guḍī temples consisted of another pillar type. Herein the square sections at the bottom and the top displayed a leaf flanked by small leaves at the corners, in place of the medallions.

The temples at Ron exhibited yet another variety. They had a square shaft at bottom while the rest of the pillar was cylindrical and bell shaped. The Mukabasavannā temple pillars at Nandavadige were composite in nature and rather resembled the Bādāmī caves' pillars. The heavy pillars with a square base were followed by multifluted shaft in the middle with an octagonal narrow band in the centre. A square block capped by a multifluted *pūrṇaghaṭā* and multifluted cushion capital topped the shaft.

The more ornate type of pillars, also primarily square, had a vertical band of indented shaft chiseled with *latā* or scroll motifs. Their lower portion was generally plain while the upper was usually divided into two horizontal sections. The upper horizontal was designed with petals and floral motifs while the lower one showed *kīrtimukha* at the top. Two loops formed by *muktāvallī* contained miniature sculptures of *yakshas*, deities or animals.

An interesting variant recalling Pallava[154] influence has been found in a smaller shrine at Sirivala. It projects a huge seated lion at the base supporting the circular shaft decorated with floral motifs, geometrical designs and *kūḍūs*. The brackets are profiled at 45 degree. Such type is not seen in any other temple in Deccan, either under the Early Western Cālukyas or the Rāṣṭrakūṭas. Another exquisitely carved pillar type belonged to the Añjaneya temple, Kadur. Made of schist, this square pillar consisted of sculptural friezes depicting deities and tales from the *Mahābhārata* in its bands. Thus, the development of pillar types in Rāṣṭrakūṭa structural edifices exhibited several variants.

Dvāraśākhās

The *garbhagṛha dvāra* usually depicted *Pañcaśākhās* decorated with motifs like *nāga-nāginī, patralatā, yakshas*, erotic figures, leaf, etc. The *pañcaśākhā* frame comprised *nāgaśākhā, ratnaśākhā, valliśākhā, mālāśākhā* and a *bahirśākhā*. The lintel in Aihoḷe and Nandavadige shrines positioned Garuḍa; elsewhere Gajalakshmī was carved. Gaṅgā and Yamunā figures in the bottom of *dvāraśākhā* were, with a few exceptions, replaced by *kuṁbha* and *padmaśaṁkha nidhis*. A noteworthy development was the shifting of *makara toraṇa* from the *garbhagṛha dvāra* to the *ardhamaṇḍapa* as an independent unit. The *kapota* above the *dvāra* was decorated with *caitya* motifs often consisting of peeping heads, *haṁsa* or flowers, and a *haṁsāvallī* underneath it.

Śikhara Constituents

Rāṣṭrakūṭas adopted both *Nāgara vimāna* and *Kadamba Nāgara* types. The former was usually *dvitala* or sometimes *ekatala* as seen at Nadara or Aihoḷe. *Kadamba-Nāgara* had two sub-types comprising heavy, medium-sized horizontal *talas* with (i) indistinct squarish or (ii) distinct triangular projections at regular intervals separated by *kaṇṭhas* as seen at Badigera Sūrya shrine or Trikūṭeśvara at Yamakāñcī.[155]

This description makes it apparent that the Rāṣṭrakūṭas, while continuing some Cālukyan traditions and introducing certain new architectural, sculptural characteristics, did contribute to the growth of temple architecture in the Karnāṭa region.

(B) Andhra Region

The Rāṣṭrakūṭas' political authority over Telangana and Western Andhra regions such as Kurnool, Mehboob Nagar, Cuddapah, etc. became instrumental for the growth of a new idiom by adopting new stylistic features and norms that prevailed in the centres of Karnataka. Instances of Rāṣṭrakūṭa monarchs, either erecting temples or giving donations to existing ones, are gleaned epigraphically[156] at Rāmeśvaram, Puṣpagiri and Ulchala.

The Ālampur *pratoli* was perhaps their earliest[157] building in the region inaugurating an era of Rāṣṭrakūṭa patronage and revealing initiation of new forms. The short *nāsikā* and small dimensions were unlike wide *nāsikā* of Cālukyan Tāraka

Brahmā shrine. *Kīrtimukha* appeared at the top of *nāsikā*, while wall *devakoṣṭhas* of different forms depicted Karnāṭa influence.

Bhavanāsī[158] Saṅgam site consisted of the Rūpala Saṅgameśvara, Bhujaṅgeśvara and the Saṅgameśvara group. The first one was a *dvitala*, lavishly ornamented lofty edifice. In plan, it comprised the *garbhagṛha, mukhamaṇḍapa, antarāla* and *mahāmaṇḍapa*. Its *pādabandha adhiṣṭhāna* consisted of *upāna, jagati, kampa, antarita,* and *kumuda* and *kapota* mouldings. The pillars were topped by *lasuṇa, kuṁbha* and *pīṭhikā*. The *devakoṣṭhas* and *jalavātāyanas* were generally crowned by *makara toraṇa*, while *citratoraṇa* and *toraṇa* with two *makaras*, their gaping jaws converging at the middle of lintel, were also popular. The Bhujaṅgeśvara was an *ektala* shrine with square *śikhara* topped by *stūpī, triśakhā dvāra* and both Maheśa image and *liṅgapīṭha* inside the *garbhagṛha*. The Śiva temple, Bandatandrapadu and Mahānandī temples belonged to the *phāṁsanā* order.

Pāpanāsī near Ālampur was another important centre where prolific occurrence of *phāṁsanā* structures revealed a variety of ground plans. Of its twenty-two shrines, three were *jātivimāna*. Pāpavināśeśvara temple, besides other regular features, exhibited carving of *candraśilā* adorned with *śaṁkha* and *padma*. Here soapstone was the major medium; therefore, both architectural and sculptural carving was less.

As to the stylistic features in the Rāṣṭrakūṭa Andhra shrines, close affinity to the Karnāṭa style was evident. The *vimāna* and *phāṁsanā* constituted principal forms of *śikhara* in the region. Configuration of two-three shrines with a common *raṅgamaṇḍapa* also became popular at Pāpanāsī, Pratakota, etc. Besides, freestanding pillars were used to demarcate the *antarāla* from *mukhamaṇḍapa*.

The decorative features mostly comprised *vidyādhara* figures, *dikpālas*, variety of *toraṇas*, carved grill windows, etc. Pillars and pilasters were largely of the *citrakaṇḍa* and *rūcaka* types with the usual *lasuṇa, kuṁbha* and *paṭṭikā* components.

The *dvāras* were exquisitely carved. *Triśākhā* and *pañcaśākhās* were common. They were generally decorated with *latāpatra, staṁbhapatra* and *ardharatna*, besides varied representations of *vyāḷa, mithuna, gāndharvas* and *dikpālas*. The lintel was invariably shaped into the *kapota*.

Ceilings, mostly flat, were carved with lotus medallions, Naṭarāja with *aṣṭadikpālas*, *Naṭarāja* with Gaṇeśa, *Kalyāṇasundara*, etc. Inside the *garbhagṛha*, the combination of Maheśamūrti and *liṅgapīṭha* was a common feature of Rāṣṭrakūṭa shrines. Temple *toraṇas* at Ālampur and Pāpanāsī resembled *pratoli*.

Thus, it may be held that Rāṣṭrakūṭa architecture in the Kṛṣṇā Tungabhadrā region revealed affinity with the Karnāṭa style.

(C) Tamil Cola Regions

The Rāṣṭrakūṭa sway had extended to the Tamil Cola regions for almost two decades after Krishna III won the battle of Takkolam (AD 944). He claimed to have founded three temples at Kāverīpakkam though none of them survive presently. The ruined Śiva temple at Peraṅgiyur (North Arcot) and Srī Mūlasthānam Uḍaiyar temple, Bāhūr, are also assignable to this phase of Rāṣṭrakūṭa occupation.

Down south, the two extant temples erected by Krishna III were rather different from both prevailing Cola and preceding Pallava styles. The Peraṅgiyur temple, a *caturārṣa vimāna* type, had a *pādabandha adhiṣṭhāna* with plain *brahmakānta* wall pilasters. Its *kapota* had a *gaṇāvarī* below. The southern *devakoṣṭha* consisted of a *dakshiṇāmūrti* while the *ardhamaṇḍapa devakoṣṭhas* contained Durgā and seated Gaṇeśa in the northern and southern ones, respectively.

The Bāhūr temple stood over a *kapotāsana upapīṭha.*[159] *Caturārṣa* in plan, it had a *pādabandha adhiṣṭhāna*, the walls consisting of *devakoṣṭhas* and *brahmakānta* pilasters with floral decoration. The figures portrayed different ethnic types while the techniques of carving sculptures betrayed Rāṣṭrakūṭa influence. This indicates that although these structural temples were produced under the aegis of Rāṣṭrakūṭa power, yet they retained their respective local influence.

Rāṣṭrakūṭa Sculptures

Sculptural art seems to have made exemplary progress under Rāṣṭrakūṭa patronage. Despite being the political successors of the Cālukyas, their sculptures were relatively free from their influence. They rather imbibed the vitality and expression potential of the Gupta sculptures. The decorative elements, deities' hands and related weapons, and subsidiary figures marked a growth along with an expansion of the subject matter.

The Rāṣṭrakūṭa sculptures were mostly produced at Ellorā,[160] Elephanta[161] and Kanherī.[162] Of these sites, Ellorā displayed the most continuous presentation of the religious and sculptural traditions from sixth to tenth centuries AD.

The Rāṣṭrakūṭas, being mainly śaivite, varied forms of Śiva, comprising both *ugra* and *saumya* aspects, were elaborately sculpted. The popular forms included *Tripurāntaka, Andhakāri, Yamāntaka, Gajāntaka, Bhairava, Rāvaṇānugraha, Kalyāṇasundara, Naṭeśa, Gaṅgādhara, Dakshiṇāmūrti, Maheśamūrti*, etc. Besides, Viṣṇu, Brahmā, Sūrya, Gaṅgā, Yamunā, Śakti, *dikpāla, dvārapāla, śālabhañjikā, śārdula* images were also carved. In addition to the images in round or relief, story panels based on the *Rāmāyaṇa, Mahābhārata* and *Kṛṣṇalīlā* were also created. Jaina images depicting Pārśvanātha, Mahāvīra, Bāhubalī, Sarvānubhūti *Yaksha, Yakshī* Aṁbikā, Cakreśvarī, Padmāvatī, etc. were also carved, especially in the Jaina caves.

The rock-cut images, in particular, were colossal in size. They manifested strength and vitality along with a sense of divinity. In spite of large dimensions, efforts were made to balance their body parts. For instance, the *Maheśamūrti, Kalyāṇasundara, Ardhanārīśvara*, Lakulīśa, etc. at Elephanta; *Rāvaṇānugraha, Tripurāntaka, Mahiṣamardinī*, Gaja-Lakshmī, etc. at Ellorā, especially the Varāha and Nṛsiṁha images in Daśāvatāra cave, despite their massiveness conveyed controlled organic proportions and an appreciable synthesis of physical and spiritual forces. The facial expressions and gestures revealed different emotions. The figures usually appeared independent in keeping with their anatomical details, but at places they were somewhat restrained, maybe due to lack of adequate space.[163]

The Rāṣṭrakūṭa images, organically heavy and broad, were similar to Bādāmī Cālukyan images, though in composition they were comparatively more underlined by delicacy, linear accuracy and an easy flow of energy. The divine figures suggested a sense of supernatural, conveyed through their multiple hands and *āyudhas*. Sculptures like the *Rāvaṇānugraha*, in particular, manifested unstinted dynamism and expression of vivid emotions. It also exhibited the artist's sense of perception.[164] One sculpture showed Rāvaṇa as equal in size to Śiva Pārvatī, while another instance had him, being in front, bigger than Śiva Pārvati seated on the high, distant mountain. The artists' expertise was conveyed by the female figures, shown with heavier lower lip, pointed chin, long eyebrows, and slender, delicate body as their prominent characteristics. Thus, the art of carving images and reliefs was carried to great heights by the Rāṣṭrakūṭa artists.

Bronzes

The early Western Cālukya art style of casting metal images probably continued under the Rāṣṭrakūṭas. A finer example of the perfect craftsmanship is the image of Bāhubalī,[165] almost a precursor of the Gomateśvara stone image at Sravaṇabelagolā (10th century AD).

Painting

Evidences of Rāṣṭrakūṭa painting art are found at Ellorā. These are visible on the *maṇḍapa* ceilings and walls. Themewise, they represented iconographic forms and floral designs with animals and birds entwined in them. An elephant, partly faded yet lively, figures amidst a lotus pattern (Pl. 9). The multi-armed Naṭarāja, dancing in reversed *bhujaṅgatrāsita* posture, is comparable to the *bhujātarūvana,* i.e. forest of arms, form of Naṭarāja found in the Cālukyan style.[166] The anatomy of the figures, the ornamentation, etc. reveal minutest details. Another significant figure was *Garuḍārūḍha* Lakshmīnārāyaṇa. The fragmented painting of *liṅgodbhava* showing Śiva emerging out of the *liṅga* with Brahmā and Viṣṇu on either side acquires great significance, both artistically as well as religiously.[167] Flying *vidyādharas* and their consorts against a background of trailing clouds and musical figures were other popular motifs. The colour patterns; arrangement of one dark figure against a fair one; the *muktāyajñopavīta* of male figures and *dhammilla* of female forms; their flying postures, etc. seemed unparalleled. The lovely contours of the slim and slender, almost weightless *ratnamakuṭa* wearing figures may be likened to the flying figures of the Gaṅgā relief at Mahābalipuram.[168]

The Jaina Indrasabhā cave at Ellorā had its entire ceiling and wall surfaces covered with painted scenes illustrating Jaina texts, floral patterns, animal and bird designs, etc. The *dikpāla* group of Yama with his consort on a buffalo, painted on the ceiling band was quite eye-captivating. Thus, the Rāṣṭrakūṭas, like their predecessor Cālukyas, patronized this fine art.

This brief outline of the art activities under the Cālukyas, Pallavas and Rāṣṭrakūṭas leaves no doubt that despite their internecine struggles ongoing, various rulers of these three ruling houses indulged in large-scale building projects. The extant monuments and their remains, as unmistakable evidences of the growth and flowering of the fine arts, bear testimony to the artistic excellence of their respective artists.

NOTES AND REFERENCES

1. For a discussion of the funerary association of stone, *cf.* K.R. Srinivasan, 1975, 'Temples of the Later Pallavas', in Chandra (ed.), *Studies in Indian Temple Architecture*, pp. 197-98; *Cf.* Srinivasan, 1998, *Temples of South India*, New Delhi, p. 30.
2. Srinivasan, 1959-60, *Some Aspects of Religion as Revealed by Early Monuments and Literature of the South*, pp. 5-6.
3. *See* Dayalan, 1992, *Early Temples of Tamil Nadu*, p. 19.
4. *Vide Śatapatha Brāhmaṇa*, VIII. 7.3.13.
5. Stella Kramrisch, *The Hindu Temple*, Vol. I, pp. 108-15.
6. *Śatapatha Brāhmaṇa*, 3.1.3.11.
7. *Cf.* Jogiraj Basu, 1969, *India of the Age of the Brāhmaṇas*, Calcutta, p. 74.
8. Expert wood workers went to the forest, selected the stately tree and felled it with their axes, (*Vanaspate Svadhitistataksha*) as given in the *Ṛgveda*, III. 8.6.
9. *Vide Śālā-Sūkta.Atharva Veda*, 9.3.11.
10. *Prajāyai Cakre* - *Cf.* V.S. Agrawala, 1965, *Indian Art*, Varanasi, p. 4
11. *Vide. Rūpa-maṇḍana*, I. 3.
12. *Cf. Viṣṇudharmottara Purāṇa*, 3.90.3-5.
13. Details being provided in Chapter 4.
14. On the basis of its cave-inscription palaeography, the cave-temple at Pillaiyārpattī is assigned to an even earlier period. *Refer to* Srinivasan, *CTP*, p. 47. However, even if the beginnings of cave architecture in Pāṇḍya country are traced to pre-Mahendra times, Mahendra's shrine could still be the first so far as the Toṇḍaimaṇḍalam region is concerned. *See* Mahalingam, 1970, *The South Indian Temple Complex*, p. 22.
15. *EI*, XVII, p. 17.
16. Inferred from the temple inscriptions of Cālukyan rulers Kirtivarman, Mangalesha, and Pulakeshin. *See* Chapter 2 for further details.
17. 'The Chālukyan architecture is but an outgrowth of the earlier Draviḍian style, so modified in its development by western temple builders as to have eventually attained a separate style in their hands'. Stated in 1926, *The Chalukyan Architecture of the Kanarese Districts*, Vol. XLII, Calcutta, p. 17.
18. *Cf.* Longhurst, 1998, *Pallava Architecture*, *MASI*, Pt. I, New Delhi (repr.), p. 3.
19. 2002, *The Hindu Temple*, Vol. I, Delhi (repr.).
20. *See* M. Rama Rao, 1963, 'Early Chālukya Architecture', *Journal of Indian History*, Silver Jubilee Number, pp. 437-38.
21. *Refer to* 1967, *The Art and Architecture of Aihoḷe*, Bombay, p. 50.
22. *Ibid.*, p. 52.
23. *Ibid.*, p. 51.
24. Geographic location of the Cālukyas, at the heart of the Deccan, must have facilitated their artistic contacts with the south and the east, leading to hybrid architecture.
25. Their detailed account follows in Chapter 4.
26. *Refer* S.R. Rao, 1972, 'A Note on the Chronology of Early Chālukyan Temples', *LK*, Vol. 15, pp. 9-18; *also* O. Divakaran, 1971, 'Les temples d' Alampur et de ses environs au temps des Chalukya de Bādāmī', *Arts Asiatiques*, Vol. XXIV, pp. 51-74. However, Gupte on the basis of its simple architectural design held the Koṇṭi-guḍī group to be the earliest at Aihoḷe in *The Art and Architecture of Aihoḷe*, p. 46.
27. As classified by Divakaran. *Vide* 1981, 'The Beginnings of Early Western Chālukya Art', Anand Krishna (ed.), *Chhavi*-2, Banaras, p. 59, fn. 1; *see* Soundara Rajan, 1978, 'Temples of

Aihoḷe and Paṭṭaḍakal', in M.S. Nagaraja Rao (ed.), *The Chalukyas of Bādāmī (Seminar Papers)*, Bangalore, pp. 258-71 for stylistic details.

28. *Refer to* Chapter 4 for its geographical location. It was perhaps the original Cālukya centre for architectural experimentations.
29. Cousens had counted and recorded some 71 of them in *The Chalukyan Architecture of the Kanarese Districts*, pl. II.
30. M.S. Mate and Shobhana Gokhale in 1971, 'Aihoḷe: An Interpretation', in Shrinivas Ritti and B.R. Gopal (eds.), *Studies in Indian History and Culture*, Dharwar, p. 504 have opined that the simple and small temple-like structures at Aihoḷe or Paṭṭaḍakal are, in fact, memorial *chatrī* type monuments found there in keeping with the religious importance of these places as *tīrthas*.
31. These have been listed in *Appendix V*.
32. The Lāḍ Khān temple, usually considered the oldest, was better conceived than Konṭiguḍī and had a *mukhamaṇḍapa* and *sabhāmaṇḍapa* suggestive of its later erection.
33. *See* R.S. Gupte, *op. cit.*, pp. 46-47.
34. It showed *varāha*, *cakra*, *śaṁkha* and lamp. Both Jayasimha and Ranaraga being feudatories, it could not have been legitimately adopted by anyone before Pulakeshin I, the first sovereign in the dynasty. Therefore, the temple is assigned to about AD 540, *Cf.* Balasubramaniam, 1961(Oct), *LK*, No. 10, pp. 41-44.
35. Protected by an *antarāla*, the *garbhagṛha*, henceforth, could not be directly entered from the *sabhāmaṇḍapa*.
36. The famous Aihoḷe *praśasti* inscribed on its eastern wall gives its creation date as Śaka era 656, i.e. AD 634-35. *See EI*, VI, pp. 4-12 for its printed version.
37. The Durgā temple with its apsidal plan and Buddhist *caitya* form suggested an imitation of rock-cut architecture in the early Cālukya structural temples. Apsidal plan was also tried at Cikka-Mahākūṭa (near Bādāmī), Trivikram temple (Ter) and Cezarla (Andhra Pradesh).
38. Highlighting its inappropriateness for Brāhmanical rituals, Percy Brown in 1965, *Indian Architecture*, p. 52 and P.L. Gupta in 1989, *Bhāratīya Vāstukalā*, Varanasi, p. 148 held it to be an adaptation of a *santhāgāra* planned for secular and civic use, though intended for a temple.
39. Named after a Muslim hermit residing there in the 19th century.
40. A stone seat with sloping back rest at the *mukhamaṇḍapa*, a probable derivation from the *santhāgāra* pattern; *kakshāsanas* are mainly seen in temples built after 7th century AD. They were, perhaps, also added to several earlier temples suggested by awkward jointing and difference in stone types and sculptural style. *Cf.* Carol Radcliffe Bolon, 1988, 'Cālukyas of Bādāmī: Karnāṭa', in Meister, Dhaky and Krishna Deva (eds.), *Encyclopaedia of Indian Temple Architecture: North India*, Vol. II, Pt. 1, Delhi, p. 282.
41. For instance, flat-roofed Gupta temples at Kuṇḍā, Mukund Darrā, Sāñcī, Tigawā, Eraṇ (Nṛsiṁha, Varāha and Viṣṇu shrines), Bhumrā, Nacnā Kuṭharā, Vidiśā, etc.
42. Had a *śikhara* been in its original plan, Lāḍ Khān's appearance would have been different from the existing broader and less vertical look. *Vide* Gupta, *Bhāratīya Vāstukalā*, p. 95.
43. An instance of such conversion may be seen in the Lāḍ Khān. It consists of a large nandī figure in the corridor, probably put later as the dedicatory block clearly revealed the shrine's Vaiṣṇavite affiliation.
44. Apparently named so as it formed part of a *durg* fortifications. It is held to be dedicated to Sūryanārāyaṇa by Cousens, K.V. Ramesh, and Padigar. *See.* C.R. Bolon, *op. cit.*, p. 300.
45. *Cf.* Percy Brown, 1965, *op. cit.*, p. 67.

46. By late 7th century, fully developed, elegantly carved Latina Nāgara *Śikharas*, with their *śukanāsā* often bearing *Naṭarāja* image, appeared. However, the early temple Latina *śikharas* did not have *śukanāsā*. *Vide* C.R. Bolon, *op. cit.*, p. 283.
47. Soundara Rajan, 1969, *Early Temple Architecture in Karnataka and Its Ramifications*, p. 10.
48. For detailed location *see* Chapter 4.
49. *Cf.* Stierlin, 1998, *Hindu India: From Khajuraho to the Temple City of Madurai*, Italy, p. 81.
50. *Ibid.*, p. 82.
51. *Cf.* George Michell, 1979, 'In Praise of Aihoḷe, Bādāmī, Mahākūṭa, Paṭṭaḍakal', *Mārg*, Bombay, p. 51. He suggests an early sixth century date for this temple on account of the well-defined parapet, emphasising the empty niches in the wall beneath. Another probable date is thirteenth century suggested on basis of *maṇḍapa* similarities with Hoysala style. *Vide* Stierlin, *op. cit.*, p. 87.
52. Several temples with half and full circles on pillar faces, on entablatures and cross-beams left incomplete at Aihoḷe betrayed political disturbance and general instability.
53. *See* Chapter 2 for details of the encounters.
54. This could be one reason for transferring their activities from Aihoḷe, known for mainly Vaiṣṇavite shrines. This may also have been the time when the Vaiṣṇava shrines of Aihoḷe were modified for Śaiva worship.
55. *Cf.* Cousens, *The Chalukyan Architecture of the Kanarese Districts*, p. 9. Though the Pallavas and Cālukyas fought constant wars, it is probable that artistic influences were also exchanged as a result of these contacts leading to a hybrid style.
56. *Ibid.*, p. 68.
57. Percy Brown, *Indian Architecture*, p. 68. The view has been duly supported by A.M. Annigeri, 1961, *A Guide to Paṭṭaḍakal Temples*, Dharwar, p. 41 and Soundara Rajan in *Early Temple Architecture in Karnataka and its Ramifications*, p. 27.
58. *See* Coomaraswamy's, 1965, *History of Indian and Indonesian Art*, Dover Edition, p. 96; this date is also confirmed by M.S. Nagaraja Rao in 1973, 'Chronology of Papanatha Temple at Paṭṭaḍakal: A Reconsideration', K.V. Ramesh (ed.), *Srikaṇṭhikā*, Mysore, p. 39.
59. Suggested by the shape of the pillars, *potikās* and half-hidden struts resembling supernatural creatures. The ponderous environment created by them must have been as elemental as the caves inside.
60. Originally it seems to have a *garbhagṛha* with frontal *maṇḍapa* (AD 720-30). First alteration (AD 730-34) perhaps modeled it on Ālampur shrines with addition of *maṇḍapa*, walls closer to *garbhagṛha* and three exterior porticos. Second alteration (AD 735-50) had a new larger eastern *maṇḍapa*, porch and sculptural elaboration. The various stages may be marked out by their sculptural styles, etc. *Cf.* C.R. Bolon, *op. cit.*, p. 305.
61. *See* Srinivasan, *Temples of South India*, p. 119.
62. As also seen in the Pallava Shore temple (Mahābalipuram) and Kailāśanātha temple (Kāñcī).
63. *Vide* Paṭṭaḍakal Inscription of Kirtivarman II in *EI*, III, p. 5. An inscription on its eastern gateway mentions Guṇḍa *Tribhuvanācārya*, the *sūtradhārī* of the southern country, as its builder. *Vide* Fleet, *IA*, X, p. 165; *also* Stella Kramrisch, *The Hindu Temple*, p. 143.
64. *Cf.* Paṭṭaḍakal Inscription of Kirtivarman II, *EI*, III, p. 5.
65. For Virūpāksha temple inscription, *Cf.* A.M. Annigeri, 1960, *Paṭṭaḍakalla Guḍigalu*, Dharwar, p. 78, No. 1; *also*, *IA*, X, p. 164.
66. The stylistic as well as epigraphic evidences indicate Pallava influence in its making. For instance, two inscriptions on the eastern gateway of Virūpāksha described the builder of Lokeśvar (Virūpāksha) as the most eminent *sūtradhārī* of the southern country whereas the

one at Pāpanātha praised Chattara Revadi Ovajja, the maker of the southern country (i.e. its temples) and belonging to the same guild of *Sarvasiddhī-ācāryas*, as the builder of Virūpāksha. This also accounted for the difference between the locally made Vijayeśvara and the Lokeśvara, made by more capable architects accustomed to the advanced southern art styles. *Refer to* Cousens, *op. cit.*, pp. 61-62. But despite all claims of similarity, the form and decoration of Rājasiṁheśvara and Virūpāksha reveal that Virūpāksha was not a mere copy of the Pallava edifice. Moreover, its patron Lokamahadevi never saw the Rājasiṁheśvara. Thus, the association seems to be hypothetical. *See also* Huntington, 1985, *The Art of Ancient India*, p. 324.

67. May be Vikramaditya's death incurred a shortage of funds.
68. Srinivasan, *Temples of South India*, p. 120.
69. *Cf.* S.R. Rao, 'A Note on the Chronology of Early Chālukyan Temples', *LK*, 15.
70. A pillar (AD 601) erected in front of the temple as a *dharmavijaystaṁbha* by Mangalesha and supplementing earlier endowments for the worship of Makuṭeśvaranātha imply the existence of a very important shrine there. Its stylistic analysis also reveals early features. *Vide* 1890, *IA*, Vol. XIX, pp. 16-20.
71. In the form of Gaṅgā, Yamunā, *mithuna* figures, northern pattern of *nāsikās*, etc.
72. The former was apparent at Lāḍ Khān, Konṭi guḍī, Megutī, etc. Of the latter, *vimāna* form was prominent in Bādāmī and Makuṭeśvara shrines, while *prāsāda* types were erected at Hucchimallīguḍī, Galaganātha, Kaśiviśveśvara and Ālampur temples.
73. *See* Chapter 4 for elaborations.
74. *Cf.* Nagaraj, 1983, 'Sculpture under the Chālukyas of Bādāmī', in A.V. Narasimha Murthy and B.K. Gururaja Rao (eds.), *Raṅgāvallī-Recent Researches in Indology*, Delhi, p. 217.
75. Discussed in Chapter 4.
76. Opined by R.S. Gupte in *The Art And Architecture of Aihoḷe*, p. 117.
77. As seen in Bādāmī cave I, Durgā temple *maṇḍapa*, and *sabhāmaṇḍapas* of Paṭṭaḍakal large temples, etc.
78. *Cf.* George Michell, 'In Praise of Aihoḷe, Bādāmī, Mahākūṭa, Paṭṭaḍakal', *Mārg*, p. 21.
79. *See* W.E. Begley's, 1973, *Vishnu's Flaming Wheel*, New York, p. 51.
80. *Refer to* Lippe, 1978, *Indian Mediaeval Sculpture*, Amsterdom/New York/Oxford, p. 140.
81. *Vide* J.C. Harle, 1970, 'Some Remarks on Early Western Chālukya Sculpture', P. Pal (ed.), *Aspects of Indian Art*, Los Angeles/Leiden.
82. Aschwin de Lippe, *Indian Mediaeval Sculpture*, *op. cit.*
83. For an analysis of the erotic motifs in Indian art, *see* Desai, 1975, *Erotic Sculpture of India*.
84. *Ibid.*, pp. 31-35.
85. Identified with Aditi, she is still ritually worshipped by women seeking fertility on January 14th every year. *Cf.* Bolon, 1988, 'Cālukyas of Bādāmī: Karnāṭa', *Encyclopaedia of Indian Temple Architecture, North India*, Vol. II, Pt. 1, p. 292.
86. For instance, mythological stories, Trivikram, Naṭarāja, Kirātārjunīya, etc., from the epics and *Purāṇas* were reproduced with a cosmic grandeur. *Cf.* Nagaraj, *op. cit.*, p. 218.
87. *See* Aihoḷe inscription of Pulakeshin II; *also* Fleet, *IA*, Vol. V, p. 47 ff.
88. N. Ramesan, 1962, *Copper Plate Inscriptions of Andhra Pradesh Government Museum*, Vol. 1, Hyderabad, pp. 42-43.
89. Divakaran, 'The Beginnings of Early Western Chālukya Art', *Chhavi-2*, p. 59.
90. *See* C. Sivaramamurti's, 1968, *South Indian Paintings*, Delhi, p. 56.
91. *Vide IA*, X, p. 58.
92. *Cf. ibid.*

93. Perhaps representing Kālidāsa's verse: *nripatayaś śataśo maruto yathā śatamakham tam akhaṇḍitapaurusham. See Raghuvaṁśa,* ix, 13.
94. *Cf.* Fleet, *Corpus Inscriptionum Indicarum,* III, p. 59.
95. The portrait probably enabled Kirtivarman, even when his physical body was no more, to pay eternal adoration to Viṣṇu. *See* C. Sivaramamurti, *South Indian Paintings,* p. 60.
96. The inscribed portraits read *Srī Siṁhaviṇṇa-pōttrā-thirājan* and *Srī Mahēndra pōttrā-thirājan. Vide* Srinivasan, *CTP*, p. 172 and pl. LV; *also* Lockwood *et al.*, 1974, *Mahābalipuram Studies,* Madras, p. 53.
97. The *Narapati Siṁha Pallava Viṣṇugṛham* with the *sarpadeham vīṇā samasthala śayāna madhamam* form of Viṣṇu, near the Shore temple and assigned to Narasimhavarman *Māmalla* has also been suggested as the first attempt at a structural temple of local granite slabs at Toṇḍaimaṇḍalam, followed by Ādikeśava Perumāl temple and Śiva temple (Kūram) by Parameshvaravarman I. *See* N. Ramesan, 1972, 'Studies in Medieval Deccan History', *A.P. Govt. Archaeological Series No. 20,* Copper-plate Inscriptions of the State Museum, Vol. III, Hyderabad, pp. 8, 9, 16 and 71; *also* Soundara Rajan, 1969, 'Cult in Pallava Temples', *TASSI,* 1962-65, Madras, p. 179 & Soundara Rajan's, 1972, *Indian Temple Styles,* New Delhi, p. 29.
98. *Vide* I.K. Sarma, 1987, 'Beginnings of Temple Architecture at Kāñchīpuram, Raw Materials and Religious Impacts', B.M. Pande and B.D. Chattopadhyaya (eds.), *Archaeology and History-Essays in Memory of Sh. A. Ghosh,* Delhi, p. 546.
99. Thus highlighting the link between availability of the material and its utilisation. It is further emphasised by the fact that despite the softer brown sandstone being a perishable material, its abundant availability facilitated the planning of grandiose creation like the Kailāśanātha.
100. *Kāncayāmahā daśmavēśma vidadhē Śailopamam Śūlin tasmāt Srī Parameśvaraḥ.* (Citrur Plates of Nripatunga) *Cf.* N. Ramesan, *op. cit.*, pp. 9, 71.
101. For a detailed analysis of the medium, *refer to* Srinivasan, *CTP*, p. 26.
102. For instance, the temples later erected under Dantivarman and Aparajitavarman.
103. G. Jouveau Dubreuil, 1972, *Draviḍian Architecture,* Varanasi, p. 24.
104. Spelled variously as Māvalipuram, Māvelipur, Māmallapuram, Mahāvalipuram, Mahābalipur, and so forth, the name is probably derived from *Māmalla*, one of Narasimhavarman I's *virūdas*.
105. The unknown Greek navigator referred to it as a port north of the Kāverī. *See* Sivaramamurti. 1978, *Mahābalipuram,* Calcutta, p. 2. Ptolemy located it as Melange or Maliarpha in the territory of the Aruvarnoi and marked it as the next emporium north of Podouke, i.e. Pondicherry. *Cf.* William Willetts, *An Annotated Bibliography*, p. 4.
106. Chambers held that as their copper coating had become incrusted with mould and verdegrease, they were no longer visible. *See* 1788, 'Some Account of the Sculptures and Ruins at Mavalipuram', *Asiatick Researches,* Vol. I, Calcutta, pp. 145-70. On the contrary, Q. Crauford (in 1792) claimed seeing the ruins of seven pagodas lying under the water when it was calm. *Cf. Sketches Chiefly Relating to the History, Religion, Learning and Manners, of the Hindoos,* 2 vols., London, Vol. I, pp. 111-12.
107. *See* Report 2005, 'Tsunami unveiled "Seven Pagodas" in Mahābalipuram', *The Times of India,* 1st March; 2005, '2 more temples found in Mahābalipuram', *TOI,* 5th April. *See also* 2005, *India Today,* 6th June issue, pp. 48-50.
108. *See* Chapter 5 for rock-cut caves.
109. An ancient sacred city known for both Vaiṣṇava and Śaiva leanings. *See Brahmāṇḍa Purāṇa,* 4.19-15. The oldest name *Kacci, Kaccippēḍu* was probably derived from *kañcī* tree, *vide* Mahalingam, 1969, *Kāñchīpuram in Early South Indian History,* Bombay, p. 5.

110. Alexander Rea, 1909, *Pallava Architecture, ASI,* New Imperial Series, Vol. XXXIV, Madras, p. 1.
111. A survey of ancient buildings in Kāñcīpuram undertaken as part of the Temple Survey Project (Southern region) in the 1980s.
112. *Cf.* Thomas Watters, 1904, *On Yuan Chwang's Travels in India,* London.
113. Figure known on basis of a survey of ancient buildings in Kāñcīpuram undertaken under Temple Survey Project (Southern Region). *Cf.* I.K. Sarma, *op. cit.*, p. 546.
114. *Cf.* Percy Brown, *Indian Architecture,* p. 81.
115. The *gaṇa* forms take the place of *nandī* invariably found on top *tala* of later Śaiva temples.
116. Srinivasan, *Temples of South India,* p. 100.
117. *See* Percy Brown, *op. cit.,* p. 81.
118. *Vide* Kailāśanātha inscription, *SII,* I, No. 27; also, *ibid.*, XII, No. 31.
119. *Cf.* Lockwood *et al., Mahābalipuram Studies*, p. 59.
120. C. Minakshi, 1941, *The Historical Sculptures in the Vaikuṇṭhaperumal Temple,* Delhi.
121. As discussed in Srinivasan's, *Temples of South India*, p. 107.
122. Probably the earlier *mūlabhera* or *garbhagṛha* deity being of stucco, wood or *somaskanda* carved on the rear wall was not required to be bathed. Even wherever *liṅga* was enshrined, may be the *abhiṣeka* water was collected inside only.
123. *See* chapter 5 for details of their rock-cut shrines.
124. *Cf.* Srinivasan, 1999, *Encyclopaedia of Indian Temple Architecture, South India,* Vol. 1, Pt. 1, p. 45.
125. *Ibid.*
126. Footnote no. 118.
127. Srinivasan, *Encyclopaedia of Indian Temple Architecture,* Vol. 1, Pt. 1, pp. 63-64.
128. The sculptured stones on the *ardhamaṇḍapa* inner wall faces and the Kailāśanātha temple complex, especially the *mālikā* shrines all around and the interspaces of the walls demonstrate this fact.
129. As held by Lippe in *Indian Mediaeval Sculpture*, p. 157.
130. Soundara Rajan, *Indian Temple Styles*, p. 105.
131. *Cf.* M.N. Tiwari and Kamalgiri, 1991, *Madhyakālīna Bhāratīya Mūrtikalā,* Varanasi, p. 30.
132. Srinivasan, 1999, *Encyclopaedia of Indian Temple Architecture,* Vol. I, Pt. I, p. 50.
133. Tiwari and Kamalgiri, *op. cit.*, p. 29.
134. *Cf.* Lippe, *Indian Mediaeval Sculpture*, p. 156.
135. *See* Srinivasan, *Temples of South India*, p. 104.
136. Tiwari and Kamalgiri, *op. cit*., p. 30.
137. *Cf.* Lippe, *op. cit.,* p. 156.
138. From Kilappuddanūr (8th century AD). It has Śiva swallowing *kālakūṭa* poison to save the world from annihilation. His *yajñopavīta* over the right arm indicates its early date. Right hand holds the poison cup while left has the snake as its source.
139. One of the finest Śiva representations. Interestingly, Śiva is shown with a single pair of arms. His *jaṭā*, anklets, *yajñopavītā*, *kaṭisūtra*, simplicity in figure modeling—all suggest early 8th century AD date.
140. From Kūram, it is a fine illustration of dancing Śiva in *urdhvājanu* pose, probably the only metallic representation of *Naṭeśa* in the pose.
141. Of 9th century AD (Tiruvalangudu, North Arcot), it probably marks a transition from Pallava to Cola phase. *Vide* Sivaramamurti, 1962, *Indian Bronzes,* Bombay, fig. 32.

142. The *vīṇādhara* in Tirumalai temple; Gaṇeśa from Velankanni; *Naṭeśa*, *Naṭarāja* at Tiruvarangulam in *catura* pose; and Kāliya-Kṛṣṇā at Chidambaram, etc. represent their artistry.
143. Two beautiful Viṣṇu bronzes (9th century AD), from Trivendrum Museum, depict Pallava influence.
144. Pallava art influence is manifested in the Kalugumalai rock temple and cave shrines at Tirumalaipuram, Cokkampaṭṭi, etc.
145. The Bodhisattva Maitreya image from Nāgapaṭṭinam is considered a rare synthesis of Pallava-Cālukya characteristics as it was a period of military strife between the two dynasties. Its *ratnayajñopavīta*, necklace, etc. are indicative of this fusion.
146. The *karmāra* or metal worker was of great importance in ancient times. Earliest (about 4000 years old) bronze image of a female dancer was excavated from Mohenjodaro. Several others from Adicanallūr, Taxilā, and Amarāvatī reveal antiquity of the art and artisan.
147. Sivaramamurti, *South Indian Paintings*, p. 63.
148. Bādāmī paintings are being described in Chapter 4.
149. *Vide Raghuvaṁśa*, III, 24.
150. A detailed account has been given in Chapter 6.
151. S. Rajasekhara, 1991, *Rashtrakuta Art in Karnataka*, Dharwad, p. 16.
152. Dhaky, *Encyclopaedia of Indian Temple Architecture, North India*, Vol. II, Pt. I, p. 346.
153. *Cf.* S. Rajasekhara, *op. cit.*, p. 26.
154. The mane of the lion is well delineated. Above its head stands the circular shaft. *See ibid.* p. 38.
155. A. Sundara, 1994, 'Some Structural Temples of the Rāṣṭrakūṭa Period in Dharwar Bijapur Area: A Preliminary Study', in B.R. Gopal (ed.), *The Rāshtrakūṭas of Malkhed: Studies in Their History and Culture*, Mysore, p. 307.
156. *Vide EI*, XXXVI, pp. 57-62.
157. Dated in the first regnal year (AD 780) of Dharavarsha Dhruva. *Cf.* B. Rajendra Prasad, 'List of Temples in Andhra Pradesh', *The Rāshtrakūṭas of Malkhed*, p. 311.
158. Confluence of the Bhavanāsī and Kṛṣṇā rivers. *See* B.R. Prasad, 'Rāṣṭrakūṭa Temples at Bhavanāsī Saṅgam', *AA*, Vol. XXXIV, pp. 211-21; *also* Prasad, 'Temples of the Rashtrakuta Period in Andhra Pradesh', in B.R. Gopal (ed.), *The Rāshtrakūṭas of Malkhed: Studies in Their History and Culture*, Mysore.
159. *Cf. Encyclopaedia of Indian Temple Architecture, South India*, Vol. I, Pt. I, p. 219.
160. In Aurangābād district of Maharashtra. From 6th to 10th centuries AD, an important centre for Buddhist, Brāhmanical and Jaina sculptures. Cave art details in Chapter 6.
161. A small island also known as Dhārāpurī or Gharāpurī, located about 10 km from Bombay. It consists of various representations of Śiva. An insight into its splendid art is given in Chapter 6.
162. In Thana district of Maharashtra. It mainly consisted of embellished Buddhist images.
163. Tewari and Kamalgiri, *op. cit.*, p. 75.
164. *Ibid.*, p. 78.
165. *See* fig. 24 on p. 37 in Sivaramamurti's, *Indian Bronzes*.
166. Sivaramamurti, *South Indian Paintings*, p. 75.
167. The arrangement highlights the special emphasis on *liṅgodbhava* form.
168. As opined by Stella Kramrisch in Sivaramamurti, *South Indian Paintings*, p. 78.

4

Evolution of Rock-cut Cave Architecture

The Cālukyan Phase

The evolution of Early Western Cālukyan architecture began in the second half of the sixth century AD. Their extant monuments are mainly found in Karnataka and Maharashtra regions. In the former, their artistic creations flourished for centuries at three sites namely, Aihoḷe, Bādāmī and Paṭṭaḍakal while in the latter, Ellorā, Aurangābād, Maṇḍapeśvara, etc., witnessed flowering of architectural expertise under Cālukyan suzerainty. As described in chapter 3, the course of structural temple construction culminated in the creation of nearly hundred temples at these sites. Likewise, the Cālukyan rock-cut activity led to the excavation of nine caves at the twin sites of Aihoḷe and Bādāmī, while at Ellorā and nearby they excavated about fifteen caves. The caves in both the regions were mainly Brāhmanical, Buddhist and Jaina in affiliations. The entire activity may chiefly be assigned to an enthusiasm that was religious in origin and in intensity of purpose.[1]

THE SITES

The Cālukyan rock-cut activities commenced at Aihoḷe and Bādāmī and passed on to Ellorā. Though there were a few small natural caverns in the sandstone outcrops along the Mālaprabhā valley which were treated as temples, the cave temple concept was fully expressed through the manually excavated grottos at Aihoḷe and Bādāmī. Aihoḷe or ancient *Ayyavoḷe*,[2] an early capital of the Western Cālukyas, is located fifteen miles east and slightly south of Bādāmī, on the Mālaprabhā river, in the Kaladgi district. Bādāmī as ancient '*Vitāpī*'[3] had been a Cālukyan stronghold in sixth century AD. It was perhaps chosen as a base from where the rival dynasties of Kadambas and Kalacurīs could be crushed. Bādāmī became the Cālukyan capital when fortified in 543 AD by Pulakeshin I:

Śaka–varṣēśu caṭuṣ-śatēṣu pañca-ṣaṣṭi-yutēśu
Aśvamēdh-ādi-yajñānāṁ yajvā śrauta-vidhānataḥ
Hiraṇyagarbha-sambhūtaś=Calikyo Vallabhēśvaraḥ
Dharādhrēndra-Vātāpim=ajēyam=bhūtayē bhuvaḥ
adhastād=Upariṣhṭāch=ca durggam=ētad=acīkarat[4]

It was further developed under Kirtivarman I, its '*prathama vidhātur*':

... *Mānavya-sagotrāṇam Hariti-putrāṇām Cilukyānām*
= *anavāye vatābyāḥ=prathama vidhātur* = ... *Kirttivarmmaṇah*...[5]

Considering the art productions therein, it is quite likely that Kirtivarman had converted Bādāmī into a political center as well as a religious seat, an *adhiṣṭhāna,* where Brāhmaṇas were settled and temples built.[6]

Both Aihoḷe and Bādāmī abounded in legendary accounts[7] highlighting their antiquity. Such legends recalled the memories of early fights between incoming northern and local southern chiefs[8] of an early age.[9] These places were also mentioned by foreign travellers.[10] These sites were eventually known for the earliest Brāhmanical cave temples excavated southwards from live rocks. The site of Ellorā, already pulsating with Buddhist and Brāhmanical excavation activities,[11] continued with the momentum.

MEDIUM

The medium of excavations at Bādāmī and Aihoḷe was the sandstone cliffs of the Kaladgi series of rocks. Ellorā caves were cut into Deccan trap rocks amidst their picturesque settings.

CHRONOLOGY

The first attempt to trace the antiquity of the Bādāmī and Aihoḷe cave temples was made by James Burgess. In his original *Report*, he dated them all in the sixth century AD.[12] He sequenced the relative development of Bādāmī caves I, II, III in the order of height along the path leading from the village below. Cave IV was dated about a century later. The Aihoḷe Śaiva cave was assigned to about 500-550 AD.[13] Later, reversing himself, he placed Bādāmī cave III first and the smaller ones later.[14] He still held cave IV to be the latest. This view found support in Percy Brown[15] and K.R.Srinivasan.[16] However R.D. Banerji, the next scholar after Burgess to study this site, placed cave III later to caves I and II.[17] Similar view was proposed by Walter Spink[18] and Gary Tarr.[19] The relative chronological development of the Cālukyan cave temples reveal that the style began with the excavations at Aihoḷe in mid-sixth century and culminated in cave III at Bādāmī, dated 578 AD. Cousens[20] also held that the initial efforts of the Cālukyas in the domain of art were represented by a considerable group of shrines and temples during 450-650 AD at Aihoḷe. Though Tarr did not support the usual dating of the earliest monuments at Aihoḷe to fifth century AD,[21] he accepted the rock-cut shrines as the earliest Cālukyan temples.[22] Technique wise also the Bādāmī caves, especially cave

Fig. 22. Aihoḷe: Rāvaṇa Phaḍi, side-shrine (after AIIS).

III, represented better contours. Therefore, it must have belonged to a later phase than the Aihoḷe ones. Thus, despite divergence in scholarly opinions regarding their chronological placement the earliest Cālukyan art may be traced to the excavated caves at Aihoḷe.

1. AIHOḶE CAVE TEMPLES

At Aihoḷe the caves were cut in two locations: (i) the renowned Rāvaṇa Phaḍi and smaller Śaiva cave to the north of the site, in the vicinity of the Durgā temple, (ii) the three Jaina caves around the Megutī hill in the center of the site.

Excavated around 550 AD, Rāvaṇa Phaḍi, also known as *Rāvel Phaḍi* and *Rājakuḷa Phaḍi*[23] was seemingly the earliest of the series.[24] Located in a very low boulder (Pl. 10), it presented striking resemblance to the earlier Gupta period Hindu excavations at Udaigiri, Vidiśā.[25] Rāvaṇa Phaḍi was originally a Śaiva temple, for the *garbhagṛha* floor, the *liṅga* and *pīṭha*, all hewn out of a single rock (Pls. 11-12),[26] ruled out any possibility of later conversion. It was a small cave, only 13′ wide at its entrance and 18′ wide and 8′9″ high in its *mahāmaṇḍapa*, with two side-shrine areas (Fig. 22) and a *garbhagṛha* with a *liṅga* at the rear. Two pillars with square *śadurams* or bases and prismatic shafts divided the front of each shrine (Fig. 23).[27]

The smaller Śaiva shrine next to the Rāvaṇa Phaḍi was the simplest of the group, cut into the rock near ground level, at a place where a seam in the rock created a natural ceiling break. The *liṅga* and *pīṭha* enshrined inside were not rock-cut but later additions. The use of local stone in its excavation and the simple form indicated its belonging to the early Cālukyan period. Considering its simple nature this has been

Fig. 23. Aihoḷe: Rāvaṇa Phaḍi, shrine pillars (after AIIS).

suggested[28] that it may have been a preliminary to the larger and extremely ornate Rāvaṇa Phaḍi.

The Jaina cave, locally called *Mīnā Bastī*, was finely wrought and rather represented a link between the Aihoḷe (Rāvaṇa Phaḍi) and the later Bādāmī forms as suggested by its plan. Its *maṇḍapa*, supported in front by four plain square pillars,[29] had the entrance 8′ wide divided by two pillars.

The double storied cave was partially cut into the hill and panels of cut stone regularized much of its interior. It had a structural façade. On the basis of the relief found on the ground floor doorways it is held to be a Buddhist structure. These reliefs have been identified by Settar[30] as incidents related with the Buddha's life. It was also suggested to be a Jaina cave.[31] A seated figure sculpture on the *mukhamaṇḍapa* ceiling of the upper floor was identified by Cousens[32] as a 'clothed *Jina*.'

The fifth cave hollowed out of a single boulder from the Megutī hill was identical to earlier excavations at Udaigiri, Vidiśā.[33]

The Development of Aihoḷe Cave Temple Form

The development of caves at Aihoḷe revealed a style derived from several traditions. The Rāvaṇa Phaḍi, the small rock-cut shrine attached to it and the Jaina cave hollowed from a single boulder, all revealed affinity to the preceding structural tradition at Udaigiri, Vidiśā.

Ground Plan

The plan of the Rāvaṇa Phaḍi may be related to a series of Hindu monuments in Maharashtra and Konkaṇ in the early and mid-sixth century.[34] It probably developed out of the interior spaces found in the Buddhist excavations of the Vākāṭakas wherein the enclosed spaces led through pillared openings to shrines, niches and cells. It appeared in a primitive form at Maṇḍapeśvara[35] and developed towards the mid-sixth century in the east wing of Elephanta,[36] and in Rāmeśvara cave at Ellorā.[37] At Aihoḷe, the cave temple plan (Fig. 24) rather took a uniquely concentric aspect with a central *maṇḍapa* opening on all four sides through horizontal frames containing a pair of pillars. The same form as the entrance, repeated in the rear of the *maṇḍapa*, served as a preliminary entrance to the shrine and its recurrence on either side served as screens for sculpture niches.

Regarding the plan's basic irregularity of form it contained several features that betrayed a definite indecision regarding its final form or executing its parts. There was a lack of right angles in the *maṇḍapa* itself and an attempt, apparently reconsidered, to expand the sculpture niche on the right into something else. The nature of this intended form is not clear. There are no parallels to compare with and it has been very irregularly worked out.[38] The imitation of structural elements like *adhiṣṭhāna*, pillars, etc., within the cave was another peculiarity of its design.

The Rāvaṇa Phaḍi façade was not full temple width and also not as distinctly detached from the rock as at Bādāmī. On the sides and above, it appeared blended into the rock rather than separated from it. It had no *kapota* or *mukhamaṇḍapa*. Tarr rather suggested the possibility of a structural façade in it.[39]

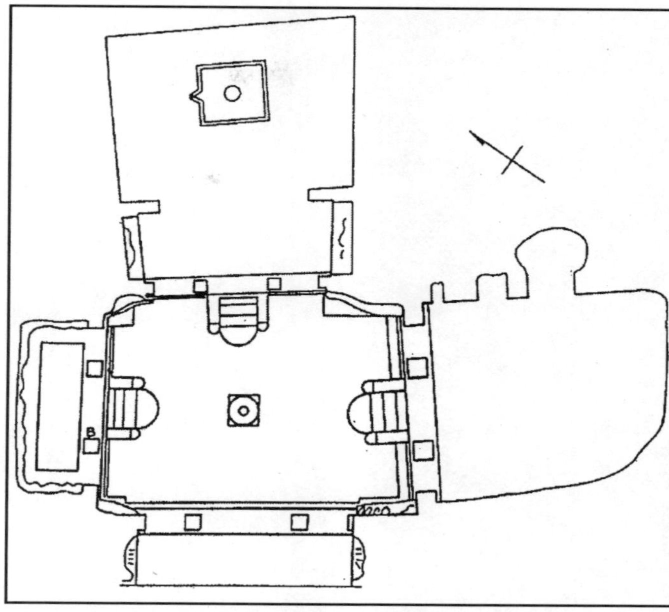

Fig. 24. Aihoḷe: Rāvaṇa Phaḍi cave, ground plan.

The extremely simple form of the smaller Śaiva shrine made it a reasonable though not certain preliminary to the Rāvaṇa Phaḍi. However, the Jaina cave, though not as impressive as the Rāvaṇa Phaḍi or later Bādāmī caves, was finely wrought and in its plan represented a transition between the Aihoḷe form as seen in Rāvaṇa Phaḍi and the later Bādāmī form.

The double storied Jaina cave ground floor had an interior consisting of three *śālās*, each lined with dressed stone, though standing beneath an overhang and cut back into the hill.[40] The upper floor contained a single rock-cut *śālā* and *ardhamaṇḍapa* corresponding to the one below. Hence homogeneity in the ground plans of the Aihoḷe rock-cut shrines.

The Aihoḷe caves' architectural details, such as the pillar, *potikā*, *garbhagṛha*, *dvāraśākhā*, and above all, sculptures, exhibited the influence of earlier traditions and styles, being discussed later in this chapter, besides reflecting the indigenous Cālukyan innovative spirit. To comprehend the extent of development of form in the early Western Cālukyan cave temples, it is desirable to analyze their architectural features.

Pillars

In the excavated temples, the pillar was the most important element of composition and over its design depended much of their architectural effect. The pillars were ponderous and massive in proportions suggestive of strength. Placed in the façade and interiors they constituted the *mahāmaṇḍapa*, *antarāla* and *mukhamaṇḍapa*. Their number varied from two to four in a row.

The Rāvaṇa Phaḍi pillars belonged to the common type seen even in the later structural temples at Aihoḷe and Mahākūṭa. As compared to those at Bādāmī their form was quite simple (Fig. 25). It was composed of a square shaft with lower and upper *śaduram* sections. The lower *śaduram* part was mostly unfinished while at times

Fig. 25. Aihoḷe: Rāvaṇa Phaḍi, pillar (after AIIS).

even the capital portion remained quite rudimentary. Its capital components consisted of the square projecting *maṇḍī*; schematically shaped square sectioned *kalaśa*, *tāḍī* and *kuṁbha*; square *vīrakaṇṭha*, topped by the beam *uttira*; followed by *valabhī* and *vājana* mouldings (Figs. 26-27). A very narrow slightly curving *potikā* above, and the octagonal necking *paṭṭikā* were the only distinctive features in its otherwise undecorated shaft. They were devoid of bases below the shaft. This type was carved at the Rāvaṇa Phaḍi in combination with similar pilasters in a three bay *maṇḍapa* entrance presenting the simplest version of the standard *maṇḍapa* entrance form. Inside the cave the pillars were similar to the type found in the *maṇḍapa* entrances of the Bādāmī caves. They constituted three different types of the simple cushion capital pillar with very narrow *taraṅga* or angular *potikās*. Towards the rear, leading to the shrine, were narrow square cushion capital pillars. At either side prismatic sided fluted pillars[41] with slightly concave faces, rose from square bases, carrying cubical shapes just below their *potikās*. Similar simple, undecorated square pillars bearing narrow curving *potikās* were carved in Bādāmī cave III. Therein the *mukhamaṇḍapa* was supported in front by four plain, square pillars while two pillars divided the entrance to the *maṇḍapa*. The *maṇḍapa* had a shrine at each side divided off by a pair of pillars in front of each.[42] Pillars in both the storeys of the double storied Jaina cave were also simple. They carried a type of bracket and lintel that was also seen in the later part of Vijayaditya's reign.[43] The façade here was composed of four pillars and two pilasters.

Decoration had been a distinctive aspect of Cālukyan pillars at Aihoḷe. The Rāvaṇa Phaḍi pillars consisted of the *kīrtimukhas* and swag motif, the standard pillar decoration in the Bādāmī caves.

Dvāraśākhās

Dvāraśākhās in some of the shrines at Aihoḷe were elaborately carved and replete with many auspicious motifs. The Rāvaṇa Phaḍi *garbhagṛha* was originally screened from the *maṇḍapa* by a structural wall that contained a single *dvāra*. Though the wall is no longer standing, its richly decorated left jamb and its lintel (Fig. 28) can still be seen lying in the *garbhagṛha*. The shrine *dvāra* was composed of simple *śākhās*, with a small framed *dvārapāla* at each base and a single vertical row of male figures joined by a row of flying garland bearers focusing on the center of the lintel. The lintel had two ascetics worshipping the *liṅga*. This *dvāraśākhā* was simpler than any doorway at Bādāmī. The

Fig. 26. Aihoḷe: Rāvaṇa Phaḍi pillars, details (after AIIS).

Fig. 27. Aihoḷe: Rāvaṇa Phaḍi pillar, shaft details (after AIIS).

ground floor of the partly structural Jaina cave at Aihoḷe consisted of two *dvāraśākhās*. The inner *dvāraśākhā* had the miniature figures of Avalokiteśvara and Padmapāṇi at the base of the doorjamb. It was decorated with mouldings and simple narrative relief. *Jātaka* scenes were represented in small panels. The outer *dvāra* carried similar decorations, and had an articulated lintel *prastara* composed of five *kūṭas* running *śālā-karṇa-śālā-karṇa-śālā-karṇa-śālā* sequence in low relief. The *dvāra* to the shrine on the upper floor was undecorated in courses, but contained a more complex *prastara* consisting *śālā-kūṭa, karṇa-kūṭa,* and *pañjara kūṭa*. These were linked by a continuous *hārāntara* that separated them with lower relief *pañjara* and itself consisted of *adhiṣṭhāna,*

Fig. 28. Aihoḷe: Rāvaṇa Phaḍi cave, doorframe fragment (after AIIS).

wall and *kapota*. The relief of the whole was low. There was a *jina* beneath the triple umbrella on the ceiling above this *dvāra*.

The fifth cave had a couple of *dvāraśākhās*. The outer simply moulded *dvāra* led to another simply moulded, decorated *dvāra* of the *śālā*. Its decoration included a square rosette at the *dvāraśākhā* base. However, decoration pattern of squares alternating with circles was different from the usual diamond and bean shapes. The *dvāra* had no *prastara*.

ADHIṢṬHĀNA

The façade *adhiṣṭhāna* components in these cave shrines comprised of *jagati*; *kaṇṭha*; *kumuda*; *paṭṭikā*; and *prati*. Its continuity was broken by the *sopāna* fronted with a *candraśilā*. The *adhiṣṭhāna* below the interior shrines in Rāvaṇa Phaḍi consisted of *upāna*; *adhopadma* shaped *jagati*; *kampa*; *kumuda*; *paṭṭikā*; and *prati* mouldings.

SCULPTURES

In these shrines sculptures emerged on the rocks with unbounded movement. The sculptural decorations in Rāvaṇa Phaḍi were placed at the corners of the *maṇḍapa*, in the sculpture shrine and in the *antarāla*. The façade contained important sculptures including large dwarfish representations of *śaṁkha* and *padma nidhi*, figures that occurred in miniature at Bādāmī. These were placed within relief niche frames, each with a paneled *adhiṣṭhāna* containing a single *gaṇa* and a domical roof. Flanking the door stood a pair of *dvārapālas* partially on the façade and partially in the entrance, in three quarter relief, notable because of their Scythian type clothing. The sculpture shrine contained images of *Naṭarāja* Śiva with Pārvatī, Gaṇeśa, Kārtikeya and Bhṛngī, surrounded by the *Saptamātṛkās*: Brāhmī, Maheśvarī and Kaumārī on the side wall, Vaiṣṇavī on the back wall to Śiva's right and Varāhī, Indrāṇī and Cāmuṇḍā on the side wall to Śiva's left. This sculpture style was closest to Bādāmī caves I, II style. The figures appeared as lined up in simple relief placed against the wall. Spatial details were not approached, as the artist seems to have confined himself to linear stylizations of the dance. The graceful poses and patterned costumes of these figures bore affinity with the style of Kārtikeya in the sculpture niche outside Bādāmī cave I.

The *antarāla* to the *garbhagṛha* contained two images of Varāha and *Mahiṣāsuramardinī* and three ceiling medallions consisting of a lotus, *garuḍārūḍha* Viṣṇu, and Indra on Airāvata. The Varāha was in a simpler form as compared to other Cālukyan examples. At Rāvaṇa Phaḍi it was framed within a rectangular panel set into the *antarāla* wall. The figure occupied the whole space inside the frame and appeared closest to the Bādāmī cave II figure. Quite unusually, it stood on the frame floor while the *nāga-nāgin* figures were pushed into the lower corner. The artist seems to have faced the problem of showing the Varāha's left arms that had to simultaneously support Bhūdevī and his conch. Here, as in Bādāmī cave II, one arm stretched parallel to the panel to support Bhūdevī's feet. The natural arm was bent at the elbow giving her a perch to sit on but leaving no support for the conch shell that floated in the air in the panel's upper corner (Fig. 29). This panel

Fig. 29. Aihoḷe: Rāvaṇa Phaḍi, Varāha, *antarāla*, north wall (after AIIS).

Fig. 30. Aihoḷe: Rāvaṇa Phaḍi cave, *Mahiṣāsurmardinī*, *antarāla*, south wall (after AIIS).

was the least impressive of the three Cālukyan Varāha versions, the other two being at Bādāmī.

The *maṇḍapa* sculptures exhibited a consistent use of the *gaṇa* dado panels. Though the sculptures within the *maṇḍapa* were devoid of architectural frames, they were raised up by means of these dado panels. There were no narrative panels in the Rāvaṇa Phaḍi cave. An attempt was also made for pillar sculpture similar to Aihoḷe Jaina and Bādāmī cave I. Rāvaṇa Phaḍi symbolized the developing tradition of Cālukyan sculptures. The Varāha and *Mahiṣāsuramardinī* both represented distinctly Cālukyan types. Similarly, the dancing *mātṛkās; Naṭarāja* of the sculpture niche; and figures with the tall crowns, were all forms cut in a strong relief that projected plastically from the wall in a way peculiar to the Cālukyan art. The figures were mainly frontally faced. The strongly projecting forms and their angular contours were marked by a robust quality. Slim and relaxed, all the figures in Rāvaṇa Phaḍi manifested dynamic and rhythmic postures. Their elongated *makuṭas* or *jaṭās*, spokes *śīrṣacakra*, oval faces, long weapons, patterned garments with sashes falling in straight folds, etc., implied a verticality unobserved elsewhere. An entirely Cālukya version of the *devī* killing Mahiṣa was carved in the *antarāla.* The smiling *Mahiṣamardinī* faced Varāha. Both, being *avatāra* to restore *dharma,* presented a symmetrical position. *Mahiṣamardinī* form reconciled vigour and serenity, movement and poise in a very skillful manner. Her sinuous bow similar to that of *Trivikrama* in Bādāmī cave II corresponded to the curves of her body. Her open arms stretched out like sunrays. In stark contrast, the long vertical thrust of her *śūla*, almost parallel to the *khaḍga*, pierced into the arched rear of the buffalo, breaking an otherwise serene harmony (Fig. 30). The composition of this panel was much more sophisticated than the *Mahiṣamardinī* in Bādāmī I. From iconographic point of view, the quick gesture of the *devī*, turning back the head of the buffalo to break his neck, became a hallmark of the Cālukya *Mahiṣamardinīs* in the seventh century.

In the Jaina cave, Supārśvanātha and Gomateśvara images were put on the *mukhamaṇḍapa*'s right and left ends, respectively. The *antarāla* ceiling bays were distinguished, but not separated, by very elegant decorative *makara* relief. The *maṇḍapa* ceiling and sculpture niches' decoration was identical to that in Rāvaṇa Phaḍi. Only the left sculpture niche was filled and the design ran around its three walls. The relief depicted royal or celestial figures including Indra attending upon Mahāvīra. The rear shrine had a seated *jina* representation. Its entrance was flanked by lotus bearing, standing *dvārapālas*, each occupying a large frame and accompanied with an attendant *gaṇa*. All the sculptures within the cave were raised off the ground but there were no *gaṇa* or other sculptured dado panels. Here too, both the placing of the figures and their general proportions were within the framework of Cālukyan art. The sculptures within the last two caves were negligible and devoid of any noteworthy features.

In the passing, it may be observed that at Aihoḷe while the Rāvaṇa Phaḍi, the small Śaiva shrine and the single boulder Jaina cave could be related to Udaigiri (Vidiśā) tradition, the double storied cave was only partially cut into the hill, its façade being fully structural. Thus, both the rock-cut as well as structural modes were followed here. The cave shrines were more remarkable for their sculptural embellishments rather than the architectural effects.

2. BĀDĀMĪ CAVE TEMPLES

The excavation activity that began at Aihoḷe passed on to neighbouring Bādāmī. Its four excavations in the cliffs beneath the south fort constituted one of the most important series of rock-cut temples in the Deccan. It was situated at the outlet between two rocky hills on its north and southeast sides.[44] All along the north side of the lake were old temples while the cave temples were excavated in the scarp of the hill to the southeast (Pl. 13).

There are three Hindu caves and one Jaina cave at Bādāmī numbering from the lowest and closest to the village as I to IV. There is a natural grotto between caves II and III, with a defaced Buddhist sculpture and a small Gaṇapati. R.D. Banerji[45] held this to be cave III and the larger Vaiṣṇava cave as no. IV. But his numbering was inconsistent. The Vaiṣṇava cave was number III while the Jaina one was cave IV.

In their general appearance and interior arrangements, the Bādāmī excavated shrines were almost uniform. Each consisted of a *mukhamaṇḍapa*, pillared *mahāmaṇḍapa* or *sabhāmaṇḍapa* and *garbhagṛha* cut deep into the rock, sans a *pradakshiṇāpatha*. Burgess has opined that the Brāhmanical shrines were excavated within a relatively short span of time while the Jaina one was added nearly a century later.[46]

Cave I

It was considerably smaller in size. Its exterior was 42′ wide while the entire depth from its front steps to the back wall of the *garbhagṛha* was over 50′. It was located about 50′ above the town (Pl. 14). The 21′ wide entrance was divided into three bays by two pillars while the *sabhāmaṇḍapa* roof supported by two rows of four pillars. The shrine, rather irregular in shape, varied from 6′11″ to 8′3″ in depth, by 9′6″ width and contained a *caturārṣa garbhagṛha* with a small *liṅga*.

This cave, presumably the earliest at Bādāmī, revealed the basic scheme of the Bādāmī cave-temples. A small *caturārṣa garbhagṛha* scooped out in the back wall, contained a monolithic *liṅga* on a *bhadrapīṭha*. It had a frontal pillared *gūdhamaṇḍapa*. A three stepped *sopāna* with a *candraśilā* provided access to the *garbhagṛha*. Longitudinally the *maṇḍapa* was divided into three separate bays or *bhadra*. The pillar schemes had their own floor settings, transversely. Carved panels inside the *maṇḍapa* and ceilings constituted sculptural ornamentation while the pillars were also intricately carved.

Cave II

It repeated the scheme of cave I, however, the internal arrangement of the *maṇḍapa* created a strong inclination towards the recessed shrine at the rear. Cave II had an exterior of 33′. The entry to the cave was also through three *mukhamaṇḍapa* bays divided by two pillars (Pl. 15). Inside, the ceiling was supported by 8 square pillars, arranged in two rows across the *mahāmaṇḍapa* which was 33′4″ wide by 23′7″ deep and 11′4″ high.[47] The shrine, approached by five stepped *sopāna* which raised its floor 3′ above that of the *mahāmaṇḍapa*, measured 8′9″ by 7′5″ and contained a *caturārṣa garbhagṛha*.

Cave III

It was perhaps the most ornate, impressive and largest of the Early Cālukya excavations. Its date is authenticated by internal evidence. A pilaster inscription flanking Varāha sculpture described the Vaiṣṇavite cave as dedicated by Mangalesha in memory of his brother Kirtivarman in the Śaka year 500, equivalent to AD 578.[48] Several other Early Western Cālukya monuments had resulted directly from patronage by the ruling family.[49] Such patronage distinguished the art of this period and region, and suggested the influence of kings and royal families over the art. The placement of the royal inscription next to a large sculpted relief showing Varāha rescuing the earth was apparently no coincidence. For, Varāha, the dynastic symbol of Early Western Cālukyas, also symbolized their own role as protectors of the earth.

The exterior width of Cave III *mukhamaṇḍapa* was nearly 70′. It was composed of an arrangement of six pillars in addition to a pilaster at each end. Its extreme depth into the rock, including the *garbhagṛha*, was 65′ but the *sabhāmaṇḍapa* with its fourteen pillars took up only half of this, thus making the shape of the *garbhagṛha* twice as wide as it was deep, not an appreciable ratio in view of its position in the plan.[50] The average height of the whole was 15′.

Jaina Cave

Executed perhaps in the mid-seventh century, the Brāhmanical group apparently inspired it and was practically their copy adapted to suit the Jaina rituals. Its dimensions were less than the others. The façade with its four pillars and *potikā* capitals was only 31′ long and 6″ wide, and the depth of the whole was 16′. Although an interesting production, it merely testified to a temporary revival of the rock-cutting art in the seventh century AD in this locality following which it seems to have entirely ceased.

Development of Temple Form in Bādāmī Caves

A basic homogeneity and distinct division pervaded the Bādāmī shrines. Within the unity of the rock-cut tradition, they represented two different styles. The style of caves I and II was relatively simple and tended towards decorative ornamentation while cave III, IV style generally inclined to more complex compositions. Sculpture herein was more dynamically and dramatically conceived than the rather static forms of caves I and II group. Besides, it was often released from the isolation and containment of wall and frame unlike the group one sculptures that were strictly confined to their architectural niches. The second style appeared to be more regular, consistent and fully developed. The notion of caves III and IV being of later conception and execution gets support from both architectural sophistication and sculptural refinement within them. Cave III was not only twice as large but far more spectacularly located higher up in the cliff than the other two Hindu caves. Its inscription stated that Mangalesha 'erected a temple, an abode of Viṣṇu, surpassing everything which is celestial or

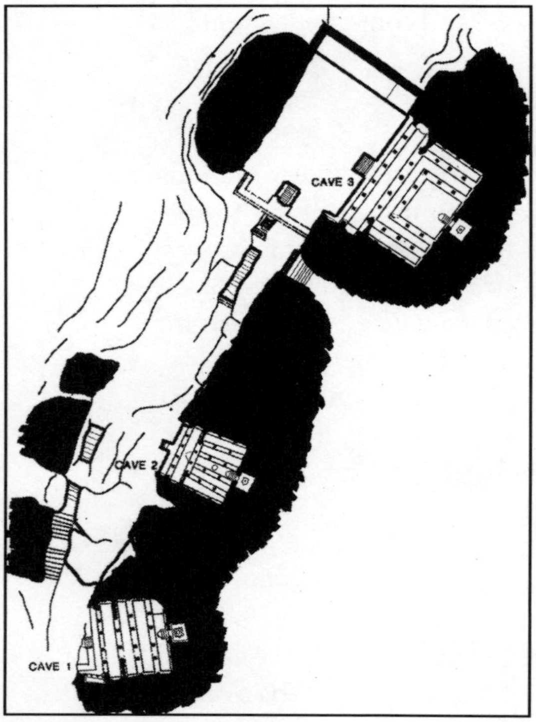

Fig. 31. Bādāmī: Rock-cut cave nos. I, II, III, plan (after Huntington 1985).

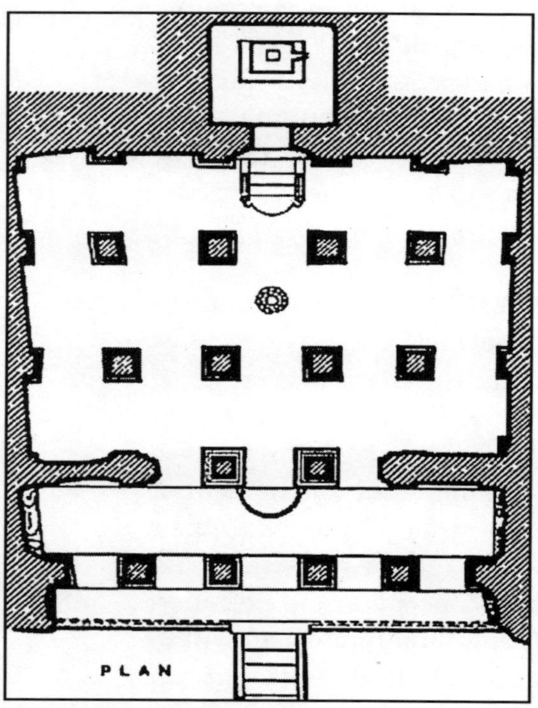

Fig. 32. Bādāmī: Rock-cut cave no. II, plan (after Soundara Rajan 1981).

human'.[51] It is then unlikely that Mangalesha or his successors would construct shrines smaller or less ambitious than those already existing at the site. Thus, the shift throughout the Cālukyan period was from modest to larger and more ornate temples, culminating in the structural Virūpāksha temple, Paṭṭaḍakal, the glory of Cālukyan architecture in the Deccan. Hence, a clear-cut evolution of which the first stage was cave I, next cave II, and the climax in cave III. This evolution coincided with the ascending topographical order also.

Ground Plan

The group at Bādāmī, by the high standard of its workmanship, proved the excellence achieved in rock-cut architecture over its initial beginnings at Aihoḷe. In their general appearance and interior arrangements, these excavated shrines represented the same type. Their exteriors displayed no outstanding architectural effect. The façade showed merely the range of pillars forming the *mukhamaṇḍapa* with a running frieze of *gaṇas*, carved in relief on the *śaduram* of each pillar. In their formal arrangements, the Bādāmī caves stood between the Buddhist *vihāra* of Ajantā and the Brāhmanical temples of Ellorā. The stressed division between their *mukhamaṇḍapa* and *mahāmaṇḍapa* was reminiscent of the Buddhist tradition. This was done by retaining a bay of stone between the pillars closest to the wall, in the second row of pillars and the wall itself. This had the same effect as closing off the whole front of a *vihāra* by a wall[52] besides setting off the *mukhamaṇḍapa* area from the *mahāmaṇḍapa* proper.

Under the basic plan of the Bādāmī cave temples (Fig. 31) a small *garbhagṛha* in the rear wall was approached through the pillared *mahāmaṇḍapa*, divided by raised floor and *uttira* beams into transverse aisles. The entrance to the hall differed from that of the Buddhist caves.[53] As a homogenous group, both caves I and II exhibited some common features (Fig. 32). Both had a façade of five bays opening into the *mukhamaṇḍapa*. The *mukhamaṇḍapa*, through the device of the blind bays at either end of

Fig. 33. Bādāmī: Cave IV, *mukhamaṇḍapa* interior, (pillars with standing *jina*), from east (after AIIS).

the second row of pillars, reduced the number of bays opening into the *mahāmaṇḍapa* to three. The *mahāmaṇḍapa* comprised of pillars in two rows of four each. The *garbhagṛha*, raised above the level of the *maṇḍapa* by stairs, was sunk in a wall with pilaster decoration. In cave I, however, the overall symmetry of the façade was broken by the addition of a large shrine niche and a sculptural panel outside the cave on the west at a right angle to the façade. There was no major deviation from symmetry in the façade of cave II except for a *gaṇa*, the only four armed one in the series. Cave II marked progress over cave I with its rational layout and its internal and external symmetry.

Cave III's dated inscription not only highlighted its royal foundation but also placed the entire series chronologically.[54] The increase in the *mahāmaṇḍapa* width proportions from four-six pillars and in the size of the sculpture panels suggested that this cave temple was an undertaking of major significance. It was not only greater in size but also in the dimensions of its parts. Its *mukhamaṇḍapa* occupied 70′ compared to 36′ and 28′, respectively, for caves I, II. The transverse aisle of the *mukhamaṇḍapa* was larger than that of the succeeding ones and of exactly the width of the central

Fig. 34. Bādāmī: Cave IV, *mukhamaṇḍapa* interior, pillar details (after AIIS).

Fig. 35. Bādāmī: Cave I, *mukhamaṇḍapa*, frontal pillar *potikā* details (after AIIS).

Fig. 36. Bādāmī: Cave I, *maṇḍapa*, interior pillar details (after AIIS).

longitudinal aisle. As wider *mahāmaṇḍapa* axis emphasized the location of the *garbhagṛha* to which it led, the equally wide *mukhamaṇḍapa* indicated the placement of major sculptural panels occupying its walls at either ends. The cave façade consisted of six pillars and two pilasters while its *mukhamaṇḍapa* opened to the outside through seven bays. The *mahāmaṇḍapa* opening was reduced to five bays by the blind bays at the back of the *mukhamaṇḍapa* proportionately. Cave III was shallower in depth than either caves I or II. The arrangement of *maṇḍapa* pillars suggested that the plan was based on the elimination of four of them to create more space in front of the shrine.[55] The cave width being greater than its depth was a feature also found in a few Hindu caves at Ellorā and some Pallava excavations in the south.[56]

The Jaina cave plan was largely based on that of the Brāhmanical ones, with one major difference. It had no *mahāmaṇḍapa* but a pair of *mukhamaṇḍapas*, one behind the other, the second opening directly into the *garbhagṛha*. Like caves I and II, it had a façade of four free standing pillars and two pilasters and also had the side pillars of the second row attached to the sidewall by blind bays (Figs. 33-34). It bore resemblance to cave III in its relative shallowness and in the pillar spacing. Similar to cave III but unlike caves I and II, the width of the aisle on the central axis of the cave was not only larger than the flanking aisles but exactly equal to the width of the transverse aisle of the *mukhamaṇḍapa*.

Fig. 37. Bādāmī: Cave I, *maṇḍapa*, interior view (after AIIS).

Pillars

At Bādāmī too, the pillar constituted an important part of the architectural scheme. The simplest and standard pillar type was a square shafted, *potikā* capital pillar in cave I façade (Figs. 35-36). It was used throughout in the *mahāmaṇḍapa* of the three Hindu caves and with the addition of a simple and relatively slight *vyāḷa potikā*, served as the façade pillar in cave II. The decoration of the pillar shaft remained an integral part of the Cālukya style (Fig. 37). Eventually, the *paṭṭikā* was reduced to a more subtly integrated octagon though the *śaduram* below, with its horizontal band and pendant droops of pearl swags emerging from the *kīrtimukhas'* mouths, remained constant.

Another pillar type consisted of a 'cushion' capital between its shaft and *taraṅga potikā* (Figs. 38-40). In cave I this form occurred in the row of two pillars and two pilasters that separated the *mukhamaṇḍapa* from the *mahāmaṇḍapa* (Fig. 41). These round cushion capitals, in some ways, were similar to those found among the Kalacuri monuments

Fig. 38. Bādāmī: Cave I, *maṇḍapa*, pillar details (after AIIS).

Fig. 39. Bādāmī: Cave II, pillar detail (after AIIS).

near Bombay[57] and several shrines ranging from mid to late sixth century at Ellorā.[58] The cushion capital pillars dividing the *mukhamaṇḍapa* and *mahāmaṇḍapa* in cave II were mainly square. Cave III contained very elaborate cushion capital pillars (Figs. 42-43), both in the round and square forms (Figs. 44-45; Pl. 16), for separation of its *mukhamaṇḍapa* and *mahāmaṇḍapa*. Here the cushion was provided a more complex form (Fig. 46). This more elaborate type, though known to the builders of caves I and II was used only in minor decorative details and less distinctively by them.

Cave III façade featured the most admirable creations of the Cālukya artist in the form of bracket figure capital (Fig. 47; Pls. 17-18).[59] These bracket figures were attached to cushion capitals of the complex types. Put atop the square pillars, they consisted primarily of *mithunas* in amorous poses. These, in a way, symbolized the transition between the vertical pillars and the often elaborately carved ceiling panels in the Early Western Cālukya monuments. The idea of putting bracket figures on façade-pillars may have been inspired by Vākāṭaka and Kalacuri examples in Ajantā cave 20, Aurangābād cave 1 and Ellorā cave 21, while the grouping of figures in elegant pairs was specifically Cālukyan. Ultimately, bracket figures became the main decorative motif in later Deccan styles as that of Kākatīyas.

Fig. 40. Bādāmī: Cave I, *mukhamaṇḍapa* pillar, pecking geese and swag, details (after AIIS).

A view down the length of the *mukhamaṇḍapa* showed the square pillars of the façade and pillars with round cushion capital and heavy vertical ridges separating the *mukhamaṇḍapa* from the *mahāmaṇḍapa*. These were similar to

Fig. 41. Bādāmī: Cave I, *maṇḍapa*, interior view (after AIIS).

Fig. 42. Bādāmī: Cave I, *maṇḍapa* pillar, cushion capital, detail (after AIIS).

the ones at Elephanta suggesting more explicitly than Rāvaṇa Phaḍi, the Cālukyan links with other Deccan traditions.[60]

The *kīrtimukha* and swag motif (Figs. 48-49) in the Bādāmī caves bore similarity to the decoration of the shaft *śadurams* of the pillars fronting the *Naṭarāja* and *mātṛkā* panel niche in Rāvaṇa Phaḍi marking the simplest and earliest usage of the motifs. In cave III, IV both the inner and outer pillars of the *mukhamaṇḍapa* represented the cushion capital types (Fig. 50).

Pillar Arrangement

The first two Brāhmanical caves, apart from being smaller, differed from cave III in the arrangement of the pillars within the *mahāmaṇḍapa*. In each instance, the pillars were eight and placed at equidistance from each other, except those in the central aisle (Fig. 51). Here the inter-columniation was slightly wider introducing a longitudinal

Fig. 43. Bādāmī: Cave II, *prastara* and pillar capital, detail (after AIIS).

Fig. 44. Bādāmī: Cave III, *mukhamaṇḍapa* pillar, type 1.

Fig. 45. Bādāmī: Cave III, *mukhamaṇḍapa* pillar, type 2.

orientation into the temple interiors. The façade of each of the smaller temples consisted of an arrangement of four pillars forming the *mukhamaṇḍapa* on the inside, of which two pillars were placed at the *mahāmaṇḍapa* entrance (Fig. 52).

The arrangement of pillars in cave III *mahāmaṇḍapa* was actually a series of rows of pillars, four of which had been eliminated to create open space in front of the shrine. The *mukhamaṇḍapa* was separated from the *mahāmaṇḍapa* by four freestanding pillars and two pilasters *in antis*, all with high bases. The two central pillars consisted of a square shaft with thin and slightly narrower slabs applied to each face. The two pillars outside these were octagons (Figs. 53-54).

The unique arrangement of pillars into a double colonnade within cave III *mahāmaṇḍapa* differentiated it from the other two Brāhmanical caves.[61] It created a large open space fronting the *garbhagṛha* comparable to the open area within a *vihāra*. It viewed quite unique when looked at from the *garbhagṛha* (Pl. 19). By this *garbhagṛha* placement at the center of pillar arrangement, an exceptional visual and spatial clarity (Pl. 20) was achieved and the great Vaiṣṇava cave at Bādāmī acquired a distinction. Standing in the Trimūrti cave *garbhagṛha* at Elephanta or in the multi-pillared halls of Ellorā or more aptly in Bādāmī caves I and II, one is surrounded by an array of pillars generally equidistant spacing right up to the *garbhagṛha* entrance. These, however, lacked the visual delight provided at Bādāmī III by the absence of the four pillars permitting one to comprehend the organization of the space occupied by him.[62] Thus, they lacked Bādāmī cave III's

Fig. 46. Bādāmī: Cave III, pillar cushion, detail (after AIIS).

Fig. 47. Bādāmī: Cave III, façade, bracketed pillars.

comprehendible interior clarity of organization while the open area unified the space and stressed the central focus on the *garbhagṛha,* further signifying its developed form.

Façade

The distinct grouping and interrelationship of Bādāmī caves was also apparent from their façades that comprised of the *adhiṣṭhāna,* pillars and *prastara.*

Fig. 48. Bādāmī: Cave I, pillar, details (after AIIS).

Fig. 49. Bādāmī: Cave II, *kīrtimukha* and swag motif, *mukhamaṇḍapa* (after AIIS).

The *adhiṣṭhāna* in caves I and II featured continuous *gaṇa* panels, framed by simple mouldings and capped by a simple *kapota*. These dado *gaṇa* panels representing the unseen categories of existence underlying and supporting the temple, were a major hallmark of the earliest style.[63] In both cases, the motif was used not only as a base for the temple as a whole but as a dado for each of the major sculptural panels as well. This conceptualization reached its peak in cave I, in the attached shrine niche of the façade.[64] In cave III, the *gaṇa* dado motif was subordinated to the architecture of the façade and to some extent, superseded and discarded. In cave IV, it was discarded altogether. In cave III, the *gaṇas* were placed within an architectural framework of pilasters. There were pairs of *gaṇas* occupying niches in the *adhiṣṭhāna* tied coherently together by pilasters that were coordinated with *kūḍūs* in the basement *kapota*. This way, the *adhiṣṭhāna* as a whole was shown as a fully elaborated microcosm, having its own basement, colonnade created in form of the pilasters and inhabited by *gaṇa* and *prastara* in the *kūḍū-kapota* which was structurally linked to basement below by the pilasters.[65] The *kūḍū-kapota* was further decorated by *haṁsa* motif alternating with the *kūḍūs* along its full extent. This *animal kūḍū-kapota* was henceforth the basic form found in most of the developed Cālukya temples. In caves I and II, *kapotas* without *kūḍūs* or animals were the usual norm.[66] These devices were rather decorative in nature than being structural components of the *kapota*.

Prastara

In caves I, II style, the *prastara* was a broad lintel overhanging the colonnade (Figs. 56-57). In cave III, this lintel remained unfinished (Pl. 21). The preliminary blocking out from the east, however, suggested that it was going to be an architecturally conceived,

Fig. 50. Bādāmī: Cave III, fore-pillar capital and bracket (after AIIS).

fully articulated *prastara* of three levels corresponding to its *adhiṣṭhāna*. A more fully worked out version may be seen in the façade of the contemporary Rameśvara cave at Ellorā.[67] Cave IV was unfinished in its façade with large ridges of stone still adhering to its *adhiṣṭhāna*.

Dvāraśākhās

The design of the *garbhagṛha dvāraśākhās* further corroborated the gradual evolution of the caves. A study of the wall separating the *mukhamaṇḍapa* from the *sabhāmaṇḍapa* reinforced the fact that cave III was posterior to the first two caves. In cave I, there was an attempt to carve a doorframe between the *mukhamaṇḍapa* and the *mahāmaṇḍapa* (Fig. 58). But only *dvāraśākhās* were carved on each side. An overdoor could not continue them because the whole bay represented too wide a space to be covered. In cave II, the width of the bay was reduced and the area of the dividing walls was correspondingly increased. By this two features were made possible: (i) a full *dvāraśākhā* was carved, and (ii) the surface of the dividing walls could be used for sculptural carvings (Fig. 59). This development of the *dvāraśākhā* and the dividing walls clearly indicated that cave

Fig. 51. Bādāmī: Cave I, *maṇḍapa* pillars (after AIIS).

II followed cave I. Cave III was a step ahead. The side panels introduced in cave II were given equal value with other panels in cave III. They were occupied by large sculptures of Varāha and Harihara. Considering the cave proportions, a *dvāraśākhā* would have appeared unrealistic. Instead, the *prastara* was kept continuous and carved with a narrative frieze.

Regarding its *garbhagṛha dvāraśākhā*, cave I was the simplest of the series. Like the other three caves its entrance was raised a few feet above the level of the *mahāmaṇḍapa*. It had a plain *prastara*. The only iconic sculptures related to the composition were the *śaṁkha* and *padma nidhis* occupying the bracket squares of the *mahāmaṇḍapa* pilasters flanking the doorway.[68]

The door to cave II, similar to cave I, was also flanked by a similar *nidhi* pair. The *dvāraśākhā* mouldings had small male and female figure bases. Cave II added an elaborate *prastara* comprising three *kūṭa* separated by single *kūḍū*. It was a very significant addition, as this *prastara* of linked pavilions became the standard over door decoration in the succeeding development of the Cālukyan temple. The fact that the three *kūṭa* of the *prastara* were more or less equal was important for establishing this as an early attempt at the motif. The later versions were usually hierarchical and complex taking several differing types of *kūṭa* in their organization. This may be seen in the *kūṭa* decorating cave III and IV lintels.

Fig. 52. Bādāmī: Cave I, *mukhamaṇḍapa*, interior view (after AIIS).

Fig. 53. Bādāmī: Cave III, *maṇḍapa*, fore-pillar base (after AIIS).

Cave III marked a tentative step toward the standard *dvāraśākhā* type found among the structural temples. Herein five *kūṭa* were arranged symmetrically (Fig. 60). The central one was a barrel-vaulted structure seen from the side *śālā-kūṭa*, and the flanking pairs were square pavilions with domed *śikhara* similar to the Draupadī *ratha* at Mahābalipuram showing *karṇakūṭa*. The outermost of these pairs was further distinguished by a second elaboration of its outer profile indicating that the full *prastara* represented a series of linked pavilions. These *kūṭa* were inhabited by *garuḍārūḍha* Viṣṇu in the central *śālā-kūṭa*, female figures in the flanking *karṇa-kūṭa* and, auspicious *mithunas* in the outer *karṇakūṭa.* This *dvāra* carried further the elaboration of cave II by adding *dvārapāla* figures, flanking the stairs, and *mithunas* flanking the *dvāra* base. The *nidhis*, each with a consort, were placed as in the other caves. Cave IV had an over door of three pavilions separated by indistinct figures, probably *nidhis*. The outer pair comprised of seated *jinas* while the central one was filled by a large empty *kūḍū*. Small *dvārapāla*, similar to those found in cave III though in much lower relief, flanked the *dvāra* base.

Sculptures

Akin to architectural elements, in sculptural component also, Bādāmī rock excavations imbibed two distinct patterns. The quality of sculptural forms and decoration

Fig. 54. Bādāmī: Cave I, pilaster, base, east end (after AIIS).

emphasized the excellence of the Cālukyan plastic art. In contrast to the unassuming exteriors, the treatment of the interiors was suggestive of the rock carver's profound skills. Passing from the outside bright sunlight into its dark pillared *maṇḍapas* one gets bewildered by the sculptural wealth of symbolism and mystical imagery prevailing on all sides. While the caves I, II style was relatively simple and tended towards decorative ornamentation emphasizing *gaṇa* panels; its sculptures were somewhat static and tightly confined to their architectural niches. The caves III, IV style was more evolved and complex including sophisticated devices as the *aṣṭadikpālas* in cave III. Cave III sculptures were more dynamic and dramatic, often breaking the isolation and containment of the wall and the frame. The area available for decoration was fully utilized. Aspects of the caves I, II style such as the use of *gaṇa* panel basements and the rigid frames for major sculptures were lacking in the caves III, IV style.

Caves I/II Sculpture

The major sculptures of caves I, II constituted panels at either end of their façade and *mukhamaṇḍapa*. In cave I, a large *dvārapāla* was placed on the east and the sculpture niche depicted dancing *Ardhanārī*. Each of these sculptures was placed within a frame over a dado panel. In every panel, except the *dvārapāla*, the dado panel contained frolicking *gaṇas*.[69] Cave II followed the same format except that the *dvārapāla* at either end of the façade faced each other. This was a somewhat unusual position, similar to

Fig. 55. Bādāmī: Cave III, *adhiṣṭhāna*, *gaṇā* frieze, left of steps (after AIIS).

Fig. 56. Bādāmī: Cave I, entablature of entrance to *maṇḍapa* (after AIIS).

that of the Rāvaṇa Phaḍi *dvārapāla* in Scythian dress. It may have been inspired by the position of Gaṅgā and Yamunā at Ellorā cave XXI. Stylistically, with their graceful modeling, relaxed pose and stylized *jaṭāmakuṭa*, the *dvārapāla* resembled those in Ellorā cave XXIX. In the *mukhamaṇḍapa*, two major Viṣṇu images of Varāha (on the east) and *Trivikrama* (on the west) faced each other. Here too, the figures stood within definite architectural frames and over dado panels, each containing sporting *gaṇas*.

Fig. 57. Bādāmī: Cave I, *prastara*, detail (after AIIS).

Fig. 58. Bādāmī: Cave I, entrance to *maṇḍapa*, details (after AIIS).

Fig. 59. Bādāmī: Cave II, pilaster and doorframe, left (after AIIS).

Caves III/IV Sculpture

The quantity and scope of the large images was greater in cave III. Besides at either ends of the façade and *mukhamaṇḍapa* figures were put in the blind bays too that were left blank under caves I, II style. Just two of them were placed over dado *gaṇa* panels, the rest all standing at a level with the floor of the cave, facing the onlooker. Distinct frames disappeared as the figures stood within the architecture of the temple. Cave IV seemed closer to cave III. The shrine image of Mahāvīra and those of Gomateśvara and Suparśvanātha were carved on the *mukhamaṇḍapa* ends. Besides, the large *jina* panel at either ends of the inner *mukhamaṇḍapa* and on the blind bays were perhaps later additions.

The figures in the caves III, IV style transcended their architectural frames in a variety of means. The cave III *Trivikrama* panel offered a clear example of the images transcending the enclosing frames of the surrounding architecture. It showed Viṣṇu's attendants shifted onto the cave ceiling while Rāhū ran around the corner of the wall and faced in toward the façade. In yet another instance the *śeṣāsana* Viṣṇu and the Varāha on the blind *mukhamaṇḍapa* bay were linked by *nāgin* figure that appeared in both the panels at the same time, thereby, ending their distinction as two separate panels.

A comparison of the *Trivikrama* panels occurring in both caves II, III enables one to comprehend the device of breaking down frame pattern in caves III, IV style. It was perhaps part of an overall tendency to bring the images into closer psychological contact with the worshipper. In cave II, the *Trivikrama* stood within a square panel framed by the pilasters of the *mukhamaṇḍapa* on the sides, a dado panel of six dancing *gaṇas* below and a decorated *kapota* carrying an image of *Naṭarāja* above. The composition of the scene emphasized both the square limits of the panel and the flat ground from which the relief was projected. The major motif of the *Trivikrama* rose in a plethora of limbs and weapons that jostled the frame and hold him within it. The *vāmana* Viṣṇu beneath his *chatra* lined up statically with the assorted demons of Bali. Forms rising from and

Fig. 60. Bādāmī: Cave III, *garbhagṛha* (after AIIS).

Fig. 61. Bādāmī: Cave II, *mukhamaṇḍapa*, west wall, *Trivikrama* (after AIIS).

Fig. 62. Bādāmī: Cave III, west wall, *Trivikrama* (after AIIS).

returning to the flat wall characterized the relief. The flat, contained and static qualities predominated the panel (Fig. 61).

In contrast, the *Trivikrama* in cave III was a different conception. Though it was twice the height and over four times the panel size in cave II, it contained fewer figures. It was neither placed above a decorative dado panel nor caught within an enclosing architectural frame. It stood on the same level as the worshipper and reached out from the pilaster that marked its connection with the façade, to overlap both the overhanging *kapota* and the ceiling above. Perhaps its most remarkable feature was that it could not be seen easily from any convenient location. Curving across the sidewall of the façade and up into the ceiling, it required that the worshipper approach it specifically to fully view it. The composition in cave II stressed half and low relief although several of its parts were nearly three-quarters free of the wall. In cave III, the three-quarters relief and deep undercut were stressed (Pl. 22). While the flat ground of the panel was stressed in cave II, cave III was predominated by the curving, rather concave movement of the figures. The background of the panel was not stressed rather obscured by the curving paths of the figures raised from it.

None of the figures in cave III *Trivikrama* panel were full front, with the single exception of Brahmā who measured the height of Viṣṇu's stride as his foot approached the severed head of Rāhū (Fig. 62).[70] As an effect, instead of being a static icon, the deity was brought out into the actual space of the worshipper.

The Varāha in caves II, III[71] showed the same basic differences as seen in the *Trivikrama* panels. The cave II Varāha was positioned within a frame on the *mukhamaṇḍapa* wall. Its controlled relief exhibited the two dimensional outlines predominating over the projection of the forms. In a *pratyālīḍha* pose, his profile form had the left leg rested on a lotus placed on the coiled *nāgarāja*, suggestive of the seas below. Bhūdevī stood on another lotus held in the Varāha's natural left hand and leaned against his snout. His natural right hand rested on hip. His second right hand held the *cakra* and second left hand held the

Fig. 63. Bādāmī: Cave I, ceiling, coiled *nāga* (after AIIS).

śaṁkha besides passing behind to support Bhūdevī's body. Each element, here, was shown clearly in profile or full front. The Varāha in cave III depicted a complex use of space. Its frame was the architecture of the cave, except for the dado panel of *gaṇas*. It was linked to the *śeṣāsana* panel by a figure that leaned across from one panel to the next. The pose of the Varāha was identical to that in cave II, with the exception of the left arms. The natural left arm was curved visibly behind Bhūdevī to hold the *śaṁkha* more explicitly than in cave II panel. The second left arm was not shown at all, but rather indicated by the hand appearing out of the neutral space of the panel to support the Bhūdevī's *padmapīṭha*. The plastic use of space was typical of the great sophistication of cave III style.

Thus, these two panels in both the caves exhibited the gradual expertise achieved by the sculptors. Cave II sculpture was the most conservative at the site while *Trivikrama* in cave III was the site's most dramatic and advanced panel. The cave I panels were cut deeper than cave II, but exhibited a basically static and removed quality. Stylistically akin to cave III, cave IV was sculpturally incomparable as Jaina art, being quite static and conservative in nature.

Fig. 64. Bādāmī: Cave II, series of ceilings (after AIIS).

Narrative Panels

Each of the caves possessed rich and varied architectural or pseudo-architectural decorations. The Hindu caves had narrative panels around the *mukhamaṇḍapa* lintels with full complement of pillar and lintel decorations throughout. In cave I, seven of the twelve surrounding lintels were decorated. In cave II, all the five panels facing out from the *mukhamaṇḍapa*'s inner side carried narrative scenes of *kshīrasāgaramanthana*. The western panel of the outer lintel consisted of *mithunas*, the remaining four inward facing lintels depicting narrative scenes derived from Kṛṣṇa legends.

Cave III exhibited full use of its fourteen lintels facing into the *mukhamaṇḍapa*. The inner seven depicted *kshīrasāgaramanthana* while the outer seven were related to the Kṛṣṇa myths. The end lintels also carried *nābhikamal* Brahmā motif which also occurred in cave II.[72] Cave IV had no narrative scenes.

Ceiling Panels

The Bādāmī caves also preserved remarkable *mukhamaṇḍapa* ceiling decorations. All, except the central ceiling of cave I, contained motifs isolated in the center of large rectangular panels. There were lotuses in the outer pair and *gāndharva-apsarā* couples flanking the central bay. The central bay was fully filled with a coiling five-hooded *nāgarāja* (Fig. 63). The ceilings of the second cave were mostly filled with overall patterns (Fig. 64). There was a *matsyacakra* in the central bay (Fig. 65) and *nandyāvartta svāstikas* in the flanking bays. The outer ceilings had raised isolated images as *gāndharva-apsarā*, *garudārūdha* Viṣṇu, etc. The *garuḍārūḍha* Viṣṇu ceiling was divided by a painted overall design consisting of a central circle with equal circles in each of the four diagonal corners. Hence, supposition that all of the ceilings once contained overall designs in which the raised central portion was surrounded by either sculptural or painted decoration.[73]

Cave III had all its seven ceilings divided geometrically into overall patterns with raised central panels featuring gods. The western-most panel was blank except for traces of paint in a similar design. The eastern ceiling contained an unidentified deity in the center of a design of nine unequal rectangles formed by four intersecting tangents of the central *puṣpāvallī*.[74]

Fig. 65. Bādāmī: Cave II, ceiling with *matsya-cakra* (after AIIS).

The five central ceilings were organized on *aṣṭadikpāla* pattern. This further testified the more complex and sophisticated planning characterizing cave III. The five ceilings ran sequence wise from west to east as: Varuṇa, Brahmā, Viṣṇu, Śiva, Indra. Varuṇa, the guardian of the west, and Indra, the guardian of east, were assigned their respective directions. Placed between them the trinity highlighted Viṣṇu, to whom the cave temple was dedicated. The *dikpālas* occupied both the Brahmā and Viṣṇu ceilings within the *mukhamaṇḍapa* and the *navamaṇḍala* ceiling of the *mahāmaṇḍapa* within the interiors.

The Brahmā ceiling was composed with a central *haṁsārūḍha* Brahmā, surrounded by eight smaller medallions consisting of Indra, Yama, Varuṇa and a male figure[75] seated on a lion, respectively on the east, south, west and north. The intervening medallions contained *mithunas*. The *mahāmaṇḍapa* also had a Brahmā ceiling.

The *mukhamaṇḍapa* Viṣṇu ceiling had the only fully enumerated series at the site. A fully worked out *aṣṭadikpāla* set comprised the eight medallions surrounding the central circle of Viṣṇu. This was a device to elevate the principal shrine deity and to distinguish the central axis of the temple with more elaborate and ornate designs. Indra, Yama, Varuṇa, and the lion seated figure were placed around Viṣṇu in the east, south, west and north, and in between them Agni, Vāyu, Īśāna and Brahmā defined the intermediate 'quarters'. This was possibly the earliest known *aṣṭadikpāla* group in a dated monument.

Fig. 66. Ellorā: Cave XVII, rear aisle sculptured pillars (after AIIS).

The Jaina cave had a single ceiling panel of a flying *gāndharva apsarā* couple in the bay opposite its shrine.

Paintings

Cave III retained some figure paintings on its *kapota*, the only surviving instance within the Cālukyan regions. They included scenes of a king's entertainment by dancers and musicians or a king in his court.[76] The paintings resembled the naturalistic style of Ajantā and Sittannavāsal caves.

3. ELLORĀ CAVE TEMPLES

At Ellorā, a site near Aurangābād, witnessing the growth of varied art traditions through the ages, cave nos. XXI, XX, XIV, XIX, XXIX, XXVI, XVII, XVIII, XXVII, XXVIII, etc., may be assigned to the Cālukya phase (Fig. 66; Pls. 23-26). Although any epigraphic evidences do not substantiate this assertion, but the artistic affinity with the Karnataka sites is quite unmistakable.

In plan, the Ellorā shrines revealed a variety. They included both *sandhāra* and *nirandhāra* types. A general tendency was to widen the *maṇḍapas* transversely. Provision for *parivārālayas* was also made as seen in cave nos. XX, XXI, XXII and XVIII. The additional shrines, suggestive of *aṣṭaparivāra* scheme, were provided for in the *maṇḍapas* or the courtyards. The usual plan arrangement comprised of façade, pillared *mahāmaṇḍapa, garbhagṛha*, and sometimes, *ardhamaṇḍapa* (Figs. 67-68). Instances of *nandīmaṇḍapa* may also be cited, though not in caves XVII and XX. In orientation, the caves generally faced west, while at Bādāmī they were north facing.

The *praṇāla*, as a water outlet, was also cut in these caves. The large *dvārapālas*, high ceiling, elaborate *dvāraśākhās*, grid pattern *dikpālas*, Gaṅgā, Yamunā figures, and above all, lavish sculptural embellishments marked out these caves as either Cālukyan or bearing Cālukyan influence.

Fig. 67. Ellorā: Cave XVII, first pillar to left of shrine, details (after AIIS).

Technical Shortcomings

Although the sculptural forms and iconographic representations and decorations bore testimony to the progress of plastic art, yet, the wealth of carving also concealed to some extent, certain shortcomings of the architectural plan. For instance, an uncertainty and indecision in the plan of these temples as a whole was quite noticeable. As the arrangements of the Brāhmanical rock-cut temple were still not final, the correct shape and disposition of its constituent parts had not yet been assured.[76] This was revealed by the inadequate proportions of the pillared *maṇḍapas*, ending at their further ends rather abruptly. This left their shape truncated as if further progress was stopped for want of explicit directions regarding its form, a condition particularly noticeable in cave III. Such uncertainty, in its turn, might have affected the columniation scheme that was not always symmetrical and betrayed some hesitation in the grouping of the pillars. For instance, a wider gap between the two middle rows suggested a central aisle while in cave III the idea of a double colonnade emerged, possibly derived from a similar disposition of pillars at Lāḍ Khān temple. In contrast, the proportions of the interiors may indicate a concession to the limitations of the rock-cut mode, there being some correlation between the wide frontage and the shallow depth, the former giving the maximum light and the latter the maximum space, with which this would efficiently illuminate.

Fig. 68. Ellorā: Cave XXI, pillar and *adhiṣṭhāna*, details.

Influence of Other Styles over Cālukyan Rock-cut Architecture

Gupta, Vākāṭaka, and Kalacuri Influences

Regarding rock-cut architecture, the Cālukyas inherited almost a thousand years old tradition of soft stone excavations. In addition, imported influences resultant from their geographical location in Deccan combined to produce hybrid architecture under them. While their structural temples depicted elements of both northern and southern styles,[77] their excavated shrines also revealed this influence. Despite their originality, the Cālukyan caves had drawn on various forms from Gupta, Vākāṭaka, and Kalacuri traditions. Several features, particularly in the three Bādāmī caves, indicated their affinity with the preceding fifth and sixth century styles in the Deccan. The stylistic ties to Vākāṭaka carvings were apparent in cave I.[78] The *Mahiṣāsurmardinī* iconography was perhaps modeled after a Gupta type.[79]

Both caves I, II at Bādāmī exhibited popularity of frolicking *gaṇas*, a favorite motif in Vākāṭaka and Kalacuri caves as Ajantā cave XXVI and Ellorā cave X. The two *dvārapālas* in cave II *mukhamaṇḍapa* positioned as facing each other bore resemblance to the Cālukyan version of Gaṅgā and Yamunā figures in Ellorā cave XXI. Inside cave III, divine images as in Cālukyan Ellorā cave XXI could be seen with the difference that here the spatial arrangement was free from the two-pillared screens. The idea of having bracket figures on façade pillars might have been inspired by Vākāṭaka and Kalacuri examples at Ajantā cave XX and Aurangābād cave I, besides Cālukyan Ellorā cave XXI. A Kalacuri touch may be detected in the figure of Bhūdevī in the Varāha panel. Above all, the tradition of colossal images was particularly in tune with the Kalacuri caves. Bādāmī cave III, wherein the pillars, sculptured panels, cave interiors and exteriors stand out as massive and powerful, betrays the predomination of the colossal.

While the Bādāmī caves, especially cave III, symbolized artistic culmination, the Rāvaṇa Phaḍi and Jaina cave at Aihoḷe, as a contrast, retained the measured grace and elegance of a slightly earlier period. Their iconography, particularly the *Naṭeśa* surrounded by *mātṛkās* and Śiva receiving the *tripathagā* Gaṅgā, may be indicative of influences from Western India.[80]

Pallava Influence

Besides above-mentioned sculptural and architectural influences, Pallava impact has also been indicated in the Cālukyan caves. The Rāvaṇa Phaḍi has been attributed to the Pallavas after their conquest of Bādāmī (642 AD).[81]The earliest version of the hypothesis advanced by J. F. Fleet (1880)[82] was that the Pallavas had originally occupied Bādāmī and were later succeeded by the Cālukyas who rose to power in the early sixth century. Henry Cousens[83] further elaborated upon the idea. Stylistically, it was justified on the basis of the tall crowns worn by Rāvaṇa Phaḍi figures. However, it is an erroneous opinion with no factual contents. The Pallava tradition of rock-cut cave temples did not take off before Mahēndravarman I (580-630 AD) and the style of his excavations can in no way be related to those at Aihoḷe.[84] Besides, the characteristic Pallava tall crowns were not in vogue before Rajasimha, i.e. before eighth century and certainly later to the Rāvaṇa Phaḍi. Above all, the Vallabheśvara inscription,[85] (543 AD) proclaiming the beginning of Cālukya history and the history of Bādāmī, has pushed back the date of Cālukyan occupation of the site. Also, except the single, indirect reference to the Pallavas in the fragmentary Tamil inscription at Bādāmī, any definite trace of the Pallavas is yet to be found in the Cālukya regions. Thus negation of the theory that the Pallavas remained in the area long enough to have created any monument of significance. The Varāha, *Mahiṣāsuramardinī* Durgā, dancing *mātṛkās*, and *Naṭarāja* were all distinctly Cālukya type figures. Technically also, the Pallava artist's tendency towards softly inflated forms, or the Pallava tableau device of corner figures in profile, or figures seen from behind was unseen in these caves.

Another view suggesting Pallava influence held that the major portions of Bādāmī cave III were altered by the Pallavas to demonstrate their triumph over the Cālukyas in 642 AD.[86] This also seems to be unfounded as it again assumed a prolonged Pallava occupation of the site or concluded that the Pallavas had carved images insulting to the Cālukyas who had allowed these images to remain in their capital. This view also ignored the very contradictory implication of Cālukya Vikramaditya's inscription[87] in the Kāñcī Kailāśanātha temple wherein he stated that the beauty of the Pallava temple was so wonderful that he returned all the spoils and booty to it. The idea of one Hindu ruler re-cutting or distorting another Hindu ruler's temple has no precedent in Indian history. Thus, the fact that the caves were originally Cālukyan, though with certain stylistic affiliations to Western Deccan temple plan stands credible.

Influence of the Artists

Artistic contacts with other parts of India are also apparent in the Early Western Cālukyan temples. These may be explained by their political position as a dominating force in the Deccan, or by the constant conflicts with neighbouring kingdoms as well as by their geographical location. Therefore, artists, sculptors, etc., together with a host of other craftsmen could be brought in from different parts and master architects encouraged to experiment with different techniques and designs. Thus, one aspect of Cālukyan architectural growth may be the influence of the artists. The unprecedented activity, particularly at Bādāmī, which resulted in the fortification of the Vātāpī hill (543 AD) and the excavation of the four caves within a span of nearly fifty years, suggested the presence of a group of skilled and experienced craftsmen, architects, masons, sculptors, stone cutters, apparently under royal patronage.

Where from did the Cālukyas muster up these craftsmen and whether they were recruited locally or accompanied the rulers from places-such elusive questions may be partially solved by the short label inscriptions,[88] about 200 in number, found inscribed on the rock boulders in the vicinity of the cave temples and the 'north fort' at Bādāmī. They seem to mostly record the names and epithets of the artisans working there as many of them are engraved on the sides or façades of the excavations, sometimes, as high as twenty-five feet, accompanied by stone working of some kind. In the vicinity of the shrines specially, the names occur with numerous inscribed vertical strokes as if indicating the number of days worked by respective craftsmen.[89]

Though the inscriptions were mostly in Telugu-Kannada characters, a few were also in *siddhamātṛkā* characters. This implied some sort of northern connection. For instance, Kirtivarman II's Paṭṭaḍakal inscription mentioned *Jñānaśivācārya*, a Śaiva priest hailing from *Mṛgathānikāhāra*, probably Sārnāth on the banks of Gaṅgā.[90] Therefore, an underlying northern component in the composition of craftsmen working at Bādāmī was quite likely.[91] Some Telugu like names with *mañcī* suffix suggested Andhra artists. A Cālukya record[92] discovered in Mehboobnagar district (Andhra Pradesh) mentioned *Cālukya viṣaya* as the province in which the donated village was located. The Cālukyas had enthusiastically undertaken temple-building activity in Ālampur,[93] also in Mehboobnagar district. In addition, the influence of locally recruited craftsmen from around Bādāmī must have also played its due role. Hence, inference follows that a guild of craftsmen, highly skilled in rock-architecture, existed at Bādāmī from the commencement of the Cālukya regime. It was apparently heterogeneous in its composition. However, the nature and exact extent of their respective influence, in the actual art specimens of the Cālukyan sites, is yet to be ascertained.

Cālukyan Art Influence on Other Styles

Some scholars[94] have credited the Cālukyas with the creation of monuments at Ajantā and Ellorā, thereby suggesting the influence of Cālukyas on other styles. However, while distinct relation did exist between the motifs at Aihoḷe or Bādāmī and, at Ajantā, the distinctness was always that the Cālukya motif seemed to have evolved from the latter form. No essentially Cālukyan device appeared in a more developed, parallel or equivalent form at Ajantā. But at Ellorā, the Cālukyas were associated with some Hindu and several Buddhist creations. Although we do not come across any particularly Cālukya forms such as the Bādāmī plan type at Ellorā, nor any inscription linking the dynasty to the site has been recovered. Despite this, Cālukyan influence and creation of art edifices bearing Cālukyan touch was evident at Ellorā. The patronage to Buddhist caves assumed significance as support to the major Hindu sects and even the heterodox Jainism was a major theme of most of their inscriptions. But within the Cālukya territory itself, we get only two references of the Buddhist faith. One was the Padmapāṇi in Bādāmī's natural grotto,[95] the other being the distinct reference to the heterodox faiths casting Śukrācārya, in the form of a Buddha or Bodhisattva in the *Trivikrama* panels of caves II and III.[96]

Cālukyan Cave Sculptural Art Influence on Structural Temple Sculpture

Bādāmī cave III had the most unique and least derivative form of the Cālukya cave sculptural tradition. It symbolized the fully integrated and uniquely Cālukya temple. The evolution of cave III sculptural ideal played little part in the stone icons of the later structural temples. The shift from inside to out and from gigantic to miniature might have been responsible for this. The post-Cālukya cave temples at Ellorā continued to develop similar devices for sculptural transcendence of architectural bounds. On the other hand, the architectural decorations that developed in the cave temples were the basis for much of the later temple decorations.

The plain *kapota* mouldings of Rāvaṇa Phaḍi, which developed eventually into the animal *kūḍū kapota* of cave III, became the established form in the structural temples. The cave III doorframe served as a model for those that followed, as did its pillar and ceiling decorations. Thus, the impact of the caves on the structural temples cannot be denied, particularly with regard to images and decorative sculptures on pillars, ceilings, etc. For instance, the Aihoḷe Durgā temple, with its *gaṇa* friezes and amorous *mithunas* on the façade pillars, revealed a dependence on themes from the Bādāmī cave temples. In the Paṭṭaḍakal Virūpāksha and Mallikārjuna temples, large-scale narrative art was carved on the pillars, together with birds and animals embellished with foliation and bejewelled garlands. The brackets above the outer pillars of Bādāmī cave III became shelter havens for amorous *mithunas* beneath. In the Paṭṭaḍakal temples, especially the Pāpanātha, as well as in those at Aihoḷe brackets were transformed into mythical beasts emerging out of *makaramukhas*, a motif first carved in the Bādāmī caves. The *garuḍārūḍha* Viṣṇu in a ceiling medallion of the Mālegittī Śivālaya was clearly derived from Bādāmī cave II. Its sudarśana *matsyacakra* carved ceiling was imitated at the Aihoḷe Durgā temple and the Jambūliṅga, Bādāmī shrine.[97]

Cave Temple Architecture v/s Structural Architecture

The caves' layout bore general resemblance to that of the prevailing structural temples. This may be understood with regard to the structural Mālegittī and its nearby temple *vis-a-vis* the rock-excavation series. The inadequate design and workmanship of their pillars and the overall inferiority of the structural productions becomes noticeable. Quality wise it is difficult to believe that the structural edifices were executed a century later to the excavations. The two different techniques were indicative of the great change-taking place in the building art at that time. Hitherto, architectural form was determined by the rock-cut method, permanence being assured by the stability of the cliff side. This method was soon about to be superseded by the use of stone masonry. The process was destined to be very gradual as rock-cut method was to persist for several succeeding centuries. The rock-architecture had already achieved a high level while the art of building with stone blocks was relatively in its infancy.

From the variance in the principles of the two modes, it seems fairly certain that each was practiced independently by a separate guild of workmen, according to their specific technique. The courses of both arts suggest that there was a mutual understanding regarding architectural style, but practically they rather progressed on parallel lines. When finally perfected, masonry buildings proved more refined, accommodating and, up to some extent, even more lasting than the sometimes crumbling rock ones. Apart from technical qualities, masonry constructions ushered in a novel architectural content into the temple scheme in the form of exterior elevation, an aspect and dimension hitherto little known to the rock-architect who dealt almost exclusively with interiors. Thus, by the beginning of the seventh century AD, the transition from the rock-cut mode to structural techniques was already underway. Within a short span of time the summits of the sandstone cliffs overlooking Aihoḷe and Bādāmī were furnished with finely wrought buildings executed in a completely new manner.

Hence, the Cālukyan rock-cut shrines formed a distinct stylistic unit of their own. They rightly occupy an integral place within the more elaborate and extensive development process of the Cālukya temple as a whole.

NOTES AND REFERENCES

1. *Cf.* Divakaran, 'The Beginnings of Early Western Chālukya Art', *Chhavi-2*, p. 59.
2. *IA*, VIII, pp. 237 and 287.
3. The name was probably related to the demons Vātāpī and Ilvala. *See footnote no. 7; also* chapter 2 for further details.
4. Bādāmī Inscription, *EI*, XVII, p. 8.
5. Ciplun plates of Pulakeshin II, *EI*, III, p. 5.

6. R.S. Panchamukhi, 1941, *Karnatak Inscriptions*, Vol. I, pp. III-V and 2-4.
7. Local legends relate the demon Ilvala to Aivalli (Aihoḷe) and Vātāpī to Bādāmī. They both wrought havoc upon the northern settlers at Daṇḍakāraṇya and were destroyed by *ṛṣi* Agastya at Mahākūṭa. *Vide IA*, VIII, p. 238.
8. *Cf. IA*, X, p. 102; *also* chapter 2.
9. Probably during the process of Āryanization, *see* chapter 2 for elaboration.
10. The Egyptian geographer Ptolemy (AD 150) mentioned five places of consequence from this region – Badiemaei, Kallingeris, Modogulla, Petirgala and Indi. His Badiemaei may have been Bādāmī. *Cf.* McCrindle, *Ancient India as Described by Ptolemy*, in S.N. Majumdar (ed.), p. 171.
11. Discussed in chapter 6.
12. *See* James Burgess, 1874, 'Report on the First Season's Operations in the Belgām and Kaladgi Districts', *ASWI*, Vol. 1, London, p. 15.
13. He put it about fifty years earlier to Bādāmī ones. *See* Fergusson and Burgess, 1880, *The Cave Temples of India*, London, p. 403.
14. *Vide* Fergusson, 1910, *History of Indian and Eastern Architecture*, (Rev. Edn.) Burgess, Vol. 1, London, p. 121.
15. Percy Brown, *Indian Architecture (Buddhist and Hindu)*, p. 54.
16. *See* Srinivasan, 1964, *Rock-cut Monuments in Archaeological Remains, Monuments and Museums*, ASI, Vol. I, p. 132.
17. Banerji, 1928, *Basreliefs of Bādāmī*, *MASI*, No. 25, p. 2.
18. *Cf.* Spink, 1967, 'Ajantā to Ellorā', *Mārg*, Bombay, pp. 5-6.
19. *Vide* Tarr, 1970, 'Chronology and Development of the Chālukya Cave Temples', *Ars Orientalis*, Vol. 8, p. 157.
20. *See* Cousens, 1911, 'Ancient Temples of Aihoḷe', *ASI Annual Report* (1907-08), Calcutta, p. 189.
21. There is no concrete evidence for any structural temple at Aihoḷe earlier than the inscribed Megutī (AD 634). None of the others can definitely be dated before eighth century. For further reading *refer to* Gary Tarr, 1969, *Architecture of the Early Western Chālukyas*, U.C.L.A, chapter 4.
22. *See* Tarr, 'Chronology and Development of the Chālukya Cave Temples', p. 171.
23. There is no unanimity amongst scholars regarding reasons or meaning for the place names. However, local traditions variously relate and identify the explicitly Śaivite cave with Rāvaṇa, himself a great Śaiva *bhakta*. Sculpturally the ten armed *Naṭarāja* sculpture inside is likened to *daśabhujī* Rāvaṇa. The enshrined liṅga, somewhat slanted, is interpreted as the *kailāśatolana*, or attempt at lifting of the Kailāśa, by Rāvaṇa. Religiously the site was a veneration centre for the Rāvels, a probable sub-sect of the Nāthapanthīs, and visited regularly by them for worship, hence *Rāvel Phaḍi*. As *Rājakuḷa Phaḍi*, it is marked as a place of royal worship. That Cālukya monarchs sponsored such ventures is attested from the Bādāmī Cave III bearing Mangalesha's inscription. Architecturally the low height boulder amidst the cliff resembles a cavern or valley, abode of Śiva. Whatever be the exact motives behind the popular names, it is apparent that this place was a symbol of Śaivite hegemony and preserves memories of Rāvaṇa as a Śaivite devotee. (Information provided by Prof. Pattar, Head, Department of History, Karnatak University, Dharwar, Karnataka on 15th January 2010.)
24. Some writers, on the basis of large crowns worn by several figures, have suggested that the cave must have been excavated after the Pallava invasion (AD 642). *Cf.* Goetz, 1960, *India:*

Five Thousand Years of Indian Art, Baden-Baden, p. 125; *See also* Gupte, 1967, *The Art and Architecture of Aihoḷe: A Study of Early Cālukyan Art through Temple Architecture and Sculpture,* Bombay, p. 70. Stylistically, this seems quite unlikely.

25. In both cases the excavators chose conservative sites in low boulders rising slightly above the caves. Also a more finely grained and harder stone than that used by the Buddhists was chosen in both the instances.
26. *See* Rajasekhara, 1973, 'Identification of the Early Cālukyan Temples', K.V. Ramesh (ed.), *Śrīkanthikā,* Mysore.
27. First Archaeological Report, Pl. XLVIII; also p. 38.
28. *Vide* Tarr, 'Chronology and Development of the Chālukya Cave Temples', p. 176.
29. *See* Fergusson and Burgess, *CTI,* p. 491.
30. *Cf.* Settar, 'A Buddhist *Vihāra* at Aihoḷe', *East and West,* New Series, Vol. 19, Nos. 1-2, pp. 134 ff.
31. *See* Tarr, 'Chronology and Development of the Chālukya Cave Temples', p. 180.
32. *Cf.* Cousens, *Chālukyan Architecture,* p. 32.
33. Similar excavations can be seen in Tāwā and its nearby caves.
34. *Vide* Tarr, 1969, 'The Śiva Temple at Dhokeśvara and the Development of the *Nidhi* Image', *Oriental Art,* Vol. 15, No. 4, pp. 269-80.
35. *See* Spink, Ajantā to Ellorā, *Mārg,* p. 21.
36. *Ibid.*
37. *Ibid.,* p. 22.
38. Burgess opined it to be later than original work in his *Report,* p. 38.
39. Tarr has suggested the possibility of a structural façade in 'Chronology and Development of the Chālukya Cave Temples', p. 171.
40. This format could be seen in the Western Cālukya structural temples of early 8th century. In each, as here, the stress was on the central shrine.
41. *See First Archaeological Report,* Pl. XLVIII; also p. 38.
42. Fergusson and Burgess, *CTI,* p. 492.
43. In about second quarter of the eighth century as held by Tarr, *Vide* 'Chronology and Development of the Chālukya Cave Temples', p. 180.
44. *See* Fergusson and Burgess, *CTI,* p. 405.
45. *Cf.* Banerji, *'Basreliefs of Bādāmī',* pp. 29 ff.
46. *See* Fergusson and Burgess, *CTI,* p. 412.
47. Plan in *Second Archaeological Report,* Pl. XXII.
48. For the inscription *see* J. Eggeling, [1874]1971, 'An Inscription from Bādāmī', *IA,* III, (repr.) Delhi, pp. 305-06; *also* (translation by J.F. Fleet) Burgess, 1877, 'Rock-cut Temples at Bādāmī in the Dekhan', *IA,* VI, pp. 363-64.
49. *Cf.* Huntington, 1985, *The Art of Ancient India,* New York – Tokyo, p. 285.
50. Brown, *op. cit.,* p. 55.
51. 1877, *IA,* VI, pp. 363-64.
52. It limits the amount of light that is allowed to penetrate to the shrine of the temple.
53. The front wall of the *vihāra* with its small windows and doors admitted little light. Herein, while retaining the veranda in front and further protecting the hall from rain and sun by projecting eaves, a large portion of the front was left open. *Vide* J. Burgess in *CTI,* pp. 415-16.
54. This inscription marks the completion of cave III in the five hundredth year following the coronation of the Śaka King (AD 578) and thus acts as an anchor for the otherwise relative

chronology of the caves. The only other date is the *terminus post-quem* of AD 543 for the Cālukya occupation of the site, *see footnote no. 5.*

55. Tarr, 'Chronology and Development of the Chālukya Cave Temples', pp. 157-60.
56. *Cf.* Huntington, *op. cit.*, p. 287.
57. *Refer to* Spink, *op. cit.*, figs. 14-17.
58. *Ibid.*, Figs. 3, 18, 19 and 24.
59. These brackets relate to the creations of the Ellorā artists of the Rāmeśvara cave. *Cf.* Heinrich Zimmer, 1960, *The Art of Indian Asia*, New York, pls. 128-131.
60. Huntington, *op. cit.*, p. 287.
61. Percy Brown has suggested that this is an adaptation of the Lāḍ Khān temple ground plan indicating an interior supported by sixteen pillars set in two concentric squares- four pillars on the inner and twelve pillars on the outer square. *Op. cit.*, p. 52.
62. *Cf.* Tarr, 'Chronology and Development of the Chālukya Cave Temples', p. 160.
63. Their function appears identical to the *yaksas* in similar locations in the Buddhist shrines.
64. In this, above the *gaṇa* dado panel supporting the temple, another panel serves as a dado for the shrine while a third panel is used as a base for the sculptures of the interior.
65. This basement, may be a later addition to the façade of the cave, is structural.
66. An exception can be seen in the narrative friezes around the attic of cave I *ardhamaṇḍapa.*
67. *Cf.* Srinivasan, *Rock-cut Monuments in Archaeological Remains, Monuments and Museums*, pl. XL.
68. This pair appears on the mouldings of the *maṇḍapa* entrance also.
69. The *dvārapāla* stands over a dado containing a buffalo and an elephant sharing a single head, a *vṛṣabha kuñjara*. *Cf.* Banerji, *op. cit.*, pl. II, fig. C.
70. This is analogous to the change of position that takes the Buddha from his frame on the face of the *stūpa* in Ajantā Cave XXVI and projects him 18′ out and onto the floor in front of the *stūpa* in Viśvakarma, Ellorā. *Vide* Tarr, 'Chronology and Development of the Chālukya Cave Temples', p. 172.
71. For the details of the Cālukyan Varāhas *see* Preeti Sharma, 2010 (July-December), 'The Meaning and Symbolism of Varāha Motif: With Special Reference to the Chālukyan Rock-cut Caves at Bādāmī', *Journal of History & Social Sciences*, Vol. I (I), pp. 1-26.
72. This seems to be the earliest version of the *nābhikamal* myth in which the lotus grows distinctly from Viṣṇu's navel.
73. There are several painting fragments left on both the sculpture and decorative carvings in all the Cālukyan caves. *Cf.* Tarr, 'Chronology and Development of the Chālukya Cave Temples', p. 166.
74. Banerji has identified this figure as Varuṇa. *See op. cit.*, p. 56.
75. Only this figure appearing in place of Kubera, the guardian of north, distinguishes this from the usual *Paurāṇic* set. Banerji identifies this as the figure of Buddha, *op. cit.*, pp. 56-57.
76. For description *see* Sivaramamurti, 1959, 'Western Chālukya Paintings at Bādāmī', *LK*, No. 5, pp. 49-58.
77. *Cf.* chapter 3 for details.
78. The delicate treatment of the pillars, the intricate tracery of floral motifs, scrolls and beaded garlands, the graceful bracket figures, use of *gaṇa, vyāḷa, makara* motifs and of the *gāndharva* couples on the ceiling, a line of tiny lion-heads on the *prastara*, etc., recall the Vākāṭaka caves, for instance Ajantā caves 16 and 19.
79. *See* details in chapter 7.

80. *Cf.* Kirit Mankodi, 1973, 'Gaṅgā Tripathagā', *AA,* Vol. XXXV, pp. 139-40.
81. Hermann Goetz, *India: Five Thousand Years of Indian Art*, p. 125; *cf. also* Ernest Hultzsch, 1890 (ed.), *SII,* Vol. I, Madras, pp. 12-13.
82. *Cf.* Fleet, 1880, 'Sanskrit and Old Kanarese Inscriptions', LXXIII, *IA,* Vol. 9, pp. 99-100.
83. Cousens, *Chālukyan Architecture of the Kanarese Districts*, p. 53.
84. *Cf.* Srinivasan, 1964, *The Cave-Temples of the Pallavas,* Madras, pp. 37-43; the stylistic treatment and placement of figures, their robust movements, angularity, etc., are unparallel with the Pallava specimens.
85. *See footnote no. 4.*
86. *Cf.* Lippe, 1964, *Unusual Icons at Bādāmī* (Summaries of Papers of the Twenty-Sixth International Congress of Orientalists), New Delhi, p. 151; *also,* 1967, 'Some Sculptural Motifs on Early Chālukya Temples', *AA,* Vol. 29, pp. 5–24.
87. *Vide* E. Hultzsch, 'The Kāñchī Inscription of Vikramaditya', *EI,* III, pp. 359-60.
88. Published in *SII,* XV, Nos. 277-400; XX, Nos. 258-273; XV, Nos. 415-477; *Karnatak Inscriptions,* I, Nos. 10-12.
89. *See* Padigar, 'Craftsmen's Inscriptions from Bādāmī: Their Significance', *ECSA,* p. 399.
90. *EI,* III, p. 1 ff.
91. The *prastara–kūṭas* of Cave II are of a kind found in association with temple *śikharas* of the northern style. This suggests that by now the difference between southern and northern styles was already recognized and both the temple styles were being used by the Cālukyas. *Vide* Tarr, 'Chronology and Development of the Chālukya Cave Temples', p. 163, fn. 26.
92. *Cf.* Tummeyanuru grant of Polekēśi II, *Copper Plate Inscriptions in Andhra Pradesh Government Museum,* I, pp. 40-45.
93. Details discussed in chapter 3.
94. Tarr, 'Chronology and Development of the Chālukya Cave Temples', p. 182.
95. Banerji, *Basreliefs of Bādāmī*, pl. XIV, fig. A.
96. Although the figure shown pouring water on the Vāmana's hands has been identified as Balī himself, his *mṛgacarm* robe as well as the simple *dhotī* indicates that he is Śukrācārya. Balī is the figure behind, who assists and is accompanied by his queen.
97. *Cf.* Divakaran, 1970, 'Le Temple de Jambuliṅga (date de 699, Ap. J.C.), ë Bādāmī', *Arts Asiatiques,* T, XXI, pp. 15-31.

5

Origin of Monolithic Architecture during the Pallavas

Parallel to the Cālukyan excavations in softer rocks, their contemporary Pallavas revived the mode of carving in hard rocks, redundant since Ashoka and Dasharatha. The Pallavas have been credited with the foundation of distinct and regular school of Draviḍian architecture. They were the first builders in stone in South India.[1] They patronized the earliest South Indian litho-monuments created in the form of cave temples, monolithic shrines, structural temples, and expansive relief panels sculpted upon the hillsides. The architectural character of these edifices was simple and severe, yet, indicative of great strength and durability due to its medium.

The various Pallava monuments may be placed into three distinct periods[2] depending on their forms and styles: (i) the earliest of rock-cut cave temples with an external façade, (ii) the intermediate comprising of cave *maṇḍapams* as well as monolithic *rathas*. It was, thus, an effort of technically excavating units inside the rock and also giving shape by cutting all around, (iii) the later period witnessed growth of structural buildings built of stone and brick. Thus created, the Pallava architecture constituted two types: fully rock-cut, i.e. excavated *maṇḍapams* or *rathas*, and fully structural.[3]

The early cave shrines were excavated during Mahendravarman I. Those belonging to intermediate period were mostly scooped out of rock during Narasimhavarman I while the structural tradition was initiated by Rajasimha.

TEMPLE SITES

The Pallava architectural activities were mainly concentrated in the regions lying immediately around Kāñcīpuram, i.e.Toṇḍaimaṇḍalam. Some artistic productions were located as far south as Tanjore and Pudukkoṭṭai. The Mahendra group *maṇḍapams* were scattered at various sites while *Māmalla* group art creations were clustered at Mahābalipuram. It was a site of a very different character unlike the rural or provincial outposts. Mahābalipuram was a Pallava port of trade and royal seaside residence.[4] Evidences of its intense trade activities are both literary and archaeological. Pallava court poet Daṇḍī[5] (late seventh century AD) and Vaiṣṇava saint Tirumāngai *Ālvār*[6] (eighth century AD) described the merchandise traffic. The *Mahāvaṁśa* also described the departure of two naval expeditions against Srī Lankā from this port during Narasimhavarman I.[7]

Located about 45 miles from the capital Kāñcī, Mahābalipuram was the nearest suitable site for setting up a naval base.[8] The archaeological evidence confirming its status as a port of trade comprises coins recovered from the sands. Some dunes along the beach were so plentifully stocked till the 19th century that they were known as *'kāsi-moḍu'*, i.e. coin mounds.[9] Along with indigenous types, Chinese and Byzantine coins have also been found, the earliest one of Theodosius I (371-395 AD).[10]

The labouriously carved cave temples at Mahābalipuram, far more embellished and sculpted than all the outlying Pallava monoliths combined, perhaps exhibited their special significance for the royal family itself. An evidence for the royal family's personal interests at Mahābalipuram is a labeled pair of royal portraits in the Ādivarāha *maṇḍapam*, which probably represented post-humus ancestral effigies, and not self portraits of the temple patrons as usually suggested.[11] This great concentration[12] of religious monuments charged with imperial content at one site distinguished Mahābalipuram as an important trading and innovative royal art center.

The site has granite cliffs and a rocky hill, rising abruptly from the sandy plain in a solid mass of bare gneiss rock to a height of nearly a hundred feet. The top and sides of this hill were carved, scored or excavated in numerous places. Several of the outlying rocks and detached boulders were hewn into shrines.

LOCATION

The usual location of the cave temples in the south indicates their invariable association with a large irrigation tank[13] or river (*tīrtha*). For instance, the Mahēndravāḍī Viṣṇugṛha near Mahendra *taṭāka*, Māmaṇḍūr cave shrine at Citramegha *taṭāka*, Tiruciráppaḷḷī cave on banks of the Kāverī; Pallāvaram, Śīyamaṅgalam, Mēlacēri and Daḷavāṇūr cave temples not only testified to the cave temples' association with public irrigation works, but also remained indicative of parallel patronage towards religious and agrarian enterprises. Perhaps the location of Pallava temples by dam sites reflected the belief recorded in the *Bṛhat Saṁhitā* that the gods always play where the lakes are.[14] The choice of Mahendra's later Śaivite cave temples was often a renowned Jaina center, probably to proclaim the ascendancy of Brāhmanical cults over the heterodox ones.

MEDIUM

The Pallava monuments, except Tirucirāppaḷḷī cave, were geographically distributed along the flat plains of the Coromandel Coast. The place abounded in low-lying hills of the metamorphic gneiss[15] rocks. The Pallavas emerged as pioneers in tackling of the harder and less tractable rocks as granite, charnockite, and gneiss for excavating cave shrines and carving of monoliths. The absence of softer rock cliffs in their area and a possible belief, as suggested by Srinivasan, in the durability and novelty of material in the local hard rocks may have been the probable reasons for this initiative.[16] Carved from the extremely hard granite gneiss the Pallava rock-cut sanctuaries were virtually impervious to weathering. Even those exposed to the corrosive sea air at Mahābalipuram were first estimated by Fergusson to be not older than five and a half centuries, due to clear crispness of their execution.[17]

However, the novel medium was not without limitations. Owing to the hardness of the material and consequently the greater time taken for working on it, the resultant excavation could only be of lesser depth, height and width compared to those of softer rocks in the Deccan and Western India. The carving and sculptural embellishments were also limited in quantity and executed in semi-relief and large size, in contrast to the numerous smaller and intricate carvings of the Deccan trap and sandstone excavations. The archaic experimental nature of the earliest efforts in carving and the region's intractable rock was apparent in the figures at Māmaṇḍūr, Tirukkaḷukkuṇṛam, Vallam and Kōṭikal *maṇḍapams*. Sometimes, the placement of figures was also conditioned by the availability of suitable rock piece.[18] As the early Pallava shrines were mainly experimental; they adapted the scale of their efforts to the natural rock formations (Pls. 27-28). Adhering strictly to the geometric forms was not deemed imperative. If a recess in the rock necessitated, the plan was accordingly adjusted to accommodate such an irregularity. At times, the natural features of the medium also contributed towards the symbolism of the carvings as exhibited in the cleft of the '*Gaṅgāvataraṇa*' relief.

SCHOLARSHIP

The Pallava monuments, especially those at Mahābalipuram, aroused keen scholarly curiosity and interest. They were first referred to by the Italian travellers[19] and were also noticed by the British when they occupied the region. Later a host of the scholars associated with the Royal Asiatic Society discussed the enigma about the monoliths.[20] Besides scholarly, the fascination became artistic too, when some European artists[21] sketched their details. The site attracted cartographers[22] from an initial phase of its European occupation. Thus, with its varied, enigmatic monuments Mahābalipuram symbolized irresistible charisma for generations of European and Indian scholars who have created a plethora of literature about the site.

NOMENCLATURE

The Pallava rock architecture took up the forms of cut in temples and cut out monoliths. The cut in temples, with shrines in their hind portions, were called *maṇḍapa* and *maṇḍakam* in Tamil[23] as mentioned epigraphically. For instance, the Sittannavāsal and Kuraṅgaṇilmuṭṭam cave temple inscriptions recorded them as *maṇḍakam* or *kal-maṇḍakam*.[24] Their traditional local names also corroborate this designation. The monolithic cave temple at Tirukkaḷukkuṇṛam is called *Orukal maṇḍapam* while several rock-cut temples in Mahābalipuram, Śāḷuvankuppam, Ariṭṭāpaṭṭī, etc., are even now known as *maṇḍapams* or *maṇḍakams*.[25]

The Pallava cut out monoliths, *ratha*, were exact copies in granite of certain structural prototypes. *Ratha*, suggesting a root meaning 'to move', is the Sanskrit word for wheeled vehicle or chariot of a deity. Its Tamil synonym is *ter*.[26] In local dialect the monoliths were popular as the 'seven pagodas' though numerically they constituted nine structures.

CHRONOLOGY

Despite the availability of vast writings, the dating or chronology as well as the sequencing of the Pallava monuments is still not unanimous. Their identification as Pallava edifices was firmly established epigraphically. Nearly half of them were engraved with dedications that identified their patrons as the Pallava kings themselves. As such, in the ongoing debate of dynastic versus regional definitions of style[27] they clearly provided evidence for the former. Such direct links between a period's monuments and its ruling house are either less abundant or non existent in other regions of India where dynastic nomenclature is nevertheless still favoured.[28] The un-inscribed examples are assignable to the same tradition by provenance, i.e. on the basis of geographical proximity to the inscribed ones.[29] For instance, the four caves at Māmaṇḍūr, just ten kilometers south of Kāñcīpuram, may be considered Pallava monuments though only one cave bears a royal dedication. Similarly, the un-inscribed cave at Kuraṅgaṇilmuṭṭam may be considered a Pallava shrine because it is even closer to Kāñcīpuram.[30] The lack of inscriptions may be attributed to their unfinished nature.

Even after their identification, the scholarly opinion remains sharply divided on the dating of these monuments. Since late nineteenth century, a vague consensus has prevailed that they probably belonged to approximately seventh century. However, Fergusson's early denial of any stylistic development among them could not initially be totally refuted. He held that:

> '...They are all of one age and probably the work of one prince...had even one been finished, or had there been any gradation of style or workmanship some chronological arrangement might easily have been traced but nothing of the sort exists...'[31]

Further R. Nagaswamy[32] (1962) proposed a radical chronological reattribution. Relying on epigraphic considerations and agreeing with Fergusson over the lack of any significant stylistic evolution among the monuments, he assigned the entire chronology to a single generation, declaring Rajasimha as the sole patron of all the Mahābalipuram monuments. His theory was widely accepted.[33] Dubreuil, Longhurst, Srinivasan and Lockwood endorsed the traditional multi-generational chronology view.[34] Another opinion[35] held Mahendravarman I as the principal creative force behind the monuments. Thus, the primary factor affecting the chronology of the Pallava temples has been the issue of their authorship.

However, in addition to epigraphic evidences, taxonomic and stylistic analysis has also been utilized to ascertain this. Taxonomy, or the dating of architecture and sculpture by classification of their ornamental motifs, has been the special forte of the French school.[36] As a pioneer of this approach to art history J. Dubreuil put forth the 'principle of the synchronism of Draviḍian styles'[37] and introduced the dynastic nomenclature. He classified the inter-generational changes in the Pallava art through the study of pillars and *dvārapāla* types.[38] Later, Lockwood and his colleagues used the computerized rigour of numerical taxonomy for the study of Pallava *Somaskandas*.[39] Besides, on the basis of architectural stylistic development, Rabe divided Pallava art into archaic, severe and classical styles[40] while Srinivasan classified the cave temples as Mahendra and *Māmalla* styles assigning them to individual rulers.[41]

ORIGIN OF THE PALLAVA ROCK-CUT ARCHITECTURE

The Pallava rock-cut architecture acquired its form under Mahendravarman I as claimed by his Maṇḍagappaṭṭū inscription.[42] Longhurst suggested that Mahendra developed the taste for rock-cut temples from the Buddhists living in the Telugu country at the beginning of his reign, during his brief sojourn there.[43] This assumption is based on the similarity between the early cave temples in Tamil regions and those at Bezwada, Mogalrājapuram, and Uṇḍavallī, which Longhurst assigned to Mahendra. But Dubreuil[44] held that Bezwada and Uṇḍavallī caves were excavations by Viṣṇukuṇḍins, who had occupied banks of Kṛṣṇā and Godāvarī and were neighbours to the Pallavas when the latter reigned over Nellore and Gunṭur towards the end of sixth century. It is likely that Pallavas may have learnt rock excavation from them. But this view is not much acceptable.

The Buddhist origin of rock-architecture in India is more favoured.[45] Its influence on the Pallava tradition, too, is apparent in several architectural features. The *caitya kūḍū* motif, floriated *toraṇas* as depicted in Draupadī *ratha* and bas-reliefs as well as the shape of some monoliths suggest Buddhist art leanings. For instance, the Sahadeva *ratha* possessed clear-cut Buddhist architectural features. Its apsidal halls and wagon roof indicated the *caitya* prototype, while the simulated *śālās* placed over the two terraces were suggestive of the *vihāra* form. Bhīma *ratha* was another classic example of such influence. These buildings resembled the Buddhist ones, both on plan and in design. However, this view is also not without reservations. Buddhism was undoubtedly a force to reckon with in Pallava times and Kāñcīpuraṁ was probably one of its leading centers. Mahendra I refer to a Buddhist monastery in the city in the *Mattavilāsaprahasana*. However, Mahābalipuram art generally betrays Hindu influence. Its makers, some of whose names are inscribed on a rock at Punjeri, were probably all Hindus.[46] It is unlikely for them to have their creations modeled on Buddhist examples when plenty of Hindu exemplars in local art and the Cālukyan triad were available. It might be more appropriate to relate the origin of the diminishing storeys in the pyramidal *śikhara* over Dharmarāja and Arjuna *rathas* to some preceding Hindu model than to the Buddhist *vihāras*. The Buddhist inspiration also gets nullified from the fact that there is just one reference to the Buddha in Pallava art and that too, incidental.[47] None of his sculptures, either anthropomorphic or symbolic, is to be found here. Thus, Mahābalipuram art appears to be purely Hindu in its origin, spirit, form and inspiration.

INFLUENCE OF WOODEN ART

The influence of prevailing wooden architecture was quite apparent in these monuments. The *rathas,* in particular, present petrified versions of existing brick and timber architecture. In the cut-in *maṇḍapams,* the interior architectural aspects of the brick and timber prototypes could be reproduced. In the cut out monoliths, the total external aspect of the brick timber originals was recreated in full with much of their interior aspects in the *maṇḍapas* and *garbhagṛhas* excavated within. The Bhīma *ratha,* particularly imitated the spirit of wooden art. The pilasters with *potikā* brackets supporting the curved *kapota* or shape of the timber framed roof with ornamental ridges and corners were a few of the wooden art features carved in these monuments. As sculptured stone replicas, they reproduced faithfully every detail of the original wooden constructions. Even those like the ribbing below the *kapota,* the nails with boss heads or the timbering and curved rafters below roofs that were functionless and therefore, unnecessary in a monolith, were also copied. Such reproduction of timbering details including the fastenings and joints of wooden originals in the living rock continued from third century BC caves at Gayā and Western India to the sixth to tenth centuries AD cave temples and even to the later structural temples, despite textual canonization of current art traditions.[48] This tendency extended to sculptures also in the form of stucco or wooden image installed as the *dhruva* or *mūlabera* inside the shrines of even the stone sanctuaries. Hence, little doubt over the *ratha* shrines reproducing the *vimānas* of prevailing wood architecture while the *maṇḍapams* imitated the halls constructed mostly of wood.

EXCAVATION TECHNIQUES

Considering the nature of formation and the hardness of the rock, the technique of excavation of the cave temples as well as carving of the monoliths was naturally different from the softer rock technique.[49] Moreover, the method of hewing the caves and the monoliths also differed. The caves were dug deep into the rock. Therein the rough work and finishing probably commenced simultaneously. In contrast, the monoliths were cut out of entire rocks, the process of cutting moving from finial to the plinth. Firstly, a suitable rock was reduced in size and shape to manageable proportions. It was stepped to provide safe footing as well as serve as rough horizontal guidelines for different levels of the building. Small socket holes cut at regular intervals supported the scaffolding. This method of excavation incurred much less labor than production by building. The activity resulted in the creation of about thirty cave shrines and nine monoliths besides bas-sculptures under Pallava patronage.

MONUMENT TYPES

Stylistically, Pallava monuments were usually designated after their patron kings. Under the Mahendra style[50] rock-architecture took up the form of *maṇḍapam,* i.e. an open pavilion excavated in the rock as a simple pillared hall with one or more shrines in the rear wall. Art creations of this style[51] were located at Maṇḍagappaṭṭū, Pallāvaram,

Māmaṇḍūr, Kuraṅgaṇilmuṭṭam, Vallam, Mahēndravāḍī, Tiruciräppaḷḷī, Śīyamaṅgalam and Daḷavāṇūr as also the Pañcapāṇḍava *maṇḍapam* at Vilāppākam and unfinished cave shrine at Aragaṇḍanallūr. Excavations were also found at Tirukkaḷukkuṉṟam, Śiṅgapērumāḷ-Kōil, Śiṅgavaram, Mēlacēri, Māmaṇḍūr, Śāḷuvankuppam, Kīlmāvilaṅgai and Vallam. The monuments assigned to *Māmalla* style and exhibiting some advanced features suggesting a later period were mostly confined to Mahābalipuram. These included the Kōnērī, Varāha, Mahiṣamardinī, Trimūrti, Ādivarāha, Rāmānuja and Yāḷi *maṇḍapams*, the last being at Śāḷuvankuppam.

1. MAṆḌAPAMS

Development of Form in the Maṇḍapams

The architectural features and sculptural representations were indicative of the evolution of art forms in the Pallava excavations. The early *maṇḍapams* were marked by simplicity of plan and ornamentation, paucity of sculptures, and the plain pillars placed therein. In contrast, the later *maṇḍapams* revealed several refined features.

Plan

In plan the early *maṇḍapams* consisted of a large *maṇḍapa* with one or more small *garbhagṛhas* in the rear or sidewall. The Vallam Vasantēśvaram, Mahēndravāḍī, Māmaṇḍūr Viṣṇu cave, and Śīyamaṅgalam *layaṇa*, each had one *garbhagṛha*, cut in the back wall. All temples at Maṇḍagappaṭṭū, Māmaṇḍūr Rudravāliśvaram and Kuraṅgaṇilmuṭṭam Kal-maṇḍakam[52] had three each, Pallāvaram had five, while Vilāppākkam unfinished cave temple consisted of seven *garbhagṛhas*. Besides, the row of pillars and pilasters on the façade, another row running parallel inside the *maṇḍapa* divided it into *ardha* and *mukha maṇḍapa*.[53] The façade faced east, west, north, or south. In the east and west facing cases, the *garbhagṛha* was cut in the back wall, while the *maṇḍapa* façade facing north or south had the shrine cut into sidewalls.

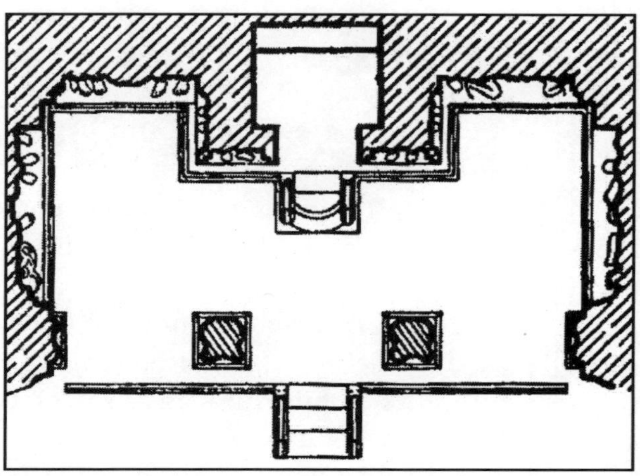

Fig. 69. Mahābalipuram: Varāha *maṇḍapam*, ground plan (after Srinivasan 1993).

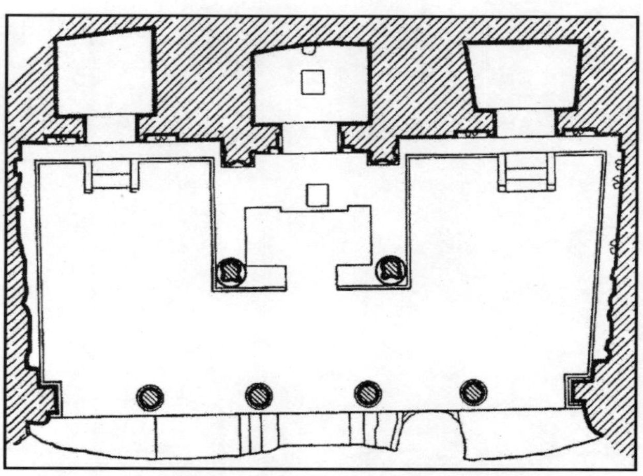

Fig. 70. Mahābalipuram: Mahiṣamardinī *maṇḍapam*, ground plan (after Srinivasan 1993).

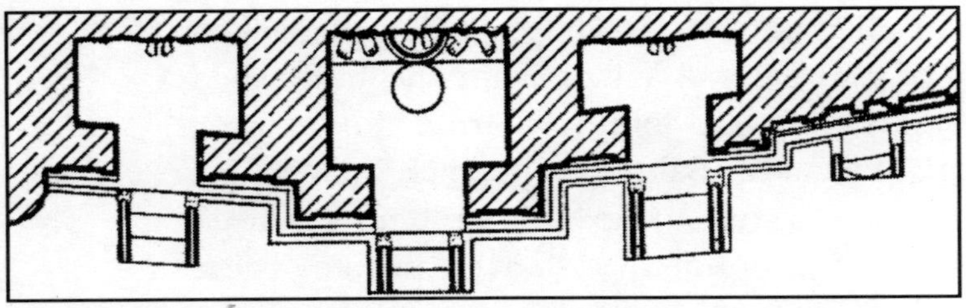

Fig. 71. Mahābalipuram: Trimūrti *maṇḍapam*, ground plan (after Srinivasan 1993).

The later examples at Mahābalipuram also represented *maṇḍapas*, divided or undivided into *mukha* and *ardhamaṇḍapa* by an inner row of pillars parallel to the façade, with one or more shrines in the rear. The shrines were mostly projected into the *maṇḍapa*. The unfinished Pañcapāṇḍava *maṇḍapam* revealed an effort to cut round with the *garbhagṛha* at the center with a pillared *maṇḍapa* all around it. The Mahiṣamardinī cave *garbhagṛha* had a monolithic pillared porch in front inside the *maṇḍapa*, a feature also seen in the early *maṇḍapa* at Daḷavāṇūr. The later excavations represented a fuller representation of the *maṇḍapa* in its frontal and interior aspects. In the early cave temples the front elevation usually ended with the *kapota* or *prastara* suggesting a flat terraced roof. But the later instances had a *hāra* with *hārāntara* connecting *śālās* and *kūṭas*, thereby forming an enclosure above the flat roof. The Trimūrti *maṇḍapam*, as an exception, had no frontal *maṇḍapa*. The practice of multiple *garbhagṛha* also continued. Varāha (Fig. 69) and Ādivarāha *maṇḍapams* each had one *garbhagṛha*; those in Mahiṣamardinī, Trimūrti and Rāmānuja *maṇḍapam* were three (Figs. 70-71), while Kōṇēri *maṇḍapam* had five *garbhagṛhas* in all (Fig. 72).

Garbhagṛha

It normally faced east or west. Pallāvaram was the only instance where the *maṇḍapa* as well as the *garbhagṛha* faced south. *Garbhagṛhas* varied in shape, for example, *āyatārṣa* at Māmaṇḍūr and Śiṅgapērumāḷ-Kōil; *caturārṣa* in Daḷavāṇūr Śatrumalla and Mahābalipuram Kōṭikal *maṇḍapam*; cubical at Vallam and Tiruchirāppaḷḷī Lalitāṅkura. The *garbhagṛhas* were cut at a level higher than the *maṇḍapa* floor and were approached by a *sopāna*. They were often cut into projected shrine fronts consisting of *adhiṣṭhāna* with *kumuda*, *upāna*, *kaṇṭha*, and *paṭṭikā* mouldings; pilasters and *prastara* portions up to the *kapota* mouldings partially anticipating the monolithic *rathas* in elevation.[54] The projected fronts of Tirukkaḷukkuṇram, Orukal and Kōṭikal *maṇḍapam garbhagṛhas* had all such architectural features of a structural temple. In the early caves, no sculptural evidence of the *garbhagṛha* deity survives. A slightly

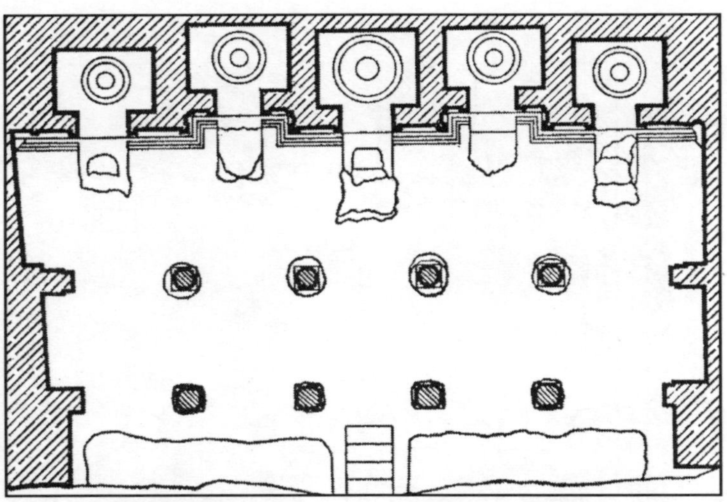

Fig. 72. Mahābalipuram: Kōṇēri *maṇḍapam*, ground plan (after Srinivasan 1993).

Fig. 73. Mahābalipuram: Varāha *maṇḍapam*, *garbhagṛha* entrance (after AIIS).

raised rock-cut platform often at the rear wall base was rather indicative of the consecration of a sculpture plaque or a stucco relief. Socket holes in the Śaivite caves, cut in the center of the floor suggested installation of detachable[55] *liṅgas*. As it was almost impossible to cut into the rock the *garbhagṛha* did not show any water outlet as *praṇāla*.[56] The *abhiṣeka*

Fig. 74. Mahābalipuram: Ramanuja *maṇḍapam*, *alpavimāna* view (after AIIS).

water and materials mentioned by popular saints[57] were probably collected in vessels inside the shrine only.

Among the later *maṇḍapams*, the *garbhagṛha* was often *āyatārṣa* in shape as seen in Kōṇēri, Varāha and Mahiṣamardinī *maṇḍapams*. Some of these, for example, in the Varāha, Ādivarāha, Mahiṣamardinī *maṇḍapams* also contained bas-reliefs of the principal deities, often in *samabhaṅga* (Fig. 73). The Kōṇēri *maṇḍapam garbhagṛhas* had socket holes for the installation of *liṅgas* with an outer circular groove suggesting the base of the *āvudaiyar*. The back walls contained square, plain niches, probably to place some wooden image or bas-reliefs in them. The projected shrine fronts stood over moulded *adhiṣṭhāna* and in elevation reached up to the *kapota*. In *trikūṭa* shrines like Trimūrti and Rāmānuja *maṇḍapams*, the central shrine was projected more than the lateral ones and also assumed greater proportions. The Rāmānuja *maṇḍapam* façade consisted of two *alpavimānas* with full frontal view on its either sides (Fig. 74).

Sopāna

Garbhagṛha was approached by a three-stepped rock-cut *sopāna*. The upper two steps were usually rectangular, while the lowest formed a semi-circular *candraśilā*. The later *maṇḍapams* exhibited *sopānas* with number of steps varying from two to four flanked by two *śurulyāḷi* parapets on either side. The three *sopānas* of Trimūrti *maṇḍapam garbhagṛha* were quite noteworthy. The proboscis of their *śurulyāḷi* parapet rising from the *vyāḷa* mouth was octagonal moulded. The steps of the central *garbhagṛha* were semi- circular, the upper two resembling *padmapīṭhas* and those of the lateral *garbhagṛhas* were *āyatārṣa*, while in all three the lower-most step constituted the *candraśilā*.

Pradakshiṇāpatha

The *garbhagṛha*, when excavated into the rear or side wall in the *maṇḍapams* left no space for a *pradakshiṇāpatha*. However, the unfinished Pañcapāṇḍava *maṇḍapam* plan (Fig. 75) reveals that had it been finished, it would have produced a rock-cut centrally placed shrine with a pillared *maṇḍapa* all around permitting circumambulation.

Adhiṣṭhāna

Adhiṣṭhāna, as base mouldings (Fig. 76), was carved below the projected shrine fronts in the *ardhamaṇḍapa*. Even for multiple *garbhagṛhas* the *adhiṣṭhāna* remained common. Mouldings, namely *upāna*, *jagati*, *tripaṭṭa kumuda*, *kaṇṭha* with *kampa* mouldings above and below it, *paṭṭikā*, and *prati* on the top, constituted its usual components. In the early *maṇḍapams*, at times, the *kumuda* was not differentiated from the *upāna* as seen in Mahēndravāḍī shrine. The Māmaṇḍūr Rudravāliśvaram *maṇḍapam* presented the fully developed

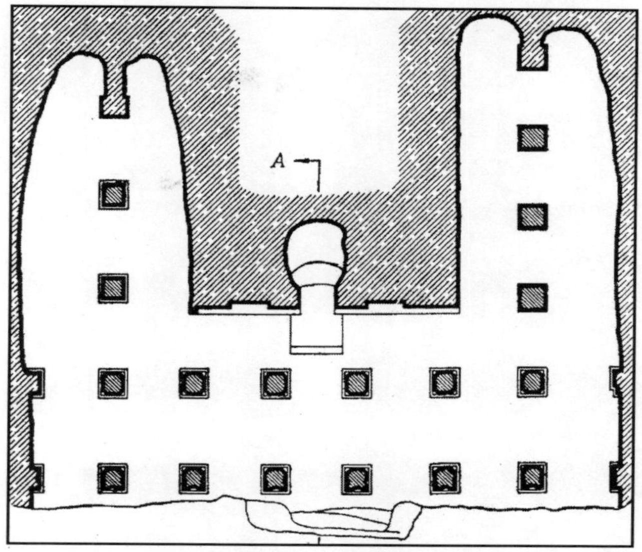

Fig. 75. Mahābalipuram: Unfinished Pañcapāṇḍava *maṇḍapam*, ground plan (after Srinivasan 1993).

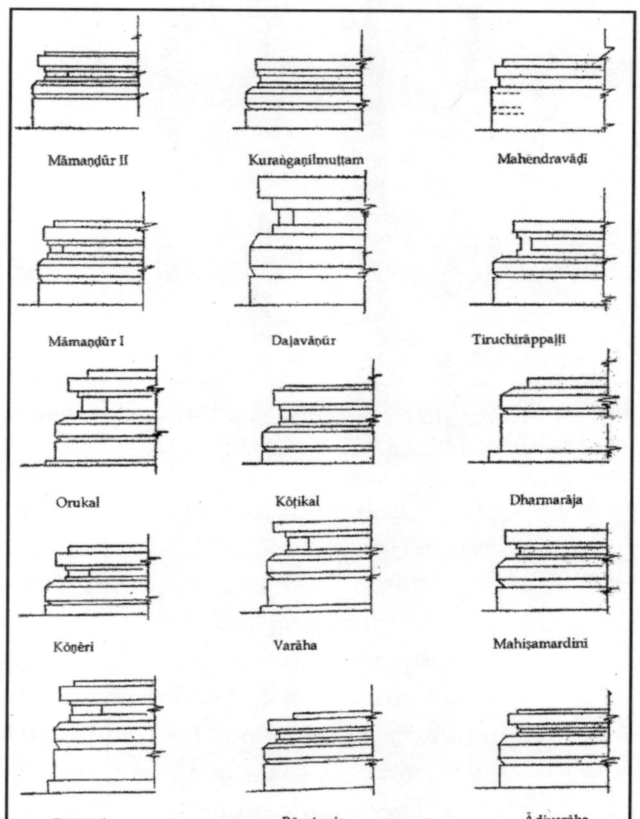

Fig. 76. Mahābalipuram: *Adhiṣṭhāna* types in Pallava cave temples (after Srinivasan 1993).

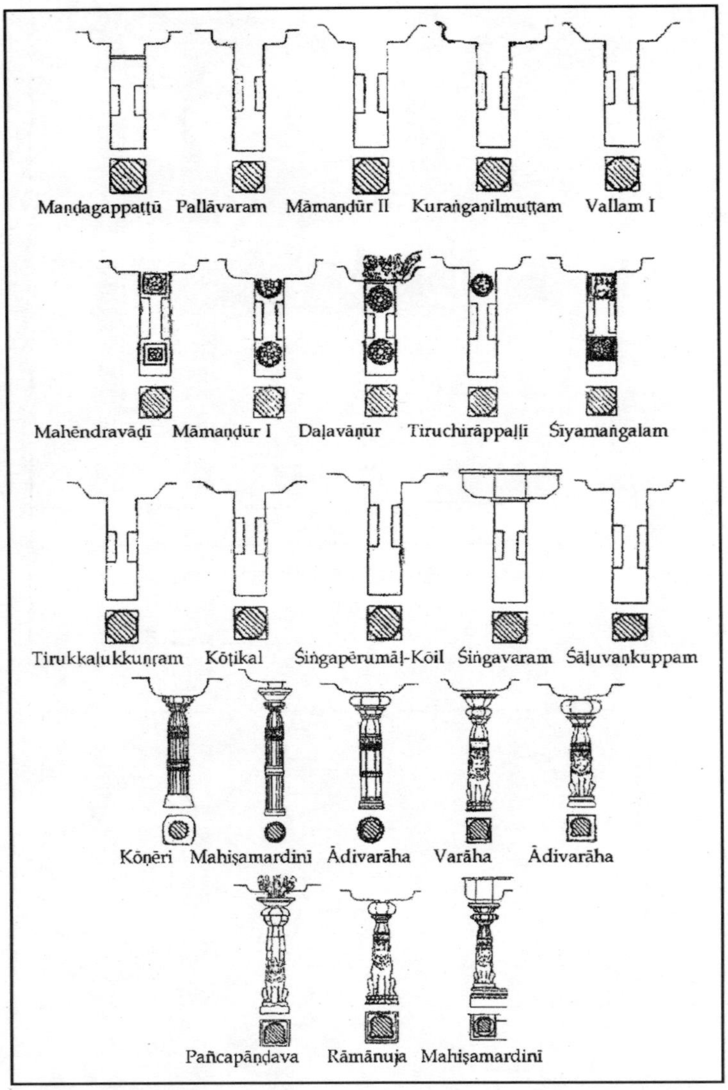

Fig. 77. Mahābalipuram: Pillar types in Pallava cave temples (after Srinivasan 1993).

adhiṣṭhāna with a vertical *jagati*, octagonal *kumuda*, and recessed *kaṇṭha* with two *kampa* mouldings, one above the other, topped by a projecting *paṭṭikā*. Above all, the *prati* carried ten pilasters spaced out almost uniformly. In the later *maṇḍapams* although the components were the same, in some instances the work remained unfinished.[58] The continuity of the *adhiṣṭhāna* was broken at the center by the *sopāna*.

Pillars

Pillars are an important aspect to assess Pallava rock-cut architectural development (Fig. 77). The early *maṇḍapam* pillars were rather short, massive, essentially square, and unornamented. Their various components were not always clearly demarcated seemingly due to the novelty, hardness and unfamiliarity with the qualities of the rock medium adopted. For similar reasons possibly, the inter columniation as well as height was much reduced in proportion to their massiveness. Gradually they evolved as taller and thinner. In the later pillars, elegant, proportionate forms, slender shafts and well-defined capital mouldings with decorative motifs could be clearly marked out. Columniation also became wider.

Pillars were usually placed in the façade and *maṇḍapa*. The *maṇḍapa* was further divided into rear *ardhamaṇḍapa* and front *mukhamaṇḍapa* by another row of pillars usually equal in number to the front row. However, in the Ādivarāha *maṇḍapam* the inner row consisted of two lateral pillars only with a wider gap in between them. Thus, the elimination of the central pair of pillars and resulting wider intercolumniation was probably to accord a full view of the façade of the inner shrine front.

The pillar numbers varied from two and four to six. The row of pillars in the façade and *maṇḍapa* running parallel usually numbered equal though exceptions were seen in Vallam, Māmaṇḍūr, Kōṭikal, Mēlacēri, Atiraṇacaṇḍa, Varāha and Rāmānuja

Fig. 78. Mahābalipuram: Ramanuja *maṇḍapam*, façade pillar, details (after AIIS).

Fig. 79. Mahābalipuram: Pañcapāṇḍava *maṇḍapam*, view (after AIIS).

maṇḍapams. Herein the *maṇḍapa* inside had no pillars. The Trimūrti *maṇḍapam* was unusual in that it contained no pillars at all.

Pillar Components

The early pillars, mainly *caturārṣa* in plan, consisted of two large cubical *śadurams*, at the base and top of the square section. The two front pillars in Śatrumalla Daḷavāṇūr garbhagṛha porch were quite unusual in having no upper *śaduram*. The intermediate portion between the *śadurams*, i.e. *kaṭṭū*, constituted an *aṣṭakoṇīya* section. In the Tiruciráppaḷḷī Lalitāṅkura *maṇḍapam* façade pillars the *kaṭṭū* was proportionately of greater height than the *śadurams*, a characteristic of later pillars. Pillars in the later *maṇḍapams* were mostly *vṛttākāra* in plan, fluted into sixteen facets. The usual type with *śadurams* at base and apex and intervening *kaṭṭū* were also in vogue as found in Kōṇēri *maṇḍapam* façade side by side with the *vṛttākāra* types inside. The Varāha and Pañcapāṇḍava *maṇḍapam* pillars had their shaft *aṣṭakoṇīya* in section. In *vyāḷa* base pillars, the major height of the shaft was often constituted by the *vyāḷa* as seen in Varāha, Ādivarāha, Rāmānuja, or Mahiṣamardinī *maṇḍapams*.

(a) Base:- The base of the early pillars was formed by the lower *śaduram*, quite plain and undecorated, and often of a slightly greater height due to the height of its plinth, *ōma*. But the later pillar bases revealed some sophisticated features. They were frequently shaped into forms of squatting lions or *vyāḷas*. The Yāḷi *maṇḍapam* at Śāḷuvaṇkuppam depicted rearing lion form with on looking riders as the pillar base. The Mahiṣamardinī *garbhagṛha* porch pillars firstly depicted sejant lions sitting with their forelegs erect on circular plinths of diameter greater than the shaft. Among others, the Varāha, Ādivarāha, Pañcapāṇḍava, and Rāmānuja *maṇḍapams* (Fig. 78) consisted of *vyāḷa*[59] based pillars.

The pillars were placed on plinth *ōma* of different shapes. The circular *ōma* in Mahiṣamardinī *maṇḍapam* looked like a *bhadrapīṭha* with three mouldings. The Pañcapāṇḍava *maṇḍapam vyāḷa* based pillars (Figs. 79-80) were placed on *caturārṣa ōmas* while those in Ādivarāha *maṇḍapam* façade on *āyatārṣa ōmas*, looking like *padmapīṭhas*.

Fig. 80. Mahābalipuram: Pañcapāṇḍava *maṇḍapam*, pillar (after AIIS).

(b) Capital: - In the initial *maṇḍapam* pillars, the capital components were not clearly developed. The capital was generally represented by the top *śaduram* occasionally with a *phalaka* and rudimentary *padma* below it. Later, almost all the pillars depicted components of the prevailing wooden capitals, viz. the *kalaśa, tāḍī, kaṇṭha, kuṁbha, padma* or *pāli, phalaka*, and a short, square *vīrakaṇṭha* (Figs. 81-82). These components were usually identical in section with the shaft and appeared polygonal. The *phalaka* and *vīrakaṇṭha* were generally square though the latter appears octagonal in Ādivarāha *maṇḍapam* façade. In a distinct feature of Pañcapāṇḍava *maṇḍapam* three rearing *vyāḷas*, one facing front and the remaining two lateral ones having riders on their back, could be seen springing from the top of the *phalaka*.

(c) Corbel *Potikā* Brackets: - The terminal *śaduram* often carried the *phalaka* moulding on its top over which the *potikā*, a massive block with curved or angular profile and size wise proportionate to the massiveness of the pillar, was carved. The angular profile *potikās* were plain and unornamented while those with curved profile often consisted of *taraṅga* roll mouldings held together by the *paṭṭā*, i.e. a median band. The former types prevailed during the subsequent period while the latter ones survived the Pallava period only. The later *maṇḍapam* corbels were quite huge in size. The *taraṅga* corbels appeared without the *paṭṭā*. The Rāmānuja *maṇḍapam* pillar *potikās* with *taraṅga* ornamentation and *paṭṭā* decorated with *patralatā* were equal in width to the diameter of the pillar.

(d) Decoration:- The early pillars as those seen at Maṇḍagappaṭṭū, Pallāvaram, Māmaṇḍūr, etc., lacked ornamentation. Those at Śīyamaṅgalam, Tiruciráppaḷḷī and Daḷavāṇūr, had large lotus or floral medallions or bas-reliefs adorning their *śaduram* sides. The lotus medallions consisted of deeply carved full blown lotuses with three seriate petals, the two alternating outer whorls spreading outwards while the innermost running round the

Fig. 81. Mahābalipuram: Varāha *maṇḍapam*, façade, through central pillars (after AIIS).

torus. The lotus was put inside two concentric circular lines with a row of beads falling between them, the whole motif carved inside beaded square frames. The Śīyamaṅgalam façade pillars' top *śaduram* portrayed a floral motif *patralatā* on the lateral sides while its front face had two standing lions carved with looped tail and bead like curled manes. At Tiruciṟāppaḷḷī, circular medallions carved in relief in concentric circles with beaded frames depicted motifs as scroll, *haṁsa*, *mātaṅganakra*, *patralatā*, *kinnarī*, etc.

Pillars in the later *maṇḍapams*, being circular and more ornate, were embellished by various motifs, such as *madhyabandha*, *padmabandha* and *patralatā*. The circular floral *madhyabandha* adorned the middle of the shaft while the *padmabandha* decoration on top of it had lotus petals above, flowers and creepers below them and hanging *mukta-saras* or *mālā-sthāna* in the lowermost portion. Thus, pillars served as an important yardstick to signify the evolution process of the *maṇḍapams*. From simple, bulky and plain to elegant, embellished from top to bottom, possessing shapely contours, they speak volumes about the Pallava artisans. The Kōṇēri *maṇḍapam* (Fig. 83) seems to

Fig. 82. Mahābalipuram: Mahiṣamardinī *maṇḍapam*, inner façade, pillar capital details (after AIIS).

have been the first step towards developed pillars with plain, early type pillars on the façade and pillars with capital components and no *vyāḷa* or lion base placed inside the *maṇḍapa*. The Mahiṣamardinī cave (Figs. 84-85) having pillars with capitals on the façade and those with lion-base inside marked the next stage; while the Varāha *maṇḍapam* (Fig. 86) façade was formed by *vyāḷa* based pillars, henceforth, a characteristic of Pallava art, especially of *Māmalla*. However, it is quite significant to note that in these excavations pillars were cut just in imitation of the prevalent wooden and structural models otherwise in a rock-cut creation technically they were of no utility (Figs. 87-88). The absence of pillars in the finely executed triple shrined Trimūrti *maṇḍapam* substantiates this fact.

Pilasters

Placement and Number

They were carved on the façades, projected shrine fronts and *ardhamaṇḍapa* walls. Two pilasters that generally formed the doorjambs flanked the shrine entrance. Their number in the façade was usually two, although in the *ardhamaṇḍapa* it went up to ten as seen in Kuraṅgaṇilmuṭṭam. In the later *maṇḍapams* too, pilasters were placed in the façade, on top of the moulded *adhiṣṭhāna* in the *ardhamaṇḍapa* and flanking the *garbhagṛha* and niches as in Varāha *maṇḍapam*. While their number in the façade was generally two, in the interiors it ranged from four to eight.

Constituent Parts

In plan the pilasters were quadrangular. In the early *maṇḍapams* they were generally not differentiated into *śadurams* and *kaṭṭū* thus having a uniform tetragonal section throughout, as seen in Maṇḍagappaṭṭū *ardhamaṇḍapa* and Māmaṇḍūr façade pilasters. As an exception Maṇḍagappaṭṭū façade and Śīyamaṅgalam façade pilasters were clearly differentiated into top and basal *śadurams* and central octagonal *kaṭṭū*. At places pilasters *in antis* exhibited all the parts of a developed pillar, i.e. a square *ōma*, a tetragonal shaft with a raised floral *madhyabandha* band in middle and a *padmabandha* with *mukta-sara* on top, and above all, the capital components. Such specimens were placed in Tiruccirāppaḷḷī Lalitāṅkura *maṇḍapa adhiṣṭhāna* or Śiṅgavaram *maṇḍapam* façade. Those in Maṇḍagappaṭṭū and Śīyamaṅgalam Avanibhājana façade were clearly differentiated into top and basal *śadurams* and middle octagonal *kaṭṭū*.

In the later instances too, pilasters were tetragonal throughout, with long slender shafts and well defined parts but the eight pilasters, four on either side of the Ādivarāha *garbhagṛha*, despite belonging to a later period, were undifferentiated into base, shaft, capital or *potikā* (Fig. 89).

(a) Bases:- The early pilasters were generally without any base. The Pallāvaram *ardhamaṇḍapa adhiṣṭhāna* pilasters depicted slight relief along the length of the *kaṇṭha* moulding below them, to mark their basal projections. Among the later *maṇḍapams* too, pilasters without base were not uncommon as seen at Kōṇēri *maṇḍapam*. But Varāha *maṇḍapam* revealed some advancement. Its façade pilasters placed on *padmapīṭha* had their *vyāḷa* shaped lower portions as high as half the shaft and facing each other rather than the front. The Mahiṣamardinī cave façade pilasters without *vyāḷa* bases were put on small square *ōma*. Inside, on the projected *garbhagṛha* wall, it had *yāḷi* base pilasters on square *ōma*. *Vyāḷa* base pilasters were also carved in Pañcapāṇḍava, Ādivarāha and Rāmānuja *maṇḍapams*.

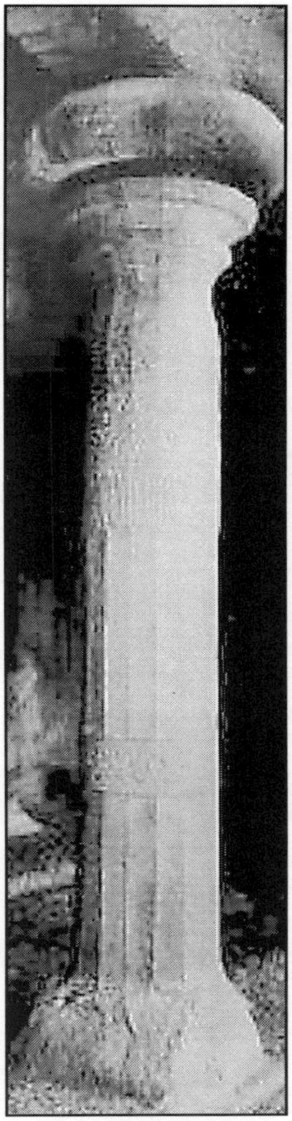

Fig. 83. Mahābalipuram: Koneri *maṇḍapa*, inner pillars, southern end (after AIIS).

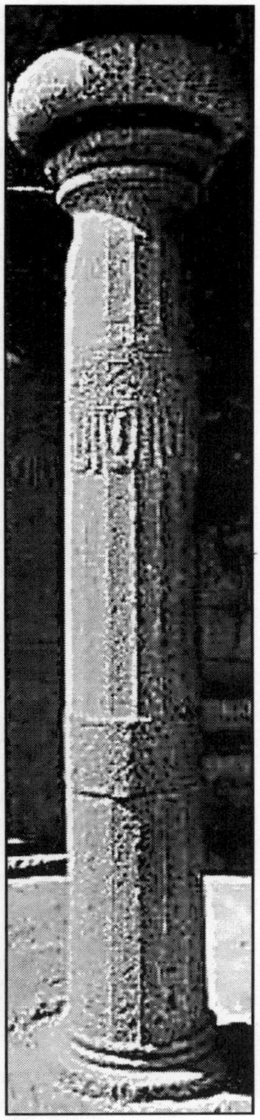

Fig. 84. Mahābalipuram: Mahiṣamardinī *maṇḍapam*, façade on east, *somakānta staṁbha* (after AIIS).

(b) Capital:- The pilasters, earlier rather plain in their form, generally consisted above the *padmabandha*, all the components of the capital, i.e. *kalaśa*, *tāḍī*, *kaṇṭha*, *kuṁbha*, *padma* or *pāli*, and *phalaka*, all usually tetragonal in section. Such differentiated capital in early cases was noticeable only in the ornamental pilasters on the *garbhagṛha* walls or those flanking *garbhagṛha* entrance or *toraṇa staṁbhas* flanking sculpture niches. At places, one or the other of these components was missing. For example, the Kōṇēri *maṇḍapam mukhamaṇḍapa* pilasters were without *padma* and *phalaka*. The pilasters had *potikās* cut on top of the *vīrakaṇṭha* placed on the *phalaka*. Over the *potikā* the beam *uttira* of almost identical height and width as the *potikā* was cut. But the Pañcapāṇḍava *maṇḍapam* pilasters in the *ardhamaṇḍapa* did not carry *potikās* and their shafts directly abutted on the ceiling. Similarly, in Kōṭikal *maṇḍapam*, the two-cantoning pilasters on *garbhagṛha* front did not carry *potikās*.

Fig. 85. Mahābalipuram: Mahiṣamardinī *maṇḍapam*, *maṇḍapa*, inner façade, *siṁhapāda staṁbha* (after AIIS).

Fig. 86. Mahābalipuram: Varāha *maṇḍapam*, façade, *vyāḷapāda* pillar, details (after AIIS).

(c) Decoration:- The Pallava *maṇḍapams* comprised of both plain and decorated pilasters. The ornamented ones often consisted of lotus medallions on their faces. The top of the shaft had the *padmabandha* decoration with *mukta-sara* as found also in the pillars. Pilasters in Śīyamaṅgalam façade depicted bas-relief sculptures of *Vṛṣabhāntika* Śiva with Pārvatī in *tribhaṅga* and dancing[60] Śiva on the lateral sides in the upper *śadurams*. The *madhyabandha* or a floral band appeared in the middle of the shaft.

Kapota, Kūḍū

Kapota was carved over the façade and projected *garbhagṛha*, above the *valabhī* moulding, sometimes extending to sections of *ardhamaṇḍapa* and *mukhamaṇḍapa* walls. It marked the last segment of the *maṇḍapam*'s front elevation. In the early *maṇḍapams* the *kapota*

Fig. 87. Mahābalipuram: Varāha *maṇḍapam*, façade, *vyāḷapāda* pillar capital, details (after AIIS).

Fig. 88. Mahābalipuram: Varāha *maṇḍapam*, pillar capital, section details (after AIIS).

was just a roughly cut eave formed by the projecting rock over the façade. At Pallāvaram it was finished into a smooth flexed straight moulding, while at Daḷavāṇūr it was also decorated by the *kūḍū* [61] motif. *Kapota* in the later *maṇḍapams* was usually more projecting and curved and consisted of ornamental *kūḍūs*, sometimes up to ten in number.

Kūḍū, a miniature *nāsikā* formed by two *toraṇas* joined on top beneath a flat finial, was carved over the *kapota* often in pairs. It usually consisted of human head inside though some *kūḍū caityas* in Varāha *maṇḍapam ardhamaṇḍapa kapota* displayed lotus designs. The *kapota kūḍūs* on *maṇḍapa* sidewalls in Ādivarāha *maṇḍapam* either had lotus medallions or were blank. Decoration on Ramanuja *maṇḍapam* façade *kapota* was in the form of *koṇapaṭṭa* or embossed scrollwork on the corners corresponding to the corners of the projecting *garbhagṛha*. In Kōṇēri *maṇḍapam* the *kapota* inside on projected shrines' wall was supported by abutting rearing *vyāḷas*, their hind legs firmly placed on the pilasters' *phalakas*, forming *koḍungai* or curved brackets.

Fig. 89. Mahābalipuram: Adi Varāha (Paramesvara) cave, façade pilaster, rear view (after AIIS).

Fig. 90. Mahābalipuram: Koneri *maṇḍapa*, *haṁsamālā* above *garbhagṛha* doorway (after AIIS).

In the later *maṇḍapams* the projected shrine fronts consisted of *vyāḷa* frieze, *vyāḷavarī*, over the *kapota* marking the ends of the terracing joists. Rāmānuja *maṇḍapam* had two *vyāḷas* between the *kūḍūs* of each lateral *garbhagṛha* while four for the central one, suggesting the corresponding number of terrace joists. In Varāha *maṇḍapam* the *vyāḷavarī* had projecting *makara* head at either end. While fully cut *vyāḷas* were seen in Kōṇēri, Ādivarāha and Rāmānuja *maṇḍapams* sometimes the *vyāḷa* figures were not clearly cut, indicating unfinished character of the process.

Beneath the *garbhagṛha kapota*, a *haṁsa* or *gaṇa* frieze marking the decorated ends of the projected joists over the *uttira*, was carved on the *valabhī* moulding placed between *vājana* courses (Fig. 90). Sometimes, it extended over sections of the *ardhamaṇḍapa* back wall. In the Ādivarāha *maṇḍapam* the corner *haṁsa* were carved frontally against a background of their spread out plumage. The number of *haṁsa* varied from twelve to thirty. The Rāmānuja *maṇḍapam* had a *gaṇāvarī* instead of the usual *haṁsāvarī*. Arranged in two symmetrical rows of twelve each, it had total twenty-seven *gaṇas*. The two left on both ends were shown supporting the *kapota* while the central one had a *kumbhodara*. Two *gaṇas* had elephant head and bull face, respectively, the rest having human faces. *Valabhī* in Varāha and Trimūrti *maṇḍapams* was internally decorated by a series of scrolls and foliage motifs.

Fig. 91. Mahābalipuram: Trimurti *maṇḍapam*, elevation details (after AIIS).

Thus, the *kapota* was apparently an important constituent of the *maṇḍapam* elevation scheme. The beam *uttira* was cut over the *potikā* while the *vājana* moulding topped it.

Hārāntara/Śālā

In the early *maṇḍapams* the front elevation ended with the *prastara kapota* suggesting a flat terraced roof. The later excavated cave shrines consisted of the *hāra* with cloister like *hārāntara* connecting a series of *śālās* or miniature oblong wagon shaped shrines forming an enclosure or parapet over edges of the flat roof (Fig. 91). Firstly seen in the Kōṇēri *maṇḍapam* it depicted a row of five projecting *śālās* with six recessed lengths of *hārāntara* connecting them. Each of the *śālās* or *koṣṭhas* had an oblong *masūraka* showing the *vyāḷavarī* with projecting *makara* heads at the corners. Each *śālā* had four *stūpīs* over the ridge while the ridge of each *hārāntara* had three *stūpīs* placed over it. The *śālās* each had *alpanāsikā* openings with frontal *kūḍūs*. Some *nāsikās* in the Ādivarāha and Rāmānuja *maṇḍapams* showed *jālaka* or trelliswork suggesting them to be reproductions of *vātāyanas* or windows. *Śālās* at the corners constituting the *karṇakūṭa* were usually square shaped.

Doorframes

The *maṇḍapam* shrine entrances were devoid of jambs, lintels and sills, and were framed only by the pilasters on the sides and *uttira* on top. At times even the flanking pilasters were missing as noticed in the Mahiṣamardinī *maṇḍapam garbhagṛha*.

Sculptures

Sculpturally the *maṇḍapams* were not very exemplary. While the early examples were bereft of any theistic sculptural representations, the later ones consisted of a few. The deity sculptures, whether standing in *samabhaṅga* or sitting, displayed an erect stiff posture. The other sculptures in the *maṇḍapas* or shrine walls displayed more graceful and easy poses coupled with the slimness of form, beautiful proportions and fineness of the sculpture. Such *vaiṇika* or lyrical forms were common to both masculine and feminine figures. Besides individual figures, large group sculptures, both synoptic and narrative, occupied entire wall spaces. The *Mahiṣamardinī* and *Anantśayīn* panels in Mahiṣamardinī *maṇḍapam*, *Ādivarāha*, *Trivikrama*, *Gajalakshmī* and Durgā panels in Varāha *maṇḍapam* were particularly noteworthy. Certain animal forms as *vyāḷa*, *gaja* and *vṛṣa* were also carved out. Sculptures were mostly in profiles, the extent of profile varying, though *tribhaṅga* frontal was not rare. They were seldom freestanding or carved in the round.

The pair of *dvārapālas* flanking the *garbhagṛha* façade was the most profusely carved form. Both were two-armed and usually front-facing though later, profiles became more customary. *Dvārapālas* in Śaiva *maṇḍapams* had a pair of curved horns[62] on the head shown laterally on either side of the crown or behind it. They also held a *gadā*. The *dvārapālas* in Vaiṣṇava *maṇḍapams* were without *gadās*. The Durgā shrines had *dvārapālikās* flanking doorways. Thus, they were generally indicative of the deities to which the respective shrines were dedicated. Sometimes, they held lotus in their inner hands as seen in Māmaṇḍūr Rudravāliśvaram *maṇḍapam*. Herein they appeared more like *ṛṣis* with the *jaṭā* prominently knotted at top, faces heavily bearded, and their *vastras* of ankle length. *Dvārapāla* figures flanking the Brahmā shrine in Trimūrti *maṇḍapam* were quite unusual in form. Placed in very narrow niches, they were in three-quarters profile. Both bearded, wore a three-tiered *sūtra yajñopavīta* and the northern one also carried a *śruk* or ladle in his right hand placed in the *kaṭyāvalaṁbita* pose.

As their regular features, the *dvārapālas* displayed a fierce look. They wore a *kirīṭa* or *karaṇḍa makuṭa* with *jaṭābhāra*, *patrakuṇḍala* earrings, a *phalaka hāra*; a *vastra yajñopavīta* in the *upavīta* or *nīvīta* style, the Kuraṅgaṇilmuṭṭam *dvārapālas* sported a *sarpa yajñopavīta* while Śīyamaṅgalam specimen had a beaded one. The outer right hand was usually placed in the *kaṭi* posture while inner left one either displayed *abhaya mudrā* or simply rested on the *gadā*. The Kōṇēri *maṇḍapam* had its central *garbhagṛha* flanking *dvārapālas* in reverse position of hands, while one *dvārapāla* in Varāha *maṇḍapam* projected both hands in *kaṭi* and another had right hand in *vismaya* or adoration pose pointing towards the *garbhagṛha*. Their legs were generally crossed and they showed *damuṣṭras* in their mouths as seen at Maṇḍagappaṭṭū, Vallam, etc. Their *gadās* sometimes consisted of intertwined serpents as at Kuraṅgaṇilmuṭṭam, Śīyamaṅgalam, etc. They wore long garlands in the *upavīta* and *prācīnivīta* manner reaching up to the ankles. The two graceful and slim *dvārapālikās* in Kōṭikal *maṇḍapam*, in addition to ornaments, carried a *khaḍga* and a bow, respectively.

Other sculptures included a relief of Gaṇeśa and Jyēṣṭhādevī in Vasantēśvaram *maṇḍapam*, Vallam. The Śiva *Gaṅgādhara* bas-relief in Lalitāṅkura *maṇḍapam*, Tirucirāppaḷḷī depicting the descent of Gaṅgā in Śiva's tresses is a fine specimen of early Pallava sculptural art. Warriors like two figures were placed inside niches with *toraṇa stambhas* in Śīyamaṅgalam façade. In Orukal *maṇḍapam* on either side niches of the *garbhagṛha* bas-reliefs of Brahmā and Viṣṇu were respectively placed. The four armed and four-faced Brahmā standing in *tribhaṅga* wore *makara kuṇḍalas* and carried a *kalaśa, akshamālā,* and lotus in three hands while fourth hand rested in *kaṭyāvalambita* pose. The Viṣṇu figure was also four armed, in *tribhaṅga*, held *śaṁkha, cakra,* and *padma* in three hands and fourth hand on *kaṭi*. The Raṅganātha *maṇḍapam*, Śiṅgavaram comprised a huge sculpture of *Anantaśayī* Viṣṇu reclining on a five-hooded śeṣa. It had four faced and four armed Brahmā seated on Viṣṇu's *nābhikamal* and the flanking figures of Garuḍa, Madhu, Kaiṭabha and Bhūdevī.

The *tribhaṅga* form of Durgā in the nearby niche was a deviation from other usual Pallava representations of Durgā standing erect in *samabhaṅga* over a buffalo head or a *padmapīṭha*. Here her left leg was put straight on the ground while the right, slightly raised and bent with the foot, trampled on a buffalo head. Two kneeling figures were seen on either side, one of who pierced his palm with a dagger as if offering blood to the deity. The Varāha *maṇḍapam*, Mahābalipuram's Varāha panel has become exemplary for the perfection and tilt of the boar's snout and its' merging with the human neck below in quite an innate manner. The same *maṇḍapam* also comprised of panels depicting *Trivikrama, Gajalakshmī* and Durgā. The composition as well as iconography in these panels corresponded to the *Āgamic* norms.[63]

A large bas-relief of *Somaskanda* group on a *siṁhāsana* in the Mahiṣamardinī *maṇḍapam*, Mahābalipuram is, probably, the only *Somaskanda* group with nandī and a devotee below identified as Caṇḍikeśvara. Behind Śiva, figures of Brahmā, Viṣṇu and Sūrya could also be seen. This might have been the earliest representation of *Caṇḍeśānugrahamūrti*.[64] Another notable sculpture in this *maṇḍapam* remarkable for its grace, beauty and virility was the *Mahiṣamardinī*. The eight armed deity as well as buffalo headed Mahiṣāsura wielding a *gadā* were portrayed in powerful pose. Opposite this panel was a panel of *Anantśayī* Viṣṇu in *Yogaśayanamūrti* form. Viṣṇu's reclining, calm figure offered sort of a contrast to the virile, dynamic portrayal of Durgā. The Ādivarāha *maṇḍapam* also consisted of several sculptures like *samabhaṅga* Viṣṇu on a *padmāsana*, Harihara, *pralambapāda* Srīdevi on a full blown lotus, Durgā, etc. The *maṇḍapam* had a couple of royal group panel also. One portrayed a king[65] in *sukhāsana*, sitting on a *siṁhāsana* escorted by two queens. Another panel had a heavily ornamented king[66] and two queens, in standing posture. These figures indicated that the practice of carving royal portraits[67] in the temples was not uncommon in the Pallava art.

Thus, it is quite evident that the Pallava *maṇḍapam* type rock-cut monuments were not bereft of sculptural embellishments, although the quality of carving may not have been uniform throughout.

2. RATHAS

Besides the cut-in *maṇḍapams* there are nine[68] freestanding, cut out monoliths or *rathas* at Mahābalipuram. Of these, the five, popularly known as Pañcapāṇḍava *rathas*,[69] are particularly noteworthy for variety in terms of plan, elevation and sculptural

Fig. 92. Mahābalipuram: Unfinished Pidari *ratha* (after AIIS).

ornamentation (Pl. 29). They were perhaps modeled after prevailing architectural forms.[70] These model structures, carved out of granite, are mostly unfinished. It seems that work on the *rathas* was abandoned once their external appearance became apparent.[71] Were they ever consecrated and used cannot be stated conclusively.[72]

Similarly, who created them[73] and to whom they were dedicated[74] - are issues that have baffled art historians long enough. Thus, they are quite enigmatic in character as well as in their forms.

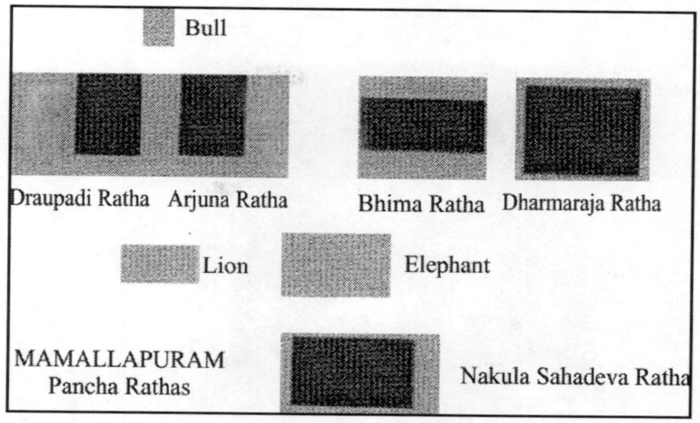

Fig. 93. Mahābalipuram: Pañcapāṇḍava *rathas*, site location.

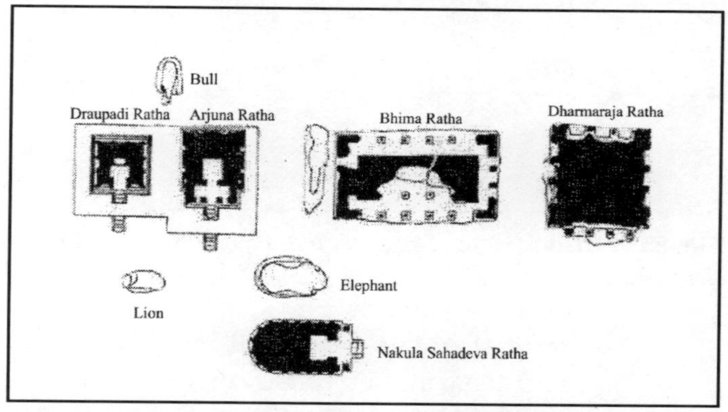

Fig. 94. Mahābalipuram: Pañcapāṇḍava *rathas*, plan (after Huntington 1985).

Development of Form in the Rathas

A typical Pallava temple may be classified into four broad division, viz. *karṇakūḍū* (arched roof), *devasthāna* (the main body), basement *adhiṣṭhāna* with *upapīṭha* pedestal and the *gopuram* (gateway).[75] The *karṇakūḍū* subdivisions were *the śikhara, stūpī, kūḍū, grīvā, hārāntara*, and *prastara*, while the *devasthāna* included the *garbhagṛha, mukhamaṇḍapa, maṇḍapa*, and façade. The *adhiṣṭhāna* consisted of several mouldings. As the *rathas* were primarily an experimental venture as indicated by their varied shapes, they did not conform strictly either to the architectural norms or to the geometric forms. If a recess in the rock made it imperative, the plan was adjusted to accommodate the irregularity. Still, the *ṣaḍvargas* of a characteristic *vimāna*, i.e. *adhiṣṭhāna, bhitti, prastara, grīvā, śikhara*, and *stūpī* were found within them in varying numbers. As already noted, the *rathas* were partly finished. While their exteriors and upper parts were usually well shaped, the lower and interior portions including *garbhagṛha, adhiṣṭhāna* details, and sculptures were generally not excavated or carved out completely. The two Piḍārī (Fig. 92) and Valaiyankuṭṭai *rathas* remained unfinished to a degree greater than the others while Draupadī and Gaṇeśa *rathas* are the most finished ones. Despite these shortcomings, the rock-cut monolithic *rathas* ushered in a novelty in Indian architecture as suggested by their ground plan and elevation schemes besides their medium.

Plan

The Nakula Sahadeva *ratha* alone faced south, while the rest of the monoliths were west facing (Fig. 93). The *rathas*, even in the incomplete instances, represented several varieties[76] of the Draviḍian *vimāna* above the *adhiṣṭhāna* such as *kūṭākāra* in Draupadī *ratha*; *śālākāra* in Bhīma and Gaṇeśa *rathas*; *gajapṛṣṭha* or *dvyārṣa* in Nakula Sahadeva *ratha*; and *miśra-Viṣṇuchanda*,[77] both *dvitala* in Arjuna *ratha* and *tritala* in Dharmarāja

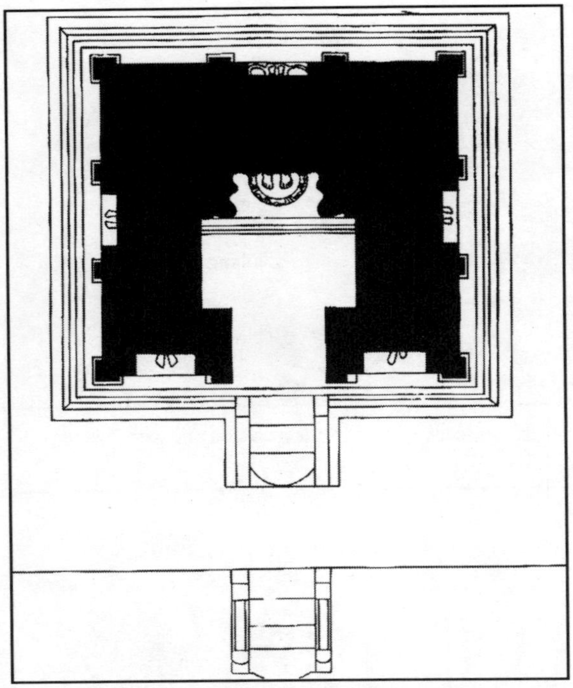

Fig. 95. Mahābalipuram: Draupadī *ratha*, ground plan (after AIIS).

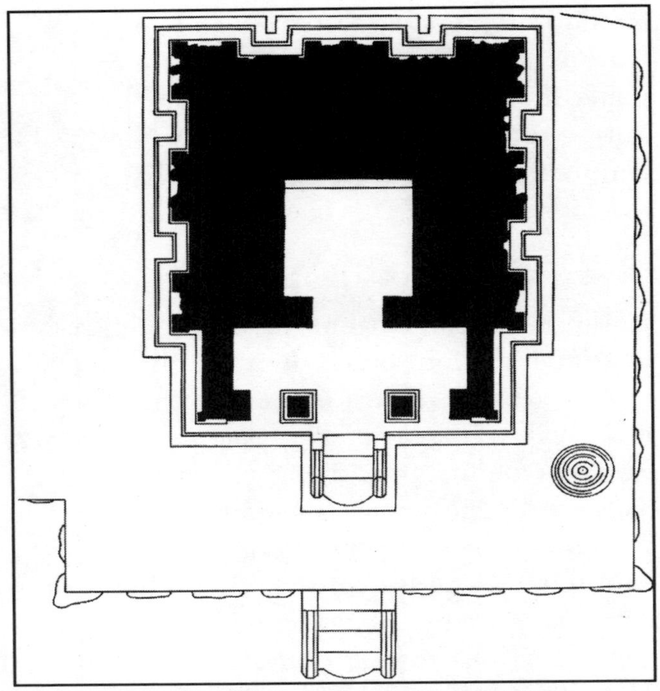

Fig. 96. Mahābalipuram: Arjuna *ratha*, ground plan (after AIIS).

ratha (Fig. 94). Draupadī and Bhīma *ratha* were *ekatala* while the rest, except Gaṇeśa and Dharmarāja *rathas*, were *dvitala*. *Caturārṣa* plan *rathas* were linked to the *vihāra*[78] model while those of *āyatārṣa* plan as Bhīma and Gaṇeśa *ratha* were likened to the *śālā caitya* type.

The *rathas*, except Draupadī (Fig. 95) and Bhīma *ratha*, consisted of a pillared *mukhamaṇḍapa* and frontal façade in one or more directions below (Fig. 96). For instance, the peripheral *maṇḍapa* around the central shrine in the Dharmarāja *ratha āditala* had openings on the four sides forming façades on the north, east, and south sides. Above this, the *talas* and *śikhara* part, mostly pyramidal in elevation, were carved (Fig. 97).

Garbhagṛha

The *garbhagṛha* in the *rathas* was not fully chiseled. For example, the interior of Dharmarāja *ratha āditala* was left largely un-worked. If finished it would have been a *sarvatobhadra* shrine as suggested by openings in all four directions. Its *madhyatala garbhagṛha*, about 4′ deep was also incomplete while the *uparītala* had 5′ deep shrine in front on the west with a *Somaskanda* relief consecrated in it. Likewise, the Arjuna and Nakula Sahadeva *ratha garbhagṛha* had been partly excavated. The Bhīma *ratha* had no *garbhagṛha* at all while the Gaṇeśa *ratha āditala* consisted of a *garbhagṛha* enshrining *liṅga*. The unfinished Valaiyankuṭṭai and Piḍārī *rathas* were also devoid of the *garbhagṛha*. The smallest and simplest Draupadī *ratha* consisted of a small *garbhagṛha* 6′6″ deep in its interior. Thus, it

Fig. 97. Mahābalipuram: Dharmarāja *ratha*, west elevation.

may be inferred that the *rathas* were scooped out externally from top to bottom and were left largely unfinished as their interior details, especially the *garbhagṛha* remains partly excavated or unexcavated, suggests.

Pillars

The *ratha* pillars placed in the façade and constituting the *maṇḍapa* bore similarities with those of the later *maṇḍapams*, discussed earlier. Their number and location was not always fixed as the *rathas* varied in form. Besides, the unfinished character of the monuments also affected the pillars most of which were largely un-worked in varying degrees, sometimes, not separated from the rock itself as seen in Dharmarāja *ratha*.

Placement and Number

The Dharmarāja *ratha* consisted of four freestanding pillars in west front, while two were carved in the rear. The two central pillars of each side had a wider bay between them than between each of them and the pilaster of that side. This feature was, perhaps, a departure from the usual equal intercolumniation of Pallava rock-cut schemes. It may be related to the possible *sarvatobhadra* form of the unfinished *garbhagṛha*. It is suggested that the lower *tala* was planned with sixteen pillars, about 6′ apart, above this, the *talas* were supported by wooden posts about 3′ far.[79] Bhīma, Arjuna, Nakula Sahadeva, Gaṇeśa and Valaiyankuṭṭai *rathas* had two frontal pillars each. Had Bhīma *ratha maṇḍapa* been opened on both ends, there would have been twelve pillars in center and two at each end (Pl. 30).

Pillar Parts

Both square and octagonal types of pillars were carved. They consisted of both square shafts as seen in Dharmarāja *ratha āditala* front and Valaiyankuṭṭai *ratha* and octagonal ones in Arjuna, Bhīma, Gaṇeśa and Nakula Sahadeva *rathas* (Pl. 31). Besides, pillars in Dharmarāja *ratha madhyatala mukhamaṇḍapa* had circular shafts or *daṇḍa*. The Gaṇeśa *ratha* in a stance of a fully developed pillar form displayed one with a square base, lower *śaduram* consisting of a standing *yāḷi*, *padmabandha* in middle *kaṭṭū*, and fluted apex *śaduram*, topped by the capital components.

(a) Base: - Pillars with basal *yāḷis* and *vyāḷas* were quite common, therefore, in the finished pillars, front faced squatting or couchant lion formed bases. The unfinished pillars too, as seen in south, north, and west façades of Dharmarāja *ratha aditala* revealed initial stage of carving lion form or *siṁhapāda* (Pl. 32) on the east and north, less finished on the west, and southwards not even roughly carved. It is equally noticeable that the rearing *vyāḷa* form found frequently in later *maṇḍapams* was conspicuously lacking in the *rathas*.

(b) Capital: - Capitals, shape wise in consonance with the shaft, were usually of the Pallava order, as found in the *maṇḍapams*. But several times, they were also left unfinished or lacked some of the usual components. For instance, pillar capitals in the Dharmarāja *ratha āditala* lacked the *phalaka* and *pāli* though showing off the *kalaśa*, *tāḍī*, *kuṁbha*, and *potikā* components. The Gaṇeśa *ratha* pillar capitals depicted all the formal components.

(c) *Potikā*: - The completed pillar instances revealed curvilinear *potikā* with *taraṅga* ornamentation. *Potikās* in Arjuna *ratha āditala* corner pillars were decorated with little rampant lion figures. These appeared as a contrast to the generally plain *potikās*.

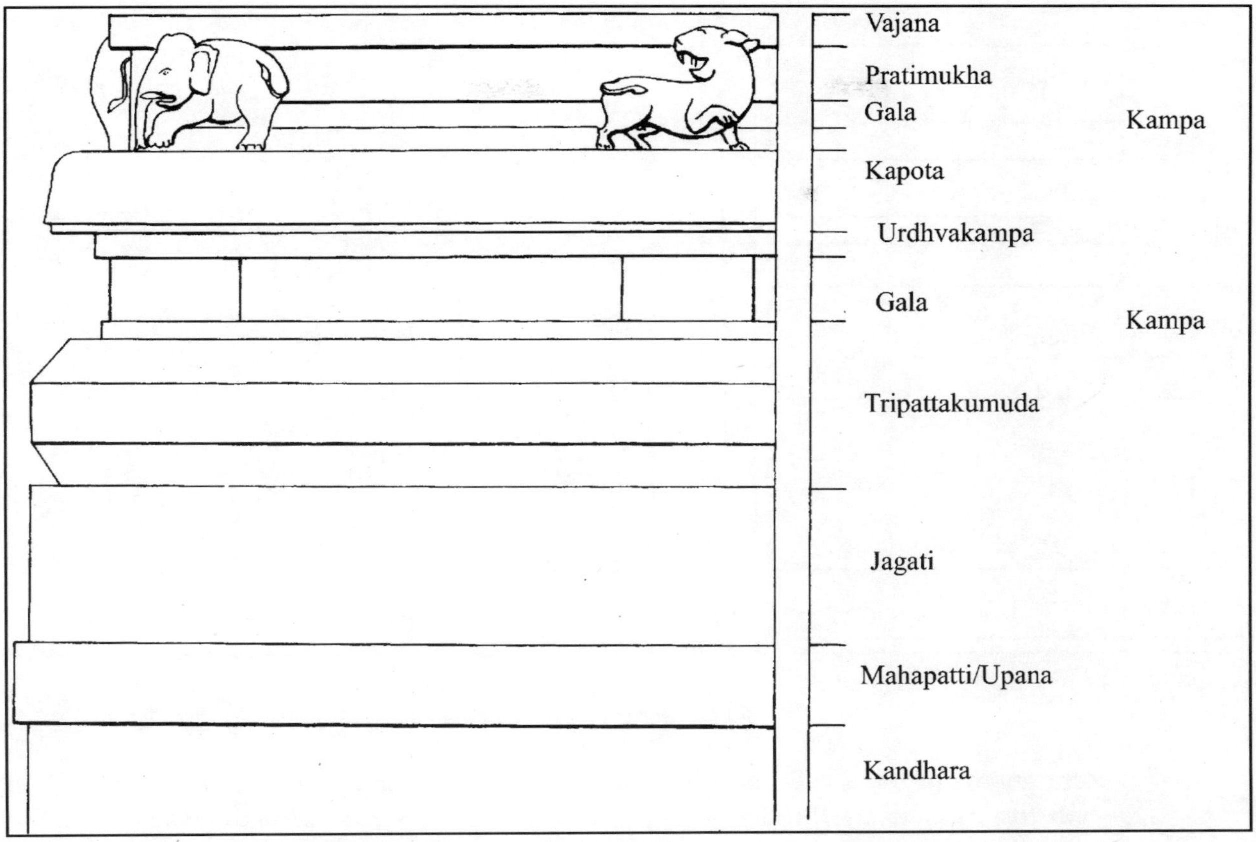

Fig. 98. Mahābalipuram: Dharmarāja *ratha*, *adhiṣṭhāna* details.

Pillars were mostly plain except for the *padmabandha* and *mālā-sthāna* motif of pendent loops of beads and pearls from the lotus petal band, found in some as those in Gaṇeśa *ratha*.

Thus, it is apparent that the pillars in the monolithic *rathas* were not always as finished or finely chiseled as those of the *maṇḍapams*. Still wherever finished, they did exhibit a similarity of style and ornamentation.

Pilasters

Their number or placement did not indicate any uniformity. They were usually found flanking the *garbhagṛha* entrance, façade sides, inside the *maṇḍapa adhiṣṭhāna* corners, and around the *bhittis*, creating panel niches or *devakoṣṭhas*. Plan wise, pilasters were mostly tetragonal or square. Even they betrayed an impact of the sudden abandonment of work on the *rathas*. Still the finished ones as seen in Dharmarāja and Arjuna *rathas* consisted of three plain but clearly fluted sections. Although the surrounding pilasters were generally plain squares at base, those at Dharmarāja and Arjuna *ratha* entrances carried *vyāḷa* base, the figures facing each other (Pl. 33). Pilasters on either side of the Nakula Sahadeva *ratha* shrine portrayed elephant bases.

The pilaster capitals in the finished instances had been exquisitely carved as seen around the Arjuna *ratha* walls and in Dharmarāja *ratha*. They consisted of all the

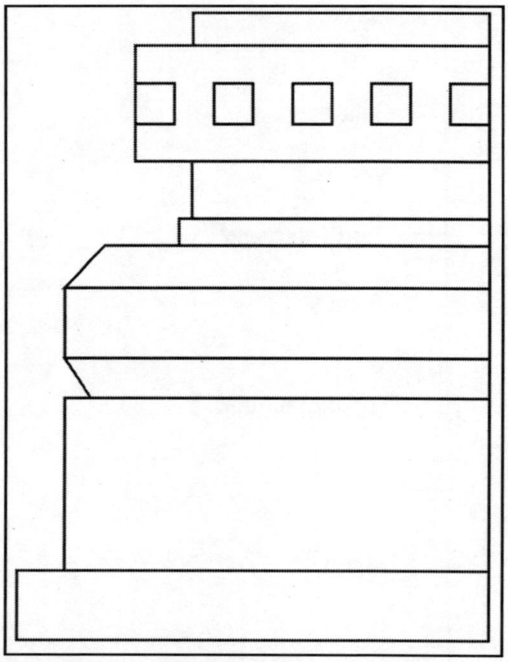

Fig. 98 (i). Mahābalipuram: *Pādabandha adhiṣṭhāna.*

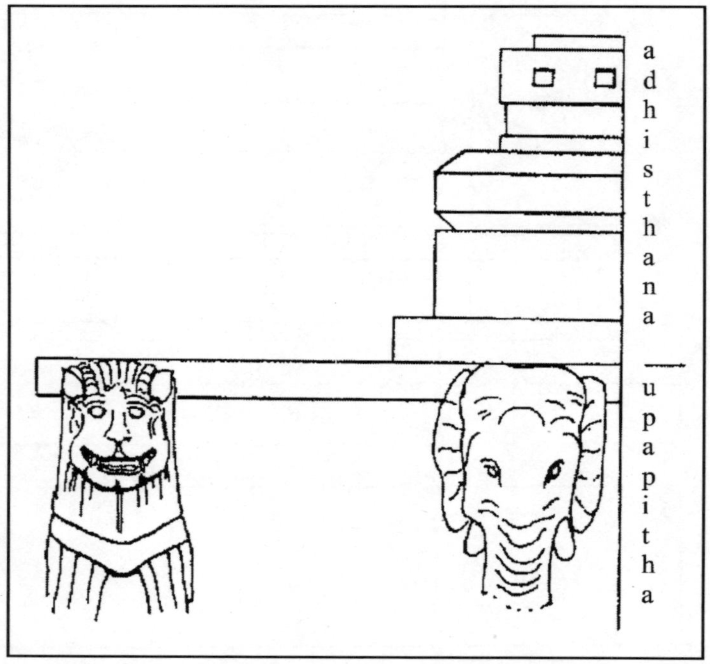

Fig. 98 (ii). Mahābalipuram: Arjuna and Draupadī *rathas, pādabandha adhiṣṭhāna.*

components of the 'order' and in shape conformed to that of the shaft or *daṇḍa*. The shaft top marked by the decorative *padmabandha* with *mālā-sthāna* had above it, the *kalaśa, tāḍī, kuṁbha, vīrakaṇṭha,* and finally, the *potikā*—both angular as well as curved with *taraṅga* mouldings. *Potikās* in the Arjuna *ratha* sported small lion figures as if supporting the *kapota* above.

Adhiṣṭhāna

The elevation of the *rathas* began from the *adhiṣṭhāna* component. It had been carved out just in five cases and was clearly demarcated only for Dharmarāja, Arjuna and Draupadī *rathas*. The former displayed a *kapotabandha adhiṣṭhāna*, probably the first of its type (Pl. 34; Fig. 98). The shape of the *kapota*, the widely spaced elephants, and *vyāḷa* figures in the *vājana* portion as well as the absence of end *makaras* typical of *kapotabandha adhiṣṭhāna* suggested its early form.

Arjuna and Draupadī *rathas* had *pādabandha adhiṣṭhāna* (Figs. 98(i)-98(ii)). Both consisted of the usual *upāna, jagati, tripaṭṭa kumuda, kampa,* and *vājana* mouldings. It is indeed noteworthy that following the mode of carving in the *rathas*, their *adhiṣṭhāna* should have been the last portion to be worked upon. But we find that in the Dharmarāja *ratha* while the *āditala* details had not been fully done, *adhiṣṭhāna*, especially on the eastern side, was clearly demarcated into precise, finished mouldings. However, westwards it had not been done even roughly, suggesting the stages of work. The uncommon *kapotabandha* type adopted here perhaps also highlights the interest and care taken in designing the *adhiṣṭhāna*.

Beneath the partially finished *adhiṣṭhāna* of Dharmarāja *ratha* and finished one of Arjuna, Draupadī *rathas*, a lower *upapīṭha* or sub-base was also carved. Incomplete in the former *ratha*, it was of the *mañca* type consisting a tall recessed *kandhara* with a *mahāpaṭṭī* platform on the top (Pl. 35) while the lowermost *kura* had not been cut out. The projecting *mahāpaṭṭī* was supported by alternating lion and elephant busts, relieved from the *kandhara* face, posed at intervals as also seen on the common *upapīṭha* of the latter two *rathas*. The rough outlines of these animals relief had been carved out of the rock mass at the north-east corner while for the rest they were either uncut or probably could not be cut for lack of sufficient rock. The square socket holes in the *mahāpaṭṭikā* moulding suggested that they were possibly to be carved separately and then inserted therein as can actually be seen in the Arjuna and Draupadī *ratha upapīṭha*. The animal supported *upapīṭha* base and the simple thatch roof like structure of Draupadī *ratha* indicates that it was probably the replica of some portable shrine taken out in processions.

Fig. 99. Mahābalipuram: Dharmarāja *ratha*, *gaṇāvarī* beneath the *kapota* (after AIIS).

Fig. 100. Mahābalipuram: Dharmarāja *ratha*, *haṁsamālā* beneath the *kapota* (after AIIS).

Kapota, Kūḍū

Fig. 101. Mahābalipuram: Dharmarāja *ratha*, prostrate monkey chutes, east side (after AIIS).

The usual *prastara* above the *potikās* was topped by the projecting roll *kapota* decorated with *kūḍū* or *alpanāsīs*. It showed *gaṇāvarī* (Fig. 99), *vyāḷavarī*, or *haṁsāvarī* (Fig. 100) over the *valabhī* moulding (Pl. 36) while the beam *uttira* ran just below the *kapota*. Dharmarāja *ratha āditala kapota* had water chute devices in prostrate human and animal forms, each as lions and monkeys with their backs ripped open to form the channels, holes cut through their head and reaching out to their open mouths (Fig. 101).

Decorative *vyāḷa* frieze over the *prastara* often terminating into *makara* ends, constituted the bearing member of the *hāra*. *Gaṇāvarī* on the *valabhī* depicted *gaṇas* in different poses of dance and merriment or carrying garland as seen in Dharmarāja *ratha āditala*. Herein they appeared closer and greater in number in contrast to the Arjuna and Draupadī *ratha valabhī* (Fig. 102). The *gaṇa* and animal motif was each representative of the carved and embellished end faces of the criss-cross joists in brick and timber plant roofing originals. Thus, despite being functionless in the rock-cut *rathas* they did find place as an obligatory decorative frieze, reminiscent of their wooden influence.

Fig. 102. Mahābalipuram: Draupadī *ratha*—detail of *toraṇa* and *bhūtamālā* (after AIIS).

The *kūḍū* motif usually consisted of a human head in relief, suggesting an inmate of the simulated building. In Valaiyankuṭṭai *ratha* it consisted of square beam ends depicted in relief.

Hārāntara

The *hāra* was an important constituent of the *rathas'* elevation scheme. It invariably ended in the *karṇakūṭas* with a number of *śālās* separated by *hārāntara* intervals in between them. The *karṇakūṭa* was a miniature replica[80] of a *samacaturārṣa vimāna* of a domical *śikhara* with a single *stūpī* while the *śālā-koṣṭha* was the miniature *āyatārṣa* shrine with a wagon shaped *śālā śikhara* having a row of *stūpīs* along its ridge. The intervening cloister or parapet *hārāntara* was lesser in width and height than the *kūṭa-śālās*, had a curved roof devoid of *stūpī*, and consisted of the *nāsikā* on its exterior wall.

The Dharmarāja *ratha* western *mukhamaṇḍapa hāra* deserves attention for the arrangement of its corner constituents. Here two collided *śālās* of the adjacent sides appeared as a *kūṭa* when viewed diagonally from an angle and as a *śālā* when viewed from the sides. This was rather a precursor to the future *karṇakūṭa* or *karṇaśālā* motif (Fig. 103). The first suggestion of the *karṇaśālā* or *lāṅgulākāra śālā* may be seen in the Trimūrti *maṇḍapam*. It consisted of two *karṇakūṭas* with a single *madhyaśālā* of two *stūpīs* in between in its *hāra* over central *vimāna* front. That of the southern front had a *karṇakūṭa* at southern corner but a truncated *śālā* with a single *stūpī* at the northern corner. It was relegated into the corner between the southern and central *vimāna* frontlines. Strangely, the northern *vimāna* had three *śālās* in line and no *karṇakūṭas*. This suggests the apparent evolutionary character of Pallava architectural forms. These instances also negated the notion of these monuments being spontaneous or whimsical creations.

Fig. 103. Mahābalipuram: Dharmarāja *ratha*, *karṇakūṭa* (after AIIS).

The number of *śālās* perhaps depended upon the length of the *prastara* which in its turn depended upon size of the *vimāna*. The Dharmarāja *ratha āditala hāra* extension over the *mukhamaṇḍapa* in the west included the *pañjara* or *nīda*, i.e. a miniature apsidal shrine of almost similar proportions as the *kūṭa* and *śālā*, introduced herein for perhaps the first time (Pl. 37). Destined to be an essential component of the later South Indian temple *hāras*, it may also be seen in south *hāra* over second *tala* of the apsidal Nakula Sahadeva *ratha*. From its position on the upper *tala* in contrast to the lowest *tala* of Dharmaraja *ratha*, this could have been its earliest occurrence. However, the other three sides of the *āditala* or the four sides of the upper two *talas* of the Dharmarāja *ratha* as well as the remaining *rathas* were devoid of the *pañjara*.

Fig. 104. Mahābalipuram: Valaiyankuṭṭai *ratha*, *śikhara* details (after AIIS).

Fig. 105. Mahābalipuram: Valaiyankuṭṭai *ratha* (after AIIS).

While full *kūṭa śālā hāra* with interconnecting *hārāntara* was carved over the *uparītala* topmost *harmya* in the Dharmarāja, Arjuna, Valaiyankuṭṭai, and South Piḍārī *rathas*, it was totally eliminated in the topmost *tala* of the Northern Piḍārī *ratha*, an *nāgara vimāna* with square *grīvā* and *śikhara*. Similar elimination of *uparītala hāra* was noticeable in the Shore temple that had squatting *gaṇas* instead, one in each corner while in Kāñcī, they consisted of recumbent nandī. This indicate that the Northern Piḍārī *ratha* was perhaps also to conform to the norm of bearing the *vāhana* or *lāñchana* of the principal deity around its *grīvā* instead of the *hāra*.

Another significant feature of the *hāra* scheme was the presence of an open *pradakshiṇāpatha - āliṅda* round the next *tala harmya*, which prevented the *hāra* of the lower *tala* from reaching up to the base of *harmya* on the next *tala*. This left the *hāra anarpita* or non-merged against the usual *arpita* condition. The probable advantage of this element was to facilitate a better view of the rear components of the *hāra* as well as to precisely carve out the *gajapṛṣṭhai* form of the apsidal *nīḍas* and symmetrically cut the rear parts of *kūṭas* and *śālās*. However, in the Dharmarāja *ratha āditala hāra* we find that the efforts of the artists to cut sufficient wide *āliṅda* within the limited rock available resulted in plain vertical forms of the *kūṭa*, *śālā*, and *pañjar* elements of the *hāra*. The *kūṭa*, *śālā pañjara* of the *ratha hāras* consisted of the four *angas*, viz. *vedī*, *galā*, *śikhara*, and *stūpī*.

Yet another important aspect of the *ratha* elevation was the *śikhara*. Generally *astārṣa Viṣṇuchanda* as in Dharmarāja, Arjuna, and South Piḍārī *rathas*, or *caturārṣa brahmakānta* in the

Fig. 106. Mahābalipuram: Bhīma *ratha*, second storey, north façade, gable roof (after AIIS).

Valaiyankuṭṭai (Figs. 104-105) and North Piḍārī *rathas*, the *śikhara* with the *grīvā* was the first component to be cut and shaped in the monoliths. Resembling the *śirodaya* position of a newborn, the monolithic *vimāna* thus emerged from womb of the parent rock with the *śikhara* followed by *aṅgas* and *anukāyas*. This mode was in contrast to the *padmopāna* type of structural *vimāna* erection. Therein the stages began from *upāna*, i.e. base to *stūpī* or top of the *śikhara*. The symbol was perhaps unfolding of lotus buds to expose the central torus.

The Bhīma and Gaṇeśa *ratha* roof was a straight line pointed both internally and externally. Adorned by *triśūla* motif at each end its ridge in Gaṇeśa *ratha* was ornamented with nine *kalaśa* shaped pinnacles. The *kalaśa* in Bhīma *ratha*, now non-existent, probably numbered eighteen. The roof at the ends constituted a gable form (Figs. 106-107; Pl. 38).

It is quite interesting to note that the *astārṣa śikharas* of Dharmarāja, Arjuna and South Piḍārī *rathas* in spite of being rock-cut were better in shape and proportions,

Fig. 107. Mahābalipuram: Bhīma *ratha*, second storey, north façade, sala miniature (after AIIS).

more indicative of elegance than the structural *astārṣa śikharas* of similar times seen in the Shore temple *vimānas* or Mukundanāyanār temple (Mahābalipuram) and the Rājasiṁheśvara, Pirāvātaneśvara and Vāliśvara temples (Kāñcī).

Mahānāsikās were carved on the *śikhara* faces all around, for instance, on the eight sides of the Dharmarāja *ratha*. They consisted of a flat, broad pilaster like strip rising from the *grīvā* as the lower member and the *toraṇa* projected from the base of the *śikhara* with a shovel-*śaktidhvaja*- at its apex as the upper member. The *mahānāsikā* in the lower *āyatārṣa grīvā* was, perhaps, a perforated window of the prevalent patterns as portrayed in the relief models of *ektala alpavimānas* in the Rāmānuja *maṇḍapam* and the Descent of Gaṅgā sculpture. The *toraṇa* part with projected joist motif of curved brackets and plank as the roof-supporting component was common. But the *āyatārṣa* Bhīma and Gaṇeśa *rathas* marked a variation in the lateral series of *nāsikās*, five each on either side of the former, and three on either side of the latter. Herein the tablet part was replaced by a niche flanked by two pilasters with full capitals, set forward of the *grīvā*. The niches were either filled with human torso as in Bhīma *ratha* or left blank. Thus, while the other *nāsikās* with joist end motifs appeared as projected entrance replicas, the ones with figures or blank with flanking pilasters of complete capitals were more like keep windows.

A comparison with the structural *vimānas* reveal that the Shore temple shrines' *astārṣa śikhara* consisted of similar *mahānāsīs* with the difference that their *toraṇa* component consisted of either a seated Gaṇeśa or *gaṇa* image, instead of the joist end carving, alternating on the cardinal and lateral faces, respectively. Another alteration seen was the replacement of the *nāsikā grīvā* by figure niches of the peeping window types in the Kailāśanātha temple, Kāñcī. Gradually these icon figures, too, became synonymous with the religious denomination of the shrine as well as their respective direction. For example, the Mukundnāyanār temple *śikhara nāsikās* in east, south, west, and north, enshrining Śiva, *Dakshiṇāmūrti* Śiva, Viṣṇu, and Brahmā icons, respectively.

Nāsikā forms also appeared as *alpanāsikās* on the *kūṭa* and *śālās* in the *hāra* portion and as *kshudranāsikās* on the *hārāntara* sections, projected with their *śikhara* and *grīvā* components. The difference was only of size. Many times the lower part revealed *jālī* work in varied patterns highlighting their window forms instead of plain tablet. Besides they were devoid of a *prastara* component in between the upper *toraṇa* and lower rectangular tablet parts, as found in the *nāsikās* and *kshudranāsikās* of the Bhīma, Gaṇeśa and Nakula Sahadeva *rathas*. This lack of *prastara* made them look like *alpanāsikās*, as could be seen in the Dharmarāja *ratha.* As *kshudranāsikās* peep window replicas were provided on the *hārāntara* wall in the form of two pilasters enclosing a *jālaka* window, surmounted by a *toraṇa* projected from the curved coping roof.

It is quite significant that the cutting of the monoliths did not begin from the *stūpī*, but from the *śikhara* below it. This was, perhaps, because the erection of the former was to coincide with the ceremonial installation of the deity in the *garbhagṛha* along with the simultaneous consecration of the *stūpī* through *aṣṭabandhana mahākumbhābhiṣeka.* As this was the last stage of the work here in the *rathas* being cut from top to bottom, it would have been against the norm to commence work from a part symbolizing its end. Thus, the *stūpī* was to be inserted separately. It is equally interesting to note that ample rock material was left uncut in the Gaṇeśa *ratha* on top, while working on the *śikhara* so as to cut *stūpīs* from the material after completion of the work. This way, probably, the artists devised a means to circumvent their difficulty.

Thus, surmise that elevation wise the *rathas* offered more preciseness, variety and development of architectural features. Although not brought to their lower culmination, they still were indicative of the formative stage of several new features, such as the *pañjara* or the *nāsikās.* Being endowed with a complete *śikhara* the Dharmarāja *ratha,* with its *tritala* scheme, heralded the southern *vimāna talachanda* pattern.

The stages of the cutting process in the Dharmarāja *ratha* may also be traced. While the *śikhara, grīvā,* and *ūparitala* might have been done in the first phase with plenty of rock available as suggested by their finished form; the second phase might have been work around the *ālinda* and *vyāḷamālā* on *āditala* top. The rock formation here must have necessitated restraint in cutting. The third phase, probably, commenced from the *āditala prastara kapota* till the *adhiṣṭhāna* sometimes finished, and mostly not even roughly hewn.

SCULPTURES

The monolithic *rathas* were attended with a lavish sculptural output, including both sculptures in relief, i.e. *citrārdha* and in the round, i.e. *citra.* The quality of the figure sculptures revealed a classical style. Most of them were relief in the rock-cut mode. While the *rathas* had sculptures in varying numbers, as exceptions the Bhīma and Nakul Sahadeva *rathas* remained bereft of them.

The *ratha* reliefs were set in shallow, rectangular panels or niches between two slender pilasters, on either side. This rectangular frame set vertically governed the composition of the relief. These were generally placed around the walls and carried large figures of deities, *dvārapālas* and adorers as seen in the Arjuna *ratha.* Wherever carved the central *bhadra* niche was provided with a *makara toraṇa* as in the Draupadī and northern Piḍārī *rathas.* Figures were also cut in Dharmarāja *ratha* upper *talas.* Thus, sculptures were placed in the *adhiṣṭhāna, prastara* friezes, in the faces of *madhya* and *ūparītala harmya,* inside the shrine and, around walls in *devakoṣṭhas.*

Architectonic in context, the figures also appeared architectonic in character with an emphasis on verticalism.[81] The tall, slender physiognomic forms and the rather pointed *makuṭa*, placed on their heads orientated the verticality. Emerging out of the rock, every form seemed to be clear here, avoiding any play of light and shade as seen in parallel excavated Ellorā caves.

Under the Pallava style the thin, elongated limbs almost tubular in shape sans the swaying grace, emphasized tall stature of the figures. The bodies seemed to retain their pliancy, while a disciplined vitality permeated the figures. In the male figures broad shoulders, supported on an elongated torso, enhanced it. Female figures were slighter in appearance with slender waists, narrow chests and shoulders, sparse ornaments, and generally submissive attitudes.

The divine figures were mostly four armed. The main *mūrtis*, whether of *pradhāndevtā* or *upadevtā*, were depicted in the *sthānakāsana* in *sambhaṅga* and *samapāda*. Dharmarāja *ratha somaskanda* was the only sitting instance. The Pallava sculptor exhibited great mastery in profiles than frontals. Simpler compositions in small groupings with perspectives and higher relief were probably also his expertise as could be seen in the *rathas*. The stances were rendered graceful by the body *bhaṅgas* accompanied by the leg postures and *hastamudrās*. Varying degrees of finish may be detected in the *ratha* sculptures. For instance, the upper *tala* sculptures in Dharmarāja *ratha* marked by *dvibhaṅga*, *tribhaṅga*, and *atibhaṅga*, finer modeling, boldly cut and rounded form, and expressive of *rasabhāvas*. Sculptural art here appears essentially personal. It dealt with single individuals or episodes. It also reflected keen observation of the surroundings and animal world in particular. The elephant was depicted quite majestically, be it stalking forward in the bas-relief, or standing near the Nakula Sahadeva *ratha*, or gamboling at the feet of its mother on a hill near Gaṇeśa *ratha*. Thus, Pallava art was subtle, sublime as well as worldly and real, sometimes humorous.

The sculptures were broadly religious, human and animal in theme. Representing Śaiva and Vaiṣṇava cults, they also portrayed Brahmā, Indra, Sūrya, Candra, and Durgā. Majority of sculptures in the Dharmarāja *ratha* were Śaivite. They portrayed iconic aspects of Śiva as *Kevala Candrasekhara*, *Kapardin*, *Kaṅkālamūrtī*, *Viṇādhara*, *Caṇḍeśānugraha*, *Gaṅgādhara*, *Kālāri*, *Vṛṣabhāntika*, *Nandisahita*, and *Somaskanda*. Synthesized forms of Harihara and *Ardhanārīśvara* were also portrayed. Viṣṇu and Kāliya Kṛṣṇa forms were also carved, while Brahmā form was carved twice in the Dharmarāja *ratha*.

The male form, be it divine, semi-divine or human, and *saumya* or *ugra*, enjoyed a preponderance in the *rathas*. Of the fifty major sculptures in the Dharmarāja *ratha*, just two, i.e. a female devotee and Umā in *Somaskanda* relief, besides the half part of *Ardhanārīśvara*, represented feminine sculptures. A royal portrait in the Dharmarāja *ratha āditala* was suggestive of the human portrayal in art. The animal motifs appear on the *upapīṭha* and *prastara* besides carved as freestanding figures.

Sculptural Technique

Carving of sculptures *in situ* position and that too, in granite rock must have entailed practical problems for the sculptors. This mode was in contrast to the usual practice of carving on quarried stone blocks. Under the latter, the sculptor could either turn the sculpture, or himself move to any convenient position required. However, in the *rathas*, limitations of postures of convenience for the craftsmen to access various parts of the sculpture, or working at varied height *talas*, or doing different portions of a group of sculptures, must have been some usual hurdles. Such immovable medium and the lack of ample working space and resultant freedom of movement were perhaps responsible for the unfinished lower portions of sculptures in Dharmarāja *ratha ūparī talas*. It seems that the only freedom of action and choice of poise for the sculptor was confined to the narrow *ālinda* part with a fixed floor. This must have hampered his reaching out to the material easily at the lower levels of the sculptures. Thus, the rock-cut technique of sculpting was much more cumbersome, required more physical labour, and was less rewarding than the quarried block mode.

In addition to the *ratha* sculptures, freestanding rock-cut figures of an elephant, bull and lion were carved in their vicinity. The unique bas-relief said to represent the *Gaṅgāvataraṇa* or *Kirātārjunīyam* myths[82] was carved on the nearby cliff face on two large boulders. It is one of the greatest masterpieces of Indian sculptural art. The relief was graded in such a manner that the figures seemed to be in a continuous process of emerging from the flat rock. The whole cosmos including deities, humans, animals, half celestials, as well as creatures from the nether world occupied place therein.

It is, therefore, apparent that the *rathas* assume importance not only as architectural innovations but also as superb sculptural and iconographic achievements. Hence, the two rock-cut monumental forms of *maṇḍapam* and *rathas* created under the Pallava rule were quite innovative and novel. They seemingly exerted influence on the structural *vimānas* upcoming simultaneously or slightly later. For instance, the now lost *śikhara* of the Viṣṇu shrine in the Shore temple was, probably, a gable roof type like the Bhīma *ratha* judging from the *Anantśayī* Viṣṇu form. The *śikhara* of the other two shrines had been derived from the Dharmarāja *ratha*. The practice of installing images in *devakoṣṭhas* on the outer walls seems to have been derived from the Dharmarāja, Arjuna and Draupadī *rathas*. The *dvārapālas* also revealed a continuity of the tradition, as also the *hāra* component above the *prastara*. Besides, the Bhīma, Nakula-Sahadeva and Gaṇeśa *rathas* with their *āyatārṣa dvyārṣa* plan, and keel roof with its pinnacles and gable ends, also gave rise to the later structural *gopurams*. The Shore temple provided an instance of the same. Thus, the *rathas* may be regarded as the prototypes of South Indian temple architecture.

Sculpturally, the *Somaskandas*, first appearing in *maṇḍapams* and Dharmarāja *ratha* in rock-cut mode, were invariably placed in the later structural Śaiva temples at Mahābalipuram and Kāñcī. It becomes apparent from this analysis that the Pallava rock-cut creations, though unfinished, proved a landmark in the making of Draviḍian architecture. Besides, the origin and evolution of new architectural elements in the *maṇḍapams* and *rathas*, we visualize quite a daring attempt on part of the artisans. The very process of copying models of prevailing architectural forms in hard rock did not end with the *rathas*. On the contrary, the Rāstrakūṭa period in the Deccan witnessed the culmination of the process in the form of the Ellorā Kailāśanātha temple.

NOTES AND REFERENCES

1. Dubreuil, 1972, *Dravidian Architecture*, (trans.) S.K. Aiyangar, Varanasi, p. 24.
2. *Vide* Longhurst, 1998, *Pallava Architecture, MASI*, No. 17, p. 8.
3. *See* Brown, 1965, *Indian Architecture*, Vol. 1, p. 77.
4. *Cf.* Rabe, 1988, *The Monolithic Temples of the Pallava Dynasty: A Chronology*, U.M.I., p. 9.
5. *Vide* Daṇḍin, 1954, *Avantisundarī*, Trivandrum Sanskrit Series, No. 172, p. 13.
6. Aiyangar, 1919, 'The Antiquities of Mahābalipura', *IA*, No. 46, p. 52.
7. *Vide* 1889, *Mahāvaṁśa*, Pt. II, Chap. 47, (trans.) L.C. Wijesinha, Colombo, pp. 43-44; the transport of elephants for the expeditions in ships from Mahābalipuram has been referred to by Tirumangi Ālvār in *Periyatirumoli*, II, VI, 6 in the hymn on Tirukkadalmallai.
8. *See* Longhurst, 1998, *Pallava Architecture, MASI*, No. 33, p. 5.
9. *Vide* Wilson, 1828, *A Descriptive Catalogue of the Oriental Manuscripts and Other Articles*, Calcutta, (cited by) W. Willetts, 1966, *An Illustrated Annotated Bibliography of Mahābalipuram*, Kuala Lumpur, p. 19, item 1821 (i).
10. *Cf.* Sewell, 1904, 'Roman Coins Found in India', *JRAS*, pp. 609, 636.
11. *Cf.* Rabe, *op. cit.*, p. 14.
12. There are 14 *maṇḍapams*, 9 monoliths, 3 structural stone temples, and 4 relief sculptured rock panels.
13. Several of these tanks in Toṇḍaimaṇḍalam, Cola and Pāṇḍya regions originated in the megalithic times. They attained sanctity and fertility value by their association with the remains of the dead. Small shrines *pallippaḍai*, monumental and funerary in nature, evolved near these tanks. The later *maṇḍapams* and structural temples perhaps marked the continuation of this tradition of sanctity. *Vide* K.R. Srinivasan, 1993, *CTP*, p. 31.
14. *Refer to* Varahamihira's *BS*, LV, 4-8 (cited by) Stella Kramrisch, *The Hindu Temple*, Vol. I, p. 4.
15. Identified as quartz felspathic gneiss by Fergusson in *CTI*.
16. Mahendravarman claimed creation of the first stone edifice without the use of perishable brick, timber, metal or mortar, for the trinity. *See* Maṇḍagappaṭṭū Inscription, *EI*, XVII, pp. 14-17.
17. *Cf.* J. Fergusson, 1846, 'On the Rock-cut Temples of India', *JRAS*, 8, p. 85.
18. For instance, the colossal, unfinished nandī at the back of Arjuna *ratha*. As there was no available rock in front of the shrine the figure could be carved only at the back.
19. Gasparo Balbi (1582) in S. Purchas, 1905, *Hakluytus Posthumus or Purchas His Pilgrimes*, 20 Vols. Glasgow; Niccolo Manucci detected a Chinese look about them, '... there is also a rock called Mavelivaro, distant four leagues from a place called Sadrastapato where there are many sculptured fragments resembling Chinese'. *Refer to* W. Irvine (ed.), 1907, *Storia do Mogor or Mogul India 1653-1708* by Niccolao Manucci Venetian, London.
20. Foremost among them being Chambers' 1788, 'Some Account of the Sculptures and Ruins at Mavalipuram, a Place a Few Miles North of Sadras, and Known to Seamen by the Name of the Seven Pagodas', *Asiatic Researches*, Vol. I, Calcutta, pp. 145-70; Goldingham's, 1798, 'Some Account of the Sculptures at Mahābalipuram, Usually Called the *Seven Pagodas*', *Asiatic Researches*, Vol. V, Calcutta, pp. 69-80; Babington's, 1830, 'An Account of the Sculptures and Inscriptions at Mahāmalaipur', *Transactions of the Royal Asiatic Society*, Vol. II, London, pp. 259-69; Newbold, 1846, *Journal of the Royal Asiatic Society of Bengal*, Vol. XV; Fergusson, 1846, *The Journal of the Royal Asiatic Society of Great Britain and Ireland*, Vol. VIII, London.
21. Among them Robert Home painted *Les Cinq Temples de Maveliewarom* (1811); William and Thomas Daniell had sketched the *rathas* in *Oriental Scenery* (1812-16); Graham's paintings

were made during 1811-14; Babington's *Monograph* (1830) and *Hindu Pantheon* (1864) by E. Moore also contained their portrayals.

22. For instance, *Les7Pagodes* as mentioned in a map of 'the Coasts of Malabar and Coromandel' presented to the king by William de I' Isle at Amsterdam, dated 1723.
23. The Sanskrit form *maṇḍapa* meant an open hall, the Tamil form *maṇḍakam* probably derived from *maṇṛakam* also meaning an open hall or *sabhā*. *Cf.* Srinivasan, *CTP*, p. 30, *footnote no. 2.*
24. *Muṇṇāl-Maṇḍagam-Kallāl-iyaṟṟi-* Sittannavāsal, 1940-41, *Annual Report on South Indian Epigraphy, 1904,* No. 368, p. 215; *Cf. also Kalmaṇḍakattālvār* – Kuraṅgaṇilmuṭṭam, *Ibid.*, 1912, No. 295.
25. For example, Kōṭikal *maṇḍapam*, Dharmarāja *maṇḍapam*, Yāḷi *maṇḍapam*, Idaici *maṇḍapam*, etc.
26. *Vide* Fergusson and Burgess, *CTI*, p. 112.
27. In tune with Dhaky and Ghosh, Pramod Chandra has rejected the persistence of dynastic appellations: '...it makes for obscurity rather than clarity for the simple basic reason that it is the region that is the basis of Indian history as well as art...' *vide* Pramod Chandra (ed.), 1975, *Studies in Indian Temple Architecture,* Delhi, p. 36; others still perpetuate the long established classifications of Indian art on dynastic basis. *See footnote no. 28.*
28. As held by Harle, 1974, *Gupta Sculpture,* Oxford; also Williams, 1982, *The Art of Gupta India: Empire and Province*, Princeton; Huntington, 1983, *Pāla-Sena Sculpture*, Leiden.
29. Attributed by Rabe, *op. cit.*, p. 5; By the same tradition, Rabe excluded the un-inscribed cave shrines in outlying districts of Bhairavakoṇḍa and Uṇḍavallī in former Pallava Empire from this category.
30. A later Rāstrakūṭa inscription within the cave referred to the site as Pallavapura, i.e. city of the Pallavas. *Vide* Srinivasan, *CTP*, p. 58.
31. *See Illustrations of the Rock-cut Temples of India,* J. Weale, 1845, London, p. 58.
32. Theory as propounded in 1962, 'New Light on Māmallapuram', *TASSI,* (repr.). From the Silver Jubilee Vol. of the Archaeological Society of South India, pp. 1-50.
33. The chief adherents included Subramaniam. *The Pallavas of Kānchī in South East Asia*; also Tarr, 1969, *Architecture of the Early Western Cālukyas,* Los Angeles, p. 327; Dehejia, 1977, *Namakkal Caves*, pp. 4-37; Ramaswami, 1975, *Māmallapuram.*
34. *Refer to* Dubreuil, 1916, *Pallava Antiquities*, London; *also* Longhurst, 1998, *Pallava Architecture, MASI*, Nos. 17, 33, 40, Delhi (repr.); Srinivasan, 1975, *The Dharmarāja Ratha and Its Sculptures,* New Delhi; Lockwood, 1974, *Mahābalipuram Studies*, Madras; Lockwood, 1982, *Māmallapuram and the Pallavas,* Madras.
35. Advocated by Hirsch, 1983, as 'Royal Implications of the Unique Subject Matter, Scale and Format in the Narrative Reliefs At Māmallapuram', *South Asian Religious Art Studies,* No. 3, pp. 56-63.
36. Expounded by Philippe Stern 1961, *Evolution du Style Indien d' Amarāvatī*, Paris.
37. *Cf. Draviḍian Architecture*, 1972, (trans.) Aiyangar, Varanasi.
38. As given by Rabe in *op. cit.*, pp. 34-35.
39. These have been discussed in 'A Numerical Taxonomic Analysis of Various Somaskandas', Michael Lockwood *et al.*, *Mahābalipuram Studies*, pp. 106-11.
40. (i) Archaic, i.e. predating Mahendra's reign; (ii) Severe-belonging to Mahendra period; (iii) Classical-of Narasimha period while (iv) Embellished style was marked by increasing proportions of ornamentation in art and poetics following the classical period. *Vide* Rabe, *op. cit.*, pp. 49-52.
41. Mahendra style consisted of earliest excavation at Maṇḍagappaṭṭū followed by those at Pallāvaram, Māmaṇḍūr, Kuraṅgaṇilmuṭṭam, Vallam, Mahēndravāḍī, Daḷavāṇūr,

Tiruciräpallī and Śīyamaṅgalam; *Māmalla* style instances were Kōṇēri, Mahiṣamardinī, Varāha, Ādivarāha, Rāmānujam, Trimūrti and Pañcapāṇḍava *maṇḍapams*, besides the monolithic *rathas*. *See* details in Srinivasan, *CTP*, pp. 37-46.

42. *EI*, XVII, pp. 14-17.
43. *Cf. Pallava Architecture*, *MASI*, No. 17, p. 5.
44. *See* Dubreuil, *The Pallavas*, pp. 33, 35.
45. The *vihāras* and *caityas* were the earliest manifestations of the activity. *Refer to* chapter 1 for details.
46. *Cf.* Ramaswami, *Seven Pagodas*, p. 33.
47. *Ibid.*, p. 34; Nagaswamy has also ruled out the Buddhist influence theory; *see A New Light on Māmallāpuram*, p. 3.
48. *Cf.* Srinivasan, *CTP*, p. 29.
49. The respective excavation techniques have been duly discussed in chapter 1.
50. Further classified into three phases: (i) contemporary to Mahendra, (ii) subsequent to Mahendra up to Rajasimha and (iii) post-Rajasimha.
51. Inscriptional evidences record their creation by the king or their being named after one of his *virūdas* or the presence of his *virūdas* therein.
52. Quite unusually it had four more *garbhagṛhas* in the two *ardhamaṇḍapa* lateral walls, thus, bringing the total number up to seven.
53. In the absence of this row of pillars, the demarcation was indicated by the different floor level of the two parts.
54. *Cf.* Srinivasan, *CTP*, p. 39
55. The absence of rock-cut *liṅgas* or their pedestal *āvudaiyār* in the *garbhagṛha* was a very peculiar feature seen in Pallava Śaiva *maṇḍapams*. A solitary example where the *liṅga* and the *āvudaiyār* were cut out from the same rock as the *maṇḍapam* is found in the Śikhari Pallaveśvaram at Mēlacēri. Moreover the *liṅga*, always of black polished charnockite or basalt, appears to be a later addition in the early cave temples as stone *liṅga* found no reference in the prevailing hymns of the *Tevāram*. *Cf.* Srinivasan, *Journal of the Madras University*, XXXII, pp. 131-98. The early absence and later insertion of *liṅgas* has also been pointed out by Soundara Rajan in 1969, 'Cult in the Pallava Temples', *TASSI (1962-65)*, Madras, pp. 144-45.
56. The painted forms on the rear wall apparently could not have ceremonial bath, i.e. *abhiṣeka*, *Cf.* Gopinatha Rao, *EHI*, I, Pt. I, p. 52.
57. *Cf.* Tirūñāna-Sambandar, *Tevāram*, I, 660; II, 1528.
58. Most of these monuments reveal an unfinished state. The reasons for their incomplete nature remain conjectural.
59. Leonine *īhā mṛga* or composite animal having lion face and three horns like projection from their foreheads. The two diverging lateral horns hold the bulging eye sockets at their bases, while the central one is an upward extension of the ridge of the nose.
60. Four-armed Śiva dancing in *bhujaṅga-trāsita* or *ānanda tāṇḍava* pose while a *gaṇa* below playing an *ūrdhva-maddala* - this is perhaps the earliest extant southern representation of dancing Śiva.
61. A Tamil word for a horseshoe shaped opening projected out of the flexed *kapota*. It was filled with human figures and usually surmounted by a *makara toraṇa*.
62. The horned *dvārapāla* was perhaps a representation of nandī, also known as *sṛṅgī*. *Cf. Annual Report on South Indian Epigraphy*, 1921-22, Pt. I, pp. 3-4; such horned *dvārapāla* was usually associated only with particular forms of Śiva enshrined in the *garbhagṛha*. *Vide* Srinivasan,

CTP, p. 36; P.R. Srinivasan in 1959, 'Beginnings of the Traditions of South Indian Temple Architecture', *Bulletin of the Madras Government Museum*, New Series, Vol. VII, No. 4, p. 34 opined that the two horns were a transformation of the multi snakehead Nāgarāja, the Buddhist *dvārapāla* motif; yet another theory related them to the horn wearing primitive Nāgā and Goṇḍ tribes. *Refer to* Lockwood and Siromoney, 'Pallava *Dvārapālas* and the Mahiṣahamardinī Cave', *Mahābalipuram Studies*, p. 9; *See also* Lockwood and Siromoney, 1971, 'Guardians of Pallava Cave Temples', *The Sunday Standard*, Madras, 14 February.

63. For instance, *Varāha* and *Trivikrama* panels corresponding to *Vaikhānasāgama* norms given in *Paṭala 56* and *Paṭala 58*; *refer also* Rao, *EHI*, Vol. I, Pt. I, pp. 132-34, 137-40 and p. 161 ff.
64. Srinivasan opines that if the object in Śiva's upper right hand be accepted as a garland or *parivaṭṭam*, then the devotee is identifiable as Caṇḍikeśvara. *Cf. CTP*, p. 153.
65. Labelled as *Srī Simhaviṇṇa-pōttrā-thirājan*. *See* Sastri, 1926, *Two Statues of Pallava Kings and Five Pallava Inscriptions in a Rock-cut Temple at Mahābalipuram*, *MASI*, No. 26, p. 3.
66. Labelled as *Srī Mahēndra pōttrā-thirājan*, *ibid*.
67. In India, royal images were often set up in temples, though always in a human form. Also suggested by Coomaraswamy in 1965. *History of Indian and Indonesian Art*, p. 185.
68. Dharmarāja, Bhīma, Arjuna, Nakula-Sahadeva, Draupadī, Gaṇeśa, Valaiyankuṭṭai and the two Piḍārī *rathas*.
69. (i) Neither they (except Draupadī *ratha*) resemble *ratha* or carts, nor are they related to the Pāṇḍavas. The designation also seems inappropriate as four monoliths are named after the five brothers, while one is assigned to their wife Draupadī due to its apparently feminine character; Their names are rather modern appellations applied from the popular belief that everything rock-cut was executed by the Pāṇḍavas during their exile. *Vide* Fergusson and Burgess, *CTI*, p. 113, (ii) The term Piḍārī suggests a village goddess, generally evil. It denotes a form of Kālī, (iii) Valaiyankuṭṭai was perhaps some village or place name (as suggested by Mr. Pattar).
70. Modelled after village *kuṭāgāra*, *vihāra*, *caitya*, etc. The fully developed forms of *rathas* along with the lack of any extant stone replicas also suggest that they were copies of prototypes in a perishable, probably wooden, medium.
71. Nagaswamy in 1962, *New Light on Māmallapuram*, p. 31 has attributed this to the chaotic circumstances within the Pallava kingdom after Rajasimha; Fergusson in *CTI*, p. 128 also held some social or political revolution responsible for abandoning work in the *maṇḍapams* and bas-reliefs. However, for the *rathas* he assigned only physical factors responsible for the incomplete state. With experience, the artisans must have realized the inadequacy of wooden forms for monolith carving and hence given up the experiments.
72. The *stūpī* placed on the *śikhara* after consecration may be seen near the Dharmarāja and Draupadī *ratha* ready to be laid in position or still undetached from rock. But Longhurst has suggested that the Arjuna *ratha garbhagṛha*, though not fully excavated, was used for worship as indicated by the *somasūtra* or water outlet made towards the north and also by traces of red colour found. *See* 1998, *Pallava Architecture*, Pt. II, *MASI*, No. 33, p. 18.
73. There is a controversy regarding their patron. Both Narasimhavarman and Rajasimha are credited with erection of these unique art creations. *Cf.* Nagasw̦amy's, *A New light on Māmallapuram*.
74. That primarily they were religious edifices is evident epigraphically. But their dedicatory deities are a matter of surmise. Architectural and sculptural evidences reveal that Draupadī *ratha* was probably dedicated to Durgā, Bhīma *ratha* to Viṣṇu *Anantśayī* while Dharmarāja *ratha* was Śaivite in nature; T.N. Ramachandran upheld that Nakula-Sahadeva *ratha* was

dedicated to Caṇḍeśa. *Cf.* 1970 (Sept.), *Mārg*, XXIII: 4, pp. 107-08; Longhurst in *Pallava Architecture*, *MASI*, Pt. II, p. 21 related it to Indra; Arjuna *ratha* is usually associated with Śiva. *Cf. Ibid.*, p. 17; It has also been linked to Murukan Skanda. *See* Srinivasan, 'Some Aspects of Religion', *Madras University Journal*, XXX II: 1, p. 173; Huntington in 'Iconographic Reflections on the Arjuna *Ratha*' in *Kalā Darśana*, p. 60 related it to Aiyanār Śāstā, an enigmatic South Indian deity; Marguerite E. Adiceam has compiled a bibliography of the deity in 1967, *Contribution a' l' Etude d' Aiyanār Śāstā*, Pondicherry; *also see* Louis Dumont, 1959, 'A Structural Definition of a Folk Deity of Tamil Nad: Aiyanar, the Lord', *Contributions to Indian Sociology*.

75. Maity, 1982, *Masterpieces of Pallava Art*, Bombay, fig. S.1-2.
76. A probable influence of the Vedic leanings of Pallava rulers. In Vedic period religious edifices of different shapes were preferred for different prayers, such as *droṇacita* (apsidal), *rathacakra cita* (wheel shape), *syenacita* and *ravega* (triangle). *Vide Taittirīya Yajurveda Saṁhitā*, 5: 4:11.
77. i.e. *samacaturārṣa* up to the *prastara* of third *tala* but *aṣṭārṣa* in its *grīvā* and *śikhara*, thereby constituting *vimāna* of the *miśra* type.
78. They probably evolved from a building composed of cells around a square courtyard which was later covered with a flat roof on pillars. In due course, several storeys were added to this, topped by a domical roof or *stūpī*. In rock-cut specimens, these cells were rather modified into ornamental turrets. *Cf.* Brown, 1965, *Indian Architecture*.
79. Fergusson and Burgess, *CTI*, pp. 126-27.
80. Amarāvatī sculptures also portray the *stūpa* in miniature forms over its slabs in relief. The practice might have had influenced the Pallava artists in creating the miniature *kūṭas* and *śālās*.
81. *Cf.* Rajeshwar, 1988, *The Pallava Sculptures*, Delhi for details.
82. A great number of scholars have associated the relief with either of the myths. For details, *refer to* Willetts, 1966, *An Illustrated Bibliography*, pp. 11, 12, 16, 25-26, 28, 31, 44-46, 48, 52, 54-56, 59-64, 66-67, and 69.

6

Development of Monolithic Architecture
Contribution of the Rāṣṭrakūṭas

Taking advantage of the incessant warfare between Cālukya and Pallava empires, Dantidurga had consolidated the Rāṣṭrakūṭa power in Deccan. The heart of the newly founded kingdom had been a flourishing center of rock-cut activities since second century BC. The experience and creativity of generations of *sthāpatis, sūtradhāras*, and *śilpins* had survived in the form of rock-cut monuments. Therefore, revival of the art under the emergent Rāṣṭrakūṭa power was easier. It was, particularly, rejuvenated at the sites of Ellorā and Elephanta besides Jogeśvarī and a solitary instance at Poonā.

1. ELLORĀ CAVES

Ellorā was a great center of artistic activity where excavations belonging to the Buddhist, Brāhmanical and Jaina faiths[1] were vigorously undertaken on live rocks. It was originally known as Elāpura,[2] while the local Maraṭhi name remained Verūl.[3] Its geographical location facilitated linkage with both North and South India. Ellorā had been a flourishing art center even during the preceding Cālukyan times.[4] Quite significantly, the Rāṣṭrakūṭa cave architecture was not a replica of its precursor. Rather it presents a heterogeneous style wherein along with structural models as in the Kailāśa temple, certain innovative measures were also undertaken. For instance, introduction of longitudinal layout in the Lankeśvara cave, or the modifications of Daśāvatāra cave from Buddhist to Brāhmanical, or the profusely carved cult sculptures with perfect iconographic details. The icons representing conventionalized *Āgamic* norms were also a distinctive feature here.

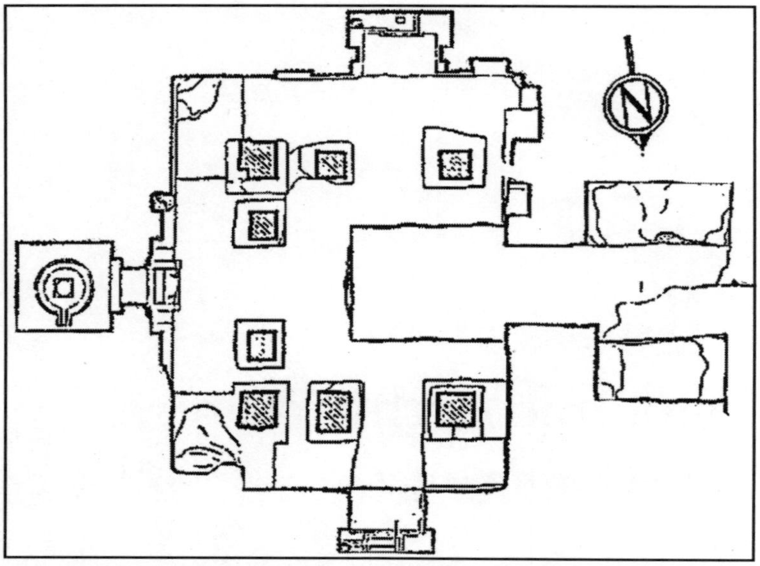

Fig. 108. Ellorā: Gaṇeśa Leṇa, Cave No.1, ground plan (after Soundara Rajan 1981).

The Rāṣṭrakūṭa creations at Ellorā included the Daśāvatāra or cave XV; cave XVI comprising of Lankeśvara shrine; *yajñaśālā* and Parlankā caves, besides the monolithic Kailāśa; the Gaṇeśa leṇa group of nineteen shrines, etc. In this chapter, the plan, development of form, and architectural features of the excavated caves are being analyzed separately from the Kailāśa owing to its monolithic character. The Elephanta caves, which due to their uncertain dating are attributed to various powers including the Rāṣṭrakūṭa,[5] have also been given due space.

Development of Form in the Rāṣṭrakūṭa Caves

Plan

The Rāṣṭrakūṭa caves exhibit meticulous attention towards their lay out scheme. The caves excavations generally reveal a uniform plan. The usual components of their plan comprised a *garbhagṛha* with a frontal pillared *ardhamaṇḍapa*, *mahāmaṇḍapa*, *mukhamaṇḍapa*, and *raṅgamaṇḍapa*. A *nandīmaṇḍapa* aligned to the main cave entrance was also cut even in closed composition as in the Lankeśvara shrine. The Gaṇeśa leṇa[6] group shrines (Figs. 108-116) exhibit three varied patterns of plan: (i) a *trikūṭacala* layout with triple shrines having a common *antarāla* with an *ardhamaṇḍapa* and façade pillared *mahāmaṇḍapa* for all three shrines, (ii) shrines for the main deity and perhaps for nandī at opposite ends with an intervening open court in between, (iii) shrines without freestanding façade pillars at the outer side of the

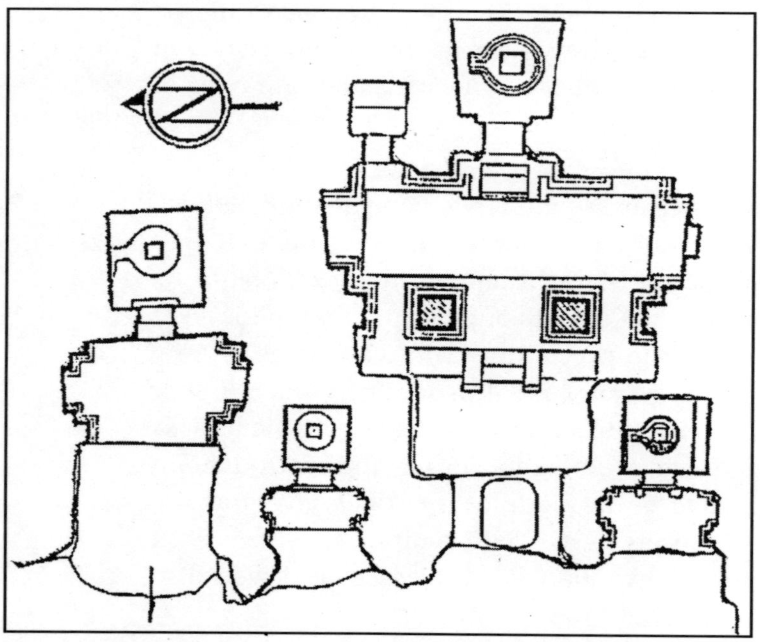

Fig. 109. Ellorā: Gaṇeśa Leṇa, Cave Nos. 2, 3, 4, 5, ground plan (after Soundara Rajan 1981).

ardhamaṇḍapa. At times, the open court with *nandīpīṭha* consisted of small cells as found in cave XXIII. The introduction of a plain *prākāra* or wall on the outer edge of this court with a *dvāra*, with or without *gopura* was also noticeable. The Pātāleśvara cave (Poonā) marked several innovations. For instance, its plan exhibited a polygonal *nandīmaṇḍapa*, *trikūṭacala* lay out in a common *sandhāra* mode, and perhaps, the beginning of a *devī* sub-shrine, separate from, but close to the *garbhagṛha*.

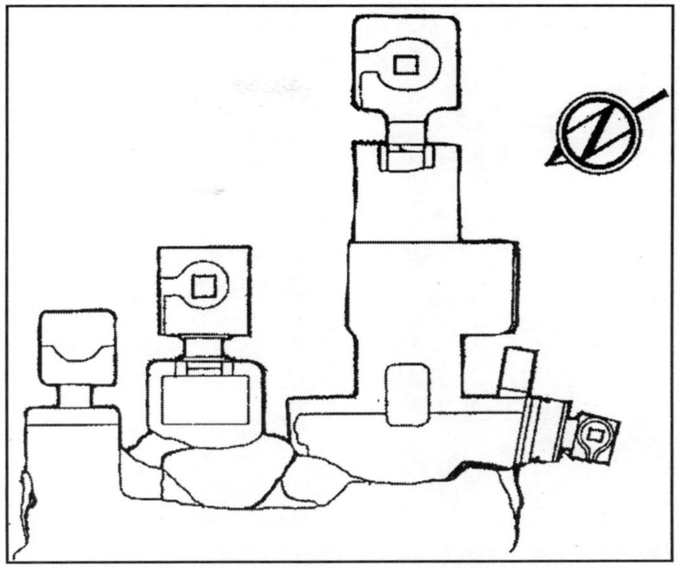

Fig. 110. Ellorā: Gaṇeśa Leṇa, Cave No. 6, ground plan (after Soundara Rajan 1981).

While the Cālukyan caves had transversely running bays, the Rāṣṭrakūṭa instances revealed preference for longitudinal layout as given in the Lankeśvara cave plan (Fig. 117). The Lankeśvara cave was the only instance at Ellorā of a *sandhāra pradakshiṇāpatha* with *vedī* around the *garbhagṛha*. This feature shared with Cālukyas puts it in the transitional phase between Cālukyan and Rāṣṭrakūṭa occupation of the site.

The Daśāvatāra cave (Fig. 118), originally Buddhist, had its upper floor converted for Brāhmanical faith indicated by the panel carvings and *garbhagṛha*. The four cells on the ground floor and the small, seated Buddha images on pillar capitals of the upper floor further corroborates this idea.[7] Besides, the monolithic *maṇḍapa* marked a departure from the usual practice of excavating cave shrines into the rocks.

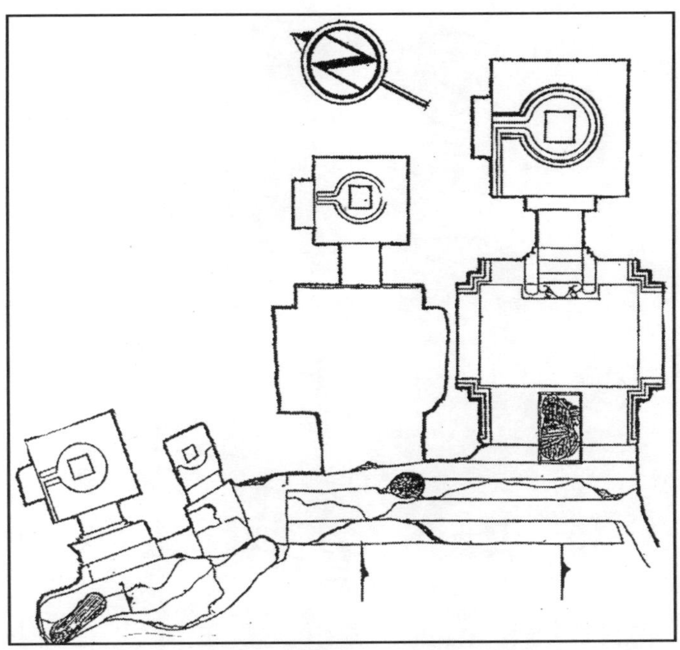

Fig. 111. Ellorā: Gaṇeśa Leṇa, Cave Nos. 8, 9, 10, 11, ground plan (after Soundara Rajan 1981).

Garbhagṛha

An integral part of the plan, the *garbhagṛha* in Rāṣṭrakūṭa caves oriented towards west, was a spacious complex (Pl. 39). It was mainly square in form, though the Daśāvatāra cave had a cubical *garbhagṛha*. The Gaṇeśa leṇa and Jogeśvarī groups provided instance of *trikūṭacala* shrines. The Maheśa relief on rear wall remained a distinctive feature of the caves.

In keeping with the size of the *garbhagṛha*, the *liṅga* and *liṅgapīṭha* placed

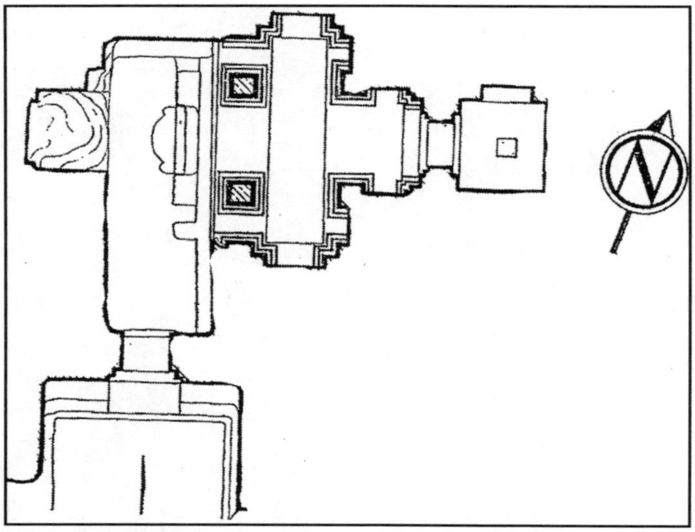

Fig. 112. Ellorā: Gaṇeśa Leṇa, Cave No. 12, ground plan (after Soundara Rajan 1981).

therein also assumed large proportions.[8] The *liṅga* shaft, be it monolithic or separately inserted, was usually square or cylindrical shaped and *mukhaliṅga* or *dhārāliṅga* form has not been found. The Cālukyan caves almost invariably consisted of detachable *ārṣa liṅgas*. In shape they were always square. The circular *liṅgapīṭha* consisted of mouldings as *upāna*, *padma*, *kaṇṭha* with *kampa* above and below, *tripaṭṭa kumuda*, *kapota*, and *prati*. Lankeśvara cave was the only exception with a square *liṅgapīṭha*, yet another indication of its nascent nature. The *liṅgapīṭha* was primarily monolithic in the shrines, though not always with a monolithic *liṅga*.

The *praṇāla*, as water outlet, lay on the north or left of the *garbhagṛha liṅga*. A variant in the Gaṇeśa leṇa group facing north showed a side *praṇāla* westwards, taken straight north along the wall in the form of a channel and out through side of the *dvāra*. This feature, unlike the Pallavas, was also detectable in the Cālukyan caves. Placed north or left to the *liṅga*, *praṇāla* in their caves was either a rectangular or round pit on the floor.

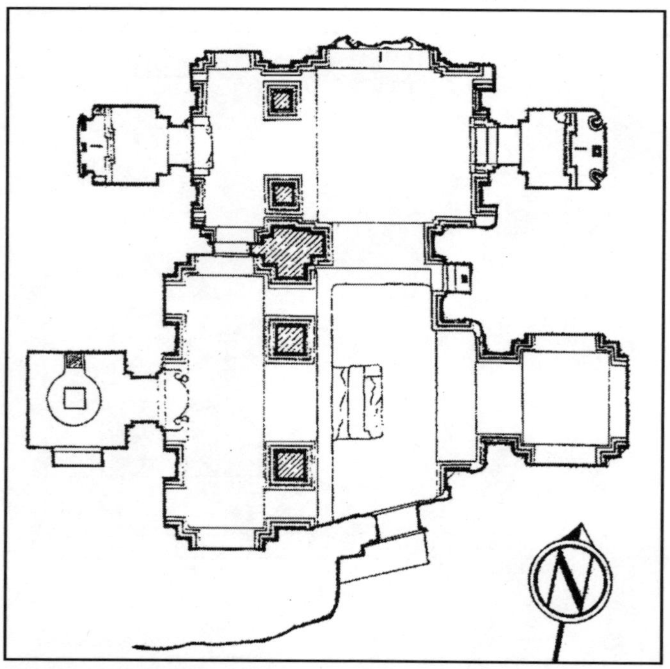

Fig. 113. Ellorā: Gaṇeśa Leṇa, Cave Nos. 13, 14, 15, 16, ground plan (after Soundara Rajan 1981).

Adhiṣṭhāna

Adhiṣṭhāna base, wherever carved, consisted of the usual mouldings - *upāna*, *padma*, *kaṇṭha*, generally *tripaṭṭa kumuda*, *kaṇṭha*, *kapota*, and *prati*. An additional *upapīṭha*, probably to enhance its height, was added to the Kailāśa. A similar elephant based *upapīṭha* was carved in the Lankeśvara cave also. This feature is not found in the Cālukyan monuments, whether rock-cut or structural, except in the outermost *adhiṣṭhāna* of Durgā temple, Aihoḷe. The frequent use of animated elephant and lion figures on the *adhiṣṭhāna* friezes also remained a unique feature of Rāṣṭrakūṭa caves. In the Cālukyan instances, we notice *gaṇa* friezes on the *kaṇṭha* moulding of the *adhiṣṭhāna* as well as of the carved wall panels.

Pillars

Placed usually in the façade, *mukhamaṇḍapa*, *mahāmaṇḍapa*, and *ardhamaṇḍapa*, the number as well as arrangement of the pillars was not uniform. For instance, a total of forty-eight pillars in eight rows of six, each placed from façade till *ardhamaṇḍapa* in the first floor of Daśāvatāra cave, while its ground floor and *nandīmaṇḍapa* had eighteen and four pillars, respectively. The first floor of Lankeśvara cave presented a scheme of eighteen pillars. Other caves, being relatively smaller, consisted of two to four pillars.

The extant instances suggest that the square and octagonal sectioned pillar (Fig. 119) with a *pīṭha* base and a *potikā* without a prominent *taraṅga* was in vogue. Separate *pīṭha* or *oma* as the pillar base was perhaps a Rāṣṭrakūṭa innovation, as we do not find it in the early Cālukyan specimens. The pillar *pīṭha*, often above the *adhiṣṭhāna*, had its own mouldings as *upāna*, *padmakaṇṭha* with a *kampa* above and below, the *tripaṭṭa kumuda*,[9] a narrow *antarita* followed by a slender *prati* and *ardhapadma* just below the pillar shaft. Such *pīṭha* bases were seen in the Lankeśvara cave (Pl. 40). The *gajamuṇḍas* kneeling from the pillar *pīṭha kaṇṭha* moulding and holding foliage in the trunks, on pillars flanking the inner *maṇḍapa adhiṣṭhāna*, appeared quite enchanting.

The pillar shaft was mostly a plain cubical lower *pāda* topped by a slightly tapering *mālā-sthāna*. Its two variants may be seen in the Lankeśvara cave: (i) a short plain base over the *pīṭha* and upwards, a *kalaśa* with multiple fluting. Above this, began the shaft square of huge dimensions, (ii) a plain cubical base with an octagonal shaft projection.

Pillar Decoration

The most distinctive feature about the Rāṣṭrakūṭa pillars was their ornamentation.

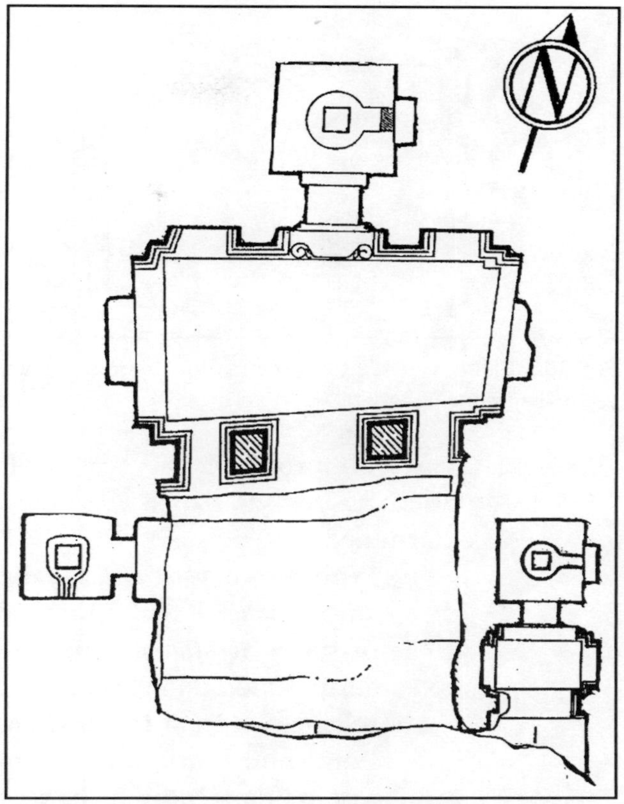

Fig. 114. Gaṇeśa Leṇa, Cave No. 17, ground plan (after Soundara Rajan 1981).

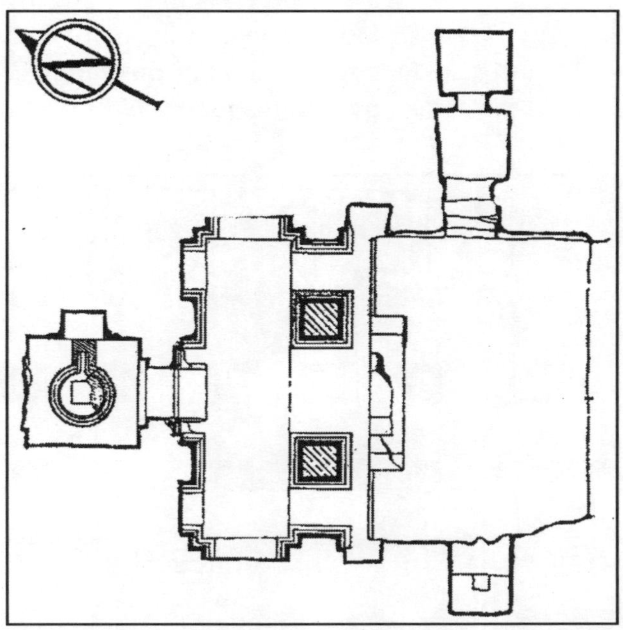

Fig. 115. Ellorā: Gaṇeśa Leṇa, Cave No. 18, ground plan (after Soundara Rajan 1981).

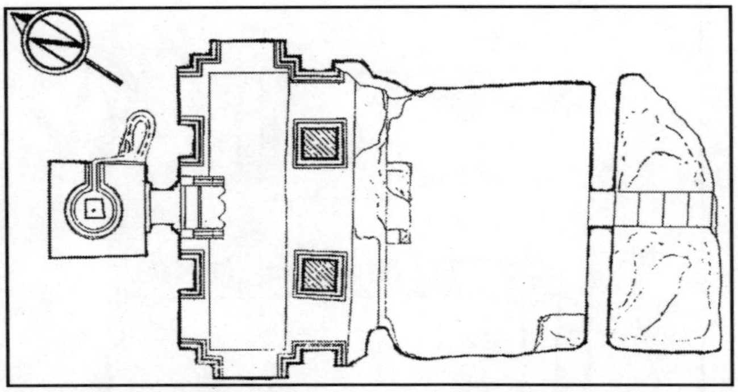

Fig. 116. Ellorā: Gaṇeśa Leṇa, Cave No. 19, ground plan (after Soundara Rajan 1981).

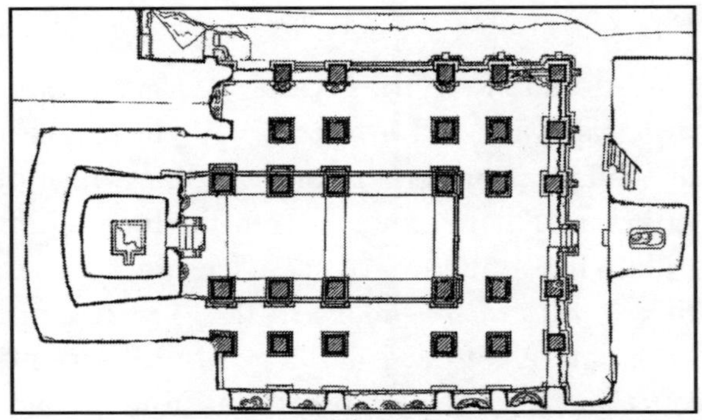

Fig. 117. Ellorā: Cave XVI (Kailāśa), Lankeśvara cave, ground plan (after Soundara Rajan 1981).

They were profusely carved with figures of various deities and *gaṇas* within floral pattern *nāsikās* and panels. On the basis of pillar embellishment, three models may be determined:

(i) With cubical *pāda* and receding *mālā-sthāna* of looped garlands emerging out of *ardhapadmas*. It had figural and floral designs inside the loops. The upper part of the *mālā-sthāna* consisted of a band of alternating *ratnas* and rosettes, surmounted on the cardinal points by the *nāsikā kūḍū* with laterally extending foliage design at the base. Within the *nāsikā*, a multi-foiled *kūḍū* outline with floral bud work stood in place of the *daṇḍikās*. The *kūḍū* enclosed a high rectangular central niche recess left in the form of a lattice window. Elsewhere it was also carved with floral and figural ornamentation. This was topped by the capital components. The *kalaśa* enclosed by the *nāsikās* had a beaded neck and flanged rim. It was surmounted by a *tāḍī* in three expanding courses, the lowest constituting a floral garland. Above this, the *kuṁbha* with sharply square edges had a flat median *paṭṭa* decorated in *patralatā* motif. It was surmounted by a thin square *vīrakaṇṭha* followed by intersecting *potikās*, *uttira*, *vājana*, and *valabhī* above them.

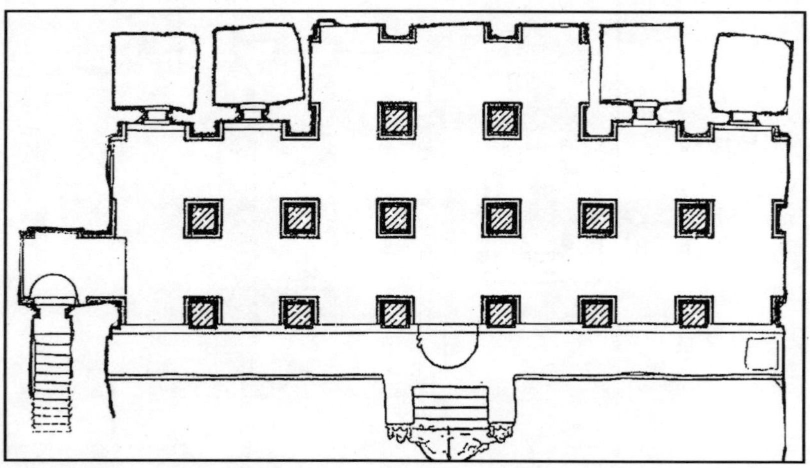

Fig. 118. Ellorā: Cave XV (*Daśāvatāra*), ground plan (after Soundara Rajan 1981).

(ii) This decoration could be seen in pillars with a multi-fluted *kalaśa*. It had the *kalaśa* over *mālā-sthāna* arrangement of floral loops covering *nāsikā* on the four sides and broad single loops joining the corners. Squatting, conch-blowing *gaṇas* with wide apart legs, their bellies pressed on the corners of the base, further embellished the angles. The main loops merged with the overflowing foliage of the *ghaṭapallava*[10] motif. Over this *nāsikā kūḍū*, the actual fluted *kalaśa* part followed by a fluted *tāḍī*, fluted *kuṁbha* with a *patralatā paṭṭa* along its circular *vīrakaṇṭha* and intersecting *potikās* were carved.

(iii) The third type of decoration had an octagonal shaft projection at its base, whose angles were decorated with looped floral arrangements in overlapping curves. The center had an *nāsikā kūḍū*. Over this, the prismatic plain shaft topped by the *mālā-sthāna* with a floral *paṭṭa* top was carved, surmounted by a triangular *nāsikā* front. The *mālā-sthāna* had an octagonal outline, thus having eight *nāsikās* flanking the *kalaśa*. The *nāsikās* hold *gaṇa* figures. Over the *kalaśa* rose the broad, fluted *tāḍī*, broad, fluted *kuṁbha*, and the whole surmounted by an oval *vīrakaṇṭha* and intersecting *potikās*. Angularly placed *śālabhañjikās* served as roof supporters.

Fig. 119. Ellorā: Cave XVI (Kailāśa), Lankeśvara section, interior row of pillars, square *Brahmakānt*, octagonal *Indrakānt* (after AIIS).

We notice that the Rāṣṭrakūṭa pillars had the *nāsikā kūḍū* component as a probable replacement for the *padmabandha* or *maṇḍī* component found in the Cālukyan style. Distinctness, particularly in sculptures carved on the pillars, was the tendency to make the background motifs rather complex. For this, features of the theme were modified to suit the background. However, the Cālukyan pillar sculptures fully emphasized their carvings and their background was rather subdued and secondary.

Pillar Potikā

Unlike their Cālukyan counterparts, the *potikā* in the Rāṣṭrakūṭa pillars did not show well marked *taraṅga* on its curved surface. But like them, they often carried figure sculptures, especially *mithunas*, in endearing postures as in the Daśāvatāra cave. The Lankeśvara cave pillars showed *potikā* figures of *madanikās* with *gaṇa* attendants rising from the *kalaśa* neck and thus, connecting the *potikās* to the main shaft. Figures normally appeared on the lateral faces of the pillars though exceptions in the Gaṇeśa leṇa cave V had them on the front and rear parts.

In contrast to the Cālukyan pillars, the Rāṣṭrakūṭa ones were more bulky, simple and rather less refined. A basic difference detected in their components is that the latter did not reveal a circular cross-section particularly for their *kalaśa* and *kuṁbha*, and were invariably square. Overall, as both bore similarity in elevation features with the Draviḍian pillar order, it is quite likely that the architectural inspiration at the site flowed from the south.

Pilasters

They were carved in the façade, *maṇḍapa*, and *ardhamaṇḍapa*; and as cantoning corner pilasters and *dvāraśākhā* pilasters, flanking the *garbhagṛha*. The latter type exhibited square, octagonal and multi-fluted sections, topped by *mālā-sthāna*, *maṇḍī* or *padmabandha*, *kalaśa*, *tāḍī*, *kuṁbha*, *padma*, *phalaka*, and *potikā*, all components of a Draviḍian pillar 'order'. By this feature the pilasters at *dvāraśākhās* also marked a variation from the pillars placed in the caves. This applied to both Cālukyan and Rāṣṭrakūṭa instances.

Pilasters mostly consisted of a square basal *pīṭha* comprising an *upāna*, *padma*, *kaṇṭha*, *kumuda*, and *prati* mouldings. Above this was a square or oblong-sectioned lower *śaduram*. The middle part comprised of a *triratha* layout as in the Daśāvatāra cave, while the apex part consisted of a surmounted *mālā-sthāna* and *padmabandha*, followed by the *kalaśa*, *tāḍī*, *kuṁbha*, *padma*, *phalaka*, and square *vīrakaṇṭha* and intersecting *potikās*. Pilasters mostly had a single *potikā* with bracket figures like the pillars.

Dvāraśākhās

Two flanking pilasters constituted the *dvāraśākhās*, mainly plain though sometimes, quite ornate. For instance, the *triśākhā* in Lankeśvara cave *garbhagṛha*. Its outermost was the pilaster *śākhā*, the next had *vidyādhara* series, while the third a *ratnaśākhā*. The pilaster *śākhā* had *dvārapālas* in the lowest portion and a *patralatā* in the middle part. It exhibited all the components of a pilaster up to the *potikās*. The next *śākhā* had two female figures holding garlands and flowers in the lowest part adjoining that of the *dvārapālas*. The lintel was constituted by a plain innermost *śākhā* of *bhāraputras* holding garlands in both hands and a plain uppermost *śākhā* corresponding to the *uttira* of the pilaster *śākhā potikā*. Over this, nine seated figures, the first and the last, respectively, Vīrabhadra and Gaṇeśa, and the intervening ones being the saptamātṛkās, surmounted the *kapota*. The Daśāvatāra *nandīmaṇḍapa dvāra* showed *makaravāhinī* Gaṅgā and *kūrmavāhinī* Yamunā flanking its sides. One cave in the Gaṇeśa leṇa group had Gajalakshmī in its *lalāṭabiṁba*. Another had a *vidyādhara* couple bearing the *uttira*. Yet another exhibited rather a southern influence in the pilaster details and *uttarāṅga* portion. A shaft of *triratha* section topped the lowest part of its pilasters consisting of Gaṅgā and Yamunā. The central part had the *patralatā* followed by a cubical *maṇḍī* and partially differentiated *kalaśa*, *tāḍī*, *kuṁbha*, *padma*, *phalaka*, and *potikā*. The whole was surmounted by *uttarāṅga* with *uttira* and *kapota* and finally, the *prastara* showing *hāra* of *kūṭa* and *śālā śikharas* with intervening *nāsikā*, one on each side.

In the Kailāśa complex towards the south, triple storied excavations presented three *trisākhā dvāras*. In all three, the inner two *śākhās* were left plain: (i) the one on the ground floor constituted by pilaster *śakhā* had the lower portion plain. Upwards, the pilasters were complete in details of capital, surmounted by *kapota* with *kūḍūs* and finally, the *prastara* with elaborate *kūṭa nāsikā śālā śikhara*. (ii) The first floor *dvāra* of slender pilaster *śākhā* had Gaṇeśa and Vīrabhadra figures at the base. The pilaster depicted *kapota* with *kūḍūs*, nandī figures on the *prastara* and Gajalakshmī in the *lalāṭabiṁba*. This was rather the most impressive of the three *dvāras*. (iii) The second floor *dvāra* was also incomplete at bottom. The simple pilaster *śākha* was less elaborate in details and finish. Complete in capital components, its *kapota* displayed two *kūḍūs*, two plain *nāsikās*, and floral design. The *prastara* above *uttira* had *kūṭa śālā śikhara*.

Cave XVI-A in the Kailāśa complex contained a rather narrow, undifferentiated, and incomplete *dvāra* with *śakhās* and niches on either side carrying Gaṅgā and Yamunā figures with their attendants. Shrine XVI-B towards the north had a better-finished *dvāra* with a regular pilaster with shaft and other components up to the *kapota kūḍūs* and *prastara*. Another doorframe in the *mukhamaṇḍapa* of the same cave showed *ghaṭadhārinī* Gaṅgā and Yamunā under *chatra* and *cāmaras*, with fully complete pilasters on either side. Doorframes in rest of the caves were either plain or incomplete. This plainness of the majority of Rāṣṭrakūṭa caves offered contrast to the lavishly embellished Cālukyan ones. Gaṇeśa and Durgā flanking the *dvāraśākhās* and occurrence of *lalāṭabiṁba* over the lintel remained the usual Rāṣṭrakūṭa features.

Elevation Details

The Rāṣṭrakūṭa structural temples, as discussed in chapter 3, almost always represented the southern *vimāna* type, with diminishing *talas* and *hāras* culminating in the *stūpī śikhara*. Their rock-cut shrines up to some extent revealed this influence marking cultural affiliations with the south. The usual height of the temple did not go beyond a *catuṣtala*, i.e. four storied structure. For instance, the Parlankā cave with *maṇḍapas* on each level, aligned and connected to form a unified temple. The *uttarāṅga* over the *dvāraśākhās* indicated not only prevalent structural models but also the elevation scheme of the caves. The *uttarāṅga*, carrying *hāra* of *kūṭa* units on the corners and *śālā* in the center or *kūṭa śālās* alternating, suggested prevalence of single floor buildings. Its placement over the *dvāra* indicated that these units probably represented the parapet of the frontal *maṇḍapa*. The *śālā* was also seen in Buddhist caves (Ajantā) while *kūṭa* appeared firstly in the Cālukyan Brāhmanical caves. Henceforth, the *hārāntara* between the *kūṭa* and *śālā* also consisted of *nāsikās*.

Important feature is that these components appeared just on the *garbhagṛha dvāra* and not on that of the exterior *maṇḍapas*. This conveys the notion that perhaps the *garbhagṛha* and adjoining *ardhamaṇḍapa* were to be the main temple part that was to carry a parapet of *kūṭas* and *śālās* all around the *prastara*, *grīvā* and a *śikhara* on top of the *garbhagṛha*. The frontal *maṇḍapas* were probably detached adjuncts. The Rāṣṭrakūṭa artists also carried this tradition of placing *hāra* on the *uttarāṅga*. Only variation was in its being more ornate and having greater number of components. Even double storied *hāra* units appeared as in first floor of triple storied excavations in *Kailāśa* complex suggesting multi *tala* buildings. These miniature models indicated the entire series of elevation components from pilasters up to the *śikhara* showing the *kapota*, *prastara*, *grīvā*, and *śikhara*, fully embellished with carvings.

Towards the exterior the beam *uttira*, followed by *vājana* and *valabhī*, could be seen over the pillar *potikās*. The Lankeśvara cave *valabhī* was reinforced by rafter projections over the pillar placements, running both axially and transversely. The corresponding inner components not visible on the ceiling part indicated that the projections were to serve as cross struts joining the *vīrakaṇṭha* to the upper components of the pillar plan after the *valabhī*. This arrangement betrays the influence of wooden technique in rock excavations.

The next component in elevation, i.e. *kapota*, was often an overhanging with a flange or flex curve. Over this, too, were indications of a wooden rafter block pattern technique. The twin units of the transverse and longitudinal rafter ends joined together by a wooden pin in the central projection indicated that the rafter course was perhaps of the *khaṇḍottara* type.[11] The *kapota* usually comprised of *nāsikā kūḍū* decoration. Above it remained the recessed *prastara*. The various mouldings, from *vājana* till *prastara* collectively forming the *prastara* area above the *potikā* and *uttira* in the inner elevation, ran as individual units around the *ardhamaṇḍapa*, *mahāmaṇḍapa*, *mukhamaṇḍapa* and *raṅgamaṇḍapa* ceilings. The ceilings were mostly flat and even, except where rafter projections were executed. The various panels sculpted on them were an evidence of their smoothness.

Sculptural Embellishment

By the time the Rāṣṭrakūṭa dynasty came into prominence, it seems that the various Hindu deities, their iconographic *lakshaṇas*, rituals, and attendant features were getting elaborated. It is desirable to analyze Rāṣṭrakūṭa caves' sculptures and see whether any variations from preceding Cālukyan art existed.

Placement of the sculptures was primarily in wall panels against the pillars, *adhiṣṭhāna* mouldings, ceiling panels, on the lintel, and also as freestanding. Mainly in relief, they were carved in the façade, *raṅgamaṇḍapa*, *mukhamaṇḍapa*, *mahāmaṇḍapa*, *ardhamaṇḍapa*, and sometimes, on the *garbhagṛha* rear wall.

Thematically, the sculptures ranged from religious, both Śaivite and Vaiṣṇavite, to secular figurines. Śaivite carvings projected both *ugra* and *saumya* aspects of the deity. The former included *andhakāsuravadhamūrti*, *tāṇḍava* Śiva in *catura* pose, *kālārimūrti*, *tripurāntaka*, and *gajāntaka* forms. *Saumya* portrayals included *kalyāṇasundara*, *gaṅgādhara*, *kailāśatolana*, *maheśamūrti*, *liṅgodbhava*, *vṛṣabhāntika*, *ardhanārī*, and Śiva Pārvatī in various poses as in *akshakrīḍā*, on the Kailāśa, etc.

Vaiṣṇavite figures, as seen in the Daśāvatāra cave and Kailāśa *prākāra*, suggested the tendency of grouping them together with Śaivite ones on the *mahāmaṇḍapa* walls. These forms consisted of Viṣṇu, *śeṣaśayī* Viṣṇu, *gajendravarada*, varāha, *trivikrama*, nṛsiṁha and *Kṛṣṇalīlā* panels. Among others, Brahmā, Sūrya, Gaṇeśa, Lakuliśa, nandī, *dvārapālas*, *nidhi* and *gaṇa*, were prominent forms. Female deities included Pārvatī, Mahiṣamardinī, Durgā, Gajalakshmī and Uṣā.

The secular figures, including *mithuna* couples in various poses, constituted the softer aspect of Rāṣṭrakūṭa sculptural art. These may be categorized as sensuous, sensual, and erotic.[12] The Lankeśvara cave façade bays and Daśāvatāra *maṇḍapa* abounded in such figures. The former exhibited nearly twenty-three *mithuna* poses,[13] their preponderance being in the interiors. The erotic figures were relatively small in size. Amongst animals, forms of elephants and lion constituted friezes on the pillar *pīṭha* and *adhiṣṭhāna* mouldings, besides occasionally forming the *upapīṭha*.

The utilization of the ceiling for decorative as well as sculptural purposes was a common feature found in both Cālukyan and Rāṣṭrakūṭa caves. But it is noteworthy that full spread decorative embellishment, as in Aihoḷe and Bādāmī cave ceilings, was markedly lacking in the early Cālukyan caves at Ellorā. The Rāṣṭrakūṭa phase, wherein elaborate ceiling ornamentation, in form of lotus medallions with circular concentric petals, or within square framework with auxiliary decoration on the corners, occurred on the bay ceilings, marked revival of the practice. Kārtikeya, *trimūrti*, *dikpāla*, *vidyādhara*, and *nāga* were other usual ceiling designs. The cave group near Gaṇeśa leṇa had a lotus medallion in the *ardhamaṇḍapa* ceiling. The Lankeśvara cave *raṅgamaṇḍapa* ceiling had a lotus medallion within a square framework, the lotus projecting down, carrying *tāṇḍava* Śiva in *lalita* pose, on its underside. The *dikpālas* were often portrayed in a grid pattern with a central deity, thereby revealing affinity with the Cālukyan style.

Sculptural Art and Style

The Rāṣṭrakūṭa sculptures appeared quite dynamic, vibrant and rigidly delineated. In this aspect they offered contrast to the soft contours and plastic sublimity of the Cālukyan specimens. The Rāṣṭrakūṭa forms were more angular and slim. They exerted tremendous force and boundless energy with a vitality of spirit. They were marked by more ornamentation and less emphasis on facial expressions or body *bhaṅga*, while aesthetic sensibility had been a keynote of the Cālukyan sculptures. The Cālukyan and even Pallava tendency of showing secondary figures such as the *dvārapālas* in mighty statures, almost touching the ceiling was lacking in the Rāṣṭrakūṭa style. Herein we find the *dvārapālas* diminutive, reduced in size, and placed in the interiors only unlike the Cālukyan ones which were placed outside the *garbhagṛha* and the *mahāmaṇḍapa*. The Rāṣṭrakūṭas also took initiative in introducing new iconographic forms[14] as the *liṅgodbhava*, the first instance in Deccan is the Daśāvatāra cave.

The sculptures corresponded to the *Āgamic* norms, as their iconographic analysis in the next chapter shall elaborate. Regarding their distinctive features, a few instances may be cited: (i) the *kalyāṇasundara* panel (Daśāvatāra cave) depicted Śiva clasping Pārvatī's hand in rather an unconventional way. It is the only stance of Śiva holding both her hands. The Lankeśvara cave *ardhamaṇḍapa* bay contained a Śiva Pārvatī panel. Showing both in *akshakrīḍā*, it had Śiva sitting left to Pārvatī whereas usually he is placed to her right. While Pārvatī was in *ardhaparyankāsana*, Śiva was shown in *utkuṭika* pose. Overall, the intimacy apparent in other such sculptures at the Kailāśa was lacking herein. (ii) The *andhakāsurāvadhamūrti* panel in same cave bore similarity to the one in Elephanta. The only distinction was the more subdued figure of Kālī in the latter. (iii) A Lankeśvara pillar panel *ardhanārīśvara* figure had the female part showing a *latā* while the male part consisted of a mango tree in full foliage. This betrayed the imagery of male *sahakāra* or mango as the eternal support of the feminine *latā*. Such imagery had not been used elsewhere for *ardhanārī* figures and revealed an application of classical imagery on ritual sculptures. (iv) The Daśāvatāra cave *kailāśatolana* panel had a composed Śiva whereas Pārvatī revealed her panic by a slight inward turn of her body while still being in the *utkuṭika* pose. Ten-armed Rāvaṇa's act of shaking the Kailāśa was schematically shown in the irregular blocks. Similar panel in the Lankeśvara cave pillar had Rāvaṇa with twenty hands. Fleeing monkeys, semi-divine beings, humans, etc., conveyed the shaking effect. (v) The Lankeśvara *kālārimūrti* depicted Śiva's emergence from a *liṅga* with a circular *pīṭha* and the *praṇāla* projecting northwards. This depiction was in consonance with the *liṅga*'s actual placement in the *garbhagṛha*. Besides, Mārkaṇḍeya was shown in a kneeling position instead of the usual stance of hugging the *liṅga*. (vi) The Maheśa figure in Lankeśvara cave had Vāmadeva to the right, Aghora to the left and Sadyojāta in the center. Even the side faces depicted a frontal aspect. The Aghora held a *kapāla* in his hand; Vāmadeva had a flower bud while Sadyojāta's three hands consisted of *nāga*, *matuluṅga*, *khaṭvāṅga* and fourth was raised in *vyākhyāmudrā*. Aghora and Sadyojāta consisted of the *trinetra*. (vii) The Govardhana Kṛṣṇa rested his left leg upon a reclining *gaṇa* while the right one was placed on a lotus. Other than this, the figure revealed the stylized form of the icon. (viii) The *gajendramoksha* panel had almost equal size anthropomorphic forms of Viṣṇu and Garuḍa. Their whole disposition and Viṣṇu's *kirīṭamakuṭa* bore resemblance to the Cālukyan and even preceding Gupta types in Central India.[15] That the Rāṣṭrakūṭa artists excelled in providing a dimension of vigorous emotion to their stone sculptures is particularly apparent in the Nṛsiṁha panels. The motif had been depicted in various forms. (ix) For instance, the Daśāvatāra cave panel portrayed Nṛsiṁha engaged in a sanguinary battle with the demon, their knees interlocked in an impressive manner. The half gyrating defensive posture of Hiraṇyakaśipu and offensive stance of Nṛsiṁha clearly indicated the winner. The leonine jaw of the deity in wide grin with the right upper arm ready to strike was very well set off by the terror stricken posture of Hiraṇyakaśipu. Another panel in Lankeśvara cave revealed Nṛsiṁha seated on a *padmapīṭha* with slain bodies of Hiraṇyakaśipu and other demons lying around.

Overall, we notice that be it the *andhakāsurāvadhamūrti*, *Mārkaṇḍeyānugrahamūrti*, *gajendramoksha* or Nṛsiṁha panels, the Rāṣṭrakūṭa sculptor usually emphasized interrelationship of two dynamic figures. The balanced forces of the two solid figures in confrontation within one field were perpetually drawn towards each other and repelled, sharing common background space and internally generating interacting energies.[16]

The form of *Mahiṣamardinī* in Lankeśvara cave had been carved on a wall face projecting from a corner pillar perhaps as it could not be accommodated on the pillar face. It remains a sequential representation of the fight showing Mahiṣa in three different forms[17] within the same panel. The figure of Sūrya in the same corridor had the *pādasaras* and a ring on the toes instead of usual stocking feet. Besides, it wore an ordinary *kirīṭamakuṭa* rather than the customary square, high crowns as seen in the *ardhamaṇḍapa* bay panel.

Gaṇeśa was a favorite motif of carving at Ellorā. A Gaṇeśa sculpture in the Gaṇeśa leṇa group belonged to the *idampuri* type with left turned trunk. Another figure in relief was placed in an *ardhamaṇḍapa* niche in the two caves' group near Gaṇeśa leṇa.

Fig. 120. Ellorā: Cave XV (*Daśāvatāra*), lintel detail, east wall, doorway (after AIIS).

The four-armed, seated figure with *nāga yajñopavīta* and leftward turned trunk had no *kirīṭa* but other ornaments. A *makara toraṇa* was raised over his head with a *padma* pendent under the central loop and *makaras* crowding in on the niche side, perhaps for lack of space. The Lankeśvara panel Gaṇeśa in *ardhaparyankāsana* was similarly four armed.

The Rāṣṭrakūṭa *dvārapāla* reflected a typical style. They were usually scooped on the sidewalls, facing inwards. Those in Daśāvatāra cave were four-armed, their upper arms holding *nāga* and *triśūla*, while the lower ones resting on *gadā* were in *kaṭihasta*. They stood upon a *padmapīṭha* consisting of lion and elephant forms on its *kapota* moulding. *Dvārapālas* in Lankeśvara cave, also four-armed with similar objects, were cross-legged in *pādasvāstika* pose. They wore high *jaṭāmakuṭa, kuṇḍalas, keyūras, udarabandha*, and *yajñopavīta* over right arm in the *nivīta* style. One of them had a garland of bells also running round to the knees and then turning up. These iconographic details were followed in almost all Rāṣṭrakūṭa *dvārapāla* figures.

The lintel *lalāṭabiṁba* (Fig. 120) often depicted two or four-armed Lakuliśa seated in *padmāsana*, attended by *gaṇas* and devotees. The Gaṇeśa leṇa *maṇḍapa* lintel had the *samudramanthana* scene. Both the groups of *devas* and *dānavas* faced each other on either side. Gajalakshmī and *bhāraputra gaṇas* were also noticeable along with floral embellishments. The *mithuna* figures in these caves, carved for whatever reasons,[18] were a prominent art motif. Seen standing or sitting, they appeared quite amorous and were sculpted in *spristaka, piḍiṭaka, ghaṭṭitaka, tilatandulaka, kshīraniraka*, and *vṛkshadhirudhaka* embraces.[19] These figure panels were mainly carved in the Lankeśvara façade, *nandīmaṇḍapa adhiṣṭhāna* and Kailāśa *mahāmaṇḍapa*.

Some instances of painting also survived in Rāṣṭrakūṭa caves at Ellorā. The last cave in the Gaṇeśa leṇa group had painted designs, quite elaborate in nature, on its *maṇḍapa* and *garbhagṛha* ceilings. These lotus medallion motifs, enclosed in rectangles, carried floral and other designs. One had *liṅgodbhava* Śiva with white drapery and body while the *liṅga* was done blue. Śiva *tāṇḍava*, musician group, candraśekhara, *apsarās* and *gāndharvas*, etc., were other themes painted there.

Thus, we may visualize phases of Rāṣṭrakūṭa rock-cut activities in Ellorā caves. The earliest Daśāvatāra cave was probably a modification of Buddhist model by adding an extra storey. Besides, the monolithic *maṇḍapa* carved in its front became a precursor for others. The Lankeśvara cave with Maheśa relief, square *liṅgapīṭha* and *sandhāra pradakshiṇā*, *maṇḍapa* with clearly demarcated central nave, a projecting frontal *nandīmaṇḍapa* recession with axial leanings, perhaps, signified a transitional phase between Cālukyan and Rāṣṭrakūṭa periods. The Pātāleśvara cave at Poonā offered some variations. Its trinity set up, *sandhāra* mode, the lack of rock-cut images in the *garbhagṛha* suggesting some portable type[20] images, an open pillared, circular *nandīmaṇḍapa* in the frontal court, were rather striking. The circular *nandīmaṇḍapa* and their *liṅgapīṭhas*, perhaps indicated their technically being of the *'kailāśa'* mode[21] of circular layout. The final phase may be seen in the Rāṣṭrakūṭa monolithic ventures. Having thus gradually succeeded in breaking the rock barrier, the artists materialized a complete structural temple elevation in a monolithic form.

We can, thus, summarize that the Rāṣṭrakūṭa cave plan type, besides specific features, consisted of a circular monolithic *liṅgapīṭha* with a *liṅga* in three parts, a Maheśa panel on *garbhagṛha* rear wall, a Lakuliśa figure as *lalāṭbiṁba*, Gaṇeśa Pārvatī in side *devakoṣṭhas*, the latter often in *pañcāgnitapas* pose. Two subsidiaries shrines, either for remaining members of the trinity or may be for some other gods, along with the shrine layout and the open front court, were also part of the plan arrangement. While the cut-in caves mostly followed this pattern, the monolithic creations as Kailāśa showed some variation, especially in the elevation scheme and sculptural carving. The Daśāvatāra cave with a variety of sculptural styles, non-Brāhmanical architecture, and a purely Brāhmanical monolithic *nandīmaṇḍapa*, was perhaps used by the artists to hone their skills before commencing work on the Kaīlāśa.[22] This brings us to our next point of analysis, i.e. the cut-out monolithic Kailāśa.

2. KAILĀŚA TEMPLE

It is a unique masterpiece of Rāṣṭrakūṭa art (Pls. 41-42). Though excavated internally as a cave, its exteriors marked the monolithic replica of a structural shrine. With the Kailāśa, the rock-cut mode reached its climax. It rather epitomizes an architectural sculpture. Assigned to Krishna I,[23] the transformation of this cave XVI into a full-scale replica of a constructed temple bespeaks genius of both the patron as well as the artisans.[24] The shrine is believed to be one of the eight *jyotirliṅga* shrines.[25] It is more like a complex of different edifices. For the vast magnitude and variety of its components, the duration[26] of its making, as also the architectural phases[27] have rather been speculative.

Mode of Carving

Once the idea of carving the monolith was conceived, the artisans must have rapidly set out on the herculean task of excavating nearly twenty million tonnes[28] of rock. The work ahead was extremely challenging. The excavation and carving, befitting a monolithic creation must have obviously started from the top.[29] As has been suggested, initially an oblong mass of rock about 200′ long and 100′ high and 100′ wide was separated in the middle of the huge cliff, made possible by vertically digging three trenches in the hill.[30] This may have been rendered easy by the configuration of rocks. Next stage was probably the hewing of this irregular rock mass into shape. For this too, beginning from the top, the rear mass of the rock was shaped into a *vimāna* to crown the *garbhagṛha* (Pl. 44). Each portion was painstakingly finished and polished before moving downwards. The carving must have been undertaken alongside the hill's slope. The work of carving might have proceeded simultaneously as indicated by the upper finished portions and lower unfinished portions of the nearby Jaina Chotā Kailāśa. This would have also prevented any possibility of cumbersome scaffolding later. Gradually, the Kailāśa and its adjuncts acquired a concrete form.

Development of Form in the Kailāśa

Plan

This unparallel edifice as a whole consisted of four main components, viz. the main shrine, *gopuram*, an intermediate *nandīmaṇḍapa*, and the surrounding cloister. In plan, it exhibited the *gopuram*, *nandīmaṇḍapa*, *raṅgamaṇḍapa*, *antarāla*, and *garbhagṛha*, thereby reflecting a dominant Draviḍian complex. On both sides of the courtyard, supplementary peripheral shrines were excavated. The north side had the Lankeśvara and river goddesses' excavations, while southwards the *yajñaśālā*, a small cave below it, and the Paralankā cave[31] were scooped. Towards the south of the *garbhagṛha* was a rectangular *śālā* type *mātṛkā* shrine facing north. It had Gaṇeśa and Durgā carved in niches for lack of adequate rock area.

The base of the *vimāna* proper measured 164′ from east to west and 109′ from north to south, and was approached by a flight of steps from both the courtyards. Through the *maṇḍapa* a door led to the flat roofed *mahāmaṇḍapa* or *raṅgamaṇḍapa* consisting of sixteen pillars. Here the *sabhāmaṇḍapa* blended with the triple *mukhacatuṣkī* openings in a *navaraṅga*[32] type layout by the pillar arrangements. Their *navaraṅga* arrangement created a big central nave and two procession paths, besides demarcation of the ceiling into nine parts. One of them, from the door to the *antarāla*, led to the *garbhagṛha* and the other approached the two side balconies. On three sides of the roof and at the two rear corners, five *parivārālayas* were placed. This feature constituted the Kailāśa into a unique *pañcāyatan* temple. In the usual *pañcāyatan* arrangement, the *parivārālaya* shrines were placed at the four corners as seen in the Gupta Deogarh temple. However, in the Kailāśa the total number of shrines including the *nandīmaṇḍapa* opposite the *garbhagṛha* is seven. Thus, the placement as well as number of shrines rendered the Kailāśa a unique character not seen elsewhere.

The 25′ square *nandīmaṇḍapa* (Pl. 45) was positioned on a highly ornamented *adhiṣṭhāna*. Flanking it two huge elephants and two *dhvajastambhas* were carved in the two courtyards (Pl. 46). The latter, about 45′ high, were quite majestic in their setting. The *nandīmaṇḍapa* was connected to the rest of the temple as well as to the *gopuram* by bridges.

Fig. 121. Ellorā: Cave XVI (Kailāśa), elephant caryatids.

In orientation, the axial alignment of the temple ran from west to east, although due to its position conditioned by the hillside, the entrance was on the west. The double storied entrance *gopuram* manifested Draviḍian influence.

Making of the Adhiṣṭhāna

While the Rāṣṭrakūṭa structural shrines revealed a preference for *kapotabandha adhiṣṭhāna,* the excavated Kailāśa complex had a *prati* or *pādabandha* type. The use of *upapīṭha* was a rare feature employed only in the Kailāśa. The *garbhagṛha*, its frontal *maṇḍapa*, subsidiary shrines, and *nandīmaṇḍapa* were all based on a 25′ high *adhiṣṭhāna*, almost constituting a ground storey. Such a massive base was created, perhaps, to uplift the whole composition out of the encompassing pit around it. Because of it, the whole temple acquired the appearance of resting on elephant and lion backs. The animals looked like *bhārvāhakas* supporting the edifice (Fig. 121). Had there been dynamism or movement in their poses, the temple would have actually emulated a chariot. It rose from the ground in a series of recessed offsets and mouldings as *upāna*, *jagati*, *kumuda*, and *galā*. Above was a spirited frieze of lions and elephants. In the *adhiṣṭhāna* mouldings we find use of *vṛtta kumuda* instead of *tripaṭṭa kumuda*.

Adhiṣṭhāna beneath the *nandīmaṇḍapa* was comprised of the usual mouldings, though the lower ones were not fully done. It consisted of pilasters flanking sculptured

Fig. 122. Ellorā: Cave XVI, Lankeśvara section, pillar details.

panels. Above these was an elephant frieze followed by the *kapota*. The *kaṇṭha* moulding reveals *mithuna* figures. The subsidiary shrines mounted over the projections of the tall base had their own *adhiṣṭhāna*.

Pillars

They were placed in the *maṇḍapa*, *nandīmaṇḍapa*, and cloisters (Pls. 47-48), while their special arrangement made the *navaraṅgamaṇḍapa* quite unique. As the temple components were of varying shapes, the number of pillars within them was not uniform either. The *raṅgamaṇḍapa* had sixteen pillars arranged in groups of four, one in each direction.

The pillars broadly represented two types:

(i) the first with a square base that first curved inward, and then outward. Above it, the square shaft was quite massive in dimensions. It consisted of floral and

Fig. 123. Ellorā: Cave XVI, Lankeśvara, pillar capital details.

bird designs in two horizontal bands. These were topped by *caitya nāsikā* motifs with *mithuna* figures, deities, *gaṇas*, and floral or animal designs carved within. They were supported by floral motifs, followed by a perpendicular floral band. Above this were the *mālā-sthāna* motif and two floral bands. Henceforth the shaft turned octagonal, then sixteen sided and fluted. At its four corners lions or *gaṇas* supported the floral band above. This was followed by a *pūrṇaghaṭa* with animal or floral designs at the corners. Hereafter the shaft was again square topped by a square capital (Fig. 122; Pls. 49-50).

(ii) The second type of pillars had a square base that was fluted upwards. The shaft above was big and square. Decorated with a floral pattern, then a band with geometrical designs with floral motifs, the shaft next consisted of *caitya kūḍū* with figures as seen in type first. Above this is the *mālā-sthāna* decoration (Pls. 51-52; Fig. 123). One such pillar in the *raṅgamaṇḍapa* had *samudramanthana* scenes carved on the four sides of its shaft.

The pillar bases in both the types consisted of various mouldings. Most of the pillars in the Kailāśa *raṅgamaṇḍapa* and Parlankā cave had bulbous *kumuda* mouldings in their bases (Pl. 53). Bases in the Lankeśvara cave pillars were more symmetrical and

Fig. 124. Ellorā: Cave XVI (Kailāśa), *śikhara vimāna* as visible from exteriors.

geometrically precise. The sixteen sided *kuṁbha* capital pillars of the Lankeśvara were not seen in either the *raṅgamaṇḍapa* or the Parlankā cave. In the pillar capitals *ghaṭapallava* gradually evolved into a fully ornamental unit with profuse foliage while the *kalaśa* was sometimes vertically fluted (Pls. 54-55). A new element of cushion capital was also introduced in form of full panels of bracket figures of graceful females. The pillars in Kailāśa were amalgamation of *ghaṭapallava* and compressed cushion types.

The two 16 metres high obelisks *'dhvajastaṁbhas'* in the courtyard had the pillars of the Draviḍian style, with a cushion capital (Pl. 56). Originally they consisted of a *triśūla* that is no longer existent.

Dvāraśākhās

They were an integral part of the architectural ensemble of rock-cut mode. The Ellorā shrines offered an amazing variety of doorways. The Kailāśa complex *dvāraśākhās* were largely similar to those in the caves. The doorframe of the *raṅgamaṇḍapa* was elaborately decorated. Two *dvārapālikās* with attendants flanked its sides. The *śākhās* depicted some very erotic *mithunas*. Two *dvārapālas*, both three-eyed, four-armed, with decorative *makuṭas*, necklaces, etc., holding serpents in their hands were seen on either side of the door reclining against their big *gadās*. Their iconography suggested as if Śiva himself was guarding the shrine.

Entrance to the small cave below the *yajñaśālā*, flanked by *dvārapālikās* on either side, was carved in the shape of an exquisitely decorated *toraṇa*. The door to the *garbhagṛha* was also intricately embellished. Pilasters in full relief were carved on the *śākhā*. The remaining *śākhās* depicted geometrical patterns and human figures. On its left, *makaravāhinī* Gaṅgā was carved, her right hand in *kaṭyāvalaṁbita* pose. To the right of the door *kūrmavāhinī* Yamunā was carved, with her left hand in *kaṭyāvalaṁbita*. Both the goddesses had *chatra* over their heads. Gaṅgā stood inclined to the left, while Yamunā was inclined to the right. Gaṇeśa and Virabhadra were seated at the base of the pilaster *śākhā* in the Parlankā cave. The placement of *nidhi* figures, *pūrṇaghaṭa*, *vidhyādharas*, Gajalakshmī, etc., in the *dvāraśākhās* had also acquired prominence. The *uttarāṅga* above with *uttira*, *kapota*, and *prastara* had been exquisitely executed depicting miniature *kūṭa-nāsikā-śālā śikhara* as seen in the caves. *Sopāna* with moulded side parapets provided entry to the *garbhagṛha*. The Kailāśa *prākāra*, too, had an elaborate *gopuram* with a passage cut through its lower part to reach the courtyard and elaborate carvings on the outer *prākāra* side.

Elevation of the Temple

The Kailāśa *vimāna* was primarily of the Draviḍa type with *caturārṣa* structure from the base to the *grīvā* and *aṣṭakoṇīya grīvā* and *śikhara* (Fig. 124). It was a *catuṣtala vimāna* rising to 95′ height. The first *tala* was a *sandhāra* type with corner *karṇakūṭas* and a central *bhadraśālā*. The inter-space between corner *kūṭa* and *bhadraśālā* was occupied by additional *śālās*. Flat slabs upon which the upper structure rested covered the *āliṅda* space between the *āditala bāhyabhitti* and *antarbhitti*. This stepping back effect gave a sense of height to the upper portions. The second *tala hāra* comprised *karṇakūṭas*,

Fig. 125. Ellorā: Cave XVI (Kailāśa), projecting *gopuram kakshāsana.*

Fig. 126. Ellorā: Cave XVI (Kailāśa), *Nandimaṇḍapa.*

bhadraśālā projection, and additional *śālās* between the *kūṭas* and *bhadra*. This arrangement continued in the next *tala* also. Thus, the *hāra* scheme of *kūṭa-śālā-bhadraśālā-śālā-kūṭa* was created. The fourth *tala* showed a deviation where four *Vṛṣas* were carved in the four corners. The *Viṣṇuchanda śikhara* above was *aṣṭakoṇīya* with frontal *nāsikās* on each side. Its *mahānāsikā* bore a *yogeśvara* Śiva image. It had no *stūpī*, thereby raising a doubt whether it was ever consecrated.[33]

The external roofs of temple *maṇḍapas* at Kailāśa consisted of a huge *padmachatra* with four encircling lions. This feature was unknown in the Cālukyan types though the *hāra* was a common element in both the styles.

Its *gopuram* had a *śālā śikhara* rising above a rectangular *grīvā* on the upper storey. It displayed a projecting overhanging balcony with *kakshāsana*, a feature also seen in *nandīmaṇḍapa* (Figs. 125-126) but not anywhere in South India.

In plan and elevation, the Kailāśa is often likened to the Cālukyan Virūpāksha temple at Paṭṭaḍakal.[34] As southern style temples, both had pyramidal *śikhara* with *kūṭa-śālā hāra*; a plan consisting of *mahāmaṇḍapa*, *garbhagṛha* with a *pradakshiṇāpatha*, a detached *nandīmaṇḍapa*, sculptured wall *devakoṣṭhas* and heavy *kapotas* with *gaṇa* motifs, etc. It has also been compared to the Pallava Kāñcīpuram Kailāśanātha shrine.[35] The layout of a typical South Indian temple complex comprising of *garbhagṛha*, a cloistered *maṇṭapam, mahāmaṇṭapam*, and entrance *kopuram* had evolved by the seventh century. At Kailāśa we find all four of these features. Besides, the *gajathara pādabandha adhiṣṭhāna*, a *catuṣtala aṣṭakoṇīya śikhara, ālinda* arrangement on the *āditala* as discussed above and sculptural affinity to be considered later. Hence the similarity.[36] The Cālukyan shrine Virūpāksha's affinity to the Kāñcī Kailāśanātha is quite apparent.[37] As the Pallava, Cālukya and Rāṣṭrakūṭa powers indulged in regular conflicts, probable cultural contacts resultant thereof and mutual influence of their art styles cannot be totally overruled. However, it goes beyond doubt that the originality of a rock-cut monolithic complex and its superb execution was entirely Rāṣṭrakūṭa innovation.

Thus, the architectural technique and carving of the monumental Kailāśa remains unparalleled in Indian art history. All its architectural components had been quite systematically integrated into a unified whole. Standing within its precincts and surrounded by its antique pavilions, one is entirely lost in a world oblivious of the present surroundings. May be in an attempt to relieve it of its dull environs, the entire complex was plastered white, a feature that led to its designation as *raṅgamahal*.

However, the crowning glory of Kailāśa lies in its sculptural ornamentation. Unrivalled as a rock-architecture, sculpturally it denoted a great spiritual achievement wherein every form pulsated with some underlying meaning and symbolism.

Sculptures

The Kailāśa, itself sculptural representation of a structural model, abounded in plastic forms (Pl. 57). The sculptures, mainly in relief, were carved as panels in the *nandīmaṇḍapa, raṅgamaṇḍapa*, surrounding cloisters and *prākāra* enclosure, in *garbhagṛha devakoṣṭhas*, under the bridge connecting the *nandīmaṇḍapa* with the *mahāmaṇḍapa*, on pillars; as *adhiṣṭhāna* friezes; as *upapīṭha* base on the pillars and pilasters; on the *candraśālās*; in the *pradakshiṇāpatha* shrines on the roof; and even on the *maṇḍapa* roof.

A plethora of Śaivite sculptures was hewn out of the live rocks in the Kailāśa complex. Dedicated to Śiva, the temple treasures his all possible manifestations. Representations with Pārvatī; his various *ugra* and *saumya* aspects; *nṛtyamūrtis* as well as anionic form leaves the spectator spellbound in the all-pervading Śiva mystique.

Amongst the Vaiṣṇavite sculptures, the *avatāras*, Śeṣaśayī, and panels from *Rāmāyaṇa* and *Mahābhārata* were prominent. Subsidiary deities, such as Brahmā, Gaṇeśa, nandī, *nidhis, gaṇas, dvārapālas, dikpālas, gāndharvas, vidyādharas, kāla*, Bhairava, etc., were carved by the sculptors in a lively manner. The female deities comprised of Durgā, Mahiṣamardinī, Pārvatī, Gaṅgā, Yamunā, Saraswatī, Kālī, Cāmuṇḍā, Mātṛkās and Gajalakshmī.

Apart from the religious sculptures, there was also a category of *mithuna* figures in the caves, as discussed earlier. Animal forms had also been carved profusely all around the *adhiṣṭhāna, upapīṭha*, at pillar bases, on the *prastara*, in friezes, and on the roof (Pls. 58-59). Above all, the temple itself emerged as a superb sculptural masterpiece.

Art in Sculptures

The reliefs were carved rather deep and high almost from all the sides. But they were not stuck on the rock surface or installed within the niches. They, in a way, seemed inseparable from the rock creating a feeling of totality. In addition to being component of the architectural scheme, the relief sculptures on the walls and pillars of Kailāśa, respectively, served three specific functions: dramatic, monumental and decorative.[38] Those carved in *nandīmaṇḍapa* and *raṅgamaṇḍapa* wall panels emphasized action and emotion as they depicted *paurāṇic* and epic scenes with theatrical vividness. The *devakoṣṭha* sculptures were rather iconic representations. Instead of depicting a specific episode, they evoked the god's presence in a timeless aspect. While these two types affirmed and represented the Brāhmanical traditions, the last type consisting of *mithunas* with varying degrees of sensuality probably served the popular folk cult tradition. Above all, the abundance of subsidiary sculptures scattered everywhere seemed to bind the whole complex as a coherent unit.

An analysis of Kailāśa sculptures may be initiated with their compositional arrangements. Figures in some of the compositions were portrayed in a tense situation, while in others they were rather tranquil. Of the former category, the most remarkable was the *rāvaṇānugraha* or *kailāśatolana* panel on *mahāmaṇḍapa adhiṣṭhāna*. Coomaraswamy underlined a powerful visual realization of geotectonic conception in the panel comparable only with the 'Elevation of Earth' in the Udaigiri Varāha sculpture.[38] It is also held to be a synthesis of the formal values with psychological elements.[39]

A comparison of the same motif in the preceding Cālukya reliefs enables us to gauge the extent of expertise achieved by the Rāṣṭrakūṭa sculptors. Similar panel in Cālukyan cave XIV divided in two equal parts had Śiva and Pārvatī in *āliṅganāmudrā* in upper half, while the lower depicted Rāvaṇa uprooting the Kailāśa. The fragile figure and awkward posture of Rāvaṇa offered contrast to the unperturbed equipoise of Śiva Pārvatī and their attendants.[40] The apparent lack of organic relation between the upper and lower parts of the panel indicated artistic weakness of the composition. Same motif from the structural Virūpāksha temple (Paṭṭaḍakal) assigned disproportionate importance to Rāvaṇa. It had an arrangement of figures suggesting the unsettled position of the divine couple. The technique of unifying composition showing varied movements highlighted in Virūpāksha shrine might have inspired the Kailāśa artisan. The affinity between Kailāśa and the Paṭṭaḍakal shrine has already been mentioned.

Sculpturally, in a southern fashion, all four representations of the motif in Kailāśa revealed prominence to Rāvaṇa, shown almost equal to Śiva. Śiva's *parśu* was also identical to the Tamil type, unseen in other *rāvaṇānugrahamūrti* instances at Ellorā. Ellorā cave XXIX panel had Śiva and Pārvatī in the central position, totally immune from the impact of the shaking mountain depicted as a flat platform of rectangular blocks. Despite overwhelming physical presence of characters, the panel in the accepted classical style failed in evoking the spontaneity of the action.

On the contrary, the Kailāśa panel imbibed a realization of the very momentousness of the action. Characters of diverse movements were presented meticulously in an integrated totality. Rāvaṇa in *garuḍasthānaka* pose, trying to lift the mountain seemed to churn the surroundings with little effort. The inertia of Śiva's poise created a reaction from the top and between these forceful acts, the atmosphere appeared quite charged and dynamic. To create such dynamism on the rock, the sculptor seemed to have shifted emphasis from mass to void and volume to linearity unlike the preceding classical Gupta portrayals. Thus, "...the action is set in a deep box-like hollow from the darkness of which the figures seem to emerge according to the depth of the relief graded into a number of planes by receding cuts".[41]

Forms and figures in the Kailāśa were rendered dynamic by the predominant use of diagonals in their setting. This was particularly visible in the *Tripurāntaka*, *Naṭarāja*, Nṛsiṁha, and Mahiṣamardinī panels, and offered advancement from the classical equipoise forms even in action packed scenes. The compositional diagonals entailed a force that directed from whichever direction created a feeling of charging motion distinguishing the Kailāśa panels from others. Movements and counter movements in different directions have enriched the choreography of these panels. Panels of Nṛsiṁha, Rāvaṇa's fight with Jaṭāyu (Fig. 127), and Hanumān crossing the sea, rank amongst the best instances of diagonal motion of forms. An enterprising use of empty space in these panels accentuated the sense of motion. This element of motion seems to have also influenced the tranquil figures. For instance, the Viṣṇu *Anantaśayī* panel when compared with that in Gupta Deogarh *Daśāvatāra* temple, or the one in Mahābalipuram Mahiṣamardinī *maṇḍapam*, clearly conveys its creativity. Although Viṣṇu was in repose, yet actions as Brahmā's emergence from his *nābhikamal*, the hoods of śeṣanāga and fingers of Lakshmī pressing Viṣṇu's legs signified movement. The *Umāsahita* panel also exhibited this new idiom quite impressively. The subtle turn of Pārvatī, seated in *ardhaparyankāsana*, towards her left to converse with Śiva, poised in *sācika mudrā* appeared rather unparallel.

Fig. 127. Ellorā: Cave XVI (Kailāśa), Jaṭāyu's attack on Rāvaṇa, southern façade (after ASI).

In a way these art creations were marked by spontaneous release of emotive forces. This not only dramatized the events but also humanized the *dramatis personae*. In Kailāśa sculptures the space in between also became a part of the sculpture. The area of the sculpture was extended further to such an extent that sometimes the onlooker becomes a part of it. For instance, the *yajñaśālā* sculptural forms extended into the open space and activated the space around them. Figures of *saptamātṛkās* in the Bhairava panel below the *nandīmaṇḍapa*, shown at Bhairava's feet, were not carved inside the niche but placed a little far off, on the ground. The figures in such reliefs moved freely in the space provided to them. Some seemed like emerging from, while some appeared receding back into the niche. Whatever their positions, these figures belonged to that space, charged and activated by their presence and activity, thus creating an otherworldly atmosphere inside the niche.

Among the *ugra* aspects of Śiva, the *Andhakāsurasaṁhāramūrti* on north wall of the *mahāmaṇḍapa* offered a contrast to the intensity and ferocity of *Daśāvatāra* cave panel. The Kailāśa Śiva conveyed a spirited, triumphant, and joyful mood. The *tripurāntaka* relief covering two wall segments at right angles represented the three cities as three blocks of small figures and columns brought into the line of Śiva's arrow. The relief marked a departure from the conventional spatial limitations of a framed niche. Quite unusually, it had Śiva with two arms and a conical *makuṭa* resembling similar features in an instance from Pāpanātha temple at Paṭṭadakal. But the balanced shapes, finer sculptural details against the plain surface, the intersecting arcs of the bow, the horses' backs, all assigned a grace and individuality to the Kailāśa panel.

The *nṛtyamūrtis* of Śiva constituted a distinct class of sculptures. Bharata's *Nāṭyaśāstra* enumerated 108 kinds of dances.[42] The *Śaivāgamas* though referred to a similar number, described just nine forms.[43] Śiva's dances symbolized both destruction and creation, life that renews itself by consuming life. As Coomaraswamy has held, 'the root idea behind all of these dances is more or less one and the same, the manifestation of primal rhythmic energy'.[44] But it seems that the concept of *naṭeśa* Śiva was still generalized at Ellorā.[45]

Śiva's dance representations in Ellorā included a sculpture in the *talasamsphoṭitam*[46] style, carved on the northern wall lower level of the *nandīmaṇḍapa*. It had Śiva putting his weight on his left leg while raising the right one higher than his left knee to be put down vehemently on the ground. The left arm was stretched across the chest in *patākā* pose. Attendant *devas* could be seen sitting on miniature shrines forming the lintel of the niche frame. Flying *gāndharvas* flanked the pilasters completing the frame. In this panel also the sculptor had projected the figure in front of the frame that could not confine his composition. Śiva's ten arms spread out like plumage of a dancing peacock, emphasizing the linear structure of the angular composition that looked like a geometric diagram of movement.

Three *nṛtyamūrtis* were placed in *vimāna devakoṣṭhas*. The eastern *koṣṭha* image on the south wall was particularly noteworthy. Movement in this sculpture was expressed by *atibhaṅga* pose as parts of the body were thrown into violent opposition to one another. Śiva's six arms all raised and bent at the elbows produced a spinning motion pulling the body into a complete turn at the waist. Resultantly, the lower half body faced into the niche while the upper half faced outwardly. Dancing upon *āpasmārapuruṣa*, this form represented the *tāṇḍava*.[47] The next *vimāna nṛtyamūrti* at north end of the east wall resembled the *lalita*[48] form. In comparison to the more obvious dancing *talasamsphoṭitam* and *tāṇḍava* forms, this form curiously had both feet firmly placed on the ground. The non-standardization of *naṭeśa* forms till then could be a probable reason behind the ambiguity of this pose.

Fig. 128. Ellorā: Cave XVI (Kailāśa), Kārtikeya and *Dikpālas*, outer screen wall (after ASI).

The Mahiṣamardinī and Nṛsiṁha panels, both narrative presentations, marked a climax in a drama of action. They had the struggle between Durgā and Mahiṣa or Nṛsiṁha and Hiraṇyakaśipu ongoing, the outcome not yet determined. Movement and energy dominated the panels, while the finality of defeat was not depicted.

Amidst the multiplicity of major gods and goddesses, the portrayal of *aṣṭadikpālas* in eight sculptural panels at Ellorā proved another landmark in art history. They were probably carved as *dramatis personae* for heightening the intensity of the event being narrated in the panels. The sculptors must have faced difficulty while sculpting in rock-cut shrines, due to the vast areas to be carved and filled. The *dikpālas* could have been instrumental not only as fillers but also for symbolizing heavenly celebrations and rejoicing. Hence, their representations whether witnessing the marriage of Śiva Pārvatī, Śiva's dance, or celebrating Durgā's victory over Mahiṣa, panicky over *kailāśatolana* by Rāvaṇa, etc. It was only on the outer *prākāra* of Kailāśa that *dikpālas* were actually represented as guardians of the quarters (Fig. 128).[49] This was quite typical of the Rāṣṭrakūṭa artists to show the *dikpālas* on the *prākāra*, unlike the Cālukya norm of portraying them on the ceiling in a grid pattern.

At Kailāśa, in tune with caves XIV, XXI or XVI-B, special shrines for *mātṛkās* were carved on the southern side of the *garbhagṛha* and facing north. Besides they were also portrayed in panels. The Kailāśa *yajñaśālā* consisted of seated *aṣṭamātṛkās* carved in full relief and detached from the wall. The *nandīmaṇḍapa* Bhairava panel depicted *saptamātṛkās*. This suggested a variance in their number.

Kailāśa also had two Lakuliśa representations, both in *samabhaṅga*. One was *dvibhujī*, while the other was *caturbhujī*. As far as rock-cut sculptures are concerned, Kailāśa has the only instance of standing Lakuliśa forms.

As mentioned earlier, Kailāśa consisted of small *mithuna* figures, sometimes in erotic postures,[50] placed throughout the temple from the *prākāra* to the *dvāraśākhās* inside. Their appearance was at times coupled with small *yogī* figures, especially on pillars and pilasters, where musicians and dancers joined them. The symbolism of these two mutually contradictory aspects is conjectural. Still elements of some folk tradition or popular cult may be traced in these figures underlined by sublimity and obscenity, keeping in view their number, and placement positions.

In the passing, some observations about the Kailāśa itself, being an exemplary sculptural monument, may also be made. The *gajathara* and *siṁhathara upapīṭha* assigned it the image of a chariot. The notion was conveyed quiet aptly by the numerous panel sculptures besides the *upapīṭha* bearers on the south side portrayed in violent struggle. The temple also symbolized image of the mountain Kailāśa, Śiva's abode. This becomes more apparent by the *rāvaṇānugrahamūrti* placement on the *adhiṣṭhāna*, manifesting Rāvaṇa's attempts to shake the mountain represented by the temple as a whole. This also entailed a unity of architectural and sculptural forms. In the excavated caves, the purely architectural features had no structural purposes. Likewise, in the monolithic Kailāśa too, they assumed rather a decorative role, freed from the limitations of support and weight.

Hence, it is evident that the Kailāśa possessed not only grand manifestations of Brāhmanical myths but also certain artistic innovations involving formal as well as emotive aspects of sculpting. By innovating dynamic compositional settings, breaking up the high sense of balance, and discarding the equipoise of the classical art, the Kailāśa artists had succeeded in creating aesthetics of their own.

3. ELEPHANTA CAVE TEMPLES

Yet another marvelous rock-cut edifice was created at the island of Elephanta (Map 8) in form of the great Śiva cave. It is a magnificent assimilation of independent freestanding sculptures and rock-cut architecture, produced probably even before the Ellorā Kailāśanātha. In the lack of any inscriptional or literary evidence, it is usually assigned to either Kalacuri Krishnaraja or Cālukya Pulakeshin I,[51] both dated to the mid-sixth century AD. However, the stylistic affinity between the art of Elephanta and the Rāṣṭrakūṭa Ellorā instances motivates us to believe in its Rāṣṭrakūṭa lineage. Therefore, during the artistic and stylistic analysis, we would try to delve upon any probable Rāṣṭrakūṭa connection with the excavated caves at the site.

Development of Form in the Main Cave

Plan

The basic plan (Fig. 129) of the main cave generally designated as cruciform was more like a stepped square. Such plan bore resemblance to the caves at Ellorā where the plan of cave no. XXIX was square with double recessed corners, i.e. with a projection in the middle of each of the three sides and an *antarāla* in front of the cave. The *Vāstupuruṣamaṇḍala* might have influenced its architecture.[52] The cave dimensions were,

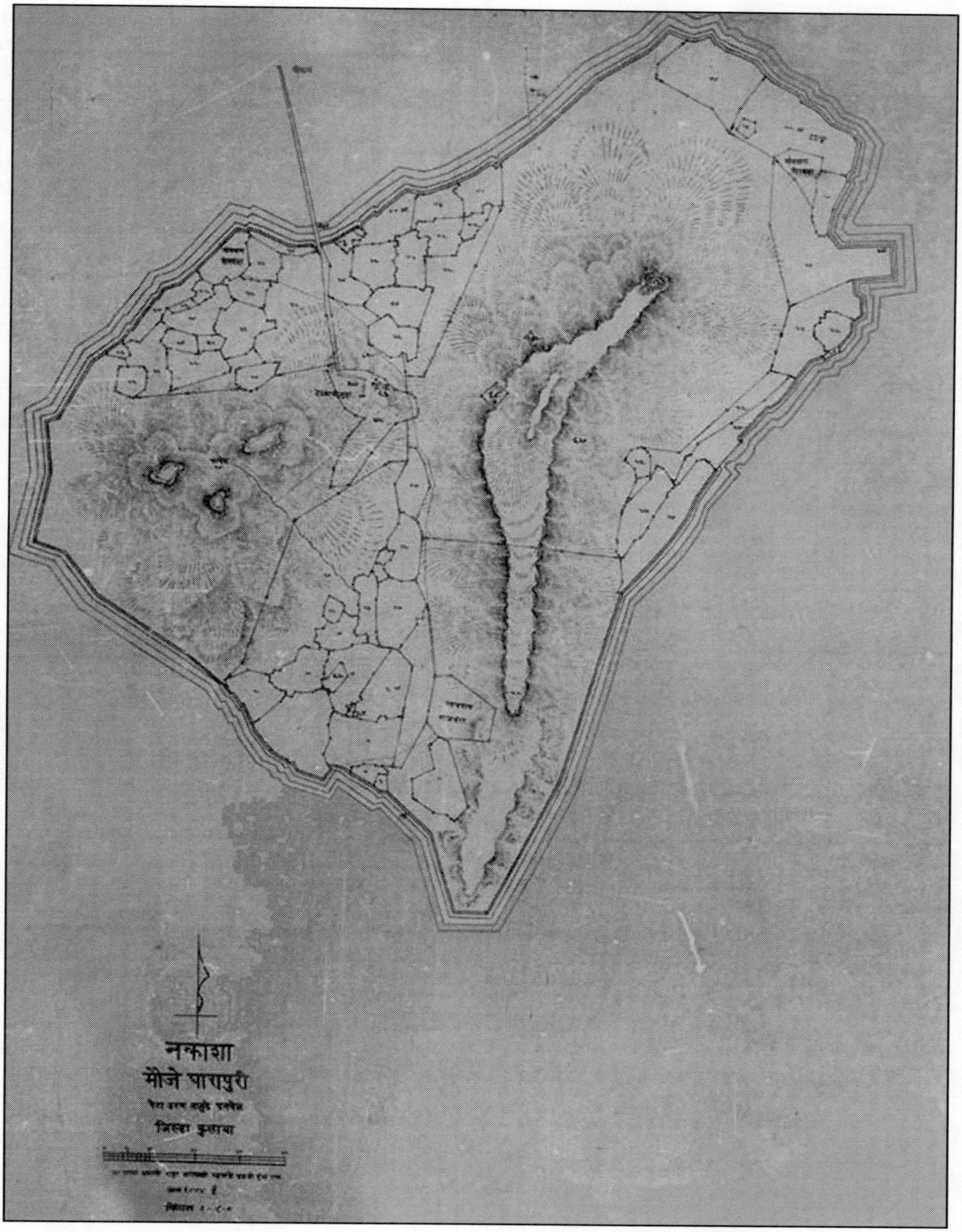

Map 8. Elephanta Island (after AIIS).

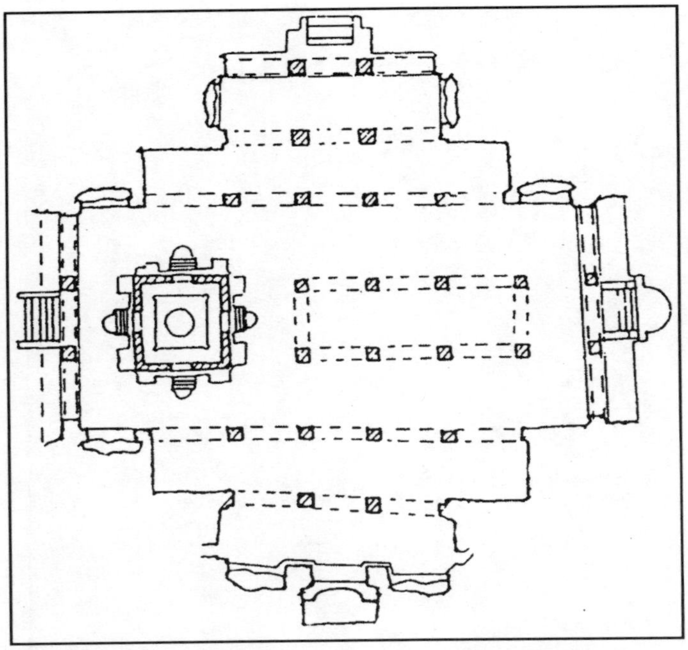

Fig. 129. Elephanta: Main cave (Cave 1), ground plan.

in height as well as in depth, rather irregular. The transverses of the main hall were each approximately 130′ long while the square formed by eliminating the porches and recesses was a little over 90′ on a side.[53] Its plan may be likened to that of the Buddhist *vihāra* consisting of rooms for the *bhikshus* aligned along three walls of the square court. Here replacement of the lateral rooms and walls of *vihāra* with *ardhamaṇḍapas* providing wall space for sculptured panels is noticeable.

Three side entrances emphasized the somewhat cruciform aspect of the main hall. This allowed more contrast of light and shade than in the usual cave temples. The now completely open northern entrance, facing Maheśamūrti, is the main entrance. However, originally the eastern entrance facing the *liṅga* shrine may have been the principal entrance.[54] In that case there would have been enough space for *pradakshiṇā* around the *liṅga* shrine, set almost at the back of the hall. This

Fig. 130. Elephanta: Main cave (Cave 1), *liṅga* shrine (after ASI).

Fig. 131. Elephanta: Main cave, *liṅga* shrine and *dvārapāla* (after AIIS).

idea also gets credence by a *nandīmaṇḍapa* in front of the eastern entrance as seen in the Rāṣṭrakūṭa caves. The *uttira* beams placed on *potikās* also hinted at east-west orientation. Had the northern entrance been the intended principal entrance, it would have entailed a deviation from the usual arrangement. In that case, the *liṅga* shrine in the east would have been a namesake shrine with *Maheśamūrti* as the focal point. This is also substantiated by the *Maheśamūrti*'s location in the south, at the natural back of the cave.

Thus, it appears that the Elephanta architects had combined two types of plans regarding the direction of entry: (i) in which the shrine was placed as attached to the very back of the wall, and (ii) in which it was at the back but detached from the wall. In the layout we observed that both the *liṅga* and the *Maheśamūrti* were geometrically linked. Two axes passed through the center of the space aligned with the cardinal points. Two concentric circles, their centers coinciding with the intersection of the axes, determined the position of the *liṅga* in the shrine on east-west axis. The circle and the north-south axis met at a point coinciding with the *Maheśamūrti*. In this manner, *the liṅga* and *Maheśamūrti* were related as the most important focal points inside the cave.

Symbolically, the east-west axis was a movement towards the shrine, a world beyond iconic forms. The north-south axis was a sort of movement from light to

Fig. 132. Elephanta: Main cave, façade (after AIIS).

darkness, from outside to interiors, as one approached the colossal *Maheśamūrti* at the back. Thus, the cave's architectural plan exhibited a duality of nature.

Fig. 133. Elephanta: Main cave, façade pillar (after AIIS).

The *garbhagṛha liṅga* shrine was square with four entrances (Pl. 60), each fronted by *sopāna* and flanked by *dvārapālas* in high relief (Figs. 130-131). Its walls were kept plain and bare. There were three *liṅga* shrines at Elephanta, suggesting a *trikūṭacala* plan, one each in the east and west courtyards and one as the main shrine with four entrances. The monolithic main *liṅga* was *brahmabhāga* at the base and *rūdrabhāga* at the top, measuring about 3′ above the *pīṭha.* The only form in the cave not cut from its live rock, it was similar to the stone of Ellorā. The square *liṅgapīṭha* consisted of *upāna*, *padma*, *vṛttakumuda*, *kaṇṭha*, *kapota*, and *paṭṭikā* mouldings.

Each of the three entrances constituting façades led from an open court, through *sopāna*, into multi-pillared *maṇḍapa*. The façades comprised of four pillars and two pilasters upon the *adhiṣṭhāna* (Figs. 132-133). The relatively high *adhiṣṭhāna* had several panel mouldings.

Pillars

The interior of the cave was divided into *maṇḍapa* shrine and stepped walls by pillars laid out on squares. The pillars, as arranged inside the main *maṇḍapa* along with the pilasters, suggested rows of squares in the sequence 3, 5, 7, 7, 7, 5, 3 starting from any side. Each row had four pillars, thus grouping thirty-seven squares. A lack of precision in the arrangement of pillars is discernible. They often appeared incorrectly aligned, besides being of varying heights. This was probably partly due to the lack of precision in rock cutting. Partly it may be assigned to Śiva's dark and dynamic world, still coming into form, inside the cave. The *Maheśamūrti* arms, suggested by the carved hands, and invisible portion below the chest indicated the ongoing process of the deity's emergence and manifestation. The dimly penetrating light in the interiors added to the sense of mystery and enigma, highlighting the potentiality of the unseen. Befitting the real yet illusive forms depicted in Elephanta sculptures, the abode of the evolving god may also not have been perfectly formed causing resultant imperfection.

Fig. 134. Elephanta: Main cave, main hall, pillar shaft details (after AIIS).

The *maṇḍapa* pillars varied in height from 15′-17′. They had a square basal *pīṭha* with a wide, slightly projecting *maṇḍī* at the top. The shaft *śaduram* (Fig. 134) was about 2″ octagonal with seated Gaṇeśa or *gaṇa* figures placed at the edges. The apex *śaduram* was also octagonal for about 6″. The intervening part showed multi-fluted *ūrdhva* and *adhopadma* petal courses. A fluted *grīvā* with the flutes ending in projecting *ratnāvallī* motif lay above the shaft. On this rested a compressed cushion capital, its center bound by a narrow flat *paṭṭā*, breaking its sixty-four flutes. A circular *kuṁbha* above it was finally surmounted by a square *phalaka*, same in width as the basal *pīṭha*. The compressed cushion capital was akin to the *āmalaka*[55] component of the North Indian temple *śikhara*.[56] A cushion shaped feature similar to the Elephanta capital in shape but decorated with floral motifs may be seen at Amarāvatī pillar bases.[57] The Elephanta pillar had semblance of partially upturned and partially down faced lotus petals directly below the *āmalaka* capital. Similar inverted lotus motif was carved on the Ashokan pillars, and pillars at Bedsā and Kārle.[58] Besides, *āmla* capital and circular fluted shaft form rising from a square *pīṭha* were common at Bādāmī in late sixth century AD and also at Ellorā in eighth century AD. In the light of these motifs, the Elephanta pillar capital assumes significant symbolism. Likewise, its shaft combining square, octagonal, and prismatic forms, all in one, also appeared quite rich in symbolic contents. This might have been an endeavor to combine the *trimūrti*

Fig. 135. Elephanta: Main cave, main hall, pillar capital details (after AIIS).

powers in the pillar form.[59] Above the capital were laterally projecting *potikā* brackets, usually simple *taraṅga* type, supporting *uttira* beam running along the ceiling (Fig. 135). The direction of *uttira* was mostly east-west creating a movement from eastern entrance towards the shrine or suggesting progression towards the *liṅga* therein. Upon the *uttira* we noticed a *valabhī* moulding of curved profile, and a *vājana*.

The pillars also help to ascertain relative chronology of the caves. As already narrated, there were similarities in Elephanta and Ellorā cave XXIX plans. Their pillar types were almost identical, but for the greater attenuation and sculptural style of the ones at Elephanta. This may mark them out as somewhat later than the Ellorā ones. This evidence also supports the Rāṣṭrakūṭas as the patrons of Elephanta caves, as Ellorā cave XXIX is definitely attributed to the Cālukyas,[60] the predecessors of Rāṣṭrakūṭas in the region.

Thus, the Elephanta pillar, massive and simple, was ideal for rock-cut architecture. Its heavy shaft and cushion capital appeared like actually bearing the weight of the mountain above (Fig. 136). Under the enormous pressure of the rock, the capitals looked lively, contained by the *paṭṭās* encircling them. We do not find any external elevation (Fig. 137) in the Elephanta caves.

There are six more caves towards the south east of the main cave, three finished (Figs. 138-139). Their architecture appeared quite plain and unassuming as compared to the latter. They did not reveal any evolutionary advancement upon or any semblance of resemblance with the main cave.

Fig. 136. Elephanta: Main cave, main hall, pillar capital details (after AIIS).

Sculptural Element

The main cave consisted of all the major Śaivite forms. Elaborate panels, nine in all, vividly illustrated Śaivite mythology. They also appeared as devotional icons with ample space remaining for related images. The sequence of the panels, considering the depth of carving, may be fixed as follows: *Gaṅgādhara, kalyāṇasundara, ardhanārīśvara, naṭarāja, lakulīśa, andhakāsurasaṁhāramūrtī*, Śiva Pārvatī in *akshakrīḍā, rāvaṇānugraha*, and *maheśamūrti*. The four-door *liṅga* shrine might have been the last creation inside.

Fig. 137. Elephanta: Cave 2, façade, unfinished pillars (after AIIS).

Panel Arrangement

Although the walls and the ceilings were undecorated, the carved panels created full visual impact. The sculptures within the cave constituted four groups: panels facing each other at the north, east, and west entrances, and three panels carved at back on the south wall. The panels were all deeply carved and framed, positioned well, back from the walls in their own space. When viewed from the front, some of the panels such as *Gaṅgādhara*, *kalyāṇasundara*, and *ardhanārīśvara* revealed a vertical arrangement, while in *the rāvaṇānugraha* and Śiva Pārvatī *krīḍā* panels horizontality predominated. However, a shift in the onlooker's position entailed changes in the compositional arrangement also. For instance, the *kalyāṇasundara* panel, when viewed from the corner, presented a row of horizontally placed figures of almost uniform size. Further, if seen from the *liṅga* shrine south door, the panel acquired a third aspect. The forms appeared in a circular pattern with Śiva Pārvatī occupying central positions. Similar changes could be felt while viewing *Gaṅgādhara*, Śiva Pārvatī *krīḍā*, and *rāvaṇānugraha* panels.

Sculptural Art Style

Elephanta marked the incorporation of three-dimensional sculptures into the walled panels. Sculptures were in relief but the emphasis seemed to be on drifting towards shrine like environments. The juxtaposition of flat and rounded dimensions appeared simultaneously within the same panel. Variations in the panels regarding levels of depth of rock penetration, or relation of volume to the background were apparent. For instance, the *Gaṅgādhara* Śiva was carved relatively flat and frontally, while opposite

Fig. 138. Elephanta: Cave 3, doorway (after AIIS).

it, the *rāvaṇānugraha* portrayal had the figures carved in the round, almost resembling freestanding sculptures. Pārvatī in the *krīḍā* panel also represented similar effect. Śiva in *andhakāsurasaṁhāramūrti* exhibited a three-dimensional form although his back was undetached from the wall.

The artists' attempt to carve three-dimensional forms also revealed evolutionary stages. For example, Bhagīratha's kneeling figure in the *Gaṅgādhara* panel was three dimensional, and isolated totally from the background. But it was not integrated with other figures. Śiva's shoulders were flat, lacking volume as compared to the *andhakāsura* panel. In the latter, the shoulders were placed one behind the other in a more balancing manner. In some panels certain figures, presenting minimal element of three-dimensionality frontally, appeared distinct from other perspectives. For instance, in *ardhanārīśvara* panel the sculptor's deep cutting in the rock created a three-dimensional

Fig. 139. Elephanta: Cave 4, façade (after AIIS).

figure on the male part. The preparation of space to be occupied by a rounded figure also attracts our attention. In this panel, space depended on the carving of *nandī* behind Śiva in a position perpendicular to the wall. Thus, it is inferred that the Elephanta artists paved way for the alliance of freestanding sculptures with a bas-relief panel idea,[61] i.e. though still attached to the wall; the figure was gradually released from its hold.

In some panels as *ardhanārīśvara, naṭarāja, andhakāsura, lakulīśa*, etc., the action was depicted as emerging out of the back wall. Though side figures existed but all actions took place within a rather shallow space from front to back. Thus, the panel assumed a shrine like character. Some of the panel figures as in the *gaṅgādhara, kalyāṇasundara, rāvaṇānugraha* panels, seemed independent of one another. But each of them was performing different functions simultaneously, and thus could also be placed in a non-static group. In such cases, a single figure may be united with an adjacent one to form an independent group or else may be seen in conjunction with another on the opposite side. For instance, in *kalyāṇasundara* panel Pārvatī may be seen as the companion of either Himālaya or of Śiva, who could otherwise also be shown entirely single. Similarly, Himālaya may have constituted a group with the *caurī* bearer or the latter with candra. These various linkages sort of activated the panel. Thus, each panel represented different assemblages from which the onlooker remained free to correlate the various forms.

The Elephanta *rāvaṇānugraha* panel, currently disfigured, portrayed an eight-armed Śiva with a prominent third eye, unperturbed by the shaking of the Kailāśa. Quite unusually, Pārvatī seated to his right, turned towards him in panic in a position similar to the Ellorā Kailāśanātha relief.

At times the groupings crossed the frame and moved out of its limits to mingle with elements outside. Sometimes, the narrative content of the panels also reflected the process of transformation. For example, in the *kalyāṇasundara* panel Pārvatī served as the very agent of transformation. She had compelled her parents to marry Śiva and performed austerities for the same. The panel showed her in the very process of becoming a wife from a daughter. Her turning figure, left shoulder forward not only suggested this transformation but also her leave taking. The figures of Pārvatī and Himālaya have been beautifully composed. Their heads inclined from each other suggested a unity and yet, the separation. A perfect idealization of the father daughter relationship at the time of daughter's marriage may be visualized here.

The *naṭarāja* figure in *lalita* pose appeared violently disengaged from the still flat background, on its right. His shoulder was depicted forcefully forward, backed by a series of rounded shoulders with upper body parts turned towards the northern entrance. The joint angles, and spread out limbs, their convulsive movements, all indicated a sense of discord, tumult, and disorder. The jewellery details of the figures in the panel reflected preciseness in carving. Śiva's face revealed a trance like expression as if he was unaffected by his own actions in the world. The figure might be viewed in a *tribhaṅga* stance from near the pillars leftwards. Although presently the figure is mutilated still the inward looking, smiling, composed face seems to be totally detached from the frenetic movements of the limbs.

The *andhakāsurasaṁhāraka* sculptural panel exhibited three-dimensionality more emphatically than the *naṭarāja* panel. The legs, now broken, were suggestive of a powerful stance. The right leg was held stiffly behind him while most of his body weight was put on the bent left leg raised up to waist. The carving of chest and diaphragm had been so perfectly executed that it gives a feeling of inner breath. The symbolism of the figure was enhanced by the use of elephant skin as a backdrop. The sun naturally appeared behind the headdress, as its rays from the west penetrated into the excavated space.

The depiction of opposites, both visually as well as narrative, was another characteristic feature of some panels. Visually for instance, while some figures merged with the parent rock, others were in the process of expanding out of the wall. In *Gaṅgādhara* panel, Śiva appeared drawn into the rock, whereas his *gaṇas* stride outwards. Similarly, the panel frames tended to draw towards the center, while the centrifugal forces pressed against the restraining frame as observed in the *naṭarāja* panel. Besides, the figures moving towards one another simultaneously appeared to be asserting their independence.

Carving of paradoxes in the narratives was apparent in several panels. The *ardhanārīśvara* was an integration of male and female energies. In the *rāvaṇānugraha* panel Rāvaṇa, attempting to uproot the Kailāśa, was finally subdued by Śiva into a repentant devotee. Similarly, the *maheśamūrti* combined the fierce male *aghora* and charming feminine *vāmadeva* aspects into the *tatpuruṣa*,[62] a symbol of totality. The

Fig. 140. Elephanta: Main cave, *Maheśamūrti* (after ASI).

Gaṅgādhara panel, in an identical portrayal, showed the forceful Gaṅgā caught in the still more forceful *jaṭās* of Śiva. The *naṭarāja* panel symbolized the eternal cycle of destruction and creation. While this panel expressed the dynamic energy of Śiva, the Lakulīśa figure facing it represented the inward drawn, contemplative energy. The energies in these two images were actually identical though presented as opposites. Besides, the dynamic and emerging *maheśamūrti* ushered with it the source of its *śakti*, and the power of its destruction, on either side. In this manner, these panels portrayed opposites, though in an integrated form.

Of the three panels on the south wall, i.e. *Gaṅgādhara*, *ardhanārīśvara*, and *maheśamūrti*, the last one assumes greater significance as the climax of sculptural art at Elephanta. It rose to 17′ 10″ height and was based on a 3′ high moulded *pīṭha*. The panel frame holding it was nearly 10½′ deep. In the sculpture Śiva appears as if emerging from the mountain with three heads visible while the fourth unseen at the back is implied into the mountain.[63] The iconography of this image has been discussed at length. *Viṣṇudharmottara* mentioned five faces of Śiva i.e. *Śambhor=vadana pañcakam*,[64] *Iśāna*, *Tatpuruṣa*, *Aghora*, *Vāmadeva*, and *Sadyojāta*.[65] These were also the name of five *mantras*.[66] It is believed that Śiva's body itself is a *mantra*, i.e. *vidyā* made visible through *liṅga*. Therefore, the *liṅga* regarded as Śiva's body represented these *mantras*, four of which occupied four regions of the manifested world. The fifth, *Iśāna*, lay above them on the top. Havell[67] had objected to representation of a five-headed deity by a three-headed image. But the iconographic details as well as symbolic contents of the sculpture disregard all such objections. It may be associated with *caturmukha liṅga*, actually representing the five faces of Śiva and quite reasonably carving three of them, as it was a relief sculpture, not a round one. Besides, the Lakulīśa panel suggested that perhaps the Pāśupata devotees of Maheśvara excavated the cave. In either case, the sculpture remains aptly identifiable as *maheśamūrti*.

In the light of this symbolism we may visualize the sculpture as a *liṅga* and image in one (Fig. 140). The concrete form of Śiva Maheśa[68] is fully manifested herein, surrounded by his *līlāmūrtis* around the *maṇḍapa* and the *garbhagṛha liṅga*. The sculpture, rising up like *mūlastaṁbha* or the central pillar, carried the frontal image as immobile, serene and self-introspective. It appeared as surging upwards, as straight and strong as a pillar. The almost straight line was emphasized by the elongated ears from the beginning of the cheeks, along the edge of the crown to the rounded portion of the top. The other heads carved in low relief, and their *makuṭas* joining the central one before its inwards sloping, emphasized the fundamental cylindrical shape. Thus, the concept of Mahādeva with *liṅga* was aptly conveyed in the sculpture.

Each of the three faces reflected a contemplative mood. The central one was sculpted in a higher relief than the other two. Rounded, brooding and tranquil, thick lipped, with heavy eyelids, elongated ears, it had a high *jaṭāmakuṭa* consisting of *ardhacandra* and *kīrtimukha* and abundant jewellery. The *makuṭas* of the other two heads sloped upwards to merge with the central pillar type image. The left *Aghora* aspect showed skull, snakes, and leaves intertwined with the matted hair. The face beneath had a vertical protuberance between the eyes indicative of a third eye and a curling moustache. *Damuṣṭras* protruded from the mouth corners while a cobra caressed the cheek. It held another cobra in hand, almost looking steadily into the third eye. The straight and rigid mouth lines mainly created the expression of sternness in this face. The *Vāmadeva* aspect on the right depicted a feminine[69] face, full cheeked, heavy lips, and curly locks of hair with pearl strings.

A pilaster with a carved *dvārapāla* framed the sculpture on either side. Leaning upon a *gaṇa*, the *dvārapāla*, almost 13′ tall, revealed a strong body with a delicate face. *Dvārapāla* figures were also carved on the main *garbhagṛha* entrances. Massive in proportions, they still exhibit slenderness and nobility of expression. They all were two armed with *śīrṣacakras* behind their heads.[70] The Elephanta artists' tendency of working with an inner conception and not mere external form was well reflected in the *dvārapālas* who represented typified forms (Fig. 141).[71]

Thus, the Elephanta sculptures, besides other qualities, were mainly remarkable for the expression of their inner spirit. Nowhere else in Indian art, such perfectly balanced mixture of sensuality and detachment is found. Figures with richly curved mouths, as if smiling to themselves and downcast eyes, appeared barely aware of the exteriors, in a bid to look within. The line under the eye was prominent to suggest its closing under heavily rounded lids. Generally no eyeballs were indicated. The heads of most of the main figures were slightly tilted may be to support their heavy *makuṭas*.[72] Each face as well as body form had been modelled in the most generalized manner possible.[73] Hair, jewellery and drapery, despite carved in relief, exhibited a clear linear

Fig. 141. Elephanta: Main cave, entrance *dvārapāla*, pillars in hall (after AIIS).

quality. Particularly the female figures had the hard precision of *mekhalās* and *hāras* emphasizing round curves of their bodies. In the actual cutting degrees of variation in relief, creating areas of light and shade, possibly to bring out the plasticity of the forms may be noticed.

Finally, the image of the cave temple itself may be considered. Besides a hub of divine manifestations, it emerges as an image of Śiva's mountain residence. It was approachable after crossing waters, climbing mountain, and entering inside a dark cave. On a still higher level of association considering the sculptural symbolism within, it might have been a reflection of the universe itself, created and destroyed by Śiva's energies.

We have already suggested that this magnificent tribute to Śiva may have been accomplished during the Rāṣṭrakūṭa period. Analysis of its architectural, sculptural and symbolical components further corroborates this idea. Architecturally, a resemblance in its ground plan layout with the Rāṣṭrakūṭa caves at Ellorā is obvious in the *trikūṭacala* shrines and *nandīmaṇḍapa* placement, fronting the entrance. The trenches like excavations at Elephanta, resulting in three side courtyards and three entrances to the cave, are akin to the excavation mode at Ellorā Kailāśanātha temple. It seems that the artists intended to carve out not just a few figures, but a whole temple from the existing layers of rock. Thus, they scooped out as much stone as possible and endowed the rest with life in accordance to the Śaivite mythology. We may infer the Kailāśanātha's full monolithic replica form as a sequel to the early attempt at Elephanta. The *āmalaka* type compressed cushion capitals over circular fluted shafts, arising from square basal *pīṭhas* are seen at both the places. Now, this is an established fact that the Kailāśa was excavated in the mid-eighth century. Its bearing affinity with Elephanta clearly indicates a common patronage. The Ellorā Cālukyan cave XXIX also presented similarity with Elephanta pillars, but its pillars were stylistically less attenuated than the ones at Elephanta suggesting an early age for the former. It is quite likely that learning from their Cālukyan specimens or contacts, the Rāṣṭrakūṭa artists elaborated the art at Elephanta and raised it to the climax in Ellorā Kailāśanātha.

Sculpturally, we observe the preponderance of mythical Śaivite figures at Elephanta as in Kailāśa.[74] The iconography at places appears quite identical. For instance, the panicky pose of Pārvatī in Elephanta *rāvaṇānugraha* panel seems identical to that in Kailāśa panel of the same theme. Stylistically, the tendency to depict power packed scenes with their outcome yet to be achieved, as noticed at Ellorā, is also noticeable in Elephanta panels. Here also violent opponent forces clashed in tumultuous and passionate confrontations, often unresolved, though final result implicit enough. The *liṅga* form at Elephanta and Ellorā Rāṣṭrakūṭa caves are circular and often not monolithic. Even the stone used for the Elephanta *liṅga* bears affinity to that in Ellorā.

Symbolically, the Elephanta cave presented itself as an exclusive home of Śiva where his still emerging form in *maheśamūrti* as well as *līlāmūrtis* manifested his all possible aspects. We have already highlighted how the Ellorā Kailāśa temple was similarly an image of Śiva's home. Thus, the architectural, iconographical, and metaphorical indicators and similarities substantiate upon the Rāṣṭrakūṭa origin of Elephanta caves.

To conclude, therefore, it may be stated that the Rāṣṭrakūṭa phase was a period of great artistic innovations. In cave excavations as well as in monolithic ventures they introduced certain creative innovative features. The circular *nandīmaṇḍapa* in Pātāleśvara cave, *sandhāra pradakshiṇā* with three-deity delineation, separate *parivārālayas*, longitudinal layouts, are a few to mention. That cave art was influenced by prevailing structural modes gets credence by the copying of one such specimen in rock in form of the Kailāśa. From Elephanta cave to Pataleśvara to Daśāvatāra cave and finally, the monolithic Kailāśa, we may visualize the stage all set for the rock-cut version of a truly evolved structural temple. The rich array of sculptured panels of cult images with interesting iconographic details remained the crowning glory of Rāṣṭrakūṭa excavations.

NOTES AND REFERENCES

1. Cave numbers 1 to 12 (fifth to seventh century AD) are Buddhist; those from 13 to 29 (eighth to ninth century AD) Brāhmanical while numbers 30 to 34 (ninth to eleventh century AD) are of Jaina affiliation.

2. As mentioned in the Rāṣṭrakūṭa records. *Cf.* Baroda copper plates, *IA*, XII, p. 228; the earliest capital was perhaps Achalapur or Elichpur in Berar till Dantidurga shifted to Elāpura as indicated by the Daśāvatāra cave inscription. Later Amoghavarsha selected Mālkheḍ as his capital. *Refer to* chapter 2 for further political details.
3. *See* T.V. Pathy, 1971, 'Verūl Śivālayamahātmya Ms and Some More Facts about Ellorā', Shrinivas Ritti and B.R. Gopal (eds.), *Studies in Indian History and Culture*, Dharwar; *See also* M.N. Deshpande, 1950, *Verulchī Leṇi*, Marathwada Diwali Issue.
4. Fergusson and Burgess have given a detailed description of the caves in 1880, *CTI*. The caves XXI, XX, XIV, XXIX, XXVI, XXVII, XXVIII, XIX, XVII, XVIII and XXII on stylistic basis have been assigned to the Cālukyas by Soundara Rajan in 1981, *CTD*; Walter Spink has attributed the Śaivites caves XXVIII, XXVII, XIX of first series and XX, XXVI, XXIX, XXI of second series to the Kalacuris of early sixth century AD. *See* 1967 (November), 'Ellorā's Earliest Phase', *Bulletin of American Academy*, Banaras, Vol. I.
5. Originally Gharapurī, meaning 'Hill of Purification' or 'Town of Excavations' or 'Fortress City,' the Portuguese named the island Elephanta as they found a stone elephant there. *Vide* Garcia Da Orta, 1563, *Coloquios dos simples e drogas... da India*, Goa, (translated as *Colloquies on the Simples and Drugs of India*, 1913, by C. Markham, London) *Cf. also* M.R. Anand, 1960 (Sept.), *Mārg*, XIII, No. 4; the site has been assigned to Cālukya Pulakeshin by Soundara Rajan, *op. cit.*; Spink suggested Kalacuri Krishnaraja as the patron of the Maheśa cave (6th cent. AD). *See* 1967, 'Ajanta to Ellora', *Mārg*, XX, No. 2, Bombay. Krishnaraja was a devout Pāśupata by birth – *Janmehaiya Pasupati Samāśraya*, *cf.* Mishra, *Sculptures of Dahala and Dakshina Kosala*; on stylistic analysis it is assignable to the Rāṣṭrakūṭas. *See* Goswami, 1958 (ed.), *Art of the Rāṣṭrakūṭas; also* details in chapter 7.
6. The series has been named after a Gaṇeśa figure on the innermost wall panel facing the entrance in shrine group 13-16.
7. *Vide* Krishna Kumar, 1976 (Sept.-December), 'Brahmanical Cave-temples at Ellorā', *East and West*, New Series, Nos. 3-4.
8. Width of the *pīṭha* varied from one third to one half of the width of the *garbhagṛha*. The height of the *liṅga* was usually equal to that of the *pīṭha*.
9. A variation found in cave XXIV shows the pillar *pīṭhas* with a *vṛtta kumuda*.
10. Seemingly a Gupta art influence. The *ghaṭa*, often fluted, was rather stylized to such an extent that it concealed its form. The *pallava* assumed the form of overflowing lotus petals touching corresponding upraised lotus petals of a *padma* below.
11. *Cf.* Soundara Rajan, *op. cit.*, p. 183.
12. Chatham, 1984, 'Myth, Cult, and *Cetanā* at the Kailāsa Temple, Ellorā', in Meister (ed.), *Discourses on Śiva*, Bombay, p. 165. But Gupte has opined that panels depicting sexual union belonged to a later date and were not incorporated in the original plan. *Vide* 1962, *Ajantā, Ellorā and Aurangābād Caves*, Bombay, p. 251.
13. R.S. Gupte and Mahajan, *Ibid.*, p. 194.
14. Elaborated in chapter 7.
15. *Cf.* K.V. Soundara Rajan, *op. cit.*, p. 180.
16. As suggested by Carmel Berkson, 1988, 'Daśāvatāra Cave: Its Importance in the History of World Art', in Ratan Parimoo *et al.* (ed.), *ECSA*, Delhi, p. 22.
17. The scene suggested Mahiṣa attacking the goddess with a *gadā* and then a *khaḍga*. Finally, Durgā was shown as resting her leg on the demon, dead after decapitation of the head. Thus, the panel indicated the levels and outcome of the contest.

18. Desai traced their portrayal to the magical-religious aspect of sex and worldly interest in sex as *bhoga*. For details, *refer to* 1975, *Erotic Sculpture of India: A Socio-Cultural Study*, p. 196; Gupte has upheld their importance as decorative motifs. *Vide, op. cit.*, p. 253.
19. R.S. Gupte, *Ibid.*, p. 251.
20. *Cf.* Soundara Rajan, 1981, *Art of South India-Deccan*, Delhi, p. 59.
21. Temple types *Vairāja* (square), *Kailāśa* (circular), *Puṣpaka* (rectangular), *Māṇika* (oval), and *Triviṣṭapa* (octagonal) are assigned respectively to Brahmā, Śiva, Kubera, Varuṇa, and Indra.
22. As opined by Deepak H. Kannal. *See* 'The Regional Lineages and Possible Masters at Kailāśanātha Temple of Ellorā', *ECSA*, p. 259.
23. *Vide* Baroda copper plate, *IA*, XII, p. 228; *Refer also* Kadaba grant of Govinda Prabhutavarsha, *EI*, IV, p. 337 and Baroda copper plate in N.B. Utgikar, 1927 (ed.), *Collected Works of R.G. Bhandarkar*, BORI, Pune; D.R. Bhandarkar, 1911, 'Epigraphic Notices and Questions, VIII-The Kailāśa Temple of Ellorā', *IA*, Vol. 40, pp. 237-38; Burgess initially held Dantidurga to be its creator owing to the stark similarity with the Paṭṭaḍakal Virūpāksha shrine. *Cf. CTI*, pp. 449-50. Later he gave up this view. *Vide* J. Fergusson, 1910, *History of Indian and Eastern Architecture*, London, p. 348.
24. Baroda Copper Plate, *op. cit.*
25. Mentioned as Ghṛṣṇeśvara in the *Dvādaśajyotirliṅgastrotraṁ*:
    Elāpure ramyavisālake' sminsamullasamtaṁ
    ca jagatvareṇyaṁ/
    Vamde mahodāratarasvabhāvaṁ
    Ghṛṣṇeśvarākhyam sāranam prapadye//12//
    See M.N. Deshpande, 'Kailāśa: A Study in its Symbolism', *ECSA*, p. 251.
26. Krishna I ruled from 757-772 AD. The common notion is that it could not be excavated fully during his fifteen years reign. *Vide* Fergusson and Burgess *CTI*, p. 462; *Also* Goetz, 'The Kailāśa of Ellorā and the Chronology of Rāṣṭrakūṭa Art', (i) Hermann Kulke, 1974 (ed.), *Studies in the History, Religion and Art of Classical and Mediaeval India*, Wiesbaden, p. 91; (ii) 1952, *AA*, Vol. 15, pp. 84-107; Brown suggested hundred years for its making in 1965, *Indian Architecture*, Vol. I, p. 74; Dhavalikar however, adhered to the fifteen years period in 1983, *Masterpieces of Rāshtrakūṭa Art*: *The Kailas*, Bombay, p. 8; Chapter 19 of the *Verūl Śivālayāmahātmya Manuscript* narrated how Elārāja invited sculptor Kokasa with 7000 artisans from Paiṭhan to carve the Kailāśa to fulfill his wife's vow. They estimated its completion within sixteen months by all 7000 artisan working day and night. The *kalaśa* part was to be done within seven days to save the life of the fasting queen. *Vide* Pathy, *op. cit.*, pp. 107-08. This story is indicative of the popular oral traditions regarding making of the shrine and echoes the epigraphic evidence of Baroda plate; Kannal also favored a lesser time span owing to the large number of artists working. *See* 'The Regional Lineages and Possible Masters', *ECSA*, pp. 260-61.
27. Hermann Goetz has suggested ten styles and seven structural phases, *vide op. cit.*, p. 95; Doris Chatham divided its architectural development into eight styles and five phases. *Cf.* 1977 (January), '*The Excavation of Cave 16, Ellorā Before the Kailāśanātha*', paper presented in American Committee for South Asian Art Symposium, Los Angeles.
28. Suggested by Satish Grover in 1980, *The Architecture of India-Buddhist and Hindu*, New Delhi, p. 121.
29. The verse in *Verūl Śivālayāmahātmya MS*, chapter 19, rather confirmed the idea:
    Ādhī Kalas Mag pāyā
    Upaharatī Mandilī Carya

The legend of the *śilpī*'s promise of carving the *śikhara*, before the base within seven days, to enable the queen end her fast lends credence to the fact of carving upside down. *See footnote no. 27.*

30. M.K. Dhavalikar in 'Kailāśa - A Structural Analysis' in *ECSA*, p. 358, has suggested that 250 laborers would have taken 5 years to dig them. However, Kannal disagrees with the 'trench' idea. As the carvers needed sufficient 'elbow space' during carving it must have been almost impossible to carve the stone vertically. Besides, separating the block on three sides from the hill would have also been impractical. *Cf. op. cit.*, pp. 268-69, *footnote no. 5.*
31. Gary Michael Tartakov has identified the cave as the *paṇam*, a place where movable *pratimā*, i.e. images for worship in the *garbhagṛha* were inspired. *Vide* 1987, 'The *Pratimā Pratiṣṭhāpaṇam* in the Kailāśa', *Kusumāñjali*, Delhi, pp. 207-09.
32. Constituted as (i) the central square (ii) space between two groups of northern pillars (iii) space between eastern pillars (iv) space between southern pillars (v) space between western pillars (vi) space between four north western pillars (vii) space between four north eastern pillars (viii) space between four south eastern pillars (ix) space between four south western pillars; The *navaraṅga* pattern is also seen in the Dilwārā Jaina shrines. The only difference being that in the Kailāśa this feature existed in the *raṅgamaṇḍapa* whereas at Dilwārā the corridor *bhamati* possessed a *navaraṅga* ceiling.
33. In the rock architecture the *stūpī or kalaśa* was generally to be made separately and fitted in at the time of *kumbhābhiṣekam*. This has been discussed in the preceding chapter also. If consecrated the Kailāśa *stūpī* might have fallen off due to ravages of time or by vandals.
34. Burgess was one of the earliest scholars to expound this notion. *Cf. CTI*, p. 450; Gupte supported the idea in *op. cit.*, p. 144; Percy Brown agreed to resemblance between the two monuments but owing to the almost double size and distinct technique of Kailāśa ruled out any mutual influence, *vide Indian Architecture*, Vol. I, p. 73.
35. *Cf.* Jeyechandrun, 'Draviḍian Influence on Ellorā Cave Temple Architecture' in *ECSA*, pp. 374-77.
36. Some variations are noticeable. For instance, the Kāñcī shrine *śikhara* consist of *kūṭa-pañjara-śālā-pañjara-śālā pañjara-kūṭa hāra* on its second *tala* unlike the Kailāśa *kūṭa-śālā hāra*. The *padmachatra* on *maṇḍapa* roof is another departure from the *Kāñcī* scheme.
37. As suggested by Doris C. Chatham, *see op. cit.*, p. 156.
38. In *History of Indian and Indonesian Art*, p. 100.
39. *See* Stella Kramrisch's 1981, *Indian Sculpture*, Delhi, p. 88.
40. *Cf.* A.K. Bhattacharyya, 'Ellorā Sculpture: A Stylistic Examination' in *ECSA*, p. 274.
41. S.K. Saraswati, 1975, *A Survey of Indian Sculpture*, Delhi, p. 167.
42. *Cf.* Manomohan Ghosh (trans.), 1967, *The Nāṭyaśāstra*, 2nd ed. rev. Calcutta, pp. 45-75.
43. *Cf.* Gopinatha Rao, 1971, *Elements of Hindu Iconography*, Vol. 2, pt. 1 (repr.), Banaras, pp. 224-29.
44. *Cf.* 'Dance of Śiva' in Gopinatha Rao, *EHI*, Vol. 2, pt. 1, p. 232.
45. Soundara Rajan held that 'true Śaivism was born only in pre-medieval times. The Gupta, Cālukya and Pallava Śiva forms do not show any example of the *ānanda tāṇḍava* types, but rather of ferocious or kinetic energy representations'. *Vide* 1981, *Glimpses of Indian Culture–Architecture, Art and Religion*, Delhi, pp. 161-69.
46. *Cf.* Doris C. Chatham, 'Myth, Cult and Cetanā', p. 161.
47. Sivaramamurti described that in this form the movements of Śiva's arms are 'so tempestuous that they create swings of air which toss about mountains, uprooted from the earth'. *See* 1974, *Naṭarāja in Art, Thought and Literature*, Delhi, p. 100.

48. The hand of the right arm stretched across the chest and pointed down to the foot placed on *apasmāra*'s back and together with a raised left arm formed the *gajahasta* pose. The leg pose *kuṭṭitam* put the weight of the body upon the left foot while the right implied a movement wherein the heel rhythmically struck the floor: As described by Gopinatha Rao in *op. cit.*, pp. 262-63.
49. *Dikpālas* and their respective directions as given in the *Purāṇas* are: Indra (east), Agni (south-east), Yama (south), Niruti (south-west), Varūṇa (west), Vāyu (north-west), Kubera (north) and Iśāna (north-east).
50. Devangana Desai, *op. cit.*, p. 36.
51. Walter Spink hailed Krishnaraja as its creator. *Cf.* 1967, *Mārg*, XX, No. 2, Bombay; Divakaran in *Chhavi-2* also assigned it to the Kalacuris; Muriel Neff and M.R. Anand in 1960, *Mārg*, XIII, No. 4, and Soundara Rajan in *CTD*, included it among Cālukyan monuments. *See also footnote no. 6.*
52. The fundamental geometry of the plan actually seems to be a *maṇḍala* providing the interior space with a cosmic dimension through mathematical arrangement. The circles were combined with the configuration of squares by diagonals passing through the squares. *Cf.* Michell, 1983, 'The Architecture of Elephantā: An Interpretation', *Elephantā—The Cave of Śiva*, New Jersey, p. 20, figs. 5-6; *See also* P.K. Acharya, *Architecture of Mānasāra*, Vol. V, plate LX; Stella Kramrisch has reproduced the model in the 1946. *Hindu Temple*, Calcutta, p. 87, no.6.
53. J. Burgess, 1871, *The Rock Temples of Elephantā*, Bombay, pl. 1.
54. *Vide* V.A. Smith, 1930, *A History of Fine Arts in India and Ceylon*, p. 90.
55. Associated with the *āmalaśilā* or pure stone *āmalaka* was a unit of complex symbolic significance. For further details *see* Stella Kramrisch. *The Hindu Temple*, p. 354; W. Simpson in 'Some Suggestions of Origin in Indian Architecture' in *JRAS*, Vol. XX has opined that the *āmalaka*'s origin may be traced to the *chatrāvalī* of Buddhist *stūpas*.
56. The *āmalaka* herein is said to represent the capital of the imagined pillar that runs through the center of the temple. *Refer* Zimmer's 1955, *The Art of Indian Asia*, New York, p. 297.
57. *See* J. Burgess, 1887, *The Buddhist Stūpas of Amarāvatī and Jaggayyapeta*, London, Fig. 25 on p. 87.
58. Its symbolism is not unanimously expounded. The motif is also likened to a bell as discussed by A.K. Mitra in 'A Bell Capital from Bhuvanesvara' in *Indian Historical Quarterly*, V, pp. 693 ff.; *also* Commaraswamy, 'Origin of the Lotus (so called Bell) Capital' in *Indian Historical Quarterly*, VI, pp. 373 ff; The motif is also assigned a Persian influence. *Vide* E.B. Havell, 1915, *Ancient and Medieval Architecture of India*, London, p. 72.
59. Reference to pillar parts as *Brahmakhaṇḍa, Viṣṇukhaṇḍa* and *Rūdrakhaṇḍa* according to their shapes. *Vide Mānasāra*, Chapter 15, *Stambhalakshaṇam*, vv.10-11.
60. A comparison with Bādāmī Cālukyan pillars reveals that both at Ellorā and Elephanta the Bādāmī pattern was followed. But the intricate decoration of the Bādāmī types was not found in the latter ones. *Refer to* P. Rambach and V.de. Golish, 1955, *The Golden Age of Indian Art*, London, pls. 31-32 for illustrations of the same.
61. *Cf.* Carmel Berkson, 1983, 'The Historical Context and Evolution of Style at Elephanta', *Elephanta—The Cave of Śiva*, p. 8.
62. Stella Kramrisch, contrary to her early identification as *Tatpuruṣa* in (July) 1946, *Ancient India*, 2, pp. 4-8 referred to the central face as *Sadyojāta* in a revised version of the paper entitled 'The Image of Mahādeva in the Cave Temple on Elephanta Island' in Miller (ed.), 1983, *Exploring India's Sacred Art*, Philadelphia; *Cf. also* her paper, 1981 (May), 'The Great

Cave Temple of Śiva, in Elephanta: Levels of Meaning and Their Form', delivered at *Śiva Symposium*, University of Pennsylvania.

63. For long the sculpture was hailed as a *Trimūrti* of Brahmā, Viṣṇu, and Śiva. Gopinatha Rao held it to be a *Maheśamūrti*, a representation of the fully manifested supreme Śiva in *EHI*, Vol. II, pt. 2, Delhi, p. 379; The same idea was expounded by Kramrisch in 'The Image of Mahādeva in the Cave Temple on Elephanta Island' in *Ancient India*, 2, pp. 4 ff.; Neff in 1960, 'Elephanta', *Mārg*, XIII. No. 4 has corroborated the notion.
64. *Viṣṇudharmottara Purāṇa*, 3. 48. 1-3.
65. Hierarchically they, thus, represented elements of the universe: Iśāna being *ākāśa* and the others respectively, *vāyu*, *jala*, *agni* and *pṛthvī*. *Vide Ibid*. The same text also expounded another series of names for Śiva's five faces, viz. Sadāśiva, Mahādeva, Bhairava, Umā and Nandī, see *ibid*., 3. 48. 4-6.
66. *Tattirīya Āraṇayaka*. 10. 43-47.
67. Havell, 1920, *Handbook of Indian Art*, p. 187; Banerjea offered some reservations to Kramrisch's analysis, *cf*. 'The So Called Trimūrti of Elephanta' in *Arts Asiatiques*, II, 2, pp. 120 ff.
68. The supreme god who is the primordial cause of the universe and also its primordial *prakṛti*. *Vide Viṣṇudharmottara*, 3. 48. 19. The combining of masculine and feminine characteristics in the image also confirmed this notion.
69. Vāmadeva is mentioned as *strīvilāsa* in *Iśānaśivagurudevapaddati*, *cf*. 3. 12. 38. The second series of names for Śiva's five faces named it as Umā, Śiva's *śakti* and an inseparable part of his nature.
70. Either in a golden *prabhāvalī* form or radiating spokes with decorative headdress arrangement. *Vide* K.V. Soundara Rajan, *CTD*, p. 91.
71. Zimmer, *The Art of Indian Asia*, plate 263.
72. Muriel Neff in *op. cit.*, p. 51.
73. *Cf*. Zimmer, *op. cit.*, pl. 211.
74. The myths associated with the sculptures have been discussed by Wendy Doniger in 1983, 'The Myths Depicted at Elephanta', *Elephanta—The Cave of Śiva*, pp. 27-39; *see also* R. von Leyden, 1960 (Sept.), 'Drama in Stone' in 'Elephanta', *Mārg*, Vol. XIII, No. 4, pp. 61 ff. for an elementary sculptural stylistic development analysis at the site.

7

South Indian Rock-cut Temples

Sculptures and Their Iconography

The art of South Indian rock-cut temples implies the creation of architectural space by the artists under Pallava, Cālukya and Rāṣṭrakūṭa patronage. As the deity's residence, rock-cut shrine was first part of an excavation. Its art could not be completed without the presence of religious sculptures within it. It is indeed a matter of fascination how the artists under various reigning dynasties manifested their mental visions in form of sculptures and endowed the temples with a real world of the Supreme Being. The rock-cut temple constituted the world of god where a regular drama was to be performed by the deities. Thus, iconography of the images symbolized the Supreme Being along with his entourage in different forms. In this sense, the art of sculptures and iconography should not be treated separately but as part of the unified whole. Therefore, after the architectural part of excavations, an overview of their sculptural component as the second part of the excavation becomes imperative.

Iconography is the science of sculptures or icons.The term icon, in Greek *eikon*, denotes a figural representation of a deity or a saint for ritualistic purposes. Its Indian synonyms are *pratimā*,[1] *arcā*,[2] *bera*, *vigraha*, *rūpa*, *biṁba*,[3] etc. In South India an image in round was termed *citra*, while a relief was *ardhacitra*. The earliest icons were, perhaps, made of wood as mentioned in the *Ṛgveda*.[4]

The art of making icons gradually evolved into a full-fledged science *pratimā lakshaṇa* or *citralakshaṇa*, elaborating the types,[5] proportions,[6] techniques and medium of carving. The forms were to convey a specific meaning through their *lakshaṇas* or characteristics, and represent a particular symbol. The science of iconography unfolds the inner meaning of the object and in the present context puts the cave temple art in its proper context.

An iconographic classification of the rock-cut sculptures leads us to their subjectivity as (i) secular - marking projections of different aspects of life in reality and (ii) theistic - comprising various sectarian images.

ŚILPAŚĀSTRIC CANONS

Of the *śilpa* or iconological texts assigned to South India - the *Āgamas*,[7] specially the *Aṁśumadbhedāgama, Kāmikāgama, Kāraṇāgama, Vaikhānasāgama, Suprabhedāgama; Śilpa Saṁgraha; Pañcarātras*,[8] mainly the *Hayaśīrṣapañcarātra; Bṛhat Saṁhitā; Mānasāra; Īśānaśivagurudevapaddhati, Śilparatnam* and *Purāṇas*,[9] - all associated with Brāhmanical cults provided theoretical ground for sculptural rock-art in terms of *pratimālakshaṇas, pratiṣṭhāvidhi* and *devagṛhanirmāṇa*. A definite terminology denoted the postures and specific meaning of the sculptures.

Postures of the palm, fingers and arms were conveyed through various *mudrās* (*abhaya, varada* or *anugraha, añjali, dhyāna, jñāna, vyākhayāna* or *cinmudrā, kaṭyāvalaṁbita, kaṭaka* or *siṁhakarṇa, sūcī, tarjañī, vismaya mudrā*, etc.); the pose of the whole arm also conveyed a particular meaning as *daṇḍahasta, gajahasta* or *kaṭihasta*. The term *āsana* (*pīṭha*) denotes a seat. Therefore, *anantāsana* (triangular), *siṁhāsana* (rectangular with four lion shaped legs), *vimalāsana* (hexagonal), *yogāsana* (octagonal), and *padmāsana* (circular) represented icon seat types. Besides, *padmāsana, cakrāsana, kūrma, mayūra, kukkuṭa, vīra, svāstika, bhadra, siṁha* and *gomukha āsanas* were important. *Paryankāsana* and *ardhaparyankāsana* suggested position of both the legs of sitting figures. Images in recumbent position, mostly of Viṣṇu *anantśayī*, represented the *śayana* category.

Curves as *samabhaṅga, dvibhaṅga, tribhaṅga* and *atibhaṅga* manifested dynamic intensity. Standing figures, especially Varāha, were also projected in *ālīḍha* and *pratyālīḍha* postures. The delicacy of the *nāṭya* style in the female figures was classified as *kaṭisama, lalita, lalāṭatilaka, catura* and *talasamsphoṭika* poses.

Icons could also be distinguished on account of the dress, ornaments and their hand objects. *Jaṭāmakuṭa, kirīṭa makuṭa, karaṇḍa makuṭa śīraṣṭraka, kuntala, keśabandha, dhammilla*, constituted various headgears. The usual ear ornaments included *patra, nakra, śaṁkha patra, ratna*, and *sarpa kuṇḍalas*, while *graiveyaka* and *vaijayantī* adorned the neck of the images. Male figures and at times females also wore the *yajñopavīta* in *upavīta* or *nivīta* style. The *kuchabandha* band was worn over female bosom. Another band *udarabandha* was tied round the stomach, especially in male figures. *Kaṭibandha, mekhalā* and *kāñcīdāma* were waist ornaments. *Kaṅkaṇa, valaya, keyūra* were worn on the hands and arms.

The usual weaponry included *cakra, gadā, daṇḍa, kheṭaka, dhanuṣ, śara, añkuśa, pāśa, khaḍga, parśu, śūla, vajra, agni, khaṭvāṅga*, etc. Objects associated with sculpted forms could be musical instruments (*vīṇā, muralī, ḍamarū, śaṁkha, ghaṇṭā, mṛdaṅga, kartāla*, etc.), birds, or animals. *Prabhāvalī* or *śīrṣacakra* symbolized the deity's aura. The former was a halo around the whole figure while the latter served as glow around the head.

SCULPTURES IN SOUTH INDIAN ROCK-CUT TEMPLES

As already indicated, the cave temples pulsated with lavish sculptural creations. Manifestations of Śiva and Viṣṇu, *Devī* forms, *upadevatās*, *gāndharva*, *yaksha* and other figures comprised a plethora of plastic forms. In the light of sculpture and iconography, the development of these religious motifs under the three respective dynasties may be analysed.

1. RELIGIOUS SCULPTURES

Śaiva Icons

Śiva

Associated with the *pañcakṛtyas* acts of *sṛṣṭi* (creation), *sthiti* (preservation), *saṁhāra* (annihilation), *anugraha* (benedictions) and *tirobhāva* (power of concealment), Śiva[10] is perhaps the most influential Brāhmanical deity. The originator of *yoga*, *śāstras*, music and dance, his projection as *yogeśvara* in *vyākhayāna mudrā* or as *naṭarāja* remained as popular as *pāśupati*, *kirāṭa*, *bhūtanātha*, *umāpati*, etc. Thus, the diverse aspects of Śiva, as pointed out by G.C. Pande, exhibit a 'syncopated *kulturgeschichte*'.[11]

Śiva's sculptures generally constitute three groups, viz. *saṁhāramūrtis*,[12] *anugrahamūrtis* and *nṛtyamūrtis*, each with specific iconographic features.

(i) *Saṁhāra/Ugramūrtis*: Constituted by the *Andhakāsurasaṁhāra*,[13] *Gajāsurasaṁhāra*, and *Tripurāntaka*. The first icon is described in the *Śiva* and *Matsya Purāṇas*.[14] Varāha *Purāṇa*[15] has associated the myth with *Gajāsurasaṁhāra*. *Śaivāgamas* have also suggested iconography for *Andhakāsurasaṁhāra* images.[16] The *Tripurāntakamūrti* myth expounded in *Matsya Purāṇa*[17] has iconographic details in *Aṁśumadbhedāgama*.[18] *Jalandharasaṁhāramūrti*[19] conveys killing the demon Jalandhara while *Brahmāśīrṣachedakamūrti*[20] relates to Brahmā beheaded by Śiva.

Among other *ugra* or *ghora* forms *Bhairava* presents a terrific appearance.[21] *Kaṅkālamūrti*[22] carries Viṣṇu's guard Viśvaksena's body on *śūla* prongs. *Bhikshāṭanamūrti* Śiva is an untouchable nude wanderer, holding a *kapāla* and at times accompanied by a deer.[23] The *Vīrabhadra*[24] form conveys his *raudra* aspect at Daksha's *yajña*. As *Kālāri*,[25] *Kāmāntaka*[26] and *Śarabheśamūrti*,[27] Śiva punished certain gods.

Ugramūrtis in Cālukya, Pallava and Rāṣṭrakūṭa Art

There is no evidence of Śaiva *ugramūrtis* in the Aihoḷe or Bādāmī Cālukyan caves. Pallava instances are more yielding. The Dharmarāja *ratha* has a *caturbhujī kālāri* Śiva on its second *tala*. Bent right leg is placed on ground while bent left leg is upraised. His upper right hand is in *mṛgaśīrṣamudrā* and upper left hand is *triśūlahasta*. The lower right hand holds a *parśu*, while lower left in *sūcīhasta* point towards *kāla*. The *jaṭāmakuṭa* has a frontal large skull. A beaded *hāra* and *rudrāksha yajñopavīta* in *upavīta* mode, a *kaṭibandha*, *kaṅkaṇas* and *bāhuvalayas* are worn by him. *Kāla* with two *damuṣṭras*, or side tusks, is depicted fallen and with bent knees.

The same *ratha* has a *caturbhujī Andhakāsurasaṁhāramūrti*. Standing *ālīḍha* as in *tribhaṅga*, Śiva's right leg behind is placed on Andhaka's back, the left kept apart and bent at the knees. The *sūtrayajñopavīta* is worn in *upavīta* manner. *Jaṭāmakuṭa* has a skull and *ardhacandra*. His upper hands hold *parśu* and *sarpa* in right and left. The lower right is in *tarjañīmudrā* while the left holds a reversed *triśūla* suggesting Andhaka's defeat. The demon is shown with a *jaṭābhāra*, *patrakuṇḍalas*, beaded *rudrāksha*, *upavīta yajñopavīta*, and *damuṣṭras*. A *caturbhujī kaṅkālamūrti* in slight profile, head turned to front and adorned by *jaṭāmakuṭa* with skull and crescent is seen in Dharmarāja *ratha āditala*. He wears a *patrakuṇḍala* in one ear, a small ring in another one. A *pāśa* like coiled object is seen in the upper right hand while the upper left holds a *cāmara*. The lower right has a *mayūrapicha daṇḍa* whereas the lower left holds a *kapāla*. Thus, we find the Pallava sculptures of *ugra* Śiva conforming considerably to *Āgamic* norms.

In the Rāṣṭrakūṭa sculptures, the Kailāśa *Gajāsurasaṁhāramūrti* is quite impressive. Although Andhaka is not seen herein the presence of Pārvatī, the *saptamātṛkās*, *gajacarm* in Śiva's hands projected as a *śīrṣacakra*, as per the *Śaivāgamas*, leaves no doubt of identity. The corresponding *Andhakāsuravadhamūrti* in cave XV included Andhaka figure, as suggested in the *Viṣṇu Purāṇa*. While the previous relief suggested final victory, here the climax was yet to be. Andhaka is shown seeking Śiva's mercy. Yogeśvarī, appearing fierce and emaciated, lies on the ground holding a *kapāla* towards the *asura* to collect his blood drops. Leftwards, she is anticipated in her *saumya Cinmayādevī* aspect to be assumed after Śiva's victory. The panel, thus, carries forward observance of *śilpaśāstrīya* norms. The *Andhakāsurasaṁhāramūrti* in Elephanta Trimūrti cave, now mutilated, is still suggestive of its art. Śiva's posture seems to be a powerful one. The right leg is held stiffly behind him, while most of his body weight is put upon the bent left leg raised to the level of his waist. Few of his *aṣṭabhujās* survive. The second right hand holds a *khaḍga* in a threatening manner, third has a *ghanṭā*. Behind and above Śiva two hands stretch up the *gajacarma*. The second left hand holds a *kapāla* to catch the blood of Andhaka. This is a variation from the usual form wherein Yogeśvari holds the *kapāla*. The small and impaled body of Andhaka is seen above the *kapāla*. Śiva is shown wearing ornaments and a skull studded *jaṭābhāra*. His enraged face shows the third eye, two swollen eyes and *damuṣṭras* associated with *Bhairava*.

A favorite theme of Rāṣṭrakūṭa Śaivite iconography was *Tripurāntaka*. The Daśāvatāra cave has *aṣṭabhujī* Śiva on the chariot in the pose of shooting the arrow at *tripuras*. His presence over the panel is overwhelming, while the *asuras* are shown on a side wall. The chariot in side profile is represented by four pilasters and top shaft, with two circular, unspoked wheels shown fixed to it. A relief in Kailāśa shows one wheel placed centrally, while Śiva is shown with full attributes shooting the arrow. Herein neither the *tripuras* nor their suggestive *asuras* are shown. The best specimen of the myth is carved on two wall segments at right angles to each other in Kailāśa. It has the three cities represented as three blocks of small figures and pillars. They have been dramatically brought into the line of Śiva's arrow. Thus, it marks a departure from the conventional spatial niche limitations. Quite unusually, Śiva is *dvibhujī* and strikes the pose of a warrior. The intersecting arcs of his *dhanuṣ*, his arm and torso and the horses' backs render this relief a distinction of its own.

Tripurāntakamūrti instances have not been cited in the Cālukya or Pallava sculptures.

(ii) *Saumya/Anugraha Mūrtis*: These highlight Śiva's tranquil aspect and benevolent grace. The *Kalyāṇasundara* or *Vaivāhikamūrti*[28] illustrates his marriage with Pārvatī. The *Āgamas* vividly delineate its iconography.[29] The *Umāsahitamūrti*,[30] Candraśekhara *ālingānāmūrti*[31] and *Somaskanda* projects Śiva-Pārvatī together.[32] Amongst *anugrahamūrtis*, the *Rāvaṇānugraha*[33] has been most popular in South India. Bestowing grace upon Caṇḍeśa[34] Viṣṇu, Nandī and Arjuna have been other aspects of the form. *Dakshiṇāmūrti* manifestations as *vyākhyānamūrti*,[35] *yogadakshiṇāmūrti*,[36] and *vīṇādharamūrti*[37] have also been popular. *Gaṅgādharamūrti*,[38] *Sadāśiva*,[39] *Ardhanārīśvara*,[40] Lakulīśa and *Kevalamūrti* are other important forms related to Śiva. The *Liṅgodbhava*[41] form, combining human and phallic aspects, perhaps, indicated the shift from aniconic to iconic representations of Śiva.

Saumyamūrtis in Cālukya, Pallava and Rāṣṭrakūṭa Art

Dakshiṇāmūrti

Cālukyan rock-cut caves do not possess any *dakshiṇāmūrti* representation. In contrast, the Pallava sculptures offer a wide range of Śaivite forms in their prescribed iconographic details. The *dakshiṇāmūrtis* carved in Dharmaraja *ratha* presents interesting details. Śiva as *vīṇādhara* holds the *vīṇā* with his main hands, while additional two hands suggest *tripatākā* and *mṛgaśīrṣa-nāṭyahastas* linking dance with music. In a peculiar manner the resonator of the *vīṇā* touches upon the upper part of the left chest creating a breast like impression as seen in *ardhanārī* figures. This placement of *vīṇā* rather makes it a unique sculpture of early Pallava art. In another panel, a cross legged Śiva holds a *vīṇā*, his one hand holding the *ḍamarū* and other resting on a *gaṇa*. The *jaṭābhāra*, crossed leg posture and *ḍamarū* indicate his *vīṇādakshiṇāmūrti* form. The nearby *gaṇa* practices his step in *kuñcita* mode. In one sculpture standing crossed legs as *vṛṣabhāntika*, Śiva faces and instructs Nandī on *nāṭya* principles. The latter's bent head and *jaṭābhāra*, Śiva's *vastra yajñopavīta* befitting a guru suggest its being a *dakshiṇāmūrti*. The drum is laid in his extra right arm and the *tripatākā* mode of left arm hint of *nṛtta* and *abhinaya*, *svara* and *sāhitya* in dance.

One representation has Śiva in *jaṭābhāra*, holding the *śūla* and *parśu*. One of his hands in *cinmudrā* is shown teaching Taṇḍu the essence of *tāṇḍava*. The various *carī* and *recita* foot movements, *karaṇas* with *nāṭyahasta* and *patākā* are carefully watched by Śiva as Taṇḍu practices. The upraised left foot is quite noteworthy. The *kinkiṇī* anklet on this leg and its absence in any other non-dancing male sculpture of the period indicate its association with male dancers. In a rare *dakshiṇāmūrti*, Śiva is in *sthānaka* form with raised right leg as if in *yogamudrā*. Generally *dakshiṇāmūrtis*, except the *vīṇādhara* type, are in seated postures. The *kapardin jaṭābhāra*, broad *yajñopavīta*, a probable *yogapaṭṭa* type cloth band, tilted contemplative head pose, the upper two hands in *cinmudrā* and *kapittha hastamudrā* indicative of *vyākhayāna*; lower right and left hands in *abhaya* and *muṣṭihastamudrā*, all render this image a rather unique character.

Śiva's representation as expounder of the *śāstras*, music and *yoga* continued in *dakshiṇāmūrtis* carved under the Rāṣṭrakūṭas.[42] A panel beneath the *Nandīmaṇḍapa* bridge in Kailāśa temple and an image placed over its *śikhara mahānāsikā* presents such instances. The former shows an *aṣṭabhujī, trinetrī* figure in *siddhāsana* seated on a *padmapīṭha* under *aśvattha* tree. The main right hand near the chest suggest *vitarkamudrā*, next is in *abhayamudrā*, while the remaining two hold *akshamālā* and *sarpa*. The left ones, two broken, show a *padma* and *abhayamudrā*. A high *jaṭāmakuṭa* with crescent and skull, *ratna yajñopavīta* and *kuṇḍala* adorn the figure flanked by five *ṛṣis* on both sides. Wearing *yogapaṭṭas* around their legs and waist, the *ṛṣis* offer a contrast to Śiva whose seat is supported by three lions. Two squatting *gaṇas* hold musical instruments on either side. Above all, the *aṣṭadikpālas* rush towards Śiva on their respective *vāhanas* making the figure somewhat unusual. Śiva's *aṣṭabhujās* and the peculiar shape of the overshadowing tree adds unconventionality to its otherwise canonical character.[43]

The *śikhara* figure does not reveal pure *śilpaśāstrīya dakshiṇāmūrti lakshaṇas* as it is sitting alone and the setting is also neutral. However, its hand attributes betray a possible *dakshiṇāmūrti* form.

Gaṅgādhara

This motif is unseen in Cālukya rock-cut sculptures, but was a favourite theme in Pallava art as proved by the magnificent bas-relief at Mahābalipuram.[44] The motif conveys both *ugra* and *anugraha* aspects: the former through Śiva's contest with Gaṅgā, while the latter by fulfilment of Bhagīratha's desire. *Caturbhujī Gaṅgādhara* is carved on a wall panel in Dharmarāja *ratha*. He holds Gaṅgā, a personified kneeling female figure with *añjalimudrā*, in his upper left hand. Śiva's *tribhaṅga* form has a *jaṭāmakuṭa*, *kaṇṭhikā* and a *vastra yajñopavīta* in *upavīta* manner. The same motif, with certain variations, may be seen in Ādivarāha *maṇḍapam*. Herein Śiva's upper right hand holds aside his hair to receive Gaṅgā descending in female form with hands in *añjalimudrā*. His *caturbhujī* form again in *tribhaṅga* has lower right hand in *patākāmudrā*, upper left holding *akshamāla*, lower left in *kaṭimudrā*.

The Dharmarāja *ratha Gaṅgādhara*, having received Gaṅgā, placed his bent right leg on a platform, while the *maṇḍapam* figure, still readying to receive Gaṅgā, has both feet firmly on the ground. The bent leg posture may also be noticed in *Gaṅgādhara* in Lalitāṅkura *maṇḍapam* at Tiruciräppaḷḷī.[45] Here his right foot rests on a crouching *kuṁbhodara gaṇa*. Gaṅgā, a small female form with *añjali* hands, has lower portions of her body merging in a cloud. A heavily ornamented Śiva has *śīrṣacakra* also. The fine execution of this relief marks it out as the forerunner of the Mahābalipuram bas-relief with almost similar style and forms. Quite interestingly, the Ādivarāha *Gaṅgādhara*'s gesture of opening tresses and the mid-air position of Gaṅgā bear resemblance to Lalitāṅkura relief. Both *maṇḍapam Gaṅgādhara* exhibit *sarpakaṭisūtra*.The Ādivarāha and Dharmarāja *ratha* figures are identical in details of drapery, ornaments, etc. Both reveal *veṣṭi* of *kaupīna* or *ūrudhagna* type while in Tiruciräppaḷḷī it is an ankle length garment. On iconographical grounds, the Tiruciräppaḷḷī form may be regarded the earliest one, to be followed by the *ratha* figure with some variants, for instance the change in drapery,

Fig. 142. Ellorā: Cave XXIX (Sitā ki Nahani/Dhumar *Leṇa*), *Kalyāṇasundara* panel (after AIIS).

elimination of *sarpa kaṭisūtra*, Ganga's position shifted from upper right to upper left hand and non-requirement of *gaṇa* support for raised right foot. The Ādivarāha form was perhaps later to both, as it exhibits features of both forms.

The Rāṣṭrakūṭa *Gaṅgādhara* sculptures exhibit certain variants, like *vṛṣabhāntika Gaṅgādhara* and Pārvatī in the Daśāvatāra cave. Gaṅgā is not shown herein, suggesting a post-descent stage. Bhagīratha is identifiable as a sage, one leg flexed, arms upraised in *añjali*, an emaciated body with *jaṭāmakuṭa*. The panel has several subsidiary figures. The Kailāśa *mahāmaṇḍapa* panel is similar to this one except for a few details. It shows Gaṅgā descending in human form; Śiva stands on a *gaṇa*, below boulder forms probably denoting the ash mounds of Sagara's sons.

A *caturbhujī Gaṅgādhara* carving at Elephanta, in consonance with *Āgamic* norms, has Śiva firmly on his right leg while left leg is slightly bent. His back left hand, now broken, was probably under Pārvatī's chin to placate her. Front right hand depicts *abhayamudrā*, while front left one is broken. Gaṅgā is shown as a three-headed figure on Śiva's head. Brahmā, Indra, Viṣṇu and Garuḍa flank the divine couple. Near Śiva's left foot the kneeling form of Bhagīratha is evident, his hands in *añjalimudrā*.

Kalyāṇasundara

Kalyāṇasundara images are generally not seen in South Indian Cālukya or Pallava rock sculptures. A solitary instance may be cited in the Ellorā cave XXIX (Fig. 142). Therein

Fig. 143. Ellorā: Cave XXIX (Sitā ki Nahani/Dhumar *Leṇa*), west wall, Śiva Pārvatī panel (after AIIS).

caturbhujī Śiva holds Pārvatī by his right hand. His upper hands hold flower and show *abhayamudrā*, respectively. Fourth hand rest on the *kaṭibandha*. Pārvati, in slight *abhaṅga*, has right knee flexed with left arm holding a *padma* to proper left of Śiva. Brahmā officiates as the priest below. Another *dvibhuji* Śiva figure, as if in contemplation, is shown behind. One male and female figure with *śīrṣacakra* and *kirīṭamakuṭa* are also seen. A *śaṁkha* like object and halo in the male's hand facilitates his identification as Viṣṇu with Lakshmī acting as the bride's parents.

The Rāṣṭrakūṭa artists have illustrated the marriage of Śiva-Pārvatī as per *śilpaśāstrīya* norms. The Daśāvatāra cave panel shows Brahmā as the officiating priest. *Kalyāṇasundara* is *caturbhujī* with right lower arm in *kaṭi*, the left upper arm holding a *padma*, the rest two arms holding Pārvatī's hands outspread with fingers turned up. This is rather an unusual pose of holding hands. A figure behind with vase in hand is probably Himālaya. Accessory figures include the *aṣṭadikpālas*, Indra, Yama, Candra and Īśāna-Śiva. They all reveal *vismaya hastamudrā*. Adherence to *Āgamic* iconography is more prominent in the Elephanta relief. Here Pārvatī, heavily ornamented, has her right hand in Śiva's hand and stands to his right side, a position seen rarely except in marriage representations. Śiva wears snakes and jewels, *yajñopavīta* and a *jaṭāmakuṭa* with *śīrṣacakra*. To his left Brahmā, as priest, crouches over the *vedī*. Viṣṇu stands behind Śiva. Candra with a crescent behind is seen getting water for the ceremony. *Gāndharvas*, forming a curve around Śiva's *śīrṣacakra*, are suggested flying.The Kailāśa sculptures also portray the theme. One *prākāra* panel shows *caturbhujī*, ornamented Śiva holding *dvibhujī* Pārvatī's right hand with his lower right hand, *muṣṭi* pose of upper right hand, a *padma* in upper left hand, while the lower left is placed over Pārvatī's shoulder. Both figures in *dvibhaṅga* have Brahmā sitting beneath in between their legs. Accessory figures are not present in the panel. Another depiction has Viṣṇu and Lakshmī as Pārvatī's parents.

Umāsahita/Umā Maheśvara

These sculptures are profuse at Ellorā (Fig. 143). Daśāvatāra cave and cave XIV panel shows the couple in *akshakrīḍā* (Fig. 144). Śiva *caturbhujī* is in the act of throwing dice with his upper left hand and holding Pārvati's right hand to prevent her picking up the dice before the symbol is seen. *Dvibhujī* Parvatī wears *kuchabandha* and all customary ornaments. Śiva's upper right hand has *nāga* curled around the forearm and held by the fingers. Two *cāmardhārī* attend upon them while *gaṇas* are seen pranking with nandī below. One *gaṇa* is adjusting Pārvatī's leg on a *padmāsana pīṭha*. Another *akshakrīḍā* panel in Lankeśvara cave has the dice board between Śiva and Pārvatī. A *gaṇa* behind Pārvatī shown in *vismaya mudrā*, Nandī below has two *gaṇas* sporting with him. The position of Śiva to the proper left of Parvatī is an unusual stance. It has the couple in *ardhaparyankāsana* with Śiva representing *utkuṭika* posture.

Lankeśvara cave panels present different forms of the motif. In one instance, Maheśvara is shown in *vāma lalitāsana*. His right hand in *abhayamudrā*, with the left he holds a *yoni* on which a *liṅga* is placed. Umā in *ardhaparyankāsana* helps Śiva with her right hand in holding it. Another scene has them in *āliṅgana* pose. Plenty of such reliefs may be seen at Ellorā. The objects in Śiva's hands in such reliefs vary from *sarpa, dhanuṣ, ḍamarū, triśūla, anugrahamudrā* or *kaṭimudrā*.

Another sculpture has Umā to the right of Śiva with the *śīrṣacakra* behind and a female *gaṇa* standing by her side. The left upper arm of Śiva is holding a *gaṇa* while the

Fig. 144. Ellorā: Cave XIV (*Rāvaṇa kā Khāi*), Śiva Pārvatī *akshakrīḍā* panel (after AIIS).

other is behind Umā's waist. Nandī stands behind them in bull form. It is a *Vṛṣabhāntika candraśekharamūrti*. In a relief from Elephanta, *caturbhujī* Śiva, seated on a projection, leans towards Pārvatī on his left, while she appears to turn slightly away from him. Female figures stand on her either side, the one on the right carrying a child, probably Kārtikeya. Bhṛngī is seen near Śiva's foot. Several flying figures in clouds are apparent above. The popularity of this motif among Rāṣṭrakūṭa artists can be gleaned from its three forms portrayed at Ellorā.

Such representations are not found in the Pallava rock art.

Somaskanda

This motif was not seen in Cālukya and Rāṣṭrakūṭa art. It was, however, frequently carved in Pallava art,[46] mainly on the *garbhagṛha* rear wall of early *maṇḍapams* and Dharmarāja *ratha ūparitala*. It represents Śiva as a father, by the side of his wife and child.[47] The *ratha* relief[48] has Śiva seated on a *bhadrapīṭha* in *ardhaparyankāsana*. His upper two hands in *patākāmudrā* suggest holding of some objects. Lower right is in *cinmudrā*, while left is *muṣṭihasta*. His head is slightly tilted towards Umā. She is in full profile, in *ardhaparyankāsana*, with baby Skanda in her lap. Her *vastra* are rather transparent. Skanda wears a *karaṇḍamakuṭa* and seems to be demanding something from his mother. The family is flanked by Viṣṇu and Brahmā, both four-armed and in *tribhaṅga*, in panels on either side. The *Somaskanda* from Mahiṣamardinī *maṇḍapam* is the sole instance showing Nandī and a devotee[49] beneath the family. The iconography of this popular motif appears more or less identical in the rock-cut monuments only to be elaborated further in later structural shrines.

Vṛṣabhāntika

A Pallava representation survives in Arjuna *ratha* southside external *devakoṣṭha*. *Caturbhujī* Śiva leaning on Nandī is flanked by *mithuna* figures on either side *devakoṣṭhas* and single male figures[50] in two outer ones. Another sculpture from Dharmarāja *ratha* has Śiva leaning affectionately over Nandī in *tribhaṅga*. His left leg placed straight, right one is slightly bent and crossed over in front with the toes resting on the left foot. *Kaupīna* is fastened around the waist by a *kaṭibandha*. A loosely coiled *sarpa kaṭi*, *upavīta vastrayajñopavīta*, *kaṇṭhikā hāra* and *jaṭāmakuṭa* are seen on the figure. In his upper right hand he holds a *ḍamarū*, upper left a *pāśa*, the lower right rest by elbow on Nandī's hump, the lower left with palm up, third finger and bent thumb forms the *mayūrahasta mudrā*. A pillar panel from Avanibhājana *maṇḍapam* (Śīyamaṅgalam) has *caturbhujī Vṛṣabhāntika*, upper two hands holding *mṛga* and *akshamālā*, lower right in *kaṭi* and lower left resting by the elbow on the interned face of nandī standing behind with his fingers caressing its snout. He has a *nivīta yajñopavīta*. The *śūla dhvaja* is placed behind him. To his left stands Pārvatī in *tribhaṅga*, one hand in *kaṭi* and other holding *līlākamal*. Wearing *jatamakuṭa* like Śiva, she stands under a tree.

Ardhanārīśvara

Under Cālukya iconography a *caturbhujī dvibhaṅga* figure with Nandī, Bhṛngī and a female attendant is carved in Bādāmī cave I (Fig. 145). The upper right and left hands hold *parśu*, *sarpa* and *padma*, respectively. The lower hands hold the *vīṇā*. The left, female hip is shown broader. The right male leg strides forward, as if to balance the

Fig. 145. Bādāmī: Cave I, standing *Ardhanārīśvara* (after AIIS).

hip movement. We observe that the body is primarily male and the two aspects have not been adequately blended. The deity's female breast, in fact, seems to be the resonator of the *vīṇā*.[51] In contrast the *dvibhujī Ardhanārī* in Rāvaṇa Phaḍi appears more graceful. It holds a *triśūla* entwined by a *sarpa* in the right hand and a lock of hair in the left hand. The right foot is partly raised off the ground, as if in a dance pose. The female breast is prominent, body tall and slender. The thick *yajñopavīta* over the upper arm is a *sarpa*. The elongated *makuṭa* and *śīrṣacakra* are clearly seen.

In Bādāmī cave III the motif is a bracket figure. Here the slender form reveals a flowing movement by the inclined head and swaying hip. But the right leg has not come forth in tune. The female breast is emphasized by the *yajñopavīta* which falls over the arms. The female side upper hand holds a *darpaṇa*. A *caturbhujī Ardhanārī* on a pillar in Durgā temple exhibits features of both Rāvaṇa Phaḍi and Bādāmī cave III. A same motif in the Saṅgameśvara shrine reveals essentially feminine characteristics. The patterns of *sarī* and *vyāgrahacarm*, underlined male chest muscle, beauty folds under the female breast and graceful posture suggest the constant efforts by Cālukya artists to evolve a conventionalized *Ardhanārīśvara* form till a later period.

Among Pallava specimens, we see a remarkable sculpture on the Dharmarāja *ratha āditala*. It marks a perfect balance of the masculine part and the graceful poise of feminine portion. Like male, the female part is unusually *dvibhujī*. This is rather contrary to the usual iconography where the *devī* has more than two arms only in *svayaṃpradhānamūrti*. This may be a device to create symmetry with the male figure. The *nara* half is *samabhaṅga* whereas *nārī* half is in *dvibhaṅga* with slightly raised hip. A *kaṭibandha* reaches *nara*'s knee and up to *devī*'s ankle. The sculpture has no *udarabandha* or *yajñopavīta*. Usually the latter starts from the left shoulders, in this case being that of the *devī* half. We do not find *yajñopavīta* over female figures in Pallava period. This explains the omission. The figure shows *nakrakuṇḍala* in right and *patrakuṇḍala* in the left ear; *jaṭāmakuṭa* on the right and *karaṇḍa makuṭa* on the left side. The upper right hand holds a *parśu* while the lower is raised in *abhayamudrā* both having male *kaṅkaṇas*. The upper left hand has a *padma* and a feminine *valaya*, while the lower hangs down in *lambahasta*. Despite emphasis on symmetry seen in the form of paired arms and lack of *yajñopavīta*, the absence of anklet on the male leg is prominently noticeable. As it occurs invariably in the later sculptures, here the absence suggests an early date. The structural Vedagiriśvara and Shore temples enshrine seated *Ardhanārī* forms perhaps of later times. They hold a *vīṇā* with Nandī sitting below and a *yogapaṭṭa* round the right leg.

This motif abounded in Rāstrakūṭa art. Lankeśvara cave has a pillar carving with *nara* half carrying a *triśūla* in the upper hand and a *nāga* in the lower one. *Devī* holds a *darpaṇa* in the upper hand and lower one in *lolahasta* touches a flower. Standing under a mango tree in *abhaṅga*, the figure is flanked by two attendants. Two *vidyādharas* are seen in the air, in *añjalihasta* and *vismayahasta*, respectively. Significantly, the *devī* part has a *latā* rising upto the *vidyādhara* figure, while *nara* part shows a mango tree in full foliage and an owl seated thereon. This is a probable influence of Gupta *sahakāra* imagery, not used elsewhere in Rāṣtrakūṭa sculptures or those of Cālukyas and Pallavas. At Kailāśa temple *Ardhanārī* is carved as *caturbhujī* with right *nara* hands holding a *triśūla* and in *kaṭyāvalaṃbita mudrā* while the left ones are shown with a *darpaṇa* and hanging loose.

Fig. 146. Aihoḷe: Rāvaṇa Phaḍi cave, rightside wall, Harihara and *Dvārapāla* (after AIIS).

The Rāṣṭrakūṭa *Ardhanārī* form was also carved at Elephanta. The perfect balance of the male-female elements here is exemplary. The left half has a full breast and broad hip. The back arm holds a *darpaṇa*, while the now broken front perhaps held folds of drapery. The *nara* side front right arm rests on Nandī's back and head. The back hand holds a *nāga*. Both right arms have *sarpa bāhuvalaya* and thick *kaṅkaṇas*. The *vastra* clasp is differentiated on both sides. Crescent moon is also visible in Śiva's *jaṭābhāra*. The figure is surrounded by *caturbhujī garudārūdha* Viṣṇu, *haṃsārūdha padmāsīna* Brahmā, Indra on Airāvata, Varuṇa, Kārtikeya, Bhṛṅgī, etc. It is an important creation of Rāṣṭrakūṭa artists.

Thus, the *Ardhanārīśvara* remained a popular motif under all three dynasties.

Harihara

Hariharamūrti is a synthesized form of Śiva and Viṣṇu. We come across this form in the Cālukyan Rāvaṇa Phaḍi cave temple (Fig. 146). The four-armed figure has Śiva with *nāga* and *akshamāla* in right hands, while Viṣṇu part holds *śaṃkha* and shows *kaṭimudrā*. Śiva has *ardhacandra jaṭāmakuṭa* while Viṣṇu has *kirīṭamakuṭa*. Śiva shows *vyāgrahacarm*, while Viṣṇu has regular drapery. They wear *sṛṅkhalā yajñopavīta*.

Pallava instances are seen in both *ratha* and *maṇḍapam*. In Ādivarāha *maṇḍapam* a *caturbhujī samabhaṅga* figure, over a *padmāsana* holds *parśu* and *prayoga cakra* in upper right and left hands. The lower right and left hands show *abhayamudrā* and *kaṭimudrā*, respectively. In Dharmarāja *ratha* the *caturbhujī* figure, also in *sambhaṅga*, has a few variations, while largely identical in details of pose, drapery, etc., with the *maṇḍapam* one. For instance, the *ratha Harihara* is not flanked by kneeling devotees and its upper left hand does not hold the *prayoga cakra* but indicates a gesture of holding some weapon. Strangely, the missing *cakra* is carved just outside on the wall panel, perhaps an afterthought. Besides, unlike the *ratha* sculpture the *maṇḍapam* one stands under a *chatra*. The kneeling devotees are also seen in the Trimūrti *maṇḍapam* Brahmā shrine and Viṣṇu panel in Ādivarāha *maṇḍapam*.

The Kailāśa temple *Harihara* form is carved in a conventional mode. The left Hari and right Hara parts show a *cakra* in upper hand while lower is in *kaṭimudrā*. The right

Fig. 147. Ellorā: Cave XXVII (Milkmaid's cave), Brahma, Viṣṇu and Śiva in niches (after AIIS).

lower hand object is not clear but upper hand holds *triśūla*. Their *vāhanas* Nandī and Garuḍa are also shown, respectively towards right and left sides. These reliefs suggest prevalence of syncretic deities (Fig. 147).

Liṅgodbhava

This is one form of Śiva specific to the Rāṣṭrakūṭa rock creations. The Daśāvatāra panel shows a massive pillar type *liṅga* with a lenticular opening in the centre. Within this, *caturbhujī samabhaṅga* standing Śiva holds *āyudhas* in the upper hands, while the lower ones are in *abhaya* and *kaṭimudrā*. He is flanked by Brahmā and Viṣṇu below in the right and left sides. Both *caturbhujī* in *añjali hasta* of lower hands holds *āyudhas* in the upper ones. In addition, a figure of varāha nugging at the pillar base on left side and Brahmā flying up on right top have also been carved. A Kailāśa temple panel projects the *liṅga* as an *agnistaṃbha* (Fig. 148). *Dvibhujī* Śiva raises his right hand in *abhayamudrā* while left is in *kaṭyāvalaṁbita* pose. Both Viṣṇu and Brahmā assume *añjalimudrā*. Their

Fig. 148. Ellorā: Cave XVI, (Kailāśa), east court, east corridor gallery, *Liṅgodbhavamurti* (after AIIS).

additional figures are seen as tracing the origin and end of the *stambha*. Thus, this important manifestation of cult images may be taken up as a mark of Śaivite supremacy over other Brāhmanical cults.

Sadāśiva

This aspect also appears to be characteristic of Rāṣṭrakūṭa images. Twenty-eight figures of Sadāśiva are carved at Ellorā. They generally show *Vāmadeva* Śiva holding *darpaṇa* in one hand, the middle smiling *Sadyojāta* and *Tatpuruṣa* or *Aghora* to the right. The best example may be cited in the Elephanta main cave.[52] The three-headed Maheśa form is also seen in Pallava *maṇḍapams* though in painted reliefs which are no longer clear.

Lakulīśa

He is believed to be an incarnation of Śiva. The founder[53] of the Pāśupata sect, Lakulīśa iconography shows a *lakuṭa*, *lakula* or *daṇḍa* in his hand. Archaeological evidences[54] of the third-second centuries BC suggest Śiva holding a *daṇḍa*. Lakulīśa is generally *dvibhujī* or *caturbhujī*, ithyphallic, wearing *yajñopavīta*, *yogapaṭṭa* and *jaṭāmakuṭa*.[55]

Cālukya or Pallava specimens of rock-cut Lakulīśa have not been traced in the south. Therefore, we confine ourselves to the Rāṣṭrakūṭa instances. Two instances are noticed at Kailāśa conforming to the *śilpaśāstrīya* details. Seated in *padmāsana*, the *caturbhujī* figure has *akshamāla* and *kuṇḍikā*, while the lower hands show *mātulunga* and *lakuṭa*. The erect phallus is particularly emphasized. The Elephanta figure is mutilated, though revealing a few details. A *kaṭibandha* and *hāra* adorn his torso. Arms are broken. Accessory figures include Viṣṇu with Garuḍa, Brahmā, etc. The figure is also likened to *yogadakshiṇāmūrti* but the two arms clearly indicate its human status. The broken hands might have consisted of the *lakula* also. Hence, the identification.

Anugrahamūrtis in Cālukya, Pallava and Rāṣṭrakūṭa Art

Caṇḍeśānugraha

Cālukyan evidences in rock-cut are not available for this motif. In Pallava art, a *Caṇḍeśānugraha* representation survives in Dharmarāja *ratha*. *Caturbhujī* Śiva, turning

Fig. 149. Ellorā: Cave XVI (Kailāśa), east court, south corridor gallery, Rāvaṇa offering his nine heads to Śiva (after AIIS).

in semi-profile towards Caṇḍeśa, holds a *cāmara* in the upper right hand and a *nāga* by its tail in the left. The lower left is placed on Caṇḍeśa's shoulder affectionately, while the right is placed in *kaṭyāvalaṁbita*. Caṇḍeśa in *bhaṅga* stance displays a forward step, right arm folded on chest and fingers almost reaching his mouth suggesting attention. The left arm folded across supports the right bent elbow, the whole posture indicating *dāsabhāva*. His *kaṅkaṇa* and *bāhuvalaya* are similar to those of Śiva.[56]

Rāvaṇānugraha

While this is portrayed in the Cālukyan and Pallava structural temples, its' rock-cut instances have not been cited. A single representation in Cālukyan cave XIV at Ellorā shows Śiva Pārvatī in *sukhāsana*, disturbed by the shake. Kailāśa is suggested by irregular quadrangular blocks actually resembling mountain form.

The Rāṣṭrakūṭa artists created a variety of such images at Ellorā and Elephanta. The Kailāśa symbolized the very theme through its *adhiṣṭhāna* panel. Its stylistic details have been discussed in Chapter 6. Daśāvatāra cave panel *caturbhujī* Śiva holds *triśūla* and *nāga* in his right hands, while the left rests at Pārvatī's waist. He is in *paryankāsana* while Pārvatī, in *ardhaparyankāsana*, has one hand over her chest as if in fear. Another sculpture in the north gallery of the Kailāśa has *caturbhujī* Śiva and *dvibhujī* Pārvatī in analogous positions. The only peculiarity is Pārvatī entwining Śiva's left hand with her right hand.

Carving in the northern gallery depicts Rāvaṇa offering his heads in sacrifice to Śiva, symbolized by a cylindrical *liṅga* placed on a *pīṭha*. On its three sides nine heads are carved. Rāvaṇa below is seated with bent knees and holding his head with his left hand. His right hand shows a sword put on the neck. There is fire in front of him and a *ghaṭa* behind him. This rock-cut representation is exclusive to Kailāśa (Fig. 149). *Rāvaṇānugraha* in the Elephanta cave, although much damaged, reveals stylistic affinity to Ellorā. Śiva's *trinetra* is very prominent. Pārvatī, quite unusually, sits to his right. Her position is similar to Śiva's except for the variation in gesture. While Śiva exhibits unconcerned relaxation, Pārvatī turned towards him bears resemblance to the Kailāśa relief. Bhṛṅgī, Gaṇeśa, *garudārūdha* Viṣṇu, *gāndharvas*, etc., are seen around. Details of the Rāvaṇa figure are damaged to derive any conclusion.

One panel in Kailāśa north gallery perhaps represents *Arjunānugrahamūrti*. It has *dvibhujī* Śiva seated to the left wearing a *jaṭāmakuṭa* and ornaments. On the right a figure is seen in *añjalimudrā*.

Thus, *saumyamūrtis* of Śiva were profusely sculpted with *śilpaśāstrīya lakshaṇas*. While some manifestations were common to all three dynasties, some were exclusive to them.

(iii) *Nṛtyamūrtis*:- Symbolizing the whole process of life and death, creation and destruction, order and chaos in their forms, *nṛtyamūrtis*[57]constituted a distinct class of their own. Dance, like *yoga*, is a means for realizing one's own self. The tradition has had antiquity in India.[58] Śiva, the *yogī*, was also the lord of dance.[59] The Śaiva *nṛtyamūrtis* exhibit a variety of techniques and their depiction accordingly. Bharata's *Nāṭyaśāstra*[60] describes 108 dance modes, but the *Śaivāgamas* refer to just nine[61] types. Of these the *nādānta* is defined symbolically as the *pañcakṛtya*[62] of Śiva. Other dance forms include the *talasamsphoṭitam, lalita, catura, lalāṭatilaka, bhujaṅgatrāsita*, etc.

Fig. 150. Bādāmī: Cave I, façade, right wall, *Naṭarāja* (after AIIS).

Depiction of Nṛtya Forms in Cālukya, Pallava and Rāṣṭrakūṭa Sculptures

Popularity of the *Naṭarāja* theme in Cālukyan sculptures gets attested by its numerous depictions in their cave temples. Instances from Bādāmī cave I and Aihoḷe Rāvaṇa Phaḍi cave offer interesting details. At Bādāmī (Fig. 150) *atibhaṅga* Śiva in *caturamudrā* raises the heel of his left foot with the toe just touching the ground in *kuṭṭitam* pose. Resolutely the left knee flexes further to the left and a prominent bend occurs at the waist. With his three left hands Śiva holds *triśūla* and *parśu*. The body movement suggests upward action. The whole weight of Śiva's body appears forcefully thrown to the left side. The movement of his seventeen[63] arms is held together by the heavy vertical *triśūla* and *parśu*. The concentration of weight is rather balanced by the right arms spread in opposite direction. Despite such forceful action of his body Śiva's head is equipoised.

In the Aihoḷe cave relief, the toe of his right foot touches the ground. Herein we get a rather different version of the theme. The sculptor has used a plethora of snakes as different ornaments for *daśabhujī* Śiva. *Sarpayajñopavīta, sarpa kaṭisūtra, valaya, sarpa* in his hand, etc., are all swaying almost like live snakes. Śiva's rather elongated cylindrical *jaṭāmakuṭa* looks different from the more natural one at Bādāmī. The halo is a ribbed *śīrṣacakra* rather than the oval shaped at the latter site. Gaṇeśa and Skanda flank Śiva while Pārvatī looks on with admiration. *Mātṛkās*, wearing *ardhorukas*, have the dancing Bhṛngī perched above their *makuṭās*. Śiva dancing amidst *mātṛkās* is uniquely noticeable here. Nandī is unseen in the Aihoḷe panel whereas the Bādāmī cave I relief has Nandī and Gaṇeśa, not Pārvatī. *Naṭarāja* figure is carved also in Bādāmī cave II in a *kūḍū* medallion showing *daśabhujī* figure; the absence of snakes may be due to the paucity of space.

In Ellorā cave XIV Nandī, Gaṇeśa and the snake behind Śiva's head are missing. Pārvatī is present with Kārtikeya and Bhṛngī. The *tribhaṅga* pose of *aṣṭabhujī* Śiva is well delineated. His powerful movement is indicated by the awful and withdrawing stance of Pārvatī. He holds *ḍamarū* and *parśu* in two right hands, the third, now broken, rested on his thighs while the fourth, also broken, was flung across the chest in *daṇḍahasta mudrā*. The foremost left hand is a *tripatākā*, the second in *pravartita hastamudrā*, the third a *patākāhasta* and the fourth stretched out with a snake. Śiva stands in *kuṭṭitam* pose, i.e. resting his weight on the left foot, raises the heel of the right to beat the rhythm.

The *Naṭarāja* form has been profusely carved in Pallava art, be it their rock-cut monuments or structural shrines. The pilaster panel from Śīyamaṅgalam cave is probably the earliest representation in *ānanda-tāṇḍava* or *bhujaṅgāñcīta*. The lower right hand shows *abhayamudrā* while the left is in *gajahasta* mode. His upper right arm holds a fire bowl, the upper left has a *parśu*. He wears a *jaṭāmakuṭa;* below the forehead is the *trinetra*. The *jaṭā* is seen whirling all around. Heavy *kiṅkiṇī* on his feet suggest the *tāla* rhythm. The snake near his feet, coiled and hood raised appears to be listening to the music beats. Apasmāra is not seen below his feet in this panel. A *gaṇa* beats *ūrdhva maddala* with both hands.

Sculptures from Dharmarāja *ratha* provide varied representations of *Naṭarāja* including dancing on Apasmāra holding *parśu* in one of the right hands while the other is held in *alapadma*. One of his left hands is in *abhayamudrā* and the next in *patākā* pose. Apasmāra below is shown larger than usual size. The moment suggested is just before Śiva lifts his leg to make it *ūrdhvājanu*. Śiva's projection as *nāṭyācārya* has already been given in his *dakshiṇāmūrtis*.

In addition to rock-cut representations, a series of sculptures in Pallava structural temples depict the deity in dance postures as *ūrdhvājanu ālīḍha, gajahasta lalāṭatilaka, pādasvāstika*, etc. It is therefore, apparent that Śiva as *naṭeśa* and *nāṭyācārya* was a favourite theme in the Pallava art.

Moving on to Rāṣṭrakūṭa art, some remarkable *naṭeśa* reliefs survive in their caves. The Lankeśvara cave Śiva dances with the posterior in, *diksvāstika* and *pṛṣṭhasvāstika* movement. Despite being fully masculine the figure exhibits a grace and smile essentially feminine. The *jaṭā* decoration is noteworthy. Another image of *aṣṭabhujī* Śiva with *jaṭābhāra*, tilted head and rather defiant look almost seems to play with his arms. Pārvatī stands to his right. A quite unusually personified Gaṅgā sits on his *jaṭā*, playing with its snake. Śiva's stance is *pratyālīḍha*. Another dance pose is struck in *Gajāsurasaṁhāramūrti*. In his *ugra* form Śiva's dance commences after the annihilation of foes like *gajāsura*, *andhaka* or *tripuras*. Sculptures in Kailāśa temple abound in his *nāṭya* forms. One shows him with right foot raised in *ūrdhvājanu* mode, almost dropping down on one leg. A ceiling pattern has him in *catura* pose, his main hands in *abhaya* and *gajahasta*, one in *recita*, one fondly caressing Pārvatī's hair, and one holding *nāga*, while the lower pair is in *kaṭyāvalaṁbita*. Apasmāra lies trampled below his foot. Two other representations show him in *ūrdhvājanu*. The Kailāśa temple *mahāmaṇḍapa* ceiling has *catura* Śiva sculpture against a *padmamaṇḍala* background indicating *maṇḍalācārī* image. A unique sculpture of Śiva seated with *ardhayogapaṭṭa* around his left knee, playing *ghaṭavādya*, eyes closed in ecstasy, is carved in the *prākāra*.

A figure in Daśāvatāra cave has Śiva's feet in *kuṭṭitam* pose, standing on right foot, left heel upraised in rhythm. *Naṭarāja* relief is also extant in Elephanta. Although mutilated, it suggests *kuṭṭitam* pose of legs. The upper body portion in strong *bhaṅga* from shoulders to hips to slightly twisted to the left by the movement of the first right arm shown in *gajahastamudrā*. The fourth right hand shows *nāga*, symbol of death and rebirth. The remaining hands are broken.

Besides these specimens there are other *nāṭya* images at Ellorā depicting similar details. It may be held that they created a treasure house of such dynamic forms in keeping with *Paurāṇic* and *Āgamic* norms.

Liṅga[64] Forms

This aspect of Śaivite iconography is integral to the rock-cut temples wherein both monolithic and *mānuṣī liṅgas* were created. The latter consisted of three parts: (i) the lowest *caturārṣa* section *brahmabhāga*, (ii) *aṣṭakoṇīya Viṣṇubhāga*, and (iii) *vṛttākāra rūdrabhāga* at top. When fluted, *rūdrabhāga* is seen as a *dhārāliṅga*, the number of vertical flutes as per the *Suprabhedāgama* being five, seven, nine, twelve, sixteen, twenty-four and twenty-eight. The *mukhaliṅgas*[65] constituted another class. They show human faces on their *rūdrabhāga*. The number of faces determines their type as *ekmukha*, *trimukha*, *caturmukha*, and *pañcamukha*. The last named symbolizes the five aspects, viz. *sadyojāta*, *vāmadeva*, *aghora*, *tatpuruṣa*, and *īśāna*. *Īśāna* is generally not shown for being *tatheśānaṁ yogīnāmapyagocaram*, i.e. beyond the comprehension of even the *yogīs*. In *mukhaliṅga* faces the third eye is usually vertical.

Depiction in Art

Generally we do not find *mukhaliṅga* type in rock-cut shrines, except the Sadāśiva relief in Elephanta cave resembling a *liṅga* form.[66] The *liṅga* form was carved under all three dynasties. *Dhāraliṅga* is the usual type in Pallava caves, while Rāṣṭrakūṭa specimens are invariably *vṛttākāra*. A novelty seen in the *liṅgodbhava* form is the combination of both aniconic and iconic representations. The *liṅga pillar* from which Śiva emerges is also *vṛttākāra* as seen in the *liṅgodbhava* and *kālāri* reliefs or Brahmā pulling out a *liṅga* in the Kailāśa temple relief. Cālukya *liṅga* is almost always of *ārṣa* type. Even its *pīṭha* is always square while that of Rāṣṭrakūṭa ones is generally cylindrical.

Other Śaiva Images

Gaṇeśa and Kārtikeya

Gaṇeśa's iconography[67] consists of an elephant faced, *trinetradhārī*, *caturbhujī kumbhodara* figure, wearing *yajñopavīta*, holding *triśūla* and *akshamāla* in right hands and *parśu* and *modakpātra* in the left ones. Kārtikeya,[68] Skanda or Kumāra is popular in South India as Subramaṇya. His usual attributes are *akshamāla*, *kheṭaka*, *vajra*, *śakti*, *kamaṇḍalu*, *kukkuṭa*, and *daṇḍa*.

Both Gaṇeśa and Kārtikeya appear in Bādāmī cave I flanking *Mahiṣamardinī*; Aihoḷe Rāvaṇa Phaḍi with *Naṭarāja* Pārvatī; and Ellorā caves XXII and XV with Lakshmī. Besides, they are also represented individually. *Dvibhujī* Gaṇeśa in Bādāmī cave I holds a *modakpātra* and tusk with his hands. A thick *ratna yajñopavīta* falls over his right arm. A similar form, but *caturbhujī* and with elaborate *makuṭa*, is seen in Cālukyan Ellorā cave XVII. A *sthānaka samabhaṅga* Gaṇeśa in Rāvaṇa Phaḍi cave wears a *ratnamakuṭa*.

Gaṇeśa is usually not seen in Pallava *rathas* or *maṇḍapams*. An exceptional, finer relief is seen in Vallam *maṇḍapam*. This *caturbhujī* form in *siṁhāsana* holds a lotus bud in one hand, while the other hand object is broken. The lower hands rest on his thigh and seat, respectively. The tusk coiled towards the right, suggest a *valampurī* form.

Rāṣṭrakūṭa art preserves several representations. Daśāvatāra cave has the biggest Gaṇeśa at Ellorā, flanking the *dvāraśākhās* with Vīrabhadra and in Śiva family panels. In a similar manner, Kārtikeya portrayals are found more in South, though his representations appear at Ellorā also.

Nandī

Often represented as a bull and sometimes bull-faced human or a duplicate of Śiva. In the last aspect, he is *caturbhujī*, *trinetradhārī*, wearing *vyāgrhacarma*, holding *parśu*, *triśūla*, and *mṛga*, his *jaṭās* depicting *ardhacandra* and Gaṅgā. He is usually seen with *Vṛṣabhāntika* Śiva or on the Kailāśa. He is mostly placed as a bull in the *nandīmaṇḍapas* at temple entrances.

From this account it goes beyond doubt that as far as Śaivite iconography is concerned, the South Indian sculptors observed the *śilpaśāstrīya* canons and created nearly all possible forms of the deity in rock-cut mode.

Vaiṣṇava Images

Viṣṇu

He finds considerable representation in South Indian rock-cut sculptures in consonance with canonical *lakshaṇas*. Viṣṇuite icongraphy[69] has been given in the *Vaikhānasāgama*,

Bṛhat Saṁhitā, Purāṇas, etc. Viṣṇu images are of *yoga, bhoga, vīra* and *abhisārikā* types while their posture constitutes *sthānaka, āsana*, and *śayana mūrtis*.

Iconographically Viṣṇu is a *dvibhujī, caturbhujī*, or *aṣṭabhujī*[70] deity. The *Dvibhujī* form holds the *śaṁkha* in left hand while raises the right in *abhayamudrā*.[71] *Caturbhujī* has the *śaṁkha, cakra, gadā*, and *padma*.[72] In *aṣṭabhujī* form his *āyudhas* are *gadā, śara, khaḍga* in right hands, the fourth being in *abhayamudrā*. The left hands hold *dhanuṣ, kheṭak, cakra*, and *śaṁkha*.[73] His usual ornaments are *kirīṭamakuṭa, kaustubhmaṇi, vaijayantī, srīvatsa, vanamālā nakra*, and *ratna kuṇḍalas, kāñcīmekhalā, keyūra, valaya kaṅkaṇ*, etc. Viṣṇu's weapons are also conceptualized as *āyudhapuruṣa*[74] in anthropomorphic form.

Viṣṇu forms in Cāḷukya, Pallava and Rāṣṭrakūṭa Art

In the rock-cut shrines Viṣṇu is generally represented in his *avatāra* forms. The *daśāvatāra* notion suggesting both anthropomorphic and zoomorphic forms remained a favourite theme. Of these the Varāha, *Trivikrama* and Nṛsiṁha motifs were frequently carved under all three dynasties.

Varāha

Of the *bhūvarāha*[75] and *yajñavarāha* forms, the former finds representation in South Indian rock art. Its iconography has been recommended[76] elaborately. The motif is firstly seen in Bādāmī cave II and III. In stance and robustness these two Cālukya *naravarāhas* almost follow the Gupta specimens from Udaigiri and Eraṇ.[77] The Gupta *ālīḍhamudrā* Varāha had the left leg on *śeṣanāga's* hoods while the right leg was held tense and erect. The *dvibhujī* figure had Bhūdevī clinging to its tusks. The Cālukyan figures present certain novelties. For instance, the figure wears a thick *ratna yajñopavita*, jewelled crown, holds *śaṁkha* and *cakra* in the additional upper hands, while lower right is *kaṭyāvalaṁbita* and left holds a *padmapīṭha* for Bhūdevī. Besides, *Bhūdevi* is provided a support under her feet by the *Varaha*'s lower left hand as prescribed by the *Viṣṇudharmottara Purāṇa*. The *śaṁkha* placement in the upper left hand behind her further consolidated her position. She stands gracefully while leaning towards the varāha's snout or shoulder in these reliefs. Within the caves we observe the composition is more diagonal in cave II. Both Varāha and Bhūdevī wear *makuṭa* unlike in the dated cave. Bhūdevī has also a *prabhāvalī*. Varāha steps on a *padmāsana* unlike on *śeṣa* hoods in cave III. The *vanamālā* is also missing in cave II.

In the Aihoḷe Rāvaṇa Phaḍi cave Varāha's foot does not rest on *padmāsana* or *śeṣanāga*. The left heel is raised from the ground in a dance pose stance. His body is more slender and flat. His lower left hand support Bhūdevī's feet seated on his upper arm, her hand resting on his shoulder. The *śaṁkha* floats in the air without any visible support, while the *cakra* is balanced on the finger tips. The Varāha wears a *yajñopavīta* and *vanamālā* as in Bādāmī cave III. Further stylistic development in the motif portrayal may be visualized in the structural Durgā temple at Aihoḷe and Makuṭeśvara temple. Therein the *cakra* is held in two extended fingers, as if in *prayoga mudrā* while Bhūdevī is perched comfortably on the upper part of Varāha's left arm folded at the elbow. Moreover, the Varāha's sniffing her with the snout reveals a subtle intimacy.

Fig. 151. Mahābalipuram: Varāha *maṇḍapam, Naravarāha.*

Composition wise in cave III the action is fully centred on the Varāha and is not contrasted by any counter movement. All the surrounding figures are not only smaller in proportion to him but also display passive attitudes. Bhūdevī herself, standing erect and vertical appears exactly in line with the upward surge of the Varāha. Reaching only up to his snout, she neither seems to weigh down his head by resting her arm upon it, nor to disturb his rising movement by any bend of body. This portrayal offers a contrast to similar motif in Cālukyan cave XIV at Ellorā. Therein it is represented as a drama with all the figures plunging into action. The Bādāmī cave III Varāha comes close to a *sthānamūrti*,[78] i.e. a freestanding image with attendant *devatās*. Quite significantly, in cave II the Varāha is drawn back to a side with his right foot placed in the right corner providing him wide range for the stride. His head is bent downwards unlike in Ellorā or Bādāmī cave III, towards his left arm. Bhūdevī is shown reclining passively[79] rather than standing with erect head, suggestive of triumph. This relief seems to portray Varāha still in the midst of the action. Thus, even at Bādāmī is a variance in execution of the motif. Cave III suggests tranquility, triumph and tenderness, while the cave II panel is full of physical action, dramatic content and dynamism. To the latter variety may also be added the Cālukya specimens at Aihoḷe and Ellorā.

The popularity of Vaiṣṇava *avatāras* influenced Pallava sculptural art. Living up to their reputation as *Āgamapriya*,[80] the Pallavas adopted *Āgamic* conventions for religious edifices and images. For instance, the Varāha in Varāha *maṇḍapam* panel presents *Vaikhānasāgamic* iconography. The *caturbhujī naravarāha* lifting Bhūdevī from *pātāla* is shown in semi-profile turned to his right and holds Bhūdevī on his *ūrdhvājanu* right knee, one hand placed around her hips while the other clasps her ankles in the pose of holding a child (Fig. 151). Their forms are tall and slender. Details like eyes, nose, ornaments, etc., both of Varāha and Bhūdevī as well as accessory figures are rather plain and general. The figure reveals contemplation and quiet stance rather than physical exertion or triumph. His snout has been modeled with full care, in accordance with *Vaikhānasāgama*, slightly tilted up, sniffing and touching Bhūdevī's bosom. She seems to express both shyness and joy while her loosened *kuchabandha* is shown fallen on her thigh. Besides, the Varāha head blending with the human part of the figure in a quite naturalistic way is noteworthy. A stucco painted bas-relief with similar iconographic details is preserved in the Ādivarāha *maṇḍapam garbhagṛha* also.

A simple relief from Rāṣṭrakūṭa Daśāvatāra cave portrays six armed Varāha with Bhūdevī on the upper left hand at the very climax of the event. He holds a *prayoga cakra* in the upper right hand, the middle right one bent at the elbow and supporting left middle, lower right in *kaṭyāvalaṁbita*. The lower left holds the *śaṁkha* by the tip while the middle one supports Bhūdevī at her back. The right leg is forcefully laid on the ground; the upraised left one, bent at the knee, is placed on a coiled *nāga* who is shown in *vismayamudrā* by the violent action of the Varāha. Bhūdevī perched on Varāha's elbow in *ardhaparyankāsana* appears in a slanting, vulnerable position. A small *nāgī* below seems to hold back Bhūdevī by clinging to the Varāha's foot. Thus, this panel highlights the spontaneity, surprise and yet ongoing rescue process, making it different from the preceding Cālukya and Pallava specimens, in composition as well as artistic treatment.

A panel in Kailāśa temple shows *caturbhujī* Varāha with Bhūdevī seated on the joint of his left hand. The Lankeśvara cave Varāha is carved quite elaborately. It shows the *caturbhujī* figure carrying Bhūdevī in his raised and flexed left upper arm. Bhūdevī's legs hanging sideward, her body faces the front and arms are raised over the head in *añjalimudrā*. She is not wearing the *kuchabandha*. The Varāha's snout supports her hip and smells it. His head is horizontally tilted, the *kirīṭamakuṭa* projecting backwards. The flexed lower left hand carries a *śaṁkha* while the corresponding right arm has a *prayoga cakra*. The lower right arm is in *kaṭi*. His right leg is firmly on the ground while the left, flexed high at waist level, is placed on *nāga* hoods. His snout, *damuṣṭras*, and the lower jaw of a half open mouth are all well delineated.

That the motif was carved by artists in their respective manner is quite apparent.

Trivikrama

These sculptures are usually of the *vāmana* and *virāṭrūpa Trivikrama* types. Canonically the former should be *pañcatāla*, *dvibhujī*, *chatradhārī*, *daṇḍa*, and of young *brahmacārī*

Fig. 152. Mahābalipuram: Varāha *maṇḍapam*, *Trivikrama*.

appearance; the latter had to be *aṣṭabhujī* or *caturbhujī*, one foot firmly on the ground and the other upwards.[81] *Vaikhānasāgama* prescribes subsidiary *devatās* as *caurī* bearer Vāyu and Varuṇa, Sūrya and Candra, Brahmā washing the upraised foot of Trivikrama, Gaṅgā; Namucī and other demons, Jāmbavān playing a drum, Garuḍa and lastly, Bālī with wife Vindhyabāli granting land to *Vāmana* and Rāhū shown near the raised foot.

Depiction in Cālukya, Pallava and Rāṣṭrakūṭa Rock Art

Bādāmī cave II *Trivikrama* corresponds to *Vaikhānasāgama* canons.The *aṣṭabhujī Trivikrama* looks dynamic and powerful. His head and body are in frontal position as if generating tremendous energy. His step is suggested by a straight, direct leg and upper arm movement. The movement is predominantly oriented towards the left. Several accessory figures are seen conforming to *Āgamic* norms. A crowned *asura* holding the deity's leg, identified as Bālī or Namucī,[82] a head-down falling figure, probably Triśanku, *dvibhujī vāmana* with a *chatra* standing left below with Bālī and his attendants around. Rāhū is shown just near the upraised leg and *Viṣṇu gaṇas* beneath are seen playing music. The *cakra* is positioned on top of his fingers. His chest muscles are slightly underlined and knees are also emphasized.

In cave III the motif gets a more lucid and dramatic treatment. Bālī wearing *sanghāṭī* and an *uṣṇīśa* resembles Buddha more than in cave II. *Aṣṭabhujī Trivikrama* holds the *cakra* by his finger tips. Surrounding figures resembling Rāhū, Candra, Jāmbavān, Garuḍa, Śukrācārya, Vindhyabāli, etc., also occupy space. A similar motif in the Virūpāksha temple has been carved in a vertical panel. Therein the leg is upraised vertically, the foot touches the outstretched hand. The diagonal position of arm and leg are balanced by the crowned head inclined to the opposite direction.

Trivikrama motif in Pallava art is also quite significant. It betrays the influence of *Vaikhānasāgama*. The *aṣṭabhujī kirīṭamakuṭadhārī Trivikrama* carved in Varāha *maṇḍapam* has taken the second step (Fig. 152). Holding the usual *āyudhas*, his fourth right hand is held up, with palm turned up as per *Vaikhānasāgama*. In accordance with the same text his fourth left hand, stretched straight towards the upraised leg, has the forefinger pointing beyond the foot. *Caturbhujī* Brahmā washing *Trivikrama*'s foot and Śiva seated on *padmāsana* can be seen flanking *Trivikrama*'s head, suggesting their position in *svarga*. A mid-air hanging figure with legs and head upside down indicate Triśanku. Bālī and his wife are missing as the panel does not represent the *vāmana* aspect. The four figures seated on the ground are, perhaps, the vanquished *asuras*. One of them expresses *vismayahaṣṭa mudrā*. Composition wise the panel represents dynamism. *Trivikrama*'s straight form with exceptional long *dhanuṣ* dominates the scene in which other figures are also actively involved. Thus, the *śilpaśāstrīya* norms have been exactly observed in the carving of this panel, be it *Trivikrama*'s hand posture and upraised leg, or Brahmā, whose *loka* has been approached. However, the number of accessory figures herein is not equivalent to the Cālukya specimen.

In Rāṣṭrakūṭa art *aṣṭabhujī Trivikrama* in the Daśāvatāra cave holds *śaṁkha, dhanuṣ, kheṭaka*, in his left hands, while *sūcī* finger points to an unseen Rāhū. The right hands show *khaḍga, gadā, cakra* and *cinmudrā*. The left leg upraised up to chest level suggests measuring of the *ākāśa*, i.e. second step taken. Below in the left corner, Bālī pours water over *vāmana*'s hands. He is accompanied by Śukrācārya and an attendant. The right corner shows Garuḍa holding Bālī by the hairs. Placed between symmetrical groups on either side, the perfectly balanced *vikram* with fine body contours exhibit Rāṣṭrakūṭa artists' mastery. Subsidiary figures are lesser in this panel than at Bādāmī. In Kailāśa temple panel *Trivikrama* has six hands. He holds the *gadā, khaḍga, cakra, kheṭaka, śaṁkha*, etc., in them. He raises his left leg up to his shoulder level. *Vāmana* in the left corner below has a *chatra* overhead. Bālī in front is being tied by Garuḍa.

This makes it quite apparent that the carving of *Trivikrama* under the three dynasties was fully conventionalized, the only variation being its stylistic treatment or the number of subsidiary figures included.

Nṛsiṁha

Iconography in the *Matsya Purāṇa*[83] prescribed the fighting deity and demon to be shown with interlocked knees, the former repeatedly attacked by tired Hiraṇyakaśipu. Quite significantly Nṛsiṁha, besides *ugra* form, also represents a god of deliverance.

Fig. 153. Bādāmī: Cave III, *Mukhamaṇḍapa*, east wall, *śeṣāsana* Viṣṇu.

Artistic Portrayals

A seated *caturbhujī* Nṛsiṁha with a *yogapaṭṭa* tied around his waist, upper hands holding the *śaṁkha* and *cakra* while the right leg is flexed high and, the right side figure in *añjalimudrā* is probably Prahlāda, is seen in Bādāmī cave II. A *caturbhujī* figure in cave III stands in *abhaṅga*, almost in *vīrasthānaka* form, while two figures placed just above his hands apparently represent the *āyudhadevatās - sudarśana cakra* and *pāñcajanya śaṁkha*. The lion face hairs have been realistically done. He is heavily ornamented with *kaṇṭha hāra*, *graiveyaka*, *keyūr valaya*, *kaṅkaṇas*, and *yajñopavīta*. The knee joint suggests a stiff leg posture. *Kaṭibandha* shows *siṁha* clasp above and *makara* clasp below. The combative Nṛsiṁha is unseen in Cālukyan rock-art.

Nṛsiṁha rock-cut sculptures are not available in Pallava regions, whereas the theme was a favourite one for the Rāṣṭrakūṭa artists.

Lankeśvara cave has *caturbhujī* Nṛsiṁha seated on *adhopadma* and *ūrdhvapadma* courses *padmapīṭha*. The figure, although mutilated, reveals some fine details. He is seated in *ardhaparyankāsana* with his right hanging leg resting on *asura* back. An *asura* body lies dead nearby; while another seen in squatting position and one hand in *vismaya mudrā* shows *damuṣṭras* and bulging eyes. Hiraṇyakaśipu's body, holding his *khaḍga* and *kheṭaka*, lies flat in Nṛsiṁha's lap who tears its' entrails with left hand's nails. A female, perhaps Hiraṇya's wife, partially supports his limp legs. Of Nṛsiṁha's four arms, two tear Hiraṇya's body and upper two hold *śaṁkha* and *prayoga cakra*. His face reveals a cavernous mouth, bulging eyes and high *karaṇḍa makuṭa*, with ears shown high in tension. The Daśāvatāra relief shows the actual fight and the interlocking of knees is a masterstroke of artistic excellence.[84] A panel in the Kailāśa temple has *caturbhujī* Nṛsiṁha in *pratyālīḍhāsana*. He tears off Hiraṇya's stomach with two hands and displays a ferocious stance.

In this manner the Nṛsiṁha motif was represented in variant modes in the Cālukya-Rāṣṭrakūṭa regions and even within the Rāṣṭrakūṭa specimens.

Fig. 154. Mahābalipuram: Mahiṣamardinī *maṇḍapam, maṇḍapa*, south wall, *śeṣaśayī* panel (after AIIS).

Śeṣaśayī/ Śeṣāsana Viṣṇu

Instances are available from all three empires. Bādāmī cave III has *caturbhujī* Viṣṇu seated upon three-coiled five-hooded śeṣanāga (Fig. 153). He holds *prayoga cakra* and *śaṁkha* in upper hands. *Kirīṭamakuṭa, makara* and *puṣpa kuṇḍala, śālagrāma hāra, graiveyaka, vanamālā, keyūr, kaṅkaṇa, udarabandha, kaṭibandha* and *kaṭisūtra*, and *yajñopavīta* adorn his form. Garuḍa with folded legs and *añjalimudrā* hands is seen to his right. Two female *caurīdhārī* flank Viṣṇu. Underneath the left side female is another seated female, the right hand placed upon *śeṣa* coil and the flexed left one taken to the breast in *kartarihasta*. She may be *Bhū* as she is positioned particularly on Viṣṇu's left side. This relief actually represents the *śeṣāsana* theme.

A deeply cut-relief in Pallava Mahiṣamardinī *maṇḍapam* has *śeṣaśayī* Viṣṇu's *yogaśayanamūrti* (Fig. 154). The *dvibhujī* figure on five-hooded *śeṣa* holds no attributes. *Asura* Madhu and Kaiṭabha equipped with *gadās* stand at his feet, almost set to strike. A female figure in profile, possibly Bhūdevī, kneels with hands in *añjalimudrā* below his feet. Two figures in her front and two flying above Viṣṇu resemble *āyudhapuruṣas*.[85] Viṣṇu exhibits a reposing pose. Even śeṣanāga appears docile, unlike in other *śeṣaśayī* portrayals. Thus, the pose and content in the relief has a variation from the usual depiction. The head and chest of Viṣṇu are a bit raised, while other body parts stretched flat, the left leg slightly bent and drawn up and placing of the panel opposite

Mahiṣamardinī fighting *asuras* - all such iconographic *lakshaṇas* indicate that Viṣṇu is about to wake from his *yoganidrā* and fight the foes. Another huge *Anantaśayī* sculpture is in Raṅganātha *maṇḍapam* (Śiṅgavaram). Besides a *caturbhujī* Viṣṇu reclining on five-hooded śeṣa it has *caturbhujī nābhikamal* Brahmā with his usual attributes. In addition Madhu, Kaiṭabha, Bhūdevī, *āyudhas* and probably Nārada are also seen in the panel.

The Rāṣṭrakūṭa Daśāvatāra cave has a reclining *caturbhujī* Viṣṇu, his one left arm stretched along the body, other bent and raised up, one flexed right arm supporting his crowned head. He does not hold *āyudha*. The wavy śeṣanāga coil forms his head support. Besides *nābhikamal* Brahmā, it has six figures including one female seated below facing front. They probably represent Bhṛgu and *pañcāyudhas* with *kaumodakī*, the female. A female figure half carved at Viṣṇu's feet represents Lakshmī. The *asuras* or śeṣa hoods as seen in Pallava instances are not seen herein. The *asuras* are also not there in the Cālukya example. *Nābhikamal* Brahmā was carved in both Pallava and Rāṣṭrakūṭa caves. The Śeṣaśayī panel in the Kailāśa temple besides regular features has a seven-hooded śeṣanāga. A damaged panel in Pātāleśvara cave (Poonā) shows separate *pīṭhas* for five similar figures suggesting their elevated status. These instances prove that the motif certainly got enriched iconographically by artists under patron dynasties.

Other Viṣṇu Forms

An *aṣṭabhujī sthānaka* Viṣṇu form at Bādāmī comprisess *cakra*, *śara*, *gadā* and *khaḍga* in four right hands, while the three left hands hold *śaṁkha*, *kheṭaka* and *dhanuṣ*. The front left hand is in *kaṭimudrā*. A bust seen atop the *kirīṭa*, resembling Nṛsiṁha led to its varied identifications as *Vaikuṇṭha* and *Virāṭapuruṣa*.[86] But the attributes clearly indicate its *aṣṭabhujī* Viṣṇu form as prescribed in the *Bṛhat Saṁhitā*. Other Viṣṇu sculptures are also carved in cave I and II with *śilpaśāstrīya* details, sometimes in *lalāṭbiṁba* or as *nāsikā*.

Vaiṣṇavite representations were quite popular with Pallava artists. Several sculptures attest to this fact: some prominent ones include those at Tirukkaḷukkuṇram and Kilmāvilaṅgai. The latter has *caturbhujī samabhaṅga* Viṣṇu holding *śaṁkha*, *prayoga cakra* in upper hands, lower hands in *abhaya* and *kaṭimudrā*. He has a *śīrṣacakra* and *nivīta yajñopavīta*, besides *valaya*, *keyūr*, *kirīṭamakuṭa*, *kuṇḍala*, etc. These regular iconographic features are seen in nearly all Viṣṇu forms sculpted under the Pallavas as seen in Trimūrti, Tirucirāppaḷḷī *maṇḍapams*, and Dharmarāja and Arjuna *rathas*. Still in comparison to rock-cut Śaivite sculptures, Viṣṇu carvings are few and of less variety suggesting the Śaivite inclinations of their patrons.

Rāṣṭrakūṭa caves abound in Viṣṇu forms. Seated on personified Garuḍa or standing in *samabhaṅga*, or with a devotee, he has the usual ornaments and *āyudhas*, *abhaya* and *varadamudrā*, and *śīrṣacakra*. Hence, Viṣṇu and his various forms were quite popular in the rock-cut shrines.

Other Brāhmanical Deities

Brahmā

His images in the rock-cut temples are primarily of a subsidiary character. He has been carved as *āvaraṇadevatā*. Brahmā representations also vary in relief compositions. He is variously seen as *nābhikamal* in the *śeṣaśayī* reliefs, soaring skywards or in *añjalimudrā* in *liṅgodbhavamūrtis*, as Śiva's charioteer in *Tripurāntakamūrti* or as officiating priest in *Kalyāṇasundara* reliefs.

Brahmā's iconography[87] was perhaps established by this time. He is usually a *caturmukha* figure holding *akshamāla, sruk, sruva* and *Vedas* in his four hands or raising two hands in *abhaya* and *varadamudrā*. Having *haṁsa vāhana*, he wears a *jaṭāmakuṭa, yajñopavīta, kaṭisūtra, kuṇḍala*, etc. These details recommended in the *Aṁśumadbhedāgaṇa, Śilparatna, Viṣṇu Purāṇa*, etc., were followed in the making of Brahmā sculptures during the period under consideration.

In Bādāmī caves II and I, Brahmā was carved with these features. In the former, he is seen with Saraswatī and Sāvitrī on a pillar face; the latter has him solemnizing Śiva-Pārvatī's marriage.

The Pallava Brahmā specimen from Ādivarāha *maṇḍapam* and Dharmarāja *ratha āditala* possess identical *lakshaṇas*. The difference being that the *ratha* Brahmā's lower right and left hands are respectively in *abhaya* and *kaṭyāvalaṁbita mudrā*. This marks reversal of *hastamudrās* from the *maṇḍapam* Brahmā. An unusual form of an *ekamukha*[88] Brahmā is seen in the Trimūrti *maṇḍapam*.

Brahmā in Rāṣṭrakūṭa sculptures is represented in all the above mentioned forms, besides a relief Brahmā in *pratyālīḍāsana* pulling the *liṅga* in Kailāśa. Thus, his iconography appears more or less standardized in the rock-cut sculptures.

Sūrya[89]

His South Indian images present a distinct iconography. Having *kirīṭamakuṭa* and *prabhāvalī*, his hands are raised to the level of the shoulders. He holds *adhopadma*, wears *udarabandha*, a legs and feet are always bare. Arūṇa and the seven horses, invariably seen in North Indian images and the are not shown in these instances. Besides, Uṣā, Pratyuṣa, Piṅgala, etc., are also missing as noticed by Gopinatha Rao.[90] A variant at Ellorā has Sūrya standing in a chariot driven by Arūṇa and drawn by seven horses. Both hands lifted till shoulders hold a *padma*. Flanked by Uṣā and Pratyuṣa, his chariot has two wheels unlike one prescribed by the *śilpaśāstras*. Another variation in Dharmarāja *ratha* has *dvibhujī* Sūrya having left hand in *kaṭyāvalaṁbita* and right holding *padma*. The sun behind his head constitutes the *śīrṣacakra*.

Dikpālas or Lokpālas

Aṣṭadikpālas, i.e. Indra, Agni, Yama, Nirrti, Varuṇa, Vāyu, Kubera and Īśāna occur in rock-cut temples almost as a regular ceiling motif. For instance, in Cālukyan caves they appear with Viṣṇu, Brahmā or Trimūrti in center. *Dikpālas* sometimes appeared in relief panels also, for example in a Lakulīśa panel at Ellorā.

Female Deities

Female deities as *devī* or *śakti* manifestations (wife, mother, creator, evil-annihilator, guardian, etc.) with iconographic elements recommended in the *śilpaśāstras* were sculpted profusely by the artists.

Fig. 155. Ellorā: Cave XXI (Rameśvara), *Mahiṣamardinī* (after ASI).

Mahiṣamardinī

Variant forms of *Mahiṣamardinī*[91] such as Caṇḍikā, Kātyāyanī, Nandā, Navadurgā and Bhadrakālī have been portrayed in sculptures.

In Bādāmī cave I the *caturbhujī* deity hold buffalo Mahiṣa by his tail, while his head is pressed down. This motif of lifting the demon's hind part was popular in Gupta art also, conforming to the *Devīmahātmya*[92] norms. But the Cālukya version marked some variations. For instance, the number of hands created is four not twelve. The *śaṁkha* and *cakra āyudhas* in *Devī*'s hands acquire same prominence and stance as

Fig. 156. Adi Varāha *maṇḍapam*: *Antarāla*, backwall, south extreme, *Mahiṣamardinī* (after AIIS).

seen earlier in the Varāha images. The manner of the upper two hands holding *āyudhas* is rather a contribution of the Cālukyas to South Indian iconography.[93] *Devī*'s *ṭanka* pierces the demon's neck instead of its back as at Udaigiri.

The Rāvaṇa Phaḍi *aṣṭabhujī Mahiṣamardinī* hold *khaḍga*, *śuka*, *cakra* and *triśūla* in her right hands. Her left hands occupy *śaṁkha*, *dhanuṣ* and *kheṭaka*. With one left hand she holds the buffalo demon by the snout and pulls it down with her left knee. She pierces its raised hind portion with the *ṭanka*, her right back exhibiting a powerful curve. Here the goddess displays a majestic, triumphant posture. Similar features, but integrated better, may be seen in the structural Durgā temple. In both Rāvaṇa Phaḍi and Durgā temple we notice her *vāhana siṁha* present as a spectator[94]

Fig. 157. Mahābalipuram: Draupadī *ratha*, *garbhagṛha*, Durgā panel (after AIIS).

while in the Pallava relief at Mahābalipuram it actually fights and steers the goddess to victory.

Mahiṣamardinī is also represented in Cālukyan caves XVII and XXI at Ellorā (Fig. 155). In iconography and position of the figures they correspond to Bādāmī specimen. Quite significantly in none of these reliefs do we see the actual demon coming out of the decapitated neck as enjoined by the *śilpaśāstras*. This hints upon an early or formative phase of these representations.

Fig. 158. Mahābalipuram: Draupadī *ratha* (after AIIS).

Fig. 159. Ellorā: Cave XVI (Kailāśa), Lankeśvara section, *Mahiṣamardinī* panel (after AIIS).

In Pallava art several manifestations of the deity survive. Mahiṣamardinī *maṇḍapam* has *siṁhavāhinī aṣṭabhujī Devī* holding *dhanuṣ* with her outstretched lower left hand. Her lower right hand is bent behind her ears as if drawing the unseen bow string. The other three right hands hold *khaḍga*, *ghanṭā* and *cakra* while three left ones have *kheṭaka*, *pāśa* and *śaṁkha* after *Suprabhedāgama*. Mahiṣa appears equally forceful with a *gadā* in his two hands. The merging of buffalo head with human form has been superbly executed. His *makuṭa* and *chatra* still seen overhead, though he fights from the ground, indicates the ongoing battle and his impending defeat. The whole scene corresponds to *Devī Mahātmya* details.[95] While Mahiṣa's energy appears *tāmasik* and heavy, that of the goddess is effortless and swift.[96]

Mahiṣamardinī panels are also carved in Siṅgāvaram, Varāha, Ādivarāha, Trimūrti *maṇḍapams*; Draupadī *ratha* and Śāḷuvankuppam boulder. The first one is a *caturbhujī* figure holding *prayoga cakra*, *śaṁkha* in upper hands, wearing large *patrakuṇḍala* and *jaṭāmakuṭa*. Her *tribhaṅga* stance differentiates it from other *sthānaka Devī* figures over buffalo head or *padmāsana*, almost always in *samabhaṅga*. We notice instance of *navkaṇḍam* depicted here symbolically.[97] In Varāha *maṇḍapam* and Draupadī *ratha* offering of the head has been depicted. The Varāha *maṇḍapam* figure also marks the association of lion and antelope figures with the deity in a typical South Indian manner. The Ādivarāha *maṇḍapam* form is also *tribhaṅga* over Mahiṣa's head, holding the usual attributes in her six hands (Fig. 156). The remaining right front hand shows a cup while the lower left is in *kaṭimudrā* with *līlāśuka*. This relief varies from Varāha *maṇḍapam samabhaṅga* form with *caturbhujī, samabhaṅga* standing over the Mahiṣa head with usual hand attributes. *Devī* panel inside the Draupadī *ratha* (Figs. 157-158) and three other panels on its exterior walls are all in *samabhaṅga* with *caturbhujās*. The inside one stands on *padmāsana* while the finished among external ones on the Mahiṣa head. The Śāḷuvankuppam boulder relief marks some changes.[98] Thus, it becomes apparent that it was a popular motif in Pallava sculptures portrayed vividly as per the *Āgamic* conventions, though the artists' imagination also played due role. It is also noticeable that the *Devī* figure in Pallava art was almost always portrayed in the vicinity of a Viṣṇu figure.[99]

In Rāṣṭrakūṭa art, a pillar panel in Lankeśvara cave depicts the deity (Fig. 159). Standing behind Mahiṣa having her left leg flexed at the knee, the deity has actually placed it on Mahiṣa. His head has been decapitated[100] as it emerges in human form from the neck and is being held by the tuft in one of her left hands. The *caturbhujī Devī* holds *khaḍga* and *kheṭaka* in two hands, one is broken. *Triśūla* stuck on Mahiṣa's back suggest it was held in her fourth hand. The *siṁha vāhana* is shown behind Mahiṣa, pouncing upon and tearing his body. Two figures seen under her *khaḍga* arm above the lion and another above the *kheṭaka* arm probably represent stages of fight with Mahiṣa. The former shows a *gadā* while the latter rises up in air with a *khaḍga.* It is, perhaps, a three sequential representation of the battle. Mahiṣa's body emerging from the buffalo is almost full with just the portion below right knee lying within. He carries a *gadā* in right hand. The decapitated buffalo head has fallen on the ground with its tongue out. Though mutilated the deity form can still be made out. She has a *śīrṣacakra* and *prabhāvalī* with *siṁhalalāṭa* and two flanking *vidyādharas* in *vismayamudrā*. It, indeed, is a very elaborate and impressive version of the motif.

On the Kailāśa temple wall *aṣṭabhujī Mahiṣamardinī* fights human Mahiṣa in a panel placed inside a decorative *toraṇa*. Her *triśūla* has pierced the *asura*. Another panel has the buffalo horned human Mahiṣa fighting her while his allies lie trampled around. The presence of divine audience in the upper section of the panel adds to the intensity of the combat. Hence, the projection of Mahiṣa, both as buffalo and human, is seen in the Rāṣṭrakūṭa reliefs suggesting an observance of the *śilpaśāstrīya* principles.

Other Devī Forms

Of her varied manifestations, Durgā[101] was a popular motif in South India. Paired mostly with Gaṇeśa, she was almost always placed in Śaiva temples. As Pārvatī standing by Śiva's side, *devī* is shown *dvibhujī*. Umā, generally *dvibhujī*, held a *śuka* or *darpaṇa* and *nīlotpala* or some *āyudha*. A specific portrayal seen in Rāṣṭrakūṭa art is the *pañcāgnimūrti* of Pārvatī. A panel in Lankeśvara cave has her *caturbhujī* form in *samabhaṅga*. She holds a *liṅga* on a *padmapīṭha* in her upper right hand; upper left hand with similar *padma* shows Gaṇeśa. The lower right hand holds *akshamāla* while the left hand is damaged. The *agnikuṇḍa* with flames rising are shown, one on each side, at her feet. *Kuṇḍas*, too, have *padmapīṭha*. Pārvatī has a *śīrṣacakra* behind her decorated with *karaṇḍa jaṭāmakuṭa*. Her upper body part appears bare while the lower has a *kaṭivastra*, *kaṭibandha* and *mekhalā*.

In *āliṅganāmūrti* the *devī* sits on Śiva's lap. When occupying a side position, she is in *paryankāsana*. The observance of these iconographic conventions in the portrayal

Fig. 160. Aihoḷe: Rāvaṇa Phaḍi cave, Śiva-Naṭarāja panel, Mātṛkā and Gaṇeśa (after AIIS).

Fig. 161. Aihoḷe: Rāvaṇa Phaḍi cave, *mātṛkā* group (after AIIS).

of *devī* forms is very prominent in the Cālukyan, Pallava and Rāṣṭrakūṭa rock-cut temples.

Mātṛkā[102]

This motif is carved profusely in Cālukya and Rāṣṭrakūṭa cave shrines. Their number varies from seven to eight. They constitute the female counterparts of Brahmā, Maheśvara, Kumāra, Viṣṇu, Varāha, Indra, and Yama - deputed to help Śiva fight *Andhakāsura*.[103] They have often been carved in relief on rectangular stone slabs and are flanked by Vīrabhadra and Gaṇeśa (Fig. 160). They are forms seated in *padmāsana*, *caturbhujī* with two hands in *abhaya* and *varadamudrā*; and two hands carrying *āyudhas* appropriate to their male counterpart.

Hailed as patron deities in Cālukyan inscriptions,[104] they appear prominently in Rāvaṇa Phaḍi cave as a rather unusual group, not flanked by Vīrabhadra and Gaṇeśa. The placement of Śiva in centre of the group is equally un-*āgamic* (Fig. 161). They are *dvibhujī*. Brāhmī is *caturmukhī*, while Varāhī has a boar head. Kaumārī and Vaiṣṇavī have the adoring Bhṛngī or Kāla placed between them. Cālukyan *saptamātṛkās* are also carved in Ellorā caves XXI, XXII and XIV. In caves XXII and XIV the *mātṛkās* are *caturbhujī*. In cave XXI only Cāmuṇḍā, Kaumārī and Brāhmī are *caturbhujī*. In the latter they all, including Cāmuṇḍā, appear as lovely, young females accompanied, except for Brāhmī, with their children. Thus, a regular variation in the *mātṛkā* motif depiction in Cālukya art indicated a non-crystallization of the forms as yet.

Saptamātṛkā portrayal is not found in Pallava rock-cut art. *Mātṛkās* in Ellorā Rāṣṭrakūṭa caves conform to the *śilpaśāstrīya* iconography. They, however, reveal certain variants. For instance, at places they all are made alike with identical faces and known only

Fig. 162. Mahābalipuram: Adi Varāha (Paramesvara) cave, Gajalakshmī, north extreme (after AIIS).

through their *lāñchanas* or *vāhanas* marked below them, not mounted on them as in caves XVI and XVI-B. Somewhere they have a child, either in the lap or standing by the side. The group is generally flanked by Vīrabhadra and Gaṇeśa. They appear in caves XV and XVI *Andhakāsura* panel as per *Devīmahātmya* version.[105] Their placement in the *saptamātṛkā* shrine near *yajñaśālā* has them standing and west facing unlike other east facing, sitting figures at Ellorā. They reveal rather unrefined forms and *bhaṅga*. Elaborate iconographic details no more remain.

Gajalakshmī/Srī[106]

Gajalakshmī was a popular motif in Indian art during the Śungan and subsequent periods. As the goddess of prosperity she was usually shown, standing or seated, with two flanking female *cāmaradhārinīs*. The post-Gupta and later periods marked the inclusion of maidens carrying *ghaṭas* which were being passed on to the respective elephants above, usually numbering four, two on each side, shown one above the other. These flanking maidens are generally identified as *apsarās* holding holy *abhiṣeka* water for the deity. Some rock-cut renderings of the motif offer important aspects regarding its iconographic evolution and identification of the flanking figures.

Fig. 163. Ellorā: Lankeśvara, entrance, Gajalakshmī panel (after AIIS).

Gajalakshmī seated on *padmāsana* with four *gajas*, two flanking and two above shown frontally, emptying *abhiṣeka jala* over her head appears on a pillar panel in Bādāmī cave II and in a bay-relief in Cave III. A rather deviant and unusually interesting form is available in Ellorā cave XIV. It has the goddess carved in a niche, seated in *lalitāsana* and flanked by *caturbhujī*, standing male *ghaṭadhārīs*, one on each side, each decked with a high crown and *prabhāvalī*, suggesting their divine status. Significantly, two of their four hands clasp the *ghaṭa* to hand it over to the *gajas* above for anointing the goddess. The figure standing to her left distinctly holds a *śaṁkha* in his lower left hand and may thus be identified as Vāsudeva Kṛṣṇa. An early medieval schist sculpture from Āmjhara (Dungarpur, Rajasthan) presents, besides regular figures similar, flanking *caturbhujī* seated male figures. They hold *hala*, *mūsala* and *gadā*, *cakra*, respectively, suggesting Balarāma and Kṛṣṇa. In this light, the Ellorā attendant figures may be *maṅgala ghaṭadhārī* Kṛṣṇa and Balarāma.

Pallava art also presents an elaborate form of Gajalakshmī in Varāha *maṇḍapam*. She is seen in *pralamba pāda padmāsana*, her legs resting on spread out lotus leaves below. She exhibits the typical Pallava *makuṭa* with a conical top looking like a *jaṭābandha*. Four *apsarās* and two *gajamuṇḍas* flank her, the one on the right pouring water over her head, while the left one suggests lifting of a *ghaṭa* from the *apsarā*'s hands. Similar iconographic *lakshaṇas* may be noticed in the relief from Ādivarāha *maṇḍapam* (Fig. 162).

The Gajalakshmī form in Rāṣṭrakūṭa sculptures appears even more evolved iconographically. The forms in Lankeśvara cave (Fig. 163) and the Kailāśa temple front *maṇḍapa* are almost identical. They show the deity in *padmāsana* over a *padmapīṭha*, four *gajas* flanking either side. The upper two are pouring water from *ghaṭas* on her head, while the lower two are lifting the *ghaṭas* from the ground. The *dvibhujī* deity holds *padma* in both hands. She wears a *kirīṭamakuṭa, kaṇṭhī, kuchabandha,* and *kaṅkaṇa*. *Vidyādharas*, three on each side, may be seen above, floating in the air. Below is a lotus pond symbolic of *kshīrasāgar* - lotus buds, leaves and flowers in perspective with playful human figures and birds. The figure in Kailāśa temple is also surmounted by a *chatra* while the flanking elephants are ornamented. The symmetry of the panel is spectacular. Lakshmī's arms, now broken, seems bent up at the elbows towards her chest. Flying *gāndharvas* and *apsarās* are seen above. Another panel in the Daśāvatāra cave has *padmapīṭhāsīna* Gajalakshmī with four elephants on top representing the four quarters. They are consecrating her with *ghaṭas* in their trunks, two *cāmaras* shown on her either side, clouds beneath and beyond the elephants. Two *āyudhapuruṣas* are shown standing on either side with *padma* held by one of them while *cakra* and *śaṁkha* are held by the other. Both of them hold *ghaṭas* in two of their hands. Lakshmī holds *mātulunga* and *padma* in her two hands.

Jyēṣṭhā[107]

She was an extremely popular, typical folk goddess in early South India, worshipped as an inauspicious deity. Her iconography as given in *Aṁśumadbhedāgama, Suprabhedāgama, Viṣṇudharmottara,* etc., elaborates upon her *alakshmī* form. She is *dvibhujī*, with a long nose, sagging lips, long breasts and belly figure; holding a *nilotpala* in the right hand, while the left rests on the *āsana*. She is *kākadhvajasamāyuktā* and has an ass as her *vāhana*.

The representation of this deity is seen only in Pallava sculptures. Vasanteśvaram *maṇḍapam* at Vallam has her now worn-out low relief form. Shown in *paryankāsana*, wearing a heavy *jaṭābhāra* with conical *makuṭa*, her exact features are presently not clear.

This analysis of theistic sculptures makes evident the provenance of general as well as cult images. To these may also be added the reliefs placed in groups as narrative, decorative or design oriented.

Narrative Reliefs

Reliefs narrating *Kṛṣṇalīlā* scenes as *Kṛṣṇajanam, Govardhanadhāraṇa, Kāliyadaman, Dhenukāvadha, Gopīvastropaharaṇa*, etc., are carved in Cālukyan Bādāmī cave II (Fig. 164). The Rāṣṭrakūṭa Kailāśa temple *mahāmaṇḍapa* has panels depicting stories from *Rāmāyaṇa* and *Mahābhārata* on its southern and northern walls. But narrative reliefs are unseen in Pallava caves. However, sculptures as *Kāliyamardana* in Dharmarāja *ratha* and *Govardhana* panel Mahābalipuram suggest their efforts to include popular myths in art.

As decorative or design oriented reliefs, the use of *gaṇa* friezes and animals as lions and elephants arranged in friezes, and also as caryatids supporting edifices is

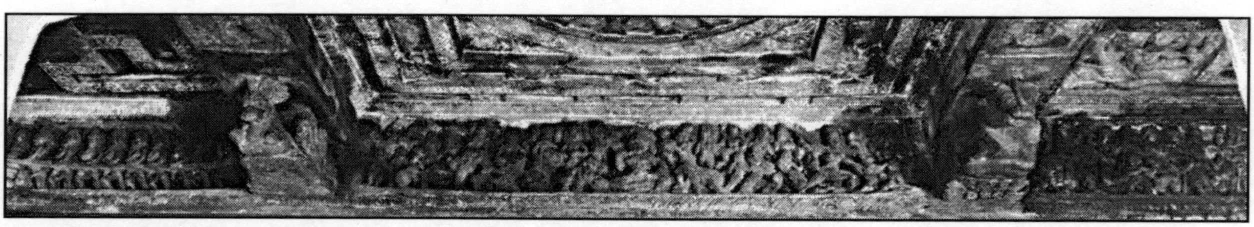

Fig. 164. Bādāmī: Cave II, *samudramanthana* motif above *prastara* (after AIIS).

Fig. 165. Bādāmī: Cave II, *matsya-cakra* in ceiling, details (after AIIS).

prominent at Ellorā and in the Arjuna and Draupadī *rathas* (Mahābalipuram).[108] The ceiling motifs, especially the flying *gāndharavas* in the Cālukyan caves, represent another

Fig. 166. Bādāmī: Cave I, *bhūmakara* bracket (after AIIS).

Fig. 167. Ellorā: Cave XVII, first pillar to right of shrine, details (after AIIS).

Fig. 168. Ellorā: Cave XVII, first pillar to right, capital detail (after AIIS).

popular sculptural motif. The *aṣṭadikpāla*, *nāga*, and auspicious symbols as *matsya* (Fig. 165), *svāstika*, etc., arranged on the ceiling are other motifs worth a mention.

Bracket Figures

Suggesting their liberation from the live rock, the bracket figures in Bādāmī cave III and at Ellorā are quite outstanding (Figs. 166-170). Mostly *mithunas*, they also consist of *Ardhanārīśvara*, Śiva-Pārvatī, and Kāma-Rati. They represent stages of the motif evolution: (i) initially standing together, (ii) indulging in interaction; (iii) intertwining of forms. The male figure is almost invariably carved in the middle of the block, as he is to be shown taller than the female and also serves as a stabilizing factor. Therefore, most of the movement as leg lifting or embracing are depicted by the female as seen in Kāma-Rati brackets (Figs. 171-172). This way, this structural architecture necessity assumes form of decorative motif in rock-cut monuments. This also hints upon the technique of carving rock-cut sculptures.

The *dvārapālas* constitute another category of sculptures in the caves. Their iconographic *lakshaṇas* included *hāra*, *keyūr*, *yajñopavīta*, *makuṭa*, *udarabandha*, *kaṭibandha*, *gadā*, and sometimes horns in Pallava instances. In size, they are rather diminutive in Rāṣṭrakūṭa instances as compared to the colossal Cālukyan[109] ones, almost touching the ceiling.

Thus, the spectrum of sculptural carvings undertaken by the three dynasties is quite varied and enriched. The early Cālukyan caves display an indiscriminate placement of sculptures. For instance, *Harihara* associated with Śiva was carved in Bādāmī Vaiṣṇava cave III. In contrast, the later ones are well classified as Śaiva and Vaiṣṇava. The former also show only *Mahiṣamardinī* among female deities, while the latter have more variety. The shift from Vaiṣṇavism to Śaivism[110] in the Cālukyan empire

Fig. 169. Ellorā: Cave XXIX (Sita Ki Nahani/Dhumar *Leṇa*), pillar-capital, *Kumara* (after AIIS).

had not yet created any sectarian narrowness, despite exclusivity of cult delineations. For instance, the pure Śaivite caves XXI and XXIX at Ellorā have no Vaiṣṇava icons. But the latter cave's *Kalyāṇasundara* panel[111] shows Viṣṇu and Lakshmī as Pārvatī's parents marrying her off to Śiva. This importance to Viṣṇu may be attributed to the growing influence of early *Āgamas*.[112] However, as their forms are not always in *śilpaśāstrīya* context they are assigned to the formative phase of the art. In contrast, the Pallava sculptures though placed in unfinished *maṇḍapams* and *rathas* are more conventional. The *śeṣaśayī* Viṣṇu in Shore temple represents the *adhama* type of *abhisārikā* form. Besides, the panel in Kāñcī Kailāśanātha depicting the disarmed Viṣṇu with two attendants bearing *śaṁkha* and *cakra* indicate their familiarity with the *āyudhapuruṣa* concept. Therefore, their artisans were rather more conversant with *śilpaśāstrīya* conventions.

Under the Rāṣṭrakūṭas, rich sculptural evolution in form of Śaivite and Vaiṣṇavite images made headway at Ellorā and Elephanta. A growing trend of adherence to *śilpaśāstrīya* norms and *Paurāṇic* versions of the myths for iconic fixation of the deities is also noticeable.

Fig. 170. Ellorā: Cave XXI, bracket sculpture (after AIIS).

Next, the secular aspect of their sculptures may be analysed, beginning with the artistic portrayal of the royal persons.

Fig. 171. Bādāmī: Cave III, *mukhamaṇḍapa*, entrance pillar bracket, Śiva-Pārvatī (after AIIS).

2. SECULAR SCULPTURES

Royal Portraits

In the rock-cut temples executed by the Cālukyas, Pallavas, and Rāṣṭrakūṭas, there are instances of or references to royal portrait sculptures (Fig. 173). Coomaraswamy[113] has noted setting up of royal images in Indian temples, though always in human form. The practice of creating images of gods which were portraits of royal persons was also flourishing in Greater India.[114]

Instances of deification of royal ancestors by setting images in South Indian temples have also been recorded.[115] With this background, wherein the temple portrait sculptures were perhaps a means for claiming divinity or affinity with gods as they were placed in the interiors, their relevance during our period of study may be discussed.

Maximum evidences of such royal portraits are in the Pallava *maṇḍapams* and Dharmarāja *ratha*. The Lalitāṅkura Tirucirāppaḷḷī *maṇḍapam* inscription[116] mentions the making of an anthropomorphic image of *Gaṅgādhara* in the form of a royal personage, suggesting immanence of God in the king. The comparison of Rajasimha and his father Parameshvara with Skanda and Śiva Parameśvara in Kailāśanātha temple and Panamalāi temple inscriptions[117] further hint upon belief in the element of divinity in kings.

The iconographic resemblance of Dharmarāja *ratha Somaskanda* with the royal figure of Simhavishnu in Ādivarāha *maṇḍapam*[118] furthers the tendency of carving gods with features akin to kings. The male figure riding an elephant and occupying central position in the Arjuna *ratha* has also been likened to a royal portrait.[119]

Fig. 172. Bādāmī: Cave III, *mukhamaṇḍapa*, entrance pillar, *mithuna* on bracket.

In Cālukyan art, it has been held that the Rāvaṇa Phaḍī cave was perhaps a royal portrait gallery, wherein Mangalesha projected himself as a deified king.[120] Similarly, in the Rāṣṭrakūṭa Elephanta cave, Śiva-Pārvatī appears undeniably human in form, with a regal quality about them. This might have been an attempt to relate the caves patron royal couple with the cosmic couple.

These instances make imperative the study of motives behind their inclusion in the shrines. Involvement with the erection and maintenance of a temple was always an effective method for the rulers to establish political control and legitimacy of their rule. "The earthly king when divinely supported spreads protection over the land" was a theme conveyed clearly in Pallava art. For instance, the *Kṛṣṇa-Govardhana* panel at Mahābalipuram symbolizes a human king[121] with god-like attributes.

Yet another angle from which to look at the issue is provided by the changes emerging in the politico-economic life of South India during this period. Legitimacy of authority was required for the Pallavas to overcome their tribal lineage. They were, perhaps, the earliest power down south to face the restricting process of royalty. The rise of *Bhakti* and consequent erection of temples under Pallava patronage was an important stage to mark this transition. That they associated their routine with that of the temple deity is indicated by the Vaikuṇṭha-Perumāl temple panels. Still, we do not see any divine attributes or *prabhāvalī* in their portraits.

Besides, a temple in this period was not merely a place of worship but also an institution of agrarian order.[122] Thus, in a polity of administratively autonomous bodies, the scope for royalty was not much, especially in the far-flung areas. There the temple deity symbolized the idealized form of the ruling king. The daily services in the temple befitting a king, *rājopacāra*, were prescribed by the *Āgamas* for the deity. The Tamil passage—*tiruvutal mannare kanal tirumale enrum*—meant seeing the king in royal attire was as good as seeing Viṣṇu himself.[123]

Thus, the portraiture in temples may be assigned to an identity between royalty of the god and resultant divinity of kingship.

Fig. 173. Mahābalipuram: Adi Varāha (Parameśvara) *maṇḍapam*, portraits of Mahendravarman II and Queens (after AIIS).

Erotic Sculptures

During the course of this study, a profusion of sexually suggestive forms in the Cālukyan and Rāṣṭrakūṭa monuments, whether structural or rock-cut, in the interiors as well as on the exteriors, has been noticed. Amorous *mithunas*, as also *maithunas*, have been placed in these shrines. Prominent among these are the Cālukyan structural temples at Aihoḷe, Bādāmī, Paṭṭaḍakal and Mahākuṭeśvara, especially the Konṭi guḍī, Lāḍ Khān and Durgā temples of former group. Bādāmī cave III consists of erotic sculptures over its pillars and pilasters (Figs. 174-178).[124] The popularity of *uttānapāda devī* was also significant. Such sculptures were not uncommon in the prevailing Buddhist creations at Ajantā, Ellorā and Aurangābād. This fact rules out any sectarian influence in their portrayal. The later Rāṣṭrakūṭa Ellorā caves (Pl. 61) also had erotic representations, notably in *kāmaśāstrīya* poses.[125]

Conventionally, the erotic figures are variously interpreted as the union of *puruṣa* and *prakṛti*; expression of *kāma puruṣārtha*; a test for one's spiritual growth,[126] etc. But these notions are not unconditionally acceptable. Rather *śilpaśāstras*[127] have highlighted the auspicious and magico-preventive role of erotic figures; the rise of tāntrism and changing socio-religious structures with the rise of aristocratic system in early medieval India. These may be up to some extent held responsible for inclusion of erotic motifs in Indian art of the times, irrespective of barriers of regions and religions.

Fig. 174. Bādāmī: Cave II, *mukhamaṇḍapa* pillar, amorous couple (after AIIS).

Fig. 175. Ellorā: Cave XIV (Rāvaṇa kā Khāi), *maṇḍapa*, pillar details, *mithuna* (after AIIS).

Gupta Influence on South Indian Sculptural Art and Iconography

This analysis may be summed up by briefly considering the Gupta influence in the evolution of South Indian rock-cut sculptures. There are clear evidences of the northern Gupta motifs making inroads into the domain of South Indian art. The Cālukyan Varāha and *Mahiṣamardinī* motifs imbibing iconographic *lakshaṇas* of Gupta instances have already been indicated. The *kshīrasāgaramanthana*, an important *dvāra* frieze at Udaigiri also occurs at Bādāmī cave II lintel.[128] Besides, the revival of Vaiṣṇavism under the Cālukyas is also synchronic with the Brāhmanical upsurge during the Guptas period. The latter were hailed as uplifters of the earth from morass.[129] Similarly, the former took up Varāha as their dynastic *lāñchana*.[130] The penetration of Gupta ideals and art into Deccan and Southern territories may have been facilitated by the Vākāṭakas, the predecessors of the Cālukyas in the region and relatives of the Guptas.[131] The Vākāṭaka dynasty's cultural influences were further expanded southwards by the Cālukyas in the wake of their political military campaigns,[132] with the Pallavas and later with the Rāṣṭrakūṭas.

The Pallavas may have imbibed this influence in a limited and distinct manner. This becomes apparent from the *Gaṅgāvataraṇa* motif being extremely popular with them, while portrayal of river goddesses in the *dvāraśākhās* did not gain much ground

Fig. 176. Bādāmī: Cave III, pillar shaft, *mithuna*.

in their rock monuments. However, personified *makaravāhinī* Gaṅgā and *kūrmavāhinī* Yamunā flanking the *dvāraśākhās* was a regular feature with the Cālukyas and Rāṣṭrakūṭas. At Ellorā, separate shrines for the river goddesses, including Saraswatī, show the influence of the Guptas. The two river goddesses were a regular *dvāraśākhā* decorative motif in Gupta art. At Udaigiri cave,[133] Besnagar,[134] Nacnā Kuṭharā,[135] Kaṅkālī Tīlā[136] and Ahichatra,[137] some marvellous manifestations of the deities survive. Therefore, the South Indian portrayals could have been a derivation of this extremely popular motif of Gupta art.

The *ālīḍha* pose warrior representation in Gupta *Tripurāvijaya* sculptures,[138] as well as in their *siṁha-vyāgrha* type coins[139] is identically seen at Ellorā, besides Pallava Kāñcī, Shore, and Olakkanātha shrines. The tendency of depicting multi-armed deities as *Tripurāntaka*, Varāha and *Mahiṣamardinī* betrays the Gupta impact.

The *siṁhāsana* seats carved at Mahābalipuram have the couchant lion's back flattened to serve as a *pīṭha*. Similar *siṁhāsanas* are seen on the Chandragupta Kumardevi type coins.[140] We may also trace a resemblance in the flying *gāndharvas* and *apsarās*. Bādāmī cave II figures suggest the movement of flying through the

Fig. 177. Bādāmī: Cave III, pillar shaft, *mithuna*.

upward diagonal posture of the torso along with flowing *dhammila* and fluttering garments. In this stance they offer sculptural parallels to the pictorial depictions in Ajantā caves.[141] To this may also be added the amorous *mithuna* motif carved in the Cālukyan and Rāṣṭrakūṭa rock-cut monuments. Although it was a popular trend, its absence in Pallava art is quite surprising. This suggest a direct contact between the Gupta and Cālukya-Rāṣṭrakūṭa regions as Gupta art also provides several instances of amatory *mithunas*.[142]

In passing, instances wherein rock-cut sculptures at Bādāmī, Ellorā and Elephanta betray iconographic features from Kālidāsa's writings may also be cited. For instance, at Bādāmī the *Naṭarāja* Śiva in *catura*, hands spread out in *bhujaṭātaruvana* mode,[143] *Kalyāṇasundara*,[144] *Tripurāntaka*,[145] *Ardhanārīśvara*,[146] Varāha,[147] *Anantśayī*,[148] *nidhis*,[149] to name a few, aptly corresponds to Kālidāsa's description.

In this way, the development of sculpture and iconography in the South Indian rock-cut temples may be visualized. Deriving features from early traditions, extant genres and *śilpaśāstrīya* texts, they created a plethora of divine and secular manifestations in their own distinct styles. From the initial ventures under the Cālukyas, to the daring artistry of the Pallavas, culminating in the highly refined and conventionalized forms of Rāṣṭrakūṭa sculptures, we may trace their evolution process coupled with innovative thought, as reflected in the concept of monolithic Kailāśa. It renders the rock-cut excavations both the aspects of architecture as well as sculpture. In this lies the novelty of this unique medium.

Fig. 178. Ellorā: Cave XVI (Kailāśa), Kāma and Rati (after ASI).

NOTES AND REFERENCES

1. An ancient term, in *Ṛgveda*, used in context of the form of *yajña*. *Cf. Ṛgveda*, X. 130. 3.
2. Patañjali has referred to some *arcās* made by Mauryan kings to beget enormous gold: *Mahābhāṣya*, p. 45.
3. Used by Śukrācārya in *Śukranīti*, IV. 4. 36.
4. *Kim svidvanam ka u sa vṛksha āsa yato dyāvāpṛthivī nistataksuh. Cf. Ṛgveda*, X. 81. 4; Varāhmihira mentions types of wood to be used by the four *varṇas* for making images. *Cf. BS*, chapter *Vanasampraveśādhyāya*, 5-6; Prevalence of stone images described in *Viṣṇudharmattara Purāṇa*, *Cf. Viṣṇudharmottara Purāṇa*, Book III, Chapter 19, *Śilāparīkshā*.
5. For instance, a three-fold classification in *Śukranīti*: (i) *sāttvika* – iv. 3. 81, (ii) *rājasika* – iv. 3. 82, (iii) *tāmasika* – iv. 3. 83.

6. The proper characteristics of images are elucidated in the *Śilpa Śāstras* by canons known as *tālamāna* or *pramāna* prescribing the ideal proportions for the deity concerned, the unit of proportion being the 'face.'
7. In total 28 *Āgamas* are mentioned – *Vide* P.K. Acharya, 1981, *A Dictionary of Hindu Architecture,* (*Mānasāra* Series), Vol. 1, Delhi, p. 750.
8. These Vaiṣṇava texts are 25 in all. *Cf.* Tarapada Bhattacharyya, *Canons of Indian Art*, p. 137.
9. Of the *Mahāpurāṇas*, viz. *Brahma, Padma, Viṣṇu, Śiva, Bhāgvata, Nārada, Mārkaṇḍeya, Agni, Bhaviṣya, Brahma Vaivarta, Liṅga, Varāha, Skanda, Vāmana, Matsya, Garuḍa, Brahmāṇḍa, Vāyu* and *Kūrma*, specially affiliated to sculpture and architecture are *Agni, Garuḍa, Nārada, Brahmāṇḍa, Matsya, Liṅga, Vāyu, Skanda* and *Viṣṇudharmottara Purāṇas.*
10. *Cf.* Arnold Kunst and J. C. Shastri, 1969 (ed.), *Śiva Purāṇa, Ancient Indian Tradition and Mythology,* Vols. 1-4, Delhi; *also* T.A. Gopinatha Rao, *EHI,* Vol. 1, Pt. 1 and Vol. 2; C. Krishnamurthy, 1985, *Śaiva Art and Architecture in South India,* Delhi.
11. As described in the 1984, *Foundations of Indian Culture: Spiritual Vision and Symbolic Forms in Ancient India,* Vol. II, Delhi, p. 297.
12. According to V.S. Agrawala each *deva* has his counterpart in an *asura.* The latter's encroachments meet retaliation by the former. Both are forms of *Prāṇic* energy whose ordained harmony is a must for life. *Cf.* 1963, *Devī Mahātmyaṁ,* Varanasi, pp. 5-8.
13. It portrays the myth of annihilation of *asura* Andhaka who tried to seduce Pārvatī. While fighting, Andhaka's blood drops created numerous replica Andhakas. Therefore, Viṣṇu came to Śiva's aid as a fierce woman who drank all the blood drops oozing out of the *asura*'s body as described in the *Śiva Purāṇa*. The myth is also described in the *Matsya* and *Varāha Purāṇas* besides the *Droṇaparva* and *Abhimanyuvadha parva* in the *Mahābhāratā*.
14. It gives another version suggesting firstly the creation of *mātṛkās* by Śiva to drink the blood. When they could not check the flow of blood, Viṣṇu created the female Śuska-Revatī and as Nṛsiṁha he created more *mātṛkās* to eliminate replica Andhaka armies. *Cf.* J.D. Akhtar, 1972, *Matsya Purāṇam,* Delhi, pp. 154-57.
15. It is said that while fighting Andhaka, Śiva was attacked by *asura* Nīla disguised as an elephant. The latter was killed with Vīrabhadra's aid. Śiva then wore the elephant skin. As explained by Gopinatha Rao in *EHI,* Vol. 1, Pt. 2, p. 379.
16. For the images the animal skin was to be held high in the two hands so as to form some sort of a *prabhāmaṇḍala. Vide Aṁśumadbhedāgam, saptatitampaṭala.*
17. Recount the destruction of the Tripura fort of *asura* Maya, Tārakāsura and Vidyunmālin by a single arrow of Śiva shot under *puṣyāyoga. See* Akhtar, *op. cit.,* Pt. 2, chaps. 129-140, pp. 1-32; the legend also finds place in *Śatapatha Brāhmaṇa,* 3.4.4.3; the *Śiva* and *Liṅga Purāṇas* and *Karṇaparva* in *Mahābhārata* also refers to it. Its iconographic features are given in the *Aṁśumadbhedāgama, Uttarakāmikāgama, Suprabhedāgama* and *Śilparatna.*
18. *Aṁśumadbhedāgama, Saptasaṣṭapaṭala.*
19. *Srītatvanidhau.*
20. *Ibid.*
21. *Vide Vaṭukbhairavakalpa* and *Rūpamaṇḍana.*
22. *Aṁśumadbhedāgama, dvisaptatitampaṭala.*
23. *Aṁśumadbhedāgama, caṭuṣsaptatitampaṭala.*
24. *UttaraKāraṇāgama.*
25. Yama for attempting *Śaivabhakta* Mārkaṇḍeya's life. *See Aṁśumadbhedāgama, satsaptatitampaṭala* and *Uttarakāmikāgama, saptapañcāśatampaṭala.*

26. Kāmadeva for inciting sensual feelings in Śiva's mind for Pārvatī. *Cf. Suprabhedāgama catuṣtriśatampaṭala*; also *Pūrva Kāraṇāgama, ekādaśapaṭala.*
27. Nṛsiṁha for killing Hiraṇyakaśipu, a *Śaiva* devotee. *Vide Uttarakāmikāgama, catuhpañcāśatampaṭala.*
28. Zimmer in 1948, *The King and the Corpse,* Washington, pp. 271 ff., has given a beautiful description of Brahmā pleading with Śiva for the union. The *Āgamic* iconography of the motif has been prescribed by the *Uttarakāmikāgama, aṣṭapañcāśatampaṭala* and *Pūrva Kāraṇāgama, ekādaśapaṭala.*
29. *Cf.* Gopinatha Rao, *EHI,* Vol. 2, Pt. 1, p. 338.
30. *Vide Śilparatna dvavinśapaṭala.*
31. *Ibid.*
32. As recommended in the *Uttarakāmikāgama, saptacatvārinśatampaṭala.*
33. It depicts the myth of shaking of Kailāśa by Rāvaṇa. The panic on Kailāśa caused by the act, the comparative poise of Śiva, final granting benefaction to repentant Rāvaṇa have been portrayed lively in the reliefs.
34. *Vide Pūrva Kāraṇāgama, ekādaśapaṭala.*
35. *Uttarakāmikāgama, ekapañcāśatampaṭala.*
36. *Vide Śilparatna dvavinśapaṭala.*
37. *Ibid.*
38. Epitomizing the myth of Gaṅgā's descent on the earth and Śiva holding her in his *jaṭās*. Its canonical iconography has been provided in the *Purva Kāraṇāgama, ekādaśapaṭala.*
39. For an iconographic description, *see Uttarakāmikāgama, tricatvārinśatampaṭala; also* B.N. Sharma, 1976, *Iconography of Sadāśiva,* Delhi.
40. Manifestation of male-female characteristics. The *Āgamic* iconographyof the motif has been prescribed by *Uttarakāmikāgama, ṣaṣṭitampaṭala.* For a contemporary work *cf.* Neeta Yadav, 2001, *Ardhanāriśvara in Art and Literature,* Delhi.
41. As given in *Aṁśumadbhedāgama, Uttarakāmikāgama, Suprabhedāgama, Kāraṇāgama,* and *Śilparatna* suggesting Candraśekhar form of Śiva emerging from middle of the *liṅga*. Śiva's presence on the *liṅga* worshipped by Arjuna and Aśvatthāma is also respectively referred to in the *Mahābhārata,* II. 39.65; X.7.13.14.
42. *Cf.* Sivaramamurti, 1974, *Naṭarāja in Art, Thought and Literature,* Delhi, p. 194.
43. Refer to Gopinatha Rao, *EHI,* Vol. 2, Pt. 2, Appendix, pp. 137-39 for iconological elements of *Dakshiṇāmūrtis;* the relief has been analysed by Alice Boner in the *Principles of Composition in Hindu Sculpture,* pp. 195-208.
44. Mistaken by some as Arjuna's Penance, it rather depicts the descent of Gaṅgā on earth as suggested by its iconography. For a further study of its symbolism, *see* the scholars mentioned in Willetts's, 1966, *An Illustrated Annotated Bibliography,* pp. 11-69.
45. Lockwood and A. Vishnu Bhat, 1974, 'Pallava *Gaṅgādhara'* in *Mahābalipuram Studies,* Madras, pp. 34-41.
46. For a detailed analysis of the motif evolution, *refer to* Lockwood's 'Pallava *Somaskanda'* in *Ibid.,* pp. 18-33.
47. *Cf.* Jouveau G. Dubreuil, 1937, *Iconography of Southern India,* Paris, p. 123.
48. K.R. Srinivasan, 1975, *Dharmarāja Ratha and Its Sculptures,* Delhi, pp. 67-71.
49. K.R. Srinivasan in *CTP,* p. 153 has identified him as Caṇḍeśa.
50. Some scholars identify these figures as royal portraits. For instance, T.N. Ramachandran in 1970 (Sept.), *Mārg,* XXIII: 4, p. 101; However, the figures lack the spontaneity and

naturalism of Pallava portraits. *Vide* Susan Huntington, *Iconographic Reflections on the Arjuna Ratha*, p. 65.

51. This figure bears affinity to the *Vīṇādhara* in Ellorā cave XXI as suggested by R.S. Gupte and B.D. Mahajan in *Ajantā, Ellorā and Aurangābād Caves*, pl. CXXIII, fig. 2.
52. *Refer to* chapter 6 for its details; *see also* Charles Dillard Collins, 1988, *The Iconography and Ritual of Śiva at Elephanta*, New York; and Stella Kramrisch, 'The Great Cave Temple of Śiva in Elephanta: Levels of Meaning and Their Form' in *Discourses on Śiva*, pp. 1-10 for further details.
53. *Mahābhārata, Śāntiparva*, 337. 59-62; *also* R.G. Bhandarkar, 1965, *Vaiṣṇavism, Śaivism and Minor Religious Systems*, pp. 115-21.
54. Ajaymitra Shastry has discussed them in 1976, 'Symbols on Tribal Coins: An Interpretative Study' in *Archaeological Studies*, Vol. 1, Mysore, p. 40; P. Bannerjee in *Early Indian Religions*, 1975, Delhi, p. 40 and J.N. Banerjea in 1974, *The Development of Hindu Iconography*, Calcutta, p. 117 have identified Śiva figure with *daṇḍa* on several Ujjaini type coins.
55. For its iconographic details, *see* U.P. Shah, 'Lakulīśa: Śaivite Saint' in *Discourses on Śiva*, pp. 92-102.
56. Identifying the serpent like object as a *dhanuṣ* Sivaramamurti has designated the figure as *Kirāṭa Śiva* with Arjuna, the latter about to receive the *Pāśupatāstra* from the former. But as given in *CaṇḍeśanāyanārPurāṇam* the object may be *śeṣavastra* presented to Śaiva devotees, hence the identification as *Caṇḍeśavaramūrti*.
57. *Viṣṇudharmottara*, III. 73.46-48 credits Śiva with the art of dancing. *Also see* Sivaramamūrti, *Naṭarāja in Art, Thought and Literature*; Vatsyayan, 1984, 'Śiva Naṭeśa: Cadence and Form' in Meister (ed.), *Discourses on Śiva*, pp. 191-201; Gaston, 1982, *Śiva in Dance, Myth and Iconography*, Delhi; Coomaraswamy, 1912 (July), 'The Dance of Śiva' in *Siddhānta Dīpikā*, Vol. XIII.
58. For instance, the *yogeśvara* seal and dancing figurine recovered from Harappa indicate prevalence of both *yoga* and *nṛtya* traditions.
59. *Cf.* Zimmer, 1946, *Myths and Symbols in Indian Art and Civilization*, New York, p. 151.
60. *See* Manomohan Ghosh, 1967, (trans. & ed.) *The Nāṭyaśāstra*, 2nd rev. ed., Calcutta, pp. 45-75; A *gopuram* in the Chidambaram temple has 108 kinds of dance forms carved on either side and corresponding largely to Bharata's account.
61. These have been described by Gopinatha Rao in *EHI*, Vol. 2, Pt. 1-2.
62. The *nāda* is a symbol of creation, *abhayamudrā* that of protection, *agni* of destruction, upraised foot of *mukti* while the encompassing *prabhāvalī* is likened to *tirobhāva*.
63. Given as eighteen by Lippe, 'Early Chālukya Icons' in *AA*, Vol. XXXIV, Switzerland, p. 288 and A. Marie Gaston, *op. cit.*, seventeen extant arms of the deity are detected.
64. *Mahābhārata*, XII 14.231-33 contains a dialogue between Upamanyu and Kṛṣṇa giving the first definite hint on *liṅga* worship; the Gudimallam *liṅga* discovered by Gopinatha Rao is perhaps the earliest archaeological instance, *vide EHI*, Vol. 2, Pt. 1, pp. 55-63. For additional details *see* Mitterwallner, 'Evolution of the Liṅga' in *Discourses on Śiva*, pp. 12-31.
65. *Īśānaśivagurudevapaddhati*, I, p. 149.
66. A detailed analysis of the relief is given in chapter 6.
67. *See* S.L. Nagar, 1992, *Cult of Vināyaka*, Delhi; Nirmala Yadav, 1997, *Gaṇeśa in Indian Art and Literature*, Jaipur.
68. For further readings *refer* Chatterjee, 1970, *The Cult of Skanda Kārttikeya in Ancient India*, Calcutta; Sinha, 1979, *Kārttikeya in Indian Art and Literature*, Delhi; Fred W. Clothey, 1978, *The Many Faces of Murukan - The History and Meaning of a South Indian God*, Hague; Thakur, 1981, *On Kārttikeya*, Varanasi.

69. For details *see* Rao, *EHI,* Vol. 1, Pt. 1; Desai, 1973, *Iconography of Viṣṇu,* Delhi; *also* R. Champakalakshmi, 1981, *Vaiṣṇava Iconography in the Tamil Country,* Delhi.
70. *BS,* 58.31.
71. *Ibid.,* 58.35.
72. *Srīmadbhāgvata,* 8.18.1.
73. *BS,* 58.33.
74. *Viṣṇudharmottara Purāṇa,* 104.46-115.
75. Earliest association of *Varāha* with earth is mentioned in *Atharvaveda, Bhūmisūkta,* XII.1.48.
76. *Matsya Purāṇa,* 260, 28-30; *Agni Purāṇa,* 49, 2-3; *Viṣṇudharmottara Purāṇa,* III, 79, 1-11; *Śilparatna,* 25, 112-116; *Devatāmūrtiprakaraṇa,* V, 72-76; *also* Nagar, 1993, *Varāha in Indian Art, Culture and Literature,* Delhi.
77. Harle, 1974, *Gupta Sculpture,* London; *also* Rangarajan, 2000, 'Varāha Images in Madhya Pradesh: An Iconographic Study' in Sinha and Dwivedi (ed.), *Proceedings of Indian Art History Congress,* Guwahati/New Delhi, pp. 135-37; Singh, 1982, *Gupta Kālīn Hindu Devapratimāyein,* Vol. I, Delhi, pl. 37; Pl. 58 (c) in Smith's, *A History of Fine Arts in India and Ceylon,* 3rd rev. ed. describes Udaigiri *Varāha.*
78. Alice Boner, 1962, *Principles of Composition in Hindu Sculpture,* Leiden, p. 119.
79. Corresponding to *Paurāṇic* details where Bhūdevī surrenders to the *Varāha, See* Wilson, (trans.) *Viṣṇu Purāṇa,* Book I, chapter 4.
80. For instance, Rajasimha's titles as *Āgampramāna, Āgamānusārī, Ācārapara, Tattvavedī,* etc. *Vide* R. Nagaswamy, 1962, *New Light on Māmallapuram* (Rprnt.), From Silver Jubilee Vol. of ASSI, p. 13. The observance of *vāstu-pādanyāsa* in Kailāśanātha by introducing *aṣṭamūrti* norm of hieratic Śaivism; the placement of *Garuḍa* or *nandī vāhanas* below *grīvā* and iconographic features betray influence of *Vaikhānasāgama, Mayamatam, Īśānaśivagurudevapaddhati,* etc.
81. *Cf.* Banerjea, 1974, *The Development of Hindu Iconography,* Delhi, pp. 418-19.
82. *See ibid*., p. 419 for Bāli and Gopinatha Rao, *EHI,* Vol. 1, Pt. 1, p. 173 for Namucī figures identification.
83. *Matsya Purāṇa,* 260. 34-35.
84. *Refer to* chapter 6 for details.
85. i.e. *sudarśana cakra* and *nandaka khaḍga* beneath as youthful forms, and dwarfish *pāñcajanya śaṁkha* and *kaumodakī gadā* flying above. Identified as Mārkaṇḍeya and Bhṛgu by Gopinatha Rao in *EHI,* Vol. 1, Pt. 1, pp. 109-10. Wearing *nivīta yajñopavīta* one of them has *jaṭāmakuṭa,* while the other a *karaṇḍamakuṭa.* The flying figures are respectively marked as a woman, i.e. *gadā* and dwarf, i.e. *śaṁkha.* This facilitates the identification of the lower ones also as *śilpaśāstrīya āyudha puruṣas.* Vogel has erroneously identified the flying female as *yoganidrā* withdrawing herself so that Viṣṇu may slay the *asuras. Vide ARASI,* 1910-11, quoted by Longhurst in *MASI,* No. 33, pp. 35-36.
86. *Cf.* Rao, *op. cit.,* Vol. 1, Pt. 1, p. 256; and Banerjee, *MASI,* No. 25, p. 31, pl. XIV b, for the respective identifications.
87. Basu, 1982, *The Concept of Brahmā,* Delhi; S.L. Nagar, 1992, *The Image of Brahmā in India and Abroad,* 2 vols., Delhi.
88. While Vogel and Sivaramamurti respectively identified it as Brahmā in *ARASI,* 1910-11, p. 58 and *Mahābalipuram,* 1978, p. 29, both Dubreuil in *Archeologie du Sud De l' Inde,* II, p. 59 and Gopinatha Rao in *op. cit.,* Vol. II, Pt. II, p. 439 disagree. Rao identified it as Brahmaśāstā, a form of Subrahmaṇya and held that Brahmā could not be represented with one head as per the *Āgama.*

89. *See* Srivastava, 1972, *Sun Worship in Ancient India*, Allahabad; Pandey, 1989, *Sūrya: Iconographical Study of the Indian Sun God*, Delhi.
90. *EHI*, Vol. 1, Pt. 1, pp. 311-12.
91. Nagar, 1988, *Mahishasuramardinī in Indian Art*, Delhi; *See* also Mehta, 1972, *Masterpieces of the Female Form in Indian Art*, Bombay.
92. As seen at Udaigiri. *Vide* Banerjea, *The Development of Hindu Iconography*, Pl. XLI, fig. 4; *Devīmahātmya* described: *Evamuktvā samutpatya sārūdhā tam mahāsuramPadenākrāmya kanthe ca sūlenainamatādayat*, III. 37.
93. *See* Parimoo, 2000, 'The Aihoḷe Sub-Style of Chālukyan Sculpture', *Studies in Indian Sculpture: Essays on New Art History*, Vol. 1, New Delhi, p. 224.
94. At Ālampur one of the reliefs has the lion actually sinking his teeth into Mahiṣa's rear. *Vide* Lippe, 1970, *The Freer Indian Sculptures*, Figs. 18-19.
95. *Mārkaṇḍeya Purāṇa*, 81-82.
96. As indicated by Zimmer in *Myths and Symbols in Indian Art and Civilization*, p. 192 the Pallava creations, though vigorous, are rather gentle in representing brutal dramatic scenes. Therefore, the moment of climax seems to have been deliberately avoided.
97. Piercing palm by a *khaḍga* for blood offering. For details of the rite, *see* chapter 2.
98. *Cf.* Katti, 1983, 'Note on the Mahishamardinī Panel at Saluvankuppam' in Narasimha Murthy and Gururaja Rao (ed.), *Raṅgāvallī-Recent Researches in Indology*, Delhi, pp. 225-28.
99. Seen in Mahiṣamardinī, Varāha, Ādivarāha, and Trimūrti *maṇḍapams*.
100. Form as described by Gopinatha Rao, *op. cit.*, Vol. 1, Pt. 2, pp. 345-46. It also conformed to *śilpaśāstrīya* details enumerated in the *Śilparatna*.
101. Identified with distinct forms and invocations as Durgāsāvitrī in *Taittirīya Saṁhitā*, 10. 1; *Durgāstotra*, *Mahābhārata*, 6. 23; *Durgāstava*, *Ibid.*, 4.5; Durgā is *bhayadām bhayanāśinīm* as described in *Harivaṁśa Purāṇa*, 2.120.10; and also described as Viṣṇu's younger, dear sister in *Suprabhedāgama satcatvārinśatampaṭala*.
102. They respectively signify *kāma*, *krodha*, *lobha*, *mada*, *moha*, *mātsarya*, *paiśunya* and *asūya* - all tendencies to be won over to dispel *andhakāra*. For additional details see Katherine Anne Harper, 1989, *The Iconography of the Saptamātṛakās*, U.S.A.
103. They caught the falling blood drops of Andhaka to prevent multiplication of secondary Andhakas.
104. As given in chapter 2.
105. Despite the presence of additional figure holding cup for blood drops, the figures are seven not eight including that of Yogeśvarī or Kālī. Thus, the artists probably didn't follow *Varāha Purāṇa* version but adhered to the *Devīmahātmya* tradition. *Cf.* Panikkar, 'Sapta-Mātṛkā Sculptures at Ellorā - An Iconological Analysis' in *ECSA*, pp. 291-307.
106. C. Sivaramamurti, 1982, *Srī Lakshmī in Indian Art and Thought*, Delhi; For identification of the flanking figures R.C. Agrawala's article 'A Note on Pitcher Carriers in Gajalakshmī Reliefs' in *Kalā*, Vol. VIII: 2001-02, pp. 5-8 may be referred.
107. For further reading *see* J.N. Banerjea, 1938, 'Some Folk Goddesses of Ancient and Medieval India' in *Indian Historical Quarterly*, XIV, pp. 107-09; Its iconography has been discussed by Gopinatha Rao in *EHI*, Vol. 1, Pt. 2, pp. 393-400.
108. The earliest example of a shrine borne on all sides by elephants occurs at the Runaweli dagoba in Shri Lankā. *See* K. Bharatha Iyer, 1977, *Animals in Indian Sculpture*, Bombay, p. 48.
109. Doris Clark Chatham has advocated the stylistic similarity between Cālukya and Rāṣṭrakūṭa *dvārapālas* in her 1981 article entitled 'Pratihāras from Paṭṭaḍakal to Ellorā: The Early Western Chālukya Basis for the Sculpture Style of the Kailāśa Temple' in *Chhavi*- 2, pp. 71-79.

110. *Refer to* chapter 2 for religious condition under the Cālukyas.
111. R. Sen Gupta has described 1960. 'The Panels of Kalyāṇasundarāmūrti at Ellorā' in *LK*, 7, pp. 14-18.
112. *Cf.* Aschwin Lippe, 'Early Chālukya Icons' in *AA*, Vol. XXXIV, Switzerland, p. 278.
113. A.K. Coomaraswamy, 1965, *History of Indian and Indonesian Art*, p. 185; *See also* Philip Rawson, 1972, *Indian Art*, London, p. 50.
114. The Hoa-Que stelae inscription is evidence from Campā. *Cf.* R.C. Majumdar, 1927, *Ancient Indian Colonies in the Far East*, Vol. II, Book II, Lahore, p. 120.
115. *Cf.* T.G. Aravamuthan, 1931, *Portrait Sculpture in South India*, London; *cf. also* A.K. Coomaraswamy, 1985, 'Votive Sculptures of Ancestors and Donors in Indian Art' in *Fundamentals of Indian Art*, Vol. 1, Jaipur, pp. 31-34; Kulke has also discussed the trend in 2001, *Kings and Cult: State Formations and Legitimation in India and Southeast Asia*, Delhi.
116. E. Hultzsch, 1890 (ed.), *SII*, Vol. 1.
117. *Cf. Ibid.*, Vol. 1, pp. 12-14 and *EI*, XIX, pp. 113-15.
118. *Cf.* Lockwood, 'God King Images and Cult Worship' in *Mahābalipuram Studies*, pp. 53-54.
119. Elephant is a symbol of royalty. For more information *cf.* Susan L. Huntington, 'Iconographic Reflections on the Arjuna *Ratha*' in *Kalā Darśana*, p. 60.
120. On the basis of the inscription reading *Srī ranavikra*...to be read as *Ranavikrantan*, Mangalesha's second name. *Cf.* K.V. Ramesh, 1984, *Chālukyas of Vātāpī*, Delhi, quoted by R. Parimoo, 2000, *Studies in Indian Sculpture*, Vol. 1, Delhi, p. 233.
121. As Kṛṣṇa holds the *Govardhana* like a *chatra*, insignia of royalty over his head. *Cf.* Marilyn Hirsch, 1983 (Oct.), 'Royal Implications of the Unique Subject Matter, Scale and Format in the Narrative Reliefs at Māmallāpuram' in T.S. Maxwell (ed.), *Saras Bulletin*, Issue 3. South Asian Religious Art Studio.
122. *Cf.* chapter 2 for details.
123. *Cf.* Rajan Gurukkal, 1987, 'From the Royalty of Icons to the Divinity of Royalty: Aspects of Vaiṣṇava Icons and Kingship in Medieval South India' in Ratan Parimoo (ed.), *Vaiṣṇavism in Indian Arts and Culture*, New Delhi, p. 123.
124. R.D. Banerji, 1998, *Basreliefs of Bādāmī*, *MASI*, No. 25, Delhi (repr.), pp. 12-13 and 32-35.
125. Devangana Desai's article 1994, 'Erotic Motifs in Rashtrakuta Art' in B.R. Gopal (ed.), *The Rāṣṭrakūṭas of Malkhed*, Mysore, p. 376 discuss the prevalence of this motif in their structural as well as rock-cut edifices.
126. *See* Devangana Desai's *Erotic Sculpture of India*, pp. 84-85 for untenability of these notions.
127. *Hayaśīrṣa Pañcarātra* in T. Bhattacharyya, *The Canons of Indian Art*, p. 232; *Matsya Purāṇa*, 258, 4-15; *Skanda Purāṇa*, *IA*, XLVII, p. 217, *BS*, etc.
128. R.D. Banerji, *Basreliefs of Bādāmī*, pp. 19-23, pl. XI. Figs. a to e.
129. Viśakhadatta compared the king in whose arms the Earth found refuge when harassed by *malecchas*, with the *Varāha*. *Cf.* H.C. Raychaudhari, 1950, *Political History of Ancient India*, p. 186.
130. Haidarabad grant of Pulakeshin II refers to the boar-crest of the dynasty. *Cf.* 1877 (March), *IA*, 6, p. 73; Carved in the Lāḍ Khān temple, Aihoḷe it consisted of *varāha*, *cakra*, *śaṁkha* and lamp and was rather an adoption of *Paurāṇic* myths to exalt their political authority.
131. Gupta Princess Prabhavati was married to Vākāṭaka ruler Rudrasena II. *See* R.C. Majumdar, 1991, *Ancient India*, Delhi (repr.), p. 235.
132. *See* chapter 2 for details of their military skirmishes.
133. It shows the goddesses descending from the sky into the sea. *Cf.* Alexander Cunningham, *ASIR*, Vol. X, p. 48, pl. XVIII.
134. *Makaravāhinī* Gaṅgā. *Cf.* Craven Roy, *Indian Art: A Concise History*, p. 118, fig. 78.

135. Appear on the lower *dvāraśākhā* for the first time as described by N.P. Joshi in *Catalogue of Brāhmanical Sculptures in the State Museum,* Lucknow, p. 71.
136. A remarkable Yamunā figure. *Cf.* R.C. Sharma, 1981, 'Gupta Sculptures from Mathurā', *BMC,* No. 27-28, pp. 101-02.
137. Both Gaṅgā and Yamunā seen on their respective *vāhanas. Cf.* J.C. Harle, *The Art and Architecture of Indian Sub-continent,* p. 117.
138. C. Sivaramamurti, 1955, *Royal Conquests and Cultural Migrations in South India and the Deccan,* Calcutta, p. 5.
139. *Cf.* S.R. Goyal, 1994, *An Introduction to Gupta Numismatics,* Jodhpur, pl. 17 and 7.
140. Pls. XX.C and text fig. 5 in C. Sivaramamurti, *Royal Conquests and Cultural Migrations in South India and the Deccan*, verify this resemblance.
141. *Cf.* Kapila Vatsyayan, 1982, *The Dance in Indian Painting,* Delhi, pp. 36-37.
142. For example Deogarh temple *Adhiṣṭhāna. Cf.* M. Vats, *MASI,* No. 70, pl. XXIV B, C, p. 20.
143. *Meghdūta,* i. 39.
144. *Kumārasambhava,* vii. 76.
145. *Meghdūta,* i. 58.
146. *Kumārasambhava,* vii. 28.
147. *Raghuvaṁśa,* xiii. 77.
148. *Meghdūta,* ii.50.
149. As seen in the Pallava sculptures at Kāverīpakkam representing Kālidāsa's imagery, *vide* C. Sivaramamurti, 1984, *Sculpture Inspired by Kālidāsa,* Delhi (repr.), Fig. 41, p. 76.

8

The Epistemology of Conservation

Mapping Challenges of Preserving Rock-cut Heritage Monuments in South India

Culture is a historically transmitted, socially constructed, shared collective structure embodied in symbols, a system of inherited conceptions expressed in symbolic forms by means of which men communicate, perpetuate, develop their knowledge about and attitude towards life.[1] For Edward Said, culture includes all those practices, like the arts of description, communication and representation, that have relative autonomy from the economic, social and political realms and that often exist in aesthetic forms, one of whose principal aims is pleasure.[2] Included, of course, are both the popular stocks of lore about the distant parts of the world, and the specialized knowledge available in such learned disciplines like, ethnography, historiography, philology, sociology and literary history. Culture also provides a standard of reference for organizing relations within and between groups and to evaluate the actions of others.[3]

Culture is a macro-structural formation that manifests in distinct patterns of micro-substructures. These distinct patterns represent discursive overtones of human creativity. Architecture is one micro-substructure of the macro-structure of culture and has witnessed a transformative evolution through the ages. This process of evolution has not been teleological, motored by the visceral processes of history. Rather, it has been dialectical, with the different methods of human intervention factoring deeply in influencing the structural transformation in the field. Although human creativity has been the underlying ontology of architecture throughout history, the post enlightenment epoch brought in a new shift in the methodology of understanding the very logic of architecture. Indicating that the epistemology of architecture witnessed a transformation from merely being a source of knowledge regarding creativity, to becoming a source of knowledge of ways in which the social histories of societies have been written and also the knowledge as to the methods of conserving the treasure of human heritage. Both emendations to the epistemology of architecture display traces of the influence of modernity and the discursivity and scientific logic imparted to it by the post enlightenment methodologies of discovering the sources of knowledge.

As a fall out of this, two significant factors emerge: Firstly, architectural structures emerge as metaphors of cultural articulation, metonymies of representing power, tropes for symbolizing social formations and instruments of historiographic illustrations. In this sense, architectural forms are not merely passive constructions of human creativity, but they epitomize a discursive space from which an active and continuous interaction between society and artistic creations takes place. Architecture, thus, is not only a monolithic construct representing creative skills of human beings but it signifies a spatial totality that is malleable by the changing tides of time and social formations. In this sense, architecture can be regarded as a metaphor of time. This means that while understanding the history of mankind, architecture acts as a metaphor for describing the nature of a particular period. Engaging architecture as a metaphor of understanding, the nature of time in history leads us to a diverse polyphony of knowledge regarding people of a specific era. For instance, temple architecture for Hindu rulers symbolized display of power, social hegemony and economic affluence. Similarly, the gothic architecture of Western European reflected upon the grand past occupied by the Roman Empire, or for that matter, the Victorian architecture demonstrating nineteenth century social ethos, morality, values and beliefs of England. Hence, architectural representations acquire interpretative capacity not merely through design and history, but the prevailing social circumstances also have a deep imprint upon it in this regard. However, there is no semantic stability to this interpretative capacity, meaning that the language of interpretation does not remain fixated but gets transformed by temporal dynamics. For instance, British attempts at interpreting architectural spaces were not characterized by any static language of the particular epoch in which those sights emerged. But, they acted as translators of Indian culture to suit the British common sense. This translation happened in the framework of the logic of enlightenment rationality professed by the English educated British. According to this, the logic of scientific rationality was absent in these creations which proved a larger point that ancient Indian civilization was bereft of any logic of scientific discovery. This placed the Indian and the European civilizations in an incommensurable position and paved the way for colonial justifications for imposing British rule in India. In this way, architectural components go beyond spatio-temporal logic of culture and history and bring in the very notion of construction of the identity of a society. In this case, architecture played a vital role in the process of the colonial *construction of the identity of the colonised periphery*.

Here, the epistemology of architecture gains a significant identity as cultural signifier and ancient India became a museum of a definite culture that has to be preserved and protected. The colonial policy of mapping the ethnography of Indian society in a manner to represent the Indian people as inferior to the Europeans was a project that was carried out on the basis of the logic of instrumental rationality of the post-enlightenment thought. Architecture, in this regard, emerged as an antique piece to be displayed in the museum, show casing ancient Indian civilization. Thus, conservation of these monuments and sights through scientific methods and logic gained prominence.

This leads to the second fall out that we are discussing. It is pertaining to the exploration of the very logic and rationale behind conservation which is a significant theme which needs to be subjected to a rigorous methodological enquiry. Conservation as a subject of examination, in this context, arises as an issue which is not merely concerned with the rote technicalities of preservation of heritage monuments. Rather, the spirit of conservation, as to depict is what to be protected and what is not to be protected, also surfaces. In this sense, the rationale behind the destruction of Buddhist statues at Bamiyan of Afghanistan by the Taliban may be understood. Here, for the Taliban, the logic of monocultural assertions entirely defeated the rationale of conservation. As dogmatic religio-civilizational affirmation necessitated the erasing of specific tropes and metonymies of socio-cultural history, the attempt is to push people into a selective amnesia, so as to write one particular kind of civilizational history. For the British in India, the scientific rationality of conservation was embodied in the colonial logic of representing the architectural antiquities of India as sketch pens to facilitate a discursive writing of India's social history. Conservation, thus, became very crucial for the British to construct not only the India before colonization but also to create India as a province of Europe by reflecting the scientific incommensurability between two civilizations.

Further, the historical transition from a colonial order to the postcolonial one was not a matter of the colonised shedding, once and for all, the multiple ways in which they are dominated by the colonizer. If decolonization refers to inspiring of anti-colonial visions of complete freedom from all possible acts of cultural and institutional acts of domination by the colonizer, that kind of decolonization did not happen in the subcontinent. That it does not happen anywhere does not take away from the political and heuristic value of a totalizing model of decolonization.[4] In an actual historical context, however, the coloniser and the colonised are often engaged in a hybridising encounter.[5] This also demonstrated the attempts of the colonized to do a kind of colonial mimicry and capitulate to the orientalist discourse of non-European peoples and cultures that were seen as far inferior to that of European culture.[6]

So, to ask how the third world writes its own history appears at first glance exceedingly naive. At best, it reaffirms the East-West and orient-occident oppositions that have shaped historical writings and seems to be a simple minded gesture of solidarity. In short, the notion of the third world writing its history seems to reek of essentialism. Seen in another way, this formulation can be construed as positing that the third world has a fixed space of its own from which it can speak in a sovereign voice. For many, this notion of a separate terrain is rendered problematic by the increasing rapidity and the voracious appetite with which the postmodern culture imperialises and devours spaces. In view of the above objections, it appears hazardous to even pose, let alone answer the question as to how the third world writes its own post orientalist history.[7] In this regard it may be argued here that the legacies of the repressive colonial past often tend persistently to keep captive the thinking and imagination of the populace of the postcolonial territories, thus leading to what has been called as the postcolonial predicament.[8] This also reinforces among the post-colonial States what has been dubbed as the predicament of culture.[9]

ONTOLOGY, EPISTEMOLOGY AND DEBATING THE METHODOLOGY OF CONSERVATION

Historical consciousness, says Hance George Gadamer in his discussions of the history of art, is always being effective. This implies that any epochal assessment of a particular social text or cultural object reveals that their effects are not confined merely to the interpretations of the civilizational dynamics of a specific era. Rather, the impact of a particular historical interpretation does not get obliterated if it is substituted by another succeeding interpretation which largely is different to that of the previous one.

Here, the question regarding conservation as being a science and history being its driving methodology assumes centrality. The question itself is entrenched in the broader question as to whether history itself is a science. Owing to this, when historians are subjected to criticism by the intellectual community, many historians have found it suitable to adopt a kind of Fabian approach to counter their critics. The tactic is simple and straightforward. If social scientists criticize them for the softness of method, the crudity of their organizing metaphors, or the ambiguity of their logical and psychological presuppositions, the most ingenuous answer some historians have is that history never claimed the status of a pure science, that it depends as much upon intuity as upon the analytical method and that historical judgments should not, therefore, be evaluated by critical standards applied in mathematical and experimental disciplines. All this symbolizes that history is an art. When reproached by literary artists for their failure to probe the more archness of human consciousness and their unwillingness to utilize contemporary modes of literary representations, historians fall back upon the view that history is all a semi-science, that historical data does not lend itself to free arts manipulation, and that the form of their narrative is not a matter of choice, but required by the nature of historical material themselves. This kind of tactic has a long record of success in disarming critiques of history, and it allowed historians to claim occupancy of an epistemologically neutral mid ground that supposedly exists between art and science.[10]

In this sense, historicism tends to get reflected into two distinct connotations: In the first, it implies towards staying away from law like generalizations specific to the natural sciences and treating each historical incident as unique. In another sense, historicism meant the belief in inexcerable historical teleology, a kind of approach adopted by Karl Popper in his cold war study *The Open Society and Its Enemies*. The second approach in this regard tends to understand social theory as a coherent whole unaffected by spatio-temporal transitions. This approach of focusing on excessive consistency has been severely criticized by Skinner.[11] In this perspective, the subtle distinctions between a historian's history and a social scientist's history must be comprehended. Here, it may also be stated that the plurality of pasts always tends to restrict the universalization of historical interpretations.

Contextualizing art history in this regard, it may be argued here that art which always plays the role of a cultural signifier carries with it the latent symbolism of the hegemony of the dominant fringe of the society. History, which continuously reinterprets the spirit of art manifest in different forms, not only attempts to comport with the hegemonic ideology that lies beneath artistic formulations but also tends to submit to the broad contours of the contemporary hegemonic culture. So, the role of culture in shaping the notions of history is as important as the role of history in the process of conditioning the contemporary cultural dispositions.

Thus, writing history in every epoch seems always inextricably laden with some kind of tendentious element. Besides, the records and documents produced at a particular point of time indubitably tend to reflect the bias of the establishment involved in the creation of these sources which are directly concerned to the problem of contemporary historical interpretation. Due to this, the explanatory potential of this archival data can be subjected to serious cognitive interrogation. With respect to the internal operations and strategies of historical consciousness, one should look at the formal characteristics of historiography. Is it structured as a narrative? If not, what does it mean for the underlying criteria of historical sense? If there is no historical representation of the past without narrative elements, where will we find these elements if important texts are structured differently? Additionally, one should therefore look for the existence and role of non-narrative elements.[12]

In the Western meta-historical discourse, there are at least four typologies of historiography.[13] Firstly, Droysen distinguishes between investigative, narrative, didactic and disputative forms of interpreting the past,[14] while Nietzsche describes three ways of representing the past which are: monumental, antiquarian and critical.[15] Hayden White offers a topology of historiography consisting of four tropes to deal with the past: metaphor, metonymy, synecdoche and irony. He then elaborates upon three parallel typologies that shape all narrations. As regards situating key events, there are four ways: romantic, tragic, comic and satirical. In so far as explanation by formal arguments is concerned, there are four modes that include: formist, mechanistic, organicistic and contextualist. With relation to the ideological implications of historical narration, White distinguishes between anarchist, radical, conservative and liberal.[16] Considering the functional and structural elements of historiography, there exist four modes of making sense of history. They are: traditional, exemplary, critical and genetic.[17]

However, while writing post-oriental histories of the third world, the key problem which is often encountered by the native authors of the post-colonial States is the diverse interpretations of historical phenomena manifest in different topoi of historiography. The most extreme asymmetry has been imposed by the dyadic contest between what could be called as the first world gesture in interpreting the history and culture of the third world and the critiques of this kind of a gesture.[18] Problematising the historicity of third world histories in this regard, it may be argued that attention to the historicity of knowledge demanded by the invitation to chart post-orientalist historiography therefore runs counter to those procedures that ground third world in essences and see history as determined by those essential elements. It requires the rejection of those modes of thinking which configure the third world in such irreducible essences as religiosity, under-development, poverty, nationhood, non-westernness and it asks that we repudiate attempts to see the third world histories in terms of these quintessential principles. This, then, tends to unsettle the calm presence that the essentialist categories, east and west, first world and third world, inhabit in our thought. This phenomenon makes it possible to treat the third world as a variety of shifting positions which have been discursively articulated in history. Viewed in this manner, the orientalist, nationalist and Marxist and other historiographies become visible as discursive attempts to constitute their objects of knowledge that is, the third world. As a result, rather than appearing as a fixed and essential object, the third world emerges as a series of historical positions, including those that enunciate essentialisms.[19]

Here lies the twin dilemma before today's social scientists: that is, on the one hand to come out of the 'iron cage' of Western notions and find genuine alternatives to understand the contours of local histories, whose nature when compared with each other are asymmetrical in character. On the other hand, the challenge is also to counter the vicious tool of bias that has plagued history writing. Due to this history has become like what Stephen Dedalus stated: 'a nightmare' from which man must awaken, if humanity is to be served and saved. Similarly, German existential philosopher Nietzsche in his book *The Birth of a Tragedy* written in 1872 included history among the many possible perversions of the apollonian faculties of man and specifically charged it with having contributed to the destruction of the mythic fundaments of both individual and communal selfhood. Further in the book *Use and Abuse of History*, he claimed that wherever the eunuchs in the harem of history flourished, art must necessarily perish. The unrestrained historical sense, pushed to its logical extreme, uproots the future, because it destroys illusions, robs the existing things of the only atmosphere in which they can live. In the same way, Paul Valery stated that history is the most dangerous product evolved from the chemistry of the intellect.

It is in this sense of historical understanding that the ontology, epistemology and the methodology of conservation must be located. Ontology is nothing but the nature of being. Viewed in this sense, use of ontology as a guide to understand conservation leads us to the positivist methodology. The positivist methodology itself views any phenomenon as natural, observable and objectively confirmable. Positivism believes in exploring the truth through a triangulation of reduction, explanation and confirmation. Thus, it places ontology at the bottom of the understanding of all social phenomenon. This is a foundationalist view and from this perspective conservation emerges as a science, possessing definite logic. Conservation, in this sense, is an objective process in which the logic of preserving any piece of antiquity is very simple. It means that for the positivist logic of conservation, preserving antiquity is part of any proper historical understanding. Here, preservation logic is not laden with any value and hence, preservation is a science. Contrary to this, the anti-foundationalist critiques of conservation can take a different position. It leads us to examine the question of the epistemology of conservation, meaning that the debate between science versus hermeneutics comes to the fore.

Science adhering to ontology believes in understanding a particular phenomenon in accordance to its inherent nature. In this sense, conservation is an objective process that cuts across subjective human interventions which implies that any monument would be preserved for the sake of its historical value. But in the hermeneutic critique of the ontological logic, preservation of a monument for the sake of history gets challenged. The hermeneutic approach seeks to establish the truth of a phenomenon not on the basis of its ontological roots, but through epistemology. Epistemology, on its part, is the theory of knowledge that leads us towards the ways of knowing the world. For this anti-foundationalist approach, the world is not known objectively through observation, but we know the world through the ways in which it is explained. Hence, we know the truths in a manner as it is constructed and explained to us. Clipped to this, the problem of epistemology also lies in the argument that as we know the truths through explanation and not objective observation and since such an explanation is not based on objectivity, the explanation itself is not perfect. Such a dual issue is called double hermeneutics. Viewing conservation in this sense, it may be argued that a hermeneutic understanding of the logic of conservation as a phenomenon constructed through explanation stands on a shaky ground. As that explanation itself is not objective, it fails to deconstruct the actual motif of conservation. For instance, the logic of preservation of Indian heritage advocated by India's first education minister K.M. Munshi, while justifying his defence of reconstructing the Somnath temple, can be explained through the problem of double hermeneutics. Since K.M. Munshi's ideological leanings clearly reflected Hindu right overtones, his explanation of the logic of preserving Indian heritage cannot be taken by its face value because the notion of heritage itself for Munshi was apparently Hindu in character. His understanding of Indian heritage in purely Hindu terms lacked objectivity and hence, the explanation also stood on faulty grounds. Rather, the first prime minister of India, Pandit Jawaharlal Nehru, gave a rationalistic response to Munshi's plea by stating that India was a secular country and the State will not involve in the construction or reconstruction of any religious structure.

Further, yet another approach adhering to epistemology is the realist critique of the positivist approach of conservation. The arguments of this school may run in these lines. Since there are some deep structures that are not observable, there always exists a divide between what is true and what actually is true. In this sense, conservation assumes a somewhat differentiated meaning. It means that conservation may not mean the same thing for everyone. Thus, what has to be conserved and why it has to be conserved and in what way it has to be done, all acquire discursive connotations. So, the British claims for conserving ancient monuments for the sake of preserving Indian culture emerge as an inverted truth. Rather, the deep structures that are not apparent were their inclination towards treating conservation as an orientalist project. Finally, if we look at this from the perspective of the post-structuralists such as Michel Foucault, conservation assumes interpretist logic. Placing the Foucaultian conception of the link between knowledge and power, it may be argued that the knowledge of conservation is always linked to the deep structures of power operating in the society.

The logic of conservation in this sense can be explained in terms of the way in which the knowledge about preserving a particular monument is transmitted by the social structures of power. Precisely in Foucaultian sense, this is called as the discourse analysis. For Foucault, the basis of knowledge is human experience and this experience is shaped by the prevalent structures of power. So, the nature of meaning and truth is always determined by the discourse that constructs them. The logic of conservation in this sense also depends on the way in which the discourse relating to it is constructed. For instance, the British wanted to preserve Indian heritage for promoting their own oriental project. Here, the interface between knowledge and power operated succinctly to determine as to how the logic of conservation had to be justified. 'The early efforts made by the British East Indian Company towards conservation of monuments in the Mughal heartland of Delhi and Agra, can be seen as mere attempts at concretizing their rule and legitimizing their claims as the successors of the Mughals. In this way, conservation for the early colonial administrators proved to be a rational choice reflecting political expediency'.[20]

Thus, the epistemological debate regarding the methodology of conservation manifests itself at multiple levels of interpretation. Since history is mainly narration, there is no certainity about its claims of the facts of the past. History also, in this sense, is a victim of presentist interpretation of the past and hence the narration of a particular time may be grounded in deep bias that aims to accomplish some present goals. Thus, a historian attempting to engage with information regarding the past through the contemporary logic of conservation must be sceptical of a singular explanation of a phenomenon. Rather, multivocal, multilingual and multiple scriptural investigations may help a historian to mitigate the narrow explanatory capacity of a single point, causal explanation model. Conservation, in this sense, cannot be thus reduced into a unified monolithic phenomenon. It must always be viewed as a multilayered process in which the logic of conservation is very much subjective. This subjectivity is not ontological, but it is epistemologically constructed through the interface between knowledge and power.

PHILOSOPHY OF CONSERVATION

The principles and ethics of conservation work, which are mandatory to be followed in the endeavours of conservation, emphasize the originality of the architectural form to be maintained. The material used in the construction of the monument, along with their texture is to be used in the repair, renovation and restoration works. The conservation measures taken should be reversible and unnecessary interference in the original structure is to be avoided totally. These basic principles of conservation are essential to preserve the originality of a monument as it reveals its contemporary social and religious history, the art and workmanship of the period, as well as the building and engineering skills of the earlier people and represent our culture and convey a definite meaning to the later generations.

The term 'Conservation' connotes different meanings in different contexts and countries. It may convey variety of philosophical stances in relation to natural, social and physical environments.[21] It may also be associated with ecological movements, energy crises, or with the fabric of historical cities. Thus, its interpretations may also range from preservation in context of destruction of fragile rain forests in Brazil to threat of pollution to the Taj Mahal, to urban revitalization and renewal of inner city areas of North America to the broader concept of sustainable development, as enunciated by Brundtland[22] and involving the use of non-renewable resources in the environment, and goes as far as the management of historical cities to accommodate new economic activities such as tourism and recreation. Thus, conservation is a connotation attached to both natural and built heritage. Scholars like Coopersmith and Hall[23] contextualized conservation with renovation, rehabilitation and reconstruction activities rather than preservation. In terms of urban forms, conservation allows for retention of edifices through renovation, restoration, alteration and modernization. At best conservation can be explained in concurrence with Burra Charter of the International Council on Monuments and Sites (ICOMOS)[24] as processes of looking after a place to retain its cultural significance. It includes maintenance and may according to circumstances involve preservation, restoration, reconstruction and adaptation. The question that arises here is: what needs to be conserved. The answer to this at the outset may be gained by citing what cultural heritage is all about, what is valued as important for history and how society should be represented in connection to its past.

CULTURAL HERITAGE

Cultural Heritage, as defined by UNESCO,[25] comprises:–

(i) *Monuments*: architectural works, works of monumental sculpture and painting, elements or structures of an archaeological nature, inscriptions, cave dwellings and combinations of features, which are of *Outstanding Universal Value* from the point of view of history, art or science;

(ii) *Groups of buildings*: groups of separate or connected buildings which, because of their architecture, their homogeneity or their place in the landscape, are of *Outstanding Universal Value* from the point of view of history, art or science; and,

(iii) *Sites*: works of man or the combined works of nature and of man, and areas including archaeological sites which are of *Outstanding Universal Value* from the historical, aesthetic, ethnological or anthropological points of view.

'Ancient Monument' as defined by the Ancient Monuments and Archaeological Sites and Remains Act, 1958 means any structure, erection or monument, or any tumulus or place of entombment, or any cavern, rock-sculpture, inscription or monolith which is of historical, archaeological or artistic interest and which has been in existence for *not less than 100 years* and includes:

1. Remains of an ancient monument
2. Site of an ancient monument;
3. Such portion of land adjoining the site of an ancient monument as may be required for fencing or covering in or otherwise preserving such monument;
4. The means of access to, and convenient inspection of, an ancient monument.

In accordance to these definitions, it may be argued that sights of architectural structures act as tropes to understand and pass on the memory of past societies to the future generations. This process of transmission is essential because civilizational histories provide us with metaphors to represent the level of artistic and philological progress of our ancestors. Passing on this information to the future generation not only enriches the civilizational stature, but also facilitates the coming generations to locate and value their own past, apart from being eclectic to other social histories. The science of conservation in this regard plays a vital role. Conservation in this sense is situated in the liberal philosophy of social construction, secular principles of assimilation and the principle of tolerance embedded in eclecticism. This is mainly because conservation in a broad sense means the preservation of past cultural creations produced by distinct religio-cultural groups. This is done not with an intention to undermine and misrepresent those communities which commend lesser social space, but to comfort greater assimilation of all the groups of the society into an organic ensemble. The Talibani destruction of Buddhist structures or the colonial representation of ancient India as a museum fell short of this spirit of conservation. Taliban on its part attempted at tearing the pages of history and the British intended to use the pages of history to artificially construct differences among two societies. Both forces used history in a manner, as to represent Foucaultian interpretation of the complex connections between power/knowledge. As Foucault had argued that knowledge cannot be independent and is deeply influenced by the archaeologies of power, the logic of scientific conservation of the British or the barbaric acts of Taliban to destroy history can be seen as attempts at constructing historical knowledge in a way to suit the stabilization and perpetuation of power.

However, the emergence of postcolonial India with a constitution providing a secular liberal State has imparted a discursive epistemology to architectural conservation, mainly because the cartography of architecture represents a microcosm of religio-cultural plurality. It marked a departure from the oriental ontology that mediated the logic of conservation during British India. Postcolonial India represented an eclectic society that provided capacious space to a grand heritage of Hindu, Islamic, Buddhist, Jain, Sikh and Christian architectures. The Archaeological Survey of India in this sense represents a secular manifestation of the institutional tolerance that deeply embeds the Indian State. To understand this very logic, the scope of conservation activities carried out under the secular liberal State of India must be analysed.

PROTECTION OF MONUMENTS

The ancient monuments, archaeological sites and remains of national importance belonging to different periods, ranging from the prehistoric period to the colonial period and located in different geographical settings, include temples, mosques, tombs, churches, cemeteries, forts, palaces, step-wells, rock-cut caves, and secular architecture as well as ancient mounds and sites representative of ancient habitation.

These monuments and sites are maintained and preserved through 24 Circles of the ASI spread all over the country. The Circles look after the research on these monuments and conservation activities; the Agra based Horticulture Branch is entrusted with the responsibility of laying out of gardens and environmental development,[26] while the ASI's Science Branch with its headquarters at Dehradun is responsible mainly for the chemical treatment and preservation of over 5000 centrally protected monuments including World Heritage Sites.

There are 30 World Heritage Properties in India out of which 24 are Cultural Properties and six are Natural Properties.[27] Of these the five rock-cut monument sites included are Ajantā caves (1983), Elephanta caves (1987), Ellorā caves (1983), Group of monuments at Mahābalipuram (1984), and rock-shelters of Bhimbhetkā (2003).

HISTORY OF CONSERVATION EFFORTS

Exploration is a prerequisite of archaeological research leading to the discovery of antiquities, artifacts and invaluable vestiges of the human times of yore. The preservation of this wealth assumes paramount importance considering their role in reconstruction of the past.

Ancient Indian Tradition

As aptly pointed out by J.N. Banerjee,[28] the builders of religious edifices paid sufficient importance to repair, restoration, and preservation of existing remains of religious art. This has been cited in several canonical texts. Texts such as *Silparatna*, *Agni Purana*, *Manasara*, *Pratimalakshanam*, etc., supplement information about replenishing the artistic vestiges of the past. Historical references of conservation efforts may be traced back to ancient times when Aśoka enlarged the Kanakmuni stupa in the fourteenth year of his coronation; Saka Rudra Daman and then Skanda Gupta renovated the Sudarshan lake; Kalinga ruler Kharvela also commissioned conservation of several edifices. Kumar Gupta gifted ten *dinars* for maintenance of perpetual alms houses.[29] Mandsor inscription of king Bandhuvarman refers to the restoration of Sun Temple.[30] Chinese traveller Hiuen Tsang had also recorded restoration of the Bodhi tree by Purnavarma, after its destruction by Sasanka of Gaud.[31]

Colonial Interventions

The beginning of documented Indian conservation may be traced to last quarter of the 18th century when famous British lexicographer Dr. Samuel Johnson asked Warren Hastings, the first Governor General of Fort William, Calcutta, "to examine nicely the tradition and histories of the East...survey the remains of the ancient edifices, and trace the vestiges of its ruined cities." The first conservation efforts in India started in 1784 with the formation of the Asiatic Society of India, Calcutta. This group, formed by Sir William Jones, surveyed and documented various monuments across India. Governmental involvement began in 1807 when it hired the services of archaeologist Francis Buchanan who surveyed the eastern Indian topography, history and antiquities. Lord Minto (1807-13) appointed a committee to take care of Taj Mahal's maintenance;

Earl Moira (1813-23) took the initiative for conservation at Sikandra, Fatehpur Sikri, while Lord Amherst (1823-28) patronised special repairs at the Qutb Minar. However, the dawn of vision for the need to preserve monuments for its worth as a monument, mainly credited to the British was not less haphazard in the earlier times. The earlier attempts to give a legal framework for preventing vandalism were the two legislations, namely the Bengal Regulation XIX of 1810 and Madras Regulation of 1817.

The explorations and excavations increased after the appointment of an Archaeological Surveyor in 1861, entrusted with the task of illustrating existing monuments by plans, measurements and drawings, etc., and to trace and record their history. The Act XX passed by government in 1863 aimed '*to prevent injury to and preserve buildings remarkable for their antiquity or for their historical or architectural value*'. The Treasure Trove Act of 1878 intended to protect findings during chance digging.

Based on the proposal submitted in 1898, five Circles were constituted to do the Archaeological work in India. These Circles were required to devote themselves entirely to conservation work. However, the actual institutionalized conservation activities could begin only with concerted efforts by Lord Curzon, resulting in founding of the Archaeological Survey of India and enactment of the Ancient Monuments Preservation Act (1904). Subsequently, extensive surveys were carried out by both ASI under Alexander Cunningham and the then provincial governments, leading to the discovery of an innumerable number of antiquities.

Marshall's Contributions

One of the leading conservators of Indian heritage, Sir John Marshall introduced several reforms including the framing of guidelines for all excavation and conservation work carried out throughout the country. These guidelines, known as the Marshall's Guide, continue to be used to date as an important guidebook for all the work done by the ASI.

However, it is very crucial to dissect the subtext of assertion of colonial culture in the code of John Marshall. The code was designed as a prescriptive colonial text and thus it constituted a text of colonial authority. It also implicitly represented the underlying tensions in the operation of colonial power in India which advocated the need for reconciling the ideas produced by metropolitan culture of contemporary Britain with the local pressures on ground in various regions and localities in India. Thus, the intentionality of the text that emerged must be understood in the context of the multiple audiences that it sought at the same time to address. It was also aimed at dealing with the ambivalence of colonial rule that was apparent in the attempts on the one hand by the colonisers to enforce the authority of the colonial State on the philosophy, principles and practice of heritage making in India and on the other hand, justifying its policies to the various watch dogs in Britain, who often tended to perceive the colonial rule in India as traditionalist and behind the time. Marshall's conservation guidelines also reveal the tension implicit in combining on one hand the notion of preserving ancient building in their state of decay, in order to preserve their historic character, and on the other hand, an energetic State driven policy that only the colonial State could apply to ensure that this is done properly. Imperial rhetoric and concerns for legitimation of rule were thus at the bottom of the logic of conservation for British administrators in India.[32]

The publication of annual reports was another major initiation. A separate branch for Arabic and Persian in Epigraphy was also created and Dr. Ross was appointed for this purpose. The most important change was the enactment of the 'Ancient Monuments Preservation Act' in 1904 that ensured legal protection for all culturally important buildings and archaeological sites in India. According to the Annual Report of the Director-General of Archaeology in India for 1918-19, Sir John Marshall was once again enabled to record much good work done, despite the absence of several of his assistants on war service and the reduction of the very small grant with which he contrived to do wonders in the way of excavation and preservation. It claimed that the 'Satanic' Government which Mr. Gandhi denounced had done far more for India's historic monuments—temples, palaces, shrines and forts— than any native rulers ever thought of attempting, and it showed complete impartiality without, of course, evoking any gratitude save from the few European and native scholars who are genuinely interested in the history of India. The Report also appreciated that some of the Native States were following the Government's good example. For instance, the Begum of Bhopal enabled Sir John Marshall to continue the work of preserving the famous Buddhist monuments at Bauchi, some of which were illustrated in the plates appended to the Report. In Hyderabad, too, the Nizam had borne the cost of putting the Ajantā caves in good order, and had authorized the employment of an Italian expert to preserve the wall-paintings from further decay. It was proposed to have the remarkable series of paintings reproduced by the three-colour process, so as to leave a complete record of them to posterity and also to facilitate their study. The total cost of the Archaeological Department for the whole, of British India appears to have been less than four lacs of rupees, or about £26,000.[33]

The years 1921-22 saw the discovery of the Indus civilization and subsequently a separate Exploration Branch with a Deputy Director General and three Assistant Superintendents was created whereby explorations and excavations were given due attention.

From the first decade of the last century therefore many monuments were taken up for conservation. Striving towards the same objective the Central Antiquity Collection (CAC) was created in 1910 to mainly house the explored antiquities from Sir Aurel Stein's Central Asian Expeditions (1906-1916). The CAC was initially established in the main building of ASI at New Delhi, which was later shifted to the Safdarjung Tomb complex in 1958 and later to the current location, i.e. Purana Qila in 1974.[34] Even before Independence, thus, the Archaeological Survey of India had developed significant expertise so much so that it was invited for conservation work in other countries. Some of the outstanding examples of such collaborative works are that of Bamiyan in Afghanistan and later in the Angkor Vat of Cambodia.

Besides the ASI, other agencies working for conservation included Department of Archaeology, State Departments of Archaeology, National Monuments Authority, the Indian National Trust for Arts and Cultural Heritage (INTACH - one of the biggest non government organizations), Indian Conservation Institute (ICI), Lucknow, etc.

Despite these endeavours, a comprehensive record in the form of database where such archaeological resources in terms of built heritage, sites and antiquities could be referred to was still lacking. Therefore, the need was felt for a proper survey of such resources, especially for the formulation of an appropriate archaeological heritage resource management and policy. Consequently, the Hon'ble Prime Minister of India announced setting up of a National Mission on India's Tangible Heritage (Independence Day, 2003).[35]

CHALLENGES OF CONSERVATION

Causes of Threat

The factors responsible for decay of monuments and edifices can be either natural or human. The first type may be caused by exposure to sun, rain, climatic effects, soil erosion, geographical location near seacoast or desert, dampness or water seepage, etc. The second type is resultant of neglect for centuries, uncared for, misuse by humans for commercial/ residential purposes, vandalism, surface vibrations due to quarrying operations undertaken near the sites, or operation of heavy machinery in the factories in vicinity. The tourists/visitors' conscious or unconscious scrapings, scratching of names, stealing away fragments of the edifice as a token of their visit are some of the common reasons posing threats to the heritage sites. Mega projects like elevated metro lines or roadways through heritage areas cause more damage than private houses 100 metres from a monument.

Bādāmī Caves

As revealed during the author's field visits, the Bādāmī caves confront several challenges towards conservation. These vary from natural processes to man generated circumstances. Exposure to light, air and humidity has proved especially fatal for the ceiling paintings made from sedimentary and vegetative colours (Pl. 62). An acute foul smell of bats abounds the environs, suggesting bat colonies therein. The bottom of pillars is stained and soiled. Marks of water seepage (Pl. 63) through crevices are also prominently noticeable. Bracket figures fallen from their place and even grinding stones used for preparing colours for ceiling paitings are lying within. As an instance of gross apathy towards heritage till they were declared protected, the Bādāmī caves were frequented by people from nearby localities who would sleep or play cards therein. Such miscreants were noticed by even Stella Kramrisch who asked them to spare this heritage site.[36] Bādāmī cave III still presents chess marks on the façade platform. There is a lack of adequate markers for the sculptures. Monkeys are is also a potent deterrent towards tourist movement (Pl. 64).

Mahābalipuram

As regards negligence towards cultural legacy, the monuments at Mahābalipuram fare no better, with scuffing seen at several places and traces of some tourists' irresponsible

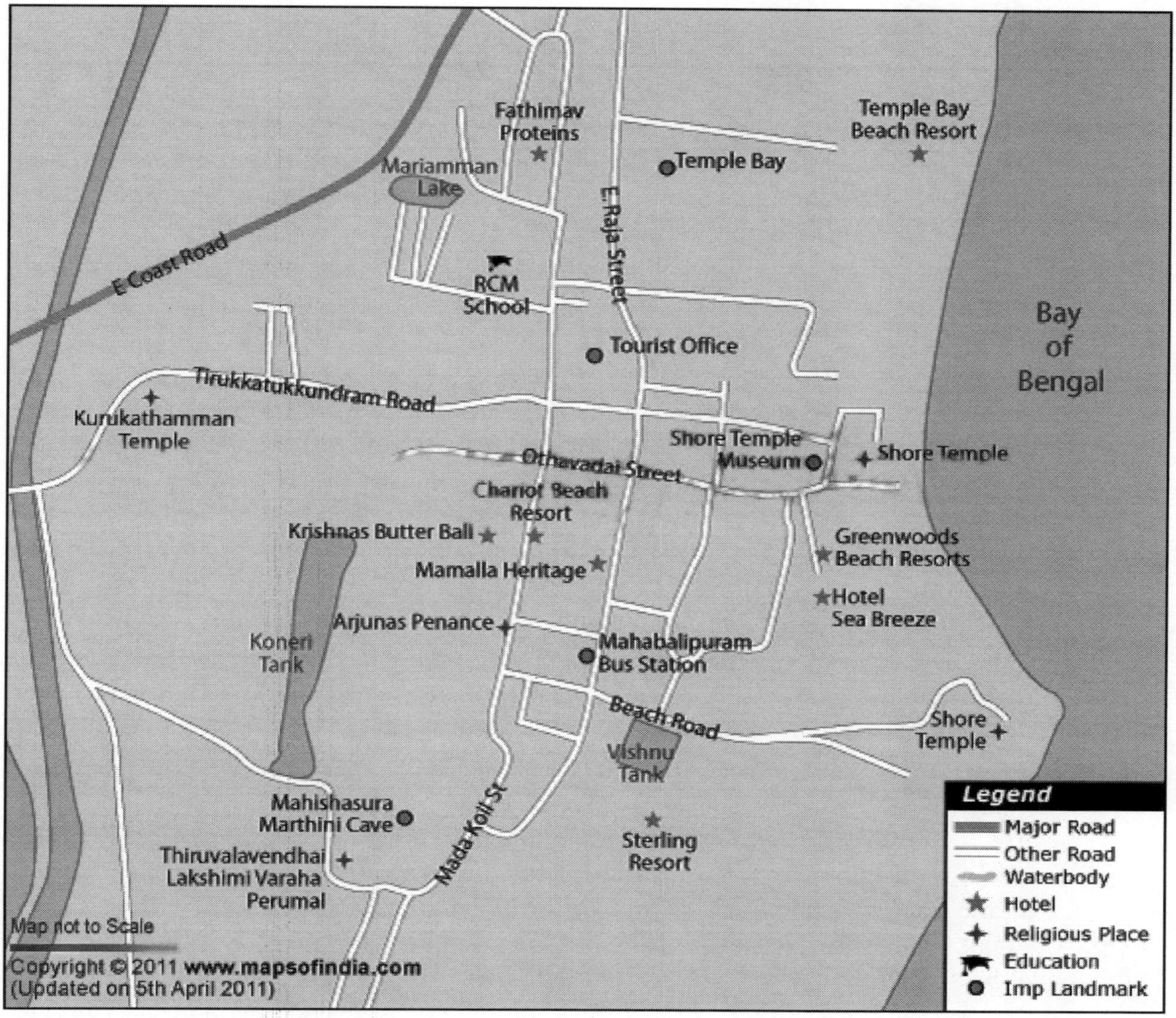

Map 9. Mahābalipuram: City map (after mapsofindia.com).

behaviour surviving. The same scenario may be witnessed at primarily all the heritage sites, varying only in degrees of callousness.

At Mahābalipuram, a world heritage site, preservation of the monuments remains a perennial challenge to the conservators because of the constant threat of salinity and abrasive action of the sand-bearing wind. What makes the task more difficult is the amorphous growth of encroachments in the form of hawkers, almost a thousand in number, besides a few hundreds shops, selling artefacts made out of sea shells, sculptures made out of granite or sandstone, ornaments including necklaces made out of beads, and toys made out of dried palmyra leaves. A number of eateries sprung up along the roadside distort the surroundings (Map 9). A score of sculptors' shops, located on the road to the five Rathas, produce exquisite sculptures but the use of chisel, hammer and power drill make the air polluted and the environment noisy. The sculptors are reluctant to shift elsewhere, fearing a slump in their business.

Under this state of affairs, the Union Ministry of Tourism and Culture, the ASI, HUDCO and the CPWD initiated a multi-crore project called the 'Integrated Development of Mamallapuram' (2003)[37] whereby they set to the task of beautifying the hillock surroundings housing the 13 monuments, the Shore Temple and the Five Rathas. The Centre, with the support of local panchayat and the State government, and prepared an action plan for the project. Amongst the early efforts, casuarinas trees were planted in the vicinity of the groin wall to prevent the salt laden sea breeze from affecting monuments; the exposed joints of the Shore temple were filled with epoxy mortar to avoid further structural damage; all age cracks on surface of the bedrock of the five Rathas, Arjuna's Penance and Kṛṣṇa Maṇḍapa have been thoroughly probed and filled with araldite mortar. Nevertheless, besides the natural and geographic constraints, the other glaring challenges still continue to be dwelling areas in the zone due to population increase and the lack of effective waste/drainage. Moreover, as highlighted in ASI's report itself, environmental pollution from vehicles is very high at Mahābalipuram and the suspension of traffic in the buffer zone may yield distinctive improvements.[38] Rising pollution levels are in fact a grave concern. Vehicular emissions with higher level of particulate matter are impacting the monuments. All of these have had an impact on monuments the world over, necessitating the use of modern conservation techniques.

Ajantā and Ellorā

At the World Heritage Sites of Ajantā and Ellorā similar negligence prevails. For instance, in Ellorā cave XVI scratch marks are noticeable on the first floor left side shrine exterior corner walls (Pl. 65). Scratching marks also exist on the frontal steps of Kailāśa main shrine garbhagrha (Pl. 66). Yet these are comparatively better off in terms of preservation initiatives (Pl. 67) though a lot remains to be accomplished towards that end. As early as 1991 a Master Plan was devised by Tata Consultancy Services, in alliance with Maharashtra Tourism Development Corporation and the Government of Japan to the tune of Rs. 817.1 million (Yen 4, 406 million).[39] The project ingredients included monument conservation, upgradation of core infrastructure in form of water supply, electricity, communication); accessibility/connectivity through airports, roads, trains; environment management by means of afforestation, low pollution local transportation, removal of encroachments; visitor management in terms of tourist circulation plans, landscaping, tourists amenities, cave illumination, directional and site signages, brochures, publicity, etc.

Despite the glaring requirements putting existence of the monuments at stake, the indifference of political parties towards heritage preservation is regrettable. As held by conservation architect AGK Menon, heritage is still seen as an abstract idea, a hurdle for development.[40]

ASI: INSTITUTION AND CHALLENGES

The Archaeological Survey of India (ASI), an attached office under the Department of Culture, Ministry of Tourism and Culture, is the premier organization for the archaeological researches and protection of the cultural heritage of the nation, celebrated its 150th anniversary in 2011. Maintenance of ancient monuments and archaeological sites and remains of national importance is the prime concern of the ASI. Besides it regulates all archaeological activities in the country as per the provisions of the Ancient Monuments and Archaeological Sites and Remains Act, 1958.

As the premier organization responsible for heritage conservation even ASI has its own limitations. While in European countries where preserving the built heritage is taken as a serious responsibility by government, multi-disciplinary specialized teams comprising architects, conservation architects, urban planners, landscape architects, urban designers, craft guilds, civil society groups, archaeologists, engineers and business interests are created at each level of government from municipality to central government to ensure effective conservation. In India, not even the ASI has access to human resources required to make conservation effective. On an institutional level, despite working in a land rich in antiquities, it faces several constraints. Without adequate funds, infrastructure and staff, ASI drags on a melancholy existence.

Government apathy also hinders ASI's functioning as in itself it is not an implementing authority. It has no demolition squads to do away with the encroachments on heritage sites. The biggest drawback for ASI is that it works with properties which have fallen out of use. Most of these properties are museums, tourist destinations or ruins which no one visits. Moreover, the ASI protects significant pieces of history, but generally it does not protect vernacular architecture. The AMASR amendment of 2010 caters to the needs of an independent India to quite some extent, yet ASI also needs to update the public communication and social media. Its website is very informative but not as comprehensive as required by the AMASR act.

Other conservation agencies use social media as a tool for raising awareness. ASI has no other way for public communication; the information provided about monuments on website is incomplete and outdated. It only provides limited information about the 'protected' heritage properties. In addition, the archaeological and architectural resources are listed together. Another important issue is that there has not been an updated survey of the properties with ASI for a long time.

As also pointed out by Irfan Habib, K.M. Shrimali, and D.N. Jha[41] the Archaeological Survey has fallen behind badly in most of the ordinary technical respects. Reports on excavated sites do not appear for decades, and when they appear, their quality often leaves much to be desired. While reports of many sites on which large funds were spent are yet to appear, even the annual survey reports of the Archaeological Survey of India (ASI) are many years in backlog, and so too the *Epigraphica Indica* and its Arabic and Persian supplements, the major source for new inscriptions discovered. *Ancient India*, the highly respected journal published by ASI in the late 1940s and the 1960s, is long defunct.

Such being the state of affairs, the gravity of the situation may further be gauged by a recent report published in the *Times of India* pertaining to a reply in the Parliament on 12 March 2013 by the ASI declaring 35 of its protected monuments as 'untraceable'.[42] Thus, natural as well as human threats loom large on the survival of heritage. However it is mainly a matter of will and since the law arms ASI with enough teeth to deter encroachers effectively, it really ought to take control of the situation. Being the central agency formed for the sole purpose of protecting and preserving monuments, ASI needs to show more confidence in its ability to conserve heritage.

DRAFTING OF NEW CONSERVATION POLICY

In the early 1920s, ASI came up with a conservation manual for ancient monuments, outlining the approach towards preserving centuries-old buildings. About 90 years later, the heritage body has prepared a draft conservation policy that incorporates new developments and technologies for monument preservation. The proposal awaits approval of the culture ministry.

With the rise in pollution, rapid encroachment and growing urbanization, there was a need to update some of the basic conservation policies. An important issue that the new proposal tackles is the use of new and more traditional building materials. The 1920s manual mentioned use of materials like 10% cement-concrete, which is not allowed by ASI anymore. The manual stresses the use of more traditional materials like lime surkhi. ASI officials say conservation techniques have evolved over the years. The draft policy still does not encourage restoration and sticks to the original principle of preserving monuments in situ. The few occasions when ASI attempted at restoration by rebuilding missing or damaged portions of a monument, the projects had stirred controversies. While many conservationists feel ASI needs to update its conservation manual, the heritage body says maintaining the aesthetics has always been a priority. 'Conservation should enhance the structure's stability and not affect the aesthetics', said an expert.[43]

POSITIVE INTERVENTIONS

Of late the grim scenario is witnessing some positive developments in form of innovative initiatives by both civil society and civic institutions. According to Ratish Nanda,[44] a conservation architect and India Projects Director for the Aga Khan Trust for Culture, conservation is possible only when we can ensure that people benefit from conservation not only through incentives but through improved quality of life such as access to health, education, sanitation, for communities residing in heritage areas. Such efforts will also encourage tourism and revenue generation, creating wealth that can be ploughed back into conservation-led development, not only for the sake of our past but for our future too.

COLLABORATIVE/PARTICIPATIVE INITIATIVES

In a novel initiative venture the Kochi Corporation, exploring possibilities of conserving the social and cultural heritage of Kochi with support from the French city of Lorient, has drafted projects to preserve the city's ancient and colonial monuments spread across Fort Kochi and Mattancherry. Marking an instance of public activism, the Bharati Vidyapeeth English medium high school, Dhankawadi has decided to observe January 12 as Heritage Day, every year.[45] Such collaborative interactions may yield positive results for the rock-cut monuments as well. Likewise, judicial interventions may play a crucial role in curbing activities detrimental to the longevity of heritage sites.

WESTERN SPECIMENS

The need for heritage conservation is realized in even the developed Western countries. For instance, the Landmarks Preservation Commission, established in 1965, is the New York City agency responsible for identifying and designating landmarks and buildings in the city's historic districts. Similarly, conservation areas in European World Heritage Cities include thousands of private buildings. Nine thousand 'conservation areas' exist in the UK alone. Even Beijing and Shanghai, which sacrificed much of their old inner city housing in the 1990s to massive redevelopment programmes, have now formulated a law that fines developers who tear down old buildings. Several cities in the world, blessed with far less than Indian cities, are achieving a great deal more through progressive and imaginative policies. Sydney, for example, held a 'History Week' in September 2012, during which citizens and tourists could choose from 250 events, including sessions on the history of the city's street names and how immigration altered Australia. Likewise, Singapore's National Heritage Board is now executing a three-year plan to create what it calls a 'museum-going culture' among its residents. As a result, the number of people who visited the city-state's museums registered a 70 per cent hike in 2005 over the previous year to 8.2 lakh. The proposals in 'Heritage Protection for the 21st Century, a joint England and Wales White Paper', recommends, inter alia, a single statute to replace England's 150 year old legal palimpsest that currently confers protection on historic buildings, landscapes, wrecks and ancient monuments.[46]

Such conscious efforts by the developed nations obviously poses the question: why as a nation that possesses a rich conservation ethic, ensuring continued existence of the country's multifaceted heritage, are we currently manifesting such disregard for our built heritage?

SUGGESTIONS FOR HERITAGE CONSERVATION

It is imperative to understand and recognize the vast reservoir of culture, traditional knowledge, philosophy and expertise within the society accountable not only for preservation of natural heritage but also of its culture and cultural artifacts. However, there now appears a fundamental lack of knowledge, understanding and, perhaps, interest in our past: in what constitutes the heritage of India, the process that governed its coming into being, and how this heritage relates to the people. Its manifestations expressed in cultural forms are losing their traditional essence in rapidly transforming lifestyles in an era of industrial growth. The real challenge is to plan the necessary measures of conservation with a view to assuring the survival of the built cultural heritage and unique symbols of civilizations for centuries to come, with as little intervention as possible but without altering or modifying in any way the authenticity of their original character. To ensure the stability as well as proper conservation of our cultural heritage, there is a need to give more thrust to the scientific research in conservation options based on a preliminary investigation which includes the knowledge of physical nature of the object (constituent materials, architectural characteristics, production techniques, state of decay) and of the factors which induce or could induce its decay. In other words, as in the case of medical study, the field of conservation therapy should be based on a correct diagnosis. The role of scientific discipline is vital to both these steps of conservation activities. Rather than restrictive conservation, practices should be based on positive intervention. Moreover, resources, expertise and practices that make the practice of conservation sustainable should be explored and identified.

This may involve environment development of monumental edifices as an important aspect that may protect them from decay. This can be achieved by improving the surroundings of edifices to enhance their architectural appeal or to save them from climatic and other natural forces and pollutants. Monuments located at the sea shore, exposed to danger of soil erosion and sea breeze injurious to stone structures, need such development more than others.

Methodology of Conservation

Technically speaking, (i) geological investigations of the caves for formulating conservation plan; (ii) structural conservation through prevention of separation of rocks, restoration of pillars, façades, and structural intergrity of cave; (iii) chemical conservation to arrest weathering of external rock surfaces and monuments, ensure slope stability; cleaning of paintings and sculptures, etc., being indispensable components of a conservation/preservation plan should be diligently followed. Conservators invariably are focused on *how* and not *why* we need conservation, so they remain uncertain and mute as decisions are made. Conservation methodology should explore the relationship between theory and practice.

Practical Approaches

Monuments and sites of cultural, historical, archaeological, or artistic interest should be recognized and preserved, irrespective of their age, currently fixed at one hundred years and above. ASI being the only agency to spearhead the conservation often acts against the life of a heritage monument. For example, the author during her stay at the Indian Institute of Advanced Study, Rashtrapati Niwas, Shimla, during the years from 2008 to 2010, found that its heritage building faces severe conservation challenges. These challenges include acute water seepage problem during rains that makes life difficult. However, no renovation can be undertaken by the authorities of the institute, without the initiation by the ASI. But, the central authority for conservation has demonstrated gross apathy towards the issue. Its negligence and inadequate conservation legislation and heritage management system are causing grave threat to this historic monument and also hampering the scholarly activities undertaken therein.

Thus, if the sites of heritage have to be made more tourist-friendly and present better environs, the following steps may be undertaken: (i) Clear demarcations and signages, both directional and site related, for easy identification of particular monuments and providing accurate historical information. (ii) Adequate visitor management provisions involving drinking water, washrooms, visitor benches, coffee shops, audio-visual aids, illumination of monuments. (iii) Battery run shuttles for reaching destination sites and preventing private vehicles beyond a certain point may help control pollution levels at the sites as well as retain their specific ambience. (iv) Proper footpath for pedestrians, cement approach roads, and landscaping around the buildings. (v) Adequate craft bazaars near the sites to arrest mushroom growth of roadside hawkers in the vicinity of the monuments. (vi) Conservation agencies may benefit from technological updates such as lasers and 3-D scanning to facilitate a non-destructive evaluation of the status of sites. (vii) Additionally, involvement of locals especially the youth should be encouraged in conservation practices. (viii) For maintenance of sites, ASI should charge more on site seeing tickets. Besides, the charges for film shoots may also be enhanced from the current Rs. 5,000 at a particular monument. (ix) Likewise, licence fee may be imposed on making sculptures based on ancient models; currently ASI issues free non-antiquity licences.[47] (x) Regular chemical treatment to stop water seepage into the rock, and put pulp on the rock, which has a tendency to absorb the salt, should be ensured especially for the excavated caves. (xi) A communication system connecting all scattered monuments, especially like the ones at Mahābalipuram, with central monitoring facilities may be quite effective in addressing the emergent requirements of day to day management of the sites whereas a co-ordination committee, the ASI and local authorities could further strengthen the monitoring system.

As suggested by historians Irfan Habib, Shrimali and Jha,[48] the ASI should be isolated from direct subordination to the government of the day. From a Department of the Ministry of Culture, Government of India, it should become an autonomous organization, directly reporting to Parliament. The ASI should have separate preservation and excavation branches under separate Directors reporting only to the Director General, on the analogy of the present Epigraphy Branch. It is also to be considered whether preservation of monuments may be entirely taken out of the purview of ASI and put under a separate national trust formed for the preservation of our architectural and art heritage. Until such a trust is created, the creation of a separate Preservation Branch is essential. All over the world preservation of monuments is a discipline by itself, and it requires recognition as a separate profession in India as well. There is also the need to decolonise the logic and principles of monument preservation in India which are still State driven, bureaucratic controlled and centralised and were introduced by the British colonial authority.[49]

Garcìa suggested that, heritage 'has to be preserved, not discussed or analysed'.[50] Appadurai and Breckenridge commented that heritage representations 'range from the problems associated with ethnicity and social identity, nostalgia, and the search for "museumized authenticity, to the tension between the interests states have in fixing local identities and the pressures localities exert in seeking to transform such identities"'.[51] As Leong stated, nation states can use tourism promotions as 'a sense of the historical past, the revival of cultural heritage'.[52]

Public Interventions

Projects, particularly those relating to heritage and culture, can take off and reach their desired end only through active governance, participation of people and effective coordination between all agencies working for it, and therefore, the committed participation of the stakeholders is very crucial. However, a legacy of colonial rule has been the legislation that relied on punishment for those who caused damage to India's built heritage. More than six decades after independence we continue to reinforce penalties - ineffective penalties - without any consideration of incentives. In India, where disregard for the law is evident everywhere, conservation can be successful only when people - owners of heritage properties, residents of conservation areas, real estate businesses, tourism industry, amongst others - can benefit from it. A cue may be taken from Chandigarh where the draft Master Plan is being given final touches and the Union Territory (UT) administration has asked the Panjab University to come up with a similar document of its own to ensure preservation of its heritage buildings.

To conclude, we also need to address certain vital questions. Does India need a separate law for archaeology and architectural conservation? Will having separate mandates provide a wider, better scope of work for the professionals? Should there be some legal protection provided to resources other than the monuments protected by ASI? Should ASI be left with administration only and outsource the enforcement to different agencies? Alternatively, more agencies like the NMA are required to cater to the conservation needs of India. Will educating people about their resources and providing them with technical skills be enough to save the heritage? Adequate concern and measures based thereupon may prevent the threat to these invaluable and irreplaceable vestiges of the times of yore, standing testimonials to the genius and ingenuity of Indian artisans and the munificence of their patrons.

NOTES AND REFERENCES

1. Clifford Geertz, 1973, *The Interpretation of Cultures: Selected Essays,* New York, p. 89.
2. Edward Said, 1994, *Culture and Imperialism,* London, pp. 12-13.
3. Avruch and Black, 1991, 'The Cultural Question and Conflict Resolution', *Peace and Change,* No. 16, p. 23.
4. Dipesh Chakrabarty, 2007, 'From the Colonial to the Postcolonial: India and Pakistan in Transition' in Dipesh Chakrabarty, Rochona Majumdar and Andrew Sartori (eds.), *From the Colonial to the Postcolonial: India and Pakistan in Transition,* New Delhi, p. 4.
5. Dipesh Chakrabarty, 2006, 'Politics Unlimited: The Global Adivasi and the Debate about the Political' in Bengt G. Karlsson and Tanka B. Subba (eds.), *Indigeneity in India,* London, p. 236.

6. Edward Said, 1978, *Orientalism*, London, p. 7.
7. Gyan Prakash, 1990, 'Writing Post-Orientalist Histories of the Third World: Perspectives from Indian Historiography', *Comparitive Studies in Society and History*, 32(2), p. 383.
8. See Carol Breckenridge and Peter van der Veer, 1993, *Orientalism and the Post-colonial Predicament, Perspectives on Orientalism and South Asia*, Philadelphia: University of Pennsylvania Press.
9. *Cf.* James Clifford, George E. Marcus, 1988, *The Predicament of Culture: Twentieth-Century Ethnography, Literature, and Art*, Harvard.
10. Hayden White, 1978, *The Burden of History, Tropics of Discourse: Essays in Cultural Criticism*, Baltimore, pp. 27-50.
11. *Vide* Quentin Skinner, 2002, 'Meaning and Understanding in the History of Ideas' in *Visions of Politics: Regarding Method*, Vol. 1, Cambridge, pp. 57-89.
12. Rousen, 1996, 'Some Theoretical Approaches to Intercultural Historiography', *History and Theory*, 35(4), p. 17.
13. *Ibid.*, pp. 15-16.
14. Droysen in Peter Leyh, 1977, *Untersuchende, Erzahlende, Didaktische und Diskussive Darstellung: Droysen Johann Gustav Historik Historisch-Kritische*, Ausgabe, Stuttgart-Bad Cannstatt, pp. 217-83 and 445-50.
15. Friedrich Nietzsche, 1993, 'On the Uses and Disadvantages of History for Life', in *Untimely Meditations*, trans. R.J. Hollingdale, Cambridge, pp. 83-100.
16. White, 1973, *Metahistory: Historical Imagination in Nineteenth Century Europe*, Baltimore, pp. 1-42.
17. Rousen, *op. cit.*, p. 18.
18. See Frederic Jameson, 1986, 'Third World Literature in the Era of Multinational Capital', *Social Text*, 15, Fall; Aijaz Ahmad, 1987, 'Jameson's Rhetoric of Otherness and the National Allegory', *Social Text*, 17, Fall.
19. Prakash, 1990, *op. cit.*, p. 384.
20. Anne-Jullie Etter, 2011, 'Antequarian Knowledge and the Preservation of Indian Monuments at the Beginning of Nineteenth Century' in Indira Sengupta and Daud Ali (eds.), *Knowledge Production, Pedagogy and Institutions in Colonial India*, New York.
21. D. Appleyard, 1979, *The Conservation in European Cities*, Cambridge, Massachusetts; P.S.A. Sundaram, 1989, 'The Future Shape of Urban Conservation in India' in B. Allchin *et al.* (eds.), *Conservation of the Indian Heritage*.
22. Brundtland Commission, 1989, *Our Common Future: Report of the World Commission on Environment and Development*, Oxford.
23. Coopersmith *et al.*, 1976, *Heritage by Design*, The MacMillan Company of Canada Ltd.
24. Bernard Feilden, 1989, *Guidelines for Conservation: A Technical Manual*, New Delhi.
25. *Operational Guidelines for the Implementation of the World Heritage Convention 2011*, pp. 13-14.
26. http://asi.nic.in/asi_monuments.asp. Accessed on 29April 2013.
27. http://whc.unesco.org/en/statesparties/IN/. Accessed 28.6.2013.
28. *Development of Hindu Iconography*, p. 569.
29. *CII*, III (8), p. 38.
30. *CII*, III (18), pp. 79-80.
31. Thomas Watters, *On Yuan Chuang Travels in India*, Vol. II, p. 115.
32. I. Sengupta, 2013, 'A Conservation Code for the Colony: John Marshall's Conservation Manual and Monument Preservation between Indian and Europe', M. Falser and M. Juneja (eds.), *'Archaeologizing' Heritage?, Transcultural Entanglements between Local Social Practices*

and Global Virtual Realities. Heidelberg Studies on Asia and Europe in a Global Context, Berlin Heidelberg: Springer-Verlag, pp. 21, 32, 35.

33. 'Indian Monuments', 1922 (14 January), Annual Report of the Director-General of Archaeology in India for 1918-19, Calcutta: Superintendent of Government Printing, p. 23. http://archive.spectator.co.uk/article/14th-january-1922/23/indian-monuments, accessed on 18.8.2013.
34. http://asi.nic.in/asi_cent_anti.asp. Accessed on 29.4.2013.
35. http://asi.nic.in/asi_mission.asp. Accessed on 29.4.2013.
36. Personal conversation with Mr. Shilakanth Pattar on 28.3.2013 at Bādāmī.
37. T.S. Subramanian, 'Conservation, a Monumental Effort', 2003, *Frontline,* Vol. 20 (23), 08-21, November.
38. 'State of Conservation of the World Heritage Properties in the Asia-Pacific Region: India Group of Monuments at Mahabalipuram'. http://whc.unesco.org/archive/periodicreporting/apa/cycle01/section2/249-summary.pdf. Accessed 22.8.2013.
39. Maharashtra Tourism Development Corporation, *Ajanta, Ellora, Conservation and Tourism Development Project, a Report.* http://aurangabad.nic.in/newsite/docs/AEDP_Phase_I_and_II.pdf. Accessed 22.8.2013
40. Nivedita Khandekar, 2012, 'Political Standoff: Conserving heritage not a priority for parties', *Hindustan Times,* New Delhi, April 8. http://www.hindustantimes.com/India-news/NewDelhi/Conserving-heritage-not-a-priority-for-parties/Article1-837592.aspx. Accessed on 22.4.2013.
41. Irfan Habib, K.M. Shrimali, and D.N. Jha, 'The ASI and Indian Archaeology Today', http://www.sahmat.org/1772000.html, accessed on 19.8.2013.
42. Atul Thakur, 2013, '35 protected monuments "untraceable"', *TOI,* April 6, pp. 1, 6.
43. Richi Verma, 2013, 'ASI drafts new conservation policy', *TOI,* Delhi, March 10. http://articles.timesofindia.indiatimes.com/2013-03-10/delhi/37597842_1_heritage-body-senior-asi-officials-structural-conservation. Accessed on 26.4.2013.
44. 'Conserve without Hurting': Ratish Nanda on preserving our conservation and heritage, November 11, 2011. http://indiatoday.intoday.in/story/ratish-nanda-on-preserving-conservation-and-heritage/1/159579.html accessed on 17.8.2013.
45. Swati Shinde, 2013, 'Students to Observe Heritage Day', *TOI,* Pune, July 30. http://timesofindia.indiatimes.com/city/pune/Students-to-observe-heritage-day/articleshow/21491249.cms? Accessed on 26.4.2013.
46. 'Heritage Protection for the 21st Century- White Paper (UK)', *CHS Newsletter,* No. 77, May 2007. www. constructionhistory.co.uk.
47. 'ASI should charge filmmakers more than just Rs. 5,000'. Interview with K.K. Mohammed by Manimugdha S. Sharma, retired ASI official, *TOI,* May 3, 2013, p. 12.
48. Irfan Habib, K.M. Shrimali and D.N. Jha, *op. cit.*
49. Indira Sengupta, 'A Conservation Code ... ', p. 23.
50. Canclini N. Garcìa, 1995, *Hybrid Cultures: Strategies for Entering and Leaving Modernity,* Minneapolis and London, p. 108.
51. Arjun Appadurai and Carol Breckenridge, 2001, 'Museums are Good to Think: Heritage on View in India', in D. Boswell and J. Evans (eds.), *Representing the Nation: A Reader, Histories, Heritage and Museums,* p. 406.
52. W.T. Leong, 1997, 'Culture and the State: Manufacturing traditions for tourism', J.T. Ong, C.K. Tong, and E.S. Tan. (eds.), *Understanding Singapore Society,* Singapore, p. 72.

9

Conclusion

Rock-cut cave temples are the most magnificent illustrations of the genius of Indian artisans in the history of Indian art. Rock-cut architecture entailed the cutting of rocks as caves or monoliths in its cut in and cut out aspects. Carved directly out of the solid rocks they epitomize not only architectural specimens but sculptural marvels too. Hollowed out of the mountains these enigmatic works of art offer a perfect amalgamation of strength with ingenuity and innovativeness.

The trend of excavations flourished in several countries such as China, Afghanistan, Tibet, Greece, Persia etc., but the cutting of religious edifices, out of the mountains, taking up the form of architectural sculpture or sculptural architecture was exclusively an Indian endeavour in its conception as well as execution. Conceived and designated variously as *guhā, layaṇa, kṛti, garbha, nidhi, hṛdaya,* mythical abode of gods, and places for realization of the self, caves in India have had an antiquity.

The rock-cut monuments were 'discovered' in the eighteenth century by a galaxy of European officials and some inquisitive travellers, for whom they remained a matter of surprise, more like monograms. As such, though initially surveyed and examined by them, the real spirit or philosophy inherent in their conception could not be comprehended. From adventurous Portuguese travellers to trained archaeologists under the East India Company, to professional art historians, these foreigners failed to grasp the myth, culture, real intent and purpose engulfing the rock creations, reducing their accounts to mere anecdotes, sketches or survey reports; seemingly due to the lack of insight into the Indian *śilpaśāstras*.

The Indian historiography of rock-cut monuments ranging from about the twentieth century is not very old. Though well acquainted with Indian mythology, the Indian scholars did not produce any serious analysis to trace the real symbolism of these art creations. Despite some pioneering works by M.N. Deshpande,

M.K. Dhavalikar, K.V. Soundara Rajan, K.R. Srinivasan, amongst others, a chronological sequence of the evolution of architectural forms in rock-cut edifices was lacking. A host of contemporary art historians are currently pursuing an interest in their art and evolution.

Considering this background and providing a historiographical sketch of rock art studies to date, the present study has attempted an art oriented analysis of various architectural aspects evolving under cave temples. It emphasizes upon rock creations as essentially sculptures on a grand scale and analyses the influence of structural architecture in their progression. It begins with the contention that the rock-cut monuments are basically different from structural monuments in their conception as well as in execution. While in the former a space or form is created inside a mountain through hollowing an excavation or subtraction technique, in the latter the monument is created by joining of stones through masonry mode. Besides, while the caves are not visible from the outside, the structural temple is seen from afar by virtue of its tall spire and other elevation components. Apart from these apparent differences, the symbolism latent in the caves is even more subtle. As a place where one may directly indulge in self realization and establish a communion with the absolute, the caves create more enigmas as compared to the structural temples, with their formal paraphernalia of ritualistic worship, as a canonized form of god's residence. Probably this very aspect of caves drew them near to the heretical sects offering contrast to ritual ridden cults.

BEGINNINGS

The first caves were excavated in the Barābar and Nāgārjunī hills near Patnā, during Mauryan period, heralding the initiation of an entirely new building form and medium. The initiative soon gained wide acceptance especially amongst the Buddhists, who undertook excavation activities to carve out their rainy season retreats, *varṣā nisidiya*. Their caves, designed as *vihāras* and *caityas* and mostly sited in Western India, served both as monastic and congregation centres. Technically they revealed gradual evolution from single cells to large-scale, multi-storeyed *vihāras*, catering to the residential as well as spiritual needs of their inmates. They were primarily architectural edifices for the fulfillment of the heretical sects' requirement of temporary dwelling places. Therefore, the sculptural element was not incorporated therein at this stage. They must have been patronized by the affluent traders and laity as suggested by epigraphic evidences, as well as their location on prominent trade routes of the times.

The activity acquired a new momentum at Ajantā, Bāgh, Aurangābād etc., in the fourth and fifth centuries AD, under the Vākāṭakas and Kalacuris. More significantly, in the wake of *paurāṇic* resurrection, the excavation idea was imbibed by the Brāhmanical sects, in all likelihood to restrain the popularity of the heretical faiths and claim their share on this popular medium. The royal benefaction, whereby monarchs immortalized their ecclesiastical inclinations, proved quite decisive. In North India, the Guptas were the first to patronize a Brāhmanical cave at Udaigiri. It is perceptible that such monastic retreats were not required in the ritualistic Brāhmanical faiths, yet they made fast inroads into these religions and that too at places like Ellorā, Aurangābād with Buddhist predominance. Southwards, the creation of excavated shrines was taken up by the Cālukyas, Pallavas and Rāṣṭrakūṭas, from the sixth century onwards.

SOUTHWARDS SCENARIO

South India, ruled by the Cera, Cola and Pāṇḍya dynasties in the early Christian centuries, enjoyed a thriving economy from early *Saṅgam* period. Flourishing agriculture, and lucrative inland and maritime trade constituted major sources of its wealth. Traders from as far as Srī Lankā, Southeast Asian countries as also from Rome reached Tamilian ports while South Indian traders organized in guilds reached these countries and carried out profitable trade, enriching their land. However, this blissful state of affairs was brought to an end in the third century AD by the Kālabhras, a northern tribe with heretical affiliations. Their encroachments dealt a jolt to the Brāhmanical traditions popularized through assimilation of Āryan and non-Āryan cultures.

For about two hundred years, the Kālabhras dismantled the established socio-political setup in the southern kingdoms, plunging them into morass. Finally recovering from the jolt, the Pallavas and Pāṇḍyas in South and Cālukyas in the Deccan regions succeeded in overpowering the foes as well as expanding the frontiers of their respective empires. Thus, began a saga of frequent conflicts between the emergent Pallava and Cālukya powers in South India, whether propelled by imperialistic or defensive designs. The Rāṣṭrakūṭas of Mālkheḍ perpetuated the struggle with Pallavas after the fall of the Cālukyas. Their continued politico-military engagements notwithstanding, these kings magnanimously sponsored temples, structural and rock-cut; or perhaps to legitimize their political authority as almost all of them had risen to sovereign status from an obscure background. The genesis of a new socio-economic formation as an integrated framework of land relationships revived economic prosperity, consolidating the material foundations for artistic growth.

Under the rising powers the Śaivite and Vaiṣṇavite faiths also witnessed resurgence. This was facilitated by the Nayanār and Ālvār saints who popularized *Bhakti* in the regions and thus created a favourable atmosphere for temple building for enshrining deities. In the wake of their strong, competent rulers and predominant religious flavour, the revival of Brāhmanical sects, especially Śaivism and Vaiṣṇavism was but natural.

SPROUTING OF ART

The new found stimulation led to the emergence of several art hubs: Aihoḷe, Bādāmī, Paṭṭaḍakal, Mahākūṭeswara, Ālampur (Cālukyan); Mahābalipuram, Kāñcī and adjoining regions (Pallava); centres in Karnāṭa and Āndhrā regions (Rāṣṭrakūṭas). The regular political patronage led to the rise of distinctive styles of architecture, sculpture and painting under these dynasties in their respective regions. They manifested the flowering of temple architecture, in particular, wherein the pace of art creation in structural modes was accelerated while initiating the most daring, ambitious, and innovative ventures in rock excavation modes.

CĀLUKYAN CAVE TEMPLES

The excavated cave shrines under the Early Western Cālukyas were harbingers of a new phase in South Indian architecture. They patronized nearly twenty caves at the sites of Aihoḷe and Bādāmī, and Ellorā, and pioneered this unique art medium in the southern regions. Considering their constant military engagements, the feat acquires even more significance.

Artistically excavated in soft sandstone, the Aihoḷe caves were quite simple and unassuming, be it in their plans, dimensions, the form of pillars or elevational aspects. At the sister site of Bādāmī, the effort proved more promising. Cave III signified an advanced stage with refined components, embellished carved forms, ambitious plans, intricately chiselled pillars, and the novel *potikā* bracket figures – all definitely marking sophistication upon the Aihoḷe specimens. The elaborately carved *dvārasākhās*; ceiling panels; treatment of the Varāha, *Trivikrama*, and *Mahiṣamardinī* sculptures, testified the enhancing expertise of the artists in the rock medium. The use of dado panels; and the placement of colossal figures; the *dikpālas*; a moulded *adhiṣṭhāna*; lack of *pradakshiṇāpatha* around the deeply cut *garbhagṛha* were other salient features of Cālukyan caves. Their structural temples, built almost in hundreds, bear out the innovativeness in their art products. Be it the stone block masonry; provision of rafter roof; *kakshāsanas*; latticed windows around the *pradaksināpathas*; use of *lañchanas* over the top; or regular variations in shrine plans, they were constantly engaged in innovative ideas.

PALLAVA ROCK-CUT SHRINES

The versatile Pallava rulers were somewhat more successful with their rock excavations. Mahendravarman I, self proclaimed *vicitracitta*, was hailed as the progenitor of rock excavations while Narasimhavarman was credited with the authorship of *Rathas* and *Maṇḍapams* located in and around Mahābalipuram, presumably named after his title *Māmalla*. The Pallava rock-cut architecture assumed the twin forms of excavated, cut-in *maṇḍapams* and monolithic, carved-out *rathas*.

Excavated from hard granitic rocks, the early *Maṇḍapams* were simple, pillared interiors with *garbhagṛhas*, ranging from one to seven, cut in the rear or side walls. They are mostly unfinished, barring derivation of any conclusive observations regarding their consecration or intended use. However, the overall projection; plan details; their *vyālapāda* pillars; *taraṅgapotikās*; a rudimentary *pradakshiṇāpatha* attempted around Pañcapāṇḍava *maṇḍapam*; and variations in elevation components like *prastara*, *uttira*; introduction of *hārāntara*, and *śālās* in place of flat roofs - suggest a constant evolution of forms. Their sculptures mostly consisted of *dvārapāla* forms and were not as impressive as those carved in the Cālukyan caves. Yet, a variety of designs, preciseness in cutting, and expansion of architectural features occurred in the *rathas*. Presenting multi *tala vimānas*, they also introduced the *pañjara*, *nāsikās*, *āliṅda* and *karṇaśālās*. Besides, the plans ranging from simple *kuṭāgāra*, to *śālākāra*, to *vihāra* type; and elaboration of *adhiṣṭhāna* in form of *kapotabanda* moulding and *vyālavarī*, *haṁsāvarī*; floriated motifs on the *kapota*; water chute device upon the roof were other prominent features of the rathas. Above all, the rathas' heralded the emergence of the southern *vimāna* form, with several of their features adopted in structural shrines, for instance, the Kāñcī Kailāśanātha temple's emulation of Dharmarāja *ratha śikhara* details.

RĀṢṬRAKŪṬA ROCK-CUT ART

Rock-cut art reached its culmination under aegis of the Rāṣṭrakūṭas, who patronized the activity through their stupendous monuments, especially at Ellorā and Elephanta. This study has recommended Rāṣṭrakūṭa origin for the Elephanta shrines on several grounds.

Excavations carried out under the Rāṣṭrakūṭas proved unprecedented in numerous respects. Elephanta claims the only island rock-cut monuments in the world, while Ellorā consists of a complete structural temple replica in rock. Excavated from soft trap stone, these art creations have immortalized the Rāṣṭrakūṭas as innovative art patrons. Elephanta Trimūrti cave is outstanding for its stepped square plan and pillars' arrangement. The silhouette and embellishment of pillars, besides the sculptural panels imbibing Śaivite mysticism are equally enchanting. Symbolically, the cave itself as an image of Śiva's mountain home bears affinity with the Kailāśa at Ellorā.

The Kailāśa, with both cut-in and cut-out aspects, represents a twofold excavation pattern. The monolith was carved out of the rock; but its external shape culminated in a pyramidal *śikhara* rising into the open air, while its interiors comprised of large *maṇḍapas* and caves. It is a unique masterpiece in itself, marking the synthesis of *Nāgara* plan and *Draviḍa* elevation. Its structural accompaniments, from *śikhara* to *adhiṣṭhāna*, remain unparalleled in the history of rock-cut architecture. The excavated caves also assume significance with their multi-storeys, pillar decoration and as hub of Śaivite sculptures.

Thus, the three dynasties proved instrumental in the perpetuation and consolidation of rock-cut architecture. The study has outlined the evolution of the ground plan - from single to multiple *garbhagṛhas*; in the provision of *antarāla*; from simple *maṇḍapa* to *mahāmaṇḍapas*; from shallow to greater depth of cutting stone; a systematic intercolumniation scheme providing better view of the *garbhagṛha*; the arrangement of *talas* in Pallava *rathas*, etc., - are all evidences of the experimental as well as developed stages of rock architecture.

ARCHITECTURAL MASTERPIECES

Gradually the excavated caves became expressive of the artists' inventive brilliance, endowing the unpretentious cave with all the characteristics of a formal, ritualistic centre. With the copying of structural forms therein, the caves no longer enclosed spaces, but acquired architectural dimensions. Plan wise the distinct evolution pattern was quite prominent. For instance, the Cālukyan caves had transversely running bays, while the Rāṣṭrakūṭa instances revealed preference for a longitudinal layout. The Pallavas ushered in their own discrete forms.

In analysing the nature of rock-cut temples, it is evident that though different from the structural mode in conception and technique, they did display considerable affinity with prevailing wooden architecture. For instance the pillars, indispensable as support in masonry construction and functionless in rock-cut mode, were carved purely in imitation of wooden forms to support the expansive ceilings. The complete lack of pillars in Pallava Trimūrti *maṇḍapam* and their absence in the interiors of Vallam, Mēlacēri, Varāha, Kōṭikal, Rāmānuja, Māmaṇḍūr and Atiraṇacaṇḍa *maṇḍapams* indicate their fundamental non-requirement and essentially decorative character in rock excavations. However, the pillar, with all the 'members' of its base, shaft and capital sections, remained the most important element of composition and over its design depended much of the rock-cut architectural effect. Initially ponderous and massive in proportions, and later slender and more decorative, pillars were suggestive of strength as well as delicacy of the rock medium. Placed in the façade and interiors, they constituted the *mahāmaṇḍapa*, *antarāla* and *mukhamaṇḍapa*, compartmentalizing the excavations, besides ensuring interplay of light and shade within the interiors.

The pilasters accordingly served a psychological, rather than physical purpose. Their presence might have added a sense of structural stability within the excavated halls, furthering the visual parallels with conventional architectural forms, besides providing space for auspicious embellishments. The shrine doorways endowed the place with special sanctity and symbolized the world within from world beyond, marking a shift from secular ground to '*Terra Sacra*'. They also exhibited the complex but essentially consistent development, moving from tentative beginnings to assured and elaborate later forms as in the case of the cave plans and pillars and other architectural elements. The *dvāraśākhās*, elaborately carved and replete with many auspicious motifs, added to the grandeur of the interiors. The base plinth, *adhiṣṭhāna*, carved in the façade and under the sanctum doorway with component mouldings, was another conventional building art device, probably to uplift the composition. The *uttira* beam, *prastara* or lintel, *kapota* cornice, *kūḍū nāsikā*, embossed nail heads, and wooden rafter placement technique were other elements of prevailing architecture incorporated as rock-cut components.

The rock-cut cave temples also emulated the plan details of structural types and adopted components as *maṇḍapa*, *mahamaṇḍapa*, *ardhamaṇḍapa*, *antarāla* and the *garbhagṛha*. Elevation wise, the multi-storeyed *talas* and *śikhara*, either symbolically in the *hāra*, or in the form of actual storeys as at Ellorā and Mahābalipuram *rathas* marking the climax of rock-cut architecture, signified the role of prevailing architectural traditions in shaping up these excavations. Thus, rock architecture in itself proved a meticulous replica of wooden forms, both vertically and horizontally, though fashioned with its own ingenuity.

For instance, the somewhat cruciform aspect of Elephanta Trimūrti cave plan allowed more contrast of light and shade than in the usual cave temples. The artisans perhaps intended to place one plan in which the shrine was attached to the very back of the wall, and the second plan in which it was detached from it. To ensure these both the *Liṅga* shrine and *Maheśamurti* were geometrically linked as the most important focal points inside the cave. The Cālukyan caves showed the *nirandhāra* type plan at Bādāmī and *sandhāra* types at Ellorā, while the Rāṣṭrakūṭa shrines bore a *trikūṭacala* aspect at Elephanta, Ellorā and Pātaleśvara. The Rāṣṭrakūṭas excavated their caves in more or less a standard layout and cult patterns of their Cālukyan predecessors in the region. But in monolithic mode, they proved more imaginative. Thus, the innovate spirit reflected also in the form of monuments created at Ellorā. Architecturally speaking, rock-cut art at Ellorā present a more compact picture. Its ritual framework was quite elaborate. Along with its structural components, the *prakāra* and *gopuram* highlighted the concept of temple complex. The assimilation of northern *pañcāyatana* pattern with southern *prākaras* and *gopuram* was a uniqueness offered by no other site.

However, the medium had its own limitations as indicated by several parameters: the initial pillars, massive in contours, revealed a lack of accuracy in their placement arrangement, maybe due to a lack of precision in the rock cutting mode. This may also be assigned to the still un-evolved arrangements of Brāhmanical rock-cut temples; the correct shape and disposition of its parts not yet being determined; or inadequate proportions of the pillared *maṇḍapas*, ending at their further ends rather abruptly. Moreover, the interior proportions further indicated limitations of the rock-cut mode, there being some correlation between the wide frontage and the shallow depth, the former giving the maximum light and the latter the maximum space which this would efficiently illuminate. The depth of sculptures, placement of objects or figural arrangements as *śaṁkha* in Varaha representations, dearth of finesse in granitic carvings, shallow heights and incomplete instances, corrosiveness of rock, bespeaks some of the technical restraints associated with this mode of erections.

EXPERIMENTAL ENTERPRISES

The essentially experimental nature of the rock creations is suggested by the variety of forms created therein under almost all the three dynasties discussed. Besides, the irregularity seen in their plan as well as incomplete instances also suggests uncertainty as to their intended shapes. For instance, as seen in the Rāvaṇa Phaḍi cave, Aihoḷe. Its shortcomings were done away with in the Bādāmī caves. Similarly, the Pallava monolithic *rathas* were a definite advancement upon the *maṇḍapams*, both in terms of plan, dimensions, elevational output as well as sculptural depictions. The experimental spirit underlined Rāṣṭrakūṭa monuments too. From the monolithic, circular *nandimaṇḍapam* in Daśāvatāra cave to the excavated caves at Elephanta, Ellorā and Pātaleśvara to the monolithic Kailāśa, a complete process of architectural evolution under them may be visualized. Moreover, the southern *vimāna* type structure; *maṇḍapa* shrine in form of Daśāvatāra *maṇḍapa;* provision of *parivārālayas;* and the apsidal river goddesses' shrines further elaborate this aspect of rock-cut art. The image of Śiva's mountain and cave abode was aptly immortalized by the Elephanta and Kailāśa caves excavated by Rāṣṭrakūṭas. Thus, the process initiated as cutting inside the womb of the mountains culminated in the shaping of whole exterior of the mountain face by the daring artisans, thereby proclaiming the culmination of the art of cave excavations.

SCULPTURAL INGREDIENT

Temple architecture constituted just the first part of the excavation wherein the deity resided. Without the presence of religious sculptures, the abode of God and the art of rock-cut temples could not be complete. Thus, sculptural art and iconography comprised the second and indispensable part of the compact rock-cut architectural whole. In this spirit the caves were intricately carved with sculptural embellishments in distinct styles. Theme wise they were mainly theistic representations although those from secular life, especially the portraits and erotic figures, also found a place. While some sculptures became synonymous dynastically, some were commonly projected. For instance, the *Rāvaṇānugraha, Kalyāṇasundara, Naṭeśa,* Nṛsiṁha, *Liṅgodbhava, Yogeśvara, Sadāśiva* and *Gajalakshmī* were identical with the Rāṣṭrakūṭas; while *Somaskanda* became the hallmark of the Pallavas; and *Saptamātṛkās, Ardhanārisvara, dikpālas* and bracket figures remained popular with the Cālukyas.

The usual motifs to be portrayed were Varāha, *Trivikrama,* Nṛsiṁha, *Anantśayi, Harihara, Gaṅgādhara, Ardhanāriśvara, Aṣṭabhujī* Viṣṇu, Durgā, Gajalakshmī - all with a plethora of their attendants and subsidiary deities. Stylistically, distinct individuality may be discerned in the carved forms. The introduction of three dimensional forms to convey dynamism, while at the same time highlighting the reflection of inner spirit on the faces as seen at Elephanta, became a characteristic of Rāṣṭrakūṭas images. The emphasis on *Āgamic* and *paurāṇic* conventionalized forms in Ellorā; experimental devices as *śaṁkha* placement behind Bhūdevī in the Cālukyan Varāha sculptures; or dynastic variations in popular motifs like Varāha, *Trivikrama, Mahiṣamardinī, Gajalakshmī, Gaṅgādhara, Naṭeśa,* etc., attest to the affluence of sculptural representations under these dynasties.

In a way the lavish sculptural embellishments on the pillars, the *maṇḍapas* and interiors, over *adhiṣṭhāna, dvāraśākhas, kapota* friezes, above the *śikhara,* etc., prove that the cave art was more of sculptural and decorative in nature, rather than architectural. The whole world of gods was recreated within the enclosed space. Appearing plain and sublime from the exteriors, it was probably a reflection of the inner spirit that is as beautiful, self contained, multi-faceted and eternal as the god dwelling within the cave temple.

Technically, the figures were cut deeper and higher within their niches. They rather appear as architectural components of the plan, besides serving the monumental, dramatic and decorative purposes. They seemed to invoke the presence of god in a timeless aspect. The use of diagonal forms further added a dynamic quality to the figures in *Tripurāntaka, Naṭarāja,* Nṛsiṁha and *Mahiṣamardinī* panels. The struggle in between the figures was always shown as approaching its culmination. Śiva's *nṛtyamūrtis* constituted another marvel of artistic creations.

Unlike the Cālukyan massive figures, the Rāṣṭrakūṭa specimens were rather diminutive. However, they reflected aggressiveness especially in the Nṛsiṁha and *Naṭeśa* representations. But the ferocity of deadly combat was not always conveyed in these creations. They rather presented the image of gods of deliverance. Overall it may be held that the Rāṣṭrakūṭa art was marked by an unprecedented dynamism wherein the figures reflected an agitated gesture in their stance, expressions and inner force, as if imbibing the renewed ascendancy of Brāhmaṇism under their patrons.

The period under consideration was also an era of gradual *Āgamic* conventionalization. The canonized forms of deities; their polarization as flanking figures; attendant or *dvārapālas;* placement in the *parivārālayas;* the extra hands and enhanced weapons, were all suggestive of the evolved pattern in the Hindu pantheon. That sculptured forms in the early period were not conventionalized is apparent from the Cālukyan instances. Herein several variants from the *paurāṇic* versions were noticeable. For example, the *Kalyāṇasundara* panel in Ellorā cave XXIX had Śiva standing to the left of Pārvatī, while figures giving away the bride to Śiva resembled Viṣṇu and Lakshmī. Even if identified as Pārvatī's father Himālaya and mother Mainā, they clearly betray a lack of canonical fixation of forms at this stage of artistic fruition. This lack of clarity in projecting canonical forms was sometimes also apparent in the Pallava monuments as suggested by the variation in the depiction of *Gaṅgādhara* motif in the *maṇḍapams* and the *rathas*.

THEISTIC HEGEMONY

Art in this era was, perhaps, a medium for the assertion of cult supremacy as revealed through the cave shrines. For instance the *Tripurāntaka* and the *Liṅgodbhava* motifs, signifying the submission of Brahmā and Viṣṇu towards Śiva, suggest that the Rāṣṭrakūṭa period was marked by hegemony of Śaivism. That it was a period of predominance of Śaivism is also apparent from the sites of Aihoḷe, Bādāmī, Mahābalipuram, Ellorā and Elephanta. Under the Rāṣṭrakūṭas, an initial division of space surfaced between the Śaiva and Vaiṣṇava images, suggesting a stage of co-existence, but in the monolithic phase Śaivite dominance exulted. A similar trend is discernible in Bādāmī caves, providing an admixture of cult images from both the sects. In the later instances, they get clearly divided into Śaiva and Vaiṣṇava groups. From the Pallava art specimens, instances of the Vaiṣṇava *maṇḍapams* taken over by the Śaivites as their places of worship by later insertion of *liṅgas* in the *garbhagṛha*, or vice-versa done by Vaiṣṇavas towards Śaivas as seen in the Rāmānuja *maṇḍapam*, exhibit an identical trend.

Thus, these art wonders provide valuable gleanings into prevailing times, in all aspects. The political stability; mutual dynastic interactions; canonization of art; theistic rivalry; evolutionary cycle of rock-cut architecture; technological and artistic background; the formation of language gauged through related epigraphs; and the initiation into stone medium from Bādāmī caves to Kailāśa replica – all phases and aspects are covered therein.

CONSERVATION STATUS

The Threats

As elaborated at length in previous chapter there appears a fundamental lack of knowledge, understanding and, perhaps, interest in our past: in what constitutes the heritage of India, the process that governed its coming into being, and how this heritage relates to the people. Its manifestations expressed in cultural forms are losing their traditional essence in rapidly transforming lifestyles in an era of industrial growth. The real challenge before us is to plan the necessary measures of conservation with a view to assuring the survival of these built cultural heritage and unique symbols of our civilizations for centuries to come, with as little intervention as possible but without altering or modifying in any way the authenticity of their original character. To ensure the stability as well as proper conservation of our cultural heritage, there is a need to give more thrust to the scientific research in conservation options based on a preliminary investigation which includes the knowledge of physical nature of the object (constituent materials, architectural characteristics, production techniques, state of decay) and of the factors which induce or could induce its decay. In other words, as in the case of medical study the field of conservation therapy to be based on a correct diagnosis.The role of scientific discipline is vital to both these steps of conservation activities. Rather than restrictive conservation, practices should be based on positive intervention. To foster conservation ethics and cross-disciplinary collaborations between academics and professionals involved in both cultural and natural heritage. Moreover, resources, expertise and practices that make the practice of conservation sustainable should be explored and identified. This is more feasible considering the current preservation status of the heritage monuments.

The factors responsible for decay of monuments and edifices are both natural and human. The first type caused by exposure to sun, rain, climatic effects, soil erosion, geographical location near seacoast or desert, dampness or water seepage, etc. The second type is resultant of neglect for centuries, uncared for, misuse by humans for commercial/ residential purposes, vandalism, surface vibrations due to quarrying operations undertaken near the sites, or operation of heavy machinery in the factories in vicinity. The tourists/visitors' conscious or unconscious scrapings, scratching of names, stealing away fragments of the edifice as a token of their visit are some of the common reasons posing threats to the art heritage sites.

As revealed during the author's field visits, the Bādāmī caves confront several challenges towards conservation. Exposure to light, air and humidity has proved especially fatal for the ceiling paintings made from sedimentary and vegetative colours. An acute foul smell of bats abounds the environs, suggesting bat colonies therein. The bottom of pillars is stained. Marks of water seepage through crevice are also prominently noticeable. Bracket figures fallen from their place and even grinding stones used for preparing colours for ceiling paitings are lying within, suggesting evidence of mismanagement and poor upkeep of the site. As an instance of gross apathy towards heritage till they were declared protected, the Bādāmī caves were frequented by people from nearby localities who would sleep or play cards therein. Monkey menace is also a potent deterrent towards tourist movement. There is a lack of markers or signboards for the sculptures. The same scenario may be witnessed at primarily all the heritage sites, varying only in degrees of callousness.

The World Heritage Sites of Ajantā and Ellorā were comparatively better off in terms of preservation initiatives though still a lot remains to be accomplished towards that end. Similar negligence is also seen therein. Scratch marks are noticeable on the Ellorā cave XVI first floor left side shrine exterior corner walls. Scratching marks also exist on the frontal steps of Kailasa main shrine garbhagrha. Yet as early as in 1991 a Master Plan was devised by Tata Consultancy Services, in alliance with Maharashtra

Tourism Development Corporation and the Government of Japan to the tune of Rs. 817.1 million (Yen 4,406 million). The project ingredients included monument conservation, upgradation of core infrastructure (water supply, electricity, communication), accessibility/connectivity (airports, roads, trains), environment management (afforestation, low pollution local transportation, removal of encroachments), visitor management (tourist circulation plans, landscaping, tourists amenities, cave illumination, directional and site signages, brochures, publicity, etc.).

At Mahābalipuram, a world heritage site, preservation of the monuments remains a perennial challenge to the conservators because of the constant threat of salinity and abrasive action of the sand-bearing wind. What makes the task more difficult is the amorphous growth of encroachments, in form of hawkers, almost a thousand in number, besides, a few hundreds shops, selling artefacts made out of sea shells, sculptures made out of granite or sandstone, ornaments including necklaces made out of beads, and toys made out of dried palmyra leaves. A number of roadside eateries have also sprung up, dirtying the surroundings. A score of sculptors' shops are located on the road to the five Rathas who make exquisite sculptures but the use of chisel, hammer and power drill make the air polluted and the environment noisy. The sculptors are reluctant to shift elsewhere, fearing slump in their business. Besides the natural and geographic constraints, the other glaring challenges continue to be dwelling areas in the zone due to population increase and the lack of effective waste/ drainage.

As highlighted in ASI's report itself, environmental pollution from vehicles is very high at Mahābalipuram and suspension of traffic in the buffer zone may yield distinctive improvements. Rising pollution levels are serious concern. Vehicular emissions are impacting the monuments. The level of particulate matter is much higher than observed a few decades ago. As regards public negligence towards cultural legacy, these monuments fare no better, with scuffing seen at several places and traces of some tourists' irresponsible behavior surviving. All of these have had an impact on monuments, necessitating the use of modern conservation techniques.

This may involve environment development of monumental edifice as an important aspect that may protect them from decay. This can be achieved by improving surroundings of edifices to enhance their architectural appeal or to save them from climatic and other natural forces and pollutants. Monuments located at the sea shore, exposed to danger of soil erosion and sea breeze injurious to stone structures need such development more than others.

Desirable Conservation Measures

Technically speaking, (i) geological investigations of the caves for formulating conservation plan; (ii) structural conservation through prevention of separation of rocks, restoration of pillars, façades, and structural intergrity of cave; (iii) chemical conservation to arrest weathering of external rock surfaces and monuments, ensure slope stability; cleaning of paintings and sculptures, etc., being indispensable components of a conservation/preservation plan should be diligently followed.

Besides, new academic and professional courses focusing on and addressing core conservation issues besides specific case studies may be introduced in universities to create more skilled hands on heritage conservation. Conservators invariably are focused on *how* and not *why* we need conservation, so they remain uncertain and mute as decisions are made. Conservation methodology should explore the relationship between theory and practice. Conservators, whether they work on delicate clocks or large wall paintings, share a common methodology and ethics. They should be trained on how conservation profession has developed over the years and examine how 'western' conservation values are deployed in the management of global cultural heritage. They should examine contentious concepts such as 'irreversibility', 'minimal intervention', value judgments and how conservators impact on the decision-making process. Research in historic interiors should be encouraged to gain an understanding of their development and serve expertise requirement criteria expected specifically from project conservators, property managers, curators, historic building inspectors, conservation officers and conservation architects. Accordingly, mechanisms and strategies for monitoring research programmes and the effective utilization of research findings to formulate conservation/representation options may be devised. In brief, courses to be designed must imbibe the history and theory of conservation and the importance of context and values in making conservation decisions.

If the sites of heritage have to be made more tourist-friendly and present better environs, the following steps may be undertaken: (i) Clear demarcations and signages, both directional and site related, for easy identification of particular monuments and providing accurate historical information. (ii) Adequate provisions for drinking water and washrooms must be made. Visitor benches, coffee shops, audio-visual aids, illumination of monuments. (iii) Battery run shuttles for reaching destination sites and preventing private vehicles beyond a certain point may also help control pollution levels at the sites as well as retain their specific ambience. (iv) Proper footpaths for pedestrians, cement approach roads, and landscaping around the buildings. (v) Adequate craft bazaars near the sites preventing mushroom growth of roadside hawkers in the vicinity of the monuments. (vi) Conservation agencies could benefit from technological updates such as lasersand 3-D scanning to facilitate a non-destructive evaluation of the status of sites. (vii) Additionally, involvement of locals especially the youth should be encouraged in conservation practices. (viii) For maintenance of sites, ASI should be permitted to charge more on site seeing tickets. Besides, the charges for film shoots may also be enhanced from the current Rs. 5,000 at a particular monument. (ix) Likewise, licence fee may be imposed on making sculptures based on ancient models (currently ASI issues free non-antiquity licences). (x) Regular chemical treatment to stop water seepage into the rock, and put pulp on the rock, which has a tendency to absorb the salt should be ensured especially for the excavetd caves. (xi) A communication system connecting all scattered monuments, especially the cave temples, with central monitoring facilities may be quite effective in addressing the emergent requirements of day to day management of thhhe sites whereas a co-ordination committee, the ASI and local authorities could further strengthen the monitoring system.

Therefore, it may be held that the rock-cut cave temple architecture of South India, spanning a period of over four hundred years and patronized by the Cālukya, Pallava, and Rāṣṭrakūṭas, as a symbol of political vitality remains a unique contribution of Indian art towards world heritage. Epitomizing Indian mysticism and philosophy besides eternalizing innovative genius of the artisans and their patrons, this mode of architecture proved to be latent with underlying symbolism of forms, a plethora of divine and worldly images pulsating with life, signify a residence place of the gods in all their glory besides highlighting the cultural ethos of the period concerned.

Appendix I

Appendix I (a): Nāgara Temples

Viśvakarma Prakāśa	*Matsya Purāṇa*	*Bṛhta-Saṁhitā*	*Samarāṅgaṇā Sutradhāra*		
				(A)	**(B) Later ones**
Merū	-	-	-	*Merū*	*Samkīrṇa*
Mandara	-	-	-	*Mandara*	*Mahānanda*
Kailāśa	-	-	-	*Kailāśa*	*Saubhāgya*
Vimānachanda	-	-	-	-	*Vibhaṅga*
Nandivardhana	-	-	-	*Nandibhadra*	*Vibhāva*
Nandana	-	-	-	*Nandyāvarta*	*Vibhātsa*
Sarvatobhadra	-	-	-	*Sarvatobhadra*	*Srī-tuṅga*
Vṛṣa	-	-	-	-	*Mānatuṅga*
Siṁha	-	-	-	-	*Vāhyodara*
Gaja	-	*Kuñjara*	*Gaja*	-	*Niryūhodara*
Kuṁbha	-	*Ghaṭa*	*Kuṁbha*	*Kuṁbhaka*	*Samodara*
Samudraka	-	*Samudgo*	*Samudra*	-	*Bhadrakośa*
Padmaka	*Padma*	*Padma*	*Padmaka*	-	*Citrakūṭa*
Suparṇa	*Garuḍa*	*Garuḍa*	-	-	*Vimala*
Haṁsa	-	-	-	-	*Harshana*
Vartula	-	*Vṛtta*	*Vartula*	-	*Bhadra samkīrṇa*
Caturārṣa	-	*Caṭuṣkoṇa*	*Caturārṣa*	-	*Bhadra-Viśāla*

Viśvakarma Prakāśa	*Matsya Purāṇa*	*Bṛhta-Saṁhitā*	*Samarāṅgaṇā Sutradhāra*		
			(A)		**(B) Later ones**
Aṣṭārṣa	-	-	*Aṣṭārṣa*	-	*Bhadra-Vishkambha*
Ṣoḍārṣa	-	-	-	-	*Ujjayanta*
Mṛgarāja / Gṛharāja / Balabhīchanda	*Mṛgarāja/ Balabhīchanda*	*Guhārāja*	*Gṛharāja*	*Gṛharāja* *Srīkūṭa* *Srīmukha* *Srīdhara* *Varada* *Priyadarśana* *Kulanandana* *Antariksha* *Puṣpabhāṣa* *Viśālaka*	

Appendix I (b): Temples in the Viṣṇudharmmottaram

Himavāna	*Subhadra*	*Alakā*	*Surarāta*
Māluavāna	*Kamala*	*Vimāna*	*Ānanda*
Sriṅgavana	*Aruṇodaya*	*Nandana*	*Śusamā*
Āgāra	*Guhā*	*Pañcata*	*Prabhañjana*
Bhavana	*Garuḍa*	*Caṭuṣkaka*	*Viśwakarmā*
Gṛha	*Sarva*	*Tribhūmi*	*Mahāsumana*
Niṣāda	*Trailokya*	*Dvibhūma*	*Chatra*
Nīla	*Liṅga*	*Ekabhauma*	*Mṛdaṅga*
Ceta	*Sarvakīta*	*Vṛtta*	*Vajra*
Vindhya	*Brahmāṇḍa*	*Naṅdi*	*Lokapāla*
Balabhī	*Sāra*	*Guhārāja*	*Digvandha*
Vṛddhida	*Caturārṣa*	*Vṛṣa*	*Sāmānya*
Triguṇa	*Sumekhala*	*Haṁsa*	*Suguha*
Balabhī (?)	*Vimekhala*	*Ghata*	*Triguṇa*
Śidhara	*Trimekhala*	*Siṁha*	*Nandaka*
Turaga	*Dhishnya*	*Maṇḍapa*	*Ākāśani*
Kuñjara	*Śalya*	*Dvādārṣi*	*Ṣoḍārṣa*
Yatheṣṭha	*Budha*	*Sadārṣī*	*Saṁkha*
Viśāla	*Indu*	*Asṭārṣi*	*Vaijayanta*
Bhadra	*Gṛha (?)*	*Kailāśa*	*Ambada*
Dvārapāla	*Bahubhūmika*	*Trikūṭa*	*Maṅgala*
Samudra	*Merū*	*Saumya (?)*	*Sawatobhadra*
Sveta	*Śuktimāna*	*Rājarāja*	(remaining 3 not
Gaṅdhamādana	*Mandāra*	*Dharamīdhara*	described in the
Saumya	*Pāriyātra*	*Vimāna (?)*	text) total 100

Appendix I (C): Early Dravida Temples (as given in Śilpa texts)

Earliest		Later		Latest	
ISGDP	***Śilpa Ratna***	***Supra-bhedāgam***	***VA***	***Ātri Saṁhitā***	***ISGDP***
Merū	*Merū*	*Merū*	*Padmakāra*	*Vṛṣabhākāra*	*Ghona*
Mandara	*Mandara*	*Mandara*	*Nandyārta*	*Kumbhākāra*	*Chandavṛtta*
Kailāśa	*Kailāśa*	*Kailāśa*	*Nalina*	*Padmakāra*	*Vedidā*
Srīkara	*Srīkara*	*Srīkara*	*Parvatākāra*	*Nandyārta*	*Siddhayoga*
Mahendra	*Mahendra*	*Mahendra*	*Vimalākṛti*	*Nalinka*	*Kūṭākāra*
Nīla	*Nīla*	*Nīla*	*Śilpa*	*Pranalinaka*	*Vilokana*
Niṣada	*Niṣadha*	*Niṣada*	*Sarvatobhadra*	*Parvatakriti*	*Kuḍyavṛtta*
Vṛṣachanda	*Vṛṣachanda*	*Vṛṣachanda*	*Caturukha*	*Tilaka*	*Trikūṭa*
Kumbha	*Kumbha*	*Nandyārta*	*Vṛttabhadra*	*Srī vatsa*	*Trikūṭaka*
Padmakānta	*Padmakānta*	*Nalina*	*Srī-Pratiṣṭha*	*Vālenduka*	*Yoga Kānta*
Garuḍachanda	*Garuḍachanda*	*Pralina*	*Svastika*	*Garūḍākāra*	*Prek Shagṛha*
Haṁsachanda	*Haṁsachanda*	*Parvata*	*Bhadra*	*Mastaka*	*Mahārājāhvaya*
Merūkūṭa	*Merūkūṭa*	*Himavān*	*Vṛtta*	*Sandhika*	*Gaṇikāviśāla*
Kailāśakānta	*Kailāśakānta*	*Srī varta*	*Caṭuṣphuṭa*	*Nandiviśāla*	*Nāgvhvaya*
Jayāṅga	*Jayāṅga*	*Padmabhadra*	*Mahāpadma*	*Koḍyavṛtta*	*Bhāgachanda*
Vimala	*Vimala*		*Udyogapadma*	*Citra Śilpa*	*Srivardhana*
Padmabhadra	*Rudrakānta*		*Vedika*	*Bhūtavaihāra*	*Padmagṛha*
Rudrakānta	*Yogabhadra*		*Yogakānta geha*	*Sarvatobhadra*	*Atyantakānta*
Skandakānta	*Maṅgala*		*Diśasvastika*	*Hastipriṣṭha*	*Bhānukānta*
Yogabhadra	*Vindhyachanda*		*Khaṇḍa*	*Caturmukha*	*Candrakānta*
Maṅgala	*Vimalaṅga*		*Harmya*	*Vṛtta-*	*Kratuvardhana*
Vindhyachanda	*Bhogichanda*		*Prekshāgṛha*	*Saubhodva*	*Mantraputa*
Vimalaṅga	*Saumukhya*		*Mahārājachanda*	*Aṣṭāṅga*	*Avantya*
Bhogichanda	*Srīmaṇḍana*		*Sanairyoga*	*Svastika*	*Mahiṣa*
Saumukhya	*Lalitākānta*		*Gaṇikā Viṣāla*	*Srimatasvastika*	*Tantrikānta*
Srīmaṇḍana	*Srīviṣāla*			*Pañjaramukha*	*Vizayāṅga*
Lalitākānta	*Vijaya*			*Utpalaphullaka*	*Viṣālabhadra*
Srīviṣāla	*Sudarśana*			*Srī-Pratiṣṭhita*	*Kamaśālaka*
Vijaya	*Jayamaṅgala*			*Bhadra*	*Padmāsana*
Sudarśana	*Citrakūṭa*			*Supauṣṭika*	*Indrakānta*
Jayamaṅgala				*Vṛtta, vṛtta*	*Savalalita*
Citrakūṭa				*Śaśivṛtta*	*Pratyantakānta*
				Somavṛtta	*Mātagṛha*
				Gandhara	*Prithvivijaya*
				Gadhara	*Nandiviśāla*

Earliest		Later		Latest	
ISGDP	*Śilpa Ratna*	*Supra-bhedāgam*	*VA*	*Ātri Saṁhitā*	*ISGDP*
				Pañcaka	*Sarvāṅgasundara*
				Somachanda	*Chāyā gṛha*
				Srīyavṛtta	*Rativardhana*
				Viṣāla,	*Viśālalaya*
				Viśālaka	*Caṭuṣpādika*
				Brahma Vṛtta	*Turaṅgavādana*
				Caṭuṣphuṭa,	*Gaṇikāpiṇḍika*
				Caṭuṣphuṭa	*Syenachanda*
				Aṅganākāra	*Utpalāgra*
				Somārdha	*Kukkuṭapuchaka*
				Mahāpadma	*Muṇḍaprāsāda*
				Ujjalapatraka	
				Utpalapatraka	
				Bahupatra	

Appendix II

Test-Results of Engineering Properties of Excavated Rocks in Present State of Preservation

	Site	Rock type	Compressive Strength	Density gm/cc	Absorption (%)
1	Ajantā	Deccan Basalt	1620	2.86	0.62
2	Ellorā	Deccan Basalt	1435	2.90	0.24
3	Udaigiri/ Khaṇḍagiri	Goṇḍwānā Sandstone	90 (wet)	2.42	7.05
4	Bāgh	Cretaceous Sandstone	65 (wet)	2.10	7.10

- Due to massive character of basalt, large chambers dug at Ajantā and Ellorā did not face roof collapse.
- Goṇḍwānā sandstone, being soft, the excavation of Udaigiri, Khaṇḍagiri caves was easier as compared to basalt. However, the height of the excavated chamber had to be less than 2 m due to close-spaced joints and low strength of rock or else the threat of roof collapse was highly imminent. High absorption of rocks necessitated special arrangement of diverting the seepage water out of the cave-interiors during rainy season.
- Cretaceous sandstone, with high porosity and softness, proved worst for construction of underground chambers. Bāgh caves, excavated in this sandstone with thin layers of pebble stones and lenses of limestone, have undergone natural ravages through the centuries.

- Vindhyan sandstone was softer than basalt but harder than Goṇḍwāna sandstone. In the *in situ* condition, the rock exhibits two important sets of joints aligned along and across the bedding planes. These structural planes influenced excavation of Udaigiri caves, M.P.
- *(Vide.* Subinoy Gangopadhyay. *Monuments of India,* pp. 81-82)

Appendix III

CAVE ENDOWMENT INSCRIPTIONS FROM KANHERĪ

Inscription No. 3, Cave II

Kaliyaṇa (nā) suvaṇako (kā) rasa Samidatasa saha sagha (ghe) na paṇi (ya) ka deyadhamma.
(A cistern, the meritorious gift of goldsmith Svamidatta of Kalyāṇa, associated with the community of ascetics and lay-brethren)

No. 7, Cave III

Deyadharmmoyam Śākya-bhiksho (r) Dharmmaguptasya
(The meritorious gift of Bauddha ascetic Dharmagupta)

No. 9, Cave III

Deyadharmmoyam ācāryya Buddhara Kshitasya...
(Meritorious gift of teacher Buddharakshita)

No. 12, near Cave VII

Sopāragā negama-Sa Samikupāsaka-Sa podhi deyadhama
(A cistern, the meritorious gift of lay worshipper Samika, a merchant of Supārā)

No. 20, Open Gallery No. XXXIX

(Sidham Sop) ārayakasa maṇikarasa Nagapalitasa saparivārasa leṇa deyadhama
(A cave, the meritorious gift of Nagapalita, a jeweller from Sorpāraka)

No. 21, near Cave XLIII

Sidha therāna bhayamta ghos(ā)na atevāsiniye
Pavaitikā P(o) nakiasanā theriya leṇa
(... Gift of female ascetic, therī Ponakiasana, the pupil of Ghosha)

No. 25, Cave LIX

Sidham kaliyiṇikiya bhikhuniya Dāmilāya leṇa deyadhamam podhi ca
(...Gift of female ascetic Damila, inhabitant of Kalyāṇa)

No. 30, between Caves XIV-XV

Kaliya (ṇa) to Nadasa kamā-Rasa patho de-Yadhama
(Gift of Nanda, blacksmith from Kalyāṇa)

Appendix IV

MONETARY CONTRIBUTIONS FOR TEMPLE BUILDING

(A) Abundant epigraphic data confirms the role of royalty and laity in constructing, renovating, or making adequate arrangements in temples. The following table gives a list of donors during the Pallava-Pāṇḍya period:

Donor	**600-700 AD**	**700-800 AD**	**800-900 AD**	**900-925 AD**	**Total**
Kings	7	4	-	-	11
Chieftain/ Royals	2	3	13	3	21
Royal Ladies	-	3	2	2	7
Officials	-	5	-	-	5
Brāhmaṇa/ Ladies	1	-	9	-	10
Merchants/ Goldsmiths	-	1	4	-	5
Priests	-	-	3	-	3
Corporate Bodies	-	-	2	-	2
Others (Male)	-	-	3	-	3
Others (Female)	-	-	1	-	1
Total	10	16	37	05	68

Vide:

1. *SII*. I. pt.11. No. 72; *SII*. XII: 8, 9, 115; *EI*. IV, pp. 152-53; *EI*. XII, pp. 225-26.
2. *SII*. XIV: 44; *SII*. XII: 45, 47; *EI*. VII, p. 26; *SII*. I: 27.
3. *SII*. I: 29, 30, 53; *SII*. III: 96.
4. *EI*. VI, p. 32; *EI*. XXXVI, p. 15.
5. *EI*. XXXII, p. 23; *SII*. VI; 287.
6. *SII*. VIII: 663; *EI*. X; p. 14.
7. *SII*. XII: 105.
8. *SII*. XIII: 314.

(B) *Cālukya Patronage*

Exact epigraphic evidences providing details of the origins of funds utilized for temple building activities are not available. However, besides the lucrative trade and agricultural productions, the booty received during their various campaigns must have also contributed. The Mahākūṭa Pillar inscription of Mangalesha, mentioning his victories over Budharaja and Kalacuris, suggest this idea:

> *...Kalaṭsūri-gaṇa sam dēvagṛha-dēvadrōṇym gatam= ima (da) ñ=ca dravyaṃ sva-dēvadrōṇyāṃ Makuṭēś (v) a ra-nāthasy=āsmākaṃ pitrā jyēṣṭhēna ch=ōpadattam (m) Srīyambātaka- Tirmmaridvenasavedve...*

(The wealth of the Kalaṭsūri has been expended in the idol procession of the temple of own god. And [therefore] this property, which at [their] own idol procession was assigned by our father and elder brother to god Makuṭēśvaranātha supplement it, by [bestowing the] enjoyment of the ten villages headed by Sriyambataka..)

(Vide. Indian Antiquary. XIX, p. 18)

(C) Amongst cross sections of the society in Deccan, the *devadāsis* also made generous donations:

> *Svasti Srī-Bijēsvarada sūle Calabbeya kamba mu ru (ii)*

(Hail the three pillars of Calabbe, the harlot of the temple of Vijayeśvara)
(Inscription No. CXIII. *Indian Antiquary*. X.)

> *...vinapotigala illiye hiraṇya garbhaṃ= ildu ellā dānamum-gottu dēvanā pīṭhamān = kisuvine katti belliyā kodeyān= ērisie Mangalulle aṣṭa-śataṃ kshētra...*

(Mahākūṭeśvara temple inscription. *Indian Antiquary*. X, p. 103)

During the Rāṣṭrakūṭa occupation of Cālukyan regions, Badippodi, a harlot of Virupāksha temple, donated a horse chariot, an elephant chariot and a land grant:

> *...Badipoddiy = embol uttama- gōsāsam – ildol*
> *śvarātha – gottol = hastiratham –ildol*
> *bhūmi-dānamum...*

(*Indian Antiquary*. XI, p. 125)

Appendix V

Dynastic Affiliations of Temples

Cālukyan:

Patron Ruler	Period	Temples/Caves
Jayasimha	Early 6th century AD	Lāḍ Khān, Konṭi-guḍī, Durgā; other old shrines at Aihoḷe
Ranaraga	Early 6th century AD	Mahākūṭeśvara
Mangalesha	578 AD	Bādāmī cave III
Pulakeshin II	610-642 AD	Megutī temple, Aihoḷe
Vinayaditya	681-96 AD	Ālampur Shrines, temples at Iṭṭagi, Aihoḷe, Paṭṭaḍakal, Mahākūṭa, Siddhankolla, Kudaveli, etc.
Vijayaditya	696-733 AD	Saṅgameśvara, Paṭṭaḍakal, Anesejjeya Basadi, Jambūliṅga Bādāmī, Hucchimallī, Aihoḷe
Vikramaditya II	733-744 AD	Virūpāksha and Mallikārjuna, Paṭṭaḍakal; additions to earlier Vijayeśvara, Pāpanātha

Pallava:

Patron Ruler	Period	Temple/Cave
Mahendravarman I	580-630 AD	Early Rock-cut *Maṇḍapams*.
Narasimhavarman I	630-668 AD	Draupadī, Arjuna, Bhīma, Dharmarāja and Nakula Sahadeva *rathas*; Kōṇēri, Varāha and *Mahiṣamardinī Maṇḍapams*.
Parameshvarman I	672-670 AD	*Rathas* as Gaṇeśa, Valaiyankuṭṭai and the Piḍārī *Rathas*; structural shrines as Vedagiriśvara, Tirukkalukunram, Śaiva apsidal shrine at Kuram, another shrine at Kalambakkam.
Rajasimha	700-728 AD	Śāḷuvankuppam *Yāḷi Maṇḍapam*; structural shrines at Olakkaneśvara, Mukundanayanār and Shore temples at Mahābalipuram, Kailāśanātha, Airāvateśvara, Pirāvataneśvara, Irāvataneśvara, Tripurāntakeśvara and Vāliśvara at Kāñcīpuram, Talagiriśvara temple at Panamalāi.
Mahendravarman III	Early 8th century (pre mature death)	Mahendravarmeśvara shrine in Kailāśanātha complex, Kāñcī.
Parameshvaraman II	728-731 AD	Vīrattāneśvara temple, Tiruvadigai.
Nandivarman II Pallavamalla	732-796 AD	Mukteśvara, Mātaṅgeśvara, Vaikuṇṭhaperumāl in Kāñcī; Kailāśanātha temple, Tirupaṭṭur.
Dantivarman	796-846 AD	Sundarāvaradaperumāl Kailāśanātha temple and Vaikuṇṭhaperumāl temple, Uttiramerur.
Nandivarman III	846-859 AD	Viṣṇu temple, Kiliyanur; and Śiva temple Sumaṅgali.
Nripatunga	859-99 AD	Viṣṇu temple, Ukkal.
Aparajitavarman	885-903 AD	Vīrattaneśvara temple, Tiruttani
Kampavarman	948-980 AD	Śolāpuram, Tiruvurriyur and Kavantaṇḍalam.

Rāṣṭrakūṭa:

Patron Ruler	Period	Temple/Cave
Krishna I	756-772AD	Ellorā Kailāśanātha and Kanneśvara

Specific information about patrons of other Rāṣṭrakūṭa temples is not authentically ascertainable.

Appendix VI

Centrally protected Brāhmanical Rock-cut Monuments

Aurangābād Circle

Sr. No.	Locality/ District	Site Name	Date
1.	Aurangābād, Aurangābād	Aurangābād Caves	8th Century AD
2.	Ellorā, Aurangābād	Ellorā Caves	
3.	Mahoor Village, Nanded	Brāhmanical caves locally known as a Pānduleni	

Chennai Circle, Tamil Nadu

Sr. No.	Locality/ District	Monument/Site Name	Date
4.	Daḷavāṇūr,Villupuram	Pallava Rock-cut Temple	Late 6th /Early 7th centuries AD
5.	Kilmavilangai, Villupuram	Pallava Rock-cut shrine	
6.	Maṇḍagappaṭṭū, Villupuram	Pallava Rock-cut Temple	
7.	Kuraṅgaṇilmuṭṭam, Tiruvannamalai	Rock-cut shrine	
8.	Mahēndravāḍī, Vellore	Rock cut Monolith	

9.	Māmaṇḍūr, Tiruvannamalai	Rock-cut caves, Sculptures and Inscriptions	
10	Śīyamaṅgalam, Tiruvannamalai	Rock-cut Temple, Sculptures	
11.	Vilappakkam, Vellore	Rock, sculptures and caves	
12.	Pallāvaram, Cingleput	Pañcapāndava Cave Temple	
13.	Māmallapuram, Kancipuram	Arjuna's Penance	First Quarter/ Mid 7th century
14.		Arjuna Ratha	
15.		Bhīma Ratha	
16.		Dharmarāja Ratha	
17.		Dharmarāja's Rock-cut Throne	
18.		Dolotsava Mantapa	
19.		Draupadī Ratha	
20.		Draupadī's Bath	
21.		Eight stone images on a masonry platform (seven Pidaris)	
22.		Huge stone figures of a lion, elephant and a bull	
23.		Kottikal Maṇḍapa	Late 7th /Early 8th centuries
24.		Krṣṇa's Butterball	First Quarter/ Mid 7th century
25.		Krṣṇa Maṇḍapa	
26.		Large unfinished rock sculptures similar to Arjuna's Penance near the lighthouse	
27.		Mahiṣamardinī Maṇḍapa	
28.		Mahishasura rock in the sea to the north of the Shore Temple	
29.		Rock-cut Gaṇeśa Temple	Late 7th century
30.		Rock-cut Varāha Temple	

31.		Rock-cut Sculpture representing a group of elephants, monkeys and peacock	Mid 7th century
32.		Royagopuram (Unfinished)	
33.		Sahadeva Ratha	
34.		Small, unfinished monolithic Valaiyankuṭṭai Ratha	
35.		Stone Sculpture representing a group of monkeys	
36.		Triple celled rock-cut shrine fronted by Gopis' churn	
37.		Two rock cut cave Temples at the north east corner of the Kōṇēri Pallam tank	
38.		Two small carved rocks to the south of Shore Temple	
39.		Two small, unfinished monolithic Piḍārī Amman Ratha Temples	
40.		Unfinished Ratha and Stone Couch	
41.		Unfinished cave Temple north of Krṣṇa Maṇḍapa	
42.	Śāḷuvaṇkuppam, Kancipuram	Rock cut Siva Temples with three lingas	Early 8th century
43.		Tiger headed rock-cut cave	
44.		Two inscribed rocks, with six and fifty lines of ancient Tamil inscriptions and remains of others ancient buildings	
45.	Tirukkalikundram, Kancipuram	Orukal Maṇḍapam	
46.	Vaigainallur, Karur	Rock (Kulithalai)	Early 9th century
47.	Kodiakkarai, Nagapattinam	Ramapada Maṇḍapam	
48.	Thirumayam, Pudukkottai	Rock-cut Siva Temple (Satyagiriswara Shrine)	
49.		Rock-cut Viṣṇu Temple (Satyamurti Shrine)	

50.	Malayadipatti, Pudukkottai	Pallava Rock-cut Siva Temple	Early 8th century
51.	Narthamalai, Pudukkottai	Rock-cut Siva Temple	Early/ Mid 9th century AD
52.		Rock-cut Viṣṇu Shrine	
53.	Kudumiyanmalai, Pudukkottai	Rock-cut shrine Melakkoil with frontal Maṇḍapa	

Dharwad Circle, Karnataka

Sr. No.	**Locality/ District**	**Monument/Site Name**	**Date**
54.	Aihoḷe, Bijapur	Jaina cave (Meena Basti)	Early to Mid 6th century
55.		Raval Phaḍi (Brahmanical Cave)	
56.		Two storeyed Jaina temple and cave at Meguti hill	
57.	Bādāmī, Bijapur	Jaina & Vaiṣṇava caves	Mid to Late 6th century

Mumbai Circle

Sr. No.	**Locality/ District**	**Monument/Site Name**	**Date**
58.	Gharapuri, Raigad	Elephanta Caves	Early 8th century

Glossary

GLOSSARY OF SOUTH INDIAN ARCHITECTURAL TERMS

Adhiṣṭhāna	: basement of a *vimāna, maṇḍapa* structure consisting of distinct moulded tiers.
Aliṅga/Antarita	: mouldings over the *kapota*.
Alpa-nāsika	: projected front-end of an apsidal shrine resembling a *kūḍū*-arch over pilasters, originally a small opening or fenestrated window.
Alpa-vimāna	: small one storeyed *vimāna*.
Antarāla	: intermediate passage between outer *maṇḍapa* and the shrine.
Ardha-maṇḍapa	: a pillared hall immediately fronting the principal shrine, with two seriate pillars.
Ayatārṣa-vimāna	: *vimāna*, oblong on plan and covered by a wagon-top roof.
Bhadra-pīṭha	: a moulded pedestal type, usually of the *mañca* variety, circular or rectilinear on plan.
Bhadra-śālā	: oblong wagon-topped miniature shrine of *ayatārṣa* type in the centre of each side of the *hāra* over the *vimāna* storeys.
Bhitti	: wall.
Bhitti-toraṇa	: ornamental festoon on the wall, usually a *makara toraṇa*, supported by two pilasters.
Bhūta/gaṇa	: goblin.
Bhūta-mālā / bhūta-vārī/ gaṇā-varī	: decorative frieze with *bhūtas/ gaṇas*, usually below the flexed cornice in the *valabhī* (eaves board),

marking decorated ends of the joists over the main beams.

Candra-śālā	: open court, usually over the terrace, surrounded by cloisters connecting *kūṭas* and *śālās*.
Candra-śilā	: crescent moon shaped lowest step in the *sopāna*.
Caturmukha	: shrine or *vimāna* with openings on all four sides.
Deva-koṣṭha	: niche of exterior shrine-wall enshrining the deity.
Galā / grīvā	: 'neck'; the clerestory raising up the *śikhara* with light and air openings (*nāsikās*) on its sides.
Garbha-gṛha	: shrine cell or *sanctum sanctorum*.
Gopura	: main gateway; storeyed structure over entrance through enclosing walls to temple premises.
Haṁsa-mālā / haṁsā-vari	: decorative frieze of geese above principal beams and below the cornice of the main shrine walls or storeys (*talas*).
Hāra/hārāntara	: string of miniature shrines over each terrace/ *tala* of the storeyed *vimāna* consisting of *kūṭas, koṣṭhas / śālās*, and *pañjaras* interconnected by cloister lengths or in its place balustrades simulating cloisters (*hārāntara*)
Iha-mṛga	: composite, fanciful animal.
Jagati	: vertical moulding of the *adhiṣṭhāna* immediately above the *upāna*, oblong in shape and in a line with the vertical norm or *māna-sutra*.
Jālaka	: window with trellis-work of different patterns.
Kal	: pillar shaft; the portion between base and capital.
Kalaśa	: wide-mouthed vase; lowermost member of pillar-capital, so called after its shape.
Kampa	: fillet shaped moulding of a minor order separating two major mouldings.
Kaṇṭha	: the major recessed basement moulding, oblong in elevation, connecting or separating other projected mouldings, viz. the *paṭṭikā* above and *kumuda* and *padma* below.
Kapota	: overhanging cornice, usually flexed, projecting beyond the principal beam to throw off water from the terrace beyond the beam and joist-end; the recesses between the joist-ends over the wall, harbouring birds protected by the projecting curved cornice.
Karṇa-kūṭa	: miniature *sama-caturārṣa* (square) shrine at the corner of each storey of the *vimāna* over the *prastara*, with a single *stūpī*.

Karṇa-śālā	: miniature *āyatārṣa* (oblong) shrine with barrel-vault roof placed at the corner of each *tala* of a structure, usual in *gopuras*.
Kaṭṭu	: intervening, octagonal or polygonal portion between the bottom and top squares of a pillar.
Kodungai	: 'bent arm'; curved bracket or eaves-bracket supporting cornice (as in original metal sheet or wooden plank cornices) or the projected eaves of the *śikhara* or roof.
Koṇa-paṭṭa	: ridge-plate, joining the adjacent edges (ribs) particularly of metal sheet or wooden plank *śikharas* or *kapotas* at the corner-junctions.
Kshudra-nāsikā	: short *nāsikā*; projected front-end of a miniature apsidal, (one or two storeyed) shrine with arch over pilasters functioning as a small opening, usually found in *hārāntara*.
Kshudra-vimāna	: miniature *viṃāna* of small dimensions of two, three, four storeys or *talas*.
Kūḍū	: 'nest'; an arched or horseshoe-shaped opening projected out of the flexed cornice, originally perhaps intended for entry of roosting birds (*kapota*) but in later examples filled with human figures surmounted by a finial of diverse shape. The arch is usually a *makara-toraṇa*.
Kuṁbha	: a member of the pillar-capital coming above the *kalaśa* and *tāḍī*, flat and bulbous in form originally a flattened carinated vase with a short, narrow mouth.
Kumuda	: three-faceted (*tri-paṭṭa*) or circular (*vṛtta*) polygonal or fluted 'torus'-like moulding of the *adhiṣṭhāna* coming over the vertical *jagati* and projected up to the vertical norm (*māna-sutra*).
Kūṭa	: square plan shrine with four-sided converging roof and single finial, or circular with domical roof and single finial or *stūpī*.
Lalāṭa-biṁba	: 'crest-figure'; chief decorative motif or figure on the frontal of any entrance or the door-lintel, sometimes extending to the overdoor.
Madhya-bandha	: raised floral or decorated band at the middle of the height of the pillar-shaft.
Mahā-maṇḍapa	: pillared hall immediately in front of the *ardha-maṇḍapa* or *antarāla* or the proximal hall of a

	maṇḍapa with two seriate pillars, closed or open, in cave-temples.
Mahā-nāsikā	: the projected (nose-like) part from the sides of the *grīvā* and *śikhara* showing the frontal aspects of apsidal *vimānas* and having pillars with surmounting arched *toraṇas*.
Makara-toraṇa	: an entrance-decoration or decorated gateway with a festoon straight or arched spanning the tops of two columns, the festoon or *toraṇa* being a decorative garland or scroll issuing from mouths of *makaras* (crocodiles), placed over the capitals of the supporting staṁbhas.
Makara-potikā	: corbel carved like a *makara*.
Mālā-sthana	: apex of pillar or pilaster shaft below capital with looped garland (*mālā*) hanging from the *padma bandha*.
Mañca	: a type of basement (*adhiṣṭhāna*) without the *kumuda*, having *upāna*, *kaṇṭha* and *paṭṭikā* and other mouldings.
Maṇḍapa	: open or closed pillared hall.
Masuraka	: basement.
Mātanga-nakra	: a decorative motif, combination of elephant and *makara*, an *iha-mṛga*.
Mukha-maṇḍapa	: the first or frontal *maṇḍapa* of a series of *maṇḍapas* at the entrance of a temple.
Muktā-sāra	: a pearl-garland or string of pearls used as adecorative motif.
Nāsikā	: 'nose'; projected arched opening (window).
Nava-raṅga	: closed or open *mahā-maṇḍapa* with four central and twelve peripheral pillars, of which eight are disposed in line with the central ones and four in diagonal lines at the corners enclosing nine *aṅkanas*, generally seen in Cālukyan shrines.
Nīda	: miniature apsidal shrine; same as *pañjara*.
Ōma	: basal *pīṭha* of pillar or pilaster.
Pāda	: pillar, *staṁbha*.
Padma	: lotus; capital member (doucene) below the *phalaka* (abacus) shaped like a lotus with petals.
Padma-bandha	: broad fillet, ringing the top of the shaft of a pillar, marked by decorative bands between rows of lotus-petals, separating the shaft from the capital.

Padma-pīṭha : lotus shaped pedestal, consisting of a prominent *padma*-moulding over the *jagati* or *upāna*, the torus forming the *vājana* on top.

Pāli : capital member, same as *padma* but without scalloped petals.

Pañjara : miniature apsidal shrine; same as *nīda*.

Patra-latā : meandering creeper-design or scroll.

Paṭṭā : plain or decorated band occupying the median face of the corbel as if binding the rolls of *taraṅga*-mouldings of the corbel.

Paṭṭikā : projected top slab of the *adhiṣṭhāna* in a line with the vertical norm or *māna-sutra*, a major moulding of considerable thickness.

Phalaka : abacus; wide plank on top of the terminal *saduram* or capital of pillar supporting the corbel or *potikā*.

Pīṭha : base, pedestal.

Potikā : corbel-bracket over pillar.

Praṇāla : chute or channel, water spout, the projecting gargoyle-like spout at the base of the wall or top of the shrine *adhiṣṭhāna* serving as an outlet for *abhiṣeka* water.

Prastara : entablature, consisting of the *uttira* (beam), *vājana*, *valabhī*, *kapota*, *āliṅga* and *antari* mouldings over the walls and pillars.

Prati : platform, crowning moulding over the *adhiṣṭhāna*, above the *paṭṭika* at the base of the wall and showing the level of the the floor inside the structure.

Ratha : 'chariot'; monolithic *vimāna*.

Saduram : square basal, intermediate or terminal section of a pillar separated by octagonal, polygonal or circular intermediary parts.

Śakti-dhvaja : flat shovel shaped finial of the *kūḍū* or *nāsikā* with two small *karṇas* at its base.

Śālā : shrine of *āyatārṣa* (oblong) type with barrel-vault roof with a series of *stūpīs* on its ridge.

Śālā-śikhara : *śikhara* peculiar to *śālā*-shrines, barrel-vaulted, wagon-top or inverted keel-shaped.

Śikhara : *vimāna* roof, domical or four sided with single finial, vaulted with many finials on the ridge, or apsidal with many finials over the horizontal part of ridge.

Staṁbha : pillar, *pāda*.

Stūpī/stūpīkā : finial, morphologically the *uṣṇiśa*, taking in later times, form of the *pūrṇaghaṭa* or *pūrṇakuṁbha*, forming the topmost or ultimate member of *vimāna*, *gopura*, etc.

Śurulyāḷi : *makara* or *vyāla* with long proboscis forming the coping of the parapet of the *sopāna* with a terminal curl of the trunk.

Tāḍī : cushion-shaped capital member above the *kalaśa* and below the *kuṁbha*.

Tala : storey of the *vimāna*.

Tali : excavated cave tomb, subsequently used to denote a cave-temple or structural shrine.

Taraṅga : 'wave'; wavy roll-ornament of the corbel, resembling the 'reed' moulding or 'reeding' of European classical architecture.

Taraṅga-potikā : corbel-bracket with a roll or *taraṅga*-moulding.

Toraṇa : free-standing ornamental foliar and floral festoon forming an entrance supported by two upright columns and often interlaced vertically, copied in wood and stone with greater elaboration and carving or taking the form of a *makara-toraṇa*, mounted on two pillars.

Trikūṭa/trikūṭācala : three *vimānas* connected by a common *adhiṣṭhāna* in a line or placed round a common *maṇḍapa*, as in Cālukyan types.

Tri-paṭṭa : three-faceted.

Upāna : lowermost part of the *adhiṣṭhāna*, projecting beyond the vertical norm and surmounted by the *jagati*. It forms the lowermost visible part of the *vimāna*, the uppermost limit of the same being the *stūpī*.

Upapīṭha : an additional moulded platform or sub-base below the *adhiṣṭhāna*, the mouldings often repeating those of the *adhiṣṭhāna*.

Uttira : principal beam.

Vājana : a top course of the *adhiṣṭhāna*, often replacing the *paṭṭikā*, and a thinner or less projected member than the *paṭṭikā*. In the entablature (*prastara*) it is a projecting member over the principal beam (and below the ceiling) with a similar member below the *kapota* bounding the *valabhī* in between.

Valabhī : a convex, sometimes concave, moulding below the cornice and above the beam, bounded above and below by *vājana*-courses, filling the interspaces between the joists and often decorated by *gaṇas* or *haṁsas*, which are the carved ends of the joists.

Vātāyana	: window.
Vedikā	: railing.
Vimāna	: the shrine from *upāna* to *stūpī* (base to finial); consisting of *adhiṣṭhāna*, *pāda* or *bhitti*, *prastara*, *grīvā*, *śikhara*, and *stūpī*, in case of simple *vimānas* (*ektala*); and with *talas* (storeys) intervening between the lowermost *prastara* below and the *grīvā*, *śikhara* and *stūpī* above in storeyed *vimānas*.
Vira-kaṇṭha	: peg or rod projecting from the centre of the top of the pillar-shaft running through the capital components, viz. *kalaśa*, *tāḍī*, *kuṁbha*, *padma* or *pāli*, and *phalaka* and inserted tenon-like into the base of the *potikā* or corbel.
Vyāla	: leonine *iha-mṛga*.
Vyāla-mālā / vyālāvarī	: decorative frieze with *vyālas* usually as a part of the *adhiṣṭhāna* and on top of the entablature of each *tala*, marking the ends of the cross-joints in original timber-work.

Bibliography

PRIMARY SOURCES

Aitareya Brāhmaṇa. 1920. (trans.) Keith. HOS, Vol. XXV. Cambridge.

Arthaśāsatra, Kautilya's text. 1919. R. Shamashastri (ed.), Mysore; *The Kautilya Arthaśāsatra*. [1960] 1986. R.P. Kangle (ed.), 3 parts. Bombay: University of Bombay (repr.). Delhi: Motilal Banarsidass.

Bhāgavata Purāṇa. [1910] 1986 (repr.). Delhi: Nag Publishers.

Bṛhadāraṇyaka Upaniṣad. 1949. Gorakhpur: Gita Press.

Bṛhat Saṁhitā. 1865. H. Kern, Calcutta; Sudhakar Dvivedi (ed.), 1895, 97. *The Bṛhat Saṁhitā by Varahamihira with the commentary of Bhattotpala*. 2 vols. Benares: E.J. Lazarus & Co.

Daśakumāracarita. [1951] 1983. Narayana Ram Acarya Kavyatirtha (ed.) *Mahākavi Daṇḍiviracitam Daśakumāracarita C*. Bombay: Nirnaya Sagar Press. Repr. New Delhi: Munshiram Manoharlal.

Gṛhya Sūtras. H. Oldenberg, (trans.). Oxford.

Jaiminīya Upaniṣad Brāhmaṇa. 1954. Raghubira and Rakesh Chandra (ed.). Nagpur.

Kumārasambhava. 1919. Commentary by Mallinath. Bombay: Nirnaya Sagar Press.

Maduraikkāñcī. 1974. U.V. Saminathier (ed.). Madras: Tiruvanniyur.

Mahābhārata. Gorakhpur: Gita Press.

Maṇimēkalai. 1985. Venkatacami Nattar and Turaicamip Pillai (eds.). Tinnevelly, Chennai: SISSW.

Nāṭyaśāstra. 1967. Manomohan Ghosh. Trans. 2nd Edn. (rev.). Calcutta.

Puranānūrū. 1971. U.V. Saminathier (ed.). Tiruvanniyur, Madras.

Rāmāyaṇa. 2 vols. Gorakhpur: Gita Press; *The Vālmiki Rāmāyaṇa: Critical Edition*. 1960–75. G.H. Bhatt and U.P. Shah (eds.) 7 vols. Baroda: Oriental Institute.

Raghuvaṁśa. 1914. G.R. Nandarkikar (ed.). Bombay.

Ṛg Veda Saṁhitā, the Sacred Hymns of the Brāhmaṇas, Together with the Commentary of Sayanacārya. 1849–74. Max. Müller (ed.), 6 vols. London: W.H. Allen.

Śatapatha Brāhmaṇa. 1885. A. Weber (ed.). London.

Śilappadikāram. 1992. Venkatacami Nattar (ed.). Tirunveli: SISSW.

Śiva Purāṇa. (V.S. 2011) 1954. (ed.). Bombay: Khemaraja Venkatesvara Press.

Srī Vātsyāyanapranita Kāmasutra. 1891. Yasodhara viracitaya Jayamangala khyaya tikayasametam. Bombay: Nirnaya Sagara Yantralaya.

Srīmad Dvaipāyanamuni pranitam Matsyapurāna. 1907. ASS 54. Poona; *Matsya Purāṇa - A Study*. 1963. Vasudeva Sharan Agrawala. Varanasi: All India Kashiraj Trust.

Subramanian, T.N. 1966. *Thirty Pallava Copper Plates*. Madras: The Tamil History Academy.

Suttanipāta. 1932. R. Chalmers (ed. and tr.). HOS. Cambridge.

Śvetāśvatara Upaniṣad. 1949. Gorakhpur: Gita Press.

Taittarīya Brāhmaṇa. 1855-70. Rajendra Lal Mitra (ed.). Calcutta.

Vāmana Purāṇa: A Study. 1943. Vasudeva Sharan Agrawala. Varanasi; *The Vāmana Purāṇa*. 1967. Anand Swarup Gupta (ed.). Varanasi: All India Kashiraj Trust.

Vāyu Purāṇa. 1880-88. Rajendra Lal Mitra (ed.). 2 vols. Calcutta.

Viṣṇudharmottara Purāṇa. 1958. Vol. 1. Priyabala Shah (ed.). Gaekwad's Oriental Series, no. 130. Baroda: Oriental Institute.

Viṣṇu Purāṇa, 1961. H.H. Wilson. Calcutta; *The Critical Edition of the Viṣṇupurāṇam*. 1997, 99. M.M. Pathak (ed.). 2 vols. Vadodara: Oriental Institute.

SPECIALIZED JOURNALS AND REPORTS (CITED VOLUMES)

Ancient India
Annals of the Bhandarkar Oriental Research Institute
Annual Reports on South Indian Epigraphy
Ars Orientalis
Arts Asiatique
Artibus Asiae
Art Bulletin
Annual Reports of the Archaeological Survey of India
Reports of the Archaeological Survey of Western India
Asiatic Researches
Bulletin of the Deccan College Research Institute
Bulletin of the Madras Government Museum
Bulletin of Museums and Archaeology in U.P.
Bulletin of the School of Oriental Studies
Corpus Inscriptionum Indicarum
East and West
Eastern Art
Epigraphia Carnatica
Epigraphia Indica
Indian Antiquary
Indian Culture
Indian Historical Quarterly
Indian Historical Review
Journal of the American Oriental Society
Journal of the Asiatic Society of Great Britain and Ireland
Journal of the Bombay Branch of the Royal Asiatic Society
Journal of Indian History
Journal of the Indian Society of Oriental Art
Journal of the Institute of Asian Studies
Journal of the Madras University

Journal of Oriental Research
Journal of the Royal Asiatic Society of Bengal
Journal of Southeast Asian Studies
Lalit Kalā
Mārg
Memoirs of Archaeological Survey of India
Oriental Art
Proceedings, Indian History Congress
Rooplekhā
Rupam
South Indian Inscriptions
Studies in History
The Indian Journal of History of Science
Transactions of the Archaeological Survey of South India
The Quarterly Journal of the Mythic Society

SECONDARY SOURCES

Abraham, Meera. 1988. *Two Medieval Merchant Guilds of South India*. New Delhi: Manohar.

Acharya, P.K. 1981. *A Dictionary of Hindu Architecture (Manasara* Series), Vol. I. Delhi: Munshiram Manoharlal.

Adiceam, Marguerite E. 1967. *Contribution a' l' Etude d' Aiyanār Śāstā*. Pondicherry: Publications de l'Institut Français d' Indologie, No. 32.

Agrawala, Vasudeva Sharan. 1963. *Devī Mahātmyaṁ-Glorification of the Great Goddess: A Study*. Varanasi: All India Kashiraja Trust.

——. 1965. *Indian Art*. Varanasi: Prithivi Prakashan.

Ahmad, Aijaz. 1996. *Lineages of the Present: Political Essays*. New Delhi: Tulika.

Altekar, A.S. 1967. *Rashtrakutas and Their Times*. Poona: Oriental Book Agency.

Annigeri, A.M. 1960. *Paṭṭaḍakalla Gudigalu* (in Kannada). Dharwar.

——. 1961. *A Guide to Paṭṭaḍakal Temples*. Dharwar.

Appleyard, D. 1979. *The Conservation in European Cities*. Cambridge, Massachusetts: MIT Press.

Aravamuthan, T.G. 1931. *Portrait Sculpture in South India*. London: India Society.

Ayyangar, M.S. Ramaswami and B.S. Rao. 1922. *Studies in South Indian Jainism*. Vizianagaram Maharaja's College Publication. Madras: Hoe & Co.

Ayyar, C.V. Narayana. 1939. *Origin and Early History of Śaivism in South India*. Madras University Historical Series No. 6. Madras: University of Madras.

Ayyar, P.V. Jagadisa. 1982. *South Indian Shrines (illustrated)*. Rev. & Enl. Ed. New Delhi: Asian Educational Services.

Balambal, V. 1978. *Feudatories of South India* (800-1070 AD). Allahabad: Chugh Publications.

Banerjea, J.N. 1974. *The Development of Hindu Iconography*. 3rd edition. New Delhi: Munshiram Manoharlal.

Banerji, R.D. [1928] 1998. *Bas Reliefs of Bādāmī*, *MASI*, no. 25. Calcutta. Repr. New Delhi: ASI.

Bannerjee, P. 1975. *Early Indian Religions*. Delhi: Orient Longmans.

Barrett, Douglas. 1957. *Elephanta Caves*. Bombay: Bhulabhai Memorial Institute.

Barthes, Roland. 1986. *The Death of the Author, from the Rustle of Language*. Trans Richard Howard. Farrer Straus INC.

Barua, B.M. and K.G. Sinha. 1929. *Bharhūt Inscriptions*. Calcutta.

Basu, S.P. 1982. *The Concept of Brahmā*. Delhi: Sundeep.

Beal, Samuel. [1884] 1969. Xuanzang's *Si-yu-ki: Buddhist Records of the Western World*. London: K. Paul, Trench, Trübner & Co. Repr. Delhi: Oriental Books Reprint Corporation.

Berkson, Carmel. 1992. *Ellora: Concept and Style*. New Delhi: Abhinav / Indira Gandhi Centre for the Arts.

——. 2000. *The Life of Form in Indian Sculpture*. New Delhi: Abhinav Publications.

Bhandarkar, D.R. 1911. *The Guide to Elephanta Island*. Bombay.

Bhandarkar, R.G. [1913] 1965. *Vaiṣṇavism, Śaivism and Minor Religious Systems*. Strassburg. Repr. Ed. Varanasi: Indological Book House.

Bhattacharya, S.K. 1996. *Krishna: Cult in Indian Art*. Delhi: M.D. Publications Pvt. Ltd.

Bhattacharyya, Haridas (ed.). 1975. *The Cultural Heritage of India*, Vol. IV. Repr. Calcutta: Ramakrishna Mission Institute of Culture.

Bhattacharyya, Tarapada. 1963. *The Canons of Indian Art: A Study on Vastuvidya*. Calcutta: Firma KLM Pvt. Ltd.

Boner, Alice. 1962. *Principles of Composition in Hindu Sculpture-Cave Temple Period*. Leiden/ Netherland: E. J. Brill.

Breckenridge, Carol and Peter van der Veer. 1993. *Orientalism and the Post-Colonial Predicament: Perspectives on Orientalism and South Asia*. Philadelphia: University of Pennsylvania Press.

Brown, Percy. 1965. *Indian Architecture: Buddhist and Hindu*. Bombay: D.B. Taraporevala.

Brundtland Commission. 1989. *Our Common Future: Report of the World Commission on Environment and Development*. Oxford: Oxford University Press.

Burgess, James. 1871. *The Rock Temples of Elephantā or Gharipuri*. Bombay: Thacker Vining & Co.

——. 1874. *Report on the First Season's Operations in the Belgām and Kaladgi Districts, ASWI*, Vol. 1. London.

——. 1877. *Rock Temples of Elurā or Verul*. Bombay: Education Society's Press Publication.

——. 1883. *Ellorā Cave Temples*, Archaeological Survey of India, Vol. V. London.

——. [1883] 1994. *Report on the Elura Cave Temples and the Brahmanical and Jaina Caves in Western India, ASWI*, Vol.V. London: Trubner & Co. Repr. New Delhi: ASI.

——. 1887. *The Buddhist Stūpas of Amarāvatī and Jaggayyapeta*. London.

——. 1957. *Elephantā Caves*. Bombay.

——. 1964. *Archaeological Survey of Western India*, Vol. IV. Varanasi: Indological Book House.

——. *A Guide to Elura Cave Temples*. Repr. The Archaeological Department H.E.H. The Nizam's Govt.

Carr, Capt. M.W. [1869] 1984. *The Seven Pagodas on the Coromandel Coast*. Madras. Repr. New Delhi: Asian Educational Services.

Champakalakshmi, R. 1981.*Vaisnava Iconography in the Tamil Country*. Delhi: Orient Longman.

——. [1996] 1999. *Trade, Ideology and Urbanization—South India 300 BC to AD 1300*. Paperback Ed. Delhi: OUP.

——. and S. Gopal (eds.). 1996. *Tradition, Dissent and Ideology*. Delhi: Oxford University Press.

Chandra, Pramod. 1957. *A Guide to Elephanta Caves*. Bombay: Bhulabhai Memorial Institute.

——. 1975. *Studies in Indian Temple Architecture*. Bombay: AIIS.

Chatterjee, A.K. 1970. *The Cult of Skanda Kārttikeya in Ancient India*. Calcutta: Punthi Pustak.

Chhabra, B.Ch. 1965. *Expansion of Indo-Aryan Culture during Pallava Rule (as evidenced by inscriptions)*. Delhi: Munshiram Manoharlal.

Clifford, James and George E. Marcus. 1988. *The Predicament of Culture: Twentieth-Century Ethnography, Literature, and Art*. Harvard: Harvard University Press.

Clothey, Fred W. 1978. *The Many Faces of Murukan: The History and Meaning of a South Indian God*. Hague: Mouton.

Collins, Charles Dillard. 1988. *The Iconography & Ritual of Śiva at Elephanta*. New York: State University of New York Press.

Coomaraswamy, Ananda K. 1956. *Medieval Sinhalese Art*. New York: Pantheon Books.

——. 1965. *History of Indian and Indonesian Art*. New York: Dover Publications, INC.

Coopersmith, *et al.* 1976. *Heritage by Design*. The MacMillan Company of Canada Ltd.

Cousens, Henry. 1926. *Chālukyan Architecture of the Kanarese Districts, ASI*, Vol. XLII, New Imperial Series. Calcutta: Govt. of India Central Publication Branch.

Dayalan, D. 1992. *Early Temples of Tamil Nadu: Their Role in Socio-Economic Life* (c. AD 550-925 AD). New Delhi: Harman Publishing House.

de Certeau, Michel. 1988. *The Writing of History*. Trans. Tom Conley. New York: Columbia University Press.

Dehejia, Vidya. 1972. *Early Buddhist Rock Temples—A Chronological Study*. London: Thames and Hudson.

——. 1977. *Namakkal Caves*. Tamil Nadu State Department of Archaeology.

——. 1997. *Indian Art*. London: Phaidon.

Desai, Devangana. 1975. *Erotic Sculpture of India: A Socio-cultural Study*. New Delhi: Tata McGraw-Hill.

Desai, Kalpana. 1973. *Iconography of Visnu*. Delhi: Abhinav Publications.

Desai, P.B. 1957. *Jainism in South India and Some Jaina Epigraphs* (Jivaraja Jaina Granthamala). Sholapur: Jaina Samskrti Samrakshaka Sangha.

——. 1970. *History of Karnataka*. Dharwar: Kannada Research Institute.

Deshpande, M.N. 1950. *Verulchī Leṇi*. Marathwada Diwali Issue.

Dhavalikar, M.K. 1983. *Masterpieces of Rashtrakuta Art—the Kailas*. Bombay: Taraporevala.

——. 2003. *Monumental Legacy ELLORA*, Monumental Legacy Series, (Series Ed.) Devangana Desai. New Delhi: Oxford University Press.

Doniger, Wendy, *et al.* 1983. *Elephantā: The Cave of Śiva*. New Jersey: Princeton University Press.

Dubreuil, G. J. 1937. *Iconography of Southern India*. Translated from French by A.C. Martin. Paris: Libraire Orientaliste Paul Geuthner.

——. 1914. *Archaeologie Du Sud De L'Inde*. Paris: Libraire Orientaliste Paul Geuthner.

——. [1917] 1972. *Draviḍian Architecture*. Madras. 2nd repr. Varanasi: Bharat Bharati.

——. 1979. *Ancient History of the Deccan*. New Delhi: Classical Publications.

Dutt, N.K. 1925. *The Aryanization of India*. Calcutta.

Dutt, Sukumar. 1962. *Buddhist Monks and Monasteries of India*. London: George Allen and Unwin.

Feilden, Bernard. 1989. *Guidelines for Conservation: A Technical Manual*. New Delhi: INTACH.

Fergusson, James and James Burgess. [1880] 1969. *The Cave Temples of India*. London: Kessinger. Repr. Delhi: Oriental Books Reprint Corporation.

Frederic, Louis. 1959. *Indian Temples and Sculpture*. London: Thames and Hudson.

Gangoly, O.C. 1954. *Indian Architecture*. 3rd Rev. Edn. Bombay: Kutub.

——. and A. Goswami. 1957. *The Art of the Pallavas*. Calcutta: Rupa & Co.

Gangopadhyay, Subinoy. 2002. *Monuments of India (Testimony of Stone-II)*. Kolkata: Dasgupta & Co. Ltd.

Gaston, Anne Marie. 1982. *Siva in Dance, Myth and Iconography*. Delhi: Oxford University Press.

Geertz, Clifford. 1973. *The Interpretation of Cultures: Selected Essays*. New York: Basic Books.

Ghosh, Leila and Dalia Roy. 1986. *Ajantā and Ellorā*. Bombay: India Book House.

Goetz, Hermann. 1960. *The Art of India: Five Thousand Years of Indian Art*. Baden-Baden: Holle (Kunst der Welt).

Goetz, Jaenicke. n.d. *Māmallapuram*. Germany: Scherpe Verlag, Krefeld.

Gopal, B.R. (ed.). 1994. *The Rashtrakutas of Malkhed: Studies in their History and Culture*. Mysore: Mythic Society.

Gopalan, R. 1928. *History of the Pallavas of Kāñcī*. Madras.

Goswami, A. 1958. *The Art of the Rashtrakutas*. Calcutta: Orient Longman.

——. 1959. *Indian Temple Sculpture*. Calcutta: Rupa & Co.

Gupta, P.L. 1989. *Bharatīya Vāstu Kalā*. Varanasi: Vishvavidyalaya Prakashana.

Gupta, S.P. 1980.*The Roots of Indian Art*. New Delhi: B.R. Publications.

Gupta, Shaktim. 1974. *Vishnu and His Incarnations*. Bombay: Somaiya Publications.

Gupte, R.S. 1967. *The Art and Architecture of Aihoḷe*. Bombay: D.B. Taraporevala.

—— and B.D. Mahajan. 1962. *Ajanta, Ellora and Aurangabad Caves*. Bombay: D.B. Taraporevala.

Hardy, Adam. 1995. *Indian Temple Architecture: Form and Transformation: The Karnata Draviḍa Tradition, 7th to 13th Centuries*. New Delhi: Indira Gandhi National Centre for Arts.

Harle, J.C. 1974. *Gupta Sculpture*. Oxford: Clarendon Press.

——. 1986. *The Art and Architecture of the Indian Subcontinent*. Harmondsworth: Penguin.

Harper, Katherine Anne. 1989. *The Iconography of the Saptamatrikas: Seven Hindu Goddesses of Spiritual Transformation*, Studies in Women and Religion, Vol. 28. U.S.A.: The Edwin Mellen Press.

Havell, E.B. 1980. *Indian Sculpture and Painting*. Repr. New Delhi: Cosmo.

Heras, H. 1933. *Studies in Pallava History*. Madras: B.G. Paul and Co.

Huntington, Susan L. 1983. *Pāla-Sena Sculpture*. Leiden: E.J. Brill.

——. 1985. *The Art of Ancient India: Buddhist, Hindu, Jain*. New York: Weatherhill.

Ions, Veronica. 1968. *Indian Mythology*. London: Paul Hamlyn.

Iyengar, P.T. Srinivasan. [1929] 1982. *History of the Tamils*. Madras. Repr. Delhi: Asian Educational Services.

Iyer, K. Bharatha. 1977. *Animals in Indian Sculpture*. Bombay: D.B. Taraporevala.

Jaiswal, Suvira. 1967. *The Origin and Development of Vaisnavism (from 200 BC to 500 AD)*. Delhi: Munshiram Manoharlal.

Jauhari, Manorama. 1969. *South India and Its Architecture*. Varanasi: Bharatiya Vidya Prakashan.

Jayaswal, K.P. [1933] 1990. *History of India, 150 AD to 350 AD*. Lahore. Repr. Delhi: Low Price Publications.

Jha, D.N. and K.M. Shrimali. 2000. *Pracīna Bhārata kā Itihāsa*. Delhi: Delhi University Hindi Directorate.

Kail, Owen C. 1975. *Buddhist Cave Temples of India*. Bombay: D.B. Taraporevala.

——. 1984. *Elephanta—The Island of Mystery*. Bombay: D.B. Taraporevala.

Kamalakar, G. and M. Veerender (eds.). 1993. *Vishnu in Art, Thought and Literature*. Hyderabad: Birla Archaeological and Cultural Research Institute.

Kramrisch, Stella. 1965. *The Art of India*. 3rd Edn. London: The Phaidon Press.

——. [1946] 2002. *The Hindu Temple*, 2 vols. Calcutta. Repr. Delhi: Motilal Banarsidass.

Krishnamurthy, C. 1985. *Śaiva Art and Architecture in South India*. Delhi: Eastern Books Corp.

Krishna Sastri and Rao Bahadur H. 1926. *Two Statues of Pallava Kings and Five Pallava Inscriptions in a Rock Temple at Mahābalipuram, MASI*, No. 26. Calcutta: Govt. of India Central Publication Branch.

Kuiper, F.B.J. 1983. *Ancient Indian Cosmogony*. New Delhi: Vikas.

Kulke, Hermann. [1993] 2001. *Kings and Cult: State Formations and Legitimation in India and Southeast Asia*. Repr. Delhi: Manohar.

Kunst, Arnold and J.C. Shastri (eds.). 1969. *Śiva Purāṇa, Ancient Indian Tradition and Mythology*. Vols. 1-4. Delhi: Motilal Banarsidass.

Legge, James. [1886] 1965. *A Record of Buddhistic Kingdoms*. New York: Paragon Book Reprint Corp.

Leyh, Peter (ed.). 1977. *Untersuchende, Erzahlende, Didaktische und Diskussive Darstellung: Droysen Johann Gustav Historik Historisch-Kritische*. Ausgabe. Stuttgart-Bad Cannstatt.

Lippe, Aschwin. 1970. *The Freer Indian Sculptures*. Washington: Smithsonian Institution.

——. 1978. *Indian Mediaeval Sculpture*. Amsterdam: North Holland Publishing.

Lockwood, Michael. 1982. *Māmallapuram and the Pallavas*. Madras: Christian Literature Society.

——. *et al.* 1974. *Mahābalipuram Studies*. Madras: The Mythic Society.

Longhurst, A.H. [1924, 1928, 1930] 1998. *Pallava Architecture*. Part I, II, III, *Memoirs of the Archaeological Survey of India*, Nos. 17, 33, 40. Calcutta. New Delhi.

Lorenzen, David N. 1972. *The Kāpālikas and Kālāmukhas—Two Lost Saivite Sects*. New Delhi: Motilal Banarsidass.

Mahalingam, T.V. 1969. *Kāñcīpuram in Early South Indian History*. Bombay: Asia Publishing Company.

——. 1970. *The South Indian Temple Complex*. Dharwar: Kannada Research Institute, Karnatak University.

——. n.d. *The Banas in South Indian History*. Sankara-Parvathi Endowment lectures.

Maity, S.K. 1982. *Masterpieces of Pallava Art*. Bombay: D.B. Taraporevala.

Majumdar, R.C. (ed.). 1962-1970. *History and Culture of the Indian People*, Vols. I-III. Bombay: Bharatiya Vidya Bhavan.

——. 1991. *Ancient India*. Delhi: Motilal Banarsidass.

Markel, Stephen. 1980. *An Iconological Assessment of the Great Relief at Mahābalipuram*. Master's Essay. The University of Michigan, Department of the History of Art.

McCrindle. 1973. *The Commerce and Navigation of the Erythraean Sea and Ancient India as Described by Ktesias, the Knidian*. Amsterdam: Philo Press. Repr. Calcutta.

Mehta, Rustam J. 1972. *Masterpieces of the Female Form in Indian Art*. Bombay: D.B. Taraporevala.

Meister, Michael W. (ed.). 1984. *Discourses on Śiva*. Bombay: Vakils, Feffer & Simons Ltd.

——. and M. A.Dhaky (eds.). [1983] 1999. *Encyclopaedia of Indian Temple Architecture, South India Lower Draviḍadesa* (200 BC-AD 1324), Vol. I, Pt. I, Repr. New Delhi: AIIS/Manohar.

——. and M. A.Dhaky (eds.). [1986] 1999. *Encyclopaedia of Indian Temple Architecture, South India Lower Draviḍadesa, Early Phase,* Vol. I, Pt. II, Repr. New Delhi: AIIS/Manohar.

Meshram, Pradip S. 1991. *Early Caves of Maharashtra—A Cultural Study*. New Delhi: Sundeep Prakashan.

Miller, Barbara Stoler (ed.). 1983. *Exploring India's Sacred Art: Selected Writings of Stella Kramrisch*. Philadelphia: University of Pennsylvania Press.

Minakshi, Cadambi. 1938. *Administration and Social Life under the Pallavas*, Madras University Historical Series, no. 13. Madras: University of Madras.

——. 1941. *The Historical Sculptures of the Vaikunthaperumal Temple, MASI*, No. 63. Delhi: ASI.

Mishra, Indumati. 1972. *Pratimā Vijñāna*. Bhopal.

Mishra, V. 1984. *Mahishamardini*. New Delhi: Rajesh Publications.

Mitra, Rajendralal. [1875] 1961-63. *Antiquities of Orissa*. Calcutta.

Mitter, Partha. 1977. *Much Maligned Monsters: A History of European Reactions to Indian Art*. Oxford: Clarendon Press.

Mizuno, Seiichi and Tosio Nagahiro. 1941. *A Study of the Buddhist Cave Temples at Lung-Men*. Tokyo.

Monod and Bruhl, Levi. 1952. *Indian Temples* (plates 83 to 100). Bombay: Oxford University Press.

Mudaliyar, Wijesinha L.C. 1889. *Mahavamsa*. Colombo, Ceylon: G.J.A. Skeen Govt. Print.

Murthy, H.V.S. and R. Ramakrishnan. 1977. *A History of Karnataka*. New Delhi: S. Chand.

Nambi, A.K. 1977. *Glimpses of Tamil Culture Based on the Periya Purāṇam*. Madurai.

Nagar, S.L. 1988. *Mahisuramardini in Indian Art*. Delhi: Aditya Prakashan.

——. 1992. *Cult of Vinayaka*. Delhi: Intellectual Publishing House.

——. 1992. *The Image of Brahmā in India and Abroad*, 2 vols. Delhi: Parimal Publications.

——. 1993. *Varaha in Indian Art, Culture and Literature*. Delhi: Aryan Books International.

Nagaraja Rao, M.S. (ed.). 1978. *The Chalukyas of Bādāmī* (Seminar Papers). Bangalore: The Mythic Society.

Nagaswamy, R. 1968. மாமல்லைடாக்டர்இராநாகசாமி . (*Māmallai*). (in Tamil). Madras: ல்பொருள்ஆய்வுத்துறைவெளியீடு .

——. (ed.). 1968. *Seminar on Inscriptions*. Madras.

Nahar and Ghosh. 1917. *Epitome of Jainism*. Calcutta.

Nandi, R.N. 1973. *Religious Institutions and Cults in the Deccan* c. AD 600-AD 1000. New Delhi: Motilal Banarsidass.

Panchamukhi, R.S. *Karnatak Inscriptions*, Vol. I. Dharwar: Kannada Research Institute.

Pande, G.C. 1984. *Foundations of Indian Culture: Spiritual Vision and Symbolic Forms in Ancient India*. New Delhi: Books and Books.

Pande, R.B. 1962. *Historical and Literary Inscriptions*. Varanasi: Chowkhamba Sanskrit Series.

Pande, Sushmita. 1982. *Birth of Bhakti in Indian Religions and Art*. New Delhi: Books and Books.

Pandey, Durga Prasad. 1989. *Sūrya—Iconographical Study of the Indian Sun God*. Delhi: Parimal.

Panikkar, Shivaji K. 1997. *Saptamātrakā Worship and Sculptures: An Iconological Interpretation of Conflicts and Resolutions in the Storied Brāhmanical Icons*. New Delhi: D.K. Print world.

Paranavitana, S. 1970. *Inscriptions of Ceylon*, Vol. I. Colombo: Department of Archaeology.

Pargiter, F.E. 1962. *Ancient Indian Historical Tradition*. Delhi-Varanasi-Patna: Motilal Banarsidass.

Parimoo, Ratan. 1987. *Vaisnavism in Indian Arts and Culture*. New Delhi: Books and Books.

——. 1988. *Ellora Caves: Sculpture and Architecture*. New Delhi: Books and Books.

——. 1991. *The Art of Ajanta: New Perspectives*, 2 vols. New Delhi: Books and Books.

——. 2000. *Studies in Indian Sculptures: Regional Genres and Interpretations, Essays on New Art History*, 2 vols. New Delhi: Books and Books.

Pathy, T.V. 1980. *Elura—Art and Culture*. New Delhi: Sterling Publishers.

Pillai, V. Kanakasabhai. [1904] 1966. *The Tamils Eighteen Hundred Years Ago*. Tirunelveli. Repr. Madras: SISSW.

Pillay, K.K. 1969. *A Social History of the Tamils*. Madras: University of Madras.

Prasad, B.R. 1980. *Art of South India: Andhra Pradesh*. Delhi: Sundeep Prakashan.

Rabe, Michael. D. 2001.*The Great Penance at Māmallapuram—Deciphering a Visual Text*, (Gen. Ed.) G. John Samuel. Chennai: Institute of Asian Studies.

Rajamanickam, M. 1972. *The Development of Saivism in South India (AD 300-1300)*. Dharmapuram. Madras: University of Madras.

Rajasekhara, S. 1991. *Rashtrakuta Art in Karnataka*. Dharwad: Sujata Publications.

Rajeshwari, D.R. 1988. *Pallava Sculptures*. New Delhi: Intellectual Publishing House.

——. 1989. *Śakti Iconography*. New Delhi: Intellectual Publishing House.

Ramachandran, K.S. 1980. *Archaeology of South India*. Delhi: Sundeep Prakashan.

Ramanujam, A.K. 1979. *Speaking of Śiva*, New York: Penguin Books.

Ramanayya, N.V. [1930] 1992. *An Essay on the Origin of the South Indian Temple*. Madras: Methodist Publishing House. Repr. New Delhi: Asian Educational Services.
Ramaswami, N.S. 1970. *Seven Pagodas, The Art and History of Mahābalipuram*. Madras: Uma Books.
——. 1980. *Māmallapuram–an Annotated Bibliography*. Madras: New Era Publications.
——. 1975. *Māmallapuram*. Tamil Nadu State Department of Archaeology.
Rambach, Pierre and Vitold De Golish. 1955. *The Golden Age of Indian Art*. London: Thames and Hudson.
Ramesh, K.V. 1984. *Chalukyas of Vatapi*. Delhi: Agam Kala Prakashan.
Rao, M.S. Nagaraja (ed.). 1978. *The Chalukyas of Bādāmī* (Seminar Papers). Bangalore: The Mythic Society.
Rao, M.V. Krishna. 1936. *The Gaṅgas of Talakad*. Madras: B.G. Paul.
Rao, T.A. Gopinatha. 1985. *Elements of Hindu Iconography*, 2 vols., 2 Pts., 2nd Edition, 2nd Repr. New Delhi: Motilal Banarsidass.
Ray, Amita. 1983. *Life and Art of Early Andhradesa*. Delhi: Agam Kala Prakashan.
Ray, H.P. 1986. *Monastery and Guild: Commerce under the Sātavāhanas*. Delhi: OUP.
Raychaudhuri, H.C. 2002. *Political History of Ancient India*. Repr. Delhi: OUP.
Rea, Alexander. 1909. *Pallava Architecture*, ASI, New Imperial Series, Vol. XXXIV. Madras: The Superintendent, Government Press.
——. 1970. *Chālukyan Architecture, Report on the Archaeological Survey of Southern India*, Vol. III, New Imperial Series, Vol. XXI. New Delhi/Varanasi: Indological Book House.
Rowland, Benjamin. 1970. *The Pelican History of Art: The Art and Architecture of India-Buddhist-Hindu-Jain*. Paperback Edn. USA: Penguin Books.
Raz, Ram. 1834. *Essay on the Architecture of the Hindus*. London: Royal Asiatic Society.
Said, Edward. 1978. *Orientalism*. London: Penguin Books.
——. 1983. *The World, the Text, the Critique*. Cambridge, Mass: Harvard University Press.
——. 1994. *Culture and Imperialism*. London: Vintage.
Saletore, B.A. 1936. *Ancient Karnataka*, Vol. I. Poona: Oriental book Agency.
Sastri, Hirananda. 1934. *A Guide to Elephanta*. New Delhi: Manager of Publications.
Sastri, K.A. Nilakanta. 1929. *The Pāndyan Kingdom from the Earliest Times to the Sixteenth Century*. London: Luzac.
——. 1948. *The Tamil Kingdom of South India*. Bombay: The National Information & Publications.
——. 1963. *Development of Religion in South India*. Bombay: Orient Longman.
——. 1964. *The Culture and History of Tamils*. Calcutta: K.L. Mukhopadhyay.
——. 1972. *Foreign Notices of South India: From Megasthenes to Ma Huan*. Madras: University of Madras.
——. [1955] 1999. *A History of South India: From Prehistoric Times to the Fall of Vijaynagar*, 4th Edn. New Delhi: Oxford University Press.
Sathianathaier, R. 1956. *Studies in the Ancient History of Tondaimandalam*. Madras.
——. 1970. 'The Pallavas' in *HCIP*, Vol. III. Bombay: Bharatiya Vidya Bhavan.
Scott, Geoffrey. 1961. *The Architecture of Humanism*. London: Methuen.
Sen, Sukumar. 1962. *Buddhist Monks and Monasteries of India*. London: George Allen & Unwin.
Sewell, R.B. 1932. *Historical Inscriptions of Southern India*. Madras: University of Madras.
Sharma, B.N. 1976. *Iconography of Sadāśiva*. Delhi: South Asia Books.
Shukla, D.N. 1968. *Prasada-Nivesha-Samarāṅgaṇa Sūtradhāra*, Pt. III (A New Light on History of Temple Art & Architecture—Brahman, Bauddha & Jaina). Chandigarh.
Sikri, Richa. 2002. *Early Brahmanical Cults and Associated Iconography*. New Delhi: Kaveri Books.
Singh, Madanjeet. 1965. *The Cave Paintings of Ajantā*. London: Thames and Hudson.

Singh, Upinder. 2009. *A History of Ancient and Early Medieval India: From the Stone Age to the 12th Century*. Delhi: Pearson.

Sinha, Kanchan. 1979. *Kārttikeya in Indian Art and Literature*. Delhi: Sandeep Prakashan.

Sivaramamurti, C. 1955. *Royal Conquests and Cultural Migration in South India and Deccan*. Calcutta: Indian Museum.

——. 1955. *Mahābalipuram*. New Delhi: ASI.

——. 1961. *Kalugumalai and Early Pandyan Rock-cut Shrines*. Bombay: N.M. Tripathi Pvt. Ltd.

——. 1961. *Indian Sculpture*. New Delhi: Allied Publishers.

——. 1963. *South Indian Bronzes*. New Delhi: Lalit Kala Akademi, Lalit Kala Series of Indian Art.

——. 1968. *South Indian Paintings*. New Delhi: National Museum.

——. 1974. *Natarāja in Art, Thought and Literature*. Delhi: National Museum.

——. 1982. *Śrī Lakshmī in Indian Art and Thought*. Delhi: Kanak Publications.

——. 1984. *Sculpture Inspired by Kālidāsa*. New Delhi: Kanak Publications.

Smith, V.A. 1908. *The Early History of India*. Oxford: The Clarendon Press.

——. *et al.* 1975. *India: Its Epigraphy, Antiquities, Archaeology, Numismatic & Architecture*. New Delhi: Ess Ess Publications.

Soundara Rajan, K.V. 1969. *Early Temple Architecture in Karnataka and its Ramifications*. Dharwar: Kannada Research Institute.

——. 1972. *Indian Temple Styles*. New Delhi: Munshiram Manoharlal.

——. 1980. *Art of South India: Tamil Nadu and Kerala*. New Delhi: Sundeep Prakashan.

——. 1980. *Art of South India: Deccan*. New Delhi: Sundeep Prakashan.

——. 1981. *Cave Temples of Deccan*, (Architectural Survey of Temples). New Delhi: ASI.

——. 1981. *Glimpses of Indian Culture–Architecture, Art and Religion*. Delhi: Sundeep Prakashan.

Spink, Walter M. 1967. Ajantā to Ellorā. *Mārg*. Bombay.

——. n.d. *Ajanta—A Brief History and Guide*. Asian Art Archives of the University of Michigan.

Srinivasan, C.R. 1979. *Kanchipuram through the Ages*. New Delhi: Agam Kala Prakashan.

Srinivasan, K.R. 1964. *Rock-cut Monuments in Archaeological Remains, Monuments and Museums*. Vol. I. Delhi: ASI.

——. [1964] 1993. *Cave Temples of Pallavas* (Architectural Survey of Temples). Repr. New Delhi: ASI.

——. 1975. *The Dharamaraja Ratha and Its Sculptures—Mahābalipuram*. New Delhi: Abhinav.

——. 1998. *Temples of South India*. Repr. Delhi: National Book Trust.

Srinivasan, P.R. 1982. *The Indian Temple Art and Architecture*. Mysore: University of Mysore.

Srivastava, V.C. 1972. *Sun Worship in Ancient India*. Allahabad: Indological Publications.

Stern, P. 1961. *Evolution du Style Indien d' Amarāvatī*. Paris: Presses Universitaires de France.

Stierlin, Henri. 1998. *Hindu India—From Khajuraho to the Temple City of Madurai*. Italy: Taschen World Architecture.

Subrahmanian, N. 1966. *Saṅgam Polity: The Administrative and Social Life of the Saṅgam Tamils*. New York.

Subramanian, T.N. 1967. *The Pallavas of Kanci in South-East Asia*.

Tarr, Gary. 1969. *Architecture of the Early Western Chalukyas*. Los Angeles: University of California.

Tewari, S.P. 1979. *Hindu Iconography Based on Anthological Verses, Literature, Art and Epigraphs*. New Delhi: Agam Kala Prakashan.

Thakur, Upendra. 1981. *On Kārttikeya*. Varanasi: Chaukhamba Orientalia.

Thapar, Romila. 1992. *A History of India*, Vol. I, repr. New Delhi: Penguin Books.

Tiwari, M.N. and Kamal Giri. 1991. *Madhyakalīna Bharatīya Mūrti Kalā*. Varanasi: Vishwavidyalaya Prakashan.

Touche, La. 1917. *A Bibliography of Indian Geology and Physical Geography*. Calcutta: GSI.

Tucci, Giuseppe. 1988. *Stūpa—Art, Architecture and Symbolism,* (trans.) Uma Marina Vesci and Lokesh Chandra (eds.). New Delhi: Aditya Prakashan.

Tyagi, I.C. 1982. *Shaivism in Ancient India*. Meerut: Meenakshi Prakashan.

Vaidya, C.V. 1989. *History of Mediaeval Hindu India, (Being a History of India from 600 to 1200 AD),* Vol. 2. Poona: Oriental Book Supply Agency.

Vakil, Kanaiyalal H. 1932. *The Rock Cut Temples Around Bombay at Elephanta and Jogeshwari, Mandapeshwar and Kanheri*. Bombay: D.B. Taraporevala.

Vansina, Jan. 1985. *Oral Tradition as History*. Madison: Wisconsin University Press.

Vasudeva Rao, T. N. 1979. *Buddhism in the Tamil Country*. Annamalainagar: Annamalai University.

Vatsyayan, Kapila. 1982. *The Dance in Indian Painting*. Delhi: Abhinav Prakashan.

Volwahsen, Andreas. 1969. *Living Architecture: Indian*. Calcutta: Oxford and IBH Publishing.

Warmington, E.H. 1974. *The Commerce between the Roman Empire and India*. Delhi: Munshiram Manoharlal.

Watt, G. 1908. *The Commercial Products of India*. London: John Murray.

Watters, T. (1904-1905) 1973. *On Yuan Chuang's Travels in India,* Vol. II. London: Royal Asiatic Society. Repr. Delhi: Munshiram Manoharlal.

Wheeler, R.E.M. 1955. *Rome Beyond The Imperial Frontiers*. London: G. Bell & Sons.

White, Hayden. 1973. *Metahistory: Historical Imagination in Nineteenth Century Europe*. Baltimore: Johns Hopkins University Press.

——. 1978. *The Burden of History, Tropics of Discourse: Essays in Cultural Criticism*. Baltimore: Johns Hopkins University Press.

Willetts, William Y. 1966. *An Illustrated Annotated Annual Bibliography of Mahābalipuram on the Coromandel Coast of India (1582-1962)*. Kuala Lumpur: Department of Indian Studies, University of Malaya.

Williams. 1982. *The Art of Gupta India: Empire and Province*. Princeton: Princeton University Press.

Yadav, Neeta. 2001. *Ardhanarisvara in Art and Literature*. New Delhi: D.K. Printworld.

Yadav, Nirmala. 1997. *Ganeśa in Indian Art and Literature*. Jaipur: Publication Scheme.

Yazdani, Ghulam. 1937. *The Rock Hewn Temples of Aurangabad*. Reprint from *Indian Art & Letters,* Vol. XI, No. 1, London: The India Society.

——. 1960. *The Early History of the Deccan*. Oxford: Oxford University Press.

Zimmer, Heinrich. 1946. *Myths and Symbols in Indian Art and Civilization*. New York: Harper & Row.

——. 1955. *The Art of Indian Asia: Its Mythology and Transformations,* 2 vols., New York: Pantheon Books.

REFERRED ARTICLES/CHAPTERS

Agrawala, R.C. 2001-02. 'A Note on Pitcher Carriers in Gajalakshmī Reliefs', *Kalā,* VIII, pp. 5-8.

Ahmad, Aijaz. 1987. 'Jameson's Rhetoric of Otherness and the National Allegory', *Social Text,* 17, Fall, pp. 3-25.

Aiyanger, S.K. 1917. 'The Antiquities of Mahābalipuram', *IA,* XLVI. Bombay, pp. 49-56.

Anandasivan, R. and K.K. Ramamurthy. 1984. 'Three Inscriptions of the Pallava period: A Study' in K.V. Ramesh (ed.), *Svāsti-Srī*. Delhi, pp. 145-49.

Annigeri, A.M. 1978. 'Religion under the Chālukyas of Bādāmī' in M.S. Nagaraja Rao (ed.), *The Chālukyas of Bādāmī* (Seminar Papers), pp. 232-39.

Appadurai, Arjun and Carol Breckenridge. 2001. 'Museums are Good to Think: Heritage on View in India' in D. Boswell and J. Evans (eds.), *Representing the Nation: A Reader, Histories, Heritage and Museums,* pp. 404-20.

Avruch, K. and P.W. Black. 1991. 'The Cultural Question and Conflict Resolution', *Peace and Change*, No. 16, pp. 22-45.

Ayyar, K.R. Venkatarama. 1947. 'Medieval Trade, Craft and Merchant Guilds in South India', *Journal of Indian History*, pp. 268-80.

——. 1956-57. 'A Note on the Kalabhras', *TASSI 1956-57*, pp. 94-100.

Babington. B.G. 1830. 'An Account of the Sculptures and Inscriptions at Mahāmalaipur', *Transactions of the Royal Asiatic Society*, Vol. II. London, pp. 259-69.

Balasubramaniam. *LK*, No. 10, Oct 1961, pp. 41-44.

Banerjea, J.N. 1938. 'Some Folk Goddesses of Ancient and Medieval India', *Indian Historical Quarterly*, XIV, pp. 107-09.

Basham, A.L. 1990. 'Geographical Factors in South Indian History' in H.M. Nayak and B.R. Gopal (eds.), *South Indian Studies (Dr. T.V. Mahalingam Commemoration Volume)*. Mysore: Geetha Book House, pp. 17-22.

Baumer, Bettina. 1988. 'From Guhā to Akāsa: The Mystical Cave in the Vedic and Saiva Traditions' in Ratan Parimoo (ed.), *ECSA*. New Delhi, pp. 59-79.

Berkson, Carmel. 1982. 'An Approach towards Examining Style in the Cave temples' in Bettina Baumer (ed.), *Rupa-Pratirupa*. Delhi, pp. 57-85.

——. 1983. 'The Historical Context and Evolution of Style at Elephanta' in Wendy Doniger O' Flaherty, George Michell and Carmel Berkson (eds.), *Elephanta—The Cave of Śiva: Essays*. New Jersey: Princeton University, pp. 3-15.

——. 1988. 'Daśāvatāra Cave: Its Importance in the History of World Art', *ECSA*. New Delhi, pp. 207-29.

Bhandarkar, D.R. 1911. 'Epigraphic Notices and Questions, VIII—The Kailāśa Temple of Ellorā', *IA*, Vol. 40, pp. 237-38.

Bhattacharyya, Asok K. 1988. 'Ellorā Sculpture: A Stylistic Examination', *ECSA*, pp. 271-77.

Bloch. 'Caves and Inscriptions in Ramgarh hills', *ARASI*, 1903/04, pp. 123-31.

Bolon, Carol Radcliffe. 1988. 'Cālukyas of Bādāmī: Karnāṭa' in M.W. Meister, M.A. Dhaky and Krishna Deva (eds.), *Encyclopaedia of Indian Temple Architecture: North India*, Vol. II, Pt. 1. Delhi: AIIS/Oxford, pp. 275-310.

Burgess, J. 1877. 'Rock-cut Temples at Bādāmī in the Dekhan', *IA*, VI, pp. 363-64.

Chakrabarty, Dipesh. 2006. 'Politics Unlimited: The Global Adivasi and the Debate about the Political' in Bengt G. Karlsson and Tanka B. Subba (eds.), *Indigeneity in India*. London: Kegan Paul, pp. 235-45.

——. 2007. 'From the Colonial to the Postcolonial: India and Pakistan in Transition' in Dipesh Chakrabarty, Rochona Majumdar and Andrew Sartori (eds.), *From the Colonial to the Postcolonial: India and Pakistan in Transition*. New Delhi: Oxford University Press, pp. 1-12.

Chambers, W. 1788. 'Some Account of the Sculptures and Ruins at Mavalipuram', *Asiatick Researches*, Vol. I. Calcutta, pp. 145-70.

Champakalakshmi, R. 1996. 'From Devotion and Dissent to Dominance: The *Bhakti* of the Tamil *Alvar* and *Nayanar*' in R. Champakalakshmi and S. Gopal (eds.), *Tradition, Dissent and Ideology*. Delhi: Oxford University Press.

——. 1991. 'Urban processes in Early Medieval Tamil Nadu' in Indu Banga (ed.), *The City in Indian History: Urban Demography History and Politics*. New Delhi: (UHAI) Manohar, pp. 47-68.

Chandra, Lokesh. 1988. 'Ellorā as Śūnyata and Rūpam' in Ratan Parimoo, *et al.* (eds.), *ECSA*, pp. 131-44.

Chandra, Pramod. 1975. 'The Study of Indian Temple Architecture' in Pramod Chandra (ed.), *Studies in Indian Temple Architecture* (Papers presented at a Seminar held in Varanasi, 1967). Bombay: AIIS, pp. 1-39.

Chatham, Doris Clark. 1981. 'Pratihāras from Paṭṭaḍakal to Ellorā: The Early Western Chālukya Basis for the Sculpture Style of the Kailāśa Temple', *Chhavi-2*, pp. 71-79.
——. 1984. 'Myth, Cult, and Cetana at the Kailasa Temple, Ellora' in Michael W. Meister (ed.), *Discourses on Śiva*. Bombay: Vakils, Feffer & Simons Ltd., pp. 156-69.
Codrington, K.de. B. 1930. 'Ancient Sites Near Ellorā, Deccan', *IA*, LIX, pp. 10-13.
Coomaraswamy, A.K. 1912 July. 'The Dance of Śiva', *Siddhanta Dipikā*, Vol. XIII.
——. 1985. 'Votive Sculptures of Ancestors and Donors in Indian Art', *Fundamentals of Indian Art*, Vol. 1, Jaipur, pp. 31-34.
Cousens, Henry. 1907-08. 'The Ancient Temples of Aihoḷe', *ASIAR*.
Desai, Devangana. 1994. 'Erotic Motifs in Rashtrakuta Art' in B.R. Gopal (ed.), *The Rāṣṭrakūṭas of Malkhed*. Mysore, pp. 374-79.
Deshpande, M.N. 1955. 'Rock-cut Caves in Western India', *Buddhist Remains in India*. Delhi: Indian Council for Cultural Relations.
——. 1959. 'The Rock Cut Caves of Pitalkhora', *Ancient India*, No. 15, pp. 46-93.
——. 1988. 'Kailāśa: A Study in its Symbolism in the Light of Contemporary Philosophical Concepts and Traditions', *ECSA*, pp. 230-54.
Dhavalikar, M.K. 1988. 'Kailāśa-A Structural Analysis', *ECSA*, pp. 351-60.
Dikshit, G.S. 1994. 'Trade under the Rashtrakutas' in B.R. Gopal (ed.), *The Rāshtrakūṭas of Malkhed: Studies in Their History and Culture*. Mysore: Geetha Book House, pp. 119-22.
Divakaran, Odile. 1971. 'Les temples d' Alampur et de ses environs au temps des Chalukya de Bādāmī', *Arts Asiatiques*, Vol. XXIV, pp. 51-74.
——. 1981. 'The Beginnings of Early Western Chalukya Art', in Ananda Krishna and Kamal Giri (eds.), *Chhavi-2, Rai Krishnadasa Felicitation Volume*. Varanasi. pp. 59-66.
——. 1987. 'Some Characteristics of the Early Brāhmanical Caves in the Pāndyan Country', M.S. Nagaraja Rao (ed.), *Kusumāñjali*, pp. 173-78.
Doniger, Wendy O' Flaherty. 1983. 'The Myths depicted at Elephanta' in Wendy Doniger O' Flaherty, George Michell and Carmel Berkson (eds.), *Elephanta—The Cave of Śiva: Essays*. New Jersey: Princeton University, pp. 27-39.
Dumont, Louis. 1959. 'A Structural Definition of a Folk Deity of Tamil Nad: Aiyanar, the Lord', in Louis Dumont and D. Pocock (eds.), *Contributions to Indian Sociology*. Paris/Hague, No. III, pp. 81-98.
Eggeling, J. [1874] 1971. 'An Inscription from Bādāmī', *IA*, III, repr. Delhi, pp. 305-06.
Erskine. 1819. 'Account of the Cave Temple of Elephanta', *Transactions of the Literary Society of Bombay*, Vol. I, London.
Etter, Anne-Jullie. 2011. 'Antequarian Knowledge and the Preservation of Indian Monuments at the Beginning of Nineteenth Century' in Indira Sengupta and Daud Ali (eds.), *Knowledge Production, Pedagogy and Institutions in Colonial India*. New York.
Ganesan, Saw. 1971. 'Fresh light on Pallava History' in Saw Ganesan (ed.), *Prof. K.A. Nilakanta Sastri Felicitation Volume*. Madras, pp. 474-78.
Goetz, Hermann. 1952. 'The Kailāśa of Ellorā and the Chronology of Rastrakūta Art', *Artibus Asiae*, Vol. XV, pp. 84-107.
Goldingham, J. 1798. 'Some Account of the Sculptures at Mahābalipuram, Usually Called the Seven Pagodas', *Asiatic Researches*, Vol. V. Calcutta, pp. 69-80.
Gurukkal, Rajan. 1981. 'Aspects of Early Iron Age Economy: Problems of Agrarian Expansion of Tamilakam', *Proceedings, Indian History Congress*, 42nd session. Bodhgaya, pp. 71-79.
——. 1986 (July-December). 'Aspects of the Reservoir System of Irrigation in the Early Pandya State', *Studies in History*, N.S., Vol. II (2), pp. 155-64.

——. 1987. 'From the Royalty of Icons to the Divinity of Royalty: Aspects of Vaiṣṇava Icons and Kingship in Medieval South India' in Ratan Parimoo (ed.), *Vaiṣṇavism in Indian Arts and Culture*. New Delhi: Books and Books, pp. 119-24.

Harle, J.C. 1963. 'Durgā: Goddess of Victory', *Artibus Asiae,* Vol. XXVI (3-4), pp. 227-46.

——. 1970. 'Some Remarks on Early Western Chālukya Sculpture' in P. Pal (ed.), *Aspects of Indian Art*. Los Angeles/Leiden.

——. 1971. 'Two Yavana *Dvārapālas* at Aihoḷe' in Saw Ganesan (ed.), *Professor K. A. Nilakanta Sastri Felicitation Volume*. Madras, pp. 210-13.

Heitzman, J. 1989 (March). 'Early Buddhism, Trade and Empire', *Journal of Southeast Asian Studies,* Vol. XX (1), pp. 121-37.

Hirsh, M. 1983. 'Royal Implication of the Unique Subject Matter, Scale and Format in the Narrative Reliefs at Māmallapuram' in T.S. Maxwell (ed.), *Saras Bulletin,* South Asian Religious Art Studies, Issue 83:3, pp. 56-63.

Huntington, J.C. 1974-75. 'The Lomas Rsi: Another Look', *Archives of Asian Art,* Vol. XXVIII, pp. 34-56.

Huntington, Susan. 1981. 'Iconographic Reflections on the Arjuna Ratha' in Joanna G. Williams (ed.), *Kala Darśana*. New Delhi, pp. 57-67.

Jameson, Frederic. 1986. 'Third World Literature in the Era of Multinational Capital', *Social Text,* 15, Fall, pp. 65-88.

Jeyechandrun, A.V. 1988. 'Draviḍian Influence on Ellorā Cave Temple Architecture', *ECSA*, pp. 372-78.

Kamat, Jyotsna K. 1978. 'Social Life and Economic Conditions under the Chalukyas of Bādāmī' in M.S. Nagaraja Rao (ed.), *The Chalukyas of Bādāmī* (Seminar Papers). Bangalore: The Mythic Society, pp. 177-85.

Kannal, Deepak H. 1988. 'The Regional Lineages and Possible Masters at Kailāśanātha Temple of Ellorā', *ECSA*, pp. 255-70.

Katti, Madhav N. 1983. 'Note on the Mahishamardinī Panel at Saluvankuppam' in Narasimha Murthy and Gururaja Rao (eds.), *Raṅgāvallī—Recent Researches in Indology*. Delhi, pp. 225-28.

Kosambi, D.D. 1955. 'Dhenukākaṭa', *Journal of the Asiatic Society of Bombay,* 30, pp. 59-60.

Kramrisch, Stella. [1946] 1983. 'The Image of Mahādeva in the Cave Temple on Elephanta Island' in Barbara Stoler Miller (ed.), *Exploring India's Sacred Art: Selected Writings of Stella Kramrisch*. Philadelphia: University of Pennsylvania Press, pp. 141-47.

——. 1984. 'The Great Cave Temple of Śiva in Elephanta: Levels of Meaning and their Form' in Michael W. Meister (ed.), *Discourses on Śiva*, pp. 1-10.

Kumar, Krishna. 1976 (Sept.-Dec.). 'Brahmanical cave-temples at Ellorā', *East and West,* N.S. (3-4).

Leong, W.T. 1997. 'Culture and the State: Manufacturing Traditions for Tourism' in J.T. Ong, C.K. Tong and E.S. Tan (eds.), *Understanding Singapore Society*. Singapore: Times Academic Press, pp. 513-34.

Leyden, R. von. 1960 (Sept). 'Drama in Stone', 'Elephanta', *Mārg,* Vol. XIII (4), pp. 61-64.

Lippe, Aschwin. 1964. 'Unusual Icons at Bādāmī', *Summaries of Paper*, XXVI International Congress of Orientalists. New Delhi, pp. 143-51.

——. 1967. 'Some Sculptural Motifs on Early Chālukya Temples', *Artibus Asiae,* Vol. XXIX (1), pp. 5-24.

——. 1975. 'Some South Indian Icons', *Artibus Asiae,* Vol. XXXVII (3), pp. 169-97.

——. 1972. 'Early Chālukya Icons', *Artibus Asiae,* Vol. XXXIV (4), pp. 273-318.

Lockwood, Michael. 1974. 'God-King Images and Cult Worship' in Michael Lockwood *et al.* (eds.), *Mahābalipuram Studies*. Madras, pp. 42-61.

——. 1974. 'A Numerical Taxonomic Analysis of Various *Somaskandas*', *Mahābalipuram Studies*, pp. 106-11.

——. and Gift Siromoney. 1974. 'Pallava *Dvārapālas* and the Mahiṣahamardinī Cave', *Mahābalipuram Studies*, pp. 7-17.

——. P. Dayanandan and Gift Siromoney. 1974. 'Pallava *Somaskanda*', *Mahābalipuram Studies*, pp. 18-33.

——. and A. Vishnu Bhat. 1974. 'Pallava *Gaṅgādhara*', *Mahābalipuram Studies*, pp. 34-41.

Mahadevan, Iravatham. 1968. 'Corpus of Tamil Brāhmī Inscriptions' in R. Nagaswamy (ed.), *Seminar on Inscriptions*. Madras, Nos. 3, 6, 71 and 76.

——. 1971. 'Pallavas and the "Jar" Legends' in Saw Ganesan (ed.), *Prof. K.A. Nilakanta Sastri Felicitation Volume*. Madras, pp. 84-88.

——. 1981. 'An Old Sinhalese Inscription from Arikamedu', *Seminar on Epigraphy, Kuppuswami Sastri Birth Centenary*. Madras.

——. 1994. 'Ancient Tamil Contacts Abroad: Recent Epigraphic Evidence', *Journal of the Institute of Asian Studies*, Vol. XII (1). Colombo, pp. 136-55.

Mankodi, Kirit. 1973. 'Gaṅgā Tripathagā', *Artibus Asiae*, Vol. XXXV, pp. 135-49.

Mate, M.S. and Shobhana Gokhale. 1971. 'Aihoḷe: An Interpretation' in Shrinivas Ritti and B.R. Gopal (eds.), *Studies in Indian History and Culture: Volume Presented to Dr. P.B. Desai*. Dharwar, pp. 501-04.

Meister, M. 1981. 'Sub-urban Planning and Rock Cut Architecture in India' in Nagaraja Rao (ed.), *Madhu: Recent Researches in Indian Archaeology and Art History, M.N. Deshpande Festschrift*, pp. 157-64.

Michell, George. 1975. 'Dating the Mahakutesvara Temple at Mahakut', *OA*, Vol. XIX (3).

——. 1983. 'The Architecture of Elephanta: An Interpretation', in *Elephanta—The Cave of Śiva*. New Jersey: Princeton University, pp. 17-26.

Mitterwallner, Gritli, v. 1984. 'Evolution of the Liṅga' in Michael W. Meister (ed.), *Discourses on Śiva*. Bombay, pp. 12-31.

Minakshi, C. 'Buddhism in South India', *South Indian Studies II*, pp. 83-131.

Mirashi, V.V. 'Rashtrakutas of Manapura', *Annals of the Bhandarkar Oriental Research Institute, Poona*, XXV, pp. 36-50.

Nagaraj, Nalini. 1983. 'Sculpture under the Chalukyas of Bādāmī' in A.V. Narasimha Murthy and B.K. Gururaja Rao (eds.), *Raṅgavalli—Recent Researches in Indology: Sri S.R. Rao Felicitation Volume*. Delhi, pp. 215-23.

Nagaraja Rao, M.S. 1973. 'Chronology of Papanatha Temple at Paṭṭaḍakal: A Reconsideration' in K.V. Ramesh (ed.), *Srikaṇṭhikā*. Mysore, pp. 36-39.

Nagaswamy, R. 1962. 'New Light on Mamallapuram', repr. from the *Silver Jubilee Volume of the Archaeological Society of South India*, pp. 1-50.

——. 1981. 'An Outstanding Epigraphical Discovery in Tamil Nadu', *Fifth International Conference Seminar on Tamil Studies*. Madurai.

Neff, Muriel. 1960 (Sept.). 'Elephantā', *Mārg*, Vol. XIII (4), pp. 1-59.

Nietzsche, Friedrich. 1983. 'On the Uses and Disadvantages of History for Life', *Untimely Meditations*, trans R.J. Hollingdale. Cambridge, pp. 83-100.

Padigar, Srinivas V. 1988. 'Craftsmen's Inscriptions from Bādāmī: Their Significance', *ECSA*, pp. 398-405.

Pande, Susmita. 1982. 'Contribution of the *Alvars* and *Nayanars*', *Birth of Bhakti in Indian Religions and Art*. New Delhi: Books & Books, pp. 112-40.

Panikkar, Shivaji. 1988. 'Sapta-Mātṛkā Sculptures at Ellorā—An Iconological Analysis', *ECSA*, pp. 291-309.

Parimoo, Ratan. 1986. 'On the Sculptures from Ellora Caves and the Problem of Deccan School' in Lokesh Chandra and Jyotindra Jain (eds.), *Dimensions of Indian Art: Pupul Jayakar Seventy*, Vol. I, Delhi, pp. 345-53.

——. 2000. 'The Aihoḷe Sub-style of Chalukyan Sculpture', *Studies in Indian Sculpture: Essays on New Art History*. Vol. I. New Delhi: Books & Books, pp. 220-35.

Pathy, T.V. 1971. 'Verūl Śivālayamahātmya Ms: And Some More Facts about Ellorā' in Shrinivas Ritti and B.R. Gopal (eds.), *Studies in Indian History and Culture: Prof. P.B. Desai Felicitation Volume*. Dharwar, pp. 105-09.

Prakash, Gyan. 1990. 'Writing Post-Orientalist Histories of the Third World: Perspectives from Indian Historiography', *Comparative Studies in Society and History*, 32(2), April, pp. 383-408.

Prasad, B.R. 'Rāṣṭrakūṭa Temples at Bhavanāsī Saṅgam', *Artibus Asiae*, Vol. XXXIV, pp. 211-21.

——. 1994. 'Temples of the Rashtrakuta Period in Andhra Pradesh' in B.R. Gopal (ed.), *The Rāshtrakūṭas of Malkhed: Studies in Their History and Culture*. Mysore: Geetha Book House, pp. 319-23.

——. 1994. 'List of Temples in Andhra Pradesh', *The Rāshtrakūṭas of Malkhed*. Mysore, pp. 309-14.

Rajasekhara, S. 1973. 'Identification of the Early Chālukyan Temples' in K.V. Ramesh (ed.), *Śrīkanthikā*. Mysore, pp. 16-22.

Rama Rao, M. 1963. 'Early Chālukya Architecture', *Journal of Indian History*, Silver Jubilee Number, pp. 437-38.

Ramesan, N. 1972. 'Studies in Medieval Deccan History', *A.P. Govt. Archaeological Series No. 20*, Copper plate Inscriptions of the State Museum, Vol. III. Hyderabad, pp. 8-71.

Rangarajan, Haripriya. 2000. 'Varāha Images in Madhya Pradesh: An Iconographic Study' in Sinha and Dwivedi (eds.), *Proceedings of Indian Art History Congress*. Guwahati/ New Delhi, pp. 129-50.

Rangaswamy, C.V. 1994. 'Some Popular Cults in the Rashtrakuta Period' in B.R. Gopal (ed.), *The Rashtrakutas of Malkhed: Studies in their History and Culture*. Mysore, pp. 138-45.

Rao, S.R. 1972. 'A Note on the Chronology of Early Chalukyan Temples', *Lalit Kala*, 15, pp. 9-18.

Rousen, Jorn. 1996. 'Some Theoretical Approaches to Intercultural Historiography', *History and Theory*, 35 (4), December, pp. 5-22.

Sarma, I.K. 1987. 'Beginnings of Temple Architecture at Kanchipuram, Raw Materials and Religious Impacts', *Archaeology and History: Essays in Memory of A.K. Ghosh*, Vol. II. Delhi, pp. 545-51.

Sastri, K.A. Nilakanta. 1960. 'The Chalukyas of Bādāmī' in G. Yazdani (ed.), *The Early History of the Deccan*. Oxford, pp. 201-32.

Sen Gupta, R. 1960. 'The Panels of Kalyāṇasundarāmūrti at Ellorā', *LK*, 7, pp. 14-18.

Sengupta, I. 2013. 'A Conservation Code for the Colony: John Marshall's Conservation Manual and Monument Preservation between Indian and Europe' in M. Falser and M. Juneja (eds.), *'Archaeologizing' Heritage?, Transcultural Entanglements between Local Social Practices and Global Virtual Realities. Heidelberg Studies on Asia and Europe in a Global Context*. Berlin Heidelberg: Springer-Verlag, pp. 21-37.

Seshadri, T.K. 1978. 'The Chālukya-Pallava Conflict' in M.S. Nagarajarao (ed.), *The Chālukyas of Bādāmī* (Seminar papers). Bangalore: The Mythic Society, pp. 207-11.

Settar, S. 'A Buddhist *vihāra* at Aihoḷe', *East and West*, N.S., Vol. 19 (1-2), pp. 134 ff.

Shah, U.P. 1984. 'Lakulīśa: Śaivite Saint' in M.W. Meister (ed.), *Discourses on Śiva*, pp. 92-102.

Shastry, Ajaymitra. 1976. 'Symbols on Tribal Coins: An Interpretative Study', *Archaeological Studies,* Vol. 1. Mysore.

Sircar, D.C. 1970. 'The Chālukyas of Bādāmī' in R.C. Majumdar (ed.), *HCIP,* Vol. III. Bombay: Bharatiya Vidya Bhavan, pp. 227-49.

Siromoney, Gift, *et al.* 1983. 'Iconometric Analysis of the Sculptures of the Dharmaraja Ratha' in K.V. Ramesh (ed.), *Srinidhih.* Madras: New Era Publications, pp. 137-50.

Sivaramamurti, C. 1959. 'Western Chālukya Paintings at Bādāmī', *LK,* 5, pp. 49-58.

Skinner, Quentin. 2002. 'Meaning and Understanding in the History of Ideas', *Visions of Politics: Regarding Method,* Vol. 1. Cambridge: Cambridge University Press, pp. 57-89.

Soundara Rajan, K.V. 1965. 'The Matrix of South Indian Architecture', Reprint from *Journal of Indian History,* Vol. XLIII, Pt. II, No. 129, pp. 783-825.

——. 1969. 'Cult in the Pallava Temples', *TASSI: 1962-65.* Madras: Archaeological Society of South India, pp. 135-88.

——. 1978. 'Temples of Aihoḷe and Paṭṭaḍakal' in M.S. Nagaraja Rao (ed.), *The Chalukyas of Bādāmī* (Seminar Papers). Bangalore: The Mythic Society, pp. 258-71.

Spink, Walter. 'On the Development of Early Buddhist Art in India', *Art Bulletin,* XL, pp. 90-109.

Srinivasan, K.R. 1958. 'The Pallava Architecture of South India', *Ancient India,* No. 14.

——. 1959-60. 'Some Aspects of Religion as Revealed by Early Monuments and Literature of the South', Sankara-Parvati Endowment Lectures, *Journal of Madras University,* Vol. XXXII (1), pp. 9-16.

——. 1975. 'Temples of the Later Pallavas' in Pramod Chandra (ed.), *Studies in Indian Temple Architecture.* Delhi, pp. 197-239.

Srinivasan, T.M. 1970. 'A Brief Account of the Ancient Irrigation Engineering Systems Prevalent in South India', *The Indian Journal of History of Science,* Vol. 5 (2).

Stevenson. 1850-52. 'The Theory of the Great Elephanta Cave', *JBBRAS,* Vol. IV (XVI), pp. 261-75.

Subramanian, T.S. 2003. 'Conservation, a Monumental Effort', *Frontline,* Vol. 20 (23), 08-21, November.

Sundara, A. 1994. 'Some Structural Temples of the Rāṣṭrakūṭa Period in Dharwar Bijapur Area: A Preliminary Study' in B.R. Gopal (ed.), *The Rāshtrakūṭas of Malkhed: Studies in Their History and Culture.* Mysore, pp. 300-11.

Sundaram, P.S.A. 1989. 'The Future Shape of Urban Conservation in India' in B. Allchin, *et al.* (eds.), *Conservation of the Indian Heritage.*

Swamy, B.G.L. 1978 (Jan-June). 'The Religion of the Pallavas of Kanchi', *Quarterly Journal of the Mythic Society,* Vol. LXIX (1-2), pp. 73-78.

Tarr, Gary. 1969. 'The Śiva Temple at Dhokeśvara and the Development of the *Nidhi* Image', *Oriental Art,* Vol. 15 (4), pp. 269-80.

——. 1970. 'Chronology and Development of the Chālukya Cave Temples', *Ars Orientalis,* Vol. 8, pp. 155-84.

Tartakov, Gary Michael. 1987. 'The *Pratimā Pratisthāpanam* in the Kailāśa', *Kusumāñjali,* pp. 201-11.

Upadhayaya, G.P. 1976. 'Origins and Functions of *Tīrthas* - Some Epic *Paurāṇic* Testimonies', *Proceedings, Indian History Congress.* Calicut, pp. 128-34.

Vatsyayan, Kapila. 1984. 'Śiva Naṭeśa: Cadence and Form' in Michael W. Meister (ed.), *Discourses on Śiva.* Bombay, pp. 191-201.

Vogel, J. Ph. 1914. 'Iconographic Note on "The Seven Pagodas"', *ARASI* (1910-11). Calcutta, pp. 49-62.

Wheeler, R.E.M., A. Ghosh and Krishna Deva. 1946 (July). 'Arikamedu: An Indo-Roman Trading Station on the East Coast of India', *Ancient India,* No. 2, pp. 17-124.

Yadava, B.N.S. 1978-1979 (July–Jan). 'The Accounts of the Kali Age and the Social Transition from Antiquity to the Middle Ages', *Indian Historical Review,* Vol. V (1-2), pp. 61-72.

PH.D. DISSERTATIONS/THESES

Chatham, Doris Clarke. 1977. Stylistic Sources and Relationships of the Kailāśa Temple at Ellorā. University of California, Berkeley.

García, Canclini N. 1995. Hybrid Cultures: Strategies for Entering and Leaving Modernity. University of Minnesota, Minneapolis and London.

Heitzman, Edward James. 1985. Gifts of Power: Temples, Politics and Economy in Medieval South India. University of Pennsylvania.

Hirsh, Marilyn. 1988. Sources for the Figural Sculptures of Māmallapuram. New York University, U.M.I. Michigan.

Maloney, Clarence. 1968. The Effect of Early Coastal Sea Traffic on the Development of Civilization in South India. University of Pennsylvania.

Rabe, Michael Dan. 1988. The Monolithic Temples of the Pallava Dynasty: A Chronology (Vols. I-III). University of Minnesota, U.M.I. Michigan.

Radcliffe, C. 1981. Early Chalukya Sculpture. New York University.

Suresh, S. 1993. A Study of the Roman Coins and other Antiquities in India with Special Reference to South India. JNU, New Delhi.

FELICITATION/COMMEMORATION VOLUMES

Bandyopadhayay, Samaresh (ed.). 1984. *Acārya-Vandanā: D. R. Bhandarkar Birth Centenary Volume.* Calcutta: University of Calcutta.

Baumer, Bettina (ed.). 1982. *Rupa-Pratirupa: Alice Boner Commemoration Volume.* New Delhi: Biblia Implex.

Chakrabarty, Jayanta and D.C. Bhattacharya (eds.). 1983. *Aspects of Indian Art and Culture: S.K. Saraswati Commemoration Volume.* Calcutta: Rddhi-India.

Chandra, Lokesh and Jyotindra Jain (eds.). 1986. *Dimensions of Indian Art: Pupul Jayakar Seventy,* Vol. I. Delhi: Agam Kala Prakashan.

Dwivedi, V.P. and G.N. Pant (eds.). 1980. *Museums and Museology: New Horizons (Essays in Honour of Dr. Grace Morley on Her 80th Birthday).* Delhi: Agam Kala Prakashan.

Ganesan, Saw (ed.). 1971. *Prof. K.A. Nilakanta Sastri Felicitation Volume.* Madras: Prof. K.A. Nilakanta Sastri Felicitation Committee.

Ganguli, K.K. and S.S. Biswas (eds.). 1986. *Rupāñjali in Memory of O.C. Gangoly.* Calcutta: O.C. Gangoly Memorial Society.

Krishna, Anand and Kamal Giri (eds.). 1981. *Chhavi-2, Rai Krishnadasa Felicitation Volume.* Varanasi: Bharat Kala Bhavan.

Nagaraja Rao, M.S. (ed.). 1981. *Madhu: Recent Researches in Indian Archaeology and Art History, M.N. Deshpande Festschrift.* Delhi: Agam Kala Prakashan.

——. (ed.). 1987. *Kusumāñjali—New Interpretations of Indian Art and Culture: C. Sivaramamurti Commemoration Volume.* Delhi: Agam Kala Prakashan.

Narasimha Murthy, A.V. and B.K. Gururaja Rao (eds.). 1983. *Rangāvalli—Recent Researches in Indology: Sri S.R. Rao Felicitation Volume.* Delhi: Sundeep Prakashan.

Narasimha Murthy, A.V. and K.V. Ramesh (eds.). 1987. *Giridharaśrī—Essays on Indology: G.S. Dikshit Felicitation Volume.* Delhi: Agam Kala Prakashan.

Pande, B.M. and B.D. Chattopadhyaya (eds.). 1987. *Archaeology and History: Essays in Memory of A.K. Ghosh*, Vol. II. Delhi: Agam Kala Prakashan.

Ramesh, K.V. 1973. *Srikaṇṭhikā: Dr. S. Srikaṇṭha Sastri Felicitation Volume*. Mysore: Geetha Book House.

——. (ed.). 1983. *Srinidhih: Perspectives in Indian Archaeology, Art and Culture: Shri K.R. Srinivasan Festschrift*. Madras: New Era Publications.

——. *et al.* (ed.). 1984. *Svāsti Sri, Dr. B. Ch. Chhabra Felicitation Volume*. Delhi: Agam Kala Prakashan.

Ritti, Shrinivas and B.R. Gopal (eds.). 1971. *Studies in Indian History and Culture: Volume presented to Dr. P.B. Desai*. Dharwar: Prof. P.B. Desai Felicitation Committee.

E-RESOURCES

American Institute of Indian Studies, Photo Archives.

http://dsal.uchicago.edu/images/aiis/aiis_search.html (accessed during January-July 2011)

2011. 'Conserve without Hurting': Ratish Nanda on preserving our conservation and heritage. November 11. *http://indiatoday.intoday.in/story/ratish-nanda-on-preserving-conservation-and-heritage/1/159579.html* Accessed on 17.8.2013.

2013. Habib, Irfan, K.M. Shrimali and D.N. Jha. *'The ASI and Indian archaeology today', http://www.sahmat.org/1772000.html*. Accessed on 19.8.2013.

2007. 'Heritage Protection for the 21st Century- White Paper (UK)', *CHS Newsletter*, No. 77. May. www. constructionhistory. co.uk. Accessed on 19.8.2013.

http://asi.nic.in/asi_cent_anti.asp.

http://asi.nic.in/asi_mission.asp.

http://asi.nic.in/asi_monuments.asp.

http://asibengalurucircle.org/list_of_monuments.html.

http://www.asichennai.gov.in/downloads/monuments-chennai-circle.pdf.

http://pib.nic.in/archieve/others/2013/aug/d2013081405.pdf.

http://whc.unesco.org/en/statesparties/IN/.

1922. 'Indian Monuments'. Annual Report of the Director-General of Archaeology in India for 1918-19, 14th January. Calcutta: Superintendent of Government Printing, p. 23. *http://archive.spectator.co.uk/article/14th-january-1922/23/indian-monuments*. Accessed on 11.8.2013.

Khandekar, Nivedita. 2012. 'Political Standoff: Conserving heritage not a priority for parties', *Hindustan Times*, New Delhi. 08th April. *http://www.hindustantimes.com/India-news/NewDelhi/Conserving-heritage-not-a-priority-for-parties/Article1-837592.aspx*. Accessed on 19.8.2013.

Maharashtra Tourism Development Corporation, *Ajanta Ellora Conservation and Tourism Development Project a Report.*

*http://aurangabad.nic.in/newsite/docs/AEDP_Phase_I_and_II.pdf.*Accessed 22.8.2013.

Sharma, Preeti. 2010 (July-December). 'The Meaning and Symbolism of Varāha Motif: with Special Reference to the Chālukyan Rock-cut Caves at Bādāmī', *Journal of History & Social Sciences*, Vol. I (I), pp. 1-26. (E-Journal) (*www.jhss.org*)

Shinde, Swati. 2013. 'Students to Observe Heritage Day', *TOI*, Pune. 30th July. *http://timesofindia.indiatimes.com/city/pune/Students-to-observe-heritage-day/articleshow/21491249.cms?* Accessed on 13.8.2013.

'State of Conservation of the World Heritage Properties in the Asia-Pacific Region: INDIA Group of Monuments at Mahabalipuram'.

http://whc.unesco.org/archive/periodicreporting/apa/cycle01/section2/249-summary.pdf. Accessed 22.8.2013.

Subramanian, T.S. 2003. 'Conservation, a Monumental Effort', *Frontline*, Vol. 20 (23), 08-21, November. *http://www.frontline.in/navigation/?type=static&page=flonnet&rdurl=fl2023/stories/20031121000107000.htm]accessed* Accessed on 22.8.2013.

Verma, Richi. 2013. 'ASI drafts new conservation policy', *TOI*, Delhi. 10th March. *http://articles.timesofindia.indiatimes.com/2013-03-10/delhi/37597842_1_heritage-body-senior-asi-officials-structural-conservation. Accessed on 19.8.2013.*

NEWSPAPERS/MAGAZINES

The Times of India. 2005. 'Tsunami unveiled "Seven Pagodas" in Mahābalipuram'. 1st March.

The Times of India. 2005. '2 more temples found in Mahābalipuram'. 5th April.

The Times of India. 2013. 'ASI should charge filmmakers more than just Rs. 5,000', Interview with retired ASI official, K.K. Mohammed by Manimugdha S. Sharma. 3rd May, p. 12.

The Times of India. 2013. Atul Thakur, '35 protected monuments "untraceable"'. 6th April, pp. 1, 6.

India Today. 2005. 6th June issue, pp. 48-50.

Index

Ādivarāha cave temple 50
Ādivarāha Gaṅgādhara 252
Āgamas 7, 48, 69, 248, 251, 289, 293
Agastya 45, 46
Aihoḷe 8, 18, 35, 48-49, 55, 70-71, 73, 76-77, 81-85, 97-100, 111-17, 121-22, 124, 147, 149-50, 202, 209, 249, 265-66, 268-69, 271, 293, 331-32, 335, 337
  caves 115, 332
  praśasti 35, 49
Ajantā 6, 8, 21, 32, 85-86, 124, 128, 144, 147, 149, 207, 293, 296, 315, 317, 320, 330, 338
Alaṁkāradevatās 93, 95
Ālampur shrines 80
Ālīḍha pose warrior 295
Āliṅganāmūrti 85, 282
Ālvār 18, 47, 49, 156, 331
Āmjhara 285
Aṁśumadbhedāgama 7, 248-49, 286
Archaeological Survey of India 314, 316-17, 321
Architectural conservation 314, 326
Ardhanārīśvara 48, 84, 86, 102, 192, 209, 233-38, 251, 257, 259-60, 288, 297
Arjuna ratha 80, 94, 159, 179, 182-84, 191, 257, 276, 291
Arjunānugraha 94
Art history 2, 159, 221, 225, 309
Ashoka 4-5, 155
Astārṣa Viṣṇuchanda 188
Atharva Veda 3
Aurangābād 6, 8, 18, 21, 111, 128, 144, 147, 293, 330
Āvaraṇadevatā 276
Āvesanin 18
Ayyavoḷe 111
Azar *Śivālaya* 78

Bādāmī 8, 18, 20-21, 32-36, 38-39, 42, 45, 48-49, 69-71, 78-82, 84-87, 95, 97, 99, 102, 111-12, 114-16, 118, 121-24, 127, 129-31, 135, 142, 145, 147-50, 209, 231, 249, 257, 259, 265-66, 268-70, 272-78, 280, 285-86, 288, 293-97, 318, 331-32, 334-35, 337-38
  Cave II Trivikrama 272
  Cave III 48, 84, 86, 112, 116, 130, 147-49, 259, 269-70, 275, 288, 293, 318
Bāgh 8, 330

Balbi 19
Banerji, R.D. 21, 112, 122
Barābar 4-6, 10, 13, 330
Benjamin 2, 20
Berkson 21
Bhāgvata Purāṇa 3
Bhairava 82, 94, 102, 221, 223, 225, 249-50
Bhājā 6, 8
Bharhūt 10-11
Bhīma *ratha* 159-60, 180, 182, 189-90, 193
Bhikshāṭana 94
Boner 20, 21
Brahmadeya(s) 32, 51, 54-55
Brahmānugraha 94
Brahmāśīrṣacedaka 94
Brāhmanical cave temples 7, 10, 19, 112
Bṛhat Saṁhitā 2, 7, 156, 248, 269, 276
Brown, Percy 2, 4, 112
Buchanan, Francis 315
Buddhist caves 10, 13-14, 18, 21, 124, 149, 207
Burgess 4, 10, 20, 112, 122

Cālukya(s)/Cālukyan 6, 8, 18, 32-36, 38-40, 42-45, 47-49, 52-53, 55, 57, 69-71, 74, 76, 78, 82, 86-87, 94, 98, 102-03, 111-12, 121, 123, 127-28, 132, 144, 146-50, 199, 221-22, 225-26, 247, 251-53, 257, 259, 262, 268-69, 271, 273-74, 276, 278-79, 283, 291, 294-97, 296, 330-31, 336, 341
  adhiṣṭhāna(s) 81, 99
  Brāhmanical caves 207
  caves XVII and XXI 280
  Mahiṣamardinīs 121
  Varāha 121, 294, 336
Caṇḍeśānugraha 94, 192, 262
Caṇḍeśānugrahamūrti 177
Caitya(s) 3-7, 11-12, 18-19, 53, 75, 77, 81, 99-100, 159, 173, 180, 216, 330
Carr 20
Castro 19
Caturārṣa brahmakānta 188
Cave I, II style 123
Cave III, IV style 123
Cave Temple 3, 6-7, 10-11, 14, 16, 19-20, 40, 50-51, 95, 78, 79, 85, 87, 97, 111-15, 122, 125, 143-44, 147-50, 155-57, 159-162, 226, 228, 240, 247, 249, 260, 265, 329-31, 334, 336, 340-41
Ceylon 4, 16, 33, 38-39, 41
Chambers 12, 19
Chatham 21
Chotā Kailāśa 213
Coomaraswamy 222, 224, 291
Coopersmith and Hall 313
Cousens 20, 70-71, 112, 114, 147
Coutto 19

Dakshiṇamūrti 94
Daḷavāṇūr 156, 161-62, 167-68, 173
Daṇḍī 39, 156
Dantidurga 36, 40, 42-43, 199
Daśāvatāra cave 102, 199, 201, 203, 205-06, 208-12, 224, 241, 250, 253, 255, 264, 267-68, 271, 273, 276, 286, 335
Daśāvatāra nandīmaṇḍapa 206
Deccan 7-8, 10, 16, 22, 32-36, 40, 42, 53, 56-57, 69-70, 97, 100, 112, 122, 124, 128-29, 146-48, 157, 193, 199, 209, 294, 331
Dehejia, Vidya 21
Deogarh temple 213
Deshpande 21, 329
Devadāna(s) 32, 51, 54-55
Devīmahātmya 284
Dharmarāja *ratha* 49, 91, 179-80, 182-88, 190-93, 249-50, 252, 257, 259-60, 262, 266, 277, 286, 291, 332
Dharmarāja *ratha āditala* 180, 182, 186-88, 192, 250, 259, 277
Dharmarāja *ratha Gaṅgādhara* 252
Dhavalikar, M.K. 22, 329
Dhenukākaṭa 17
Dhruva 43, 160
Dikpāla(s) 85, 95, 101-03, 143, 145, 209, 221, 225, 277, 332, 336
Draupadī *ratha(s)* 51, 135, 159, 179-80, 184-86, 193, 281-82, 287
Draviḍa/Draviḍian 7, 70, 78-81, 87-89, 91-93, 155, 159, 179, 193, 206, 213-14, 218, 333
  architecture 89, 155, 193
  pillar order 206
  śikhara 79-80
  style 78-80, 87, 218
Droysen 309
Dubreuil 4, 20, 88, 97, 158-59
Durgā temple 73, 75, 81-85, 113, 149, 150, 202, 259, 269, 279

Elephanta (caves) 8, 10, 19-22, 52, 85, 97, 102, 114, 129-30, 199-200, 209, 226, 229-31, 233-34, 236, 238-41, 250, 253, 255-60, 262, 264, 267, 289, 292, 296, 315, 333-37
  pillar capital 231
Ellorā 2, 6-8, 10, 16, 18-22, 36, 42-43, 52, 85, 97, 102-03, 111-12, 114, 124, 126, 128, 130, 133, 137, 144, 147, 149, 192-93, 199-201, 209-12, 218, 222, 224-26, 230-31, 233, 237, 240-41, 253, 255, 257, 262, 264, 266-68, 270, 271, 277, 280, 283-85, 287-89, 293, 295-96, 315, 320, 330, 332-38
  Kailāśanātha temple 52, 193, 240
Elāpura 199
Epistemology of architecture 305-06
Eraṇ 269
Erotic mithunas 218
Erskine 19
Excavated *maṇḍapams* 39, 155

Fergusson 4, 7, 20, 157-58
Foucault, Michel 311

Gadamer, Hance George 308
Gaṇeśa *leṇa* group 200, 202, 206, 210-11
Gaṇeśa *ratha(s)* 179-80, 182-83, 189-93
Gaṅgas 34, 36, 38, 40-41, 43, 45
Gaṅgādhara 94, 102, 176, 192, 208, 233-35, 237-38, 252-53, 291, 336-37
Gaṅgāvataraṇa relief 157
Gajalakshmī 82, 94, 100, 176-77, 206-08, 211, 218, 221, 285-86, 336
Gajāsurasaṁhāra 94-95, 249
Garuḍārūḍha Viṣṇu 95, 118, 135, 142, 150
Ghaṭapallava motif 205
Ghaṭikā 40
Goldingham 19
Gough 19
Govinda III 40, 43
Grīvādevatās 94-95
Greater India 291
Guhā 1-4, 6, 19, 329
Guhārāja 3
Gupta, S.P. 4-5, 22

Haṁsamālā 99
Hamilton 19
Hariharamūrti 260
Havell 20
Hirsch, Marilyn 21

Īśānaśivagurudevapaddhati 7, 248

Jalandhara 94, 249
Johnson, Dr. Samuel 315
Jones, William 315
Junnār 17
Jyēṣṭhā 50
Jyotirliṅga shrines 212

Kadungon 32
Kail 21
Kailāśa temple 18, 199, 241, 252, 259-61, 267-68, 271, 273-74, 276, 282, 285-86
  complex 206-07, 214, 218, 221
  mahāmaṇḍapa 267, 286
  prākāra 208, 218
  raṅgamaṇḍapa 216
Kakshāsana 83, 220
Kālabhras 32, 36, 39, 47, 54, 331
Kalacuri(s) 18, 34, 71, 85, 127-28, 146-47, 226, 330
Kālidāsa 85, 296-97
Kalyāṇasundara 94, 101-02, 208-09, 233-34, 236-37, 251, 253, 255, 277, 289, 297, 336-37
Kāmikāgama 7, 248
Kāmānugraha 94
Kāñcī Kailāśanātha temple 36, 148, 332
Kāñcīpuram 33, 35-36, 39-40, 45, 88-89, 92-95, 97, 155, 158-59, 220
Kanherī 5, 8, 16, 18, 52, 102
Kannal, Deepak 22
Kapotabandha adhiṣṭhāna 184, 214
Kāraṇāgama 7, 248
Kārle 6, 8, 14, 17, 231
Karṇakūṭa or *karṇaśālā* 187
Kauṇḍiṇya ṛṣi 46
Khaṭvāṅga 49, 210, 248
Khaṇḍottara type 208
Kilmāvilaṅgai 276
Kirtivarman I 34, 112
Kirātārjunīyam 193
Koṇḍane 6, 8
Kōṇēri *maṇḍapam* 162, 164, 167, 169, 171, 173, 175-76
Kosambi 14

Kōṭikal *maṇḍapam* 157, 162, 171, 176
Kramrisch 20, 70, 318
Krishna 21, 43-44, 101-02, 212
Kshudranāsikās 190-91
Kudā 16
Kūḍū 7, 79, 81, 84-86, 96, 99-100, 132, 134-35, 149, 159, 173-75, 179, 186, 204-05, 207-08, 216, 266, 334
Kuraṅgaṇilmuṭṭam cave temple 157
Kūrmavāhinī Yamunā 206, 218, 295

Lāḍ Khān temple 71, 74, 76, 81, 145
Lalāṭabiṁba 81, 96, 206-07, 211
Lankeśvara cave 199, 201-03, 205-06, 208-12, 216, 255, 259, 267, 271, 274, 282, 285
Layaṇa or *leṇa* 1
Liṅgapīṭha 101, 201, 202, 212, 230
Liṅgodbhava 84, 94, 103, 208-09, 212, 251, 261, 268, 336-37
Linschoten, Van 19
Lippe, Aschwin de 48
Lockwood 21, 158-59
Lomaś *Ṛṣi* 4
Longhurst 20, 70, 158-59
Loval *Śivālaya* 79
Lūpadakhe 18

Maṇḍagappaṭṭū 7, 70, 159-61, 168, 170-71, 176
Madurai 31, 33, 50
Mahēndravāḍī 51, 156, 161, 165
Mahēndravāḍī *Viṣṇugṛha* 156
Mahābalipuram 7-8, 12, 19-22, 39, 50-51, 80, 87-89, 91, 94-96, 103, 135, 156-59, 161-62, 177, 190, 193, 223, 252, 280, 286-87, 292, 295, 315, 318-20, 325, 331-32, 334, 337, 339
Mahendra group *maṇḍapams* 155
Mahendravarman I 35, 38, 49-51, 70, 155, 158-59, 332
Maheśamūrti 52, 101-02, 208, 228-31, 237-39, 241
Mahiṣamardinī cave 162, 170-71
Mahākūṭa 34, 48, 70-71, 82, 84-86, 97-98, 115
Mahānāsikās 190
Makaravāhinī Gaṅgā 206, 218, 295
Malayadippaṭṭi 40
Mālegittī *Śivālaya* 79, 84-85, 150
Malet 19
Mālkheḍ 42, 56, 331
Mallikārjuna 38, 48, 77, 79-81, 83-84, 149
Māmaṇḍūr cave 156
Māmaṇḍūr Rudravāliśvaram *maṇḍapam* 165, 176
Māmalla 35, 39, 51, 57, 156, 159, 161, 170, 332
Mānasāra 7, 248
Mangalesha 34, 48-49, 70-71, 79, 87, 123-24, 292
Manucci 19
Mānyakheṭa 33, 42, 44-45, 69
Mārg 22, 44
Mārkaṇḍeyānugrahamūrti 210
Markel 21
Marshall, Sir John 316-17
Mātṛkās 52, 121, 147, 221, 225, 266, 283
Matsya Purāṇa 2, 46, 249, 273
Mayamatam, Viśvakarmaśilpa 7
Megutī *Jinālaya* 49
Megutī temple 71, 73, 75, 85
Mithikās 18
Mithuna couples 208
Mitter, Partha 22
Monolithic Kailāśa 43, 200, 212, 226, 241, 297, 335
Monolithic *rathas* 19, 39, 94, 155, 162, 179, 183, 191, 335
Munshi, K.M. 311

Nāgārjunī 4-5, 10, 330
Nagaswamy 21, 158
Nakula Sahadeva *ratha* 179-80, 182-83, 187, 190, 192
Narasimhavarman I 35, 38, 79, 155, 156
Navakārmika 18
Navaraṅga 98, 213
Nayanmār 18, 47, 49, 50
Nāsik 6, 16, 42, 86, 100-101, 173, 175, 187, 190-91, 204-08, 216, 218, 220, 252, 276, 332, 334
Naṭeśa 94-96, 102, 147, 224, 267, 336
Nietzsche 309-10
Nṛsiṁha 85, 93, 95, 102, 208, 210, 223, 225, 269, 273, 274, 276, 336
Nṛtyamūrti(s) 95, 221, 224, 249, 264, 336

Orta, Garcia Da 19
Orukal *maṇḍapam* 157, 177
Ovington 19

Pādabandha adhiṣṭhāna 93, 101-02, 184, 221
Pallava(s) 6, 8, 10, 12-13, 18, 20-22, 32-33, 35-43, 45, 47, 49-55, 57, 69-71, 79-80, 82, 87-89, 92-97, 102-03, 126, 147-48, 155-61, 166, 168-70, 172, 177, 179, 182, 187, 192-93, 199, 202, 209, 220-21, 247, 249-53, 257, 259-60, 262, 264-69, 271-77, 280-83, 285-86, 288-89, 291-92, 294-97, 330-337, 341
  monuments 70, 88, 155-58, 160, 337
Panamalāi (temple) 51, 87, 91, 93, 97, 291
Pañcāgnimūrti 282
Pañcapāṇḍava *maṇḍapam* 161-62, 165, 167-68, 171, 332
Pañcapāṇḍava *rathas* 177
Pāñcarātra 7
Pañcāyatan temple 213
Pande, G.C. 2, 249
Pāṇḍya(s) 13, 31-32, 34-36, 38-41, 43, 47, 50, 53-55, 96, 331
Parimoo, Ratan 22
Parśurāma 46
Pātāleśvara cave 201, 212, 241, 276
Pathy, T.V. 22
Paṭṭaḍakal 48-49, 70-71, 77, 79-85, 97-99, 111, 124, 148-49, 220, 222, 224, 293, 331
Pitalkhorā 6
Popper, Karl 308
Pradakshiṇāpatha - ālinda 188
Pulakeshin I 34, 48, 49, 71, 112, 226
Pulakeshin II 33-34, 38, 71, 73, 79
Pyke, Capt. 19

Rabe 21, 159
Rajan, K.V. Soundara 22, 329
Rajasimha 21, 39, 49, 51, 57, 70, 87-88, 92, 96-97, 147, 155, 158, 291
Ramachandran, T.N. 22
Ramanayya 21
Rāmānuja *maṇḍapam* 162, 164, 166, 168, 171, 174-75, 190, 337
Ramaswami 22
Rangapataka 39, 51-52, 92
Rao, Gopinatha 277
Rāṣṭrakūṭa(s) 6, 8, 21-22, 33, 36, 40, 42-45, 47, 52-53, 56, 69, 97-103, 199-203, 205-12, 214, 221-22, 225-26, 229, 233, 240-41, 247, 250, 252-53, 255, 257, 259-62, 264, 267-68, 271, 273-74, 276-77, 282-83, 285-86, 288-89, 291-97, 330-31, 333-37, 341
  creations 200
  Gaṅgādhara 253
Rūpakāra 18
Rāvaṇa Phaḍi 48, 73, 82, 84, 113-16, 118, 121, 129, 137, 147, 149, 259-60, 265, 268-69, 279, 283, 335
  façade 115
  pillars 115-16
Rāvaṇānugraha 94-95, 102-03, 222, 233-37, 241, 264, 336
Ravikirti 49
Rea, Alexander 20
Rock-cut architecture 1, 4, 21, 22, 51, 73, 87, 124, 146, 159, 226, 233, 329, 332-34, 337
Rock-cut Lakulīśa 262
Rock-cut mode 5, 145, 150, 191, 193, 212, 218, 268, 333, 335
Rowland 2, 20
Royal portraits 87, 94, 156, 291

Sadāśiva 251, 262, 267, 336
Sahadeva *ratha* 159, 179-80, 182-83, 187, 190-92
Said, Edward 305
Śaivite 47-49, 77, 79-80, 85, 94, 156, 163, 192, 208, 221, 233, 241, 250-51, 262, 267-68, 276, 289, 331, 333, 337
Śālabhañjikā(s) 102, 205
Śāḷuvankuppam 51, 158, 161, 281, 282
Samarāngaṇa Sūtradhāra 7
Samudramanthana 95, 211, 216
Saṅgam 31-32, 37, 45, 47, 50, 53, 56, 97, 101, 331
Saṅgameśvara temple 48, 80, 84
Sastri, Hirananda 21
Śatapatha Brāhmaṇa 3, 46, 69
Sātavāhana(s) 5, 32, 37, 56, 86, 96
Sathianathaier 35
Selakamma 2
Selavadhakins 18
Sen, Sukumar 21
Settar, S. 22
Seven pagodas 88, 158
Shore temple 87-91, 93-94, 188, 190, 193, 289, 320

Śilparatnam 7, 248
Śilpasaṁgṛha 7
Siṁhavishnu 32
Śiva Pārvatī krīḍā 234
Śīyamaṅgalam *layaṇa* 161
Skinner 308
Somaskanda 92, 94, 96-97, 177, 180, 192, 251, 257, 291, 336
South India 7, 16, 18-20, 31-32, 38, 45-48, 51, 53-54, 69, 82, 97, 155, 199, 220, 247-48, 251, 268, 282, 286, 292, 305, 331, 341
Spink, Walter 22, 112
Srinivasan, K.R. 13, 21, 112, 157-59, 329
Stevenson 19
Structural techniques 71, 82, 150
Suprabhedāgama 7, 248, 267, 281, 286

Tarr, Gary 21, 112, 115
Tirucirāppaḷḷī cave 156
Tirucirāppaḷḷī Lalitāṅkura 162, 167, 170
Toṇḍaimaṇḍalam 36-37, 40-41, 44, 50, 87, 155
Trikūṭacala plan 230
Trimūrti *maṇḍapam* 162, 165, 167, 170, 174, 176, 187, 260, 277, 281, 334
Tripurāntaka 94, 96, 102, 208, 223-24, 249-50, 295, 297, 336-37
Trivikrama 95, 121, 137-38, 140-41, 149, 176-77, 208, 269, 271-73, 332, 336
Tṛṣtā 10

Udaigiri 8, 113-14, 121-22, 269, 279, 294-95, 330
Umāsahita 94, 96, 223, 255
Uraiyūr 31, 39, 53
Uttānapāda devī 293

Vaiṣṇava *avatāras* 271
Vaiṣṇavite 47-48, 50-51, 70, 80, 92, 123, 208, 221, 276, 289, 331
Vaikhānasāgama 7, 248, 268, 271-73
Vaikuṇṭha 37, 39-40, 51, 92-96, 276, 292
Vaikuṇṭha-perumāl temple 37, 39-40, 51, 92, 94-95, 292
Vākāṭaka(s) 18, 32, 71, 85-86, 114, 128, 146, 147, 294, 330
Valaiyankuṭṭai *rathas* 179, 182
Vallam Vasantēśvaram 161
Vañci 53
Vardhakis 18
Varāha 48, 50-51, 71, 84, 87, 94-95, 102, 118, 121, 123, 134, 137-38, 140-41, 147, 161-62, 164, 166-68, 170-71, 173-74, 176-77, 208, 222, 248-49, 261, 269-71, 273, 279, 281, 283, 285, 294-95, 297, 332, 334, 336
Varāha *maṇḍapam* 50-51, 170-71, 173-74, 176-77, 271, 273, 281, 285
Varāha with Bhūdevī 271
Varāha-*lañchana* 48
Vāstupuruṣamaṇḍala 226
Vātāpī 34, 35, 148
Vāyu Purāṇa 3, 46
Vēḷāḷar 53, 55
Vendārs 31, 53
Vengī 33, 43-44
Verūl 199
Vihāra(s) 4-6, 19, 52-53, 124, 130, 159, 228, 330, 332
Vikramaditya I 35, 39, 48, 79
Vilandai 39
Vimāna(s) 7, 77, 80, 89, 91-94, 100-02, 160, 179, 186-91, 193, 207, 213, 218, 224, 332, 335
Viṇādhara 94, 192
Virāṭapuruṣa 276
Virūpāksha 77, 79-81, 83-84, 86, 124, 149, 220, 222, 273
Viṣṇuchanda śikhara 220
Viśvakarmaprakāśa 7
Viśvakarmaśilpa 7
Vitāpī 111
Vogel 20
Vṛṣabha lāñchana 49

White, Hayden 309
Willetts 20

Yajñaśālā 200, 213, 218, 223, 225, 284
Yāḷi maṇḍapam at Śāḷuvaṇkuppam 167
Yogaśayanamūrti 177, 275

Zimmer 20